THE MACKENZIE KING RECORD

Volume 3

THE MACKENZIE KING RECORD

Volume 1: 1939–1944

Volume 2: 1944–1945

Volume 3: 1945–1946

Volume 4: 1947–1948

The Rt. Hon. W. L. Mackenzie King
arrives at Bayeux, Normandy, August 1946

THE
MACKENZIE KING
RECORD

VOLUME 3
1945-1946

J. W. Pickersgill
and
D. F. Forster

UNIVERSITY OF TORONTO PRESS

© University of Toronto Press 1970
Printed in Canada by
University of Toronto Press, Toronto and Buffalo
Reprinted in 2018
ISBN 0-8020-1655-3
ISBN 978-1-4875-8126-8 (paper)

Preface

I DO NOT BELIEVE it is necessary in this third volume of the Mackenzie King Record to repeat much of what is to be found in the prefaces to volumes 1 and 2. However, for the convenience of readers who do not have the earlier volumes, certain points should be made again.

The Mackenzie King Record is not intended to be a biography. It does constitute, however, for the period from September 1, 1939, to November 15, 1948, when Mackenzie King retired as Prime Minister, an integral part of the biographical project sponsored by his Literary Executors, and they do not intend to sponsor an official biography for the war and postwar years.

As explained in the prefaces to the earlier volumes, virtually the sole source for this book is the unrevised record of events and impressions kept by Mackenzie King himself. This diary was kept largely to serve as a record from which he could recount and explain his conduct of public affairs. He had told all the original Literary Executors he intended to use the diaries for this purpose.

I wish to indicate once more the basis on which I have selected the extracts from the diary for inclusion in this volume. It is precisely the same basis as that followed in the first and second volumes. I have tried, within the limits of space feasible for this project, to select what seemed to Mackenzie King most important, and, as far as possible, to preserve his own sense of relative importance.

In doing so, I have set myself certain criteria. Since I was seeking to present Mackenzie King's public life, not his private life, the references to his private life have been confined to extracts from the diaries which seemed to bear essentially on his public conduct. I have sought to present Mackenzie King's record of events made at the time, not to write the history of the period or to present the views of his contemporaries.

Mackenzie King usually referred to his diaries as the "record." Hence the title of this book. It is not intended to be the final verdict of history, nor even my own verdict, but simply a part of the raw material for the history of the period.

The diaries for the post-war period were dictated to a secretary, subsequently typewritten, and rarely revised. For that reason, in quoting them, I have not hesitated to correct obvious mistakes in form and even in sense, where what was really meant is clear to me. The extracts from the relatively rare portions of the diaries which were handwritten by Mackenzie King are reproduced unchanged. Omissions from sentences and paragraphs are indicated by ellipses. Apart from comparatively few cases where I felt extracts should be excluded because of references to persons still living or because I believed Mackenzie King himself would not have wished them to be published, the omissions consist of irrelevancies, repetitions, or trivia and were made to save precious space.

For the period from November 10 to December 31, 1945, the diaries have been lost. We have endeavoured to provide some continuity to fill that gap. The exceedingly thin narrative for that period will be found, I believe, to underline the historical value of the record provided, day by day, by Mackenzie King.

The Literary Executors were faced with a difficult problem by the terms of the Prime Minister's will. The relevant clauses read:

"8. I direct my Trustees to transfer to my Literary Executors all of my books, papers, correspondence, memoranda, state papers, diaries and unpublished material of any kind whatsoever and also the copyrights in any of my published works.

"9. I give to my said Literary Executors full power in their discretion

A to retain and deposit as they may deem fit in the Archives of Canada or in the Library of Parliament or at my present place of residence now known as Laurier House, such of my books, papers, correspondence, memoranda, state papers, diaries and unpublished materials as I have not directed to be destroyed or otherwise disposed of; or to present any of them to individuals, institutions, public bodies or places of personal association with my life or work;

B to publish, subject to the reservation herein made, such of my books, papers, correspondence, memoranda, state papers, diaries and unpublished material, as they may deem fit;

C to destroy such of my books, papers, correspondence, memoranda, state papers, diaries and unpublished material, as they may deem fit.

"10. I direct my Literary Executors to destroy all of my diaries except those parts which I have indicated are and shall be available for publication or use."

We sought legal advice as to the precise significance of the word "indicated" in clause ten of Mackenzie King's will. The advice we received was

Preface

that the clause was to be interpreted as an expression of his wishes and that it was in order for the Literary Executors to preserve and make available for publication and use such parts of the diaries as they were satisfied he wished to have preserved.

Two choices for the disposition of the diaries, therefore, seemed open to us. One was to destroy the diaries without examining them; and the other was to use them in the way we believed Mackenzie King wished them to be used. We chose the second course. Since the Prime Minister had left no written indication of what portions of the diary he wished to have used, and what portions he would not have used, we had to rely on our recollections of several oral indications each of us had had of his own wishes, in using the diaries, both for the biography for the period prior to September 1, 1939, and in the volumes of this book. However, no portion of the diary has been destroyed and one day the Literary Executors will have to face the question as to whether any part of it should be destroyed.

Fortunately, under the will, provision was made for the perpetuation of the Literary Executors and, as long as that provision is followed, a legal entity will exist with authority to make this decision. Shortly before the publication of volume 2 of the Mackenzie King Record, Mr. N. A. Robertson died. The remaining Literary Executors have since elected in his place Mr. R. Gordon Robertson, Clerk of the Privy Council and Secretary to the Cabinet, who was a member of the Prime Minister's staff from mid-1945 until his retirement.

In the case of volume 3 as of volume 2, I had already made the selections from the diaries and provided a little in the way of rough continuity, before Professor Forster of the University of Toronto began to collaborate with me. In this volume, even more than in volume 2, Professor Forster's editing and revision have given form and continuity to the record of a period which lacked the natural coherence and unity provided by the war. As with volume 2, I assembled the building materials and drew a very rough plan for the structure. Professor Forster has fashioned a book with shape and form, and the continuity he has provided is obviously more objective than mine could have been, in view of my close association with Mackenzie King, particularly in the period covered in this volume. For me, collaboration with Professor Forster has been a happy experience.

As head of the Prime Minister's Office throughout the whole of this period, my personal knowledge of the events recorded in this volume is even closer than it was of those recorded in volume 2. As the person who selected the material to be included, and as co-author, I take full responsibility for everything chosen for inclusion, though I am indebted to my fellow Literary Executors, and especially to Dr. W. Kaye Lamb, who recently retired as head of the Public Archives, for advice.

In this volume of the Mackenzie King Record, I repeat my warm gratitude for the understanding help of the University of Toronto Press, and particularly of Miss Francess Halpenny.

I wish also to express again my thanks to Miss Florence Moore, Miss Shirley Tink and my wife for the hours they spent working on the first draft of this volume, and to my secretary, Miss Audrey McQuarrie, for her help in checking the final revision.

Apart from Mackenzie King himself, no person is entitled to more credit for making this book possible than Mr. J. E. Handy, who, throughout the whole period, was personal secretary to the Prime Minister. Mackenzie King dictated the greater part of the "record" to Mr. Handy. So great was the Prime Minister's confidence in the trustworthiness of his personal secretary that he dictated this record almost as freely as he would have written it himself and, without this help, the physical labour of producing the "record" would have been far beyond the powers even of Mackenzie King.

J. W. P.

Ottawa, May 1969

There is little I can add to the comments made by Mr. Pickersgill but I can wholeheartedly repeat his appreciation of the assistance given us by the University of Toronto Press, particularly Miss Francess Halpenny. My collaboration with the senior author of this volume has been a pleasant and rewarding experience and I am grateful to him and to Mackenzie King's other Literary Executors for the opportunity to participate in the publication of the major part of a fascinating and important political diary. Many of my colleagues at the University of Toronto tolerated frequent lunch hour excursions into the intricacies of Canadian politics in the 1940s and, for their forebearance, I am thankful. I owe special debts of gratitude to my secretary, Miss Freda Chayka, to Mr. Frank Felkai who burrowed into Hansard on several occasions checking references and documentation, to Professor H. Blair Neatby who, between 1958 and 1960, stimulated my interest in Mackenzie King and his times, and, finally, to my parents for their interest and support.

D.F.F.

Toronto, May 1969

The index for this volume has been prepared by Mr. and Mrs. John Bryden.

Contents

	PREFACE	v
I	Introduction	3
II	The Gouzenko Affair	6
III	Mackenzie King in London, 1945	46
IV	A Winter of Discontent	103
V	The British Loan Negotiations	159
VI	Post-War Economic Problems	187
VII	The Heart of Empire	223
VIII	An Ottawa Interlude	257
IX	The Paris Conference	287
X	The Shift in External Affairs	328
XI	Dominion-Provincial Battles and Cabinet Shuffles	371
	APPENDIX	407
	INDEX	409

Illustrations

FRONTISPIECE

Mackenzie King in France, August 1946

FOLLOWING PAGE 102

A conference at the White House on atomic energy, November 1945

The departure of the Earl and Countess of Athlone from Ottawa, March 1946

The arrival of the new Governor-General, Viscount Alexander, April 1946

The Victory Parade, London, June 1946

The Paris Peace Conference, July-August 1946

Mackenzie King visits the Normandy battlefields, August 1946

Field Marshal Montgomery visits Laurier House, September 1946

Public Archives of Canada

THE MACKENZIE KING RECORD

Volume 3

CHAPTER ONE

Introduction

THIS VOLUME is a record, made largely by Mackenzie King himself, of his leadership of the Government of Canada from the close of the Second World War at the beginning of September 1945 until the end of 1946. The final volume takes the record to his retirement as Prime Minister on November 15, 1948.

When the war ended, with the surrender of Japan on September 1, 1945, Mackenzie King was in his seventy-first year. He had been Prime Minister for eighteen of the previous twenty-four years, the last six during the greatest war in history. In the year preceding the end of the war, he had surmounted the most serious crisis of his public life; led the Canadian delegation to the Conference at San Francisco for the founding of the United Nations; reconstructed his government and led it to victory in a general election in which he met personal defeat in his own constituency; and found a new seat in the post-war Parliament which was about to open for its first session on September 6, 1945. Although he continued to follow his regime of taking a little exercise nearly every day and a great deal of rest, the last year of the war had affected his health and he often suffered from fatigue which led him increasingly to shrink from contacts with new people and new problems, and to seek more frequent relief from the day-to-day burdens of office. One task he never neglected was the dictation of the diaries which continued to be an amazing combination of intimate personal observations with the most careful and painstakingly accurate reporting of his participation in public affairs.

Though Mackenzie King still felt that he was inadequately served by his secretarial staff, he made little effort to change its personnel and showed increasing distaste for new faces, particularly in the immediate group surrounding him at Laurier House where J. E. Handy remained the central figure. During this period, James Gibson, now President of Brock University at St. Catharines, left the public service to enter the academic world. Since Mackenzie King ceased, during the post-war period, to be Secretary of State for External Affairs, Gibson was not replaced.

Until early September 1946, Norman Robertson continued as Under-Secretary of State for External Affairs and as the Prime Minister's closest adviser. When Louis St. Laurent became Secretary of State for External Affairs in September, 1946, Norman Robertson was appointed High Commissioner in London and L. B. Pearson succeeded him as Under-Secretary. Arnold Heeney remained in the office of Clerk of the Privy Council and Secretary to the Cabinet during the whole of the period covered by this volume and continued to increase the efficiency of that office as the centre of the executive.

In the Prime Minister's office, J. W. Pickersgill succeeded Walter Turnbull, who was appointed Deputy Postmaster-General, as head of the office with the title of Special Assistant, a description chosen to enable him to avoid the day-to-day contacts of a Private Secretary. These duties were undertaken by Gideon Matte, who had been in charge of the Prime Minister's last election campaign in Prince Albert. The two other members of the Prime Minister's secretariat who had the most frequent contacts with Mackenzie King during this period were Gordon Robertson, now Clerk of the Privy Council and Secretary to the Cabinet, and Ross Martin, now Registrar of Canadian Citizenship, both of whom were seconded from the Department of External Affairs.

Because of his former association as Parliamentary Assistant to Mackenzie King and because of his encyclopaedic concern with questions of policy and political organization, Brooke Claxton continued, after joining the Cabinet, to have a close and special relationship with the Prime Minister. The member of the Cabinet who had the greatest influence on Mackenzie King and on whose judgment he relied most during the whole period covered by this volume was St. Laurent. The other senior Ministers with the greatest influence were J. L. Ilsley and C. D. Howe. Although J. G. Gardiner was a considerable figure in the government, his personal relations with the Prime Minister were not close and, indeed, were often strained. Ian Mackenzie continued to have a close personal relationship with the Prime Minister until shortly before his retirement from the Cabinet, but his influence on affairs declined rapidly. J. A. MacKinnon and Humphrey Mitchell had good personal relations with Mackenzie King, though their weight in the Cabinet was not great.

Of the newer members of the Cabinet, three men, in addition to Claxton, had a steadily growing influence on the Prime Minister and increasing weight in the Cabinet. They were D. C. Abbott, Lionel Chevrier and Paul Martin.

The first session of the new Parliament elected on June 11, 1945, was to open on September 6, 1945, and the customary agonizing preparations for the session were under way. In the new Parliament, the government had a small majority of about ten Members over all Opposition parties. John Bracken had been elected to Parliament and was about to assume the duties of Leader of the Opposition with a substantially larger number of Conservative Members than there had been in the two previous Parliaments. The C.C.F. had elected the largest number of Members it had achieved up to that time or since. The Social Credit membership was virtually unchanged by the election.

The government and the new Parliament were faced with the problems of demobilization and reconstruction for which most of the foundations had been laid during the closing months of the war. For Mackenzie King the whole perspective of the immediate post-war months was suddenly changed by the defection of a young cipher clerk from the Soviet Embassy. For many months the Gouzenko affair and relations between the Western world and the Soviet Union became Mackenzie King's main preoccupations. During this period, St. Laurent soon came to be, in fact though not in name, the Deputy Prime Minister.

THE MACKENZIE KING MINISTRY, AUGUST 1945

Prime Minister, President of the Privy Council and Secretary of State for External Affairs	W. L. Mackenzie King
Minister of Veterans Affairs	Ian A. Mackenzie
Minister of Finance and Receiver General	J. L. Ilsley
Minister of Munitions and Supply and Minister of Reconstruction	C. D. Howe
Minister of Agriculture	James G. Gardiner
Minister of Trade and Commerce	James A. MacKinnon
Minister of National Defence for Air	Colin W. G. Gibson
Minister of Justice and Attorney General	Louis S. St. Laurent
Minister of Labour	Humphrey Mitchell
Minister of Public Works	Alphonse Fournier
Postmaster General	Ernest Bertrand
Minister of National Health and Welfare	Brooke Claxton
Minister of Mines and Resources	James A. Glen
Solicitor General	Joseph Jean
Minister of Transport	Lionel Chevrier
Secretary of State of Canada	Paul Martin
Minister of National Defence and Minister of National Defence for Naval Service	Douglas C. Abbott
Minister of National Revenue and Minister of National War Services	J. J. McCann
Minister of Fisheries	H. F. G. Bridges
Minister without Portfolio and Leader of the Government in the Senate	Wishart McL. Robertson

CHAPTER TWO

The Gouzenko Affair

MACKENZIE KING's diary entries for August 1945 reflected great weariness and something approaching dread at the prospect of meeting the new Parliament. He also foresaw the possibility of having to go abroad while the session was under way. A despatch from the British Prime Minister, which Mackenzie King read on August 26, suggested that the Commonwealth prime ministers might come to the United Kingdom when the Council of Foreign Ministers met to discuss a European peace settlement. "This communication may be viewed from two sides," the Prime Minister wrote. "First, it is in part an effort to meet Evatt in his very right but very abrupt and outspoken attacks on the way Britain has ignored Australia. On the other hand, it is clearly an effort to work into one foreign policy. The use of the words 'Identical view' makes that quite clear. I do not intend being pulled away from our Parliament again just as soon as it reassembles though I confess that a trip overseas with a comparatively easy month in Britain would afford a real rest now that the war is over. I am inclined, however, in planning, to think of something that might take me to South America instead. I really need a complete rest and change."

Two days later he worked with Robertson and Wrong on a draft reply to Attlee's despatch. "They had drafted something along the lines I had indicated. A rather strong message in one particular, letting the British see quite clearly I did not think it was good enough to have Canada sit on the sidelines to be called if and when it suited the U.K. government to confer on something; particularly after Canada's part in the war we really deserved to be represented on the Council of Foreign Ministers, which would be making the preparations for the peace.

"It stressed particularly the necessity of Cabinets making decisions, not individuals. Also the desire of Canada not to have followed in postwar matters the pattern of a big 3, 4 or 5, to make everything themselves in advance of final settlement." But Mackenzie King did not put the idea of going to the United Kingdom entirely out of his head.

He spent September 3 working on the Speech from the Throne for the session due to open three days later. In the speech, he wrote, "I have embodied pretty well the main thesis underlying my 'Industry and Humanity.' I have managed to insert as the Government's policy the promotion of peace, work and health. Also references to both 'Industry and Humanity' and other references to vision. I feel greatly pleased at having decided to include in the Speech from the Throne a paragraph regarding a Canadian flag; also a reference to the improvement of the Capital as a national memorial, and a paragraph regarding Canadian citizenship. This all helps to round out in good fashion policies that have been nearest to my heart: first in regard to Canada's position as a nation in all respects equal as far as status goes to that of any other nation, and furthering international peace, social security, equality of opportunity, and improvement of the standard of living for all the people. I have reason to be deeply grateful for the opportunity of furthering these great purposes. I have sought to make the most of it in the present speech. Also the speech itself contains a profession of my belief in this world being ruled by moral law and what has been achieved of victory in the recent war we owe to God's mercy. I have tried to have the speech follow logically on those which have preceded it and which, taken altogether, reveal a fine programme of state policy."

The labour of revision took most of September 4. The Prime Minister read the speech to the Cabinet in the late afternoon. "There were very few suggested changes or additions. I myself was determined to get another paragraph on the programme regarding health and welfare; also something more in the way of recognition of labour workers, and people in the war services. Ilsley strongly opposed making any reference to lessening of taxation, except mentioning that taxation matters would be dealt with in the budget – which is quite right." At this meeting also, he "got through an Order in Council regarding the flag, which I had asked Arnold Heeney to prepare a little earlier. This will mean that the Canadian red ensign will be on the peace tower the day on which the 20th Parliament opens. I think this matter has been brought along by stages very successfully." The final text of the speech was not finished until after 10 o'clock that night.

Parliament was to meet at 11.00 A.M. on September 6 so that the House of Commons could elect a speaker before the formal opening that afternoon. When the Prime Minister arrived at his office about 10.45 A.M. he was surprised to find Robertson and Wrong waiting for him. In his special secret diary he noted that both were looking very serious. "Robertson said to me that a most terrible thing had happened. It was like a bomb on top of everything and one could not say how serious it might be or to what it might lead. He then told me that this morning, just half an hour or so earlier, a man had turned up, with his wife, at the office of the Minister of Justice. He asked to see the Minister. He said he was from the Russian Embassy. That he was threatened with deportation and that once he was deported, that would mean certain death. That the Russian democracy was different than ours.

"He went on to say that he had in his possession documents that he had taken from the Embassy and was prepared to give to the Government. They would be seen to disclose that Russia had her spies and secret service people in Canada and in the U.S. and was practising a species of espionage. That some of these men were around Stettinius in the States, and that one was in our own Research Laboratories here (assumedly seeking to get secret information with regard to the atomic bomb). He indicated that he had had to do with the cyphering of messages. Robertson was not sure that he did not have the cypher code book with him. At any rate, he said that he had enough evidence there to prove that instead of being friends, the Russians were really enemies.

"The Secretary [in the office of the Minister of Justice] had talked with Mr. St. Laurent who thought it best not to see him. Robertson and Wrong were asking my advice, whether they should not have the mounted police take him in hand and secure the documents which he had. The man when he was told that the Minister of Justice would not see him, then said that he would have to commit suicide right there. There could be no hope for him because when the vault was opened at the Embassy, they would discover there that the papers had gone and would know that he had taken them. I said to both Robertson and Wrong that I thought we should be extremely careful in becoming a party to any course of action which would link the Government of Canada up with this matter in a manner which might cause Russia to feel that we had performed an unfriendly act. That to seek to gather information in any underhand way would make clear that we did not trust the Embassy. The man might be only a crank trying to preserve his own life. If he had information of the kind in his possession during the war, he should have given it to us at that time, if he had wanted to help the Government. It looked as though he was trying to make out a case which would cause our Government to protect him which, of course, he admitted was what he wanted.

"Robertson seemed to feel that the information might be so important both to the States and to ourselves and to Britain that it would be in their interests for us to seize it no matter how it was obtained. He did not say this but asked my opinion. I was strongly against any step of the kind as certain to create an issue between Russia and Canada, this leading to severance of diplomatic relations and as Robertson pointed out, might have consequences on the meeting of the Council of Foreign Ministers which might lead even to the breaking up of that organization."

After the proceedings in the House were concluded in the afternoon, St. Laurent remained behind at the House of Commons to tell the Prime Minister about what had taken place at his office. "I had Robertson come over," Mackenzie King wrote. "We learned later that the Russian man had left saying he was going to his own flat; that there was nothing but suicide ahead of him. Again, Robertson thought of getting the police to seize the papers. I suggested that a Secret Service man in plain clothes watch the premises. If suicide took place let the city police take charge and this man to follow in and secure what there was in the way of documents, but on no account for us to take the initiative. Robertson then thought of himself going to the Embassy and stating what this man had said. Both St. Laurent and I counselled against that course. We felt it was better to let things come out wholly apart from the Government itself. Robertson seemed to feel there was a danger of the press obtaining the information and it might spread to anywhere. Both St. Laurent and I felt that no matter what happened we should not let it be assumed that the Government of Canada had itself sought to spy on the Embassy or to take advantage of a situation of the kind to find out something against a trusted ally. As Robertson says, however, it makes the whole question of suspicion of Russia greater than ever.

"Later in the day we learned that the man had gone to the Supreme Court and had sought to become naturalized. He had told the Secretary of a Judge who was there the same story he told the Justice Department. While he was telling the story to the Secretary, a man named O'Meara a loose-footed [*sic*] journalist was in the room and heard the conversation. Robertson wondered if the press should be warned. Both St. Laurent and I felt it would be unwise for us to be a party in any way. The press would have to realize they might be involved in a libel action if they published material that was libelous. Robertson at one stage expressed the situation as that of the possibility of our being a party to suicide on one hand if we did not get the papers, and protect the man, and murder on the other if we allowed him to fall into the hands of the Embassy which would send him back to Russia where he would be executed. There was this aspect to consider, but it was clear that we could not save the individual situation by any course we could take, but we might involve the countries in an open breach. . . .

"My own feeling is that the individual has incurred the displeasure of the Embassy and is really seeking to shield himself. I do not believe his story about their having avowed treachery. There is no doubt that most countries have their secret spies, but that is another matter. For us to come into possession of a secret code book – of a Russian secret code book – would be a source of major complications."

The next day (September 7) the Prime Minister telephoned Robertson to get the latest information. "I said to him I was 'phoning to find out if he was still alive. He told me he was but that the night's events had not given him much rest. He then told me that the man from the Russian Embassy had gone to his flat at night, but that he and his family had gone over later to another flat. The behaviour of the man in his own flat had caused the occupants of the other apartments to send for the city police. They had a car patrolling around in readiness to take the man anywhere.

"At 12 midnight four men from the Embassy, two from the staff and two others, came to the apartment and not getting a reply they forced the door open and got in. They made a search but were not able to discover anything. It was at this stage that the local police asked the assistance of the R.C.M.P. – of this I am not certain. At any rate, it was between 2 and 3 A.M. that word was sent to Robertson that the man wanted to make some statement to the R.C.M.P. This was arranged for and this morning at an early hour his statement was taken and the whole matter has been brought officially by the police to the attention of the Minister of Justice. When Robertson 'phoned me no word had been sent to the Embassy by our Government but once the Minister of Justice has concluded the review – I am dictating this at 11 A.M. – the Ambassador will be asked to come over or to send someone and he will be told of the information given the Government.

"I asked about the documents. Robertson said they were still in the man's possession. They might be turned over by him to the police. If they were they would be given back to the Embassy and possibly the police, meanwhile, might photostat copies. He did not say they would or that they had been instructed so to do.

"Someone at the head of the British Secret Intelligence had come to the Seigniory Club yesterday [Sir William Stephenson, head of British Security Coordination in New York]. He came up and saw Robertson last night. Robertson will a little later tell me of his talks with him on the whole situation. This man returned to the Seigniory Club at night. I am glad I insisted on Robertson not going down but having him come up. Robertson obviously is greatly fatigued. I will get further developments later. Dictated this while it was in my mind."

The proceedings of the second day of the session were brief; much of the day was taken up by a Cabinet meeting, a garden party at Earnscliffe, and a private dinner at Government House in the evening. Before the Prime Minister went to Government House, Robertson came to Laurier House. He "said that during the day the police kept questioning the man. He had not in the afternoon heard what had come out of the questioning, but fortunately we were in the position that seizure had been made by the local police who had called in assistance of R.C.M.P., and that now the R.C.M.P. were guarding the situation. They would see that the man and his family were secreted and would not be seized.

"After I got back from the garden party at Earnscliffe – it is always the way – the moment I take an hour or two off for social events, most important events come up. I would have given much to have been free of both Earnscliffe and Government House today – saw Robertson. His voice betrayed a tremendous concern. He said he had got particulars of what the police had and that everything was much worse than we would have believed. First of all he mentioned that all the documents had been photostated. The originals were with the Police still but we would have records now, and knew what was in them. They disclose an espionage system on a large scale. He said that it went lengths we could not have believed. Not only had Stettinius been surrounded by spies, etc., and the Russian Government been kept informed of all that was being done from that source, but that things came right into our own country to a degree we could not have believed possible. He then told me that they went into our own Department of External Affairs, that in the cypher room there was an agent of the Russians who had seen and knew all our cyphers and had known what they contained. The same was true at Earnscliffe. In the cypher room at Earnscliffe M. MacDonald's despatches were all seen, read and known. In our Research Laboratories here at Ottawa, where we had been working on the atomic bomb, there is a scientist who is a Russian agent. In the Research Laboratories in Montreal where most of the work was done there is an English scientist who is pro Russian and acting as a Russian agent.

"He said at the Russian agency [sic] the man said there was the freest talk among themselves about the next war. He also said it was the Military Attaché of the Embassy [Colonel Nicolai Zabotin] who had really been a direct agent of the Russian Government and was directing the proceedings for the Government in Canada. This man had been one of the pleasantest men that he, Robertson, had had to deal with. He said he thought he would try to get in touch with Stephenson in New York, along with F.B.I. men from the United States. He felt that what we had discovered might affect the whole meeting of the Council of Foreign Ministers; that if publicity were given to this it might necessarily lead to a break in diplomatic relations between Canada and Russia and might also lead to that in regard to other nations as well, the U.S. and the U.K. All of this might occasion a complete break-up of the relations that we have been counting upon to make the peace. There was no saying to what terrible lengths this whole thing might go."

The Prime Minister authorized Robertson to inform the British High Commissioner and the American Ambassador of the situation "at a proper time" but "advised very strongly ... against taking any quick steps, any public disclosures, at any early moment. We must get the whole case as fully worked out as we possibly can. Avoid arrests, etc. Keeping an eye on everything and everyone.

"Robertson said he had never been suspicious in his life. He felt now there was something that was real which had to be faced. What he felt most of all was that the people who were helping in this kind of thing were people supposed to be of the highest types of character. He doubted in some cases if it was at all for money. There was a sort of idealism of the Russian revolution which sought to get human rights for the masses of the people and this became a religion with some persons and they were prepared to do anything to further that movement. I think myself it is of course all part of a world revolution – a world communist movement to get on the part of workers a control of the Government completely out of the hands of those who have privilege, power, etc. But he, Robertson, says that democracy in Russia is not understood by our people. It is really a Russian imperialism – an autocracy of the most desperate and wicked kind, but they are using the language of idealism and words and symbols which while being used and understood by us in one way have a different meaning to them and have become symbols for this power of the world-controlled business."

Mackenzie King went out to Kingsmere that night and the next morning (September 8) got in touch with Robertson again. "He told me that the Embassy was now demanding to know where this man was and wanted to get hold of him. I told him to make sure that they [the Russian Embassy] did not get out some writ of habeas corpus which might compel the officers to deliver them up. . . . He did not tell me where the man and his family were secreted, but I said I felt that at all costs we must not let him come into the hands of the Embassy people. He said there is no doubt that the police feel that the man would have been killed or would allegedly have committed suicide, had the two men from the Embassy and the two others that had been with them been able to get hold of him the night before last. He said this man is telling them everything and we will have a very full and complete story. Robertson said that Stephenson and F.B.I. representatives would be here tonight. I told him I would be available to come in from Kingsmere at any moment."

In the evening the Prime Minister telephoned Robertson again, who reported that he had seen Malcolm MacDonald, the British High Commissioner, that morning. "He said he was calling Mackenzie [president of the National Research Council] this moment to let him know what relates to our own Research Department. Two on the British side will be coming up tonight and F.B.I. men will be here in Ottawa on Monday morning. Meanwhile a letter had come today from the Russian Embassy asking for the man, claiming that he had stolen money from the Embassy and I think Robertson said should be held for capital punishment. He says the man is out in the country. We have him secure. Robertson suggested we send no answer to the Russian note until Monday. I have asked him to see if, meanwhile, some steps cannot be taken whereby this man can be held by the Crown in a way that will prevent the Russians getting near him at all. Robertson said of course the man himself is clinging to us, would not leave on any account. To do so would mean certain death for him. Robertson feels, with the background of what we know, the letter from the Embassy is impudent."

The day before, at the garden party at Earnscliffe, Mackenzie King had chatted with the Soviet Ambassador and his wife. "I spoke to both of them and talked in a very natural and free way. I thought he looked quite concerned. Indeed, he had a very anxious look on his face.

"Zaroubin told me he had received from his Government a communication – from Stalin – indicating that Stalin wished to confer on General Crerar some high order from Russia for his service in the war. He asked me if there would be any objection at all. He told me he would be writing me on it. I said I thought it was exceedingly kind of the Russian Government. I could not see there would be any objection. It was an honour that I thought could be bestowed, but said I would look into the matter more when the letter was received.

"I talked with Olga [a secretary of the Russian Embassy] and her husband. . . . They both seemed quite cheerful. It is extraordinary that we should meet right in the U.K. grounds at Earnscliffe."

On Sunday, September 9, immediately after breakfast, Mackenzie King had another telephone conversation with Robertson and discovered that the Soviet Embassy was still pressing the Department of External Affairs for help in finding Igor Gouzenko. "Later tonight I 'phoned Robertson after returning to Laurier House. He had told Malcolm MacDonald and they had agreed on a communication to the British Foreign Office giving outline of what we knew and suggesting that at my instance Byrnes, the

U.S. Secretary of State, should be advised, so as to have this knowledge before the Council of Foreign Ministers met. Robertson and I both agreed that great caution must be used from now on in the matter of avoiding any kind of publicity, hoping that matters can be straightened out without the public ever becoming aware of what had taken place."

The Prime Minister was scheduled to reply to John Bracken in the debate on the Speech from the Throne on September 10 but the Gouzenko affair continued to be his main preoccupation. He met Robertson and Malcolm MacDonald at the House of Commons before the opening of proceedings. They told him that "on Sunday night the head of the Research work in Montreal was here to confer with them concerning the member of the Research Department there who was named by the Russian as being in communication with Russian agents. Gusenko [sic] is the name of the member of the Russian Embassy who has given the Government the information. Apparently he is not on the regular staff of the Embassy, but was associated with the Military Attaché of the Embassy.

"Professor A. N. May, a graduate of Cambridge University, England, a physicist of high repute, one who is almost second in the knowledge pertaining to the atomic bomb, and who knows practically all that has been done in Canada and the United States is the one in question at Montreal. He came out to further this research work shortly after beginning of the war. It was clear from information that has come into the Government's hands that he has been communicating with Moscow and that he may be leaving at any time. Robertson and Malcolm both represented that if he got away to Moscow he would be able to inform the authorities there of everything within his knowledge. He already has priorities on a plane leaving for England this week. The question was what should be done with him. Robertson strongly advised the passing of a special Order in Council very secretly which would re-enact certain clauses of the Defence of Canada Regulations, so far as May was personally concerned, which would enable us to have him watched by the police and if necessary arrest him; also to see that he did not get away with papers, etc. To this I agreed and signed the recommendation to Council which was to get the signatures of four Ministers: Ilsley, Howe, Abbott and myself – only enough to be told the others to justify their signing. Nothing to be said to the rest of the Cabinet. The Order to be kept in the vault of the Clerk of the Council. I immediately signed the recommendation which was subsequently signed by other Ministers. First copy made by Heeney of the Order passed and then signed by myself. Having completed the conversation with Robertson and MacDonald, I went into the House.

"Robertson told me that the head of the British Secret Service had sent two of his men to Ottawa. They had been given particulars and one at least was leaving by 'plane to give the information to Cadogan, the Under-Secretary of the Foreign Office, the Foreign Minister to be advised, and he to advise Mr. Byrnes, Secretary of State of the U.S. The F.B.I. representatives arrived this morning and were given information by Robertson."

In the circumstances, Mackenzie King was quite unhappy about his speech in the House. "Altogether," he wrote, "I was never less prepared for a speech which, having regard to the war and the opportunities that were offered by the cessation of the war should have been an historic one. I spoke for exactly an hour. Made a few points but was far from happy about the way in which I expressed myself and I am sure the speech was a disappointment to all on our side. However I noticed that the Conservatives did not interrupt me once. Having made a brief speech it was that much to the good. Before I had finished I found my mind getting so completely weary it would have been useless to try to go on and say anything about either the war memorial, citizenship, flag or any of these matters. Indeed when I saw that Bracken and Coldwell both endorsed the idea of beautification of the Capital and that no one made a reference to the flag, I thought it just as well not to stir up discussion on either of these subjects. Speaking was so brief that for a time it looked as though the debate might end today if we had had our men here; it would have been good policy to have brought it to a close. Unfortunately several were away. The French boys were not here and others also were away and if a division had come and the Opposition had united we would have been defeated. In the circumstances, it seemed best to keep the debate going until later this evening."

"I feel very strongly this evening," he added later in the day, "as though I should drop out of public life at once. Not attempt to go on. I can see that there is going to be nothing but embarrassment of the Government from day to day and week to week. I am too weary to be able to meet situations as they arise. The things that I was wholly familiar with this afternoon, I could not find strength to express. This is a condition which no responsible leader should be in in times like the present."

The domestic political situation could give Mackenzie King no comfort. With the end of the war, trade union militancy had re-emerged and left-wing leaders became prominent in assaults on the federal government's economic policies. Maintenance of war-time controls was attacked and a wave of strikes hit many sectors of the economy. On the morning of September 11 the Prime Minister was surprised to discover that he was scheduled to meet a delegation of trade union leaders with some of his Cabinet colleagues. "The press is making a terrible mistake in lending itself to the kind of demonstrations that have been started. However, I felt it would only be giving the agitators what they wanted if I did not turn up, so decided to be present. I 'phoned Mitchell and Howe. Both agreed and I met with them and Martin and Claxton in the Labour Department. It was interesting to see how the furnishings in the Minister's room there do not look a bit different than when I ordered them for the Government forty-five years ago. Not a scratch on one as far as I could see.

"As I went into the Confederation Block – the meeting was held in the Minister's office – I met all the Committee at the entrance of the building. To their surprise I shook hands with them all. At the meeting I spoke briefly of the manner in which their request for a meeting had been sent. I spoke of Howe's position, also of the Government's desire to help in a period of difficulty, pointing out that there must be co-operation and the right kind of an approach. I stayed for an hour and listened to their representations and then left.

"One of the members of the delegation extended thanks . . . [for] my presence and shook hands as I went out. I am sure it was wise to have turned up.

"This, however, I want to record. I am told that all who were present were communists. Jackson, who did much of the speaking, was interned for three years during the war. Also one or two others were interned. One had just been dismissed from a position in a Labour Union. All had very dour and bitter countenances. I thought Jackson very skilful. On the other hand, I did feel, by trying to be as sympathetic as possible, that they were a hard and dangerous lot. Their presence in Ottawa and the kind of demonstrations they had been making, along with the presence today of another group of the seaman's union, demanding the retention of war bonus in time of peace, with what I learn of other movements, makes clear that Canada is more or less honeycombed with communist leaders who have a close association with the movement in the U.S. and that all are very closely associated with the movement in Russia. I became more convinced of this than ever when, after this meeting, I had a long talk with Robertson about the Russian Embassy situation."

Robertson gave the Prime Minister a complete account of what had taken place so far in the Gouzenko case. Gouzenko, himself, according to Robertson, "was for two years in the inner secret service at Moscow. He is one of three men who apparently know the whole method of espionage. He came out here with the Military Attaché of the Embassy a couple of years ago. He says that in Moscow their secret work is divided into three main divisions: (1) related to the political field; (2) to the scientific field, and the other, to the army. They have a secret service in their own service which spies upon its members. Even here, at Ottawa, there is one member who secretly watches the movements of all connected with the Embassy.

"Robertson thinks that this man, having seen how decently and fairly Canada had helped in the war, felt that he could not bear the burden of knowing what was going on and for that reason, wished to make a clean breast of things. More probably, he has in some way been suspected by the Embassy and was about to be sent back which, as he said, would mean certain death. He has tried to make it necessary for Canadian authorities to shield him, thereby saving his life. In this, he has succeeded. He has taken a desperate chance by bringing with him, out of the vault of the Russian Embassy, material which is beyond peradventure and which reveals the extent to which the Russians have the control of men in key positions in Canada.

"There are two at Montreal, one in the Research Laboratories here, and a woman in our External Affairs. Another in the High Commissioner's Office. Others in other positions. He has given us the names, places, etc. . . .

"This man, Gouzenko, had said that the day the atomic bomb was first used, there was tremendous excitement at the Embassy. They were accustomed there to talking about the next war. This had seemed to anticipate and possibly delay what might have been part of the plan. Combined with what Stalin had said at Potsdam, it would look as though the Russians had in mind no delay in asserting their further power. One of the most serious of all the documents found revealed that they had been asking for their men in the secret service here to give them a report on the strength of the American army and forces. The extent of demobilization; where they are and where located today, to give also strength as regards other of the Defence services. Robertson pointed out getting this information from Canada may have been to check on reports they were getting from other sources in the U.S. Perhaps the most serious thing of what he told me was that this man, May, the scientist at McGill, was preparing to leave this week-end. They have the papers which make clear that May is going over in connection with the atomic bomb plant which is about to be started in England. He is to have the direction of that plant. He has been asked to give the Russians full particulars of the localities where they will be established, mentioning the hills and areas round about. He has the information needed to start such a plant. Were his plans not to be interrupted, that would be the task now before him.

"In the papers seized, our Government now has the directions given him which show he is in contact with Moscow. He is, on reaching London, to go on a certain day to the front of the British Museum where he will contact the medium who is to carry the information to Moscow. He is to have in his pocket a certain magazine. The man he is to meet will have another magazine, name given, in his pocket. They will meet casually. Converse about certain subjects. Each has been advised that the other will know the subjects to be talked about. They will then arrange to meet elsewhere and to exchange information.

"We propose allowing May to leave on the 'plane, putting a secret service man with him. He will be followed when he reaches London and will be shadowed when this meeting is to take place so that the other man may also be known. Whether the meeting will take place now that these papers have been stolen from the safe is considered a chance. The Russians will know they are gone but they do not know they are in the hands of the Government. They might suspect this and not carry on further.

"This scientist, May, is a Britisher himself; distinguished graduate of Cambridge University. A man of about 45. It does not seem that money would be the attraction with him. Some belief in world revolution for the masses or something of the kind which is the kind of thing that large numbers of so-called idealists or others who have a hatred against social order as it exists, are prepared to take any steps to effect change. We have copies of excerpts. Also a statement compiled from our telegraphic despatches which have been made up by a woman in our cypher room. I asked Robertson who she is. Apparently she was a married woman; born in Canada of Russian parentage in the West. She was employed in the passport office. When passports were done away with and the need of cyphering became very great, she was one of twenty-five or thirty who were moved into External Affairs. She gives her information to some third party who gives it to the Russian Embassy. I pointed out to Robertson we had sent no messages that we need be concerned about. He agreed with that. On the other hand, we have received very full reports from the British Government of some conversations with Americans, which imply distrust of the Russians in regard to the European situation and how they are likely to act. This is the kind of thing that has been passed on.

"The whole business makes clear a vast espionage system. Among others in the Canadian service is someone in the engineering branch of the Army who has to do with the appliances used for military purposes. Gouzenko has been taken away by the Mounted Police. They have him, his wife and child in some unknown part, being guarded. He will be transferred to some other place later. In the meantime, additional information is being secured from him. The documents are all in the possession of the police. It is fortunate that at the start, we took the line we did."

The Prime Minister's first reaction was that he should see President Truman "and tell him what we knew. Robertson had yesterday on my authorization seen Atherton [the American Ambassador] but advised him to send nothing to the States but to allow matters to reach the President via the route we have chosen through the British Foreign Office, through Byrnes, Secretary of State. The State Department will then communicate with the President. We have not had any acknowledgment of any word which has been sent, thus far. The information will have been in the hands of the British Government and of the Americans before the meeting of the Council of Foreign Ministers today. I agreed it was all important we should not allow anything to be known, making no arrests but hold everything till the possibility of preventing disclosure no longer exists.

"Coming along with evidences of communistic tactics developing across Canada and as seen right in the city of Ottawa today, with cars labelled with attacks on the Government, other cars with loudspeakers spreading views as to what should be done to protect seamen's unions, etc., it is all very significant and very dangerous. There is a condition of social revolution which cannot be obliterated. Also with what we have discovered in Canada is going on here to the extent it appears to have gone, it is wholly certain that in the U.S. and in Britain something on a proportionate scale will also exist. This means that from now on, one must be guided in many things more by one's suspicions than by one's faith in certain people. I am greatly afraid that, without knowing it, Coldwell and his party have been lending themselves, unconsciously perhaps, to the spread of this old kind of communist influence. These men, I am sure, are planted in factories, etc. As Robertson says, the alleged abolishing of the Comintern is all nonsense. Theoretically, it may have been abolished but what we have seen shows it is in practice today as a world organization, powerfully financed and very skilfully directed.

"Churchill was right when he said it would not do to let the Russians have the secret of the atomic bomb. I thought Roosevelt was right when he said he felt an ally should know what we are doing in that regard. I can see that Churchill had the sounder judgment; had keener perceptions of what was at stake, what was going on.

"Robertson felt that at any moment word might come for us to go across to England. I hope this may not be necessary but if the request comes, one will have to meet it. After realizing how the war with Germany, Italy and Japan all came into being, one sees in this revelation a repetition of similar tactics but so far as any one nation goes, on a vaster scale than that planned by any one of the other three. Indeed this revelation gives one a new and more appalling outlook on the world than one has ever had before. Combined with the atomic bomb and what it may yet lead to, causes one to feel physically actually older in years than one has felt before. I cannot believe that this information has come to me as a matter of chance. I can only pray for God's guidance that I may be able to be an instrument in the control of powers beyond to help save a desperate situation, to maintain peace now that it has at least been nominally established."

On September 12 the Prime Minister went to the Liberal caucus and was given a fine reception by the members. "What struck me . . . when I began to speak was how relatively smaller the Caucus was than the ones of the last few years. There is a considerable diminution in our numbers. I began by nominating Golding as Chairman of the Caucus. Then spoke of Weir's appointment as Chief Whip. Of Blanchette's appointment as assistant Chief Whip. Then addressed the Caucus at some length speaking of my thoughts of uncertainty at the last Caucus as to where those present might be when today's Caucus was held. Expressed pleasure at return of many of the old Members. Regretted the loss of some of them. Extended a very cordial welcome to the new Members and congratulations on their win. Then spoke of the complexion of the House. Our small majority. What it meant in the way of necessity of attendance of Members; unwillingness of the Conservatives to grant continuing pairs for the session. The desirability of having our differences fought out in Caucus and to maintain unity in the House.

"Spoke particularly about this Parliament. How serious these problems would be. Spoke specially of social unrest and of there being a world movement which would manifest itself more clearly as the years went by. Spoke of relief at being free from war. . . .

"When Caucus was thrown open, there was much straight talking and criticizing of the Government by older Members. It began by Tommy Reid [MP for New Westminster]. There was particular criticism of the Tory appointees. Some of their actions during the election. Of the Wartime Prices and Trade Board. Much said against bureaucracy or officials. Government not paying attention to private Members. Customs officials described as gestapo. Some strange instances of unnecessary interference cited. Outspoken criticism of the rationing. Demand for increased indemnity, etc., etc. Caucus concluded at 1.00 P.M.

"I made a short speech in which I promised as had been agreed in Cabinet that something would be done in the way of improving the indemnities at this session. I felt that the Caucus had been a real success and was glad that this first step at party organization was over."

A long discussion on rationing in the Cabinet meeting on September 13 was stimulated by indications that the American government was planning an early end to most types of commodity rationing. "If they do, we will have to," Mackenzie King wrote. "It is a very difficult question. No doubt Europe needs help tremendously in the way of food. Whether our people can now be persuaded to do what they did in time of war it is difficult to say. We are beginning to see what limitations are placed on the Government with no War Measures Act and with a Party following that will not be too strictly obedient or subject to Party discipline. I think the control will more and more have to go."

An infinitely more serious problem, in the Prime Minister's judgment, was the implication for Canadian wheat sales and general price stability of the decision by the American government to allow the price of wheat to rise to $2.00 per bushel. "Our Board is advocating a like course in view of what the United States has done. Ilsley wants to hold the price at $1.55 [per bushel] for a period of years, in order to have wheat available for a long time and to have more of export credit stocks available for purchase of other commodities; also to prevent additional rises in the price of grain, etc. It is a sort of breaking of the price ceiling which may lead almost anywhere. It is the largest and most difficult problem the Government has had to decide. I am afraid there is no escaping a decision on the line that will allow the Government to continue in office, which means that the farmers must be given the same chance in Canada as in the States. I do not see at the moment how we can well control the situation otherwise, though I do believe the long-range view is more truly the correct one, from the ideal point of what is economically wise and the right one. The only thing is that it will probably never be reached because of the inevitable chaos that would follow the attempt meanwhile." The worsening labour situation was also discussed in the Cabinet. "Today, a large strike of 10,000 men at the Windsor Ford works has taken place. I notice one of the leaders speaks about it being a fight against poverty, oppression, etc. Those words are very significant, uttered at a time when men have never been as prosperous as they are today. I have no doubt the employers are to blame for chiselling down the collective bargain agreement. Unless the companies are prepared to be perfectly straight on collective bargaining, I think the whole business of industry will increasingly become socialized."

Mackenzie King reported on September 13 that he had been told that Senator Haig, the new leader of the Conservatives in the Senate, had praised the government's war effort quite highly, "and both he and Ballantyne made pleasant references to myself. Once I go out of public life the whole cry will be that the strength of the Party was in myself and that strength has now gone. I was pleased to read Arsenault's speech, in which a former Conservative, who is now on our side, referred to what I had done in keeping Canada united during the war as being marvellous. The Tories in attacking Quebec have overplayed their hand prior to and during the last election. They are in large part responsible for keeping themselves out of office. They themselves have done more in this way than any other force, just as our own men by internal dissensions, Hepburn, Ralston, and the like, have done more to weaken our position than aught else."

Mackenzie King was impressed by J. M. Macdonnell's maiden speech which he thought "remarkably good. Simply phrased and well arranged, given in a straightforward way. It is clear that he realizes the danger of socialism in its battle against free enterprise. I had him come to my office to extend personal congratulations to him."

At the Cabinet meeting on September 14, wheat policy was again discussed. "The United States are allowing the price of wheat to be sold to England to go from $1.50 to $2. Were we to do the same would mean allowing barley to increase, also other stocks. This would mean increase in price of livestock or increase in price of barley used in feeding. There would come also inability to hold the wage standard, and altogether the result would be very shortly the bursting of the price ceiling with rapid inflation of prices. Against that we have to consider holding the price of wheat where we now have it at $1.55 as the price fixed for sale to Britain, keeping it there while the American market, just beside us, will allow for a steady rise in the price of wheat. This to the benefit of American farmers. It seemed to be a question of whether we could count on our own party supporting us in such a policy. They could claim that we had no right to hold down our agricultural producers and unless the Members from agricultural industries stay by us the Government would not be able to hold its own in Parliament and might have to suffer defeat.

"After listening to all the pros and cons, I told the Cabinet frankly what the situation was and said we must be prepared to make a major decision. I pointed out it might be better to suffer defeat and leave it to another Government to bear the burden of consequences of the crash of the price ceiling, and that it would lead in Canada to inflation and later its consequences – to do this rather than take a step which would bring that situation down upon our own heads. I made clear my own view as I came to feel it more and more strongly that it would be better to hold at all costs to our anti-inflation policy which, as much as anything else, had won us the support and confidence of the Canadian people.

"Fortunately, Gardiner had suggested endeavouring to get a five-year contract with the British at the $1.55 price. He felt that if the farmers were guaranteed that price for five years that the wheat might go to that and had a guarantee we would not allow it to drop below a dollar they would gladly accept that situation. In the meantime it would help secure us a market in Europe. It would also help to have our credit given to England and European countries; used only in part on wheat, leaving much else for purchase of other commodities. It was felt that to make such an agreement might take some time, perhaps a year or two. When finally Ilsley said he was prepared to make the statement that apart from the agreement altogether, it would be our policy, all Council agreed to the course being adopted. For a time, however, it looked as if the whole business of price control might have to go completely.

"Howe said he could not hold his controls if controls on wheat were to go followed by other controls on agriculture, etc. This along with the meat rationing problem has given us much anxious thought. I was, however, tremendously relieved when we found a solution to what, at one moment, threatened to be the worst problem with which we have been faced. The United States should, as a matter of fact, have tried to work with us on this sale of wheat policy. There is now very little wheat left. The whole market has become a monopoly market. I recall years ago resenting strongly our trying to reduce acreage for growing of wheat and not developing every bit of ground we could get. I said the war would not be over before the demand would be very great. I could not get a majority of Council to support me but today they see how true that position was. It was part of the madness of the American policy of reducing acreage, burning surpluses, etc. – something equivalent to blasphemy."

On September 15 the Prime Minister took time to attend the wedding of Norman McLarty's daughter and was delighted to see how well the former Minister looked. The next morning he was shocked to learn that McLarty had died during the night. His sudden death and funeral added to Mackenzie King's growing concern over his own fatigue and depression. On September 19 he read a letter from T. V. Soong which the Chinese Ambassador had handed to him the previous day at McLarty's funeral. Soong, who was returning to China, warned the Prime Minister to watch his health and advised a complete rest. The letter made a great impression. "I really should plan to get away without further delay," Mackenzie King wrote. "I have felt this morning more depressed and used up than I have for a long time past. So much so that I doubt if I could have gone into a meeting of the Cabinet and stood any kind of discussion there without breaking down. I feel that my nerves are already exhausted and that somehow somewhere I must get some change. Physically I am and look in the best of condition but I am very weary and I feel a tremendous reaction from the strain of the last few years and this year in particular. I simply cannot abide the contention of the House of Commons or indeed that of the country where the Government is being criticized for unpreparedness and strikes are threatening and the like, when I know that what we have done has been the best record of any government anywhere and I believe at any time so far as our country's name and place in the world is concerned."

The choice was between a complete rest in the south and going across the Atlantic. He realized that "there would be much advantage in going to England and to Europe at this time, first to talk over matters with the British Government, to get an insight into conditions as they are there, and really discover trends with respect to the making of peace; also to visit Europe and see conditions at first hand as they have resulted from the war and as they bear upon such problems as that of relief to be sent from Canada, etc. There would not be an actual physical rest in a trip of the kind. It is not, however, physical rest that I need so much as getting away from the things that arouse fresh complexes in one's mind and which unfit one for work. A completely new centre of interests for a time would do much I believe to refresh one's mind, to be able to contact public men in a quiet way, not with some overhanging obligation, will enable me to get a knowledge of affairs that I could not well secure in other ways. One thing I feel is certain. I cannot hope to go on through this Parliament, to take any real part in its discussions, and avoid something in the nature of a breakdown. The slightest effort at speaking in public today seems to completely undermine me. I am getting no real joy out of my work or personal or social contacts, simply jaded and exhausted nervously.

"On thinking matters over, I decided I would talk things over with R. [Robertson] and we had an hour and a half together. I told him of what was in my mind but said at the same time I thought what applied to me applied, if not in equal, in a larger measure to him. I felt he should take some kind of a trip and a change, whether along the lines I had suggested or not. I would like him to decide himself. I asked him to be perfectly frank in saying whether he would rather take a trip on his own or whether he would care to join in a trip with myself along the lines I had indicated, feeling of course free to make his own engagements as we went along but working together in connection with departmental and governmental matters while we were away. I could see a visible change in R's expression when I spoke to him. He said he doubted the wisdom of a trip to the South at this time but he very strongly favoured a trip to Europe. He said he would much prefer going with me to going alone and felt that it would be a distinct advantage to him and to the Department if we could take up a number of matters at first hand in England and on the Continent which eally needed looking into. Referred among other things to the Council of Foreign Ministers and probable developments re the Peace Conference.

"The position of our Legations, their staffs and need of men. Need for opening an Embassy in Berlin. I suggested talks with Attlee, [Lord] Addison, the new Minister and others as well as a visit to France and Germany and possibly to Italy so as to really see what has taken place during the war and to get fresh knowledge and inspiration with regard to the problems facing Europe this winter and which are linked so closely to policies on this side. Other matters such as financial relations with Britain and the like needed looking into. I suggested a visit to Washington in the first instance and crossing by steamer rather than by plane, and that on one of the Queen boats from New York if accommodation were better in that way. We could return by the South if the season were bad. R. was all for a trip by sea and named many matters which he thought we could work out together."

After his talk with Robertson, the Prime Minister saw St. Laurent, showed him the letter from Soong, and outlined his plans. "St. Laurent responded as I felt he would by saying that, of course, one should not delay if one felt consequences might be serious. He said that at this session, redistribution would not come up. He thought most of the questions would be financial ones with Ilsley. The biggest one of all would be Canada's loan to Britain and that might not take final shape until next session. If redistribution could stand until then, he thought that perhaps I should settle the Members' indemnity with Ilsley before I left. He himself rather favoured Ilsley's suggestion to increase indemnities to $5,000 – $3,000 to be regarded as indemnity, and $2,000 for living expenses during the session. This would mean that men with small incomes would get a reasonable indemnity. Those with large incomes would not profit any by the increase."

Discussion then turned to "the larger question of the future. I told him he is the one I would like to have succeed me. He at once said that was out of the question. That in the interests of the party and the country, it was desirable to have a younger man. I asked him how old he was. He said: 65. He thought the party might well stay its years of this Parliament. Would probably go into opposition afterwards. A man should be chosen who is young enough to come back after a few years in opposition.

"I said I agreed that that was probably what would be best. I thought the Conservative party had made a mistake in having Bracken at his years undertake the leadership. He would be too old when it came to the next election if he has not changed meanwhile. St. Laurent said he thought I should ask Ilsley to be acting Prime Minister while I was away. I said that as Ilsley had most of the programme, it was best perhaps to do that but I would like him to more or less take my place in the House. He said something about Mackenzie having taken the lead in Council as the oldest P.C. in running through the programme. I said I thought he St. Laurent had better do that. But he said, no. It was best to let Ilsley take that on. It may be I shall have to arrange to have Mackenzie act as President of the Council. I told St. Laurent I would like him to take External Affairs which he said he would be ready to do. Wrong would be here and would give him the material on the San Francisco Conference, etc."

That evening the Liberal Members from Quebec gave a dinner for the Prime Minister. After the new Members had been called on, Mackenzie King was asked to speak and, in his judgment, "made . . . perhaps the most effective speech I have made within the Halls of Parliament in years. I discarded what had been suggested and took up principally the position of the party last autumn; how near we were to chaos in Canada and complete disruption of the party. Spoke of St. Laurent and the French Ministers having saved the situation. Dwelt on what I owed to Quebec by way of the numbers returned at present, arising out of a remark by the Member for Wright hoping I might be one of his constituents for many years. Told him I had had land in Quebec for forty-five years past and had four hundred acres there now. That Kingsmere meant everything to me. I then spoke of Laurier House and what it meant; then of Sir Wilfrid and the talk we had together the time that he spoke of my succeeding him. I mentioned to them how I had said that I would not be able to have any following, and that he had replied to me that as long as I lived, I would have the Province of Quebec at my back. I then went on to say that it was because of my loyalty to him in 1917 when all others were deserting him. I then spoke of loyalty. In referring to the men who left us last autumn, who had gone to the other side, etc., I quoted a passage from the Scriptures that there was more joy in the presence of angels over one sinner [who repents] than ninety-nine just men who had no need for repentance. There were at least a dozen of them present. I went on to say that while we welcomed them back, I hoped that none of them would ever cross the floor again. I then spoke of the need of French Canadians regarding themselves as Canadians in the big sense of the word. Referred to their years in Canada and of asserting their rights as Canadians but also of taking a large view of Canada to get over the provincialism.

"I spoke of the change that had come over the world from the moment the atomic bomb fell over a city in Japan and that the past and the future were divided by a line which would mean that in the future, no province could stay by itself, and no country. We had better realize that our security was bound up in world co-operation and friendship with all nations. I spoke quite a bit of a political party and what it meant. Told them what I was most concerned about last autumn was not the loss of power myself but seeing a great instrument for benefit of my fellow-men being destroyed. I mentioned I came from a stock that had been prepared to give its all for developing responsible government in Canada. Prepared to face exile and if need be execution in standing for their rights and as I saw the Liberal party, it had developed from the struggle of that hour to this when the Red Ensign was flying on the Tower of the Parliament Buildings. I pointed in that direction. I really felt myself inspired when I was speaking and there was tremendous applause.

"I then pointed out how Liberalism stood for the people, increasing the opportunities of the people. Referred to the Victorian era and the luxury, etc., of the few being based on the toil of the many. Said I was glad the many were now asserting their rights and spoke of the mission which newer M.P.'s would have in Parliament in furthering Liberal traditions. I kept emphasizing the party being an intangible reality and of the advantages it afforded for companionship, friendship, etc. Next only to what one found in one's own home. It was quite touching the way Members one after the other spoke in affectionate terms of myself. Some, quite openly. Said they had been wrong in their views last year. Others that they hoped I would continue to lead for many years to come, etc. There was an impressive silence when I got up to speak, and at the end, I was given a real ovation, all Members standing and cheering."

On September 20, Mackenzie King informed J. L. Ilsley of his intention to go abroad and asked him to become Acting Prime Minister for the period. "His face lighted up with a joyous expression when I made this suggestion. He did not seem too depressed at the thought of my being absent though he did say that there were a number of important matters to be decided. He assumed these might be settled before I left. He mentioned what he thought right on the tax deduction. Personally I was surprised he was prepared to go as far as he is. Howe thinks it is not far enough. Towers of the Bank thinks it is too much. I asked him about the indemnity. His thought is to have the matter settled by a Bill and leave the indemnity where it is but make an allowance for living expenses of so much per year to date from the time a Member officially is sworn in. I think he has worked out an excellent solution. I pointed out that most of the work of the session was financial measures which would come under him."

On Saturday, September 22, Mackenzie King drove from Montreal with Ernest Bertrand to Godbout's farm at Frelighsburg for a huge and highly political picnic in honour of the Quebec Liberal leader's birthday. He drove back to Montreal with Claxton who, on the way, suggested the appointment of A. D. Dunton as president of the Canadian Broadcasting Corporation. "I told him to feel him out to see if he would be interested."

Back in Ottawa, Mackenzie King kept an appointment at Earnscliffe on Sunday evening to discuss the Gouzenko case with Sir William Stephenson and several other Canadian and British intelligence officers. "The first question discussed was the alternative method re security; one was to allow everything to be hushed up and not proceeded further; another was to take action at once and let the British and U.S. governments know the situation with a view to taking what steps might be best to prevent further developments. The third was adopting a course which would make the whole thing public, immediate arrests made and getting additional information at trials, etc. My own view was that the second course was the appropriate one, and I found that that was the view that appeared to be generally held. It was discussed in relation to the larger question of what was wisest from the diplomatic and political points of view. We all agreed it would not do to let the matter pass as though it were something which should not be disclosed to the Russians, nor would it do to have publicity given to the whole business at this time. That the best course would be to have the British and United States Governments and ourselves work together on the highest level, and let the Russians know what we know with a view to discovering from them whether they intended to really try to be friends and work for a peaceful world or whether a course should be taken toward them which would lead to having all nations against them.

"I strongly favoured the direct approach to them, once everything had been worked out at the highest level.

"The question then came about sending word to the British and to the Americans. A telegram went some days ago to the British Government but no reply has come yet. We do not know whether Byrnes, the United States Secretary of State, has been informed of what was sent to Bevin. The President knows nothing thus far."

According to Mackenzie King, there was general agreement that he should see President Truman before he went to England. "Wrong suggested he himself or Robertson might go in advance to acquaint Pearson [Canada's ambassador in Washington] with the situation so that he could let the Secretary of State Department know. I rather hesitated in giving a final answer saying I would want to consider how my going to Washington before leaving for England might appear in the eyes of our own public and how the British Ministers might view this course. I said I thought our attitude should be to keep both the Americans and the British properly informed. It was apparent from what the English specialist . . . said that the Russians have got a lot of information on the atomic bomb. It is apparent that it has come through their system of espionage. The head of our own Secret Service spoke of what was to be gained by making the whole business public in the way of stopping the Communist movement on the Continent. That to expose the whole thing might cause our people to cut away from the Russian influence altogether. While I feel this effect might be produced in small part, I believe the movement is much deeper and farther reaching than we imagine. I rather think that within the C.I.O. and other organizations, there is a determination to bring about a complete change whereby Labour will have control of Government. That the strikes today are symptomatic of the determination to force the issue. I really think that Labour throughout the world has come to believe as the Communists have stated, that its interests are one as against all other classes in society, and that in large part they are to hold to Marxian doctrines. The war itself I think has perhaps for the moment halted open co-operation on these lines but I believe that in another way it has helped to make co-operation underground more effective than it was even before. I regret to come to have the distrust that I have of any people. It is apparent, however, that the Russians have got as part of their Government, an organization which goes right to the top, a system of espionage in other countries, allies included, and have been gathering information which could hardly be expected for the service of an ally and of a character to be used against him when the moment comes. As Malcolm MacDonald said, by telling the Russians what we knew, if this had no effect, there would still be the way open to make the whole business public and let the whole world know the situation with which it is faced. I personally feel a great alarm at the encroachment which Russia is making in different parts of the world. So far as this continent is concerned, their possession now of part of the Kuriles, etc., makes clear their arm reaches right over our continent. Their agreement with China is, I think, only a paper affair. Either they will seek to control China through Communism at the right moment and have China as an ally for their purpose, or they will ignore her altogether, knowing how weak she is in the matter of effective organization. I have no doubt that Russia intends to develop the atomic bomb and to go all lengths in doing this. It looks to me as though she was already very far along the road. To try to fight a war with atomic bombs is just too appalling a thought for words. We are at the edge of a situation of the kind at this very hour."

Mackenzie King added: "I am dictating this today the *24th*. This morning before and after lunch, I spent in all two hours reading the complete statement of what the Secret Service men have secured. The names of those who are agents of the Russian service for espionage purposes, copies of documents that have passed to and fro, etc. They lead right into the Research Buildings here in Ottawa, the Laboratories in Montreal, to British scientists working there who have even more knowledge of the atomic bomb developments than almost anyone; to persons in our own External Affairs Department and in the Registry Office in Earnscliffe where all documents of a most secret sort have passed through the hands of one person in particular who has been supplying information. To Rose, a Member of Parliament; to editors of Canadian affairs, and to many other persons. The only explanation is the ideological one, which causes one to think deeply, namely, that large numbers of men and women have their hand out against society as it is constructed today, whereby there are certain leisure classes too largely controlling the government and industry, and a readiness to go any lengths in gaining for working men and women the fullest opportunities possible. The aim is all right but the terrible part is that with the Russians, use is made of that great human, one might even say Christian, desire for equality and freedom of all, to gain an imperialist control – a world control – the German conception of welt-politic. It is all very terrible and frightening. It is strange how this business should have come right into my room in the East Block on the morning of the Opening of the 20th Parliament. I can see that from now until the end of my days, it will be with this problem more than with any other that, in all probability, I shall be mostly concerned....

"As I dictate this note, I think of the Russian Embassy being only a few doors away and of there being there a centre of intrigue. During this period of war, while Canada has been helping Russia and doing all we can to foment Canada-Russian Friendship, there has been one branch of the Russian service that has been spying on all matters relating to location of American troops, atomic bombs, processes, etc. This first having to do with the army – reporting to army circles; another branch having to do with diplomatic and political questions, keeping headquarters of Russia informed of what might be going around by way of communication between the Americans, the British and ourselves, and yet another branch intended as a secret service, spying on themselves. It seems perfectly clear that chauffeurs, messengers, etc., are all a part of a political organization related to a great system of espionage. The amazing thing is how many contacts have been successfully made with people in key positions in government and industrial circles. I am sure the whole business extends much further than we begin to know. I am also sure that what has taken place in Canada, is taking place even under a vaster scale in the United States and Britain. I am almost certain also in other countries as well.

All this helps to explain the Russian attitude at the Council of Foreign Ministers. Something very sinister there. Also at San Francisco in blocking whatever seemed to stand in Russia's way to increase her power and world control."

On September 25, the Prime Minister received from Malcolm MacDonald "a communication from Lord Addison expressing appreciation on his own behalf and on that of Mr. Bevin of my readiness to come to England; a communication which referred to how serious the situation was as affecting the whole Commonwealth. It is a significant document in more ways than one."

The nagging, but politically sensitive, issue of an increase in the members' sessional indemnity continued to divert the Prime Minister's attention from the Gouzenko affair as he made preparations for his trip. The restiveness of the Liberal caucus was quite apparent at a meeting on September 26 which Mackenzie King attended. Most members had agreed to press for a taxable indemnity of $4,000 with an additional $2,000 free of tax to cover expenses connected with House business. The Minister of Finance was prepared to make some minor concessions on the non-taxable portion of the indemnity but, according to Mackenzie King, "dwelt on the difficulties to which a change ... would give rise, in the way of making it hard to hold ceilings of salaries, wages, etc. What he said was received in silence. There was no applause. I admire Ilsley for his courage but he lacks political judgment and wisdom. He may find he will break through refusing to bend before a storm. I thought the case they [the members of caucus] made out today in the light of what is being done in other countries, was a very strong one."

The Prime Minister informed the caucus of his decision to go abroad. "I explained to them the nature of the invitation from Attlee, the reasons it was not accepted – of my unwillingness simply to be present, not to be consulted and participate fully in the discussions. There was applause at this and also because of the invitation before the House had met. I stated I could not possibly leave a first session of a new Parliament until the vote on the Address had been agreed to and I was sure the Government commanded the confidence of the House. I then told them they could see for themselves in the Council of Nations how difficult the situation was becoming in regard to the making of the peace and the organization of the United Nations. I said to them I hoped they would not put their faith in any organization as to world security; that I greatly feared the new organization might in some circumstances be as much of a blind as the League of Nations. That there was a bad spirit abroad and an underground around the world movement which might lead to years of unrest, and that we could not tell what attitude might be taken by nations against each other until we were rid of hate and be prepared to get good-will on all sides. . . .

"I then indicated what I felt about the necessity of going to England and conferring with members of the new Government, getting an understanding of the problems there. . . . I also told them that having had the responsibility of directing the war effort through the whole of the war, I felt I would not like to return without visiting the battlefields and seeing what our men had had to endure. I spoke too of the conditions of famine, starvation, etc., wishing to get this information first hand. I then said what I really felt I should do was to ask the party to let me go away for a month's vacation. They all applauded that. I did not say I was very tired but mentioned I had not had hardly what could be called a day's vacation in the past seven years. Whenever I was away, I had my work with me and had gone in order to get through more of it. I said now I felt that situations were mounting up too rapidly and I had better go at once. If I did not go now, there would be no chance between the end of this session and the beginning of another and I might not through the rest of my days get the opportunity of doing the things I had spoken of to them. I also spoke about the suggestion that I should send someone to speak for me. I was out to fight against any one man speaking for an entire party. Even a Cabinet had no business to do much in an arbitrary way unless they were sure it was in accord with the will of the people. We were getting away from democracy. We must get back to it in a manner which will let the people's voice as a whole be heard.

"I then spoke of leaving with a sense of complete confidence in the men who were in the Government, controlling things in my absence, and also confidence in the Members, in their ability to meet the situation in the House. I did not ask them to keep what I said confidential. I think it best that the public mind should gradually be prepared for my leaving but I think it was a bit of a shock to them all today when they found what I had in mind was really to be absent for the rest of this session. It will do no harm for them to learn to manage things themselves and particularly the Ministers to realize what responsibility I have been carrying over the years. I must say that Ilsley, Howe and St. Laurent have had equal burdens but they are younger men and are better able to carry them. Some of the other colleagues also have had all they can do. Indeed with the exception of a very few, they have been all exceedingly faithful, able and hard working lot of men."

After a brief visit that afternoon to a country fair in Glengarry constituency, Mackenzie King returned to Ottawa and met with Norman Robertson. "I could see he was greatly concerned. He showed me a telegram which had come from Cadogan (Foreign Office, London) which indicated that the British were prepared to arrest Primrose [Professor Alan Nunn May] at once and suggesting that arrests might be made here immediately and possibly pursued in the United States. It is apparent that the United States have discovered there has been similar penetration into the bomb business as has taken place here.

"Robertson felt, as I felt, that to have arrests made at once would be a mistake. I said before I saw the telegram that I saw that the British had become exasperated at Molotov's behaviour at the Council of Foreign Ministers. The telegram stated that H.M.G. was prepared to take the step and all that might grow out of it and asked whether we would agree to a similar step and the United States taking a similar step.

"Robertson and I conferred together and after conference together, we held the same view as Robertson had set out in a message in reply, stressing that it would be unwise to take this step before we could get the whole case worked out by our police and had further evidence, but also that there should first be a conference between myself, the President or the Secretary of State, and Bevin as to how the whole matter would shape up.

"Word had come that the President has to fill a long standing engagement, to be in Missouri on Sunday, and may be leaving Washington Saturday afternoon. He would welcome my flying from Ottawa on Friday and spend the night at the White House to talk over matters together. Byrnes is not yet back. Will be back probably tomorrow. I told R. I thought it was impossible for me to start off on the English journey by beginning with flying to Washington. Moreover with the debate having gone the length it has, I could not possibly arrange to leave here Friday afternoon either by plane or train. I thought we should hold to my leaving on Saturday afternoon which was what I had decided this morning.

"I should have mentioned this in the early part of the diary. R. suggested he might go himself and see Byrnes a day in advance. I did not think this wise. It seemed to me that Byrnes was my opposite number as Secretary of State and it would be best for me perhaps to go to Washington to see him. He will just have returned from the Council of United Nations and I could get the latest word from him and be able to take the latest word to Britain. I told R. it was useless for us otherwise to discuss these great questions in the over-fatigued and bedraggled conditions in which we are. That we needed the ocean voyage and a clear mind as the whole Russian matter is opening out in a way which will completely change the United Nations organization and Russia's place in it. It may result in her being ruled out of the organization altogether. That might be a terrible thing, particularly if she has the atomic bomb secret in her possession and is planning for something in the way of world conquest on her own. The whole thing seemed so fantastic as to be inconceivable. When one thinks back, however, of what happened out of Hitler's tactics and Japan's fanatical ideas, anything might happen today unless this whole situation is handled with the utmost care. I had a feeling when the whole matter came upon us at the start that perhaps this was the big mission that I may have after all to perform. To use the judgment that may be necessary to help to avoid a break which might lead to another war very shortly, and to find some better means of coping with the situation. That is where we stand tonight."

Robertson was instructed "to let the President know through Atherton I could not hope to get away Friday but would go to see Byrnes. I am sure this is a wise procedure. I cannot leave Parliament, the Cabinet, Laurier House with all that there is to do before starting off for England without breathing space of an additional day and getting together papers and documents it will be necessary to have while abroad."

The next morning (September 27) Mackenzie King met Ilsley, Howe and Abbott and, with Robertson and Wrong present, told them the whole story of the Gouzenko defection. "The three Ministers were naturally greatly surprised and impressed. I let them know that my first information came the day of the opening of Parliament. That I had been carrying the secret ever since – known only to St. Laurent. That it was really the factor which made it necessary for me to leave immediately. They all appreciated the situation." A meeting of the full Cabinet followed immediately and the main issue was again the indemnity question. The Minister of Finance was now prepared to concede a $1,500 tax-free allowance, $500 below the amount demanded by the Liberal caucus. The issue remained unresolved in the face of Ilsley's determination "to protect the Treasury," as Mackenzie King put it. After some general discussion of possible tax relief in the budget, the Prime Minister urged the appointment of Dunton to the C.B.C. and secured Cabinet approval of a statement announcing his trip to the United Kingdom.

He read the statement in the House of Commons after lunch. "It was received with applause on all sides. Coldwell was quick in recognizing it should not be allowed to pass without some comment. That Bracken had evidently not known what to say. Coldwell made a very nice reply approving strongly the statement of my going. Bracken then followed and was followed by Solon Low.

"Later in the afternoon, I saw all three and thanked them for their words of approval. Spoke to Bracken and Coldwell about the Russian situation being serious and in strict confidence told them we had some unpleasant features right here in Ottawa which I did not wish to disclose but which I wanted them to know existed. They both seemed to share strongly the feeling that the Russians were being very difficult.

"I did not say anything to Low about there being a situation here but he too spoke of the Russians as being very difficult. I showed both Bracken and Coldwell the passage in my statement that I had struck out at the last minute, in which I said that there were additional reasons which had arisen since Attlee's invitation which made it imperative for me to go at once. I thought that would create curiosity. I wanted them to see there were further reasons. I spoke to all three leaders about the indemnity. They agreed they would back up whatever we did. Coldwell said the only one who was hesitant in their group was McInnis but he might not be so now."

At the end of the afternoon Mackenzie King went to tea at Earnscliffe with Malcolm MacDonald who was anxious to speak to him about the future of Newfoundland. "I told him it would never do to compel Newfoundland to come into Confederation or to show a desire to have them come in. On the other hand, we should let them know we would be willing to have them consider favourably their coming into the Confederation at any time. He thought possibly next summer the British Government would take some steps toward having Newfoundland seek to come into Confederation. I told him what was really needed was a new province which would combine the three maritime provinces and Newfoundland. I stressed the importance of not crowding the matter too greatly."

Late that evening, the Prime Minister was informed that President Truman had decided to cancel his trip to Missouri "and suggested my coming down by plane Saturday afternoon – if I could not get away Friday – and spend the night at the White House, also Sunday morning. I told R. I would not on any consideration think of leaving by plane. The alternative was to go on my car at night and have it picked up at 4 in the morning, travel through the day to New York and arrive at night to Washington. Go to the White House immediately after breakfast. I felt the pressure of this but R. urged very strongly and rightly that this was a case where it seemed imperative to see the President. Undoubtedly what was of concern to him was the matter we have been concerned about, and that I should see the President before crossing over. I then consented to this arrangement."

As usual, these arrangements did not prove to be as simple as they sounded for the next day (September 28), after a Cabinet meeting, Mackenzie King consulted the train schedules and "was amazed when I found that what was proposed was a transfer of my car from Grand Central

Station to Penn Station which meant an expenditure of $300 for that purpose, going to Hells Gate and back. I recalled how strongly I spoke of that once before and said I would not consider it on any account. I then rang up the U.S. Ambassador myself, Atherton, and told him I had just seen what was proposed. I had been up to that minute with the Cabinet. There were matters arising out of the Cabinet which I had still to work on and I was afraid I would have to forego going to Washington. Certainly I would not incur that expenditure with my private car. It would create a scandal, etc. Atherton said it should be done in a way that no one would know about it. I told him these things should not and could not likely be concealed. At any rate, I would take no chances. I asked if it were not possible for the President to delay until 2. I thought half an hour might serve. Leaving Saturday afternoon, I could be in at Washington at 1.15 P.M. Atherton said he would see what could be done. Robertson had been out at the time. When he came in, he urged me very strongly to hold on to this other arrangement. He thought it would be quite justifiable even if it were to cost $300 for the transfer; on a mission such as I had, it was nothing. I told him I did not wish my reputation to be damaged by any false step. I would go the next day if it could be arranged. Otherwise we might have to give up the trip altogether. I said to R. I would think of the possibility of flying but that would have to wait over until we saw what the weather was like for flying the next day.

"It was quite late in the evening before Atherton got word that it would not be possible for the President to delay longer as he was going to Missouri."

Meanwhile, the debate on the Address had concluded on the evening of September 27. On the divisions, the Prime Minister noted, "all opposition parties and a couple of independents lined up against our Party. Fortunately our men had stayed well and also fortunately Bracken and Coldwell both agreed to taking the vote tonight. If it had had to come tomorrow or Monday, that would have been terrible.

"It took until 11.30 before different votes were taken. We had a majority of twenty-seven on the first and twenty-five on the second against all the combined opposition. The Address passed on division. Immediately after I moved the appointment of Ross Macdonald as Deputy Speaker which was carried unanimously. It was really a tremendous day and I marvelled at the strength given to me to go through it until after midnight which was the time I arrived back at Laurier House."

Mackenzie King did not go into the House the next day. Having "said good-bye to the House last night at a triumphal moment," he "did not wish to go in for a half day today." He did, however, get the indemnity question settled before his departure. In an interview with Ilsley on September 28, the Prime Minister discovered that the Minister of Finance was now prepared to concede an $1,800 allowance. Mackenzie King continued to press for $2,000 arguing that the "Members would be satisfied. They would feel more kindly toward Ilsley himself. Would support his budget even if he had to give less than was anticipated in the way of reductions on income tax. The Treasury would be saved large sums through the good-will thus secured. Told him of my talks with the leaders of the other parties and their readiness to support whatever we did. His eyes filled with tears when I said even in his own interests I thought it would be well to do this. I said I knew he did not care for that but as Minister of Finance he had to be able to carry the House with him on his measures. I was afraid if he did not meet them at this time, he would find there was a perpetual feud." Ilsley finally agreed and the Cabinet approved the $2,000 allowance later in the day. The Prime Minister also secured Cabinet approval for Dunton's appointment while explaining that "on these key appointments, it was important that the Prime Minister should make the decision. Also that of course he would confer with his colleagues but he had to take the ultimate responsibility."

At the end of the meeting, Mackenzie King told his colleagues he "was sorry to be leaving them with such a load but, however, when one was past 70, one had to have regard to what he, himself, could do, and I thanked God that they had youth still on their side. I then let them know that it would be the last opportunity I would have of saying good-bye. When I had concluded, Mackenzie made a nice little speech in which on behalf of the Cabinet he wished I might have a successful trip and have an opportunity to rest, etc. He is always thoughtful in these things. Cabinet all rose and expressed their approval in that way. Then they came one by one to shake hands.

"As Gardiner was leaving, he said in a low breath would I if chance offered try and visit Edwin's grave [Gardiner's son killed in action] while I was away. What a load that little man is carrying in his heart! I promised to do all I could toward that end."

The next morning, September 29, the Prime Minister decided that he should go to Washington by plane. He arranged to leave at 2.00 P.M. and arrived in Washington three hours later. Mackenzie King and Robertson spent a quiet evening with Pearson at the Canadian Embassy and later Pearson and Robertson saw Dean Acheson, the Assistant Secretary of State.

Mackenzie King made a detailed record of his conversations with President Truman in his secret diary. "My decision to see the President before leaving for Europe was the outcome of my feeling that we owed it to the United States as well as to the United Kingdom to let those highest in authority in these two countries know all that we possessed in the way of information regarding R.E. [Russian espionage].

"There were other reasons which made it obviously desirable in the national interest that I should see the President before going abroad so that the country might know of my acceptance of his invitation. Just how matters were finally arranged I do not know and Robertson did not seem himself to clearly recollect whether the invitation which the President had renewed on Wednesday or Thursday last to stay at the White House, was the result of the President's initiative or of some word sent through Atherton that I would like to see him before going abroad. However, my position is that I was accepting the President's invitation. While it could not be for an overnight visit, it was wise to have at least a conversation before going abroad. Arrangements were made through Atherton.

"In conversation with Atherton toward the last, in his way of speaking, one might have thought that the going to Washington was rather something for which I was asking rather than something which I felt was in part acceptance of the President's invitation and in part obligation which Canada owed to an ally. I personally do not like that kind of effort to gain a certain position for the other party, either in conversation or in posture when talking to another. I am open and above board in everything, not attaching importance to individual words or gestures but in the open between individuals as far as that is possible in matters that have to be concealed from the public. . . .

"Robertson brought with him on the plane in a green folder – No. 10 – a copy of the statement prepared by our police of the statements of information secured from examination of CORBY [Igor Gouzenko] and other sources. I spent the time on the 'plane between Ottawa and Washington re-reading much of this material. I continued re-reading some of it on Sunday morning at the Embassy immediately after breakfast before going to see the President. Robertson suggested I take the book with me which I did, in an ordinary brown envelope, under my arm. Was photographed at the entrance of the White House with this document under my arm.

"Before leaving Ottawa, Robertson had received a message from Cadogan saying that the British Government thought they should arrest Primrose very soon and that they assumed the Canadian Government would wish to make arrests in Canada and that the United States would also agree to this course. The message indicated that H.M.G. was prepared to meet whatever situation might arise out of these arrests. Robertson had talked this over with me and I agreed with him this was not the course to pursue.

We must move very slowly and cautiously. We were not ready in Canada to take proceedings and our leading advisers up to the present say it would be very difficult to get a conviction on material we have considering its source, etc. We agreed the course to be taken should be on the top level. That Attlee, Truman and myself should agree on the course to be taken. A message was drafted to send to Cadogan to this effect. I went over it at the Embassy with Pearson, Robertson between 8 and 9 making a few changes in the language but agreeing to this course. It was sent off at night. . . .

"Robertson and Pearson went to see Acheson at the Secretary of State's office. They showed him the message that we were proposing to send. Acheson said it seemed to him it was sound common sense. He did not at all approve of that action by the British Government or the United States Government. Felt that the whole case should be worked out at the highest level and that we should see the probable end from the beginning as far as possible. This I learned later. The British Government had sent a message to the United States Government similar to the one sent to us. Halifax had delivered it and a reply was to be sent as soon as possible giving the United States view on Sunday. Robertson told me on Sunday morning of the talk with Acheson and of his (A's) full agreement with our point of view. Pearson at first was going to go with me to the White House but they decided it was better for them to wait at the Embassy and I would 'phone later if it was desired to have them come over."

At the White House, the Prime Minister "was pleased to see as the first picture on entering, a painting of Roosevelt which I liked very much. It was painted some years ago. I confess, however, that I felt the house sort of empty. Between the Sunday morning and the absence of persons about, it was very much so. I was taken up the lift by the chief usher. Being a few minutes before 10, we talked in the upstairs hall largely about President Roosevelt. The usher told me Mr. Truman is occupying the same rooms.

"At 10, the usher went to the circular room and asked if the President would receive me. . . . Mr. Truman who was in the centre of the room, came forward and shook hands very cordially. Then Mr. Acheson came forward and shook hands. The President asked me to be seated on the large sofa and he took a chair immediately opposite. Acheson pulling in a chair making a triangle. It was rather singular that the seat I had been given was the one where President Roosevelt usually sat and where I last saw him and said good-bye to him.

"Mr. Truman extended a cordial welcome. Said he was glad to see me and he hoped relations between us might be the same as they had been between President Roosevelt and myself. That he would welcome that sort of relationship. Was sorry that it had not been possible to have an earlier interview. He hoped I would come to stay after my return. He made some reference about our meeting at San Francisco and I then said I was sorry I could not accept the invitation for Friday night. That I had to be in Parliament until expressions of confidence on the Speech from the Throne were over. Told him what the divisions were. He turned to Acheson and said he wished he could be sure of twenty-seven of a majority over all."

After a few more social preliminaries, Mackenzie King "then said to the President that he would know something of what I was anxious to give him particulars of. He said that Acheson had given him some information. I then said I had felt it my duty to see that he was fully informed and that he was given the same information as I wished to give to the British Government. That I felt we were all equally concerned. I then said perhaps it would be better if I were to run over the whole business from the start; as I had learned of it at different stages. The President said that would be best and I then began with Robertson and Wrong coming to see me in my office at 11. on the day of the Opening of Parliament. Narrated the incidents regarding Corby. What had subsequently been obtained in the way of information. Told them of the extent of espionage in Canada. What we had learned about espionage in the United States. Mentioned particularly request as to information as to United States troops, etc., shipping to Russia; of information regarding the atomic bomb. The visit of a courier to the United States by one who turned out to be Inspector of the Red Army and of his having sized up the espionage system in the United States. Had sent out his report from Ottawa. Spoke of the Consul at New York who apparently had charge of the espionage business in the United States. Of the connection of that office with the organization in Switzerland; of large sums of money having gone from that office to Switzerland, etc.

"While proceeding with the discussion and speaking of our view of being careful not to disclose anything until the situation had been worked out, the President of his own volition said he felt every care must be taken to get full information before anything at all was disclosed. He said he assumed there must be similar penetration by the Russians into the conditions in the United States and that he would want to have this gone into very fully before any action was taken. The President also volunteered the statement that he thought the matter should be discussed between Attlee, himself and myself. That we should all be agreed on the course that was to be taken. Two or three times he repeated his view that nothing should be done without agreement between the three and above all nothing should be done which might result in premature action in any direction. He also said two or three times that he was particularly interested in anything I could tell him of what had happened in the United States or would give evidence of espionage there. I then said perhaps it would be best were I to read from the report I had with me; give him from the document I had with me the information I had. If he were agreeable, I would read it aloud. This the President said he would be pleased to have me do.

"I then read the preliminary statement concerning the espionage system in Russia. Read early portions about the system as it worked at the Embassy. Read about Primrose and others in key positions. Went particularly to the passages concerning the Russian Consulate in New York. The statements re the atomic bomb; information gained from the United States. What was thought to have gone from Chicago. Also the statement that an assistant secretary of the Secretary of State's Department was supposed to be implicated though I made perfectly clear this was only what Corby had said but I had no information to back it up. The President did not seem surprised. He turned to Acheson and said something to the effect that it would not be surprising. Acheson then said that they had thought the report had reference to an assistant to an assistant secretary. I said of course I knew nothing but what was in the statement as recorded there. Probably he was right and there might even be no foundation.

"I felt the reading was rather long and two or three times suggested abbreviations. The President said he was most interested. Finally I felt I had covered main points and put the book back into the envelope. I had kept emphasizing I was using the book because I wanted to give exactly the same information to Attlee. I told the President of my mission to England at the instance of Theodore Roosevelt in regard to Japan; of my having seized passports in Vancouver; of Edward Grey's passing on to Komura, information, etc. I told him I thought there was a possibility if Russians were confronted in a similar way with known facts that it might help to steady things and that might be a means of meeting the situation. How much farther we should go would depend on consultation. The President agreed with this and I said to him I thought we should relate the information we have to the question of the veto on the Security Council of the U.N. organization. If at all possible, we should get the Russians to realize there must be confidence all in all or not at all and that their insistence on agreement on the part of the Great Powers to any action or use of force, was creating suspicion in itself. That they should be willing to do in the matter of the action to be taken, what the other four Great Powers were prepared to do. One must know the kind of a world we wanted to live in and be assured they were prepared to help to co-operate in furthering a similar kind of world. . . . He said something about Attlee coming out to have a talk with him. I was careful to explain about my going to England and its relation to conference with the British Government and about this coming up after I had first declined to go for purposes of consultation merely before Parliament met.

"As it got on toward 12, I felt I should not detain the President longer and said that I knew his time was very precious and I thought I should not press him longer. This was the second or third time I had said this and the President then seemed to acquiesce so I rose at once. When I saw Acheson there, I had mentioned that Robertson and Pearson could come over if the President wished it. He and Acheson spoke between themselves as to whether it was desirable or not without being committal. I saw apparently they preferred the three of us might speak first. I said we might leave that until after if it was desirable to have them come. Before we left the circular room, the President again repeated what he had said about hoping I would come and see him when I got back and that we might have the same kind of relationship that had been shared between President Roosevelt and myself. I was sorry not to have had a chance to talk with him quite alone as I had meant to say something about the impressions he himself had made in the handling of affairs; also a word about Canadian-U.S. relations."

After the interview with President Truman, Acheson drove Mackenzie King to the Canadian Embassy. In Acheson's view, the British government was pressing for immediate arrests and disclosure of Gouzenko's information because "they had gotten fed up with the Russians and were prepared to take any chance. That was all very well so far as Britain was concerned but that we were in the Western Hemisphere and we had to consider our position. He felt that the United States and Canada would be more immediately affected by consequences of any action which severed relations with Russia, than even the U.K. He thought the position we had taken was the only sound one. He spoke about the possibility of war and certainly if war came of it coming on this continent with Canada as the battleground. I agreed that would be inevitable; this continent would be the one in which war would take place. He did not say he believed war itself was inevitable. He did think we ought to try and have the same types of weapons used on this continent for quick exchange. Atherton had said the same thing to Robertson. I said I thought it was desirable that the British and all of us should have the same type. That he agreed to as the really wise thing.

"I went over with him the President's attitude and it was as set forth above. At the Embassy I gave an outline of the interview, stressing what I had read and said it was also the President's view that whatever action should be taken, it should be at the highest level – between Attlee, himself and myself. It was not desirable to have precipitate action. Everything should be most carefully explored in the first instance.

"Acheson then himself repeated in his view what the President had said and what he himself would report to Halifax this afternoon. I said I thought I ought to see Halifax and had Pearson ring up the Embassy. There was to be a garden party in the afternoon – some Scotch songs. Halifax said he would like very much to have me come and if convenient at once."

At the British Embassy the Prime Minister met Lord Halifax in his library. "Took a message from Acheson to him that he would be in touch with him later in the afternoon. Halifax invited me to be seated on a sofa and took a seat to the right of the sofa. When I was seated, I found the light was shining from the windows in my eyes; so much so I could not see the features of his face. I felt a bit offended at this. It seemed to be a poor type of practice for a man like Halifax to adopt. It is I know a way that some people of the Mussolini type and others take. They must watch the countenance of the men they are talking to and have their own in the dark. I put my hands over my eyes so as to shade them and so that I could look closely into his face. There was not much time to review the situation. Said he knew particulars from what Malcolm had told him. I was meeting the President's wish to pay him a visit. I felt I should give the same information of what we knew as we were prepared to give England. Halifax said he was sure that was right. He then asked me about the President's views. I gave them to him. He said that would be the message Acheson would give him to send to London. I said I was sure it was. Halifax himself said that he agreed that that was the wise course.

"He asked me if I knew whether Attlee had sent a letter saying anything about his coming over. When he, Halifax, was in England, Attlee had written he would come over to discuss the atomic bomb policy but he, Halifax, did not think the letter had been sent. I said I did not recollect any word about that but that the President had said something about a conference later.

"Halifax then said he was sure that Attlee and the President should work out the matter between them. I at once interjected I thought it should be worked out with Canada as well. That the three of us were equally interested and added that perhaps we were in the most serious position of all as information was coming from Canada and if there was to be suffering from consequences, we would get most of it. Halifax later took care to refer to the three as being essential.

"I spoke to him about my view as to using this evidence to help to secure a removal of the right of the Russians to veto any course of action which implied use of force against one of the Great Five. Said it seemed to me that they could have to do something which would let us see that they merited our confidence. This espionage system had shaken that completely especially when it was carried on during the years that we were fighting together as allies and seemed to be intensified now up to the end of the present year. Halifax seemed interested in this point of view. He agreed the secret of the atomic bomb would probably become known to the Russians. I pointed out it would have to be shared. I said I thought it would have to be shared ultimately and all of it might as well be made part of one piece. Halifax expressed a real interest in what I had suggested. Evidently he had not been thinking on those lines."

Before leaving Washington, Mackenzie King also saw his old friend Cordell Hull and "felt a great rejoicing" at seeing how much his health had improved. "Mr. Hull began by speaking of the little biography of myself. I assumed it was Ludwig's. He said you ought to get someone to write your biography in a large way while you can direct it. Otherwise later on people will write what they think themselves. I told him I thought that applied to him. He said he intended to do a few pages every day. Had to take things easily but would write out certain subjects. He went on to say that 'they' meaning the State Department came and consulted him every now and then. He said I will tell you what I would not tell others because you and I are so close friends. They were going to let Hirohito off very easily. Going to retain a sort of monarchy in Japan. Preserve him and certain prerogatives and rights. Byrnes was about to start on his mission to Japan. I told him this was all wrong. They could not afford to be easy with the Japanese. That they would misunderstand it altogether. They ought to be treated with great severity. That no lenience should be shown. That pacifist ideas were not good in dealings with people like the Japanese. He said I think I got the whole policy changed in that particular just in time.

"Next he said he thought at the State Department they had made a big mistake with Argentine. That young Nelson Rockefeller had ideas of friendship with all the South American Republics but did not understand the Argentine mentality. Indeed Rockefeller had put it over Stettinius at San Francisco. That Argentine should never have been admitted into the U.N. conference. He felt there again pacifist ideas would only lead to further trouble. Fortunately the State Department had dropped Rockefeller and his South American co-operation. Mr. Hull thought that the whole policy in that particular had been too soft. At the same time, he felt that we must foster good-will between nations and do all possible toward that end. That we must be patient, particularly with peoples whose mentality was different than our own. I said that was true but that some things were very difficult to understand. That I thought our people were finding the Russians difficult; that with what we had seen at the Council of Foreign Ministers, it was apparent that the Russians were being difficult. Did not look as though they really were intent on furthering good-will themselves.

"Mr. Hull then said that someone from the State Department had been in talking with him – either from or associated with the State Department. I thought he had said something in reference to Communism. However what he really dwelt on was that while it was very difficult to understand the Russian attitude, we would have to be very patient with them. Little by little, show them where they were in the wrong. He said some people want to take drastic measures, go too far. That would be a great mistake. He began to put out his hands and move his fingers as though looking into the future. He said we must see that unless we can get others to understand us and our people to understand others, there would be nothing left but another terrible war. If there is, that would be the end of everything. We must try to show them where they are in the wrong, show them what we think is the right way of proceeding. This was all very remarkable to me as I had not said a word about any inside situation, just made this general remark. The way he spoke, it would almost seem as if whoever talked with him must have been speaking in regard to policy in the light of knowledge that I had though this can hardly be the case.

"I had mentioned to him that Mr. Acheson told me he had been in to see him yesterday. This caused him to remark that they came to consult him from time to time. It may well be that Acheson may have indirectly consulted him about Russia though my impression is he told me what it was Acheson had come to speak about; that, I cannot recall. Mr. Hull has a very wise and sagacious outlook."

When he got to New York on the evening of September 30, Mackenzie King had a half-hour talk at the Harvard Club with Jacques Greber and E. P. Murphy, the Deputy Minister of Public Works, about the development of the national capital. Thoroughly exhausted, and looking forward to a leisurely voyage, the Prime Minister and Norman Robertson sailed on the *Queen Mary* the following day.

CHAPTER THREE

Mackenzie King in London, 1945

MUCH OF Mackenzie King's time on board ship was devoted to revising for publication the speeches he had made during the election campaign. Daily contact was maintained with Ottawa and on October 3 the Prime Minister received word that President Truman had announced a conference of the United States, the United Kingdom and Canada on atomic energy and its utilization. This led him to reflect on the future of the United Nations. "I am more and more of the opinion that the proposed U.N. organization will be worse than nothing unless Russia can be brought to the point where she will agree to allow the Security Council to investigate conditions in Russia which may occasion suspicion and also agree to do away with the veto by one of the Great Five on action proposed by the Security Council. If that is not done, Russia will be able to prepare for war and bring on war herself without warning to others. She will not observe any pledge on paper. I am sure of that. Mere promises in writing mean nothing unless there is means for all nations to keep fretful nations in order."

Mackenzie King felt that it would be better "to look the situation squarely in the face and if Russia is unwilling to demonstrate her will to co-operation and the maintenance of peace, to the degree that the other Four Great Powers do so, it would be better to form a U.N. organization which could leave her ostracized altogether. A course of procedure which would be in accordance with Christ's teachings where conciliation, arbitration and investigation fails, as recorded in my Industry and Humanity. There must be a willingness on the part of every nation to permit investigation of conditions which give rise to suspicion. I told Robertson I thought the statement prepared for the House of Commons was weak in that it appeared apologetic for our acceptance of the veto clause instead of defending the acceptance by saying that the Great Powers had promised to use their power with due regard to the right of others. We should make it plain that we accept it only because there is no alternative. I am beginning to question whether in the light of what we know, it should be accepted at all. Robertson thinks that the sharing of scientific knowledge regarding the atomic bomb by all scientists might of itself prove sufficient to prevent any one country taking the advantage of the secret once it is known to that country. I, myself, doubt if that is enough. I am sure there is no justification for delay in getting this matter settled. Scientists themselves believe that further developments might make a bomb sufficiently powerful to destroy the entire world."

The *Queen Mary* reached Southampton on Sunday, October 7, at noon and Mackenzie King was immediately shown a telegram from the British Ambassador in Washington, Lord Halifax, to the Foreign Office "stating that Acheson . . . had given him a message from the President to say that the President was anxious that Primrose should not be arrested unless it was obviously necessary for security reasons and then only if he were discovered to be communicating some document of a Top Secret nature to the man he was to meet tonight in London. That the President felt very strongly that there should be agreement on the matter. That every effort should be made to secure further information in the U.S. and also in Britain before action was precipitated. Also most important to have complete understanding between the countries immediately concerned first.

"The Foreign Office wished to know if I would give approval to an arrest being made tonight. I stressed my agreement with the point expressed by the President and said, as he did, that I would not stand in the way of an arrest being made if the conditions mentioned were to be found to exist and observed. . . ."

Information that Professor May might be arrested on the evening of October 7 had been communicated to Ottawa earlier and, under the authority of the War Measures Act, the government adopted on October 6 a secret order-in-council, P.C. 6444, empowering the R.C.M.P. to detain persons suspected of communicating information to a foreign power and to interrogate them under conditions determined by the Minister of Justice. Even though the British authorities decided against May's immediate arrest, the order was not revoked and the Canadian government proceeded to secure the advice of E. K. Williams, the President of the Canadian Bar Association. After an examination of the R.C.M.P. transcript of Gouzenko's disclosures, Williams recommended the appointment of a royal commission, composed of justices of the Supreme Court of Canada, to investigate the case. No action was taken on his recommendation until February 1946 when some details of the case became public knowledge in the United States.

Mackenzie King travelled to London by train. Among those who met him at Waterloo Station was Martin Attlee, the son of the British Prime Minister, who was then a midshipman in the navy. They drove directly to

Chequers and Mackenzie King found "young Attlee quite attractive, highly intelligent and well informed. He had just returned from Halifax where he had been on two journeys. Liked Halifax very much."

The Prime Minister found his first evening at Chequers "most pleasant." "Attlee looked very happy. I was struck with his fine, clear appearance. His face was almost radiant as he came in from having read the lessons at St. Margaret's at the opening of the H. of C. Church. I congratulated him on his victory telling him at the same time that I had not expected it but rather counted on there being a condition of uncertainty as I thought there would be in Canada as well. Attlee said to me that he, himself, had not expected it and Peck told me that both Churchill and Attlee were immensely surprised at the result. Churchill had expected to win by 50 or 60 or even up to 90. Attlee had thought there would be a stalemate."

After the other members of the Attlee family had retired, Mackenzie King reviewed with the British Prime Minister the events which had taken place in Ottawa and the extent of the Soviet espionage system which Igor Gouzenko's information had revealed. "I then outlined my talk with the President and the view that the President held, with which Attlee said he was in entire agreement, namely, that as much information should be secured both in the U.S. and here before the case was opened up to the public. Attlee also agreed that an approach should be made in the first instance to the Russians themselves.

"I spoke of linking up this matter of espionage with the atomic bomb secret and also the veto of the United Nations Security Council plans. I found that in this, Attlee was also in entire agreement. He used the expression that he felt the time had come when there must be a 'show-down' with the Russians. He said he thought the meeting of Council of Foreign Ministers had been brought on a little too soon; nothing had been really prepared. He said he really could not understand the Russians or what was behind their line of action. They were exceedingly difficult. He said Stalin was the only one who had a final say. Molotov could not go any distance in anything. Kept getting authority from Stalin. He said he did not think there was anything in the statement that Stalin was going to retire because of ill-health. He thought that the Russian successes had gone a little bit to their head; also that they had a strong inferiority complex. That both forces were operating to make things difficult. He added that they really had not any true conception of democracy. That both were talking about different things while they used the same words."

Mackenzie King had a wretched night as he was catching a cold. He drove to London with Attlee immediately after breakfast and went to his customary suite at the Dorchester.

Lord Addison, the Secretary of State for Dominion Affairs called on him that afternoon (October 8), and after some social preliminaries, Mackenzie King proceeded to review the Gouzenko affair again. "Lord Addison said he would say to me what he would not say to anyone else excepting a few of his colleagues, which was that he really felt that the present situation was quite as bad, if not worse, than the situation which the world was faced with before Hitler declared war. That Russia's policy seems to be one of power politics, pure and simple. That he felt they did not understand us and still were very suspicious of us, believed we were seeking an Empire, etc. Also they had a very strong inferiority complex. He said that Bevin had worked with Molotov one night until 4 in the morning before he could get him to bend at all, toward helping to meet a difficult situation. That Molotov had said to him in plain language: the truth is you people do not regard us as your equals and look down on us. You still think we are inferior to you, etc. Lord Addison agreed that this kind of feeling, once men had power, would invariably find expression in showing the others just where they stood. He apparently had not caught that one of these agents (couriers) had taken back to Russia a bit of uranium from Canada. It may have been something that was acquired in Chicago. He said he felt quite sure that Russia would very soon come to acquire the secret of the atomic bomb. That scientists, once they were working on a matter which had been successful elsewhere, were pretty certain to discover the processes which led to their final result. He believes we must count on Russia getting that secret.

"He told me as a significant fact that in all the parts of Germany which are occupied by the Russians and which include many of the former great centres where research was carried on, the Russians had taken all the scientists and their equipment, etc., away and removed it to Russia. He was amazed at the extent of their organization for espionage purposes. Said he felt perfectly sure it existed here and in the U.S. as we had discovered in Canada. He could not explain the whole Russian attitude on any basis other than one of real opposition."

Mackenzie King then set out three possible alternative strategies: "one, indifference; the other, extreme publicity at once; and the third, confronting the Russians with the information we had and seeking to work out a basis of co-operation.

"He was sure that the last of the three was the preferable course. He said we must remember they are Orientals. (Montgomery had told Salisbury that he regards them as still savages.)

"Lord Addison thought we must be infinitely patient. He felt sure, however, that if we did not let the Russians see that we were in earnest, where a wrong had been done, they would think we were soft and themselves take advantage of the situation. He agreed that the President and Attlee and Canada should agree on a course of procedure and that nothing should be done which would endanger the situation until that course was agreed upon. He regarded as the main factor in a situation of the kind what was in the mind of the other man; how he really thought and felt.

"I had been mentioning that at San Francisco, Molotov was like a bit of bronze or more accurately like a bit of marble in his appearance and attitude. I said I thought at first it was due to his determination to see that Russia was put on an equality with every country, which I thought was right enough. I told him how completely he changed when a certain knotty question had been gotten out of the way. He said of the two men, he himself thinks better of Stalin, who sees things more quickly than Molotov, has a larger vision.

"I explained about not getting over earlier due to elections; also an unwillingness to sit on the doorstep so to speak to be called in for consultation. He said he entirely agreed with that point of view. Saw it. He then spoke about the difficulty of arranging some things. Said he would tell me privately that Evatt [Australia's Minister for External Affairs] was very difficult. He had said one or two things to him in confidence and that Evatt had subsequently published what had been said. I told him that President Roosevelt had said to me that that was the difficulty at meetings of the Pacific Council. He could say nothing that Evatt might not give to the press shortly after.

"I told Lord Addison I had no desire for self-aggrandizement or appearing at all in these matters. All I was over for was to be as helpful as I could in what was a difficult situation. He said to me that the situation was a very difficult one. No Government had ever had a more difficult time than what they are now faced with. He went on to say and repeated when I was leaving the room that I could be very helpful. I told him that was all I wanted and that I would be available to see him or see others he wished me to see at any time. . . .

"He spoke of the real problem of getting a concerted view or getting someone to say that is what we all think. I told him that he must remember there were two schools in relation to Imperial politics – one, that was always seeking to centralize; the other, that believed in decentralization and assertion of equality of status. That only the latter view would satisfy the Dominions today. He himself thought we should not be in too great a hurry in arranging conferences. I told him no conference should be arranged until there were grounds for believing that the problems that would come before it would be satisfactorily solved. Work should be done in the meantime by officials guided by their governments."

Mackenzie King was impressed by Addison. "I felt he was a very wise man. A good counsellor for a government. I also felt, however, that the British Government has really not as yet wholly tackled this problem or realized or begun to realize the implications of the whole espionage system."

Norman Robertson had met that morning with officials of the Dominions and Foreign Offices and, according to the Prime Minister, discovered that "they had not been thinking beyond the arrest of criminals as something which came as a matter of course, finding some official guilty of particular crimes, but they had never asked themselves how this all related itself to the atomic bomb. Robertson has suggested lines of thought which they are now exploring and may present formal paper for purposes of consideration and discussion by the Cabinet.

"As I think over the significant stages, I can come to only one result which is that the Russians do not intend to co-operate but to become increasingly a vast power in the Orient set against all Western powers. At first they refused to come into the organization to control aviation, the excuse being that Spain had been invited. This is clearly a mere pretext. The real purpose is that they do not wish to allow outside countries to fly their planes over Russian territory, thereby gaining a knowledge of what is taking place in industrial areas. Second, the unwillingness to come to San Francisco until world opinion compelled Molotov's presence as a gesture arising out of respect to the memory of President Roosevelt at the time of his death. Third, objection to everything proposed at San Francisco yielding only trivial points that it was obviously essential to yield, at the same time politically taking the course which before the world would seem to be the one likely to gain popular favour as, for example, opposing Argentine coming into the United Nations organization; the readiness to admit the International Labour Conference people as if to give Labour a wider voice in shaping treaties whereas it was really a form of Soviet penetration, etc.

"Then came Yalta at which time they were unwilling to agree to the investigation of conditions liable to give rise to war and further insistence on having the power of veto in regard to anything which implied the use of armies against Russia itself. It gave them a complete whip hand. Then the Conference of Council of Foreign Ministers, opposing almost everything that arose there.

"Lord Addison told me that Bevin had said plainly to Molotov when we wish to move into certain countries to exercise a certain authority there, you tell us we have no right to go there. The country is under your control and influence. On the other hand, when you wish to move into countries and to control them for the period that you think you should have control of or influence in, you say we have no right to exclude you. He agreed it was throughout a 'Heads I win; Tails you lose' proposition. I pointed out the difficulty of arranging a meeting between Stalin, the President and Attlee; how they were to meet, who was to come to meet the others, etc. Addison agreed this was something which had to be faced and up to the present time, did not know how it could be met.

"Lord Addison agrees, however, and we come back to that, that another war would mean total destruction and this must be worked against at all costs. This is the view that Attlee also holds. It is quite an appalling outlook."

His cold made Mackenzie King's first day in London thoroughly miserable. The next day, October 9, brought no improvement and he began to doubt the wisdom of attempting a trip to the Continent or even staying in England very long in view of the difficulty in securing transportation back to Canada. His conversation with Addison had convinced him that "the situation really was much more serious than perhaps even thus far I, myself, had supposed. His words that the Russian attitude was a repetition of the Nazi attitude and that things were in some respect worse than when Hitler was preparing for his world domination, had made a very deep impression. He told me that he would not say that to others but would tell me what he felt." The Prime Minister was beginning to feel that "it will mean far more in the end for me to return early and be in Washington with Attlee, if he is to cross soon. I firmly decided before getting out of bed that I would begin immediately to discover how soon he might be crossing and would try to arrange my return accordingly, either by plane or ship."

On October 10 Mackenzie King and Robertson had dinner with Ernest Bevin, the British Foreign Secretary. During the morning he and Robertson went over a memorandum outlining the latter's talks at the Foreign Office the day before. The Prime Minister "approved of the line taken; stated that I thought there should be no readiness to allow the Russians to have knowledge of the atomic energy which they do not already possess until some means have been devised of Russia agreeing to the same conditions as the other countries on a matter of allowing her own doings to be investigated and not to be able to veto investigation.

"During the afternoon, I read with great care Bevin's speech in the House yesterday and later the address made by the Secretary of State, Byrnes, at the Congress. I thought both were moderate and wise; of the two, Byrnes' seemed to me the abler statement. They both make clear that owing to Russia's attitude, the first stages of peace making have been a failure, have broken down. I pointed out to Robertson that there might be some significance in the fact that while the Conference opened on the

10th, they broke down on the 20th. That in the interval, the Russians may have come to know about the material that is now in our possession. That they might be waiting to present a case, to say that they had learned of what the three nations had been doing in spying on them, instead of coming to them at once with the knowledge they had. Naturally were unwilling to proceed further. It is quite significant that the change of attitude came on directions from Moscow.

"I told Robertson I thought Britain and the U.S. and Canada should all get together just as quickly as possible on defining the policy that is to be adopted and confronting the Soviet Union with the material we have. Not to do this is to allow ourselves to be put in a false light. If anything, the matter of exposure to the Russians themselves, though not to the public has been delayed too long, and the reason of the delay is the unwillingness to disclose anything to the public which Russia would resent above all else.

"I myself believe that the wise course for Canada to take would be to appoint a Royal Commission and summon before it all whose names we have. At what stage this step should be taken is, of course, a matter for careful and wise decision."

The dinner was at the Berkeley and Bevin himself was the last to arrive. Before dinner Mackenzie King had a pleasant talk with Lord Addison whom he liked "exceedingly." The next guest to arrive, Hugh Dalton, the Chancellor of the Exchequer, did not particularly impress the Prime Minister. To him Dalton was "still a little too full of himself and his position. Talks too much. Inclined to throw on the dog a bit. Was exceedingly pleasant, however. His father was Canon Dalton. I liked his quite evident affection for his father and his influence on his life." Bevin looked quite tired, Mackenzie King reported. He was "very heavy in build. Probably could not endure what he is going through. Has a pleasant voice and manner but uses from time to time the vernacular of the men with whom he was most associated from early life. He was very cordial in his welcome. We had a few words of general conversation before being seated."

The conversation at dinner covered a wide range of subjects including the results of the recent Canadian election. "All present seemed to have met Coldwell and the members of his party when they visited England last year. They spoke highly of him personally and of the address he had given to the Parliamentary Association. They also thought well of the different members of their party. Quite clearly, Coldwell had left the impression the C.C.F. fully expected to win. It was a surprise the Liberal party had come back. Bevin told me privately that he was very fond of Churchill. That he had begged of him not to have the elections until after the end of the Japanese war and then for him to step out of the party ranks altogether and be available to make important statements to the world, and to assume the role of a world statesman – outside party controversy. He said that he had fully expected Churchill to win the elections and thought his (Churchill's) majority would be about 40.

"When Attlee came in, he indicated to Attlee that he would like to be Chancellor of the Exchequer. He had told his wife when the elections were over that the party would probably be defeated. Churchill would win and they would have a chance for a little holiday together. He had then hoped to be appointed Chancellor of the Exchequer. Attlee told him he wanted him for Foreign Affairs. He said I went home and said: Old Girl, there is no Brighton Beach for us. It is Potsdam instead."

The British Foreign Secretary also reviewed some of his experiences with the Soviet delegates at the Potsdam Conference in July 1945. Bevin had been "determined that neither the U.S. nor Great Britain should, if possible, be responsible for the break-up of the Council. He thought the Russians were anxious that one or the other or both should say that they would have to leave. He, himself, however, persuaded Byrnes they should continue to hold out indefinitely. Matters were so arranged that the Chinese representative was the one who would be presiding at the time when the final break came.

"He told of his intimate talk with Molotov near the end when Molotov told him that the British always looked down on Russia. Thought they were inferior, etc., and that Russia was determined that they would be dealt with as equals in everything. He, Bevin, had assured him that England did not have any attitude of the kind. All she wanted was friendly relations with all countries."

Mackenzie King then asked Bevin to account for the abrupt change in the Russian attitude on September 22. "I was wondering if it might have been because of knowledge of what had taken place in Ottawa. He thought it was wholly because of one of the treaty agreements. He said quite clearly that what Russia was after was to get into the Congo in Africa. That there were large deposits of uranium there. This was her reason for wanting to get a foothold in that country.

"Lord Addison was the first to ask to be excused at dinner. I took advantage of this to say to Bevin that I hoped we would have a word together before he left. He then again suggested that perhaps the others should go and he and I retired to a sofa at the end of the room to talk together. Robertson remained to talk with Butler. Dixon was with Eden.

"I then spoke to him about the espionage matter and of how important I felt it to be that the United States, Britain and Canada should have a definite agreement on the steps to be taken and that without further delay. I found that Bevin seemed to have very little knowledge or appreciation of the situation in a large way. He was inclined to think that an arrest of two or three might be made here and he assumed that we would adopt a similar course. I told him that I had seen the President on the way through and that Truman was strongly of the view that all three countries should meet together and decide the course they should take. That he agreed with the American feeling that Attlee and himself and myself should meet together and decide on what was to be done and in that connection, the best course would be to confront the Russians with what we knew and directing the question of how impossible it was to go on with co-operation in the United Nations if we did not have a complete understanding as to the bona fides of all concerned."

At the end of the conversation, Bevin "quite changed his attitude. Said that he would see Attlee in the morning. Present to him the line that I had presented and, if need be, would come back from Brighton any day to meet with Attlee and myself. He asked me if I had talked to Attlee about the situation. I told him I had and that I thought Attlee agreed with the line I had suggested. I stressed the importance of not letting us get too far away from the date on which we came into possession of the documents we have. Also the importance of linking all this up with the policy on the atomic bomb and on the obligation on Russia's part to permit investigation of conditions in her country if other countries were to be permitted to have investigations in theirs. He agreed with this and himself volunteered the statement that he did not think Russia should be permitted to have any rights that others did not have. It was apparent that he feels very strongly about Russia's whole attitude. I said to him that I would tell him something which I would not wish to say except in the most intimate way to himself.

"I then said that once the statement were publicly made, the motive would be misinterpreted and it would be said that I was trying to further annexation views but it was this. That I was certain that unless we secured in some satisfactory way the relations with Russia – in a manner which would remove fear, our own people in British Columbia and on the Prairies, Alta., Saskatchewan, etc., would all become very strong for looking to the U.S. for the protection that we needed. That this would inevitably lead to annexation movement which it might be hard to control. Bevin had said that he thought perhaps the best thing to do was to have an Imperial Conference fairly soon and bring the Dominions together. I said to him at once that that did not seem to me to be the step most necessary. That this Russian situation could not be met by Britain and the Dominions.

It could only be met by closer relations and understanding of the United States and the British Commonwealth.

"At dinner, Bevin had spoken of how the United States were pressing them unduly in the matter of obligations growing out of lend-lease. That they were getting tired of the way the United States was seeking to bind them in different directions. His attitude of mind semed to be combative. He, himself, thought that what they should do was to give the British credit over a number of years to give Britain time to get on her feet. If the credit could be paid back, well and good; if not, it could be extended. He said that unless they would do that, he himself felt the only alternative was frankly to tell the British people they must pull in their belts and get to work, economize and work in every way until they once again got back on their feet in world competition. It might take many years.

"I told him I thought the United States were much concerned over the Russian situation and that to work with the United States on the solution of that problem was to the mutual interest of Britain and the United States. A more generous attitude might develop on the part of the United States. I said at all costs to hold to friendship with the United States. Not to let antagonism develop there on any consideration. Bevin was most receptive of what I said. Before the night broke up, he replied that he had in the back of his head all that I had mentioned to him. That he would follow it up at once. He stated again that he would come back if necessary. What, however, is clearly most on his mind is the situation vis-à-vis Palestine. He told me he had been working on this and outlined what the policy was which is not to let the United States throw the whole burden onto Britain in trying to solve a question which was bound up with politics but to bring them toward effecting a solution. That he proposed to suggest a commission of enquiry at which the United States as well as Britain would be represented. It would meet in three stages: (1) enquiry; (2) careful study of situation in informing itself and numbers that could be accommodated there; and (3) leaving the final solution to the United Nations Organization once it came into being."

Mackenzie King was particularly interested to hear "how strongly Bevin spoke of Anthony Eden as being a great citizen and a great patriot – a noble man, a noble character. He felt sure he could count on Eden to help him in all his work. He had shown that sort of an attitude.

"He also spoke very feelingly of Churchill and of his qualities as a great statesman above party. One cannot but be impressed by this finer relationship between men in public life here as contrasted with the personal bitterness of political opponents in Canada; also the extent to which Ministers were prepared to take over those who were private secretaries to predecessors. Here was Bevin having as private secretary, Mr. Dixon, who had been with Eden at San Francisco and elsewhere. I am sure my talk tonight came just at the right moment; also that my presence in England at this time is exceptionally fortunate as it is clear that both Attlee and Bevin have been so pressed with other matters that they have not seen the necessity of working out as quickly and conclusively as possible some understanding with Russia which will enable the Big Five to function with some degree of confidence in the United Nations.

"I begin to feel that what Russia perhaps is aiming at is to get outside of the United Nations altogether, just as Germany and Japan and Italy did in the League of Nations in the years preceding the last war. They are determined to let the rest of the world know that what they are capable of doing is to go back into power politics and with greater vengeance than ever."

October 11 was really the first day Mackenzie King saw much of central London. On his way to and from lunch at *The Times* with Major Astor he had some opportunity to observe the war damage and sense the mood of the people. To him "the whole city has a gloomy bewildering sort of look about it. I see it through eyes wholly different from those in which I looked at London when I first came here in 1900 and indeed at different times since. A certain glory has passed away. One feels that the masses of people are struggling. One wonders how they manage at all. Food is at impossible prices. Clothing hardly obtainable. I personally feel uncomfortable having a large apartment as I have at the Dorchester. It is, I presume, necessary, however, for the position I hold."

Late that afternoon the Prime Minister went to Downing Street for a talk with Attlee which lasted about an hour. "He was very cordial in his welcome," Mackenzie King wrote. "Then spoke to me about a letter he had written the President around the 20th of September on the atomic bomb. It was a long letter – one of the best letters I have ever read. It spoke about the complete change the existence of the atomic bomb had made in world affairs. The necessity now of finding some way to good-will between nations which would save the world from complete destruction. He made it clear that another war would mean the end of the world. If we had to face that possibility, men would now have to prepare for people to live in caverns. He spoke of the need of a control that would admit of no uncertainty as to the use of the atomic energy for destructive purposes.

"The letter indicated that Attlee would be prepared to come to see him to get his views on the subject and to work toward ensuring peace. No answer has yet come from the President to this letter. Meanwhile Truman has made a statement to the effect that the United States will not give up the secret and he believes the United Kingdom and Canada will take the same position. Attlee said after I had finished reading the letter that scientists had told him that they saw no possibility of a secret of the kind being kept; that the Russians would certainly secure it. He felt once they secured it, it would become a weapon of power politics. That our only hope lay in fostering good-will with Russia.

"He then spoke about the question of his going over to America. He said he could not go without the press making a tremendous sensation of his going. It might look as if his visit had to do with financial matters which he would not want. He asked me if the President had told me of the letter. I said no but that he had intimated to me that Attlee would be coming over and was strongly of the view that the three of us should meet together to discuss the whole question of espionage, the atomic bomb and the United Nations Conference. I asked if he had made a further enquiry as to finding out if the President had received his letter and making a special request for an answer. He said that was being done now. I agreed that he should have an answer from the President which could be made the basis of his crossing. He was not sure that meeting the President might not risk further suspicion in the eyes of the Russians. I said if it were known that the atomic bomb was a matter being considered and how nations could be brought to closer and friendlier relations, that would do no harm and might do much good. He said they had been considering the matter in the Cabinet and had thought of Sir John Anderson being sent over to talk with the President. That he knew more about the development of the atomic bomb, etc., than any member of the Government. I told him it was not for me to express opinions of any member of the government but I questioned whether on the matter of promoting good-will between the U.S. and the U.K., Sir John would be as effective as he Attlee himself would be with the President. I said I thought that he and Truman would get along well together. Attlee agreed and said he liked Truman very much. I said they both had the same purpose and motive and would understand each other fully."

Conversation then turned to the Gouzenko case and, according to Mackenzie King, Attlee still favoured the immediate arrest of Professor May. "He stated that this could not be a matter of surprise to the Russians. As a matter of fact, they would come back with the reply that Britain herself had her spies. Was getting all the information she could about Russia. Russia also would say she had not kept her promise as an ally in not letting

Russia know that she was developing the atomic bomb and had found the secret before using the bomb itself. He said he thought it was a mistake not to have told the Russians. I said that President Roosevelt had said the same thing to me. He thought Stalin ought to be told that I had agreed with him.

"Attlee added that Winston was adamant on the matter and had felt he had a weapon there which could end all war. Attlee repeated he did not believe a secret of the kind could be kept. If it were kept away from the Russians, they would some day by action let us know that they possessed it.

"He then asked me if I had talked to the President about this and I told him of the three courses that had been considered, telling him that we had given the President the same information we had sent first to Bevin to pass on to Byrnes. I said we had given all the information we had. That the President had strongly expressed the view that no arrest should be made without giving both the United States and the United Kingdom authorities ample opportunity to get such additional information as was possible, and that the right way to proceed was to have a showdown with the Russians by Truman himself as well as Attlee and along with Canada, letting them know what we had of knowledge and of the extent of their spying procedure. I stressed this point to Attlee."

Eventually the British Prime Minister agreed and suggested further talks between Robertson and British officials before any firm decision was made. As they talked, Mackenzie King found Attlee "becoming increasingly tired and really very worried and exhausted. As he came to the door with me, he could not have done so in a kinder, gentler manner. I spoke to him of the pleasure of the night at Chequers and having meant to write Mrs. Attlee before this but of my cold having prevented that.

"As he opened the door of the Cabinet Council to let me into the hall, it seemed to me as if he was hardly able to stand on his feet. This perhaps is exaggerated view but I am beginning to wonder whether the load so suddenly placed upon him and upon Bevin may not be heavier than these two men can bear. The press reports that Stalin is away on a first real vacation. Greenwood says he knows positively, I do not know how, that Stalin is very seriously ill. . . . If that is so, the situation will be more difficult than ever. Stalin at least has shown he is prepared to meet situations in a way that will help to preserve peace.

"Attlee did say that he thought the Russians were intent on showing their power. That their successes had gone to their head. That they had an inferiority complex, very strong, and one could not say what they might do. I mentioned to Attlee what I had said to Barrington Ward last night and to Bevin about the situation that would develop in Canada once the people of our country and of the United States became alarmed at the Russians.

"That Russia was very near to Canada. Could bomb us from across the North Pole. Her hand was reaching out toward Alaska in the possession they had gained of the Kuriles Islands. Her route to the States would be through Canada and if the Americans felt security required it, would take peaceful possession of part of Canada with a welcome of the people of B.C., Alta., and Saskatchewan who would become terrified. I thought the only hope of meeting the Russian situation was at all costs for the United Kingdom and the United States to keep friendly and to have common policies on foreign relations.

"Attlee at one stage had spoken to me of what he had been told about the possibility of atomic bomb being sent high into the stratosphere to circle around there dropping at any moment on any part of the world, America, Asia, Britain or elsewhere and helping to make a total destruction. The whole business is the most frightful and frightening thing which has yet come to the world. Again how strange it is that I should find myself at the very centre of this problem through Canada possessing uranium, having contributed to the production of the bomb, being recognized as one of the three countries to hold most of the secrets and with knowledge of the United States and Canada having more in my possession of the Russian system of espionage and what it may affect at any moment than anyone living excepting the men whose duty it is to keep me informed. I am particularly sorry I am laid up with a heavy cold at this time and that I am war weary.

"Evatt spoke in the same way of himself. Robertson feels the same; finds it in all the departments over here. Everyone is tired out; not ready to tackle new problems. Another great world problem. However, it must be done and I am convinced with Attlee if it cannot be saved along the lines of Christian teaching, the world itself is doomed and that ere very long. I pray I may regain my health and vigour."

During Mackenzie King's stay in London delegates from the fourteen nations, including Canada, who had served on the Executive Committee of the San Francisco Conference were meeting to prepare plans for the first meetings of the United Nations General Assembly and other UN organizations. The committee had convened on August 16 and worked until October 27 on a series of recommendations which, in November, were presented to the Preparatory Commission, on which all UN members were represented. Lester Pearson represented Canada in the discussions until late in September when he was replaced by W. F. A. Turgeon, the Canadian Ambassador in Brussels. Since the committee's work was primarily organizational, the atmosphere was less tense and more productive than at other conferences in the immediate post-war period where the Great Powers jockeyed for position. On October 12 the Prime Minister received a report on the committee's work from the chief American delegate, Edward Stettinius, who called on him at the Dorchester. "We had an exceedingly pleasant talk together," Mackenzie King wrote. "Hopes to have final settlement of all matters pertaining to the organization of the U.N. over before Christmas. He told me there was great difficulty making much headway here. Had to keep pushing things along. I said I found everyone very tired and I thought it was better not to crowd things too rapidly. Explained how Bevin and others were used up with the pressure of the matters that followed so quickly upon them. Also lack of preparation in advance was responsible for not much success once meetings took place. He thought that by March or April, the Assembly itself would meet."

Stettinius asked the Prime Minister about his views on an appropriate place for the first meeting of the Assembly. "I told him it was so difficult to separate one's personal feelings – arising out of convenience, associations, etc., from a judgment wholly detached. It was difficult to say. My own preference frankly was for Geneva because I thought the place was such a suitable one for gatherings of the kind. On the other hand, Stettinius at once said that Geneva was out of the question. Russia could not consider it and spoke of two or three other States that were opposed. He then asked what about Canada or America or South America. I said I did not think other places in Europe would be as satisfactory, e.g., Vienna and the like, nor did I think South America was any good. That the difficulty with Canada was our cold climate in winter. Difficulty of getting hotel accommodation, etc. I said that some place in the States would be my second choice. I said, however, I did not like San Francisco, the city. If they were going to California, to try and get to Pasadena or somewhere other than that great city. He spoke of opening up a great area beyond the Golden Gate. He said it was imperative to be near a large city though not in it. Because of the need for concert hall, music places, etc. Also entertainment. He then said that there was no commitment as between one part of the U.N. rather than another. In that event, I said somewhere along the Atlantic seaboard would seem to me to be best. I did not think European nations should be asked to make that long journey across the whole Continent of the United States. The number of nations to be suited on the other side was more limited. He then told me they were quite open to consider sites in New England or Southern States; in any of the States along the Eastern border. I said that would suit us in Canada splendidly. Naturally I would be prepared to support that. I did not say to him what was most in my mind, namely, that I feel it very important to get U.N. conference tied down to U.S. in a way which would make them feel responsibility for its success. They are the most powerful nation and strong in shaping opinion of the nations."

Conversation then turned to the appointment of a Secretary General. Stettinius argued that if a European site was chosen for the United Nations "they could not choose a European for that position. If in the States, it should be someone of another country. He then spoke to me very confidentially about different names. Said there were two names in particular that he thought there would be strong likelihood of agreement upon. I knew at once who he meant. He followed it by saying: Pearson and Robertson. I said I agreed they were the best men we had. It would be a great loss to Canada to lose either of them but I would not stand in their way though I doubted if Robertson himself would be interested. Stettinius questioned me somewhat on Pearson's abilities as a scholar as well as diplomat. . . . I was able to speak in the highest terms of both. Van Kleffens' name [the Foreign Minister of the Netherlands] was mentioned. I did not think he would do. There was agreement between us on that. There were names of a few others mentioned. One or two prominent in Scandinavia. I said I doubted the wisdom of choosing one from a small country."

The following day (October 13) Mackenzie King was considerably irritated by a letter from Hugh Dalton inviting him to a meeting two days later to discuss Commonwealth trade preferences. Just after he had read the letter, his secretary came in with a note from the Chancellor's office requesting an immediate reply by telephone. "I felt I would have to make a decision at once. First of all, I am not in a position to discuss financial and trade questions. I have not come over for that purpose and I should not, without having had a prior conference with my colleagues in the Cabinet, wish to undertake so great a responsibility. . . ."

Dalton's indication that Dr. H. V. Evatt, the Australian Minister of External Affairs, would also be present only increased Mackenzie King's reluctance to attend. "Robertson had told me late last night that the meeting had been fixed for yesterday at Dominions Office to discuss matters with Evatt but he had not turned up. This meeting was being arranged so as to meet his convenience on Monday as he leaves for Washington a day or two afterwards." The Prime Minister decided to call Dalton to explain his inability to attend the meeting but only succeeded in getting through to the Chancellor's somewhat persistent private secretary. "The Private Secretary whoever he was said that the Chancellor would be very disappointed and I rather inferred from his remarks it was up to me to meet the Chancellor's wishes once they had been expressed. I replied I also regretted not being able to be present. I added to what I had said that I had come over on other matters which were not connected with trade or financial questions at all. I also was very tired. In fact, was used up and did not feel in shape to undertake discussion of a matter as important as that to which the Chancellor's letter referred.

"The Private Secretary still persisted in saying the Chancellor would be sorry to hear I could not come which caused me to repeat with a bit of insistence that I, too, was sorry but I had to consider my position and that of the Government."

Finally it was arranged that Norman Robertson would attend in the Prime Minister's place. On the morning of October 15 Mackenzie King decided to dictate a letter to the Chancellor of the Exchequer explaining his position again. "Robertson had thought it would not be necessary for me to do this but I thought I wished to have my position registered and protected, also to have on record what I could show my colleagues of my attitude on attempting as one member of the Government to settle or influence, even remotely, matters which have not been discussed by the Cabinet as a whole.

"Robertson told me tonight that he felt it was fortunate I had not gone to the meeting, that it developed into a sort of Party discussion with Evatt putting forward some views of his own and that the British Government did not seem to have its own mind made up. That altogether the discussion was futile. He thought that Cripps was the best informed person. He did not think that Dalton the Chancellor handled himself any too well.

"Robertson stated that he knew my view to be that it was very desirable that America and Britain should keep together as closely as possible and that we would be prepared to give most careful consideration to any proposals that would serve that end. I am sure my judgment was right in not being drawn into this discussion. Moreover there was no Prime Minister from any of the other Dominions. I think he said Hofmeyr was there with Evatt. At the end there was a question as to whether an announcement should be made of the meeting. R. counselled against any announcement. I think he was right. The whole purpose of this kind of a meeting was make believe and have the public think the Dominions are being consulted, etc."

Obviously upset by this incident, Mackenzie King had recorded in his diary on October 13 that he felt "a great sense of loneliness" in London and "thought a good deal about getting back to Canada as soon as possible." This feeling seemed to vanish on Sunday, October 14, which he spent with Mr. and Mrs. Frank Salisbury. During the afternoon, Salisbury's wife suggested that the Prime Minister should have his portrait painted. "This caused me to say that there is nothing I would value more than having a painting by Frank but there was only one condition on which I could consider it at all which was that he would treat me in the same way he would any other sitter. That Sir William Mulock had left me a very handsome bequest and that I had felt when I received it that out of part of it I should like to get a painting of myself which could be left to the country, one which would really portray the side of my nature which I thought Frank knew perhaps better than any other artists. I told them that J. [Mrs. Patteson] had spoken of being anxious I should be painted by Salisbury. I then said something about sometime when he was out I would like to have this done if he could arrange it. He then asked me about the present and finally indicated that he would be ready to put off all sitters excepting one man and give his entire time to a portrait while I am here. He stressed the importance of the present as against any other time. I have been feeling so tired, so depressed and, of late, so unworthy at anything that I rather questioned the wisdom of sitting for a portrait at this time. He went on, however, to say that a cold would not make any difference, that he had watched my different expressions, knew my features and would be glad to go right ahead. And then said a word about the style of portrait. He asked me if I had any gowns or robes with me. I said I had not. I described the Orpen painting, how it came to be done. This was at Beaverbrook's instance and it was loaned to me for my life or given to me to keep for my life, or otherwise for the nation. I then said I thought it would be better to just have ordinary dress. He himself said he believed that what the people themselves would like best of all would be ordinary dress and thought that the suit I was in would be quite good. He had also liked the brown suit I had been wearing yesterday. He thought it would be best to have a portrait painted, seated. Indeed, while we were talking we were looking at one of his paintings of President Roosevelt, one the President liked best and which is in plain dress. Frank thought that something on that line would be best.

"I then told him that I could not think of having anything of the kind done if it were not that after all I was the one Prime Minister who had gone through the whole period of the war – before its beginning until after its close – that I had now a record of nearly nineteen years as Prime Minister and was in my twenty-seventh year as Leader of the Party, with other years in Parliament as well. Also I was now in my seventieth year and had been in ten General Elections in Canada, seven while myself Leader of the Party, and had won six out of the seven. It seemed to me that this might be an excuse for having a painting made.

"Frank spoke of it as something for the Houses of Parliament. I said

I felt I ought to give it to the Houses of Parliament or to the National Art Gallery. Of course the Houses of Parliament would be preferable. He would not discuss any question of arrangement. I repeated I would only allow him to do it on the condition it would be treated as a business matter and that he would treat me as he would others in the manner I described. We then discussed the possibility of beginning this week. He thought, too, he would probably finish it by the end of the week if I could give him pretty continuous sittings. I could run away to keep any engagements. Everything considered I felt perhaps that such an opportunity would never come again and I accordingly arranged to have the first sitting on Wednesday.... The painting, I think, is more important than anything else...."

Sittings began on October 16 and continued daily until the 20th. The hours he spent in Salisbury's studio gave Mackenzie King great pleasure. In a telephone conversation with Salisbury on October 22 he told him that "the past week had been as happy as any week in my life. That it was something I would never forget. That I should never forget its days and what they had meant to me quite apart from the portrait altogether. So far as the portrait is concerned, it seemed to mark a completion of something that I had hoped for most in my life – a permanent record of which I was wholly satisfied to bring it to the country. I was glad in his letter that he added that my argument about having the portrait regarded as a business matter was so convincing that he would allow it to be so, much as it was against his wish. This gives me the feeling that I am most anxious to have for the portrait being my very own – something which I can personally bequeath to Parliament and in particular to the House."

When the Prime Minister returned to the Dorchester on October 16 after a pleasant talk with Neville Chamberlain's widow, he found a call from Mr. Attlee. The British Prime Minister told him that he had received a reply from President Truman to his earlier letter. Truman was "interested in the points raised and would be glad to go into them later. Attlee said this was not very satisfactory. Each of us found it difficult to understand.

"Regarding the man tomorrow ... night [Professor May's next meeting with his Soviet contact], I said it was quite all right to go ahead with him but that we could not take similar action [in arresting the Canadian citizens implicated by Igor Gouzenko]. That was based on the idea of a plan arranged as a result of a meeting between Attlee, the President and ourselves."

Early the next evening Robertson delivered another communication from Attlee to Mackenzie King. "When I opened it, I found it contained the letter from Prime Minister Attlee to the President on the atomic bomb which had been written on the 26th of September. There was an acknowledgment from Mr. Truman, dated the 5th of October. This was the acknowledgment which Mr. Attlee referred to in my talk over the 'phone with him on Monday night, the 16th, and which Attlee said was not very satisfactory. Evidently the acknowledgment must have come by mail. It referred to Attlee's letter as a thoughtful letter on the atomic bomb problem. Says there can be no division of opinion regarding the gravity of the problem which presses for a solution and the President would talk with Mr. Byrnes informing himself further in regard to Mr. Attlee's further thoughts on the problem. I have no doubt this refers to R.E. [Russian espionage] as well and adds: later I shall of course be very pleased to discuss the question with you at a time and place that is convenient to both of us.

"Mr. Attlee had received that letter only on the 15th and on the 16th wrote the President acknowledging it, expressing his desire to see the President before making further statements in Parliament on the subject of the atomic bomb. Says that he had been discussing the matter with me here, who takes the same view as he does of the urgency of the problem and adds: I should like to receive your views and I think it important that you and I and Mackenzie King should have a discussion as soon as possible. I need hardly say I am prepared to come over as soon as convenient.

"Robertson told me that he had, only a few minutes before handing me this confidential letter, heard from Attlee's Secretary, Rowan, to the effect that Mr. Attlee had received this afternoon a further letter from the President in which the President expressed the hope that he, Attlee, would come over to the U.S. and that he, Attlee and myself might meet together at the White House to consider the whole situation.

"The President said he would be there any time before the 27th of the present month or any time after the 6th of November. Rowan had been asked by Attlee to tell me of this communication and to let him have my views upon it. I told Robertson to reply, which he did in my room, while I was here to the effect that I was prepared to do whatever Mr. Attlee wished to do. To go at whatever time and by whatever route might be necessary."

Mackenzie King and Robertson had a preliminary discussion of alternative travel arrangements which would bring them back to Canada in time to attend the conference in Washington with Attlee and Truman. Both preferred either November 10 or 11 for the conference itself but a final decision on their departure date was postponed. The Prime Minister realized that this development "puts the Continent off the map as far as a visit there at this time is concerned. Gives me the best of reasons for not going over there. Attlee has fixed Wednesday of next week for a dinner at the House of Commons with himself and some colleagues. That will keep the Canadian public informed of my continuing to be in touch with the Government here. There will be a real world sensation when it is announced that the President, Attlee and myself are together in Washington and there follows probably immediately thereafter some disclosure of the R.E. matter."

On October 18 Mackenzie King had what he described as "a most delightful and refreshing conversation" with Lord Addison at the Dominions Office. Addison "wished to discuss the situation in Newfoundland and presented a case much as we have known it would be presented. In a word, the British Government are to allow the people of Newfoundland to decide on its future in some convention to be held in the coming year. Newfoundland has been prosperous through the war but it is unlikely that she will be able to continue that prosperity for long. The British Government are unable to make large expenditures on the Island and it is doubtful if the people governing themselves may not again fall into bankruptcy.

"The Government here would like to see Newfoundland a part of Confederation. They do not wish to see the Island fall into the hands of the U.S. They realize that unless the Newfoundland Government itself wishes to join Confederation, there would be no possibility of bringing it about.

"I expressed the view that it was regarded as a financial liability. We recognized, however, there were strategic reasons why it was desirable it should come to be a part of the Dominion. If our arrangements with the provinces at the Dominion-Provincial Conference were successful, it might be that we would be willing to make terms for Newfoundland similar to what we were doing for each of the other provinces; that would mean we would not have much difficulty with other provinces of getting their consent to having Newfoundland enter Confederation. Both Lord Addison and I said we were simply thinking aloud and were committing no one to anything but the British Government wished to be able to see their way. All that was being said amounted to Canada not objecting to the British Government lending such encouragement as it might find it possible to lend to the Island to make overtures to the Dominion if it so desired.

"Lord Addison brought up the question of conference. Mentioned that he and his colleagues had been talking over matters quite evidently as the result of the meeting suggested last week with Evatt. Lord Addison told me that when it was suggested to hold the meeting and to bring me in, he himself had said: I bet my bottom dollar Mackenzie King won't come to that meeting. He thought I was entirely right in staying away. That no one should be expected to discuss a big problem without being notified in advance and having a chance to confer with his colleagues, etc. I stressed strongly my point of view with Lord Addison as to ending this business of one man making decisions for his country without consulting with his colleagues. Lord Addison told me I was 100% right...."

That evening the Prime Minister was the guest of Lord Moran at the Harveian dinner. Aneuran Bevan was present and Mackenzie King found him unimpressive, "a rather rough and tumble sort of man, without depth or dignity." During dinner Attlee told Mackenzie King he intended to cross the Atlantic by plane and expected to be in Washington on either November 10 or 11. Mackenzie King told Attlee that he planned to sail on the *Queen Mary* on November 4.

Late in the afternoon on October 19 the Prime Minister went to Marlborough House to see Lord Athlone and Princess Alice, who were on leave in England, and to have an audience with Queen Mary. Athlone seemed to be a somewhat fussy host. The two men exchanged information on their respective colds and then Athlone "skirmished around the house to bring a little table which he could put between two chairs, which were on opposite sides of the fireplace. He was going to light the fireplace but I told him not to think of it, the room was quite warm." According to Mackenzie King's account, their conversation "was quite general."

"After a short time Queen Mary came in dressed in a blue suit – dressed as though she had been out walking or driving. She spoke very pleasantly about meeting again and enquired as to my cold. She then spoke about Lord Athlone's cold, referring to him as her brother, and it being nice for them to be together there. We had quite a nice talk.... Queen Mary looks considerably older. A little anxious in appearance. Is bent more than she was. I notice while talking she was continually moving her fingers of both hands. She sat, though, remarkably erect."

Almost the only reference in Mackenzie King's English diary to events in Canada was an entry on October 20. He was "much annoyed to find that the Government had decided to put a duty on some commodities to help an industry in Welland. Had divided with a majority of one. This should never have been permitted and would not have been had I been in Ottawa. I learned tonight that the charter approving the U.N. organization – the resolution approving the U.N. charter – has been passed by the Canadian Parliament."

On Sunday evening, October 21, Mackenzie King dined with the Attlee family at 10 Downing Street. Apparently it was a delightfully relaxing evening. "I was surprised and felt much honoured to discover that I was the only guest and that the dinner was one of the first which Mr. and Mrs. Attlee had in their new home. . . . They have had the top floor of 10 Downing St. done over like a large apartment. Everything fresh and clean, walls a light green in colour. A fine sitting room. A sloping roof at one end overlooking the Horse Guards parade ground. At another end of one of the passages, the dining room with the kitchen and serving pantry off.

"On the floor beneath, the P.M. has his library. It is the room which was used by Baldwin for a similar purpose when he and his family were occupying the lower floor as their home. I had not known until tonight there was a little elevator from the main hall to the top floor. I was a minute or two ahead of time. The P.M. and Martin were waiting in the drawing room. A few minutes later, Miss Felicity Attlee came in. A fine looking young girl who is doing some nursing at one of the hospitals and a moment later, Mrs. Attlee looking very sweet and gentle as she does. . . .

"The conversation at dinner was a pleasant family conversation on a variety of subjects. . . . After dinner, we returned to the drawing room. Felicity Attlee left to return to her work. The P.M. took me downstairs to his library. I was interested in noticing how it included some of the books that he had had at College and those which he had studied and worked over during recent years. Before the evening was over, he drew my attention to 'Industry and Humanity' being among the number. I drew his attention to the quotation from Pasteur. He later read to me the last part of an address he had made in '35 or '36 published in his book on the Labour Party and its aims. He had quoted this yesterday in his speech in Scotland to make clear that what he is now doing is to seek to carry out the views set forth at that time."

During their conversation, Attlee re-opened the question of immediately arresting "Primrose," Professor A. N. May. "That he had not turned up on Wednesday evening and their intelligence officials were feeling that they ought to disassociate him from the work that he is doing in connection with atomic energy and that if there was a much longer delay, the whole business would be getting cold and blame might attach for not having taken some immediate action. They proposed as what they would like to do, to examine him privately under some military protectionist measure – I have forgotten the name of it, not with a view to publicity being given but simply to bring out information which would be helpful in discussing the matter later with the Russians. He thought it was as well to have the information first.

"He then asked me if we could not begin an immediate enquiry. I told him that I agreed it was not well to delay much longer the getting of information. I doubted, however, if we had the same authority at law for examining individuals on the score of suspicion. Attlee himself referred to the girl in the High Commissioner's Office and I mentioned the clerk in our own External Affairs and said that quite recently, we had found that some papers in our passport office were missing which we had been a little suspicious about. I told him I would communicate with the Minister of Justice and see if some way could not be arranged whereby we could immediately question the different persons involved in what we had discovered. Attlee stressed the point of not giving publicity to the matter at present but of having the information where it could be given to the Russians.

"We both agreed that they probably already were aware of my having some of the information. I spoke particularly in this connection of the fact that Gousev [the Russian Ambassador in London] had not called on me nor had he come to speak to me at the dinner of the Harveian Society at which he was present. That I thought was significant. . . .

"I said then to Attlee that I thought it was important before we did anything or he did anything, that we should let the President know at once of what we planned; that I had promised him that we would not act without letting him know and that what we had really thought was the best way of proceeding was to do nothing at all until after he, Attlee, and the President and myself had had a talk together and were mutually agreed upon the plan.

"This brought up at once the question of the time at which the talk would be possible. Attlee said that he was planning to be at the White House on the 11th which is Armistice Day. Might stay a few days. There were a number of things he would like to talk about.

"He then told me that cables had been exchanged in the last day or two as to what was best as to the announcement of his visit and the time of it. He said that the President seemed to have been in favour of giving it a slant away altogether from the Russian situation and the atomic bomb. He, Attlee, did not think that that would be wise. It was much better to have it known at once he was coming to talk over the bomb problem. That sooner or later the facts would come out and he saw no reason why the public should not know that they were discussing among other things the atomic bomb.

"I said I agreed with him in that. He then told me that Halifax had, he thought, persuaded the President that it was best not to do other than have it known publicly the exact purpose of the meeting. I said to Attlee after all it was known everywhere that Britain, the U.S. and Canada had had most to do with the matter of the use of atomic energy for war purposes, and that nothing could be more natural than that we should meet to discuss that situation and to deal with the Russian situation in relation to it. He said moreover he had to make a statement in Parliament about Britain's policy and did not want to delay too long. He proposed perhaps within the next day or two to say he had been in communication with the President and the Dominions on the matter; was going to have the conference at Washington and felt that would avoid making any further statement in Parliament at once. He told me that he did not know exactly what was happening to Stalin.

"That it looked as though Stalin was really seriously ill; might be a break-up after the war. After all he was not young and had been through a terrible strain. But they could get no information. He agreed that if anything happened to Stalin, it would probably delay any hasty action on the part of the Russians against other parts of the world but we also agreed that there were forces other than the government that controlled situations there.

"Attlee said that he, for a long time past, had thought and spoken of the Russians as ideological Imperialists. They were out for power and they were using their ideologies with the masses to secure that end. The masses themselves did not realize the significance of it all. He felt very concerned about the use of the atomic energy and what might develop through the discoveries that have been made. There are two articles in today's Sunday Times which are most significant and important on this subject."

Mackenzie King "repeated to Attlee that what I proposed to do was to let the President know of our talk together. Say that we felt Primrose should be apprehended for questioning without delay and that we should seek to verify through examination of witnesses in Ottawa, the information we already have so that this might be available before the conference at Washington. But that I wished to get the President made aware of this before taking any action. Also ascertain his views. This Attlee agreed to. I shall get off a telegram in the morning.

"He, Attlee, told me that among other reasons why he did not wish to cross before the later date mentioned by the President, was that there is an important gathering at the Guildhall which he wished to have over before he left. He thought we could easily arrange for the recall of the Ambassador and others from Ottawa quietly, without disclosing the reason. I am not so sure that this will be as easy to arrange and that that step may not be the occasion of publicity which might throw the main onus of everything on Canada.

"I told Attlee I was deeply concerned about Canada's position in the event of any trouble arising between Russia and other countries. That I believed it would be the battleground; that they were near neighbours of ours and to reach America, would come across Canadian territory.

"I also added that I felt perfectly sure that once the Western provinces became alarmed in the matter of their security, they would look to the United States for protection; not to Canada itself or the Commonwealth. This was something to keep in mind. I again stressed the necessity at all costs of being patient with the U.S. in the matter of reaching an agreement; let nothing come up which would cause these two countries to get apart but to keep on working close together on the policy on which they were both agreed. Attlee said he was sure that that was right. I said we must be patient, too, with Russia but be careful and seek to obtain the right of investigation into matters which threatened danger to other countries."

The Prime Minister felt obliged to explain to Attlee personally the reasons for his refusal to attend the meeting called by the Chancellor of the Exchequer. "Attlee said that he fully understood and that all the others did." Conversation then turned to the problems of the "public service, particularly men in foreign affairs. He told me that there had been a real shaking up in the Foreign Office, giving younger men a chance, etc. That there was a terrible tendency particularly under Tory Ministers who liked ease, to have their own time, in their own way; to leave very much to their officials and the officials got, after a time, where they began to control matters themselves.

"This was true of all departments. That recently one of his own Ministers – a young man in charge of a department – had had to argue at length with his officials about certain things being done and had finally said he wanted a certain thing done and done at once; that he, himself, was directing. The matter had brought a sort of feud. Attlee said he commended his Minister very strongly and said that was what he wanted his Ministers to do. Take responsibility and see that it was carried out. He was very strong on the kind of bureaucracy that soon develops in government departments, unless there are Ministers who are really capable of exerting their authority and are prepared to exercise it."

Much to Mackenzie King's "surprise and delight" the British Prime Minister gave him a letter outlining arrangements for the repatriation of Canadian troops in the United Kingdom and on the Continent, a politically sensitive issue in Canada. The letter made "clear that according to present plans the British Government shall repatriate to Canada 162,000 men between July and December 1945 and hope that repatriation will be complete by the 30th of April, 1946. The letter made clear that I had been anxious over this problem and that the letter was to relieve that anxiety and to give the assurances necessary which included the reference to the Americans returning to the British the Queen Elizabeth and the Aquitania which had been lent to them until the end of 1945; also referred to the repatriation of prisoners of war and internees from the Far East. The letter concludes with assurance that the government is most anxious to get our men home as soon as possible and that it is endeavouring to allocate the ships available as fairly as possible between all requirements.

"I thanked Attlee warmly for this letter and recalled our talk together regarding the repatriation of our men as we drove into the city from Chequers on the morning after my arrival. This was before the Queen Elizabeth had been turned over. I asked him if it were the case that Canada's action in furthering the transportation of British troops from the Far East across the Dominion and my talk with him had been factors which contributed to this arrangement. The P.M. replied that such was the case. He authorized me to have this made clear. I told him I thought it would be helpful to both his government and our own to have that known and understood; that, in fact, a section of the Canadian Press had already made that statement without any inspiration or knowledge on my part. I then asked if I might make public the letter which he had given to me. It is not marked private. He stated that I might. I then spoke as to the time. He thought it would be best to wait until my return and give it to Parliament after my arrival. Nothing surely could be better than this. Mr. Attlee then talked to me about questions in the Far East. What Mountbatten had accomplished. . . .

"In the course of the conversation, reference was made to Winston's speech of yesterday in which Churchill spoke of the gulf possibly widening between Attlee's government and Churchill's party. He said in a few words: He is the one who widened the gulf. He spoke of the advantage it had been to be in the coalition for years and get the knowledge and background of conditions in the world but agreed that coalitions themselves were a mistake except for special purposes. I said I thought it was possible the war might never have come on had there been a strong government and a strong opposition. That a Tory government would have gone in for arming; a liberal radical government for settlement by peaceful means of outstanding difficulties.

"Attlee said he agreed entirely; that the period of Baldwin, who was a man who liked peace and quiet, and Ramsay MacDonald who could not arrive at a real decision on anything, had been an unfortunate period for Britain."

After their private conversation in the library, the two men returned to the drawing room. "Martin and his mother were having a new game of rummy quietly together, with the radio on. I said goodnight almost at once. Martin took the little dog King out for a walk in the park. Attlee came with me to the front door. Going down the lift, I thanked him for the invitation to meet members of the Government at dinner in the House of Commons on Wednesday. He told me that it was the first time that this had been arranged. That it was an innovation. He had enquired of the chefs as to whether they could carry out a dinner there. They had told him they certainly could. He said he had said to them he was sure I would enjoy dining in the Commons and then mentioned that it left the evening quite free so that if a division bell rang, Members could slip into the House to vote without going out of the buildings.

"I told him it was a distinct honour to be associated with a departure of the kind which will probably become a feature of the Commons life.

"The last time I walked out of 10 Downing Street, at the end of a visit, Mary Churchill had come to the door with me to say good-bye. Mary was in a uniform. Tonight, Martin was dressed in his midshipman uniform and was taking out the little dog."

Early the next morning, October 22, Mackenzie King met Norman Robertson and reviewed his conversation with Attlee, particularly the British Prime Minister's anxiety about early action on Gouzenko's disclosures. "I told him I thought we should get off immediately a telegram to the President telling him of my talk with Attlee, of my intention to communicate with the Minister of Justice in Canada as to examining persons whose names we have before us with a view to having as much information as possible when we arrive at Washington, and let the President know of my plans for sailing on the Queen Mary and being in Washington on the eve of Armistice Day; of my asking for his approval of the course proposed by Attlee before finally acquiescing in it. Also the drafting of a telegram to St. Laurent as to what was being proposed. I find Robertson hesitant on these matters, timid about taking positive action, and this quite rightly so. There cannot be too much caution. At the same time, I share absolutely Attlee's view that to leave the Primrose and other matters too long is to let the whole thing get cold and to risk being blamed by the public for not having taken action at once or at least sooner. I stressed the importance of getting information but not making arrests. Also the necessity of getting people out of the positions they are in who have been guilty of espionage. They can be apprehended later.

"Robertson spoke of searching their premises, seizing material in their rooms, etc. I said there was no reason why this could not be done in the same manner that I had handled the question of passports with the (Japanese) Nippon Supply Co., years ago, namely asking them to permit a search at once. In the event of any resistance, taking the step under a warrant, etc., letting them know it would be all to the good for them to give evidence very quietly. Another thing Robertson suggested was for me to let my colleagues know at once. I told him I thought it would be inadvisable to be in haste about having colleagues know anything that they do not already know. That I would have to take the decisions myself. They would have to trust me as they have in the past and I knew would be prepared to do. I can see in Robertson always a tendency to get things into the hands of the permanent officials rather than to leave them to the judgment of the government. That is all right enough but the two have to be kept in balance. I do not propose to yield my own judgment to any man living. I have not been given the place I occupy at the head of the country without the people trusting my judgment in their interests in these matters.

"I told Robertson to see that any telegrams before they were sent were shown to Attlee and approved by him.

"(Later in the day – 8.00 P.M.) Spent a considerable time with Robertson going over what should be done at Ottawa regarding R.E. He is working on a draft to be sent Wrong and a communication supplementing it to Pearson at Washington. I am anxious to have Attlee see both communications before they are sent. It is important they should meet with his approval. I am strongly taking the position that we should not attempt any arrests at the outset but have employees of the Government questioned in the presence of the Minister of Justice. If they refused to allow searching to be made, then they should be apprehended under warrants. I doubt the wisdom of attempting any general enquiry by a Royal Commission until we got some evidence other than that of Corby's on which has been based the line of action to be taken when the conference is held in Washington between Attlee and the President.

"The letter I sent to Attlee today made clear the desirability of my going to Washington with him and of the conference we were having together."

On October 23, Mackenzie King lunched at Buckingham Palace with the King and Queen and the two Princesses. He was taken by the King's Equerry "to one of the drawing rooms on the second floor which, he said, they were just beginning to use. In a few minutes, the King and Queen came in with the two Princesses immediately behind them. I shook hands first with the Queen who came forward a little before the King and then with the King and then with the Princesses. They asked me about my stay in London; my cold; spoke of Lord Athlone having had a similar experience. Also of the pleasure to meet again and we then went in to a smaller room adjoining in which there was a round table. The King sat on the far side with Princess Elizabeth next to him. I was placed next to Princess Elizabeth with the Queen to my right, and the little Princess Margaret Rose sat between the Queen and the King. It seemed very natural to be again sharing a pleasant hour with the King and Queen. They were as natural and friendly as could be. I spoke to the Queen of the message she had sent to the Queen Elizabeth and of her reference to coming to Canada again. She said she hoped very much to do so. Both she and the King spoke of what the Scottish regiment had meant in England from the beginning of the war, with the Canadian troops being practically the only ones in England, that it was their presence here which enabled England to send some of her troops to the near East. Then of the nearness of the call at different times in the course of the war especially of Germany's great strength. I spoke of their own great example and how it had helped to buoy up others. The King told me that he felt very tired. That he sometimes felt as though everything had gone out from under him. There was a curious sort of feeling. Kind of unreality. The symptoms as he described them were very similar to what I myself feel. Kind of great exhaustion after a tremendous strain. McNaughton's name was mentioned and how well he had done over here. I spoke of the new Governor General. Mentioned I had not seen him thus far. The King spoke of him as a great personal friend of his own; one who was very wise and thoughtful. . . .

"We talked a little of the new Government; and of Churchill's defeat. The King said that he had asked Attlee to make Bevin Foreign Minister. That Attlee had spoken of him for Chancellor. He mentioned something of this at the table and repeated to me after when we were alone that he had felt that Bevin was the better man for Foreign Minister. Not Dalton. I noticed that the Queen seemed a little surprised when the King used the expression he had secured Bevin as Foreign Minister which I think was what caused him to tell me later that Dalton had been proposed for that post. The King thought Bevin was doing very well; was very patriotic. Something was said about Russia being exceedingly difficult and the King asked me if I knew what had happened to Stalin. I told him Attlee had said to me he did not know. Both the King and Queen thought it was strange that Stalin should be away with his daughter getting a rest and the public not informed when there were rumours he was very ill and might be dead. The King spoke of the dual kind of government there was at Moscow. One did not know whether they were dealing with Stalin or whether with some other group that was really controlling things. At all events it was always in evidence directing certain courses. It is clear that the Palace is concerned about Russia though nothing in particular was said about possible use of the atomic bomb. The King thought Russia would probably have learned something from Molotov going back and having to acknowledge to their people that the Council of Ministers had been a failure and that America and Britain were united in their views that Russia was in the wrong.

"Something was said about Americans being difficult in financial arrangements. The King thought three millions of them in the country would have gathered some things about the British which they would take back.

"I said it was to be remembered the Government itself had difficulties with its own people; large numbers of foreigners, etc. But emphasized the necessity of England and America keeping together and especially re Russia.

"Some mention was made of Hitler. When the King was speaking of not knowing whether Stalin was dead or alive, in addition to not knowing whether Hitler was dead or alive, the King said something about it being a pity that Hitler had not been shot. Princess Elizabeth said she would have been prepared to shoot him...."

After luncheon, "the Queen spoke about her reviewing the Canadian W.D.s this afternoon," an engagement which Mackenzie King missed so that he could have a longer talk with the King. "He asked me what I thought of Attlee. I told him I liked Attlee very much. Had known him for some years. Thought he was modest but quiet and able. The King said he found it very hard to talk to him. He would just say a sentence or two. Would then be quiet. Did not seem to get far in conversation. (I recall the King making a somewhat similar remark about Eden at Hyde Park saying the only difference was that Eden seemed to read answers from a paper or to be so careful about what he said.)

"The King then said to me: You know, of course, that my brother [the Duke of Windsor] has been over here. He stayed with my mother. I was over and talked with him. He is not coming to live in England. We would not have his wife here. He understands that. France is not a place that he can very well live in long. Things are very unsettled there. We talked of the possibility of his going to live in America. He said he would like to help to further friendly relations between United States, Britain and Canada. (I recall Edward having said to me much the same thing when he was anxious to go to Hollywood.) He could not, of course, be given an official post. He has many friends in America. Knows many of the Americans who have been over here. He could receive people from here at his home there and have them meet others in America. He could not, of course, have an official position but being who he is, could perhaps render a helpful service that way. The King then asked me what I thought of that.

I replied that I did not see there was any official post that could be given to the Duke of Windsor very well. He had been asked if he would be prepared to accept the position of Governor General of Canada. Replied he would. I had received a number of letters protesting against the thought of it. Of course the people of Canada would not have thought of having him in such a position. We would do nothing that would be other than making clear that we stood solidly behind the King himself. I felt, however, I could see no reason why he should not live in the United States if he wished to do so. He had been at his ranch a couple of times in Canada. He would always be welcome there. He had I thought made a good impression in America. Recalled having met him at the White House when Churchill was there. The King then said he, of course, would have to get some word to the President and to the Secretary of State to see what they thought about it. He said that their meeting had been very friendly; since he had gone back to France he had written a very nice letter to him, the King. That he, the King, had told him he did not like his earlier letters. There were passages in them that he thought had been written by lawyers, not by himself; Edward said that was true. His whole tone and attitude, however, were quite different on this occasion. The King said that of course his wife was the trouble, the bone of contention. I said to him that I certainly felt that the only attitude that he, the King, could take was a brotherly attitude and if it were known that he, the King, was anxious that the Duke of Windsor should be well received in America, that would go far. He said he rather hesitated to talk to Attlee about it. . . .

"The King spoke of expenses in America being pretty costly. He said that with regard to the visit [of the Duke in England] he was a little anxious about it before it came off but felt it had been all to the good and felt different about things. Said the bitterness of the past was over. He said he would have, of course, to speak to Halifax and satisfy him that it was all right for the Duke of Windsor to go to America. It was clear that what the King was trying to gain for him was to be a sort of unofficial Ambassador. I said to the King I thought Winant [J. G. Winant, the American Ambassador in London] might be a better person to speak to, to take any messages to Washington. The King said he did not know Winant very well. He thought it might be all right to talk with Churchill about him. I said I saw no reason why he should not. He told me I was the only person he had spoken to thus far and would ask me to keep the matter confidential. When I was coming away, I said if there was anything I could do in any way at any time to not hesitate to let me know."

The Prime Minister thought the King looked very well. "Had gained in force and strength. He remembers incidents of the past well and is remarkably free in his speech from any stammering. He spoke with some interest and enthusiasm of the time he had getting off to Scotland when the change of Government took place and of having to make the speech from the Throne in the afternoon and a broadcast of it at night."

After leaving the Palace in mid-afternoon, Mackenzie King was driven to Westminster and ushered into the section of the Commons Gallery reserved for Dominion representatives. "The first person I saw in the House was Churchill who was immediately opposite to where I was standing. The Chancellor had just begun his budget address. The House was filled to capacity. I figured that there must be about 600 on the floor. Members were crowded against each other on the benches. The whole proceedings were very orderly. I thought Dalton read his material very well. Had many humorous touches. While he was speaking, about the middle of the speech, Eden, who was seated next to Churchill, smiled and then nudged Churchill who looked up and when he saw me, nodded and then put up his hand and waved. It was quite an experience to have had in the British House of Commons. Churchill's reply was exceedingly well made. He spoke slowly, giving careful attention and thought to each word; using the right word. Light touches all the way through. A great deal of humour; befitting commendation to his opponents. Altogether I thought a very excellent introduction to the debate.

"I was interested to see how rapidly the proceedings were conducted. Instead of water, Dalton drank what looked like milk while he was speaking.

"Oliver Lyttelton was sitting on the other side of Churchill. I did not know most of the other ones on the Government benches. Attlee had his feet on the table most of the time and at one time, at least six of the opposition side including Churchill put their feet up against the edge of the table. I am sure that the compact house is a better house for purposes of debate than what we have. The whole decorum was much finer though I know it is not always what it was today. There were substantial reductions in the income tax; for persons in lower brackets; some increase in the surtax. Excess profits tax lowered. I noticed that the Opposition favoured a good deal of what was proposed in the budget.

"Churchill made the most of getting people producing goods; not keeping them in the army, etc. Beverley Baxter came up to shake hands with me; downstairs, Clement Davies, leader of the Liberal party, shook hands and said he would like to come and have a talk. Hopes some time to get the old party going again."

When he returned to his hotel Mackenzie King had Robertson in to hear the details of his interviews about the Gouzenko affair during the day.

Robertson had met that afternoon with two representatives of the British Secret Service and had "gone over the draft which he had prepared this morning but had come to the conclusion that we might question the few men without danger of publicity but where there were 18, it was almost certain there would be publicity. Also they thought that an effort should be made to capture the principal persons who would be Rose and Kerr. In fact, the conversation indicated that they felt it was wiser to defer any action until after we had met at Washington. That we could take the posiion that instead of having delayed matters, thereby endangering a situation, we had purposely waited until the President and Attlee had conferred together, and the whole atomic bomb question had been taken up before giving any publicity to the R.E. matter. To have given publicity before this interview would have been to prejudice whatever joint action the different countries might wish to take toward Russia. This has been our view from the start but Attlee had represented on Sunday night that M.I. 5 [the British Intelligence Service] were anxious to apprehend criminals at once, and had asked if we could not proceed at once. It was clear the only way we could proceed at once was by voluntary questioning unless we wanted to give publicity to the whole business.

"Robertson reported that the President had at first thought it was better to make no mention of the atomic bomb at all but as Attlee stated to me on Sunday night, Halifax had persuaded him it was best to have it known that the atomic bomb was one of the subjects to be discussed. It is now definitely fixed that the meeting will take place in Washington on Monday the 12th instead of Sunday the 11th. That has been to meet Byrnes, Secretary of State of the U.S., convenience, who will be present. No date has yet been fixed for announcement but it will probably be about the 4th which will be about the time that we sail. I should be happy if it could be announced just as we were leaving.

"The announcement will, of course, have reference to Attlee and myself both meeting in Washington. This will fit in perfectly with our going back on the Queen Mary; indeed here again it would almost seem as if some unseen hands had planned the whole arrangements. Attlee is to see me probably in the morning as a result of the talk Robertson had today with M.I. 5 people and at the Foreign Office along with Rowan.

"Robertson feels very strongly even yet they have not got hold of the whole significance of the situation here. Cadogan has been away on a holiday. Bevin has been absent. The whole business has been allowed to drift so far as the U.K. is concerned. It is now, however, taking definite shape."

On October 24, while Mackenzie King was at Salisbury's house for a final sitting, Field Marshal Montgomery came in to view his own portrait.

"I enjoyed immensely the talk we had together," the Prime Minister wrote. "He began speaking about Germany. . . . He is in charge of the whole civil organization. Says he has learned much about the government of men. Is also commander in chief of the occupation area and is a member of the Council which has to deal with future organization, etc. He says the conditions are going to be very difficult this winter. That in the first place he will not have enough food for the people. That the best he can do in the way of rations is to give them half the amount of rations which is allowed to the people in Britain who are being inadequately fed at present. He said there is very little clothing and that worst of all, the houses are cold. Many of them will have no fuel at all. He also fears there will be much disease. If they can get through the winter and the spring and begin with gardening again, there may be some chance but he fears the loss of life will be very heavy. He told me he believed the only settlement that would be any good would be for the French and other powers to take possession of German territory right up to the Rhine, internationalize the Ruhr by taking off German territory of the Rhine. They would only be doing what Russia had done on the other side.

"He feels that he is seeking to carry out Potsdam decisions. Asked if I would come to Berlin to see the troops; offered to do anything he could to make the visit worthwhile. He asked me how long we wanted to keep our men there. I told him we wanted them back as soon as possible. He asked if we did not wish to keep a brigade so as to have a sort of British Empire force controlling. I replied we were very short of men for agriculture and for building and other purposes and unless they were absolutely required, we would wish to have them back. Our contribution from now on would be in food and the like and they were needed for all purposes.

"He asked about shipping. I said I thought we would have additional shipping in the spring. He seemed to feel they could be kept on until later in the year. I told him I was not giving a government decision; but now the Government already had expressed the hope that we might get our men out of Europe just as quickly as could conveniently be arranged.

"Montgomery spoke of coming to Canada. Would be delighted to come when invited. I told him that we had thought it was well for Crerar to come first and now that the new Governor General was appointed, it would be an advantage for Alexander to be in Ottawa when Montgomery arrived. He said Alexander was a friend of his. Went on to say he would be kept busy in Germany until spring. Asked if the month of May would be convenient. I assured him it would and he would be given a hearty welcome. He spoke about McGill wishing to give him a degree. I told him the Government would like to have him as a guest of the country, to travel across Canada to B.C. He asked if he would have to speak. I said to the extent that he was willing. Spoke of three weeks and I said longer if he wished. He seemed quite pleased. Will expect a formal invitation. . . .

"Attention was then given to my painting. The general liked it very much. Thought it was excellent. Indeed I rather sensed in his words of appreciation that he might well have wished to have been painted after the style in which my own painting had been made. I know he is entirely satisfied with his own. He thought every feature of my portrait was excellent. I showed him the photograph of the painting of mother. He was much taken with that. I told him he ought to have his own mother painted. I had cut her picture from the papers, liking so much her appearance, thinking of how lovely she was at her age. He told me he had stood nine hours while Frank was painting his portrait."

After this "memorable hour" with Montgomery and tea with the Salisburys, Mackenzie King returned to his hotel to prepare for a dinner party in his honour given by the British Prime Minister in the Chess Room of the House of Commons. Most of the members of the British Cabinet were present plus Lord Cranborne and Sir John Anderson. "I had exceedingly pleasant talks with the Prime Minister, Cranborne, Bevin, Morrison, Sir Stafford Cripps, Lord Addison, Alexander and others. Robertson and Hudd [the Acting Canadian High Commissioner] were present. Attlee made an exceedingly nice little speech of welcome. Beautifully worded and happily phrased and most cordial.

"My reply was quite offhand taking up some of the points that Attlee had mentioned as to not inflicting guests with speeches; something about the Kitchen Committee; body organized to give this dinner which was the first that has been given in the Commons private dining room since the war. I mentioned there were different ways of obtaining fame and to be the first to be honoured in this way was one of them. Spoke of the privilege of meeting those present and replied to what Attlee had said about Canada's effort in the war; how much more impressed one felt today with the justice of the cause being the preservation of freedom. Also the need for giving assistance in food and other ways. My being able to speak with greater conviction in Parliament of what we should be doing in the way of helping those in distress here and in Europe.

"I then spoke of what was more needed today than concrete policies, etc., was attitude and objectives. Attitude of understanding, of good-will between members of political parties and different parts of the Empire and spoke particularly of the U.S. and the U.K. Importance of infinite patience; also the need of patience in dealing with even more serious problems that might arise and spoke particularly of the problems which they all had. Made humorous references to my coming over partly at Attlee's invitation for purposes of consultation but also after having served the country so long, I thought the time had come when I should have a bit of a change and rest at the public expense. Also the advantage of informal conversation as against conferences. Told them I was sick of conferences. We had too many of them. It was desirable for Ministers and their officials to do some of the business of their own countries. Concluded by taking up a word which Attlee had used about nobody having a good word to say about something I have forgotten what it was. I stated that had been my lot for 20 years but that I have come to the point that whatever they thought of me in Canada, I can go back and tell them I was a big dog when in London. The remarks were well received and I think they were deemed appropriate by those who were present. Robertson and Hudd both seemed to be quite satisfied. Attlee could not have been pleasanter or kinder than he was or more attentive. He came with me to the door when we left.

"At dinner, he told me about the history of the different men who were seated at the table. It made me proud indeed of these men having risen as they had from the ranks. All of them practically self made and having come into the positions they had. It was that which will save England from revolution and will help to further a true democracy in other parts of the world."

Thursday, October 25, was a quiet day. "This evening," Mackenzie King wrote, "I had a talk with Robertson who began by telling me that he had been talking with the Chief of the Secret Service here and they had now come to the conclusion it was better not to take any action on R.E. until after the meeting in Washington; also that it was felt if we took action before, especially giving publicity, it might spoil the chance of getting a settlement on the atomic bomb and might rouse public opinion in a very serious way. It is curious Robertson's mind was quite the opposite to what it was before. . . . I am sure that the course of caution, secrecy, etc., is the right one. Direct approach to the Russians is the right thing.

"I tried to emphasize to Robertson that there would be great difficulty in getting proof and that unless we had entire proof, the whole thing would backfire in a very serious way whereas I thought members of the service should be questioned but care taken not to start any legal proceedings or enquiry by a Royal Commission. Apparently there are to be no further talks this week but next week some discussion of Defence measures with Attlee, Addison and one other Minister."

Mackenzie King lunched with Winston Churchill on October 26. As he drove up to Churchill's new home on Hyde Park Gate, "who should appear on the sidewalk but Randolph without any hat on, looking very well and strong, and Mary. They both gave me a very warm welcome. When the front door was opened Winston came along from the front of the hall to the steps to meet me. He could not have given me a warmer or more friendly greeting.

"After the butler had taken my overcoat, hat and umbrella he opened the door into the drawing room where Mrs. Churchill was waiting and came forward. She also greeted me in the warmest way, saying Dear Mr. King, how glad we are to have you with us again. Glasses of sherry were passed around and we all had a little talk together. There was a question as to whether Randolph would wait for luncheon. Churchill told him they had only so many snipe for luncheon but that he could arrange a seat for him. Randolph said, however, he had just come up with Mary but he was not staying for lunch. He left almost immediately, and after we had had a few words in what would be Winston's library, the shelves are in but books are not there yet, we went downstairs to luncheon – a lovely room looking out onto a little garden at the back with a brick wall covered with vines – a crystal globe on the little statue.

"Mrs. Churchill told me that she had gone to pick out the snipe herself. There was another delicious dish and there was some debate whether it should come first or last. The first dish was caviar which I think he said Randolph had procured somewhere. Churchill persisted in adding more to the dish. This, when I was helping myself modestly.

"A little wine was served, also some vodka, and port. The vodka had been brought from Russia. Mrs. Churchill told the waiter not to use it but to throw it out. She said brandy was a better substitute. It was clear that the vodka had been brought on with a view to discussing Russian conditions.

"In the course of the conversation Mrs. Churchill told me of the reception she had in Russia. With what meticulous care they did everything to make a guest feel much at home. She spoke of Stalin keeping Mrs. Stalin in the background but of Molotov having Madame Molotov taking a most important part as a hostess. She evidently had been quite beautiful and was a person of strong personality. When she, Mrs. Churchill, had gone in they had asked her if she would like a little music before luncheon. Music was played just sufficiently long to make the atmosphere pleasant and harmonious. Attentions were also paid in other ways. For example, when she acquiesced in the music, servants came in with their hair powdered, etc., brought the piano in and moved furniture to one side. Everything was done in the style that would have taught Buckingham Palace lessons in how to delight guests. She spoke of the courses that were served as being no end in number and delicious in the dishes served, etc. The whole business had been to impress her with the refinement and culture and high quality of living which was the order of things for the Russians."

During lunch, Mackenzie King reported, Churchill "did most of the talking in an exceedingly nice way. He has a marvellous mind, ranges from one subject to another with perfect ease and adequate expression.

"Winston spoke quite frankly about the elections. He said it had been the greatest surprise to him and quite a blow. That he feared conditions were going to be pretty serious in England as a consequence of the policy of destroying the rich to equalize incomes of all. That he himself would have been prepared to take three quarters of the income of wealthy men but he would have left them enough to have an incentive to work. He was afraid lawyers who would take great cases would simply take a limited number and not bother with the rest. Same would govern the actions of men generally and the wealth of the country would be lessened. He spoke particularly about Cripps as being the one mostly responsible. . . .

"I spoke to Churchill about enjoying the debate. He told me that his action from the benches in waving to me had been quite spontaneous. He asked me if I had been there while he was speaking. He said you have not heard me speak impromptu before. I said to him I thought his words were so well chosen that he must have given thought to them in advance. He said, no, he had no intent to say more than just a word. That the whole speech was spontaneous. He seemed anxious to know that it was along the right lines. I told him I liked the moderation of it, the courtesy extended, etc. He said that was traditional. He did intend some day soon to go very hard after the Government. To move a vote of censure, in fact, for the length of time they were taking to demobilize men. He thought these men should not be doing nothing all round England and far too many of them on the Continent. They should be employed in industry and helping to get on with the work of production.

"Churchill then got on to the question of Russia. He said that Russia was grabbing one country after another – one Capital after another. He said that all these different countries, naming the lot of the Balkans, including Berlin, would be under their control. He thought they should have been stood up to more than they were. I asked him if it was true that Stalin had told them at one time that if need be settlements would have to be made by force. He said no, that was not true, though he had had some pretty stiff talks with Stalin. He did not know what was the truth about Stalin's position. Whether he was sick or well. The Government had told him nothing.

"He spoke about the Russian regime as being very difficult but said there was nothing to be gained by not letting them know that we were not afraid of them. That they would not thank us for lying down before them at any stage. He said that he had strongly pressed before the war to make no settlements or awards until the armies were holding all the positions they had taken. He stressed very strongly what realists they were. He called them 'realist lizards,' all belonging to the crocodile family. He said they would be as pleasant with you as they could be, although prepared to destroy you. That sentiment meant nothing to them – morals meant nothing. They were hard realists, out for themselves and for no one else and would be governed only in that way. I asked him how they got the money to develop the power they have. He said to me that they had quantities of gold and platinum in Russia. That was one source and they had paid for nothing that had been given to them. He then spoke of the difference between the people and the militarist regime. He said that the militarist regime were a class by themselves and were the controlling factor."

Mackenzie King noted that "as Churchill and I talked I felt I would like to get his views on the situation with which we are faced. I said to him; would you think it disloyalty to the Government if I were to tell you of a situation which I had come over about which was one that concerned us all. (We were both Privy Councillors.) It was not a party matter but something that I felt he ought to know about. I would be glad to have his view on it. He said certainly he would keep in strict confidence anything I might say to him. I then told him about the happening at Ottawa and one or two aspects of it. He said this is indeed interesting and most important. It did not, however, seem to take him by surprise. He said you must remember that with the Communists, Communism is a religion. One could say if one were using an expression that should not be misunderstood that some men would call them Jesuits without Jesus in the relationship. What he meant was that they were using any means to gain an end without that end being the end of Christianity, of Christian purposes. He said that it was impossible to view them in any other than a most realistic way. They were realists to the extreme. He said to me he thought that where men had done what was wrong the wrong should be exposed but he agreed that it would be better not to do anything without exploring the situation very carefully at first. He strongly approved of the President, Britain and Canada all acting together in the matter. He thought it would be as well to delay action until a careful plan had been worked out but that is should not be allowed to go by default. He felt it was right to talk to the Ambassador but to leave it there would be a mistake. That the world ought to know where there was espionage and that the Russians would not mind that; they had been exposed time and again. He felt that the Communist movement was spreading everywhere and that those who were Communists would do anything for their cause, deceive everybody. They had no religion or religious belief beyond that of what they were seeking in their cause.

"He then went on to speak about the U.S. and the U.K. He said to me he hoped I would do all I could to keep the two together. I said to him I did not think the British Commonwealth of Nations could compete with the Russian situation itself nor did I think the U.S. could. That I believed that it would require the two and they must be kept together. He said to me, that is the thing you must work for above everything else if you can pull off a continued alliance between the U.S. and Britain. It must not be written, it must be understood. But if you can get them to preserve the Joint Chiefs of Staff arrangement and have plans made to keep the two together you will be doing the greatest service that can be done the world and that is your particular mission. I asked him if he did not think there should be uniformity of arms used in time of war. He said he was altogether of that view and that in all particulars we must keep together as one people against the rest of the world. He stressed this again when I was leaving, stating to me that my mission was to get that alliance between the U.K. and the U.S. He asked me if I had spoken to the Government here on those lines. I told him it was precisely the line I was emphasizing to everyone. He said you have the key position and you can do more than any other man toward bringing this about."

Churchill told the Prime Minister that he had received several invitations to visit North America, one from the University of Missouri "to give a course of lectures on European conditions. . . . Truman had scribbled in his own hand across the letter that he would like very much to see him come and deliver the course. He mentioned a large honorarium, etc. He said that he thought he might go and deliver one lecture on the conditions of the world. He would not wish any honorarium but this might give him a chance to talk with Truman and he might be helpful to British and American relations in that way."

As he was leaving, Mackenzie King again asked Churchill "to keep to himself what I had said about Russia until the Government spoke to him of it. He assured me that he would not mention it to another person. I feel quite justified at having spoken to him as this is something much apart from any party affair. He stressed how anti-Communist he knew Bevin was and also said he was glad Bevin had got the Foreign Office rather than Dalton.

"When I was coming away he spoke to me about the elections in Canada. Earlier I had told him about the results in three provincial elections and of the Conservative party being completely wiped out in each provincial seat. I said the truth was that the word Conservative did not suit this present age. That Liberal had come to mean what Liberal-Conservatives really stood for. That the C.C.F. or Socialist party represented the other extreme. . . .

"When I was leaving he said to me, in reference to the elections, other men are as children in the leadership of the party as compared to yourself. You have shown understanding and capacity to lead that other men have not got, or words to this effect. He used the expression that he hoped that God would bless me. No words could have been kinder than his as we parted. It was the sweetest side of his nature throughout – a really beautiful side. One cannot help loving him when that side of his nature is to the fore."

After dinner on Saturday evening (October 27), Mackenzie King read the text of a speech President Truman had delivered the day before "which, reading between the lines, refers to Canada, U.S. and U.K. on the atomic bomb, all of which emphasizes the importance of peace being secured by means that make for peace. Makes clear that the U.S. will not give up keeping up its power in the world. I like the emphasis which the President puts on Christian behaviour in the world. More and more I feel that my Industry and Humanity has in it everything that is applicable in the most immediate way to the present situation. All things, however, are moving to the preparation of the world for a meeting in Washington of the President, Attlee and myself which will be taken by the world as most significant. I will go back from England ready to enter on a larger sphere of work than ever – a sphere of work which will identify me with this new age of atomic energy and world peace. It is the thing that I am sure is a part of the purpose of my life. All that I get from my own inner feeling through psychic sources, etc., stresses this very clearly. I must go back prepared to let lesser things be dealt with by others and devote the remainder of my life more earnestly than ever to the ways of establishing good-will between nations and peace as the fruit thereof."

Two days later the Prime Minister called on Mrs. Neville Chamberlain again and met the historian, Keith Feiling, who had just completed Chamberlain's biography. Their conversation was interrupted by the arrival of Norman Robertson who informed Mackenzie King that the news of Attlee's visit to Washington had leaked to the press. "That the Evening Standard had the whole story but indicated a number of subjects that Attlee was supposed to be going over to discuss, such as finance and trade, etc. Did not mention the bomb particularly. He said that Attlee would have to make a statement and was anxious to confer with me about it. He thought it important that I should go to Downing Street immediately where Attlee was waiting.

"I introduced Robertson to Feiling and Mrs. Chamberlain, and we then started off together for Downing Street. After waiting a few minutes in a room adjoining the Cabinet Council Chamber where, by the way, we saw a painting by Mr. Pickersgill, 1825, Rowan came to take me in to the Cabinet Council. I thought it was a good chance for Robertson to be brought into the Conference."

He reported that "Attlee was seated alone when Robertson and I were taken in to Cabinet Council by Rowan. Attlee asked me to sit beside him and then turned to me and said: 'The Washington papers have published information about my going to Washington. They have been speculating on the matters to be discussed. It is quite clear I shall have to make a statement in Parliament at once. I will be questioned. I cannot delay the announcement until later.'

"He then said: 'I will have to tell the President this' and picked up a typed sheet from which he read the communication he was sending to the President which was to the effect that messages had come from Washington which were in the evening papers here, making mention of his visit. He did not think he could delay longer in making a public statement in Parliament. That he would have to do so tomorrow. The statement which he proposed to make was to the effect that it was true he had arranged to go to Washington for a conference with Truman and myself in regard to matters connected with the atomic bomb. These were not the exact words. It also gave the date of his arrival which will be: to be in Washington around November the 12th. He asked me what I thought of the statement. I told him I thought it was all right. He arranged to have it sent off at once.

"When we left the room, Robertson told me he thought the statement covered the ground satisfactorily.

"I then said to Attlee that he would have no trouble making it clear in the House that the matter was one he had been seeking to arrange for some time past, showing it was not connected with the failure of the Council of Foreign Ministers as he had sent the letter to President Truman regarding the atomic bomb while the Conference was on. That that letter would show that he had been the one who had sought to initiate the discussion.

"I suggested he have his secretary prepare a chronological statement which would show that he had set apart a day for the discussion of the Palestine question – Thursday of this week. Also other questions as to when they have been discussed, etc., and making clear that he had planned to leave after the Guildhall address. He accepted this suggestion quickly. I said it would be all to the good for him to have his letter produced later. It would make the record very clear. (Also though I did not mention this, it would show Attlee's letter had gone before the President made his statement about not disclosing the secret re manufacture.)

"Attlee then picked up the file of blue typewritten papers and said regarding the espionage matter that he evidently concluded 'You could not pick up the men in Canada simultaneously with our taking action here.' Robertson chimed in and said we could not do it without publicity and that their police as well as we, ourselves, felt it would be better not to have any publicity in the matter until after Attlee had had a talk with the President. Attlee then said: You think it best to wait until after the talks with the President. I said I thought that was all to the good. Otherwise the publicity on the espionage matter might prejudice any talks which it might be thought advisable to have with the Russians.

"Robertson asked whether the Russians had been told of Attlee's visit to Washington. He very wisely felt that they should have been told before the Russians would get information in the press. Attlee said they were looking into that matter at present. The truth is over here there has not been the appreciation of the seriousness of the Russian situation vis-à-vis the atomic bomb – atomic energy, espionage, etc., that one would expect to find. Attlee then said to me, looking across in a pretty anxious way: There are so many questions that are coming up in all parts of the world. There are questions that are causing great trouble. I felt the deepest sympathy for him.

"I asked myself the question whether he would be able to stand the load which is on his shoulders. He looks so slight – almost diminutive for the burdens that he is called upon to bear. Is always so gentle and kind. A very true soul. I pray he may be given the strength and guidance needed. I told him I would be on hand here, anywhere, at any moment that he wanted me for any purpose."

Undoubtedly the most incongruous engagement during Mackenzie King's visit to London was a luncheon at the Soviet Embassy on October 31. The Ambassador, Mr. Gusev, gave the Prime Minister "a very warm welcome" when he arrived. "Mrs. Gusev also came running along the hall and extended an equally cordial welcome. We went upstairs in a lift and were shown into an ante-room where sherry was served. I was introduced to the commercial representative of the Embassy – the opposite number to Krotov, in Ottawa – quite a pleasant substantial fellow. After a few minutes' talk, the four of us went into the dining room...." In the course of conversation, the Ambassador raised the subject of scientific research and referred to Attlee's statement about the meeting in Washington with President Truman.

"Gusev said to me something to the following effect: Canada had a good deal to do with the making of the atomic bomb; also Canada knew the secret. He said there has been a lot of research work done at McGill University; British scientists and American scientists and Canadians all met together there to work out the plans or to do research, I have forgotten which. I said to him that I knew there had been research into the discovery of release of atomic energy both at our research laboratories at Ottawa and at the universities. That they had been working on this apart altogether from anything related to the construction of a bomb. That for a long time there had been researches in all of the leading countries on atomic energy. So far as Canada was concerned, however, it was not correct to say that we had the secret of the bomb because we had not had to do with its manufacture at all. I thought the scientists everywhere knew pretty much what there was to be known about release of atomic energy but that the question of manufacturing for purposes of destruction – the process of manufacture – was something that we had no knowledge of. I said at Petawawa, we had been working on some of the substances that had to do with the release of atomic energy but this was only incidental to general research.

"(An amazing thing is that . . . R. [Robertson] said to me that the subject would be brought up at luncheon. That the Ambassador had an inkling of what had taken place – not to express any surprise but to be guarded in what was said.)

"I was careful in speaking not to go beyond any information that had been given out in Howe's statement. The Commercial Attaché asked me if I had seen Low's cartoon – picture of Truman carrying a little bomb under his arm – bomb marked 'secret.' I said I recalled having seen something the night before but was not too clear about it.

"Before coming away, I said to Gusev: you and I are old friends. We must do all we possibly can to see that good-will is promoted between different countries – particularly our respective countries. Spoke of our being near neighbours. Also of the great part Russia had taken in the war, etc. Gusev himself had proposed a toast to the friendship of our two countries. At luncheon, he had every kind of wine served: sherry, white wine, vodka, champagne, etc. I was careful not to do more than taste some of the wines that were served.

"I felt a certain restraint in conversation. A sort of silence after talking about the investigation of the scientists at Montreal. I felt sure he knew about Primrose and he must have known that I did, too. From what he said, I could see that the Russians may come back on any disclosure we make, presenting the view that the bomb was really conceived in Canada and worked out there by scientists of Britain and the U.S. That this was done at Montreal. This will be the excuse they will make for having found it necessary to have espionage."

On Friday, November 2, Mackenzie King went to Downing Street at noon to say good-bye to Attlee. He "was shown into the Cabinet Council at Downing Street and had a quiet talk with Mr. Attlee, who was seated alone in front of the fire. He later was joined by Lord Addison. The subject they had wished to discuss was the question of strengthening up the more effective co-ordination of the defence of the Empire. Reference was made to the Imperial Council of Defence. I had been forewarned by Robertson about what was coming up so said immediately that at all the conferences I had attended in 1923 and since, this question of Imperial Defence came up. That I had always to take exception to Canada being represented on that body. That I thought I should make very clear that the word 'Imperial' was a word which to members of our party and the C.C.F. and other parties in Canada, denoted centralization in matters of defence; being drawn into all kinds of conflicts in all quarters of the world, etc. That, as a matter of fact, we had not been represented on the Imperial Council at any time, nor was it of the slightest use during the war. That I might say at once our Government would not be favourable to Canada taking a different course at this time in regard to an Imperial Council of Defence than that taken on any previous occasion.

"I went on to say that anything in the nature of exchange of officials so as to have all parts familiar with methods, etc., of other parts, was all right. That what I thought was needed was an inter-change of views and knowledge on matters related to defence plans, etc. That Canada would gladly co-operate in matters of that kind. What I did think was most needed was standardization of equipment in training and military research between U.S. and the U.K. and Canada. That I thought our Chiefs of Staff would recommend that we standardize our equipment, etc., with that of the U.S., having in mind experience of fitting our men for the Pacific. That I would strongly recommend maintaining the combined Chiefs of Staff Board at Washington. It was very desirable to keep the U.S. and U.K. together on all military as well as other matters. This need not be done in an open, formal way but could be done by understandings, etc. I found both Attlee and Lord Addison quite receptive of this last suggestion and quite prepared to accept what I said about the former matters.

"I spoke about the Imperialistic scheme being stock in trade of the Tories, etc.

"When I said I did not quite understand what Churchill meant when he talked about the Empire and the Commonwealth business, Attlee said that he himself was responsible for that phrase. He regarded the Commonwealth as a self-governing part of the Empire – and the British Empire, Britain and her dependencies and colonies, etc. I did not go into the fact that Britain, in this way, figured twice. It was interesting to hear Attlee say he himself had been responsible for the distinction. I then spoke about the position of the Dominions as self-governing nations. Said they would find that Australia, for example, would be more emphatic on being regarded as a country in all respects, equal in status to the U.K. That I felt that in dealing with the Dominions, there were underlying bonds of common institutions, etc. They should be regarded in their own rights as completely self-governing and as independent as Holland, Belgium and any other country. This must be kept in mind."

In the course of the conversation, Attlee mentioned that Lord Addison "had brought up the question of Privy Councillors and said that Hofmeyer had been made an Imperial P.C. There were now two in Africa; mentioned there were two or three in Australia and only one in Canada: myself. He thought there might be others. I assumed he had reference to the leader of the opposition and began speaking of there being two oppositions. Bracken would be thought of; also that Coldwell who had been much longer leader of the C.C.F. party would have to be thought of. I gave no expression for or against that aspect as the P.M. said it was in relation rather to the govt. side that they had been considering the matter. I thanked them very much for having thought of this and they asked me what men I thought it would be best to have considered. I said undoubtedly Ilsley, Minister of Finance, and St. Laurent, Minister of Justice. Lord Addison then said that Malcolm MacDonald had put forth the suggestion and these were the two names he had mentioned. I said I would be very pleased if they could be recognized.

"I then told them about feeling they were both well worthy of such a recognition, if they could receive it. . . .

"At the Cabinet Council table, I extended a very hearty invitation to Attlee to come and visit Canada while he was in Washington. Told him I thought the visit would be tremendously appreciated by the people of Canada. I thought it would do him good personally and his government and I did hope he would accept. To my great delight he said he thought he should accept; would be glad to do this if it could be arranged. I repeated the invitation in Lord Addison's presence and got an acceptance from Attlee and his permission to announce that he would come during or at the end of the Washington Conference. He seemed quite pleased about the invitation.

"Later I expressed to Mrs. Attlee the hope that she might some time also pay us a visit. She is a very sweet person – a charming companion to

Attlee, of whom I think more and more as I listen to him in conversation. He is very humble minded; very clear minded. This visit was an exceptional pleasure."

Sir Harold and Lady Margaret Alexander lunched with Mackenzie King at the Dorchester on November 3. They had just returned from Ireland. Alexander impressed the Prime Minister "as a very able man, not unlike Lord Byng in appearance at the side of his face and his manner, quiet, thoughtful, but quite clearly a character welded together. Is rather shy. I thought he was splendid in conversation. Anything he undertakes, I am sure, he will go through in a most efficient way. Will have Government House well regulated.

"I gather from what he said that he was ready to come in January or February and that the delay was due to the desire of the Athlones to stay on until early March. He told me he was a bit indefinite about time. I said I would try to find out what their plans would be and let him know as soon as I could.

"He then spoke to me about his staff. Said he felt that his secretary should be chosen by the Canadian Government. That would be a real link between the Government and himself. He did not think it was wise to have a secretary go on from one régime to another and he thought a man around 40 years of age who would be young enough to be active and old enough to have judgment would be the best type. He, himself, says he intends to have only men who have served in the war on his staff. I suggested he should have some Canadians among the number. He said he would. He would like me to tell him whom to appoint as a secretary and also to name the secretary. I was not sure myself who pays the secretary or what the arrangements are. He said of all positions he would rather have this one than any. Said he might have succeeded Sir Alan Brooke as Chief of Staff in England and other posts had been thought of but he thought Canada was the most important of any post. He is keenly looking forward to being in the country. I told him about the Byng incident; about the effect of the photograph of himself and the little boy in the swing [see vol. 2, p. 437]. He is looking forward to travelling through many parts of Canada. Says Massey has given him many books to read. I suggested his adding Parkman's works to the number.

"I asked him about his religion. He told me he was Anglican. Had no patience himself with people who were intolerant in religious matters. Many of his friends were Catholics and he would himself not allow any thoughts of differences of religion to alter his mind. One can see he is broad minded and sensible. We discussed a good deal the Russian situation. He is not afraid of Russia. Feels they had started on a five-year plan.

It was broken up by war. They want to go back to something of the kind. They had taken up all the supplies and all the men they can get. Feels they have their own inner problems to deal with. Says they want to get a band around their country . . . until they complete the whole plan.

"Stalin had said they had lost five million men in the war which he thought was true. He said it would not do to be afraid of them in any way. They were much behind in development, as individuals and as a nation. He was against giving them any atomic bomb secret. He thought it would take four or five years for any country to work out similar plants to those in the U.S. Indeed only a certain number of bombs could be manufactured within a year. At the same time, he did feel the necessity of doing all possible to allay suspicion.

" I felt the talk with him on the Russian situation rather reassuring. I felt as we discussed conditions that he was extremely well versed and would be most helpful.

"He spoke about our taking walks in the woods together [at Kingsmere]. Evidently the Athlones have been referring to that. I told him something about the other Governors. When I talked about Byng he said there were military men and military men. . . . It was clear he desires to be as tactful as a man can be. . . . Lady Margaret was very quiet. Seems most natural and friendly; of a kind nature. . . . After luncheon, I went with Field Marshal Alexander to his car as far as the front of the hotel. I am sure he will be a real success in Canada. As a man, he is one of the most manly men I have met and clearly one of the best informed."

Mackenzie King sailed from Southampton that evening. He had every reason to be satisfied with the results of his visit to London. "There is no doubt," he wrote on November 4, "that the talk I had with the President and with Attlee over the question I went to Washington about has been the main factor in effecting this meeting at this particular time though Attlee had been ready for some time to go over. There is no doubt that my association with these men and the atomic bomb problem has given me a place in world recognition that even years of war themselves did not begin to give."

The voyage across the Atlantic was uneventful. On his last day at sea (November 8) Mackenzie King wrote: "Looking back on the visit, I feel it has been well worth while in many ways, particularly as affording much needed change and helping to fill one's mind with fresh interest and a truer appreciation of conditions. It is hard to believe it is not part of some larger design to help in keeping the English-speaking peoples together and of furthering international good-will at a time when that would seem to be more necessary even than before the beginning of the last Great War. The atomic bomb has brought the world into an entirely new era – one which might precipitate its destruction even in the lifetime of men of my years. My prayer as I leave this ship is that I may be guided to help others in finding a way of preventing its further use for purposes of destruction and utilizing possibilities of the invention to the greater benefit of mankind."

The Prime Minister had been informed that morning that President Truman had announced that he, Attlee and Mackenzie King would meet in Washington the following Sunday. "Later Robertson read and gave me a telegram from Pearson through Wrong stating that the Secretary of State's Department had placed Blair House at the disposal of myself and party during our stay in Washington and announcing that there would be a State dinner at the White House on Saturday night, attendance at an Armistice Day service on Sunday morning and later the day to be spent aboard the President's yacht in company with President Truman and Mr. Attlee, mentioning dinner with Lord Halifax on Monday or Tuesday; invitation to President's Press Dinner on one or other of these nights; a Dinner to be given at the Embassy on Thursday. Attlee is to broadcast an address to both Houses in Congress; also a press conference. Mention of his leaving on Friday which means dinners, etc., in Ottawa; probability, before the week is out, of his addressing both Houses of Parliament before returning to England. This means a pretty strenuous week."

Still suffering from a heavy cold, Mackenzie King landed in New York the next day. His diary for 1945 ends on November 9.

Mackenzie King's diaries for the period from November 10 to December 31, 1945, could not be found after his death, despite repeated searches through all his papers. A skeleton record has been prepared from his engagement sheets and from Hansard.

For the visit to Washington, the record has been supplemented, with the permission of the Rt. Hon. L. B. Pearson, by references to his own record of that visit. Pearson was, at the time, Canadian Ambassador to the United States and, as such, he had a unique opportunity to observe and record Mackenzie King's discussions with President Truman and Prime Minister Attlee.

On November 10, Mackenzie King arrived in Washington on his private railway car and almost immediately left for Blair House where he stayed throughout his visit. Attlee arrived in Washington by air and later that morning, accompanied by the British Ambassador, Lord Halifax, met Mackenzie King, Pearson, President Truman, the Secretary of State, Byrnes, and Admiral Leahy at the White House. The President described the arrangements for the ensuing talks on co-operation in the development and exploitation of atomic energy and for the Armistice Memorial Service to be held the next day. Those who participated in this first meeting were invited to remain for lunch at the White House. This was a purely social occasion and no official business was discussed.

That evening, the President entertained the visiting prime ministers and their advisers, as well as members and officials of the United States government, at a state dinner, during which he and Mr. Attlee spoke briefly.

On November 11, at 11.00 A.M., wreaths were laid at the Tomb of the Unknown Soldier in Arlington cemetery. As each head of government moved forward to the tomb, the National Anthem of that country was played, and the guard of honour presented arms. Afterwards, Mackenzie King laid a wreath at the Canadian Cross of Sacrifice and Attlee, a wreath on Sir John Dill's grave. The President, Attlee, Mackenzie King, Byrnes, Admiral Leahy, Sir John Anderson, the United Kingdom and Canadian ambassadors, and Rowan, Attlee's private secretary, then motored to the Navy Yard, where they boarded the *Sequoia*, the Secretary of the Navy's yacht.

They sailed about noon and returned to Washington the same evening. By agreement, no transcript was made of the discussions that took place, though most of the participants probably made some record subsequently. The President and the two prime ministers had a discussion before luncheon on the use of atomic energy for destructive purposes and found themselves in general agreement on the main principles which should govern national and international action on this matter. After luncheon, they were joined by their advisers and each member of the party was invited to express his views as to how the problem should be dealt with. There was complete agreement on the fundamental and far-reaching nature of the problem, on the necessity of an international approach to its solution, on the importance which the world attached to these discussions, and the desirability of issuing a joint statement, embodying an agreement, as quickly as possible.

The meeting broke up that day without reaching an understanding on procedures for the next stage of the discussions. The following morning the British delegation prepared a paper for circulation and consideration. That evening, the Secretary of State, James Byrnes, entertained Attlee and Mackenzie King and their parties to dinner. After the dinner, Pearson, Hume Wrong and Norman Robertson exchanged views with the Under Secretary of State, Dean Acheson, and subsequently prepared a Canadian draft of a joint statement which was submitted to Mackenzie King on Tuesday morning, November 13. Discussions between the President and the two prime ministers were resumed that afternoon. At this meeting, Byrnes produced a draft statement which did not prove to be entirely suitable and the Canadian group drew up a re-draft of the Byrnes statement on Wednesday morning. A second United States draft was also drawn up and discussed at the White House that afternoon. On this occasion, Mackenzie King suggested certain changes in the document, two of which were of particular importance. He argued that the reference to the appointment of a commission under the United Nations should follow the specific recommendations of the three signatories on immediate action. He also suggested that, at the end of the paragraph, "We are not convinced that the spreading of the specialized information regarding the practical application of atomic energy before it is possible to devise . . . safeguards . . . would contribute to a constructive solution of the problem of the atomic bomb," there should be added the following sentences: "On the contrary, we think it might have the opposite effect. We are, however, prepared to share on a reciprocal basis with other United Nations detailed information concerning the practical industrial application of atomic energy just as soon as effective and enforceable safeguards against its use for destructive purposes can be devised." Such a change made this crucial part of the statement positive rather than negative. Both these changes were warmly supported by the President and Prime Minister Attlee. Mackenzie King also suggested the removal of all words and phrases from the document which implied that, in accepting the agreement, the signatories were acting for their respective governments. As finally approved, the agreement was between heads of governments and not between the governments themselves.

Pearson considered that the general effect of the changes proposed by Mackenzie King removed the impression that the three conferees were shelving the problem by sending it to a commission and that they had no fixed ideas about it themselves. In Pearson's view there was a general understanding that referral of the problem to a commission of the United Nations meant that the world organization was being given a very severe test at the outset of its existence and that the three powers were now obligated more than ever to strengthen and develop the United Nations organization so that it could successfully meet this and other tests.

The British draft was also discussed and a drafting committee consisting of Pearson, Sir John Anderson and Dr. Vannevar Bush, subsequently chairman of the U.S. Atomic Energy Commission, was appointed to prepare a new draft. This committee met at 5:30 P.M. at the White House and again later in the evening. At 10:00 P.M., the President and the prime ministers met to go over the draft sentence by sentence, a task which was completed by midnight. The statement was signed by the three heads of government on Thursday morning (November 15) at 11:00 and immediately read to the White House press correspondents by the President.

Mackenzie King paid a farewell visit to the President on Thursday afternoon and left for Ottawa on the afternoon train, accompanied by Prime Minister Attlee. Meanwhile, Ilsley, the Acting Prime Minister, had announced on November 15 that Mackenzie King would return to Ottawa on Saturday, November 17, and that Attlee would address both Houses of Parliament on November 19. In addition, St. Laurent, as Acting Secretary of State for External Affairs, had read the statement agreed upon in Washington to the House of Commons.

Mackenzie King and Attlee arrived in the capital shortly after noon on November 17. The British Prime Minister lunched at Laurier House and that afternoon met with the Cabinet. A government dinner in Attlee's honour was given at the Country Club that evening. Mackenzie King took his guest to tea at Kingsmere on Sunday afternoon. On Monday, November 19, the usual wreath-laying ceremony at the War Memorial was followed by a luncheon at Earnscliffe and Attlee's speech to both Houses of Parliament in the afternoon. The Prime Minister left for England by air the same day.

Mackenzie King took his customary place in the House of Commons on Tuesday, November 20, and was welcomed by the Leader of the Opposition, and by Coldwell and Low. In responding, he told the House that he believed "the visit which Prime Minister Attlee and I had together at Washington was not only of great service to the three countries represented at the conferences we had with the President of the United States, but will prove to have been of real service to the world itself. Certainly I feel very strongly that the conferences in England and in Washington have helped, if such were needed at this time, to strengthen the bonds of friendship between the peoples of the British commonwealth of nations and of the United States. I am sure that nothing in this world is more needed for the preservation of peace itself than the maintenance of the relations that were so firmly established between those peoples at a time of war, and their continuation throughout the period of postwar reconstruction."

The Prime Minister's list of engagements for the next few days indicates that he was plunged at once into activities related to the concluding phases of the parliamentary session. On Monday, November 26, at 10:00 A.M., the Co-ordinating Committee of the Dominion-Provincial Conference met and continued in session each morning and afternoon until Thursday, November 29. On Wednesday morning, Mackenzie King was annoyed by a report in the *Ottawa Journal* on the conference which stated that proceedings had been slowed by disagreement between the Prime Minister and several of his colleagues. He referred to the matter in a statement on a question of Privilege in the House of Commons. "The entire membership of the conference took strong exception to this article and desired that I should make a statement to the House of Commons on behalf of all who are present at the conference," he stated.

"May I say that all provincial premiers and all members of the dominion government who were present at the conference are united in saying that they know nothing of a clash having taken place between myself and any of my colleagues. As a matter of fact, there has been nothing of the kind. I make that statement emphatically. May I add that there has been nothing that I am aware of, and that I think any of the premiers on the co-ordinating committee are aware of, which has in any way complicated the proceedings that have been, I am happy to say, going forward so amicably and splendidly since the opening of the conference."

Two days later, the Prime Minister told the House that, during the meeting, "questions related to the dominion proposals and proposals that have been submitted by some of the provinces were very fully discussed, together with questions arising out of those proposals as well as questions quite apart from anything specifically set forth in the proposals but dealing with matters relating to other aspects of dominion-provincial relations. The conference proceedings throughout, may I say, were characterized by the utmost harmony. As I said to the press at the end of the first meeting, the meeting itself was interesting and profitable. As the proceedings continued from day to day, I think I added the word 'most' before the words 'interesting' and 'profitable.' I would say I could not imagine a better series of meetings than those of the co-ordinating committee."

He then placed on Hansard the text of a statement which all participants had agreed on. It read in part: "It has been decided to establish immediately a dominion-provincial economic committee, the members of which will examine and report to their respective governments upon the economic factors affecting dominion and provincial proposals and relations. The economic committee will proceed forthwith and will hold its first formal meeting on Tuesday, December 4. The dominion and each of the provincial governments will have three members. The chairman of the economic committee will be the senior dominion member." The statement also indicated that the full Co-ordinating Committee would meet again on January 28, 1946.

In late November, the government became greatly concerned about a sudden decision by the United States to end meat rationing and its effect upon rationing and price control policy in Canada. An unsuccessful attempt was made to arrange prior consultation between the two governments, the Prime Minister indicated in the House on November 29. "As I explained in my statement to the house on Friday afternoon, there are fundamental differences between the problems of control confronting a country like the United States which normally exports some five per cent of its meat production and those in a country like Canada where thirty per cent to forty per cent of output finds its way into export markets. Both governments have made commitments to allied and liberated countries where the average level of food consumption is very much lower than on this continent. Both countries are determined to carry out these promises, though methods and arrangements by which they implement them will naturally differ.

"Since my suggestion to the President was, in fact, received too late for consideration, and since the position of our own government was made clear to the house at the first opportunity, I do not think there is any purpose in my taking up at this stage with President Truman the question of our making public the actual texts of the messages exchanged."

While the provincial premiers were in Ottawa, a bill to extend certain of the wartime emergency powers was before Parliament and some of the premiers had taken strong exception to several of its provisions. As a result, the bill was substantially revised and, replying to the Acting Leader of the Opposition on December 30, Mackenzie King explained that during "the sittings of the co-ordinating committee of the dominion-provincial conference some of the provisions of the bill were under discussion. There were certain objections by some of the premiers to powers that were being requested under the bill. The government undertook to consider the objections that were raised. That has been done, and important amendments have been drafted which we believe and expect will help to meet the objections that have been raised, and incidentally help to meet objections that otherwise might have been raised by hon. gentlemen opposite."

During the first week of December, the Prime Minister had one or two conversations with Garfield Weston in the hope, which was not realized, of arranging for the removal of the Eddy paper mill from Hull to a site farther down the Ottawa River, as a contribution to the development of the national capital.

Earlier in the session, while Mackenzie King was in England, there had been a minor revolt of the Liberal members from Manitoba over certain tariff increases which had been proposed in the budget. The Prime Minister had some sympathy with the rebels and an excuse was found to withdraw the proposed changes. In a statement the Prime Minister made in Parliament on December 12 outlining proposals by the United States government for an international conference on the expansion of world trade and employment, he stated: "These proposals have been prepared for consideration by an international conference on trade and employment, which the United States government suggests should be convened by the united nations organization for the summer of 1946.

"The government of the United States has proposed that all countries should concert their efforts in the sphere of their international economic relations, with a view to expanding the volume of world trade and maintaining high and stable levels of national employment. The specific suggestions for achieving these ends, set forth in the document which is now being tabled for the consideration of members of parliament, deserve our most careful study, for no country has a greater interest than Canada in the realization of these objectives.

"Members of the house will recall that in withdrawing, on November 12 last, such tariff changes as had been incorporated in the budget resolutions the Minister of Finance stated that 'within the last few days we have been given substantial ground for believing that the prospects of early international action for the reduction of tariffs and other barriers to world trade are considerably improved.' The documents I am tabling today indicate that in the four weeks that have intervened, material progress has been made and that what was then a mere hope or expectation has become, to quote from the joint statement by President Truman and Prime Minister Attlee, 'agreement on the broad principles of commercial policy for which the two governments will seek international support.' "

A good deal of Mackenzie King's time was taken up in early December conferring with Senators, members and his colleagues about the proposals to increase parliamentary sessional allowances which had been agreed upon earlier in the year. After much discussion and with some misgivings, the Prime Minister introduced the resolution on December 13 and the bill was passed the following day with little opposition.

Monday, December 17, was Mackenzie King's birthday. He was presented with an engraved silver case by his colleagues in the Cabinet, warmly congratulated by the Opposition leaders in the House of Commons, and given a dinner by the Liberal Members of Parliament.

The first session of the post-war Parliament prorogued the next afternoon. That day, the Prime Minister's brother-in-law, H. M. Lay, died at Barrie, Ontario. Mackenzie King left for Toronto on the evening of December 19, attended the funeral on December 20, and returned to Ottawa the following day. The list of his engagements, which were mainly social, indicates that the rest of December 1945 was an uneventful period for the Prime Minister.

Mackenzie King visits a cemetery in Normandy where Canadian soldiers are buried, August 1946

Below: The visit to Normandy, August 1946. Colonel C. P. Stacey, who accompanied the Prime Minister, appears in the background

Right and far right: The Victory Parade, London, June 8, 1946. Mackenzie King rides with Field Marshal Jan Smuts; Canadian troops pass the reviewing stand before King George VI and Queen Elizabeth

ft: Mackenzie King with
nadian correspondents in
rmandy, August 1946; from
t, the Prime Minister, Marcel
imet, Matthew Halton, Ross
nro

The Prime Minister reads an address of welcome to Viscount Alexander of Tunis in the Senate Chamber, April 12, 1946

Members of the Canadian Delegation, Paris Peace Conference, August 1946. *Left to right*: General Georges Vanier, Norman Robertson, Mackenzie King, Brooke Claxton, Arnold Heeney, Dana Wilgress

Below: Norman Robertson, Mackenzie King, Brooke Claxton, Arnold Heeney

Members of the Canadian delegation, Paris Peace Conference, August 1946. *Left to right*: General Georges Vanier, Norman Robertson, Mackenzie King, Brooke Claxton, Arnold Heeney, Dana Wilgress

Below: Norman Robertson, Mackenzie King, Brooke Claxton, Arnold Heeney

A Washington conference on the atomic bomb, November 1945. Seated are Prime Minister Clement Attlee of Great Britain, President Harry S. Truman of the United States, and Mackenzie King of Canada. Among those standing are Dr. Vannevar Bush; Representative C. A. Eaton of New Jersey; Senator Brien McMahon of Connecticut; Lester Pearson, Canada's Ambassador in Washington; James F. Byrnes, the Secretary of State; Representative Sol Bloom of New York; Admiral William Leahy

The Prime Minister entertains Field Marshal Bernard Montgomery at tea, Laurier House, September 9, 1946

CHAPTER FOUR

A Winter of Discontent

DESPITE HIS GREAT WEARINESS in the months after the election, Mackenzie King was reasonably satisfied with 1945. "I shall always feel," he wrote in beginning his 1946 diary on January 1, "that 1945 was the best year of my life. I hope and pray that the new year may, in an equally significant way, afford opportunities for service to the world as great, if not greater, than those of 1945. It will have, I believe, so far as my own life is concerned, real national and international significance."

These hopes were not to be realized. Although high honours and a greater measure of recognition came to him in 1946 than ever before, it was not a happy year for the Prime Minister. Being intensely human, he blamed much of his disenchantment on others; but, underlying it, as his diary clearly shows, was a growing realization that he no longer had the resources of will and energy to bear the heavy burdens of office. Psychologically, he undoubtedly missed the incentive of a future contest for political power, once he had decided not to face another general election campaign. Although he had high hopes for his younger colleagues in 1945, it became more and more difficult for Mackenzie King to adjust to new faces and new styles. Yet he recognized that most of his older colleagues, like himself, were no longer able to face the complex problems of peacetime administration. For a time even C. D. Howe seemed afflicted by the prevailing war weariness and loss of a sense of direction. Of all Mackenzie King's older colleagues, only St. Laurent attacked problems of government with real zest; yet even he remained determined to retire to private life at the first convenient opportunity. Among the more recent appointees to the cabinet, the Prime Minister grew steadily more dependent on Claxton and Abbott.

In view of all these unfavourable circumstances, what was actually accomplished during 1946 was all the more remarkable.

Of course, there were many disappointments. On January 1, 1946, the first words Mackenzie King heard when he turned on his bed-side radio were " 'The Maple Leaf Our Emblem Dear' . . . I thought at once of the national flag for Canada as being one of the events of the new year. My own thought is that it might be better to have the maple leaf on the red field instead of the coat of arms of Canada, though I should be wholly content with either. Instead, however, of a green maple leaf, I should like to see one of the golden red type, which we see in the autumn. The maple leaf is, indeed, a national emblem. Canada's autumnal glory and the colouring of the maple leaves of autumn is something not to be surpassed in any country in the world. A beautiful golden maple leaf with tinges of red, with other autumn shades, would look very well, on a red field."

The Prime Minister instructed his butler to fly the Canadian red ensign on the Laurier House flag pole for New Year's day. "As I looked at it from my library, the flag floating in the sun, it was indeed beautiful. The shield was quite effective with its colouring of gold and red and green. Its one drawback is that it is not distinguishable at a distance. Also there may be changes in the coat of arms from time to time.

"I told Pickersgill over the 'phone what I had in mind, and of my thought in presenting this suggestion to the Committee [the House of Commons committee on the flag question] myself. He thought the idea an excellent one. It is something I have had in mind for some time. It may be given to me in the course of my days to make this suggestion and to see it accepted. I am sure our national flag will be one or the other: the red ensign with the coat of arms or with the maple leaf."

Mackenzie King was to return to the flag question many times during 1946 and, by the end of the year, had evidently come to the conclusion that he could never finally settle it.

One very disagreeable and embarrassing problem plagued the Prime Minister during the early months of the year. A few days before he left London in November 1945 Mackenzie King had concurred in a suggestion by the British Prime Minister that Ilsley and St. Laurent be made United Kingdom Privy Councillors. Their names were included in the New Year's honours list issued on December 31, 1945. After his usual New Year's reception at Laurier House, Mackenzie King was surprised to receive "a very impulsive and hot-headed" telegram from Ian Mackenzie protesting his colleagues' appointments, "referring to the matter as an insult to himself and tendering his resignation . . . saying he intended to cross the floor and fight. I was amazed when I read it, but saw at once it was the outcome of his Highland pride and a feeling he has had that as senior P.C. he should be acting P.M. or President of the Cabinet, etc., when I went away. No man sees his own faults or his own limitations as he ought to see them. Mackenzie has only himself to blame. Had his habits not been what they had been, things might have been different. I have been his truest friend and have saved him many situations. I could see at once that he had mistaken the whole situation. He had been under the impression that I had made the recommendations for the Privy Councillorships. That particularly would occasion intense feeling on his part. The fact that he sent the telegram that he did showed that he was either too excitable in his present condition or had been taking too much of New Year's festivities. In neither case was he doing justice to himself as a Minister to the Crown.

"I drafted an answer immediately and by its wording sought to remove the cause of his worries. His message reminds me a little of the one McNaughton sent in reference to Ralston. Practically all the trouble we have had in the Cabinet stems from that particular feud. I have no concern as to how Mackenzie is likely to behave in the end. His telegram makes impossible for all time any recognition of his part in Parliament or before the country. Its publication would settle him for good."

Mackenzie was away from Ottawa on holiday and the Prime Minister spoke to him by telephone. However, relations between the two men were clearly not restored to their former cordiality. Mackenzie King received two letters from his colleague on January 8, "one making out a list of things he thought should be done by the Government; helpful enough in the way of suggestion but quite clearly seeking to get himself on record. The other, a saving of his own face in regard to the telegram he had sent to me but not making the *amende honorable* which he should have made. I can, however, afford to let him overlook anything in that way. He will not last very long."

Ian Mackenzie was not the only member of the Cabinet who was hurt by Ilsley's and St. Laurent's appointment. C. D. Howe, who had been in Cuba for the holiday season, called on the Prime Minister on January 15. Mackenzie King was "quite sure in my own mind that he probably had some grievance that he wanted to discuss," and brought up at once "the appointment of Ilsley and St. Laurent as Privy Councillors. I told Howe of the letter received from Mackenzie, and more particularly of my own part in merely approving the addition of two members of the Government to the British Privy Council, at the request of Attlee and Lord Addison, stating that I had approved the addition, not wishing to monopolize the title myself. I had made no suggestion of names, but had approved the two names mentioned to me. To my surprise, Howe said that he had felt very bitterly about it for some time, but he had gotten over that. He felt that he was the one man who had carried the heaviest load in the war effort and spoke of Ilsley as not being as deserving as himself and also of St. Laurent as being quite new. I was much surprised to hear him say that he had been assured by a couple of British Ministers that he would receive an Imperial Privy Councillorship, and the worst of it was he had told his wife and daughters who now very greatly shared his disappointment. Later I said to him I could not understand how any Ministers could give that assurance except the Prime Minister, which caused him to say they had told him they had recommended him for an Imperial P.C. He then said that what he had really come to talk about was that he felt he ought to give up continuing on as a Minister. He was now sixty years of age and found he had not come back as well as he should have after the absences he has had. He was very tired and the work of the office irritated him. The reconstruction business was of a character that no one could make a success of. However, it could run itself. It was now on the lines of a pattern 'a bit contradictory.' He said that he liked 'straight businesses.' Could not stand being a member of committees. I told him I thought he should not entertain any idea of the kind. That the country needed his services, particularly at this time; that I am sure many of us felt the way he did. I said a rest and change would be welcome. I myself was in my seventy-second year; he was sixty. He replied that I had given my life to politics; his was more a business life. I said I could well understand his feeling that the war had been a great strain, his own narrow escape, his boy in peril, apart from all the work; there was bound to be that reaction. I said I thought no one should make a decision when they were tired. What I would strongly advise him to do was to take a prolonged rest, make his decision after he was completely rested.

"I told him that St. Laurent had told me about wanting to return to his practice, on account of having a son he wanted to start in practice, and not be too long away from the law himself; which caused Howe to say he would like to start one of his boys in his business at Port Arthur. Also he had another boy he ought to be looking after, and his daughters who were growing up. This caused me to see he was looking around for excuses."

The Prime Minister kept stressing "the idea that he must not in any way consider dropping out for at least another year or two. [Howe] said now that things were smooth we might get into a difficult place and it would be awkward then to withdraw. He did not want to go through another election and had not wished to go through the last. I am afraid that what he foresees is that there is likely to be much discussion in the House on salvage work, and that the reconstruction job is not going to be too easy and would like to get out before this comes out. He said he thought the country would be going ahead all right. I said it would as long as the Government in whom the people had confidence kept intact. If there was a break in one part others would follow and it might well be that the Government itself might not be able to cope with the situation that might arise. I said it was too important at this stage to allow anything of the kind to occur. I also said to him if he got out at the moment it would be said it was because of his feeling of not having received an Imperial P.C. In this connection he had mentioned he had received a couple of hundred letters about the matter. All of this makes me feel that that is what has caused him to feel as he does. I can now see quite clearly that my unwillingness to make any recommendation myself, or to do more than just approve names I was asked about has really occasioned a deeper resentment than I had thought it would. Perhaps too in my high regard for St. Laurent I have not sufficiently considered the length of service of other colleagues. I certainly did not feel enthusiastic about having Ilsley appointed, but agreed to this simply because I did not wish my own personal feelings to stand in the way of any recognition which might come his way through his efforts over the years. It is only too true that personal jealousies count for more than almost anything else in the actions of men. It is going to be a little more difficult to hold colleagues together now that the glamour of war no longer enshrines their actions and service for the sake of service comes to be the necessity of the times."

After they had talked for some time, Howe then asked if he "could have back his old Department of Transport. I said that certainly anything of that kind I would be prepared to consider. That as an older Minister, one who had worked so strenuously over the years, he was entitled to have things made easier and more to his liking if that could be arranged. I asked how Chevrier might do in the Department. He was not too sure. He was afraid that he would find the pressure of Members very great, though he would be sterling in his integrity. I then spoke about giving the job to McCann. He thought McCann could handle it very well. That he would be very strong in resisting pressure. He doubted if he would altogether welcome the change. I said that all Ministers must be prepared to shift about, that I thought I had perhaps made a mistake in not changing Ministers oftener. Howe replied that now that the war was over the civil servants were taking far too much into their own hands, trying to run things and Ministers were giving them far too much freedom in that way. I agreed he is right in this.

"As soon as he mentioned wanting his old Department back, I could see that his coming today was the outcome of feelings he has had over the P.C. matter and probably what came up with respect to his Department during his absence. Indeed he said he felt he had not been properly protected in the House. It so happened that McIlraith [Howe's Parliamentary Assistant] was away because of the death of his father-in-law.

Mackenzie had promised he would look after things but had not given the attention he should. He felt he should have been more protected. The truth is Howe should, of course, have stayed here to look after his own Department.

"Howe added further that when he dropped out of public life, the position he would like would be that of President of Trans-Canada Airways. That he liked that kind of constructive business work. I told him I did not know anyone who was better qualified or would be more deserving for that particular post. By this time, it was wholly apparent to me he did not intend to get out but had rather come to carry out what he has probably told others he would do in the way of tendering his resignation. I can make all allowances for a man's feelings. What I would like better, however, is if anyone would come out frankly and state the cause of resentment but not come and talk resignation where there is owing to the country what Howe must know what is owing on his part at this time.

"Before he left Howe said to me he thought he would perhaps go out to B.C. and stay a month or two, in about another month's time. That in the interval he would stay around. I told him I thought that would be the wise thing to do. Take a real rest but to abandon any thought of not continuing on in the Ministry. His mood changed completely during the time when we were talking together and I felt as he went away he was really much happier at heart. I am glad of this as I should naturally be very sorry to lose him as a colleague. His loss would be a real one to the Ministry. One of the secrets of successful government is not to allow breaches to be made in the Cabinet where it is possible to avoid anything of the kind."

The next day (January 16) the Prime Minister became convinced that the origin of Howe's problem "lay in not having been made a P.C. and in a desire to put a certain premium on himself. The thing that would have surprised him most and pleased him least would have been willingness on my part to accept his resignation. It was a sort of trying out of my attitude towards himself. At heart some of these men are little conscious still of where they stood when the Government was in danger. With all this I still can see wherein I myself in similar circumstances should have felt indignant at the recognition of Ilsley and St. Laurent to the exclusion of one's self, had there been reason to believe that this was a deliberate action on my part. What I should have done was to follow my own inner judgment and not agreed to any appointments to the Imperial Privy Council at this time."

To add to his worries about Howe and Mackenzie, the Prime Minister received word on January 17 that Ilsley was anxious to see him before the Cabinet meeting that day. "The impression I got at the moment the message came was that the subject probably relates to his own health. I confess that my thoughts dwell upon the difficulties that I see ahead with respect to the Cabinet now that the first year of the new Government is over. To have Ilsley drop out even temporarily would make the situation very difficult. It may be difficult if he remains with the frame of mind which he has come to have. . . .

"This afternoon, I received a letter from Frank Ross, Montreal, saying he was going to resign from Howe's Department because of the injustice done Howe in not being made a P.C. Howe had been pleading for Ross to be given some British honour, when we were last discussing honours. Ross would know that I had opposed any honours being given by the British Government to him, until Canadians were given civilian honours.

"Mackenzie has left his resignation in my hands because he was overlooked. The fact in reality is he is tired out and not equal to business of his office. Were it not for the risks that are run through vacancies arising out of resignations, I would not be much concerned at the loss of any of these Ministers though Howe and Ilsley have still an important part to play. Replacements create jealousies, etc. St. Laurent is the one man above all I would not wish to lose. He, too, is getting anxious about the years passing and holding on to his practice. It may be that I am facing a situation of the kind which will be difficult. I shall, however, seek, as I have in the past, to do my best to keep the Government together. When I find that the time comes that I cannot do this any longer without impairment of health, I shall ask the party to find another leader. It might well be that some defeat would come in the House which might make this step advisable. I can see that Members generally, those of the older stock in particular, are beginning to put a price on their support."

Mackenzie King saw Ilsley later in the day at Laurier House. "I lighted the fire in the grate and we had a cup of tea together in the library. He is so very quiet, it was a little difficult to get started on conversation while the maid was still in the room. When she left Ilsley said: It is about myself that I have to speak. He then went on to say he was finding it increasingly difficult to do any work. He could not be enthusiastic about anything. It was all a heavy burden. He envied Claxton very much – the optimism that he had that it was going to be possible to meet the problems. They just needed to be tackled, etc. He had felt that way some years ago himself but had come to feel the problems could not be solved. At any rate, he was not the one to try to work out the solution further. He went back to prior to the last election. He said that in the election he did strike the optimistic note that was necessary but he did not himself really believe that much that he was saying could be achieved. He had intended to speak to me about this before he went to New York for his holiday but thought he had better wait until he came back. On coming back, he had found himself quite unable to work with any zest at all. He did not want to embarrass me. He knew the load I was carrying and the worries of Ministers and others that I had to contend with but he felt that, sooner or later, he would have to give up. He went on to say that he felt he perhaps owed it to me and to the Government to stick on, through this session, no matter how hard it was going to be. To just make up his mind he would go through with the session and then drop out after it was over. He said he could, of course, return to his practice of law. He did not know, however, whether or not I might feel he was suited for a position on the Bench. That, if so, such a position he would feel would give him all that he could do. He said there was a vacancy on the Supreme Court in Nova Scotia or would be because of Chisholm's age and illness. He wondered if that post might not be kept open until the end of the session. He did not think the Court would suffer any if the position were kept open that much longer. He then would be able to go back and live among the people he had been brought up with and would feel quite happy.

"I said to him that I was very glad he had come to speak to me. That on coming out of Council yesterday I had remarked he had looked quite worn. He would recall I had expressed surprise that he had come back so soon. . . . That, naturally, I had been right along watching what he was doing and the effect it was having on his health. That I had hesitated to speak myself lest he might think in some ways I was not wholly satisfied, etc. I said I was not the least surprised he felt as he did. It was an evidence of nerve exhaustion, not at all surprising, but wholly natural. I felt what he should do was to take a good rest; make no decision at all while he was tired; get away for a couple of months. Much better we should do the best we could without him than he should have a break in which event we would have a longer strain in the end. His health is more important than anything else.

"I went on to say I thought he should get on an ocean liner and get away from this continent altogether. He did not know how this could be done. I said we would have to get on without him if he were broken up in health and better avoid that and make some other provision.

"Ilsley spoke about how heavy the Finance Department was. I said I thought there were some phases of it he should get rid of. Spoke of housing in particular. He said he thought that could be arranged under the company that had been formed. Turned over to Howe, who would take it.

"He referred to Mackenzie's letter regarding the things to be done and said that was an extraordinary letter of Mackenzie's, which gave me a

A Winter of Discontent   111

chance to say it was a build-up, in the light of his annoyance at not having been made an Imperial P.C. That he had written me a shocking letter in that connection. Ilsley looked surprised at that and a little contemptuous. I said Mackenzie seemed to think that years in government were the ground for preferment, not realizing that he had in many ways been kept on and shown every consideration. He seemed to feel he should have been the leader while I was away. Ilsley said he announced himself that he was. I said I did not mean leader of the House, but acting Prime Minister. Ilsley then said that Mackenzie had had no word with him about acting as leader in the House. I said neither had he with me. He took that on himself. I said, however, I thought he had done what services he could there. Had done a lot of good work in connection with veterans affairs, etc.

"I then told him that Howe also had felt disappointed about the Imperial P.C., and of Howe's desire to drop out. He, too, felt very fatigued. He said he understood that Howe was talking of going to the Coast for a month. I said Howe had spoken to me of it. I thought it was better he could take a rest at once as well. I also mentioned to him the note I had received today from Frank Ross. The more I think of that note the more indignant I feel about it. I should have asked him in my letter if he wished to have his letter forwarded to the British Government. He is looking for recognition from them. ..."

Ilsley then reviewed some of the major problems which would have to be dealt with during the next few months. Of top priority was the second meeting of the Co-ordinating Committee established by the Dominion-Provincial Conference in August 1945. The meeting was scheduled to begin on January 28 and Mackenzie King assured Ilsley that St. Laurent, who was then in London leading the Canadian delegation to the First Session of the United Nations General Assembly, would return to Ottawa to take part in the discussions with the provincial premiers. Also on the Minister's priority list were amendments to the Income Tax Act, a budget, housing legislation, financial negotiations with the British government, and a series of new trade agreements.

"He spoke about Dr. Clark [the Deputy Minister of Finance] being in good condition now, having been away for nine months. Said that at times Clark had gotten where he could not think at all. Was quite incapable of constructive thought which I am not surprised at. Says he is a bit highly strung yet which, of course, Ilsley himself is to the degree of almost no other Minister. He also said that he thought no Minister of Finance should stay longer than five years. . . . I said perhaps we had made a mistake in not shifting portfolios about more. I asked what Ministers could take his portfolio. He spoke very highly of Claxton. Said, of course, St. Laurent was the best of all and that Abbott was also good. They were the only three. I asked him how he would like to take over Justice. His face lighted up at once and he said that would please him immensely. He would like that very much. What he feels is the terrible pressure from every side. I then told him about having St. Laurent in mind for External Affairs but that St. Laurent too had spoken to me about feeling that the time had come for him to drop out and to get back to his law practice. Ilsley said: How you stand it, I don't know. I told him my only desire now was to get things in such a shape that the party could continue on; to bring it as much up to the mark as possible, believing honestly there was no place for the Conservative party in Canada, and that Socialism meant dictatorship which would be most unfortunate. He agreed.

"Ilsley could not have been nicer than he was in the way he spoke, nor clearly could he have been less concerned about anything for himself. It is a singular thing which I never thought of while talking to him that not a word was said about the desirability of his remaining, with a view to possibly succeeding to my position. Evidently he sees that is not going to be possible, probably for two reasons; first, of health; and second, very doubtful if he could get the nomination from the party. The truth is all these older men see that their chances of leadership are fading before those of younger men coming on which is as it should be. What is odd to me is that I never seemed to entertain the thought that I should suggest to him seeking to continue on with the prospect of what some future Convention might do as to the leadership. It is perhaps just as well that I did not. I have never discussed that matter wtih a single colleague in relation to himself. My own impression is that St. Laurent is in every way the best equipped but would not, I believe, himself entertain the possibility. Claxton is the ablest and best equipped in outlook and knowledge but has not the personality that Abbott has. Abbott would probably be the choice of the party today. Whether he is strong enough physically to undertake the task is open to question.

"When Ilsley left, it was understood between us that we would talk freely over the matter from time to time and that meantime I would keep in mind what he said. My own feeling is that a complete re-arrangement of portfolios may be desirable."

In Cabinet the next afternoon, Mackenzie King decided to raise the question of honours and awards. "As Ilsley and Howe were both in the Cabinet, I thought it well to speak in the presence of each and such Ministers as were there. They included Robertson, of the Senate, Claxton, Mitchell, McCann, Jean, Bridges, Glen and Bertrand.

"I took up first the Imperial Privy Councillorships. Told the Cabinet of my being asked if I would agree to extra appointments from Canada. Later asked if I would approve of Ilsley and St. Laurent. Pointed out that Ilsley was acting Prime Minister at the time; also that Hofmeyer, Deputy Prime Minister of South Africa, had just been made an Imperial Privy Councillor. That St. Laurent was doubtless thought of as representing the French element in Canada as Hofmeyer had been the Dutch in South Africa. I stressed that the United Kingdom Government controlled their own Cabinet. That I had made no recommendations. If I had declined to agree to more being appointed, it would have been said I wished the position for myself, etc.

"I was quite amazed when, all of a sudden, Howe burst out by asking who this lecture was intended for and saying that he had felt very much annoyed at what had taken place and was spending his time answering letters about it. Did not see why we had to continue discussing it. I think all members of the Cabinet were very much surprised. I said to him he clearly was taking me up the wrong way. I was simply seeking to make clear to the Cabinet the position irrespective of the powers of the Prime Minister, etc. I pointed out I myself was experiencing a good deal of unpleasantness and misunderstanding as to my position. I thought that should be explained. It is clear, however, that Howe and his associates have been talking this matter over at some length and have really been very exasperated about it. To me, this is hardly understandable."

After the Cabinet meeting the Prime Minister learned that Ian Mackenzie had just returned to his Ottawa apartment after a period in hospital. He immediately telephoned and discovered that Mackenzie "was clearly in a mood of defiance and resentment. His letter had been signed 'Yours truly.' Evidently as men, when they are in the wrong, do, seeking to find a grievance against myself. When I told him I had not known he had been in the city, he said he had sent word to Heeney a week ago that he was here. I repeated I knew nothing of that and certainly would have been out to have seen him or have had a talk with him, or made enquiries at once. Was under the impression he had gone to the West. He got on to the Imperial Privy Councillorship business. He said it raised a very serious constitutional question which was that of the precedence of Ministers going from Canada to functions in England. That an Imperial P.C. gained a precedence there over what they would have because of seniority here. I told him I was not aware of any such precedence. All of us who were 'Rt. Hon.' did not carry any precedence. He said it did tell at social functions, etc. It seemed to me the thing [was] too trivial to discuss. I merely said with equality of status, I felt that Ministers from different parts of the

Empire took their place in accordance with what might be arranged as obviously satisfactory. Precedence after all is only a matter of arranging things in decency and order to prevent confusion. He then asked me to listen a moment and said he knew who was responsible for this business and anathemized Malcolm MacDonald very strongly, saying he was deceitful, etc. Where he ever heard of Malcolm having made a recommendation to the British Government I don't know. I don't know of any source it could have come from which had been traced back to myself. It might, of course, have been found out from some of Mackenzie's friends in the Old Country or friends of Howe or his associates. It reminds me that Howe again told the Cabinet he had been assured by two British Ministers that he would receive a P.C. I asked him when he said that to me the other day, how British Ministers could give him any such assurance. It shows how completely astray these men are in their appreciation of the right way of proceeding in such things.

"It is altogether probable that Mackenzie and Howe and others have been checking up on who made the recommendations to the British Government. How the British Government came to select the two they did and there is little doubt they would learn that the High Commissioner for Canada had been the one who had sent over the names.

"I was horrified at the way Mackenzie spoke but I urged him very strongly not to go on with his meetings [a series of speaking engagements] in the West but to take a rest immediately. However he persists he must have these meetings, etc. The impression that I get of him is that he is like a drowning man catching at straws. That he is breaking up completely but trying to keep a certain assurance before the public. The whole thing is appearance rather than reality. I thought he had a profounder sense of reality than he is exhibiting. He wanted to decide when he came back to Ottawa, when he should resign. I told him that I was not seeking the resignation of any Ministers. I had not sought them at any time. What I think is almost certain to happen is that he will come down with a crash at some moment of excitement or stress. Whether it will finish him or make him an invalid, for a long time, I cannot say. If I could spare him this fate, I would, but I am afraid he will take counsel or advice from no one."

Late the next afternoon, January 19, the Prime Minister had Ian Mackenzie to Laurier House for tea. "He was very formal and stiff in his manner at the outset. Spoke to little Pat in a friendly way in the hall. Addressed me as 'Sir,' etc. When I asked if he would like a cup of tea, he declined it. Equally cigarette which he said he did not smoke. I sought to put him at his ease by speaking at once of my regret at not having known he was in Hospital. I sought to clear that up. . . . I could see that he had been thinking I was deliberately leaving him to himself.

"I next went on to the question of the Imperial P.C., repeating what I had said. Beyond touching on what the matter involved on the matter of my surrendering a certain precedence of Canadian Ministers at international gatherings in London, he did not try to pursue the matter at all. He said that personally he had no ambitions to satisfy. It was quite clear that the constitutional thing is all a make-believe. . . ."

Mackenzie persisted in saying he would resign after he returned from his western trip or after the proposed veterans legislation had been prepared but, as the two men talked, he "gradually lost his austere manner. He had earlier said something about having learned how very indignant Howe was and that he was going to resign. . . . I said Howe had talked with me. Said he was very tired. I had I thought persuaded him he should take a long rest. . . . I said I could understand the fatigue he [Mackenzie] must feel. I then said what I felt very much and very deeply was that any colleague of mine would wish to hold me responsible for taking a step which would injure their feelings or fail to ask for recognition which he deserved. I said Mackenzie knew perhaps as well as anyone how consistently in all the years I have been in office I have tried to advance the position of my colleagues in the eyes of my fellowmen to protect them in every way and to gain for them as much in the way of recognition as possible. He had to admit that this was true."

After an hour's conversation and several cups of tea, Mackenzie had "become quite natural and normal" but as the Prime Minister escorted him to his car he could "see how much he has changed, even in his walk. The truth is he has been really destroying himself. It is a great pity. Had he left liquor alone, as I recall his ability when he came into the House and his popularity, he might easily have been my successor in the position.

"How long Mackenzie may last I of course cannot say. It is clear, however, that his usefulness as a Minister of the Crown is at an end. I propose, however, that the end comes through some action of his own, not of mine."

The subject continued to preoccupy Mackenzie King and by January 20 he had decided "to let these men see that I am wholly indifferent to what they do. If Howe wishes to leave the Ministry I intend to let him go. I shall also let Mackenzie go at the first opportunity. I am, however, not going to allow Howe or Ross or others to get away with the idea that they have been injured through some action of mine. It is a dastardly deed for a man like Ross to express regret for not continuing his services voluntarily for the country's work of reconstruction because of his feeling about the extent to which his Minister has suffered an injury, when he is leaving because the glamour has gone off the job and he himself is disappointed at not having got from the British Government some honours in the New Year's list, Howe too is interested mainly in power that the position gives him, not in public service for its sake. While it may make matters more difficult in some respects it will help to remove a reactionary Tory influence from the Government to have Howe out. The same would be true in another way should Ilsley drop out. They are the two men who the real Liberals in the party object to. What I have to consider is our limited majority and the difficulty of obtaining their support in the House once they are out of the Ministry and the uncertainty of electing someone in their place should they give up Parliament as well. But for these factors, I would gladly dispose of Howe and Mackenzie in no time whatever. My feeling toward Howe has changed entirely because of his attitude over this wretched business of recognition by titles and what appears to have been going on behind the scenes in seeking to arrange this kind of thing with the British Government. I have decided definitely not to go on with the Canadian order of chivalry but from now on to take the stand that I want nothing of the kind for Canada. The Canada Medal would be different as a form of recognition to McNaughton and Crerar, though apart from that I see no need for it. Some day in Parliament, if not there, in anything I shall be privileged to write in my memoirs, I will make known my feeling about the false and the true in the way of recognition. It is something I have felt more deeply than anything else in my life. In regard to university degrees and all the rest of it."

The following afternoon Howe telephoned to ask Mackenzie King to attend a dinner the next evening in honour of former members of the Department of Munitions and Supply. The Prime Minister refused to attend "a gathering of which Mr. Frank Ross was a prominent member. . . . Howe replied that he hoped I would not hold Ross's action against him. That Ross was a hot-headed Scotchman and when he had resigned he (Howe) had accepted it. . . . Howe said Ross's letter had been written before he was back from the South. I replied that it had not been received until after he had been in to talk with me. I added that it was Ross's second letter which caused me to say what I had said in the Cabinet at its last meeting. I said I had reason to feel that the Department had been worked up over the question of honours and that I was being made responsible for the disappointment which members of the staff had felt; that he (Howe) knew as I did that this was no more the case than that I was responsible for the troops overseas not getting to the front as soon as they expected, but they had been led to believe that I was responsible. I told Howe I had looked forward with pleasure to an opportunity of thanking the men in the Department of Munitions and Supply for their services, but the letter received from Mr. Ross had given me quite a different feeling about the whole business and that I really could not see how I could bring myself to attend and make the sort of address expected of me."

The Prime Minister seemed even more upset on January 22. He felt "indifferent to Mackenzie's attitude. I had expected something different from Howe. The fact that the only word that came to me about the dinner was through Pickersgill from Howe's Secretary and was not in the nature of an invitation but rather something left to myself to come if I liked was evidence itself of some feeling that had arisen. For a meeting of that importance I should have had a letter from Howe himself with a request to speak.... With the feeling of indignation I have about matters of recognition I would have found it difficult not to have expressed some of my views pretty plainly at the dinner and that was the last thing that would be wanted there.... At the same time, the occasion is one which, had these incidents not arisen, I would have greatly welcomed [as] a chance to thank those who had given their services during the war in the Department ... and [say] a word about carrying co-operation of wartime into peacetime efforts."

Reading about the dinner in the morning paper on January 23 did not improve Mackenzie King's mood. It was "described as the greatest show and Howe himself as the ringleader of a circus. I was not altogether sorry I had missed the occasion. At the same time I do feel perhaps I should have gone and ignored everything and spoken as Prime Minister." At the Cabinet meeting that afternoon, the Prime Minister reported, Howe "looked very tired and worn. I asked him how his party went. He said very well, but was sorry I had not been there. I said I also was sorry as I would have liked to have participated in it. I added that I really knew very little about it until immediately before; that I had got no information, and I might have added or any real invitation. He said he was sorry for this. He had been away and left the things to others. I asked him if he would let me have a copy of Ross's resignation and his acceptance of it. I asked if Ross had mentioned his reason for resigning other than that which he had given to me. Howe said he did not think he had. That everyone knew what his reason was. He wanted to take life easier. He had been intending to resign. He [Howe] said he had refused to read his letters to me when they were written. This contradicts what he [Howe] says and what he himself told me, which was that letters had been written before his return, the inference being that he had not been shown them at all. He also said he refused to read them when Pickersgill took them to him. I said I did not propose to have Ross lie to me or to get away with any lies concerning myself as a subterfuge for his dropping out of public service. I could see from Howe's face that he had felt considerably upset over the whole business. It has been a great strain to myself. Had matters gone differently, the occasion might have been made one for me to speak of Howe's services as well as of the others. Also to have been given some mention in connection with the Government's part in assisting or furthering of work of the Department of Munitions and Supply. I notice that all that was said by way of credit was to Ilsley for being lavish in the funds given and to Mitchell in regard to Labour. The whole thing was about as badly messed up as it could be. I felt very tired and depressed all day myself."

After the Cabinet meeting on January 24, Howe raised the matter again with the Prime Minister and "said he did not believe that his name had not been put forward. He had been told that that was not true. I said to him I had merely been asked if I would agree to two additional P.C.'s. The reason given was that I was the only one in the Canadian Government who was a P.C. I was later asked if I would approve of Ilsley and St. Laurent. That I had agreed to them. I had understood the number was restricted to two and these were the names which were put forward. Evidently, someone is supplying Howe with different information – someone who cannot possibly know as only Attlee, Lord Addison and myself were present at the conversation. It was Malcolm MacDonald who sent over the names. The two he sent were Ilsley and St. Laurent. This Malcolm told me himself and it was what was told me by the Secretary of State. It was also what Lord Addison told me MacDonald had sent. I did not bring MacDonald's name into the conversation with Howe. I can see he is still very much put out. Felt that he should have been so recognized and evidently wished recognition very much."

There the matter rested until February 13 when Mackenzie King had a further talk with Howe and discovered that he had given up the idea of switching to the Transport portfolio. "That is a great relief. He said he thought he ought to get out about the middle of the summer. Feels his boys are growing up, etc. He added he hoped I would not make it too hard for him to get out. I told him I would do anything I could to meet his wishes. Fully understood how he felt. Spoke of Trans-Continental Airways. Howe said there was no salary attached to that position. I said I thought it might be properly made a salaried position; either one or the other, he would be glad to have it. Spoke about C.P.R. ships on the Pacific. He thought this might well be left alone for a while with other expenditures more important. As to branch lines for aviation – the matter Neal [President of the C.P.R.] was interested in – he said private firms were not offering and he thought for a year it would be well to just allow C.P.R.

to continue for that time. They would need it to get equipment. I said to bring that matter before Cabinet; not to have a decision for which he and I would be responsible. Spoke about housing. He said he might be ready to take the job on after his holiday if he felt differently but would not like to touch it at present. He feels when war veterans affairs are investigated, there will be a bad showing there on the housing business."

His difficulties with Howe and Mackenzie obviously coloured the Prime Minister's attitude during a long discussion on honours and decorations at a Cabinet meeting on March 6. "Gibson wanted to know if we had not agreed on the Canada Medal and a Canadian Order. I told the Cabinet I had never experienced more pain and anguish over any public matter than I have on anything that has to do with decorations and honours. I said that personally I was all against them and upon conviction, for honours that were done one multitudes were ignored who were more worthy. That, for instance, a man who had escaped injury or death could not be regarded as being more worthy of decoration than one who had given his life. Parents were really more entitled to be honoured where they had lost their son than some man who had been fortunate enough to perform a noble deed and get credit for it and escape with his life. I did not say anything about service for service's sake, which comprised readiness to serve without recognition, but I did say that I had made up my mind as to the Canadian Order. While I thought it looked better than British orders, I did not wish to have my name or a Ministry of which I had been a member identified with the establishment of an order of decoration in Canada. That I would not approve any recourse to that end. Equally I would not favour a Canada Medal until it was known to whom the medal would be given. That I was not particularly anxious to see any form of that kind of recognition. Some subsequent Ministry could introduce these two things but I would not as long as I was at the Council table." And to that decision he stuck.

A visit to Ottawa by General and Mrs. Eisenhower gave Mackenzie King real pleasure early in 1946. However, after meeting them at the station on January 9, he characteristically began to worry about what he would say at the government dinner that evening at the Country Club. Mrs. Patteson made "a very helpful suggestion, which was to look at the Foch speech made twenty-five years ago and to repeat its thought, and I did. At the last moment, I decided not only to do this but to read what I had said about Foch, substituting Eisenhower's name for Foch's. It was astonishing how completely accurate the description was and how much more appropriate even to Eisenhower than to Foch."

At the dinner, Eisenhower "made an exceptionally favourable impression, as he does I think at all events. What appealed to me most, in reading his own speeches, is his humility and sincerity, the absence of affectation, and belief in his fellow-men. Also his strong family feeling: what he owes to his parents, and his readiness to make this apparent. There has been no effort in anything he has said to help embellish himself. He has expressed in words what I have often thought to express but have not thus far been able to – how wrong it is for a man to seek out of the blood and sacrifice of others to have himself glorified."

The next morning, Mackenzie King became even more worried "about how I would meet the obligation I had assumed to reply to Eisenhower's speech at the Canadian Club luncheon. Happily, two days ago, Brockington had suggested to Pickersgill that I might like to have the name of Castle Mountain changed to Mount Eisenhower. The idea appealed to me instantly and I at once had the Geographic Board meet and take action in the matter. This was arranged in time to get from Glen, the Minister of Mines and Resources, a certified copy of the decision of the Geographic Board. I had had in mind a few thoughts I might express. Realizing how tired I was I decided not to trust to the moment to say what I wished but to write out in the form of a letter to Eisenhower what I thought it advisable to say in bringing about the change of name. . . .

"As matters turned out, I found it quite easy to say a few words of appreciation of his visit, and then I changed quickly to a reference to the presentation of the castle made to him in Scotland, and from this referred to the change in the name of Castle Mountain in Banff to that of Mount Eisenhower. I then read the letter and handed it to him with the enclosure from the Geographic Board. The whole business was received with tremendous enthusiasm by the Club.

"Eisenhower was taken completely by surprise. I noticed that his eyes filled with tears, as he made a reference to what it meant to have his family name go down through centuries to come. He caught the significance of the whole thing in a moment. He ended up with a very happy reference of being sure that the mountain had a bald peak, owing to what appeared to be baldness of his own head.

"I have never seen any single act which was received with more enthusiasm than was this giving of Eisenhower's name to this particular mountain, which is located at a point where there are more American tourists than anywhere else in Canada. My own feeling is that we have got far ahead of the United States Government in taking this step. Indeed, I have known of few happier ideas being brought forward at any time or received with equal enthusiasm. Everyone seemed to feel that the right thing and an exceptional thing had been done."

After the visit, Mackenzie King wrote a memorandum outlining his talks with Eisenhower. "I was impressed with the genuineness of his naturalness, of his real belief in and desire for peace and good-will among men and nations. Of all this being the outgrowth of his early training. I said to him at the Embassy that I had been impressed with the way in which he had referred to his parents and what he owed to their teaching, etc. I asked him if he did not think that was the main influence in the lives of men who had achieved real things. In an instant he turned and spread out one hand until about the height of his knee and said most decidedly so. A man is made when he is that high. It was the influence of parents upbringing he was emphasizing this way. . . .

"Another significant thing he said was that he had learned early in life that it never did to lose control of oneself. That his father, and he also spoke of some other persons, had spoken to him very strongly of the importance of this. The other person had said he learned to manage himself, not bother about others. That he had kept this before him through his life. I asked him if he did not think that anger was a very destructive thing. He said there was nothing so destructive. It destroys the man himself and all he was seeking to deal with. He clearly attributed the success he had to his readiness to co-operate with all who displayed a willingness toward that end. He also attached real importance to his own views where he felt they were the result of careful study and long experience. This he brought out very clearly in what he told me of some conversations he had had with Churchill.

"Churchill, he said, was terribly tenacious of his own view. Used every method conceivable to have his own wishes prevail. It was, I think, over the question of seeking to penetrate Germany through the Balkans which Churchill had most at heart as against coming in across the Channel that their greatest difference in attitude and of view re strategy, etc., had asserted itself. He said Churchill one day had argued, he thought, for seven hours, using every conceivable weapon. That he would be emotional at times. At other times would seek to bludgeon. Would then fall back on his knowledge of history and recite what had taken place here and there. Would flatter, sympathize, etc. Do anything to have his view prevail. At one stage he said to Eisenhower he was putting forth the view he did because America had a larger number of troops, whereupon Eisenhower had said to him at once 'you cannot talk that way to me.' He did not say 'you can have my resignation' but said, 'if he held the view that he, Eisenhower,' was taking the position he was for any reason other than that of higher strategy the sooner Churchill was advised by someone else the better.' Churchill instantly withdrew what he said and apologized for it. Eisenhower said he had on one or two other occasions to tell him he thought he, Eisenhower, should resign. Churchill had said to him that was not fair. He had no right to even think of such a thing. They were there to work out what was best and to trust each other, etc. He likes Churchill very much on a certain side, but recognizes the other side as well. He was determined to prevent interference in his own field by Churchill. I said to him I thought the greatest thing Churchill had done was holding back the crossing of the Channel and thereby saving many lives, and possibly losses had the crossing been made too soon. Eisenhower said something about in the long run he felt perhaps Churchill had the larger vision on some things. Whether it was this or not I did not catch, but that history might justify him. He did not say that it was not wise to have held back.

"Now I recall how Eisenhower had said at Ascot that if we had a few more men to penetrate from other sides, he would go into the invasion smiling. Churchill had replied I have been telling you that right along. I think probably there was some difference of view there, but it was the Balkan situation that I know Eisenhower felt so strongly on. The whole question of invasion from the south rather than from the north. He thought Churchill's desire to go through the Balkans was his fear of Russia and of gaining a control of that area for that reason. There is no doubt that this is so. Churchill's remark to me at luncheon at his home in London that all these smaller states would become Russian satellites, that Russia's influence would extend right up to the middle of Europe, bears that out. It is conceivable that it was to this that Eisenhower had reference when he spoke about history some time in the future bearing out Churchill's judgment. Of this I am not sure. He himself has real concern about Russia and also is genuinely concerned about the atomic bomb and other mass destruction of forces that may be brought into play. I wish Eisenhower could see his way to become Secretary of the United Nations. He would be the right man for that task.

"He told me of a talk he had had with Coldwell in which he had said to Coldwell that he did not see how the socialistic ideas could end up in anything but dictatorship. If the state kept taking over industry after industry and owned them all then it meant that the few men controlling the state would be virtually dictators and have the nation enthralled. I think this is a far-sighted view. With the power that Labour has today as exhibited by the strikes in the U.S. – almost a million men on strike now in the meat packing industry, electrical workers, etc., one sees how appalling the problem is ahead. If industrial relations could be made those that grew out of co-operative organizations the whole situation might be changed. I am afraid, however, that Labour as a party has become too conscious of its power . . . to determine its own monopoly of control to make this possible.

"Eisenhower's visit to me was a real inspiration. I saw in him the marks of true greatness, in his sense of values, in human relationship. He is not an egotist nor an exhibitionist but a genuine man. True lover of his fellow-men."

Before leaving for the United Kingdom on leave, Malcolm MacDonald lunched at Laurier House on January 11. Mackenzie King told him that he had suggested his name for the position of Secretary General of the United Nations. "It is doubtful, however, if other countries would agree to give him this appointment. It looks very much as though Pearson would be the one to be selected, especially if Eisenhower refuses to allow his name to be considered.

"Malcolm brought up the question of our continuing to have our troops remain in the occupation zone for another year. I had gone carefully over a long despatch which Attlee had sent me, pointing out that Britain would have to take on this obligation in large extent. I told Malcolm quite frankly that our obligation there was to furnish food and supplies to Britain and to the occupied territories and that he would have to tell his Government that in furnishing the United Kingdom not only with supplies on credit but giving them money with which to make purchases from other countries we were assuming an obligation which the United Kingdom Government itself was not; that we needed our men back to produce and that by remaining abroad, instead of helping us to meet the need of added supplies, they were making a demand on that. I had fully expected this appeal from Attlee, but told Malcolm that I would have to remain adamant in declining. I fought this thing all along in the Cabinet, and Abbott told me that the more he had gone into the matter of keeping our troops longer in Europe the more he was convinced this would be a very great mistake. In these matters we have been far too lax in protecting the interests of our own people and the burdens they were bearing in the way of taxation."

After Malcolm MacDonald left, Lester Pearson, who was visiting Ottawa, arrived at Laurier House for a talk. "Amongst other things," the Prime Minister wrote, "I can see that what was most on Pearson's mind was his possible appointment as Secretary General of the United Nations Organization. I felt quite sure from the way he spoke that he intended to accept the appointment, if offered, though he said there were some things he would want to know first. I told him that of course we would not wish to stand in his way if he were inclined to accept the appointment. I told him, however, that if I were similarly situated I would prefer freedom of the position of an Ambassador in a country in the position Canada was to that of an official of an international organization, as important as that was. I thought he would find a great difference in trying to serve many masters instead of one master.

"Pearson mentioned to me that he had very much in mind entering

Canadian public life; that, at most, he would take on the Secretary Generalship for five years. I told him I was delighted to hear that he had public life in mind. The best preparation for that would have been in my office in the last few years and to have run in the last general election. However, he might have a chance in the future, as he is still young, and that I would be glad to see him in Parliament. My own feeling, however, is that should he be appointed to the Secretaryship of the United Nations his chances of ever getting into public life would lessen materially. It would be much greater if he remained in the Canadian service as an Ambassador. He would have a fine opportunity in Canada, but may overreach himself in the step now being contemplated should it come his way. That is my feeling and judgment."

The most important domestic problem the government faced in 1946 was devising new fiscal arrangements acceptable to the provincial governments. Mackenzie King, though his distaste for the subject was profound, found himself more and more drawn into the details of the negotiations. Under his chairmanship, the Co-ordinating Committee established by the Dominion-Provincial Conference of August 1945 had met in Ottawa from November 26 to November 30, 1945, to continue discussion of the "Green Book" proposals made by the federal government [see vol. 2, pp. 448-9] and met again on January 28, 1946. The federal government had proposed that it alone should levy personal and corporate income taxes and collect all succession duties in return for unconditional annual subsidies to the provinces which would not fall below a guaranteed minimum and which would rise with increases in per capita gross national product. The federal government also offered to assume nearly all responsibility for unemployment relief, introduce a wholly federal old-age pension scheme, and give to the provinces a package of matching grants covering transportation, public works, natural resources, development, vocational education, health services, and aid to the indigent, aged and physically handicapped. These proposals were developed and clarified in meetings of the Economic Committee, consisting of technical representatives of the different governments, during December 1945 and early January 1946. W. C. Clark, W. A. Mackintosh and Alex Skelton were the principal federal spokesmen in these meetings.

After some years of relatively high revenues and restrictions on expenditures imposed by war-time conditions, the provincial governments could afford a much more independent posture and, with the exception of Manitoba, all the provinces greeted the federal proposals with varying degrees of coolness. Maurice Duplessis, the Premier of Quebec, adopted the most uncompromising stance during the negotiations, with Premier Drew of Ontario only slightly less unenthusiastic.

In preparation for the second meeting of the Co-ordinating Committee, the federal Cabinet reviewed the progress of the negotiations on January 23. Mackenzie King reported that "the committee of experts, Clark, Mackintosh, Skelton, etc., have found it necessary to make an increase in the amount the Dominion should be prepared to pay – if agreement is to be reached with the provinces to increase from 12 to 15 millions the amounts to be given the provinces in lieu of their surrendering some sources of taxation. This was a compromise as between demand for 18 millions. I voiced again my feeling of concern at the method of federal proposed finances which made one Government the taxing power and the other Governments the spending power. From the Federal Government's point of view this is a double concern as taxing business is the unpopular end. From the point of view of economic and public finance I do not see how the system can be defended.

"Ilsley spoke of a skilful defence made by Garson of Manitoba. He admitted that he himself found it difficult to be convinced. This illustrates Ilsley's attitude. He does not decide these matters on his own judgment. Almost invariably he takes the advice given by officials, then holds tenaciously to it at all costs. The experts seem to think, and this includes Claxton, that Drew will have to yield his point of view to pressure from the Provinces. I am pretty sure Drew will follow Duplessis in opposing the other Provinces. It will mean the whole business will fall through, if he does. Drew's statement, that we must succeed at all cost, may be the reason which in the end he might assign for changing his attitude and joining in with the others.

"The argument that our taxes may still be lowered, notwithstanding these increases in contributions to the Provinces, is that by this method production can be kept at a high level. That will permit of increased volume of taxation. If production gets on a low level, taxes will have to be higher or the Dominion or the Provinces will come into a state of bankruptcy. The whole business is terribly involved. My own feeling is that, sooner than later, and perhaps sooner than expected, there will be a complete collapse and depression, as a result of the war financing and the liabilities it has left. Much in the way of total cessation of work by strikes on large scale would soon bring all of this about. There will then be a financial crisis, something like what overcame the United States after the civil war with repudiation, etc.

"I strongly opposed going on with the construction of another highway to Alaska in B.C., simply because requested by one of their Senators. I am amazed at how difficult it is to get our people to think of 'Canada First.' The British have come back again with a request for retaining our troops longer in occupation zone, the claim being that they have so much to do in distant countries, etc. In these things they have an interest which we have not at all. Our whole plan of finance rests on getting sufficient in the way of production in Canada. To have this we must have our Canadians at home."

With the meeting imminent, the Prime Minister was relieved when St. Laurent returned from the United Nations General Assembly meeting in London. They had a brief talk on January 28 during which St. Laurent told Mackenzie King "of his talk with Attlee, who spent some time explaining Britain's many obligations, urging our men should stay longer in occupation zones. He said he had to speak out and pointed out our conception of the Empire was not based on an undertaking of responsibility for all parts of the Commonwealth. We had our own contribution as a nation to make. It is clear the present government [in the United Kingdom] is even worse than the last on recognition of Canada's part as a nation."

That afternoon the Co-ordinating Committee met in camera in Room 16 of the House of Commons. All the provincial premiers were in attendance and Mackenzie King "opened the Conference in an informal way at the outset and then read the statement which had been prepared. Some exception was taken to one or two statements in it and strong exception to the request it contained to allow the statement to be made public at any time in the proceedings. I had no sooner finished the reading than I felt these criticisms were quite right and I immediately said that I would not have any statement given out without the consent of the gathering. To my mind it would have been better if no statement had been typed at all, and I had just spoken in a simple, introductory sort of way. This is the difference between dealing with a matter of this kind where one is experienced in public affairs, and following the official lead which is put forth in trying to prove a case, etc. I let the proceedings evolve gradually and before we adjourned at 8.30 [P.M.] felt a real headway had been made in getting our revised proposals put in the proper light before the Committee, and also making clear that Drew's proposals were ones that had a different line of approach – and if persisted in would mean that Ontario would not yield up certain sources of revenue, corporation, income tax and succession duties – would probably mean that the Conference would fail altogether. I sought to let the Premiers and Ministers do the discussing and to say as little as possible."

The premiers came to dinner at Laurier House that evening. "I do not think ever before in Canadian history have the Premiers of all the Provinces and the Dominion Prime Minister sat down and had a meal in any private home," Mackenzie King wrote. "Drew was most observant of the house, and I found Duplessis rather remarkably pleasant to talk with. Since he has given up drinking he is an entirely different man. Sort of shrewd, cunning person. Is on the surface all the time, but one can see how he could get a certain following."

Next morning (January 29) there was a meeting of the federal Ministers attending the meeting, Ilsley, St. Laurent and Howe, to decide on the day's procedure. Mackenzie King noted that "At the close of last night's meeting the question was whether we would present our own programme, as revised first and have it discussed, the provinces finding out exactly where they would be, or, whether, as our Cabinet seemed to have wished, we would get Drew's proposal taken up first with a view to exposing the shortcoming, and having the Conference end at once if he were unwilling to yield up the three sources of revenue. I decided myself the thing to do was to have our own proposals put forward. Ilsley and St. Laurent agreed with me. Howe was opposed, but I am sure we took the right course. When the Conference opened, I said I had been thinking over the matter. It was like having to render a Solomon's judgment as to which thing was to be dealt with first. I thought, as we had put our proposals first we should take our infant into our arms and go ahead with our programme first. This clearly was the right course to pursue. The discussion took all forenoon on our proposals. I could see as I thought would be the case that one after the other of the Provinces seemed more drawn to our side than ever, as well they might be from the liberality of the proposals. Even Drew, it was apparent, was not anxious to go on with his.

"In the afternoon I suggested we might take up Drew's proposals, but he said there were still some questions to be answered as to the remaining proposals so I let the thing go on these lines and the entire day was taken up in discussing how far we were prepared to go. My own feeling is that Drew is quite prepared to let us have personal and corporation sources of revenue. He may hold back on succession duties, which I think we could afford to let the Provinces collect. Also I think they are right in seeking to get an undertaking which would not invade the direct tax field one way or another beyond what we have already gone and I should think we might well afford to have certain definite taxes exclusively, deducting of course from the subsidies to be given them what we grant in that way. This matter has to be decided in the morning."

In the Prime Minister's judgment, "the spirit of the Conference was very good during the day and I am decidedly hopeful that we will reach an agreement. Indeed, Drew repeated today that the Conference must succeed, and also he was open-minded about his own proposals and our proposals. He is clearly retiring from the position he took at the start."

The following morning the federal Ministers and the Prime Minister met again to discuss strategy. "It was a line shaped out pretty much by Clark, after conference with Towers [the Governor of the Bank of Canada]. I personally felt they were going rather too far in the way of sticking all but irrevocably to the position we had taken. Fortunately, when asked if the attitude was irrevocable, with regard to succession duties, Ilsley said: Nothing is irrevocable.

"We conferred for three-quarters of an hour, then shortly after 10.30 Ilsley presented the views which we had agreed to to the Conference. The rest of the morning and all the afternoon was taken up in discussing them. I was agreeably surprised on finding no sudden outspoken opposition, but rather a continuous questioning of the implications. I rather felt that the Provinces were prepared to let us have personal and corporation income taxes and even the succession duties. Drew, for the first time, added mention of them to the income taxes, but insisted very strongly on the Provinces being given the very definite field of taxation reserved for themselves – to give them elbow room to meet situations which might have to be faced. This particularly true re taxes on gasoline, electricity – the point being that this was the kind of thing with which the Provinces were in immediate contact from day to day."

Drew also argued for a "definite statement, and made out the case against the Dominion as not having made good on some undertakings they had previously been given. I felt very strongly that so long as the Federal Government declared its intention in case of national emergency, to use whatever tax field was necessary, it was doing all that was needed to protect itself, in the light of making a declaration that it would not go further than it had up to the present. I felt so strongly about the justice of the situation and the political wisdom of the course to be pursued that after the meeting I had St. Laurent come to the office and gave him my impressions. I found he felt the same as I did. I later had Claxton come in and gave him my impressions and found that he also was in agreement with myself. Both Claxton and St. Laurent said that Ilsley felt as we did but was fearful because of Clark and Towers feeling they could not map out the budget unless we had absolute control of the whole field of taxation. I had Claxton work tonight on preparing something along the lines that he, St. Laurent and I had talked together. I feel that if we take this line we can get a settlement tomorrow, which will cover the matter for the next three years. Drew has been steadily retreating from his position and I think should be allowed to get out of it gracefully, so long as we get ourselves what we are after."

At the federal Ministers' strategy meeting the next morning (January

31), both Clark and Skelton were present. "I expressed the view," Mackenzie King wrote, "I thought there were certain positions we were taking which we could not defend. The first was in not being prepared to state definitely we did not intend to go further. Not mere intention, but to say definitely there were certain sources of taxation we would not take up in the next three years; also that we would not go further in some directions with others, reserving, however, in the event of some national emergency, the Dominion's right to take whatever action it thought best, informing the Provinces of the same in advance.

"I found that last night officials were going over the matter with Claxton and Ilsley. Following my talk with Claxton, they had agreed to this. That removed one problem. I later said I thought there was much in the argument that they needed extra elbow room and that they might be certain of the Provincial sources that we might let them have exclusively, which we now have, provided of course that the source of revenue was made up by a lowering of the subsidies. McCann, who was present, came out strongly for Provinces to have exclusive field of gasoline and electricity. Those were the fields I had intended to suggest. There was objection to this by Dr. Clark. I could see that Clark is in very poor shape, he is highly strung. He realizes the terrible extent of obligations which the Dominion has undertaken to assume and realizes that it is going to be almost impossible to meet these obligations. . . . It just excites him tremendously. I felt we had to be very careful with him. He is liable to break down completely at any moment. Ilsley is not far from the same position. For these reasons I did not press particularly the points raised as another statement had been drafted. However, when the Committee assembled, I stated I thought the time thus far had been taken up in pressing on Dominion proposals. I thought now we should decide at once whether agreement could be reached within the framework of Dominion proposals. If not consider whatever alternative proposals might be presented. The discussion followed on these lines, Drew still taking the position that he had not got full information as to the Dominion's proposals, but indicating he was prepared to work out something within the framework of the Federal proposals and inferring he would not press his own.

"Duplessis came out strongly against allowing the Dominion to have the succession duties and before the morning meeting was over, Drew took a similar stand. Macdonald made a series of suggestions of which at least four out of five could be accepted at once – the fifth, about giving the Provinces lesser sources of revenue, could not, but they would accept one or two and let the rest go. Macdonald was for an acceptance of the Dominion proposals as framework, including personal and corporation income tax and succession duties. Garson made clear he was prepared to work within the Dominion framework. Manning did the same. McNair too, talking a good deal about further proposals for financial need [but] that he would be equally prepared to [accept the federal proposals as the basis of negotiations]. Douglas I should think ditto. John Hart would be met by Angus Macdonald's suggestion on which different Provinces should receive their subsidies."

In the afternoon discussion returned to the question of succession duties and, to Mackenzie King, it was "quite apparent neither Ontario nor Quebec will give up this field. Personally I do not blame them. I find myself very strongly of the position that Ontario and Nova Scotia are taking, namely, that Provinces should be left with certain definite fields of taxation, the Dominion ditto, and subsidies reduced to as small a margin as possible. The Finance Department, behind which is the Bank of Canada, have completely changed the generally accepted procedure which has been to keep as largely as possible the spending authority responsible for the tax-raising. I think their effort is in the direction of centralization of financial control. That may be desirable from the point of view of more effective administration, etc., from Ottawa's end, but politically it will not be possible I believe for a long time to come. Much better to get services under Dominion control but not to seek to keep under Provincial control with subsidies."

At the morning meeting of federal Ministers on February 1, the Prime Minister "spoke about what I thought was a mistake of the Dominion stating it did not intend to use certain taxes, but that they would, if they thought it necessary, call the Provinces in, tell them so and then go ahead and take the course they intended. As Drew said, this means absolutely nothing. I contended that they should simply make it clear they would not go into certain fields. If a national emergency arose the Federal Government would take any course the emergency commanded under its general powers. Why the Finance Department could not agree to that I could not understand. Also I asked for a clear definition of the meaning of gross national production. They keep referring to some letter written with a definition in it which only aggravates everybody. I got this statement finally today in a form which was generally accepted by the Conference. Personally I sympathize strongly with the Provinces for wishing to retain succession duties. I could see that it may not be at all possible for the Dominion to balance its budget if it [gives up] this field. Having both authorities enter the same field is I think a great mistake, if it can be avoided. I would like to see the Provinces yield up the succession duties and the Dominion yield up the minor sources of taxation now that the

Dominion is assured of personal and corporation income taxes. At the morning Conference the question came up of admitting advisers. I was pleased on the whole to get Clark and Mackintosh in that they might hear for themselves what was the Dominion-Provincial point of view.

"Drew spoke at great length and I think exceedingly well on the Provincial point of view. Duplessis was vague and general and smart, etc. He, however, stated definitely that the succession duties, so far as Quebec was concerned, would not be yielded up. I think the reason is that these two large provinces are afraid if a socialist government came in that that would make it impossible for the people to leave much for their children. . . ."

After lunch the Co-ordinating Committee reconvened to discuss the date of the next meeting. "Discussion came up at once about question of holding over until next week or having an adjournment for some months. Drew suggested April 25. That was the Thursday following Easter vacation. It seemed to me that was on the whole a good date. We would have the days previous for a vacation to prepare; also House could be brought together following Monday, so that we would have part of the time at least without Parliament sitting while having next meeting. I allowed the debate to flow back and forth. I myself felt we would be wiser not to try to reach a final agreement at present and this largely because I feel our own people have not worked out as carefully as they should the implications of their own suggestions. I find also in Claxton and some of the others a strong political feeling against Drew and Duplessis that they do not themselves see the larger political aspects of what has to be considered. I had a very difficult decision to make at the close. Clark, Skelton and Towers who are advising Ilsley all wanted the Dominion so-called offers to be made public at once. Drew was strongly against this, so was Macdonald and, of course, Duplessis. I felt that all our proceedings were in camera and were not concluded, and that it would be wrong to have this statement given out and discussions in Legislatures take place upon it. Also in the Federal Parliament.

"Drew had stated his position pretty clearly but I made the additional point that we were a co-ordinating committee and were not the Conference reporting proceedings in the open, and until the Conference met, I thought all negotiations should be regarded as confidential and no statement given out other than that proceedings were going satisfactorily. I felt and said quite openly that I thought all the federal ministers and secretarial staff had a different view than myself and would like to publish the statement immediately but I could not agree that that was the right thing to do. That I thought in Legislature and in our Parliament we should take the view that negotiations were proceeding and that nothing had been finalized. We did not want resolutions passed which would bring back some of the Premiers with their hands tied. I had in the back of my mind too that when we meet in April, most, if not all the Legislatures will be through with their sessions which will give to the Premiers a much freer hand in accepting Dominion positions than otherwise they would have. Also that we would avoid having a discussion in our own Parliament which would lead to opposing points of view. I felt that Ilsley and Howe were very tired, so tired as to be willing to drop everything rather than discuss further. Skelton, I do not think, has the experience or the judgment or the ability to really guide matters of the kind. Clark has embarked on a financial policy [such] that we have almost gone too far, I think, in the way of permitting expenditures to ever hope to recover the ground needed to balance budgets. . . . The collapse will not come in the next couple of years unless something unforeseen takes place but that it will come in the 50's, if not a year or two before, I feel pretty sure. When it does come, there will be an appallingly difficult situation to meet, one which conceivably might bring on another world war. By that time, I think, Communism will have permeated the different countries of the globe. It has a subterranean foothold already that few realize. I think had we gone on with the conference, the chances are no agreement would have been reached and the Dominion would have decided to abandon the effort to make any agreement for three years. I believe I saved that situation by keeping things in such shape that there was no finality. No doors were closed, and I now really think that when we do meet in April, we shall work out some agreement which will give to the Dominion the personal and corporation income taxes which is a great field of taxation though by no means a popular one. We will get a situation that will hold for the next three years during which time there can be continuous conferences at the technical end and also occasionally at the ministerial level which will help to prepare the way for what may be needed from the 50's on. While I am wholly sympathetic with doing everything to promote health and welfare matters, I do feel that this will have to come very gradually and that people in Canada are in a more fortunate position in dealing with these questions than are the peoples of any other country.

"Altogether the temper of the Conference had been remarkably good throughout. It was really remarkable that we had carried on almost for one week with very little of recrimination. Drew has kept himself in good check and I must confess has impressed me with his ability as a leader and clear thinker. If he could only hold his tongue in check when he gets on to the platform! It was after 6 when we broke up."

With few firm decisions made except agreement to meet again on April 25, Mackenzie King felt quite satisfied with the results of the meeting and put the subject of dominion-provincial financial relations well to the back of his mind.

During the early months of 1946 the Prime Minister became increasingly concerned about finding time to write his memoirs and organize his private papers. Hugh Keenleyside, who was then the Canadian Ambassador in Mexico, came to Laurier House on January 25 and the subject came up in conversation. Mackenzie King found Keenleyside "extremely pleasant and very thoughtful in his way of expressing himself. . . . I was interested in hearing him say that if I wanted assistance in working up my own memoirs he felt that the material would be of such value to Canada generally that he would be prepared to give up his representation of Canada abroad and devote his time, should he be so assigned by External Affairs, to assisting me in the sorting of the material. He would be interested in doing this as an historian by profession, and one deeply concerned in Canada's future. I told him I had been most anxious to get some young man or some woman, with that aim, who would come in at once and help."

On February 1, the day the Co-ordinating Committee adjourned, Admiral Leahy visited Ottawa and Mackenzie King had him to lunch alone. "In the course of the conversation, I spoke to him about the atomic bomb," the Prime Minister wrote. "He was quite outspoken in saying that he did not think it ever should have been used as the United States had used it, against defenceless women and children which was the case in the two cities that were bombed. He also stated the destruction was due more to intense heat than to explosion. He told me how examination had revealed curious evidences of this. Believed that only the U.K., the U.S. and Canada should for the present know the effect of the use of the atomic bomb, at sea, against ships, etc. He felt that the whole system of warfare might have to be changed.

"We talked a little of the Corby case. He felt that we ought to go on with our enquiry if it involved our own civil servants. He also agreed that it might have far-reaching repercussions. I asked him his feelings about the U.S.S.R. He said some people thought that war with the U.S.S.R. was inevitable. He did not accept that feeling. Others thought that war with U.S.S.R. was a real possibility and we must do all we can to prevent it. This was his view. He also felt that another world war would be between Russia and other parts, particularly the U.S. and the U.K., but that Canada would in all probability be the battlefield. This is what I myself believe as he said: Germany can do nothing and Japan can do nothing. The only power capable of another world war is Russia. I expressed the view that Russia would come to have great internal problems of her own that might prevent a world war. He agreed as to that."

Three days later some sketchy details of the Gouzenko case finally became public knowledge. During the afternoon of February 4, Robertson telephoned to inform the Prime Minister that, the previous evening, an American broadcaster, Drew Pearson, "had stated I had gone to Washington some time ago to tell President Truman about a situation in Canada which disclosed Russian intrigue, etc., and had spent the night at the White House. The report went on to speak of the Russians making plans of rivers, etc., round about Calgary. . . . Also the facts about the Russian business as disclosed to Truman, before I left for England. As Robertson said this business has become known to too many people – the President's office, the Secretary of State's office, the F.B.I., etc. However, this may be all for the best, as it gives us a special reason for starting immediately with our investigation."

Robertson added that he had met during the morning with senior officers of the R.C.M.P., the British High Commissioner, and E. K. Williams, the President of the Canadian Bar Association, who had, of course, known about the details of the case for some time. Mackenzie King "suggested having the Commission appointed at once, to take evidence in secret wherever Corby may be. Then make the arrests necessary of our own people and defer to that moment my having a word with the Russian Ambassador." Even though Colonel Zabotin, the Soviet Military Attaché, and two of his principal associates had returned to Russia, the Prime Minister was convinced that "the business of espionage is still going on actively." A few days earlier, the new Military Attaché had been arrested in Toronto on a charge of drunkenness and, according to Mackenzie King, was "found to be carrying a loaded revolver" and "a receipt for money paid over to one of the persons whose name appears in the record." He was sure that the Soviet government was "pretty well aware that we have knowledge of some of the things which have been going on which could not stand the light of day. What may grow out of the enquiry we shall have in Canada, I cannot say, but there can be little doubt that a very heavy responsibility is now on our shoulders, and that it will grow into one of the major sensations of the day."

On February 5 the Prime Minister reviewed the whole situation with Robertson who told him that "suspicions are directed right up to the top of the treasury [in the United States], naming the person; also that it is directed against another person who was very close to Stettinius at San Francisco and who took a prominent part in matters there. I said in regard to the latter I was not personally surprised. I confess I was surprised when I saw the particular person he mentioned filling the position he did. . . . The lady Corby [named] had for two years been employed as liaison between the Soviet headquarters in New York and officials in different government departments, from whom she was securing documents. These documents were taken to New York, copied there and then returned to departmental files, so that there was nothing to show they had been abstracted. The evidence went to show that the Russians knew everything about the invasion of Europe before it took place. Material apparently had come from the service departments. There was also evidence of expenditure of much money."

Mackenzie King also read the actual text of Drew Pearson's statement and felt that it had "in some way been inspired. I may be wrong but I have a feeling that there is a desire at Washington that this information should get out; that Canada should start the enquiry and that we should have the responsibility for beginning it and that the way should be paved for it being continued into the U.S. This may be all wrong, but I have that intuition very strongly. It is the way in which a certain kind of politics is played by a certain type of man."

At the Cabinet meeting that day, the Prime Minister finally told his colleagues most of the story. "I said little about the source of the discovery but mentioned that we had the documentary evidence. I read through the order-in-council appointing Judge R. Taschereau and Judge R. L. Kellock of the Supreme Court as Commissioners to take evidence. It was decided the taking of evidence would begin tomorrow. E. K. Williams, Counsel, is in the city and will assist the commissioners. Corby will be brought to the Justice Department or the Commissioners will go where he is located to get evidence. It is most important his evidence should be gotten at once in case anything should happen to him. It is all-important we should have his statements re documents, etc. When the report is concluded it will be published and we will then take into custody certain members of the service who will have to stand trial." Gerald Fauteux, a Montreal lawyer, and D. M. Mundell, of the Department of Justice, were also appointed to serve as counsel to the Commission.

Mackenzie King added that "in speaking to the Cabinet of this matter I said I had been deeply concerned in the responsibility I had in advising the Government to have Canada declare that a state of war existed between our country and Germany. I did not feel, however, as great a responsibility or as much concerned as I did over this matter. In the case of war, I was convinced there was only one course to take, which was the one we took. That it was either to take that course or risk the existence of the country; that in this matter I was far from sure what the consequences would be. They might help to set aflame a controversy of extensive and bitter proportions, throughout this country and the U.S., and also to further suspicion and unrest in other countries. That Canada would be a marked country, so far as Russia was concerned in the future. We were the most vulnerable of any country in our proximity to the U.S.S.R. That I had hoped, and had so said to the President and Bevin, that we might find a way of communicating the facts to the Russian government itself without disclosing them in court, giving the government a chance to clean up the situation itself. I pointed out, however, that on the other hand there was the need to clean up our own service, and that now that Drew Pearson's statement was out, there would be questioning and we would not be able to conceal the situation effectively. Howe asked whether it was Drew Pearson's disclosure that was responsible for the timing. I replied it was not. That the timing was based on the return of Mr. St. Laurent after his talks with both Bevin and Byrnes in London [during the meetings of the United Nations General Assembly]. St. Laurent then reported on these conversations and stated that both Bevin and Byrnes thought we ought to make an enquiry. It was of course our own business to decide, but it was their view that the matter should be gone on with now.

"I explained that we had waited to give the U.S. an opportunity to follow up the revelations that they had received. They had now told us it was better we should proceed without delay. They were of the view that the U.S.S.R. might not take the matter too seriously. That they might simply feel that spying was a practice all countries adopted and that they had done nothing more than what other countries might be doing. My own feeling is that this whole business goes much further than any one of us begins to realize."

The taking of evidence in the Gouzenko case began the morning of February 13, Mackenzie King noted in his diary for the day. "It will probably be continued through the week. Arrests will have to follow at the end of the week. I can see where a great cry will be raised, having had a Commission sit in secret, and men and women arrested and detained under an order in council passed really under War Measures powers [the order of October 6, 1945]. I will be held up to the world as the very opposite of a democrat. It is part of the inevitable."

On February 14 Robertson told the Prime Minister that "examination of Corby was proceeding morning, noon and night and will probably be concluded tonight, and tomorrow a number of civil servants will be taken into custody. A statement will have to be given out in the evening. We discussed the contents of it. R. wonders if it would not be better given out by the Minister of Justice. I told him no. That while I would personally prefer the Minister of Justice doing it, not to forget that the Catholic Church was a bitter enemy of the Soviets and this would add fuel to the flames. I better take full responsibility. I could of course mention legal actions being taken at the instance of the Minister. The Russian Ambassador is not yet back, nor have I yet replied to communication regarding Popov in Toronto which has come from the Embassy. A terrible document they have sent.... Typical Soviet method of doing things."

At the Cabinet meeting that afternoon, the Minister of Justice "informed Council of action about to be taken in detaining and interrogating members of the service. The Commission has been much impressed with Corby's evidence and with the whole situation. We discussed statement to be given out. Agreed that this should be done by myself tomorrow afternoon."

The next morning (February 15) the Prime Minister telephoned Robertson to check on the statement for the press which had been "carefully prepared in combination with St. Laurent and Williams. ... It came to me as a surprise, though I should have remembered it, that the civil servants involved had all been rounded up early this morning. I suggested yesterday that the young woman in the High Commissioner's office should be brought in among the number. It was arranged Malcolm MacDonald himself would write and say he understood she was suspected and request that she should be taken into custody for detention. The police had planned to make arrests at 3 this morning but fortunately this was caught in time and the different persons were rounded up at 7.00 o'clock. They were taken to police barracks at Rockcliffe where they are now being detained. Will be questioned forthwith by the Commission and, if evidence justifies it, will be then brought up for trial where it is clear they have been disclosing material to the Russian Embassy. There are about 14 altogether under arrest, the authority being the order in council passed last year under the War Measures Act and there may be some questioning as to this but this whole matter is so serious that I think there will be disposition by Parliament to agree that the right course in the circumstances has been taken as the evidence is so strong."

Among the group arrested that morning were Dr. Raymond Boyer, a scientist with the National Research Council who had worked on the development of explosives; two engineers employed by the NRC, S. W. Mazerall and Durnford Smith; J. S. Benning, an official in the Department of Munitions and Supply; Emma Woikin, a code clerk in the Department of External Affairs; and Captain Gordon Lunan, an army officer on loan to the Wartime Information Board. Miss Kathleen Willsher, the deputy registrar of the office of the United Kingdom High Commissioner, was also detained at Malcolm MacDonald's request.

To Mackenzie King, the case had now become "a situation of world significance. Although no mention specifically made of the U.S.S.R.

Embassy, the public will gather at once that that is the Embassy to whom disclosures have been made. When the report of the Commission itself is made public, it will of course create a stir in all parts of the world. A very great stir in Russia itself and also in U.S., Canada and England. I think on the whole all has worked out for the best in that this business has not become a matter of public knowledge before the conclusion of the first meeting of the Assembly and the Security Council of the U.N.O. It cannot be said that in any way the position of the U.S.S.R. was prejudiced through these disclosures being made at an earlier time. I told Robertson I thought we should try to have a reply to the U.S.S.R. written regarding the arrest of the Military Attaché, ready for me to give the Chargé d'Affaires this afternoon before giving him a copy of the statement to the press which I shall have to give him letting him know it has reference to the U.S.S.R. Most of the persons involved so far as the Embassy is concerned have melted away and the Ambassador himself has not yet come back from Russia though it was said by the Embassy that we were asked to arrange for his getting transportation some ten or twelve days ago. It is beginning to look as though his remaining away was intentional. The U.S.S.R. themselves may break off relations with Canada. This remains, of course, to be seen. We are, I think, proceeding in the right way in dealing only for the present with our own civil servants.

"Primrose of the Montreal Research Laboratories will be apprehended in London today and questioned. There seems to be a difference of view as to what can be done concerning him, should he refuse to make any statements that might implicate himself."

At his office that afternoon, the Prime Minister met with the Leader of the Opposition, John Bracken. "I tried to get Coldwell, but he is out of the City. I also tried to reach B. K. Sandwell, of *Saturday Night*, to give him an inside story so as not to have the Civil Liberties body begin to criticize without knowing of the retention of civil servants. He was in Regina. Robertson was in my room when I talked with Bracken. I reminded him of my having told him in a general way, when I left for Washington and England, that there was a situation that was so serious I could not tell him of it but would later. I wanted him to remember my having spoken of it and had given him to understand it related to the Soviet Embassy. He recalled I had spoken in general terms but not specifically. I then told him about the Corby episode, of my speaking to the President and Bevin, and gave him information about appointment of Commission. Told him of the detention of members of the service. Also told him of the secret session of the House [at the time of the reinforcement crisis;

see vol. 2, chapter VI] which had been reported and which linked up with one of the Members [Fred Rose, Labour-Progressive M.P. for Montreal Cartier]. Gave him a general idea of what was at stake. I told him of Primrose and let him know the reason we had not acted sooner was because of the Americans not wishing us to act until they had a chance to explore their own situation. I said we had reason to believe there was a very serious situation there as well as here.

"Bracken said he thought it was all to the good that this whole business be exposed. He made no adverse criticism of anything. I told him about orders in council passed while I was in England. Of St. Laurent acting under one of them at this time. We had a talk of three quarters of an hour."

A few minutes after 4.00 P.M. the Prime Minister met the Chargé d'Affaires of the Russian Embassy, Mr. Belokhvostikov, and the Second Secretary, Mr. Pavlov, at his office. Robertson was present for the interview. "I gave to the Chargé d'Affaires a copy of the statement which I was issuing to the press at 5.00 P.M. The two members of the Embassy sat on opposite sides of my table. Robertson was seated on the sofa near the window. My first words were to ask the Chargé d'Affaires if he had had any word of the Ambassador as to when he was to arrive. He replied that about a week or ten days ago they had received word from London that he was coming, but that nothing had come since. He could not say when he would arrive. I said I had hoped to be able to see him and speak to him direct about the matter I was going to speak of. Would he please let the Ambassador know this as soon as he came, that I was anxious to see him.

"I then said to them that I wanted to speak of a very important matter on which I was issuing a statement to the press later in the day and which I would like to read to them. I then began reading the press statement, in which mention was made of a foreign mission in Ottawa. I said to them I had purposely refrained from making any statement as to the mission referred to but I thought they should know it was the U.S.S.R. Embassy. I then continued the reading of the statement.... I observed that he would notice that we were dealing only with members of our own civil service. I said that the statement would not go beyond reference to our own people except in the particular I had mentioned, which was to a foreign mission. (Pavlov [who was the representative of the N.K.V.D. in the Embassy] figures pretty largely in the evidence of Corby as the one who has a good deal to say – is ready to argue, etc.)

"The Chargé d'Affaires looked the statement over. He had a word with Pavlov, talking to him in Russian. The Russian Chargé d'Affaires then said that this was a surprise to him, that it was not a matter of which he knew anything. As it of course concerned his government he would report the matter at once to them.

"When I began to read the statement, I noticed the young Chargé d'Affaires coloured up quite perceptibly. His countenance became very pink. There was no other evidence of particular emotion and his face gradually assumed its natural colour. The other man, Pavlov, however, sat throughout with his hands clenched tight and with a sort of dour, determined, indifferent appearance. I noticed that he kept pressing his thumbs on his fingers as I was reading. He had a way of throwing back his head and looking more or less into the open.

"When I had finished this statement, I spoke of the incident in Toronto where a member of the Embassy, Popov, was arrested. I said that Mr. Robertson had a reply to the communication which we had received.

"Robertson asked me if he would read it which he did. Again Pavlov spoke to the Chargé d'Affaires in Russian. We could not, of course, make out what was said but the Chargé d'Affaires immediately stated that he would see that the government was immediately informed of what was stated in the papers. I had urged on Robertson to get this Toronto incident cleaned up at this time, not to have a further communication coming later. He had to press the matter along during the day. I had no chance to more than read it over before the two young men came into the office. My own feeling was it went a little far in expressing an apology to the Russians for the detention of a member of the staff by the police. It was right in admitting that what had been done was not in accord with procedure and the immunity given members of foreign missions, but knowing all we know I felt that apology was too strong a word to use. However, Robertson seemed to think it would be better to err on that side and leave no ground for complaint that we were not observing amenities, etc. . . . Gouzenko's statement and other evidence were so convincing themselves that we could afford to go that far.

"The young men were about to rise when I stopped them for a moment to say how sorry Robertson and I were that it was necessary to speak of these matters at all; that we were all close friends, and that nothing should destroy that relationship. I wanted to repeat again what I said about the care we had taken not to deal with other than members of our own public service. Disclosed nothing further than what was essential to indicate the seriousness of the offence which justified the action we had found it necessary to take against them. Robertson and I then shook hands with both of them.

"The Chargé d'Affaires I know quite well and have always joked a little with him about his marriage to Olga, who was an attractive secretary at the Embassy under Gousev. He had his happy smile in shaking hands. The other man was quite indifferent. When we closed the door, Robertson said to me 'Pavlov is the villain of the piece.' He did not think the Chargé d'Affaires knew much about the situation."

Robertson was concerned about informing Dana Wilgress, Canada's Ambassador in Moscow, of the situation as soon as possible. "Two or three times referred to the hope that our mission in Moscow would be safe and secure. Also he spoke of sending me a volume of the evidence to read over as soon as possible. He mentioned the judges might not sit Monday or Tuesday. I said it was most important that civil servants should not be detained any longer than necessary. It was a pity Sunday intervened; also that one hoped the judges would go on Monday or Tuesday. Otherwise we would be faced with a writ of habeas corpus and would give grounds for real attack on the administration for star chamber methods. He said he would speak to counsel about the matter. The need for delay is that the statements of those who have been taken in custody will have to be carefully scrutinized, and matters made in readiness for continued examination of the witnesses."

The statement issued by the Department of External Affairs in the Prime Minister's name, though cautious and guarded, created a major sensation in Canada and elsewhere. It read:

> Information of undoubted authenticity has reached the Canadian Government which establishes that there have been disclosures of secret and confidental information to unauthorized persons, including some members of the staff of a foreign mission in Ottawa. In order to make possible the full investigation which the seriousness of this information demands, the Government has appointed Mr. Justice Taschereau and Mr. Justice Kellock of the Supreme Court of Canada to act as Royal Commissioners to hear evidence and to present a report which will be made public. The Commissioners have appointed as their Counsel Mr. E. K. Williams, K.C., of Winnipeg, Mr. Gerald Fauteux, K.C., of Montreal, and Mr. D. W. Mundell of the Department of Justice; the Commission has already commenced its investigation, which is proceeding in camera.
>
> Upon the application of Counsel, and having regard to the serious nature of the evidence already adduced before the Commission, the Commissioners recommended Counsel to apply to the Minister of Justice for orders for the Interrogation and detention for that purpose of a number of persons known or suspected to be implicated. This action has been taken today. The persons involved include some now employed or who have been employed in a number of Departments and agencies of the Government.
>
> It is the intention of the Government that, after the report of the Royal Commissioners has been received, prosecution will be instituted in cases in which the evidence warrants it. It would not be proper at this stage to make

a more complete statement or, in particular, to make public the names of those concerned. Some of them appear to have been far more deeply and consciously involved than others. Some will probably be found to be more or less innocent instruments in furthering activities much more serious than they may have imagined. Obviously, the whole matter should be treated with caution and reserve, pending the time when it will be possible to issue a fuller statement. Until the investigation by the Royal Commissioners has been completed the case remains sub judice.

Although the statement did not explicitly mention the "foreign mission" involved, the press needed no great wit to make a connection between the Canadian government's actions and Drew Pearson's earlier disclosures about Soviet espionage activity. Mackenzie King was very upset by a Pearson article which appeared in the *Montreal Gazette* on February 16. To him, the article "made perfectly clear . . . that I was right in believing that his previous article had been inspired by the State Department. It had all been done to cause U.S.S.R. feeling to be diverted from State Department and to have it appear, first, that Canada and not the U.S. had taken initiative in this matter and, secondly, that the Justice Department of the U.S. was more responsible than the State Department. Third, that there was the desire to get information, where there had been much delay, to have it appear that this had been due to indecision of Canadian officials, as between Justice and External Affairs, when, as we knew, the whole effort of the State Department and the policy had been to get things under way quickly. We have held back at the request of the U.S. to let them get further information. All this side of things which Robertson and others seemed to think I was unduly suspicious of are proving to be absolutely correct. When I went to talk with Heeney he spoke of not liking the Gazette article because it did not feature the Prime Minister of Canada's statement but gave prominence to Drew Pearson's statement. I told him at once, which is very true, that I doubted if he and others realized the significance of this whole business; that what the Gazette was interested in was the fight of Capitalism vs. Communism. From their point of view they were doing the right thing in featuring that aspect as it was featured in Drew Pearson's article. My statement was naturally restrained and as far as circumstances would permit colourless. I said to Heeney, which I believe to be true, that the real significance of the disclosures that we had made is that we have now entered upon phase 3 of the battle, which has been waged over the quarter of a century – the effort toward world conquest by other powers. Germany and Japan have had their try. Britain has been mistress of the seas, controlled the world herself, in the eyes of the U.S. Germany and Japan have tried to share world conquest, before the U.S. became powerful enough to play Britain's role in the world. Now the conflict is whether the

U.S. or Russia shall control the world. What has now been disclosed must inevitably lead either to world war No. 3, in which Russia will seek to destroy the States, and of course Canada, and of which Canada will become the battlefield, or whether by these disclosures the Russian people themselves may come to have their eyes opened and decide they will not be made victims of the new military power that has gained control there and which elections of a few days ago make clear that Stalin has all but absolute authority. I cannot interpret these events and how all of this has come direct to my own doorstep in any way other than in the play of world forces and unseen forces beyond that I have been somehow singled out as an instrument on the part of unseen forces to bring about the exposure that has now taken place. There has never been anything in the world's history more complete than what we will reveal of the Russian method to control the continent as a result of Corby fleeing to the Department of Justice and the course then taken, which has been taken under direction of my office. As Prime Minister I have had to take the responsibility. The world now knows that I went to see the President and that I also went to see Bevin. They do not know that I have had to hold this whole business for five months. It has now broken into the light of day. The forces it will arouse are more terrific than any of us begin to comprehend.

"I am a great believer in the power of truth and, having the truth, I feel certain that we shall win, and that now we may find the real path of peace which will be letting the masses of the people know how they are controlled by the few and bringing about a real brotherhood among the common people of the earth. To help toward that end is unquestionably my mission and the thing for which I was born. It is my grandfather's life effort only on the arena of the world instead of the small arena to which in his day his efforts were necessarily confined."

First thing next morning (February 17) Mackenzie King read parts of Gouzenko's testimony before the Commissioners and, to him, it was "an astounding revelation. It will be a terrible shock to the free nations of the world. I think even more to Russia for it discloses their whole method of espionage in a more convincing manner than it has ever been exposed.

"On listening to the radio, I heard that demands are being made by American Senators for following up what has been announced in Canada to see what has been going on in the States. There seems to be little doubt that the U.S. will find it impossible not to have a pretty telling investigation there, whether they like it or not. Once they get at it in Congress or the Courts it is certain to be pretty thorough. I think we struck the psychological moment in beginning our inquiry just before the proceedings of assembly of the U.N.O. were concluded and my statement came out immediately after. We might have been accused of breaking up co-operation with Russia had this revelation come sooner. It really is a terrifying business in what it reveals of a diabolical planned effort to produce a fifth column within a friendly country and to have all plans laid in readiness for another war. Russia is not in a position to begin anything at once. This revelation has come in time to permit of other forces exerting themselves to preserve peace. Russia has begun by being most disagreeable and assertive since the war ended. She will be on the defensive from now on."

Later in the day he "was interested in hearing over the radio the expression used that others should have the initiative and courage Canada has shown. It can be honestly said that few more courageous acts have ever been performed by leaders of the government than my own in the Russian intrigue against the Christian world and the manner in which I have fearlessly taken up and have begun to expose the whole of it. I see the full significance. I am certain that America now cannot hold back, but I myself know of what has taken place there. Britain cannot hold back what is known to the British Government with respect to Primrose, which links him up to what pertains to disclosures regarding the atomic bomb. What has been unearthed in Canada will lead each country to begin to examine its conditions in the light of this evidence. We are only at the beginning of the real disclosures. . . . There will be certain major sensations. Of course there is the evidence of how completely the Embassy in Ottawa is headquarters of a spying regime. I have come to the conclusion that a break between Russia's and Canada's diplomatic relations is wholly inevitable. It will probably be made by the Russian government itself as a means of saving further disclosures and trying to turn the tables on us."

On February 18 the Prime Minister observed that had Gouzenko defected "a month or two sooner it would have been too early. What we got in the last few weeks of cables to and from headquarters at Moscow brings in the U.S., Britain, as well as disclosing how far espionage had gone in Canada and how substantial were the beginnings of the fifth column organization here. When the evidence is published, and that must be as soon as possible, it will fairly tear the roof off the American nation. It will rouse public opinion as nothing has done since the beginning of the war. The great danger is of course that Russia may sever her relationship not only with Canada but with one or two other countries, and then try to develop great power internally. Drew Pearson is right in saying that the only way in which the situation can be saved is by believing in the people themselves, having contact made with them and exposing in their eyes the militarist regime which is using them as tools for world conquest as Hitler and Mussolini used the peoples of their countries. Robertson said Primrose had been picked up in London on Friday but had denied any part in these doings. There can be no escape for him when the evidence is produced. What has come to light will bring to light much that at present is unseen and unknown."

In the newspapers on February 19 Mackenzie King "was particularly struck . . . to see the defence that ex-Ambassador Davies gives Russia. He claims they have a perfect right to try and get all the information they can about the atomic bomb, that it is recognized that Missions of the kind do this sort of thing. I can see that pro-Russians are going to take the line that this business is largely the result of not sharing atomic bomb secret. It is important, therefore, that it should be brought out clearly in the report that this espionage business started on a big scale two years before the end of the war before anything was known of the bomb. . . .

"I was interested to see a despatch based on information from the Russian Embassy in Washington, disclosing that there were two phases of their representation work: (1) relating to political policies; (2) the other on a different level, relating to military secrets. It is that part of things which will be brought out so clearly in our report. That of itself will be a revelation to the world. It was only yesterday that the Russians broadcast my statement. They made no comment. What I now am perfectly sure of is that when Zaroubin left Ottawa with another member of the Embassy he knew we had the material we had, or at all events, had got the inside of things that were going on. The subsequent departure of Zabotin also was to enable him to get away and the fact that Zaroubin himself has not yet returned is due, I think, in part, to afford an excuse for not having a reception on Red Army Day, and it may well be that he may not return at all. Somehow I believe he will, but not until after Red Army Day. At any rate, I think the Russians have been fully aware that Corby had made some disclosures. Robertson tells me that of those who have been taken up it does not appear that the Russians have put them at all wise of our knowing anything about their actions. I told Robertson today that the evidence will have to be published. He seemed to be surprised at that and not to like the thought of it. I think the time for publication is a factor. Nothing should be given away pending the prosecutions that will arise, but later we must see to it that the Government has been fully justified in every step it has taken."

Later in the day Mackenzie King discussed the Gouzenko affair with M. J. Coldwell, who had just returned to Ottawa. "He remembered distinctly I had told him before I went to England that there was a situation in the Russian Embassy, etc., I let him know I had been trying to see him and to show him a copy of my statement. I outlined a few aspects of the situation. In particular, I told him of the steps we had taken to have the parties examined taken into custody, etc. He said he thought that was all right. He had been in St. Louis when the papers came out. He had been asked whether this was a witch hunt. I told him he would find it was anything but that. I told him that the only ones examined up to the present were persons against whom we held documentary evidence."

On February 20, the Prime Minister, commenting on the evidence, wrote: "I was immensely pleased with what Corby said of his motives in taking the course he has. Also immensely impressed at what happened from the time he left the Embassy, until the time he came under the protection of the police. I cannot account for either on any score, other than unseen forces granting protection that was essential to preserve his life and to enable the documents which he brought forth to be disclosed. I believe the man to have been genuinely sincere. That it is a case of a man's soul and conscience being roused and that, through guidance and inspiration, he has taken a position which was that of a true world patriot. I have read nothing which seemed to me more dramatic in every way than what occurred in those 48 hours and what appears in his own statement of his readiness to let his life be taken so long as Canada was saved a third war, which he said would come out of what was being plotted by Russia. It interested me immensely to read that what had brought him to the decision to expose the whole Russian scheme was the effect our elections had upon him. He saw a real democracy at work in Canada – people freely choosing their own government. He contrasted it with the mock sham of Russia where people are allowed to vote for only one candidate. He brings out what a complete tyranny there is there.

"I am somewhat amazed at some of the statements coming from the U.S., Byrnes in particular, which would seem to indicate that they have no knowledge of a similar situation in the U.S. I am afraid it will come as a terrific blow to the administration when, inevitably, what they do know now, comes to be disclosed. I am coming to feel that the Democratic party have allowed themselves to be too greatly controlled by the Jews and Jewish influence and that Russia has sympathizers in high and influential places to a much greater number than has been believed. Indeed, I used to feel that even with Franklin Roosevelt, he was perhaps trusting Russia far too much, sympathizing of course with the mass of the people. When we speak of democracy and freedom, the words have different meanings to us than they have to the Russians, although the people at heart are the same."

The next day (February 21) Mackenzie King reported that Robertson "came to me with the best bit of news we have had yet. He told me that Primrose who had denied any knowledge of contact with Communists when first picked up had now, since the Royal Commission had been appointed, made a full confession. Even admitting he had given some of the samples of uranium to Russian agents to take to Moscow in connection with the atomic bomb research, giving as his reason that he felt they had a right to share in the secret. . . . I said to Robertson I thought it would be best to arrange for his trial in England. Let them see that everything is not put off on Canadians. When he is arrested, and his trial comes, bring home Britain's responsibility and this is certain to lead very far in the U.S."

On February 22 the Prime Minister saw Williams, the Commission's chief counsel, and "told him that I had been talking with Robertson. Felt that Robertson was inclined to think it was best to confine the findings of the Commission entirely to the guilt of our own people. I said that unless this was accompanied by something that would disclose that our own people had been drawn into a net by the Russians, which explained their actions, the Commission would be only lending emphasis to what Russia was seeking to have made the public impression, namely, that Canadians were the guilty persons and not the Russians, who have organized their complete system of espionage throughout all Canada. I think Robertson had come to see that in the light of the messages that are now coming out from Russia.

"After I told Robertson we did not want to have people say it is too bad this has all happened in Canada, and Canadians have made a mistake, etc., and thought it was entirely the other way. It was fortunate it had happened here; that we had the courage and initiative to expose the whole business. The despatches from Russia make clear that my name is now anathema throughout the whole Russian Empire, in the manner in which the Government has disclosed matters through its controlled press. Williams read me a statement that will be given to the press. He asked whether it should be sent to me from the Commission, or to Mr. St. Laurent. I told him I thought having regard to what it contained I thought it better to have it sent to Mr. St. Laurent."

Since the Prime Minister's sketchy statement on February 15, Canadian public opinion had swung from shock and confusion to a degree of disbelief that the situation was as serious as the government implied it was. Thus Mackenzie King was anxious for a full interim report from the Commission which would illustrate the range of Soviet espionage activity in Canada and its ramifications in both the United States and the United Kingdom. In some quarters there was regret that Soviet-Canadian relations had been damaged but others saw increased justification for an anti-communist and anti-Russian stance. Contrary to the Prime Minister's prediction, the Soviet government did not break off diplomatic relations with Canada although Ambassador Zaroubin did not return to Ottawa and was not replaced for some time. In a statement issued on February 20, the Soviet government attempted to minimize the importance of the affair while admitting the "inadmissibility of the acts" of some of the Embassy's officers. Of particular concern to Mackenzie King was growing criticism of the government's action in detaining suspected persons without formal charges and without allowing them to communicate wtih each other, with their relatives or with their counsel. The Prime Minister was upset on February 27 to discover that no reply had been sent by his office to a letter from the wife of one of those detained. He spoke to Robertson "about the general impression the public was getting of the whole Commission's enquiry. I said I thought it was wrong that those who are suspected should be detained indefinitely and that some way should be found to shorten the enquiry and give them the full rights of protection which the law allows them. I said I wished he would speak at once to the Government Counsel and tell him this. I asked him to have a word with the Judges; also to meet with Mr. St. Laurent and myself this afternoon at the end of the examination to discuss this aspect of affairs. I said at the beginning unless this part was carefully handled we would create a worse situation than the one we were trying to remedy. People will not stand for individual liberty being curtailed or men being detained and denied counsel and fair trial before being kept in prison. The whole proceedings are far too much like those of Russia itself. I stressed this very strongly in conversation with Robertson; also asked to have a letter prepared at once to be sent to the woman who had complained about not seeing her husband. Learned for the first time that some other woman had written me a letter which I had not seen and who also had not been replied to. Was also annoyed to see an item in the press that someone on my staff had said that I had not received the letter of the woman; that care was taken by the staff that I was properly protected in these matters. It sounds like something said in a casual way but certainly wholly wrong and will create trouble in itself. These are the things that get one down. I tried to keep calm this morning."

At five o'clock that afternoon, Mackenzie King met with St. Laurent, Williams, Fauteux, and Robertson. "Spoke of desirability of having enquiry expedited as much as possible and discussed possibility of admitting wives to see their husbands and also lawyers to see clients, etc. In the light of statements made by Counsel, I felt we would have to leave to the Commissioners letting them know our wishes to have procedure as little arbitrary and as summary as possible.

"Williams says by Friday and Saturday, he thinks there will be at least five or six who will have admitted their guilt. Will not wish to retain counsel and that an announcement can be made of their arrests so as to permit of Court procedure thereafter. Most gratifying was the word that the legal authorities in the U.K. feel that 'Primrose,' on his own conviction, has gone far enough to warrant his arrest and trial. It was thought advisable to wait until Canadian arrests were made and to have the one in England made simultaneously. That will satisfy public opinion for a time and by Thursday of next week, examination should be through with all who are detained and report by Commissioners ready before Parliament opens."

On the morning of March 2 the Prime Minister received an advance copy of the Royal Commission's first interim report. He was not entirely satisfied. "It is short but quite enough to stimulate a fresh interest and activity and also to justify in the minds of the public generally the steps taken in secrecy to discover the extent of espionage. What I regret is the examination has only proceeded far enough thus far to justify the arrest of four persons. That one of them – the first on the list – should be a woman in the Department of External Affairs [Emma Woikin]. The worst feature about her is that she should ever have been employed seeing that she is of Russian descent but of course she was sent by the Civil Service Commission to the Department. It will, however, afford room for an attack on the Department and the Opposition will say that I have been taking on too much to give the supervision needed to the Department. I am glad along with her is an employee of the British Government [Kathleen Willsher] which brings the British into the picture and also that the report draws attention to efforts being made to secure secrets with respect to U.S. Army and Navy as well as our own.

"Robertson told me there was some hesitation about the British to be ready to proceed against Primrose on Monday. I told him to have Counsel press very strongly so that such arrests would be simultaneous – that there should be an arrest in Britain and a trial in Britain simultaneous with an arrest and trial here. What worried me most is the detaining of persons without permitting them counsel and the long detention. I am so afraid that by the time Parliament meets to deal with this question, I will be completely used up and in no shape to handle myself in debate. I can only pray it may be otherwise and do my best to prevent it. Told Robertson to see that a copy of the report was sent to the Soviet Embassy and that it is given to the press if possible by noon on Monday.

"I read the report in Council. Was interested in watching the reaction of Ministers. Most of them were perfectly silent. Ilsley asked a question as to whether publication of the report in advance of trial might not be in the nature of a judgment in advance. It was clear, however, that the persons mentioned have already been given a chance of counsel and do not intend to deny the information contained therein. At the same time, there might be criticism on this score. I think the report will alarm the Continent considerably and possibly also the people of Britain but I think the consensus will be that having in hand the material it discloses, we would have been particularly wrong had we not taken the course we did."

The next day the Prime Minister learned from Lester Pearson that the American Secretary of State had been given a copy of the report. Pearson "had felt we owed that to the U.S. and Britain, so that they would not be taken by surprise at what would appear in the newspapers. Byrnes had made no comment to the reference which the report contained to what information had been sought in the U.S., etc. What he seemed more concerned about was how everything was focussing up pretty strongly these days against Russia, so much so that it might be thought matters might be prearranged. There was a situation in Iran, where Russia was refusing to withdraw her troops. There was also a situation in Manchuria, where Russia was keeping her troops. The U.S. were sending Consuls to Manchuria tomorrow. Churchill would be speaking with the President on Tuesday, which would be the strongest statement of all. The report of the Commissioners coming in between would be a tremendous sensation, and Byrnes had wondered if, instead of issuing the report, we might not make an abstract of it and simply issue a statement, mentioning that it was an interim report. Pearson said he would not press this and would not ask me to do anything of the kind. He recognized we should deal with the matter as we thought best. I had talked this over with Robertson and we agreed that the one thing to do was to let the document speak for itself and not for us to put any interpretations upon it.

"After my talk with Pearson, I had another talk with Robertson, and we agreed that I was right. We had a further word or two about the report itself. Also I insisted on Robertson sending another wire to Britain to urge that there should be no delay in Primrose's arrest. He told me that the British had allowed our having the statement of this person at Earnscliffe being given out along with names of some of our own civil servants but not to get final word about Primrose. The British had been hoping to hold the announcement re Miss Willsher and Primrose until Wednesday. I felt this would not be right, that it was important that the public should see that British servants and scientists were involved and that the whole burden was not on the shoulders of the Canadian Government in relation to its own civil servants. Moreover, the statement would make clear too that the Russian espionage was not restricted to Canada or Britain but extended also to them and the U.S. It was all-important that this larger aspect of the situation should be made clear at once."

With the first interim report scheduled for release at noon, Mackenzie King was relieved to receive word from Robertson during the morning of March 4 that Professor May would be arrested almost immediately. "I am dictating this diary between 12 noon and 20 past," he wrote. "The report of the Commissioners will have now been in the hands of the press for 20 minutes. I have just said to H. [Handy] that I imagine telegraph wires all over the world will be alive with the information it contains as they have not been in days since the beginning of the last war. I have just been handed a copy of the Commissioners' statement as it has been sent out from me at 12 o'clock today and delivered at the Russian Embassy. It names several members of the Embassy staff and brings the whole business to a direct issue wtih Russia. Up to the present the name of the Embassy had not been specified. By this time too four civil servants will have been charged with having violated the Act respecting Public Secrets and will have been arrested. Trials will open in Ottawa before long. Primrose the scientist will have been arrested in London and trials will open there. It is a moment in the history of international relations, the importance and evidence of which cannot be overemphasized. I am only too conscious of the great gravity of the whole situation and of the tremendous responsibility that has come on my shoulders without any wish or desire on my part but solely discharge of my public duties at a moment when I should have been happy to have been relieved of them altogether."

Reviewing the reception of the report by the press on March 5, the Prime Minister "felt relieved to see from editorial comment, news items, etc., that the public were now getting some real impression of the seriousness of the investigation and with it justification for the Government's action in courses which I myself dislike above everything else. The attacks from Russia on myself are going to prove in the end one of the best things that could possibly have happened. They are so completely the opposite of all that everyone who knows my public life knows to be true."

At the Cabinet meeting on March 12, strategy for handling questions about the affair in the House of Commons was discussed. "Agreed later with St. Laurent I would state the case generally; he would assist in legal matters. I think this is best. I should, perhaps, deal with the main speech on the Address; and anticipate others, and arrange for copies being printed. This will take up procedure for the first days.

"St. Laurent and I feel very indignant at the length of time the Commissioners are taking in detaining men; also we were both astonished that Kellock was going to adjourn sittings for some days to keep some engagement with a Y.M.C.A. meeting. . . . It seems to me that everybody is going crazy these days. One cannot understand how they could take or propose some of the actions they do. Another report will appear Wednesday night. Three more arrests will be made. St. Laurent says the police say that Rose and Sam Carr [secretary of the Canadian Labour-Progressive party] have not been heard of for the past week. They believe they have left the country altogether. I hope this is true but I will be surprised if Rose does not turn up. If he has left, it is pretty clear his extent of the degree of guilt perhaps is filling him with alarm."

The Commission's second interim report, to which the Prime Minister was referring, was expected on March 13 but was actually not ready for release until March 14, the day the session of Parliament opened. It implicated both Fred Rose, M.P., and Sam Carr. Shortly after noon on March 14, St. Laurent telephoned the Prime Minister. "Seemed to be unduly concerned and excited. He had just finished reading the Report. He had received letters from three counsel associated with the Commission giving it as their opinion that the Report of the Commission, linking one of the names with the cover name of Fred Rose, M.P., in the conspiracy, necessitated the arrest of Rose. St. Laurent was disturbed lest it might be thought that the timing had been so arranged as to have Rose arrested just as the House was opening. He said, however, he did not see how he could do other than act in accordance with the opinion he had received and which he believed to be right. He wanted to know if I would take responsibility for having Rose arrested. After listening to all he had to say, I stated that I agreed with him it was the only course which in justice and right could be taken, and said I would be prepared to take with him the responsibility involved. The Police had expressed the view that Rose had been out of the country for a week past. I had said right along I was sure he would be in Parliament today and in Parliament he was when we met this afternoon. The warrants for his arrest had to be sworn out in Montreal and sent to Ottawa. There were four persons whom the Commission felt should be taken into custody at once. Rose would make a fifth. St. Laurent seemed to think that the arrest should be made forthwith; that I should announce the arrest, etc. on tabling the report."

When he reached his office in the House of Commons that afternoon, Mackenzie King found St. Laurent, Robertson, Pickersgill and Wrong "all more or less in a state of subdued excitement. Robertson and Wrong were concerned lest Rose, whom they learned had turned up, would stay in the Buildings, thereby defying arrest and that a scene might be created which would throw him and the proceedings generally into undue prominence. That involved a consideration as to whether the Second Report should not be held until Rose was arrested, which would have to be outside of Parliament Hill grounds. Unless the whole question of arrest of a

A Winter of Discontent   153

Member of Parliament for a crime were to come up, in which case it would be for parliament to decide. I had everything in readiness to table: the two reports and a motion to ask the House to order their printing. Just before going to the House, decided in the circumstances that the arrest had better be made first. At all events the arrest of Rose and the second report to be tabled thereafter. Hansard proceedings will show the questions that were asked and my answers.

"From the way the Tories applauded the question asked by Bracken as to the detention of persons I could see that they are getting ready to champion the liberty of the subject. I took one glance up the House to see if Rose was in his seat and he was there, sitting very quietly. I mentioned that a Second Report had been received and I expected to table it tomorrow. Also that I would speak on the matter on Monday."

In the evening, Robertson telephoned the Prime Minister and told him that Rose was staying in the House of Commons. "We discussed together what the procedure might be if he remained all night, which is quite possible, seeing that he might not wish to go to a hotel or boarding house for the one night, as he would probably be leaving for Montreal again tomorrow. We decided not to have the interim report published until after he was arrested. The police have the warrant and there is legal authority which would justify an arrest in the House of a Member charged with a criminal offence, but both Robertson and I agreed that the police should be instructed to make no arrest excepting outside the grounds of Parliament. We can see tomorrow what the next course is. Meanwhile the report which has been mimeographed will be held back from the press. There are four other persons to be arrested. That means some concern tomorrow, unless perchance Rose should leave the building tonight, in which event there will be another major sensation."

Listening to the early morning news broadcast on March 15, Mackenzie King learned that Rose had been arrested about 10.30 P.M. when he had left the Parliament buildings and had been taken to Montreal. "When I rang up Robertson this morning to arrange about giving publicity to the second report at once, he had not seen anything in the papers. He evidently reads the Gazette first. But was about to tell me of Rose's arrest last night. I told him of the word the morning's papers contained."

Just after the House of Commons had been called to order that afternoon, M. J. Coldwell "was at once on his feet wanting to know about the arrest of Rose," Mackenzie King wrote. "Fortunately I had together certain papers but had not intended to bring up this question until after tabling the many reports. However, I dealt with it at once. Very fortunately, just as I was going into the House I remembered I wanted to use the concluding paragraph of the Report by the Commissioners, in explaining the reason for persons being detained incommunicado. This proved to be the salvation of the situation. Robertson had fortunately anticipated the necessity of my making an immediate explanation to the House, about the arrest of a Member. Coldwell rather stole Bracken's thunder, but I let the House know that Bracken had previously sent me word of his question."

The Prime Minister spent most of the morning of March 18 "very quietly going over in my own mind the outline I had prepared on Sunday" of a major speech on the espionage case for the House. He felt "it was providential that I reserved for the day that statement re espionage and not to have to labour over a mass of material, as I have in other years, for the debate on the speech [from the Throne]. I read over the two interim reports again, also particulars regarding Gouzenko and the documents and his own written statements. Decided not to quote from either, particularly the latter, as it is almost alarmist in some of the particulars and is strong indictment of the Russian government. It is better it should come out in evidence from Gouzenko himself. I have quite decided to speak without notes and not attempt to read the material prepared for me."

When the Prime Minister got to the House of Commons early in the afternoon, there was a good deal of speculation that Fred Rose, who had been released on bail, would take his seat. "A few minutes after Parliament opened he came in," Mackenzie King wrote, "but there was no recognition from any source of the fact he was in the Chamber. It was all for the best that this was so." The Conservative leader opened the debate and spoke for over two hours, criticizing the government's performance on a range of issues including the espionage affair. Mackenzie King found Bracken "very tiresome to listen to. Everything he said was read. . . . Fortunately he left me a little time before 6. I spoke with great ease and was given much applause, both on rising and when concluding. I could see the House noticed very definitely the contrast between his voice and manner and reading and my own speaking without notes, and clearly in reply. I found, however, when it got to 10 to 6 that I was beginning to tire, and as I was just starting on the espionage matter I mentioned this to the House and there was a feeling it should be called 6 o'clock."

The Prime Minister had a light dinner and then looked over his material to refresh his mind on Gouzenko's statements. "I had hoped that the rest would give me just what was needed. However, when I got up to speak, after the House resumed its sitting, I was horrified to find that I was excessively tired. I could feel the whole weight of my body from my neck down and also the drawing of my throat from fatigue which made it very difficult for me to raise my voice and speak out clearly. I had hoped that this might pass but it did not and I had to keep the one tone pretty much through the entire evening. What distressed me even more in speaking was that I saw clearly my mind would get just a little clouded at times from weariness. I was not quite sure I was using the right words and not feeling sure of the points which I wanted to develop. Indeed, when I got to the end of the speech, I had had nothing particularly in mind and felt really too tired to attempt any real expression of feelings or of giving to the entire statement the emphasis that I wished to give to certain sides of it. Speaking without notes and also to parts that it was a little difficult to recall. Other parts I had in mind were not decided upon before speaking. I had to keep feeling all along the way lest I should say things that would be taken up in the wrong way in other countries than our own, or prejudice the trials which are now taking place. There was a dead silence in the House throughout the time I was speaking. The galleries applauded. Altogether the scene was quite an impressive one, I did feel however at the close that I had not done myself justice or the subject justice. I might have made a very great speech. As a matter of fact I confined what I said to the simple record and that not too well expressed. However, it may be that my own subjective feelings deceive me in what may be the real effect. The matter was as serious a one as this country has had to face and in its international bearings very far-reaching indeed.

"I tried to prepare the ground for the future by separating any knowledge of this business from Stalin, and expressing a certain confidence in him. Also every confidence in the Russian people and my own determination not to allow what had been disclosed to affect the relations of the two countries, but rather be made the instrument for drawing us closer together. That course alone will save the world. An opposite course, one of antagonism and fight, would very soon provoke an appalling situation. If war ever comes between Russia and any part of the British Commonwealth and the United States this country would be the battlefield and everything we value here would be obliterated. I might have dwelt on that side last night, but did not think it was wise to link up that possibility in any way as being related to what I was discussing. I tried to shape matters so that it would be regarded as incidental."

Debate continued the next day and Mackenzie King was particularly impressed by Arthur Smith, the Conservative M.P. for Calgary West, "who surprised me very much in his delightful and clever way of speaking. A real acquisition to the House and his party." In his judgment, Smith made an effective attack on the government's procedures in handling the espionage affair "but went just a little too far in one or two remarks.

St. Laurent, who was beside me, kept taking notes. We discussed whether he should follow immediately. I thought he should and I could see he was anxious to, so arranged to call Gardiner off a little later in the evening. St. Laurent made a most effective speech – a model really in every way. I have noticed during the last few days that he seemed to have been very anxious. I think he has felt sensitive about an attack on himself over the procedure and over not having disclosed – quite innocently – the secret order under which the arrests have been made for the spy enquiry. He really electrified the House while he was speaking and I thought met the situation perfectly. I am annoyed that the Police should have done some of the things they have done. . . . This kind of thing would exasperate anyone. Also I think there had been much too long a delay in detaining some of those who were held for the purpose of enquiry. However, St. Laurent cleared up the situation very well."

Mackenzie King was also more satisfied, in retrospect, with his own contribution to the debate the day before. To him it was "a kind Providence that confined me in my statement to a mere narration, simple in words, but quite clearly along the right lines in what was said, especially in regard to maintaining good relations with Russia."

On March 22 the Prime Minister had a short talk with St. Laurent who was speaking the next day at the Forum Club in Montreal. "Told him I thought we should repeal order in council [of October 6, 1945] just as soon as the [Commission] made its next interim report and the last man was examined. He seemed to think that I wanted to repeal it at once and I could see was quite concerned about it. Felt we ought to hold on and not admit for a moment directly or indirectly that the right course had not been taken. I told him I was quite prepared to agree to that but I thought the matter would have run its course when the last of the present persons were taken up. He had not caught that significance at the start and seemed prepared to consider that next week."

Many of the speeches during the debate simply reflected and reinforced a growing chorus of criticism from civil liberties groups and legal associations of the government's action in detaining suspects without charge and without access to counsel. Mackenzie King thought that John Diefenbaker had made "an effective speech" on this theme the day before as had Chubby Power. "I myself share that view," he wrote on March 22, "and do not see the necessity for holding these men longer. The three or four men that are still incommunicado. It is unfair that counsel and the Commissioners should let the Liberal party get into the position where it may take a long time for the party itself to be freed of the charge of having acted in a very arbitrary manner with respect to civil liberties. It is pretty difficult to have people see that to preserve the larger liberty of the nation itself, the liberty of a few individuals has been thus thwarted."

During the evening sitting of the House on March 28 Mackenzie King again discussed with St. Laurent "the importance of cancelling the order in council giving power to detain persons brought before the Royal Commission. I personally would like to cancel the order the moment we receive the report from the Commissioners when they are through the examination of persons detained. St. Laurent I could see was for retaining the order for some time longer. He spoke of a man to be brought up in connection with a passport case which is Sam Carr. I told him there was no reason why it should be kept for that purpose. He could be brought up in the regular way. St. Laurent thought if we acted at once it might look as though the Commission itself felt we were in the wrong. I do not agree with this. I told him I felt we should make it clear we did not want to exercise powers interfering with individual liberty that could possibly be avoided without prejudice to the well-being of the State. After discussing matters for a time, St. Laurent thought the best course to pursue would be for himself to write to Counsel for the Commission as soon as the report was received, asking if the Commissioners felt it was necessary to retain this order any longer. He would then receive a reply from the Commission itself and cancel the order. I told him I thought this was all right but I feared that someone of the Opposition would anticipate our action and get credit for it by asking in the House for the immediate cancellation of the order. It would then appear that our hands had been forced by the Opposition. I have, of course, to consider St. Laurent in this matter as he has had to stand to the attack and we all agreed to his action. What I am very much concerned about is that discussion does not go a stage further and our position come to be prejudiced on the ground that St. Laurent's action may be believed to be influenced by his being a Roman Catholic and the known attitude of the Church toward Communism. That phase we must keep out of discussion and from beginning an issue."

The Commission's third interim report was tabled on March 29 and on April 1 the Prime Minister informed the House that the order-in-council of October 6, 1945, had been revoked. He "also made statement that permanent civil servants were not involved. Also statement on Mrs. Woikin who got a position in External Affairs Department. It is an immense relief to have that Order in Council cancelled. I feel the Commissioners have thought more of themselves and doing a fine bit and of the report they are making than of the position in which they have placed the Government and our party. It will always be held against us and the Liberal party that we sanctioned anything that meant so much in the way of deprivation of liberty for a number of people. Moreover, as I saw at the start, it has raised an issue in the minds of the people even more important than that of the espionage and will probably result in several of the persons being freed altogether when they come before the Court, or given trifling sentences. It will be an interesting study in the power of public opinion and the preservation of freedom."

Mackenzie King returned to this theme on Sunday, April 7. "I continue to feel more and more put out at the course adopted by the espionage Commission in detaining the persons whom they had before them. It has done irreparable harm to the party and my own name will not escape responsibility. Only the documentary knowledge I had in advance and its bearing on the safety of the State could have excused the course taken. Even there I think the ends of justice would have been better served by risking more in the way of possible loss of conviction."

CHAPTER FIVE

The British Loan Negotiations

APART FROM DOMINION-PROVINCIAL RELATIONS and the Gouzenko case, the great issue for the government in the early months of 1946 was the shape of Canada's future economic relations with the United Kingdom and more particularly a proposed loan to finance British purchases in Canada. There was also some question of reducing the Canadian butter ration to provide additional stocks for Britain. While this question was being discussed at the Cabinet meeting on February 7, the Minister of Agriculture, who had just returned from London, joined the meeting. "I asked him whether the Lord had sent him or whether he had come on his own account," Mackenzie King wrote. "He was the one man needed at that moment. Cabinet all felt that the distress in Britain being what it is, Canada must make some further sacrifice to help keep the people from starving. I was surprised to hear Gardiner say he did not think conditions were nearly as bad from that point of view as they were represented, either on the continent or in Europe. I told him he had not been moving in starvation circles and that poverty hides its head. Men generalize from too small a premise. I am afraid the suffering is going to be great indeed, famine conditions. Certainly all this justifies the fight I made years ago in the Cabinet, not to be in haste to part with our grain or to cut down areas of seeding. Everything today is urgently demanding the opposite."

With the termination of Lend Lease and Mutual Aid on September 2, 1945, the United Kingdom had to devise a policy which would lead to rapid economic recovery while reducing a massive deficit in its international payments position. A British financial mission had visited Ottawa in September, en route to Washington, and made it quite clear to the Canadian government that British purchases abroad would be strictly limited to essential products until the prospects for securing interim financial assistance from both the United States and Canada were clarified. If rigidly interpreted, such a policy could have an obvious impact on Canadian exports of a number of natural and manufactured products. A statement by the Minister of Trade and Commerce in the House of

Commons on December 15 had only partially reassured the Canadian export community. MacKinnon promised that the government would "press on as quickly as possible" with discussions "having in mind that we must reach the earliest possible solution of our United Kingdom–Canada trade arrangements which are so vital to our whole trading position."

It was announced on December 16, 1945, that the United States had agreed to lend Britain $3,750 million, drawable to the end of 1951, with a schedule of repayments over fifty years at an interest rate of 2 per cent. A few days later, Ilsley indicated that the Canadian government had received a detailed explanation of the new agreement from British representatives and that preliminary talks concerning a similar loan by Canada were under way. With the arrival of the British delegation imminent, Mackenzie King spent most of the morning on February 8 with Ilsley, St. Laurent, Howe, Mackenzie, Clark, Towers and Robertson, considering the position the government would adopt in the discussions. "St. Laurent was very outspoken against allowing the British to retain about two million dollars of our securities – C.P.R. and others – and not have them written off against what the U.K. already owes us on war account, or to be set off against the loan we may make to Britain. The British evidently wish to keep the securities and have us pay the interest on them, which means a charge of some fifty million dollars interest to be taken account of in the budget. Another question to be carefully considered is whether we can decide on our loan until definite decision has been reached by U.S. as to making its loan to Britain [the American loan agreement was contingent on congressional approval]. The whole business is very involved. The discussion as delicate and involved as any that has yet come forward. My own feeling is that we are mortgaging Canada's future far too much. On top of all else are these enormous loans to China and other countries, many of which I do not believe will ever be repaid."

Discussion resumed the next morning. "I thought it advisable not to act as chairman, as suggested by Ilsley," the Prime Minister wrote, "but simply to be present [during the meetings] and keep myself free for possible communications direct with Attlee on the question of the loan. This matter likely to take up most of next week." In fact, of course, the negotiations took far longer than one week.

The formal discussions began on Monday, February 11. Mackenzie King, Ilsley, St. Laurent and Gardiner represented the Canadian government and the British delegation was led by Sir Wilfred Eady. Eady "gave a review of the British situation explaining the country's losses through the war; present indebtedness of different countries outlining negotiations with U.S. government, etc. He made an exceptionally fine address. Spoke for almost two hours with very little in the way of notes; logical, closely reasoned sequence of arguments. It reminded me of Lord Curzon's review of foreign affairs at the Imperial Conference of 1923. When he concluded, I felt I should say a few words and mentioned this. Thanked him for his very remarkable presentation and his moving remarks at the close. I thought it was an exceptionally fine bit of work.

"We went in the little room reserved for External Affairs downstairs. I thought the arrangements were very bad. No attention paid to chairs, drinking water, tables, etc. Also room filled with horrible modernistic pictures which should be burned rather than hung on walls as samples of Canadian art. One picture supposed to represent trees in a rocky quarter. One of the British delegates thought they were representations of oil wells."

During the afternoon session, "St. Laurent presented pretty strongly difficulties we have with our people. We feel Canadian securities in Britain should be owned by Canada, or the income from the securities which are in the hands of the British used to purchase sterling which we could use in Britain for Canadian purposes, as, for example, extension of Canada House.

"Sir Wilfred Eady made it clear that the British Government would probably not wish to make any loan [agreement] at all if it had to be contingent on the U.S. loan going through with the educational work which would be done in the U.S. from different sources. I asked if it would be helpful to the British to have us make the loan before the U.S. loan was through or have it in any way contingent upon the U.S. loan.

"Malcolm MacDonald replied for the delegation by saying he thought it would be distinctly helpful with the U.S. loan to have agreement regarding our loan signed. That it would be detrimental to the U.S. loan if one was made contingent on the other."

Reporting on the February 12 meeting, Mackenzie King felt that the British officials had "been quite taken aback at the suggestion that we should wish to have the proceeds of our own securities credited to Canadian account. To them it seemed to defeat part of their object in trying to get money up to a certain amount. They indicated, too, that it would embarrass their situation in their relations with the other Dominions and the countries of which they were holding certain securities.

"I pointed out there were still considerable American securities in British hands and that this point had not been raised by the U.S. Something in the nature of an accommodation between the two governments over this question was hinted at as a possibility."

To illustrate the potential political difficulties his government faced, the Prime Minister quoted from a recent speech by Jean-François Pouliot, the Independent Liberal Member for Témiscouata, in which he had stated that "Chinese, Dutch, Belgian, English, etc., could get anything from this Government but if one were a Canadian, one could get nothing for our own purpose.

"I made it clear that we were far from being sure in Parliament of sufficient support to let us put through a loan of a vast amount without interest. We all pointed out the difficulty in making clear to the Parliament and the country that Canada's prosperity depended upon Britain having the wherewithal to develop her export trade and get imports from us. All our officials – Clark, Towers, Mackintosh, Robertson, etc. – seemed to be in entire agreement with the British and to feel that the argument St. Laurent was putting forward would not be carried out if an agreement was reached.

"At one, it was decided to leave matters over for further consideration until the morning."

Sir Wilfred Eady led off the session on February 13 by replying to the points St. Laurent had raised and, at the Prime Minister's request, Cobbold, the Governor of the Bank of England, spoke "on what would be the consequences if Britain failed to get a loan from us and America. I confess I was very deeply impressed by the statements of both gentlemen. Eady made it quite clear that if we pressed for being credited with the income on our securities it would open up the whole agreement with the U.S. on that score. It would also make difficult settlements with other countries. It was pointed out too that they had been counting on these assets in basing their calculations as to what could be done. Cobbold's statement, in a word, was that the British through holding too much in the way of sterling in other countries had a stranglehold upon all of them in the matter of compelling the direction which trade should take and this stranglehold would have to be exercised if there was no agreement with Canada. For a couple of years England would necessarily continue to buy from us but if it was apparent that she had to tighten her belt and work out her own economy without a loan from U.S. and Canada it would mean that she would have to direct her trade to those countries which had quantities of sterling in England and exercise a rigid direction of industry, commerce, etc. It would probably be disastrous for Britain, but equally disastrous for other countries. Cobbold made it plain that he was not making any threat but was simply, at our request, citing the case as they saw it.

"I intervened at the close of his argument to say that if the consequences he foresaw were realities there was a further one which would certainly follow, which would be that if this continent became dependent on herself,

Canada would soon be out of the British Commonwealth of Nations. All three Englishmen nodded assent to this remark. I did not say it at the time, but said it privately to them afterwards, that I felt a very deep concern about Canada's future. I felt the great menace was from the U.S.S.R. and of having little doubt that the fear of Russian aggression would create a strong continental feeling which might inevitably make this continent one. I felt pretty sure that in the next war Canada would become the battlefield in an attempt at conquest of the world by the U.S.S.R. I made these remarks to St. Laurent privately. He told me he thought the Russian policy was really to drive the European countries out of Asia; that the trouble over the Dutch possessions, etc., had that at the heart of it. It is equally true, I think, that Russia is pulling into her orbit all the countries that surround her. I feel very strongly that China will be completely controlled by Russia before long. We may witness a rise of the old Asiatic power which with the use of new weapons of war may become terrifically powerful. I have come to think that the whole business may break much sooner than the world expects. I doubt if the U.N.O. would ever be other than a creaking house with nothing of a solid structure about it. It will be used by different nations to serve their ends, so long as it serves them. Indeed, I almost feel that what we have had in the first war and second war is only leading up to the third and that another world war is almost inevitable. Great cities like New York, San Francisco, were never intended to be the habitation of the children of God. All that kind of abnormal living will be wiped out some day. I greatly fear that until men and women are brought to their knees and made to acknowledge the Omnipotence of God there shall be no peace restored in this world. It is an appalling prospect and one hates to entertain it. It is not looking realities in the face to fail to do so."

At the Cabinet meeting that afternoon, Mackenzie King commented that Ilsley made an excellent report on the British loan negotiations. He noted that "St. Laurent and Gardiner who have been following the meetings seemed to feel deeply the force of what had been said to us. I myself said that the impression that the talks had made on me was to cause me to feel very sad – to see a great world power, like Britain, really suppliant for help to restore its place as a producing and manufacturing exporting country. The picture that was painted of chaotic conditions of affairs in Europe – the extent to which [the stability of] currencies of other countries [depended] on stabilizing the pound sterling and making it convertible multilaterally – altogether one saw a picture of possible complete collapse in Europe unless the situation were met. If treaties did not go through with U.S. and Canada, and I think they will hang together, I can only see the development of continentalism here and the breakup of the British

Commonwealth of Nations. With the growing power of Russia what it is, the control of oriental people and the like, it began to look to me as though the war had started in 1914. We had been through the first phase to 1918. The second phase was just ending now and a world war on more devastating scale than ever was inevitable unless Europe became in some way stabilized in the next few years. Whether that can be done or not I cannot say. I felt too that communism had spread much more throughout the world than many of us realized. We did not know just where we were in dealing with some of these terrible situations. I felt that we should go ahead and work towards some agreement.

"St. Laurent who had presented some of the strongest arguments against the financial agreements and for something different, I think felt that the argument presented by the British was a complete answer. He I think shares my view. Certainly Ilsley and Gardiner do, that the situation is the gravest that the world has faced at any time and that the need for action on our part is imperative. It will be very difficult to put over in Parliament, but the situation is clear.

"We discussed possible propositions to put up to the British delegates, so as to get enough to present something to Parliament; for example, some interest payment on the loan, even possible forgiving of all war debt, the purchasing of Canadian securities, loaning them the purchase money in the next few years, etc. These and other suggestions were left to the others to be thought over and considered by the experts and ourselves within the next day or two. We decided to call off the meeting fixed for tomorrow morning."

On Sunday, February 17, the Prime Minister finally read the full text of Sir Wilfred Eady's statement of the British Treasury's position. Basically the British negotiators were repeating in Ottawa the request they had made unsuccessfully in Washington, an interest-free loan and cancellation of British indebtedness incurred during the war years. Mackenzie King was not impressed. To him, "it amounts to asking Canada, on top of all we have done in the war, and what we have given of free gifts of a couple of billion dollars, to make now a free loan without interest with no consideration in any particular. I do not believe the Parliament of Canada would agree to such a loan. It makes me a bit indignant that the British should not seek to make the way possible for us but to simply attempt, by use of words, to get what they are after regardless of the position in which Canada may be placed. I think we will have to consider most carefully our trusteeship to the nation. Governments are apt to forget what they owe to the people, through their members, thinking mostly in terms of what they should be doing for their opposite numbers in negotiations. There might have been no negotiations at all, but much better a straight request, than to have to yield on what has thus far been presented, with great force it is true, but with almost exclusive benefits to the British."

In his diary for February 18, the Prime Minister noted that Graham Towers, the Governor of the Bank of Canada, had asked for an appointment, "saying I had said to him at one time if there was ever a critical matter on which he thought he could be helpful not to hesitate to speak to me himself privately. He had some notes prepared. Had evidently known of negotiations going on. Was evidently wholly familiar with the talks Clark and Ilsley had been having with the British Treasury officials, Eady and others. I told him I had not talked with them myself. Towers went over some of the ground which Treasury officials had put before us. I could see he was clearly behind them and had come to strengthen their position, if possible in the face of the objections which Clark and Ilsley had raised. What he really wanted to say, and did say at the end, was that the loan should be made without interest; that a loan with interest would make very great difficulties, etc. He said he had not given this as advice to either Clark or Ilsley. It was evident that he was reserving making any final advice but was anxious for me to have this word. I let him see that I saw great difficulties in anything of the kind. I asked him what there was in the way of negotiations where the request was simply made for a loan – to all intents and purposes a gift. Should it not be paid back but without any consideration. I asked if interest could not be paid back, how could we ever expect the principal to be paid back? He indicated if we got everything going well that a loan without interest would help to get the money, to get things started, and that if everything went well, of course the principal would be sure to be paid, whereas if things did not get rightly started any situation might develop. I confess that Towers' statement did not impress me. What did impress me was that as Governor of the Bank of Canada he was really under the influence of large financial banking world. It was clear he was influenced by their environment."

At the Cabinet meeting that day, "Ilsley went over the talks that he and Clark had had. He said that now we were all further apart than ever. He pointed out that the British were pressing for an arrangement – for giving of more in the way of indebtedness and placing a heavier obligation than ever. He did not see what could be done. I told him I was not sorry to hear him speak in that way, as I had read over the two memoranda and they had given me a feeling of deep indignation. I read bits to Council where Eady had said they would examine the proposals and a statement would be made that they did not wish to be haunted with obligations, etc. I said they must take us for a lot of infants and children to present a document of that kind to a government; that my colleagues knew I had been very deeply impressed by statements made but I felt indignant when we received a document which implied that we were gullible and, as I saw it, not in the nature of negotiation, but a demand for something for nothing and the equivalent of, and going the length of, even stating that if this were not done we would be responsible for failure in the case of the U.S. loan and in the case of negotiations with other creditor nations. I did not use the expression but it kept coming into my mind of there being a threat of blackmail in the whole attitude.

"St. Laurent was not there and I insisted that no final agreement should be reached without the whole Cabinet having a chance to discuss the matter fully. That was definitely understood. It was also understood that there would be no loan without interest. We might consider a plan which was put forward, which was to charge no interest for the first few years. If there was evidence of Britain gaining in their export position, etc., they should pay interest of one percent and increase it up to two or three percent, making the interest dependent on the business they were doing. This was discussed in the light of U.S. terms and it was thought the British would not accept it. While I would have been prepared to have gone far and to go comfortably for a loan at one percent with certain other conditions and understandings, I have now come to feel that we should take the position that we cannot get through our Parliament a loan on terms less favourable than those which have been given to the U.S. In other words we owe an obligation to our own people to protect their interests. We could defend that. To begin with we are under no obligation to make any loan and it would be indefensible were it not that the money would be used to create a demand for products of our own farms, fields, manufacturers, etc. What we would really be doing would be to save money for our farmers and others for goods they would sell to Britain. This to keep a high standard of employment at the present time. Where the country will be landed eventually is what causes me very grave concern. I think the Government must have regard for future generations as well as its own."

On the evening of February 19 the Canadian government gave a dinner at the Country Club for the British delegation. "In the course of the evening," Mackenzie King wrote, "I talked with Sir Wilfred Eady . . . and after dinner with Brand and later with Cobbold; also had pleasant talk at dinner with Malcolm [MacDonald]. . . . I gave each of the three in turn reason to feel they could not take a 'take it or leave it' attitude which their memorandum proposed. Not in these terms but I pointed out to them that with the best will in the world, we could not get our House of Commons to pass what they wanted. I might have added we could not get the Cabinet."

The Minister of Finance again reported at length on the progress of the negotiations during the Cabinet meeting on February 21. Mackenzie

King noted that the British officials "having learned that the Government would not consider a loan without interest, have agreed to pay same interest as [in the U.S. agreement]. They want, however, to have us write off the 400 million dollars owing as Britain's share of the air training plan. They want the other war debt to be freed of all interest.

"St. Laurent fought vigorously for interest on war debt to be continued though allowing it to be foregone for 5 years and the matter to be looked at later. Also to hold to what was owing on the air training account but to accept interest payment thereon in sterling instead of dollars and agreeing to use sterling for investment in Britain. I asked pointedly what was the reason for not simply agreeing to do what the Americans had done. Neither more nor less and leaving other matters as they were to be considered later. Ilsley could give no reason for this beyond he would not like 5 years hence to have it said if Canada had not been so hard in her position at this time that things would have gone better.

"All of Council excepting Ilsley were for St. Laurent's point of view. Ready to go that length. I pointed out to the Cabinet that we seemed all to be forgetting what difficulty we were likely to have when we got into Parliament to get a loan of a billion and a half, at 2 per cent, put through – money that was not likely to be paid back. Having it run for 50 years – until the year 2,000. It did not seem to me it was fair to future generations to mortgage the future in that way though I was prepared to agree that had Britain become a debtor nation in the war, and we had become a creditor nation, that we must recognize an obligation to help to restore Britain's future. This did not mean our going the length of risking the defeat of the Government itself. I said at the time of reciprocity [1911] the Government had taken nearly one or two years to consider the agreement. We all felt familiar with it and its terms and argued ourselves into supporting it, when it got to the country. It was new to the people. They had not the knowledge that we had and cries were raised in Quebec that Laurier was too Imperialist and Ontario, not Imperialist enough – exactly the same thing might happen again in our own Parliament and this over a loan of this sort with the small majority we had and with a lack of effective organization on the part of Whips in the House. I said it was my first duty to see that the Government was sustained. It would be little help to Britain or anybody else if we were out of office.

"Ilsley very reluctantly took the Government's position before British negotiators. Word came they would like to meet the Committee that had dealt with them at 2.30 tomorrow afternoon. That will be a difficult final round. St. Laurent has a very fine mind. Very true instinct. Very honourable in every way."

The next day was not the final round in the negotiations. Writing on

February 22, Mackenzie King fully expected that "the meeting . . . this afternoon will be a very trying affair. The political equation is even more important than the agreement itself. I have strongly in mind what happened to the government in the reciprocity campaign, the public not accepting what the government knew in its own mind was advisable."

In the afternoon, the Prime Minister reported, "Eady looked very depressed. . . . Cobbold friendly, but also looking serious. The financial officials – Towers of the Bank in particular – rather concerned. When we met in Ilsley's room St. Laurent and I were the only two members of the Government with him. Before going in Malcolm MacDonald came to me and said he felt pretty concerned about the loan. Was afraid that things were going to break up. I said I hoped not, but they might and that could not be helped.

"I begin to see now the significance of Towers' remark when he told me he thought it was advisable to not have any interest in the loan. He did not think it could be arranged with interest, but added that he had not so advised Clark or Ilsley. That he was trying to get me to give in to bring pressure on others to do away with the interest. They have all come around now to seeing and being able to understand our position and really feeling that we should have interest as there was interest on the U.S.

"Of course I feel that Clark and all his group and all the Finance Department and the Bank people, the big trade interests and so forth have only one point of view and really are a world of finance – feeling a greater common interest in finance than they do any interest in common with the political world. Eady went at length on arguments he had used before, becoming increasingly threatening in his attitude and just saving himself with a word here and there from having the door absolutely closed. Continuously saying he did not think his Ministers could entertain this. They would want to go before Parliament with such a measure and it would be putting Canada in a false light; changing public opinion against the Dominion, etc., not what they had expected, etc. He was referring to what Ilsley had told them last night of the Cabinet's decision. Ilsley I thought defended our position very well with the one exception that he indicated that he would not like five years from now to feel that perhaps had they taken a different stand a certain situation would have been saved. St. Laurent said nothing.

"Malcolm MacDonald unfortunately overplayed his hand today. He said a little too much at the start about the difficulties of the British Government. Also spoke of himself as an interpreter of Canadian opinion and British opinion. It was quite evident before we were met with at all, it was to be arranged that he would come in in this fashion, pretty strongly on the British side and that we would be prepared to accept what he would say. Finally Eady made mention of what we were proposing now of being even harsher than the U.S. He talked about the U.S. not having asked them to bring back their securities; that it would be all right if it were general policy, but that we were asking England to do something that we had not asked any other country. I might have said we will make it a matter of general policy right now; that when making vast loans to other countries, we would wish to bring back to our own any investments that might be held in the country seeking the loan. It was this kind of argument which makes one annoyed because it implies an absolute lack of intelligence on the part of those to whom it was addressed. Malcolm made his great mistake by taking up this particular point of Sir Wilfred Eady's and stressing it, saying that it was something that was very true.

"St. Laurent finally came in and took strong exception to what had been said in that way. Asked MacDonald how it was true that when we were easing an existing burden we were making something more difficult? Malcolm was of course obviously taken aback. He tried to explain, but I thought his explanation very far-fetched. It was clear he had intended only to help the British delegation. Eady said he was sending Cobbold back to England by 'plane to explain the position, instead of having a lot of telegramming. Asked for our statement in writing, etc."

Just before the meeting broke up, the Prime Minister decided to intervene. "I . . . said I had been listening to everything very carefully; that I thought what Sir Wilfred Eady had said about the necessity of care being taken as to the proposition that was to be put before Parliament by the Ministers, and the need . . . to assist in getting the main proposition through was very true. I said the same applied to our position. That we had to be very careful as Ministers about what we attempted to do in Parliament and that we too needed a cushion that would help us get through the proposal of making a loan to Britain, and feel in the light of all Canada had done that the Cabinet had been united in not seeing how we could go farther than approve a loan at a low rate of interest. That I doubted if we could not get the matter through the Cabinet we could get it through the House of Commons. Also, I thought my intelligence was at least average and my not being able to see the justice of the arguments that were put forward I did not see how it would be possible to present them through the House of Commons in a manner that would convince others there. I then said that all the gentlemen in the room, excepting myself, were men who understood great world financial transactions and who were looking at matters in the light of world financiers and traders. Unfortunately the average man did not possess that great ability. That the whole matter was so much above their heads, it was unreasonable to expect them to understand something that was next to impossible to explain. I said if Sir Wilfred Eady were P.M. he might be able to persuade the House of Commons of the argument that he had presented to us. But I did not know how even Mr. Ilsley would be able to present a strong enough argument to get any appreciative following for going beyond what we had proposed. I said they must remember they were a highly specialized group and that we were dealing with men of all classes. I then told them I recalled very vividly when I was in the Laurier Cabinet what happened when we were defeated on the reciprocity issue. . . .

"I foresaw the same sort of thing were we to attempt to go too far in the matter of the loan. That our difficulty would be in getting a loan through at all, let alone other features. I then spoke very plainly and said that we would be asked if we were sure our country would ever get back the loan. The only support that could be given to this was that Britain honoured her obligations. I then asked how can we say that, though, when Britain made the solemn obligation to us to pay back a certain part of the war expenditures, interest to begin after the war, and we had not had any interest up to the present. Also they were now telling us we must forego interest for all time, but get rid of the principal as well, or else we would be destroying the future of the British Commonwealth, and driving Britain into a position where she would have to close her markets to us. It was a strange thing, I could not understand it.

"Later when Eady was replying a little further, he said something about not wanting to put his Ministers where they would have to apologize for bringing the measure in and risking a change in public opinion toward Canada. I said in conclusion: Sir Wilfred Eady and myself would not apologize to the Canadian Parliament, nor would I apologize to the British Parliament for what we are offering to do to help Britain as far as we can in her difficulties at this time. I felt incensed at his talking of apology in reference to what Canada was ready to do, on top of all we had done. When the meeting broke up, Brand said to me he did not like to hear me say that Britain would not honour her obligations. I had said to him that I had not said she would not, but that the first question we would be asked would be how could we expect she could when the condition of her doing so was that we were told we must agree to breaking a solemn obligation she had already entered into. I was asked by Eady if it was all right for them to consult with Clark as to the statement to be made re Cobbold going to England. He did not want to have it appear that he was going because of any break. I said I thought it was the natural and right course and would be so regarded. Verbal explanations, instead of attempting to do too much by cable."

The British Loan Negotiations 171

The next day, Saturday, February 23, Malcolm MacDonald, looking "very worried and distressed," came to see the Prime Minister. "I could see he realized he made a serious mistake in what he had said yesterday. Both St. Laurent and I had taken him up before the others pretty sharply, and roundly combatted the argument he tried to present. I could not but feel a little pained at his expression and his lack of merriment. . . . I told him quite frankly how shocked and amazed I had been, both at the memo which Eady had given Ilsley some days ago with its references to examining the form, etc., and its argument which seemed to imply that Canada was to pay tribute for all time to come to Britain, investment situation, etc. I was horrified when I heard it said, on top of all we had done and were prepared to do, that we will have to be apologized for in the British Parliament, when we were offering a 2 billion dollar loan, on top of the 2 billion they had had as gifts before, we were told we were making the situation more difficult with the U.S., and possibly helping to break up the Empire, through not going further and asking Britain to just help us to do what we wanted to do for her by making it clear that she was prepared to keep her word in regard to previous loans.

"Malcolm then said that there would be no difficulty, he did not think, about the previous loan. That the difficulty was rather with the Air Training Scheme and payment for that. Well, I said: Look at that. First of all we were told that to start this Plan we would be making the greatest contribution to the war. Britain was to do so much. She started out by doing nothing. We could not even get from her the engines and the equipment which had been promised. We had taken that over ourselves. We had developed the Scheme beyond all proportions in seeking to give help in many parts of the world. We had taken over payments we had never expected to take – payments for this, and payments for that, we had never been expected to pay for. I said I had fought the battle about getting a gift of 2 billion to Britain, but against what had been said at the time, and what I myself had said, to allow the debt to accumulate in sterling and forgive it all when the war was over. If we did not do this, we would get no credit for anything that we might give. It would all be forgotten. I said it made me feel very cynical to discover what I had said at the time and was prepared to overlook, was turning out to be the case, only in a worse form than I had ever imagined. I did not spare my words and feelings in what I said. I spoke of the other men from the Treasury that have wanted me to give the French gold over to Britain and when I had held to an honourable trust and obligation, said they would have to tell Churchill about it. Now, I said, we were being told that the Ministers in England will all have to apologize for us. I told Malcolm that that sort of thing was not good enough. I felt about this matter as I felt about the

Russian situation: that it was for us to stand for what we thought was right, regardless of all consequences.

"I then said to Malcolm he knew as well as I did, that when they talked about England and saving situations, etc., it was not the great masses of the common people that were considered; that when we talked of these investments it was the privileged ones generally that were seeking to hold their own against all the rest of the world. It was that kind of thing that was responsible for the growth of Communism, for the war, and all the rest of it. Malcolm said he knew how I felt about what I was saying in that connection; it was also, of course, what he felt himself. I said that for my part I was prepared to further that sort of thing regardless of consequences. He is leaving for London on Monday. Said he would help all he could to explain matters to Attlee, Bevin and others. I gave him plenty to tell them. I think it will have its effect. In the back of my mind I have the thought, if they come to accept what we have proposed in the right spirit and attitude, of suggesting to the Cabinet that we change the two percent to one percent. I have already made that suggestion to St. Laurent and will be prepared to do this as an evidence of our readiness to go further than stated, but I have said nothing of this to any of them meanwhile. However, today Malcolm has yielded up on their behalf. Without doubt the question of the obligations which I said involved Britain's honour, namely, the debt to be repaid and the interest on it, has had its effect. That leaves the Training Scheme, as he says, and the investment. I think Britain will even forego the Training Scheme business. She will fight to the last ditch with regard to investments."

On February 25, the Cabinet discussed the British loan for over three hours. Mackenzie King reported that "Ilsley had been working on something with Clark and St. Laurent over Sunday – something which involved without any interest but which would bring more in the way of money into our treasury over some of the years. I thought the proposal was altogether too involved and said to the Cabinet anything which was next to impossible of explanation would do more harm than good. Ilsley, Clark and St. Laurent were all agreed I think that the British will not agree to a 2% loan and to our holding them to the war loan of some $500,000 [*sic*] with interest contracted in 1942. (Interest free up to five years and to payment of $425 millions on remaining indebtedness for air training.) Also making no change in their determination not to part with further Canadian securities. This would mean there would be no loan made. The effect of this might be prejudicial, if not disastrous to the success of the American loan. Clark and Ilsley were emphatic that this was really a harder bargain than the bargain with the U.S. inasmuch as the U.S. had written off an amount relatively equivalent to ours on account of certain war charges which the U.S. had against the British. We had nothing corresponding to that. I did feel that we should not make a bargain which would be more difficult for the British than the American. That might prejudice the success of the American loan and would certainly lead to the Government being criticized in our own press – so largely British controlled. It might, too, offset the position which Canada holds in the eyes of the British and others. Accordingly I made the suggestion that we might consider holding everything as it is for the next five years, to be reviewed at that time, which is something the British do not want as they feel it is going to make settlement with other creditors very difficult – but letting them have the loan at 1%. Clark and Ilsley seemed to think that this would be still everything considered 'tougher' than the American loan or at least quite as tough. I pointed out that whatever was done, it was desirable that it was made very simple. That the public would understand Britain asking us for a loan and our lending our money at 1% seeing that practically all of the loan would be made to purchase Canadian products within the next couple of years. They could understand a review of 5 years hence. This seemed to meet with the general approval of the Cabinet, the more it was discussed. At one moment, we came to the conclusion that that was the wisest course to pursue.

"St. Laurent then pointed out that a 1% loan would be pretty difficult for him to defend. It would be pointed out we would be lending money to Britain at 1%. It would cost us 3% to raise it from our own people. He also figured out what this would come to in the way of loss of money. I then said we might consider, as an alternative, holding the loan at 2%. It was certain that we could not ask for a higher percentage than the Americans but I suggested that this being conceded – also the British being willing to forego their request for us to abandon the 1942 loan of $500 millions and undertaking on their part to see that it was paid off part every year, paid off through the sale of certain securities with which we would be credited – that we might agree to forego the amount owing on account of air training. That being clearly a war expenditure and similar in its nature to what the Americans had themselves foregone. It seemed to me that Canada would never have the British pay this amount in any event. If it were carried for five years without interest, at the end of that time it would be written off. Meanwhile it would be like a sore thumb; as a liability with which Britain would have to reckon in her negotiations with other countries.

"St. Laurent thought this was better and other members of the Cabinet came to share that view after there had been a good deal of figuring back and forth. While Clark thought that a loan without interest was best financially, all Cabinet felt it would be more difficult politically. . . . The Cabinet, as I said, would have favoured 1% had I held out for that, but felt 2%, dropping the British obligations on account of Air Training, was perhaps, everything considered, best of all. Clark and Ilsley both thought the British would now accept these terms though they would not have done so a night or two ago. They had come to feel pretty much concerned lest they could not get any loan at all from Canada. While it was not what they wished, or what they had expected, they wanted the loan free of interest. They both believed they would accept it now. It was agreed that this proposal was the one which the Cabinet was prepared to have now considered. I said I hoped they would clear up at the same time all outstanding obligations to the British, so that there was no further excessively hard driving on their part. This proposal must be linked up with decent treatment in other outstanding amounts and also be made in the light of expectations that the terms for the purchase of Gardiner's bacon and eggs should be dealt with in a manner fair to the Canadian taxpayers.

"I felt pretty tired at the end of the afternoon's long session, but believe we have got the best it is possible to secure. Clark who knows most about the whole business is certain of this. . . ."

The Canadian loan to the United Kingdom in the amount of $1,250 million paralleled the American in duration, interest rate, and terms of repayment. In addition, the Canadian government agreed to cancel the $425 million balance due from Britain for its share of the costs of the Air Training Plan and to accept a lump sum of $150 million in gold in lieu of collecting the outstanding indebtedness for essential purchases made by Britain from the termination of Mutual Aid to the end of February 1946. Under the agreement, an earlier interest-free loan of $700 million, which had been reduced by some $161 million through the sale of Canadian securities in London, was to continue free of interest until payments of interest and principal on the new loan commenced.

On March 2 the Prime Minister informed the Cabinet that the British government had accepted the loan agreement that morning. "The only real question outstanding related to some tanks amounting to some forty million dollars or more which our army had ordered but which subsequently it was decided to discard and use American tanks instead as being safer for the men. The British had taken these over from Canada. The question was whether they should now be charged for them; our people had discarded them.

"This illustrates the kind of waste there is in war. Ilsley felt, and I think rightly, that if they had been completely discarded by our people, and used by the British under the circumstances, it would not be fair to charge them until we got a settlement which, apart from that, would clear up all outstanding accounts both ways.

"The truth is these accounts have never been kept up to date as they should have been and I am told it will take a year or two to have the whole business worked out in detail, knowing that it is doubtful how much will ever be paid back by the British at any time, setting this off against the extent to which Britain has suffered and the certain knowledge that none of us would have been free if Britain had gone down. It seemed, on the whole, to be advisable not to let this item stand in the way of final settlement."

Mackenzie King spent part of the morning on March 6 reading over the text of the loan agreement and the press statement to be released later in the day. "It is a tremendous transaction comparable to some of the largest in the war. I believe we have done what is right and what is best but I confess that in these great transactions, far too much centres around a very few officials. I have great misgivings as to the ultimate effect of some of our financial policies. I question if enough thought has been given to the position of Canada some years hence."

Next day the Prime Minister was pleased to see that the evening papers "gave a great prominence to the signing of the British agreement. During the evening I received a nice cable from Attlee on the result of the negotiations. The papers announced the agreement was received with great enthusiasm by the British House. This may not make it easier of enactment in Canada but I am now convinced that what we have done, has been the best possible and all for the good. It certainly will be difficult for my political opponents through generations to come to say that I have been anti-British with what has been done for Britain under my administrations in the war and post-war years.

"Indeed I feel that in these very large issues and transactions of the present, I am given a place in the public life of Canada which will mean in the eyes of future generations, one of world significance."

With no appeal to imperial sentimentality but a strong emphasis on the importance of the British market to Canadian trade, the Minister of Finance presented the agreement to the House of Commons on April 11. The debate was spread over five days and ended with approval of the loan by an overwhelming majority. Despite Mackenzie King's forebodings, only a few members of the Bloc Populaire, Independent Liberals and Independents voted against approval although their position had wide support in the French-Canadian press and the St. Jean Baptiste Society.

Closely connected in the Prime Minister's mind with the British loan was the question of the repatriation of Canadian troops from Germany. Like many Canadians, Mackenzie King felt they were there merely to shift part of the financial burdens of occupation from the United Kingdom to Canada. For weeks he had been urging an acceleration of repatriation and his anxiety was only increased by reports of deteriorating morale and discipline in the Canadian units. On February 13, the Prime Minister helped to revise a statement of government policy on the question, noting that Abbott had told him "there had been a 'sit-down' strike in the occupation zone yesterday by some of our men. Foulkes had handled it tactfully but there was danger of this spreading. I could not help saying . . . that I hoped they would remember I had been pressing for this matter to be settled months ago; in fact, even before the war was over I had made clear the position Canada should take. We had allowed ourselves to be dragged along and used by the British army.

"Abbott was quite concerned. He feels the situation might get out of hand if word does not go out at once to have all these men brought back. I took out certain apologizing sentences which had been inserted in the draft. For instance that we were assisting in other ways by finances, etc. I felt we needed no apologies; that we had gone further than we should. These other matters can be mentioned in rebuttal if there is any questioning, but I am sure Canadian opinion is all for having our last man in Europe return as soon as possible." Later the Cabinet approved a message to Attlee "about return of our men in the army. Gibson wants additional messages regarding men of air force. Gibson also said he had received a letter from me and spoke of different services that had been wished on to the Air Force which he thought could be discontinued. Council decided in most of these cases to discontinue them. Also all very firm on cutting down numbers."

On February 19 the Prime Minister spoke to Abbott about repatriating a small number of Canadian servicemen who were stationed in Jamaica. He pointed out "how I had tried months ago to get them back before they would become involved in a strike, mounted police duty, etc. He said he thought they were all back. Later he 'phoned to say he had found that some of them were still there and had been called out by the Government to maintain order. As I pointed out to him this is a scandalous business that the Canadian taxpayers' money should be used to have our troops keep order in Jamaica. In all these things, I have exerted my utmost strength to prevent wasteful expenditures of the kind. After getting decisions and assuming that they would be carried out, they have been sidetracked or ignored by Departments. What I have said has come true both from the air force of England and other forces in Jamaica and is now true with the men now in Jamaica. Their job in part is rounding out lunatics."

At this time, Mackenzie King was greatly touched by a visit from J. W. McConnell, the publisher of the *Montreal Star*, who had tea with him at Laurier House on February 12. He reported that McConnell "talked to me about myself and his desire to see that I should be free of anxiety once I was out of public office. He mentioned having spoken of it to me some time ago and that I had said not to pay any attention to that. There would be time to talk of that again. I had to admit I had forgotten he had even spoken of the matter. I told him he must not think of anything of the kind. He spoke about my services to the state throughout the whole of my life and that he felt I would live longer and could do effective work and enjoy the last of life if I felt secure. I told him I was much better off than he realized and mentioned the Mulock gift. He told me in case the books of his companies relating to sugar were ever examined it would be found that every cent of profit that had been made out of sugar because of war had gone into a foundation fund to be used for public and charitable purposes. That he had not got a cent of it for his private use and fortune. He spoke about having been fortunate in his life. He said there was nothing he could wish from any one, nothing that the Government could give him, or anything of the kind. He said he was going South for a little time with his wife to take a rest, but hoped to see me in the summer at his country home.

"McConnell's whole purpose in calling had been to speak about myself. I confess I was deeply touched in the way in which he spoke to me."

On February 21, the Prime Minister received two letters from Vincent Massey "one intended for publication, the other, a personal letter, asking to be relieved of the position of High Commissioner in the month of May. I think he is probably wise in giving up at this time. He has done yeoman service and I am sure feels a genuine longing to be at his own home and in his library. Is probably anxious to get to work on his memoirs. This raises another problem in External Affairs. Robertson may wish to go to London. It might be wise to have Pearson go there except that he is doing very well where he is.

"I would not mind having Wrong go to London though I feel Robertson is entitled to the preference if he wishes it. It would be hard to refuse him. I told St. Laurent today we must have a talk together about the coming months and the session. I am thinking of asking him to take over External Affairs."

On February 26, Mackenzie King returned to this theme. "This morning I have been thinking, as I have been for some time past, of the change to be made in the portfolio of Minister of External Affairs. I would like St. Laurent to take it, but do not know who to make Minister of Justice. The thought occurred to me that I might put Paul Martin into that position and make Gibson Secretary of State, though I do not particularly care for Martin as Minister of Justice. Abbott would make a good man for that post if we had someone else for Defence. If I could get Pearson into the Government, I would have him for Minister of External Affairs. Claxton would probably be preferable as Minister of Justice. Martin might do for Claxton's present work.

"The Journal editorial of last night stresses the obvious need of my giving up the portfolio of External Affairs, which would greatly lessen the load. This has become imperative."

The next day the Prime Minister raised the subject with St. Laurent who "spoke of finding it necessary to leave at the end of the year. Thought it would create wrong impression if he took it over. It would look as though he intended to remain [in the Cabinet]. He was ready to help in any way and was willing to take on as Acting Minister for a time. We will discuss these matters further." Earlier in the month, on February 7, Mackenzie King had noted that St. Laurent "wanted advice as to accepting invitations to speak. He is sensitive about having colleagues feel that he is thinking of leadership, etc. I told him not to be concerned about that; not to take too much time off for public addresses."

During the Cabinet meeting on March 12 it was decided "to amend the External Affairs Act so as to do away with necessity of Prime Minister acting as Minister of External Affairs. Two years ago, made arrangements for separate salary for Minister of External Affairs. Had thought appointment of separate Minister could be made by simple designation or appointment, but found that the Act needs to eliminate the [section] referred to. This is my way of replying to Graydon. The Bill will be through before his resolution is reached. I can however continue on for such time as may be necessary for Conferences, treaties, etc., until remainder of the year.

"Massey's resignation is announced today. When I spoke in Council about the Bill I asked Ministers if they had any suggestions to make. No one said anything except Martin who did not see any need for the appointment of a separate Minister at present. I told the Cabinet I was not anxious to carry any heavier load than was necessary. I would be glad to make this change at the right moment." A resolution preceding introduction of the bill to amend the External Affairs Act was introduced in the House by the Prime Minister on March 18.

A good deal of Mackenzie King's time in late February and early March was taken up with the departure of the Athlones. The Prime Minister greatly enjoyed the farewell dinner at Government House on February 22 but, as usual, he was apprehensive about arrangements for the government's dinner in the Athlones' honour at the Country Club on February 28. "I have been deeply conscious in the last two weeks that tonight's occasion . . . was really an important national event for which I could not escape all but complete responsibility. Also that the years they had spent in Canada had to be reviewed with some discernment as to their contribution to our national life. As a consequence, I put a lot of time and thought into what I was to say. The dinner itself and the evening altogether went off exceedingly well. The guests began arriving before 8 and by special direction, went into the room adjoining the lounge where cocktails were served. Then lined up in order of precedence and after being presented, took their places at the table before H.E. and H.R.H. came in. They were a little late in arriving. I could see, too, that they had evidently had an anxious time. They have had two days of investiture ceremonies, quite fatiguing in themselves and, of course, with packing up as well.

"Princess Alice seemed quite tired but at dinner became quite animated and was cheerful and exceedingly pleasant throughout the evening. Madame Fournier presented a little bouquet specially arranged. Looked quite pretty. H.E. and H.R.H. and myself sat at a triangular end of two tables which stretched the full length of the verandah. The sight was really a very beautiful one. I am sure that both H.E. and H.R.H. were impressed with the way in which everything had been arranged and with the number of guests present. I made the speech I had prepared with considerable ease and effect. It was, as I said, at the time, perhaps longer than it should be but I felt that H.E. and H.R.H. should not be allowed to leave without knowing what we felt of what their lives had meant to us in times of strain and stress. What their contribution had been to the national war effort in strengthening the country's morale; in visiting different parts of Canada, in the hospitality they have extended in so many directions, and knowing how pleased we were that they had lived to see victory crown our efforts and were leaving now at a time when a new order was being shaped.

"I spoke also of their lives at Government House, of H.E. adhering in spirit and word to constitutional practice. In referring to the Royal Family, I remarked how interesting it is for me, the grandson of a rebel, to find myself seated with the uncle of the present King, to my right, and the granddaughter of Queen Victoria to my left. Also in the light of a bounty of a thousand pounds placed in the name of Queen Victoria on my grandfather's head, expressing the affection which I felt for both of them and which was shared by all present. This reference made quite a hit and was enjoyed by all. It caused H.E. to refer to one of his ancestors in the Georgian line and a contrast with his own life.

"H.E. read his reply for the most part. In it he referred in a very likable way to his 13 years of service as G.G. and having as his advisers General Smuts and myself. He made a reference to the length of years of each of us in the public service and to my nearly 20 years in my office of P.M. and being the one Prime Minister in office today who had been in office at the beginning of the war. I know they both feel genuinely sorry to be leaving Canada at this time. The scene was quite a beautiful one as all at the time rose and applauded H.E. when he finished his speech.

"We then adjourned to the lounge in the adjoining room for conversation. It must have been after ten o'clock when we left the dining room. As the evening was drawing on, when I looked at the clock I was amazed to see both hands together at 12 midnight. It was another 20 minutes or so before H. E. and H. R. H. felt they must leave. I then suggested we should all join together in the singing of Auld Lang Syne. H.R.H. said to me could we not get the Government together in an inner circle. This we did. The singing went very well. It was really a fine evening altogether. Princess Alice said to me she thought we had outdone her party. I am glad she felt that way about it. She spoke most appreciatively of the book I gave her on her birthday. Indeed, in every way, both H.E. and H.R.H. showed their feelings of genuine friendship and regard.

"Olga and her husband from the Russian Embassy were present. I told them I was glad they had been able to come and asked about Mrs. Zaroubin. She told me Mrs. Z. sent her kindest regards but was sorry she was not feeling well enough to come. I asked that all kind remembrances be extended to her. I thought Olga and her husband were quite courageous in the way they turned up.

"It was quite pleasant to see old colleagues, Mulock and his wife, Chubby Power and his wife, Crerar and his wife, Thorson and his wife. It was the right thing to include them all. I had pleasant talks with most of the guests, just a few words. Before leaving, had a remarkably pleasant chat with Mrs. Paul Martin, who had been regretting Paul's long absence. I drove Chief Justice Duff home."

During February 1946, Winston Churchill was staying with friends in Miami and Mackenzie King had been giving some thought to visiting him in Florida. On February 28, Churchill telephoned. "It was very pleasant to hear Churchill's voice," Mackenzie King wrote. "He started by saying: How are you, my friend? When I asked him about himself, he said he was unfortunately not feeling too well. I said I had enjoyed hearing his voice again.... He seemed to have a little cough. He said: it is not bad but I will tell you myself later what it is. He sounded just a little disappointed on that score. He then asked me if there was any chance of my coming down to see him. That he was giving this address which would be very important and would like to have a word with me about it. I explained that I had planned to go down but had to cancel everything because of the espionage matter which had reached an acute stage here and which I had to follow closely. He wondered whether I could see him in Washington and gave me the dates he would be there – until March 3. I said I would like very much to come down but I felt concerned about going to Washington at this time. Everything was being related, in the public mind, to espionage, and I did not know how much the Americans would like my coming to Washington, just at this moment. A wrong construction might be given to my being there. Churchill said he quite understood this. I asked if he could trust anything to the mail. He said he doubted if time would permit. He said he intended to speak on closer American-British relations and question of bases. He said he would follow along lines he believed I would approve of. In regard to the espionage matter he said it was a very serious matter – regarding the larger question of Russia's relations generally.

"When we concluded, Mrs. Churchill came to the 'phone, just to say a few words and to exchange greetings. In explaining I had to mention among other things the departure of the G.G. and the Government's engagements in connection therewith, also meeting of Parliament. As regards coming to Canada Churchill said he would rather come out again in the summertime. He would go to Toronto then. That the cold here just now would be a little hard after the South. Curiously enough, I had been thinking of writing him just when I got word of his 'phoning me this morning."

The next morning (March 1) the Prime Minister had another call from Churchill who had discovered that there was a private line between Washington and Ottawa and "that he, if I agreed, would read over it what he proposed saying. He said he was going to speak on an agreement between the British Commonwealth and the U.S. on defence along lines of our Permanent Joint Board on Defence. He thought if that could be arranged it would be a steadying force in the world. I said that I thought that was excellent. He said I will, of course, not commit you in any way in anything I say and you will not be responsible, but felt he would like to have my opinion on the speech.

"I spoke to him about reasons for not going to Washington. He said he saw quite clearly I was right. He had not thought of that aspect until I told him of it. I mentioned I might see him in New York before he left; would try to do so. He said at once that would be splendid. I shall be in New York for a few days. You will have to come and stay the night with us at the Hotel. It would be fine to have a good talk together there. He could not have been more pleasant.

"After conversation ended, I recalled my speech on the Ogdensburg Agreement. Felt that it might be of service to him. On reading it through, I was amazed to discover how very apposite it was and how very helpful it would be to him. It really would be an anticipation in large part of what he had to say. He probably has not seen it and will be surprised when he does. I am sure he will be grateful for it. I sent copies to Miami and also to Washington."

On March 3, Mackenzie King had another telephone conversation with Churchill. "He had received my letter and enclosure and had had a talk earlier in the day with Pearson," the Prime Minister wrote. "I had 'phoned Pearson yesterday to New York, and Robertson had also 'phoned him asking him to see Churchill.... I thought it better to have Pearson go over Churchill's manuscript with him instead of his trying to read it over to me over what he thought a direct line but what was a line which might easily be cut into by others along the way. I did not want to be responsible to have him risk leakages before his speech was delivered. Pearson had told me it was as fine a speech as Churchill had ever made. The first part of it dealt with Canada–U.S. Joint Defence Board, the basis of which he expands into a wider relationship. This is what I myself have, time and time again, suggested and have suggested I know to Churchill as well. Fortunately, the whole story is of record in my 'Canada at Britain's Side' in the chapter on the Ogdensburg Agreement. Pearson had been able to get him to strike out that this was a military agreement. It was fortunate on this score that Pearson had a chance of going over the material. He told me that when he had a chance of seeing Churchill in the morning he was in bed propped up on pillows and was going through the Hansard copy of my speech which I had sent to him.

"It was about 5 when I called Churchill this afternoon. He was most appreciative of my having rung him up and was glad I had suggested Pearson going over the material with him. I told him that Pearson thought it was excellent. Pearson had assured me that such was the case, particularly with the first part. He felt that Churchill was using pretty strong language in the second part but that, so far as we were concerned, our end was protected, and that he of course was speaking for himself. In the second part, he was speaking as he did because of having no responsibility to any government, giving his own views and impressions. These will be given at Fulton, Missouri, on Tuesday.

"When talking with Churchill, I mentioned that we would be having a pretty strong statement coming out from the Commissioners [Royal Commission on Espionage] tomorrow. He said to me: 'Oh you are so completely right' or words to that effect. He went on to say that if a similar course had been adopted when Britain learned that Germany was re-arming this last war might never have taken place. Someone at that time should have drawn the attention of the League of Nations to what Germany was doing and have had the whole matter thoroughly exposed to the whole world. He went on to repeat: 'Do not hold back anything – go ahead.' 'Keep firm to the position you have taken. I am sure that it is the only thing that will save the situation as it has been developing. It is the same tactics all over again.' Churchill could not have been more emphatic or stronger than he was. He then asked me if I could not come and spend a day and a night as his guest in New York before he left. He said that Clemmie would be there, also Mrs. Oliver and Randolph. It would be so fine if we could have a day together. He would give me different dates. I thanked him warmly and told him I would certainly accept the invitation if at all possible to get away when the time came. I thought we would be through with the opening of the House before he left. If so, I would seek to get down for a day."

On the afternoon of March 5 Mackenzie King listened to the broadcast of the ceremonies at Westminster College, Fulton, Missouri at which Winston Churchill and President Truman received honorary degrees. It was on this occasion that Churchill delivered his famous "Iron Curtain" speech warning against the dangers of Soviet expansionism in Europe. "On listening to the preliminary," the Prime Minister wrote, "I felt how wise it was to have the address delivered in the middle U.S. and at one of the smaller colleges and communities. Also in selecting the home town of the President for the event. The President, accompanying Churchill, was a very wise arrangement.

"The President was wholly natural, . . . simple and unconventional in his speaking and in the brevity of his remarks. It was interesting to notice the intonation of other citizens of Missouri – one in particular whose voice was hardly distinguishable from that of the President. Churchill was in every way at his best. He sounded fresh and vigorous and less hesitant in speaking than I have ever heard him before. His introduction was very clever – full of wit and humour. He led into his subject in an admirable manner. It was the most courageous speech I have ever listened to, considering what we know of Russia's behaviour in Europe and in Asia since the war and what has been disclosed here in Ottawa, much of which is not yet public, I think it was in every way most opportune. I confess I personally believe that as regards Russia the rest of the world is not in a very different position than other countries in Europe were when Hitler had made up his mind to aim at the conquest of Europe. The tragic part is that the true position of the rest of the world never reaches the people in Russia. The Government controlling the press, having a single party, makes it possible for unscrupulous men to inflame the passions of the people against others. The kind of thing being done by the Russian press in reference to myself who has only the kindest of feelings towards the people of Russia is the best evidence of what a handful of unscrupulous persons in office are able to accomplish. What makes Churchill's address so impressive is that what he says is true, but the truth represents possibilities greater than anything the world has had hitherto to face.

"[Pickersgill, Gibson and Handy] and I were all seated together in the sunroom while the President, Churchill and others were speaking. We were all profoundly impressed by what was said. I confess it gave me very much the feeling that I had not made the use of my life that I should have made, being my grandfather's grandson and having had the advantages I have had. I should today be speaking out to the countries of the world as Churchill himself was speaking and should have been able had I applied my time and talents to really equipping myself for public life, – to speak if not with the same eloquence and words at least with a like power of influence on world problems. Perhaps the mistake was not marrying early in life and having a home where my whole thoughts could have been centred in a great public mission. But if I had had the problems of a home I might not have been able to give the public life and work the time I have. What distresses me most is that this year I seem through the overcrowding at the Christmas season to have lost a certain calmness and resolution which I had gained and held to after returning from Britain and visiting Washington. My mind is not as calm as it was and I do not begin to have the grasp of the questions I should have in anticipation of the coming session of Parliament. I am really getting most anxious.

"With Smuts and Churchill I am pretty much today in the position of one of the few remaining men who stand out in their separate countries as the older statesmen. I should be more worthy of being so classed. I never feel that I am doing justice to the position I hold. Addresses like Churchill's on questions of the day, which give expression to thoughts, feelings and convictions I so strongly feel and entertain, but to which I give such little expression in public always cause me to feel a bit disappointed and sad. I might have done so much better. Churchill's address today was all built around the Ogdensburg agreement, which was essentially and wholly something worked out by myself. At San Francisco and elsewhere I have thought of putting forward what Canada has done in the Rush-Bagot self-denying ordinance, the International Joint Commission – the settlement of international issues by investigation and the Permanent Joint Board on matters of defence as examples to the entire world. They keep presenting themselves to my mind but somehow or other I never seem to be able to give public utterance to them. The same is true with what is set forth in my Industry and Humanity. I am prevented from preaching the doctrine there set forth which bears immediately on today's questions simply because I am so cluttered up with many, many things which come up from day to day and which have to be dealt with to the exclusion of some of the profounder and more necessary issues."

Mackenzie King decided to telephone Churchill and Truman and managed to get through. "He and the President were together. He was obviously both relieved and greatly pleased that I had rung him up. I told him what I thought about his speech, being, all circumstances considered, the most courageous made by any man at any time, having regard to what it signifies at the moment and for the future. That I agreed with what he had said, etc. He thanked me very warmly, said it was so kind to let him know. He was so glad that I felt as I did. He then asked me if it came over clearly. I told him his voice was better than I had ever heard it. I could feel he had gained new strength by the rest he had had by the seaside. Two or three times he repeated how grateful he was to me for letting him know that I felt that what he had said was all right. He later asked me if I would be willing to send word to Attlee. That he had not had a chance to talk with Attlee, but if I thought it all right to let him know how I felt the speech had gone and the impression he had made, he would be very pleased. He said of course he had been careful to say that he had been speaking only for himself but he did not think that he had said anything which would embarrass Attlee. I told him it would be a pleasure for me to do so and I sent off a cable later in the evening.... What he did say most emphatically was something to this effect: 'I have followed your career over so many years and have been impressed so deeply with it, with your political wisdom and sound judgment that I value very deeply your approval of what I have said.' The significance of this statement was that the President was with him while he was talking. He then said to me previously the President was here with me and then told me not to stop until I had had a word with him."

President Truman then came on the line "and I congratulated him on receiving a degree and on his speech. I also told him how glad I was to hear his voice again. He spoke of it being nice to hear my voice and asked was that not a fine speech, a great speech, delivered by Mr. Churchill? I told him the whole proceedings were intensely interesting and that I felt we must all work very closely together naming the U.S., the U.K., Canada and other parts, to see that our position was made secure. That I felt what Churchill had said was most opportune and needed saying very much at this time.

"When Churchill got back to the 'phone he again spoke of my coming to spend a night with himself and Mrs. Churchill and the other members of the family who are on this side. He said it would be awfully fine if we could have part of a day together and I would stay the night as their guest. He said he would send me alternate dates as soon as he got to Washington. Hoped very much that I would come, etc. I promised that I would come if it could possibly be arranged. I am very glad I rang him up when I did. It was most fortunate in every way as I know he was very anxious to have a word before making the speech and would feel it was not lack of sympathy or aught else that prevented my having the chance to see and discuss its contents with him. The truth is with the President gone, Smuts in Africa and Eden in England, I can see wherein, excepting Halifax, I am about the only one he has to counsel with of those who have been nearest to him in critical times."

With great reluctance, Mackenzie King finally decided that he could not take the time to see Churchill in New York and so informed him by letter on March 16. However, they had another telephone conversation on March 20. "Winston was evidently pleased that I had rung him up. He spoke about his speeches and said if matters did not turn out well, it could not be said that he had not at least sounded a warning in time; spoken out at this time. If all turned out well, it could do no harm. He seemed to indicate that he did not know whether on the whole they had been good or not.

"I told him I thought the speeches were all right; were needed and in the end would do good. He quite understood about my having to be here. He said he followed with the greatest interest what we were doing. It was most important certain people should not get into positions of trust. Spoke about going aboard a large ship. Would have plenty to eat, probably for the last time for a while. Asked when I was coming over. I told him about beginning of May. He said we will be there when you come. He also said to me he thought he might accept Alexander's invitation to come to Canada in the summer or later. I said by all means to do so. He would get a great welcome in all parts of the country. He then turned over the 'phone to Mrs. Churchill who seemed to be impressed with my voice sounding as though I were very well. I told her I was in splendid shape. We were having an interesting, vigorous time...."

CHAPTER SIX

Post-War Economic Problems

PERHAPS BECAUSE of the extraordinary pressures in the early months of 1946 Mackenzie King, by early March, was suffering through a severe case of pre-session jitters, an even worse attack than usual. On March 9 he was pleased to receive "sharp at ten o'clock" a copy of the draft Speech from the Throne minus the crucial concluding paragraphs "which I find exceedingly difficult to write." Pickersgill and Gibson came to Laurier House later in the morning and worked on revisions until almost 5.00 P.M. "I had asked [Heeney] to find the Speech from the Throne in which reference was made to Lord Grey's departure, and reference to the help his wife and daughters had been to him throughout his term of office. No such speech could be found, but H. discovered a farewell address which Sir Wilfrid had moved and which was approved by both Houses. I felt almost as if I had, or was about to have, a paralytic stroke. I saw in an instant that it would be a terrible omission if a farewell address were not given to Lord Athlone; also it seemed to me to be the one thing that he and Princess Alice would really prize above everything else, and that I could make no farewell gift to him which would be as appropriate. I felt there was but one thing to do, and that was not to lose a moment and begin on an address at once. Called in H. and dictated an outline based on what appeared in Sir Wilfrid's address to Lord Grey; then sent for the material which I had prepared for the dinner at the Country Club, and began to weld its features into concise form. After doing this, I went for a short rest.

"After the rest, I spoke to Pickersgill about proceeding with this address rather than doing more on the Speech from the Throne. We got down at it in earnest fashion and continued to work out paragraphs until ... a quarter to five. By that time I found myself wrought up – by that I mean highly pitched in conversation, not calm and reflective. We were far from completing even the outline, but dropped everything."

The Prime Minister took a copy of the Speech from the Throne to Government House on March 11. He reported that Athlone read it "through quietly and with care. When he came to the concluding part he said he liked that very much. He then opened the side drawer of his desk and drew out a paragraph that he had himself drafted. He said: I have made a modest little effort of my own. I think yours is better. You have expressed things much better. Mine will not be necessary. He then referred to the words 'proud privilege' in the draft, and said he liked that way of expressing himself. He then showed me his little draft which referred to his having been offered the governor-generalship before. It contained a very nice paragraph in reference to his association with the P.M., Ministers, etc. Other parts were similar to my own draft. I said that easily I would be delighted to work into my draft what he had himself prepared. I thought there was plenty of room for both.

"Later when Princess Alice came in she spoke of hoping that I was retaining the personal reference to himself as a soldier; that is to the previous offer of the governor general. I could see at once that they were both anxious for this. I said, O certainly, that should be included. H.E. then said: I am very grateful to the King – and then stopped and said – to you and to the King for my appointment. It is clear to me that what has naturally been in his mind is his desire to make clear that the appointment was on his own merit, that he had been offered the position years ago and had been offered it again. In talking with him I spoke very frankly about how helpful he had been and of his not having made any slips of any kind in speech or otherwise."

The session of Parliament opened on March 14. Although the opening days were complicated by the arrest of Fred Rose, far more significant to the Prime Minister on March 15 was "the announcement by Attlee of the British Government's willingness to give India complete independence, if she so desires. That is the right course. Were any other course taken it is almost certain that India, sooner or later, would join with the other Eastern powers in helping to overthrow British rule."

The first Liberal caucus of the new session took place on March 20 and Mackenzie King "was given quite an ovation on coming in. I let the Members talk for a while themselves and then spoke for about an hour. I outlined what I thought most important for the session. Stressed, above all, the need for Members attending the House and spoke of their having received an extra two thousand dollars last year. Said they were honour bound to the Government and the Party to attend. I spoke particularly to those accustomed to leave on Fridays until Mondays. It was not fair to others to have us handicapped in any way. Spoke of the desire to end the debate soon and of the talks with other leaders. Received authority to say our party will be prepared to take a vote Thursday night. If not then at the earliest date thereafter. I spoke at some length about the international situation, stressing the importance of it and how dangerous I felt the whole world situation to be. I went on to the necessity of strengthening Britain's position as a steady force in the world, and laid the background for gaining support for the $1,250,000,000 loan. I also spoke on redistribution. Need for properly organizing the Liberal office and arranging for study groups. Spoke about Ilsley's and St. Laurent's appointment to the P.C. Made clear how that came about. . . . I spoke, too, at length, of the espionage matter and gave them the background. Told them what I felt about the significance of it all. I found it very easy to speak and I think I made a real impression on the Members present."

Later that day, the Prime Minister made a point of being in the House while Howe spoke in the debate on the Address. "He did it very well. He has shown great improvement as a speaker. Also while Graydon spoke on foreign affairs. It was a school boy venture, ending up with Tennyson: 'Ring out wild bells.' It is that kind of thing that makes for unreality and deceives people. I have been greatly disappointed in Graydon. His manner is changing for the worse, rather than for the better, although in debate today he was very mild. It is a piece of impertinent rudeness, his undertaking to tell the Government what they should do about having a separate Minister for External Affairs, when he himself owes all the prominence he has got in External Affairs to myself."

Despite his other preoccupations, Mackenzie King still found considerable time to devote to his favourite subject, national capital improvements. On March 21 he met with the Mayor of Ottawa, the chairman of the Federal District Commission, and Jacques Greber, the French town planning expert who had developed the original master plan for the capital area. After the meeting, one or two of those present suggested that the Prime Minister should become Chairman of the Commission and write his memoirs after he left public life. He "told them about Sir Wilfrid having made that very suggestion to me as something that he himself would be interested in doing. I told all present to remember that if they would begin to co-operate now firmly and work as a great single team, seeking this vast improvement, there was not a man in the room whose name would not go down in history as a part of history itself with honour to the individual concerned. That this was something all Canada would be proud of for all time to come."

Earlier in the year, on February 6, the Prime Minister had tried to get the Cabinet interested in the "improvement of the Capital – in particular the purchase of properties in Hull. . . . I tried to have them see the vision of larger Ottawa and the importance of taking the step now, if it is to be taken at all. Ilsley said nothing. St. Laurent asked if anything had been done. I thought not. Howe said he had begun some enquiries. Later he offered to take the matter in hand himself by asking Garfield Weston to make an offer. He is going to Vancouver next week and will see Weston when he is there. It may be that we shall yet succeed in breaking the ice and getting a beginning made on the other side of the river. (Apparently Murphy, the Deputy Minister of Public Works, is sold on the idea of the Government forming a corporation and purchasing property in Hull.) Our men ought to take a larger view of the situation. They are prepared to take a world view when it comes to spending money outside Canada, but when it comes to helping ours it is very hard to get anything done."

An unusual development on March 29 raised his hopes considerably. While he was correcting Hansard proofs in his House of Commons office, his secretary "noticed what looked like a fire in Hull. We watched it for a short time. It then began to develop rapidly and finally it turned out that a considerable part of the Alexandra Bridge was burned. The wind driving the fire toward the Eddy works; piles of pulpwood took fire. Altogether a tremendous fire through the evening. I was mean enough in my own heart, while regretting the fire and what it might occasion for a moment of unemployment, to almost wish that the plants opposite might be totally destroyed so as to make possible their complete removal at an early date. There is something very singular about the fact that when we were trying to improve Ottawa as a Capital, the improvement started through a fire in a tobacco store on Elgin Street which led to that block being expropriated.

"Then the fire destroyed the Russell House and theatre, and then the City Hall; also there had been a fire in the Post Office Building. Now in that area that I am most anxious to clear comes a fire to prepare the way for preserving the waterfront on the opposite side of the Ottawa River and making a really fine Capital." The efficiency of the Hull fire department dashed Mackenzie King's hopes.

On March 21 the Prime Minister had a talk with Ilsley who had just returned from a meeting in Savannah, Georgia, of the governors of the International Bank for Reconstruction and Development. The Minister of Finance had asked for the interview to tell Mackenzie King that the new American Secretary of the Treasury had asked him to accept the position of Manager of the new World Bank. "It is the highest financial position in the world. Ilsley said the salary was between thirty and forty thousand dollars. The Americans had wanted to make it more, but Canada stood for having it come down. They had made the offer to Towers, who felt he was much freer as the head of the Bank here than he would be as head of the new International Bank; might find there that the directors were difficult. Ilsley said the same would apply to him. He did not know whether he had the ability to do the managing or the technical knowledge. Vinson [U.S.

Secretary of the Treasury] had said to him there would be plenty of assistance given him. He said as soon as the offer was made to him he had rejected it outright. Vinson would not hear of that. He said he must give it consideration and continued to press him, pointing out that an American would be President of the Bank; they could not have an American as Manager; also they did not want anyone from Europe, as Europe would be drawing from the bank all the time. Vinson said what was needed was someone who could hold situations in reserve. He had also said he had been watching him throughout the week and felt he was the man they would like to have. Ilsley said he had really felt he should not consider it, but to get away had promised he would talk it over after he got here, and would send word to Washington. He said he had not spoken to anyone excepting Clark. That he talked about many things to St. Laurent but had not even told him. He did not wish to have St. Laurent know that the offer had ever been made to him. I told him I would be very sorry if that were so. It might not be advisable to have anything known at present but once he gave up public life, if he should do so, and go on to the judiciary or elsewhere, I should not like to feel, if he rejected this offer, that the country would not know it had been made to him. He told me he did not think he would be staying on long, as he had told me, in politics. The thing had got too heavy. Whether it would be wiser to accept this or later take a position on the Bench, as he had spoken of, he did not really know.

"I said to Ilsley it was a very difficult matter on which to advise – it was so personal. He would realize I would be thinking of Canada; that there was no disguising the fact that if he left it would be a serious loss to our country. I thought he should consider very carefully how he would feel when he made the change. I explained that he would find himself less his own master than he is here and find his life narrowed down to purely financial matters. I did not think he cared about money; that that was quite secondary in his life. Ilsley agreed with that when I spoke of it but indicated that the salary was a large one and free of all taxation. He also said that at the conference Canada, the U.S. and Britain were the only countries that really had a voice or spoke out; that the U.S. dominated everything. South American states were all creatures of the U.S. Europeans, even when they thought Canada was right, hesitated in following but would wait for the U.S. I said to Ilsley that I thought this would be one of the great dangers of the world. We had not men big enough in different countries to have the ideas and judgment that was needed and the courage to express their views. I told him of the offer Mr. Rockefeller made to me before I was chosen leader of the party and of the conversation I had with Sir Wilfrid. I said I told Mr. Rockefeller that nothing he could offer me would cause me to live in New York. I said I should never have been happy there. I mentioned that the Carnegie Corporation had also given me an offer and I could not think of accepting either, although I might have gone into pretty high figures at that time. I said, as a man got older, he found himself part of what his life had had relation to; that he, Ilsley, had a great place in Canada as a part of the country. Were he to leave it to take a financial post elsewhere, great as the post was, he might not be happy in it, and if he were not happy nothing else would serve as a reward. I said to him that anything was open to him here. If he did not wish to stay on in politics, and did not care anything about High Commissionership or Ambassadorship, but preferred the Bench instead, for him just to say what he wanted. I told him I admired very much his attitude toward this in rejecting it, but also felt a deep concern for him, knowing how very difficult the decision was that he had to make. He did not try to play up what he would be giving up by not accepting it. He seemed very happy when I was saying good-bye at simply having had the offer and being prepared to reject it. I have no doubt in the world he will not accept. He said something of between now and Saturday having to make the final decision but that he would write at once and say he had talked the matter over – I think he means to say with myself – and had reached the decision that he could not consider the post. He really is a man of fine integrity."

Before Ilsley left, conversation turned to the housing situation which had become a major problem for the government. The housing needs of returning veterans simply aggravated an acute shortage partly caused by wartime restrictions on construction. Housing policy remained the responsibility of the Minister of Finance even though the National Housing Act of 1944 had been administered since January 1, 1946, by the new Central Mortgage and Housing Corporation. Ilsley wondered whether "he should turn everything over to Howe at once. I told him I thought it would be wise if he did that; it would relieve him tremendously, and that Howe was now ready where he will accept. He said I think I will do that, because things are becoming intolerable here in that connection just now. He asked me if he had better speak to Howe or would I. I said I had already had a word with Howe and had wished him to have a talk with him. He then said he would talk with Howe at once. Ilsley looks much better for his little stay in the South but it is only the result of a few days rest. One can see he is pretty used up. I really think he would be making a mistake to accept that post. He is too high strung. He would not have at his side men like Clark and other advisers he has had: Towers, etc. He would be in the hands of strangers and powerful financial interests and groups – the most powerful in the world. He himself said the whole business might collapse inside of five years, if all nations did not work together as it is hoped they would, which is very true. I think, at his age, with his temperament, and his health, what they are, he would be foolish indeed to accept the position at any price. It made me very proud to feel I had men of that stamp around me. Certainly, this Government has men in it of fine integrity. St. Laurent is another who cares nothing about money and gives his whole service at a great financial sacrifice. The country owes much to these two men. Gardiner is poor, loves spending the public money, but has never enriched himself a cent. Others, too, have been most honourable."

That did not end the matter. Late in the evening on April 10, Mackenzie King received a telephone call from President Truman "to say that they in the U.S. were most anxious to have either Towers, of the Bank of Canada, or Ilsley, become, in the case of the first, a managing director of a certain fund, or in the case of the latter, President of the Development Bank. The President said that those who had been at Savannah liked very much the way we did things in Canada and the way the Government was managing. He said they were very anxious to have one or the other of these men for this all-important work. He said something about the Secretary of the Treasury being most anxious. I told the President Ilsley's position was, as he knew, pretty important to the Government, pretty much the whole business of government hung around the neck of the Minister of Finance at this time. I also said that Towers had a very important position as Governor of the Bank of Canada. I did not think that either was anxious to leave. I doubted if either could be persuaded to accept. I thought their minds were pretty well made up. Said I would have a word with them and would send him word later. I could not gather from the President's message whether he wanted me to communicate with him or with the Secretary of the Treasury."

Next day the Prime Minister informed Ilsley of his talk with Truman. "He indicated to me that he had not finally shut the door. It may well be that the President's message was owing to some indecision on his part. However, he said to me that he felt he ought to decide definitely not to accept and went on to say his strongest reason was because he had grave doubts as to whether he could fill the position. He said he doubted that very much. I told him if he felt that way he would be unwise to accept. That it was a position in which he would have to make decisions. If he worried about each decision he would soon be completely knocked out. He said he felt that way himself. I told him I had seen Fielding suffer for a couple of years, just from the nervous strain in the Finance Department. I thought he had taken about all the strain he could. That the rest of his life he had to consider. If his health broke down there would be no happiness. Here he had his friends around him and the assistance he needed and could have whatever post he wanted. He said he thought I was right. When I asked him again could I give the word finally that he would not consider the matter further, he said yes, do that. He also told me Towers had felt he would be simply a prisoner, or slave or a servant in the hands of 21 directors. He would not have any freedom and would not be able to control the situation. Decided definitely against becoming Managing Director of the fund. The salaries in both cases were very great. Our people voted against them.

"Later when I got Towers on the 'phone he told me that Harry White was one of the Directors. He was pleasant as long as you agreed with him, but could be very obnoxious. Had been so to Keynes in the presence of the Committee. He did not feel that he, Towers, could stay any time with him. Also he felt there was too much in American control all through. I told him what I had said to Ilsley about decisions, etc. He said Ilsley had talked to him about it and while he had not said just the same thing to him he had used the same language or the equivalent of it. He said he felt I was right in advising Ilsley not to accept the position. I was told this afternoon they were quite anxious about Ilsley's health in the Department. I could see at Council today he was very nervous. In the House he seemed quite tired."

That evening Mackenzie King telephoned the White House and "dictated a message to a clerk there to give to Mr. Truman, letting him know the decision of Ilsley and Towers. It would be a great misfortune if Canada lost either of those men. Others can be found for the job they are being sought for, but others cannot so easily be found to replace them here."

With the debate on the Address successfully and safely concluded on March 28, Mackenzie King's interest in the proceedings of the House of Commons seemed to wane. However, a potentially troublesome issue came up in the House on April 4. Philias Côté, the Liberal member for Matapedia-Matane, had introduced a private bill to change the name of Dominion Day to Canada Day and the Prime Minister, who was not in the House, learned that the Progressive Conservatives had moved the six months hoist. He telephoned to tell the Liberal House leader "to go right ahead and put the Bill through. In the meantime there had been a motion to adjourn which, however, was voted down in the House. Second reading was carried by a good majority, and tonight the third reading also by a good majority.

"I rang up Cote . . . and congratulated him very warmly. He told me if he had not embarrassed me in any way he would be content now to die happy. I told him far from embarrassing me I was very pleased that the

Bill had gone through. . . . He said I will be your servant all my life – do anything you wish. He had felt a little concerned lest he had gone counter to the wishes of the Government. He said all of them had gathered from what I said at Caucus yesterday that I would favour the Bill, which I certainly do. I am pleased at this being a part of what has been achieved in rounding out Canada as a country in the years of my administration." In the event, the bill did not pass the Senate.

To add to the government's problems, labour unrest in Canada had been increasing steadily during the early months of 1946. Union membership had risen dramatically during the war years and formal collective bargaining procedures had been adopted in many leading corporations and mass production industries by 1946. Despite greater union security, guaranteed by legislation, most industrial unions became more militant and aggressive after the war, a product of the stresses of reconstruction and readjustment to a peace-time economy. In addition, the self-consciousness of and internal strains in some newly organized industrial unions tended to push union leaders into pressing demands which appeared extravagant to management and government. Aggressiveness and militancy were the main features of the annual brief to the Cabinet presented by the Canadian Congress of Labour on April 5. "The statement," Mackenzie King wrote, "was so written as to be defiant of the Government and calculated to stir up industrial unrest in the country. Mitchell made a rather poor speech I thought. Ilsley spoke very well. The others declined to speak. Conroy when asked to speak made a sort of apology for the language in the presentation. Said I had done a magnificent job but went on to criticize the rest. I debated much while listening to the reading of the memo and the speeches whether I would say anything or sail into the gathering. I decided to let them see just what I thought of any labour organization approaching the Government in the way they had. When I got up I spoke to them about writing 'Industry and Humanity' after the last war and finding in a sun-dial the key to what position meant in human relations. Then spoke of the kind of approach they had made which was intended to be provocative. Conroy had spoken of the possibility of our being angry at what they had said. I told him I was not angry but I felt sad at heart to think of what it means to Labour to have its case presented in the way in which their case had been. I referred to a couple of paragraphs in their statement: one which said the Government had not tried to do anything but was prepared to let things drift to get into the worst depression. I told Mosher if that was what he thought of me and the Government we would have to part company. I spoke about the use of rough language and how it had helped to bring on the last war and of human reactions to that kind of thing. I went pretty strong, though careful in the choice of my words. Conroy felt it necessary to try and get in a last word and said something about their having to put forward their presentation in frank, brutal workingmen's language.

"The Ministers were apparently quite delighted with what I said. I understand the pressmen felt the same. They were all a bit surprised, but several of them said they wished Hansard had been there to get down what I said. The suggestion was made by some of them that I should accompany them to the front of the Parliament Buildings where a photograph was to be taken. I did not feel I should, so went directly to the Cabinet meeting."

Social life in the capital became increasingly active during these months and one departure from the Ottawa diplomatic corps particularly affected Mackenzie King. On April 3 he had a farewell dinner for Malcolm MacDonald who was retiring as British High Commissioner in Ottawa. MacDonald arrived at Laurier House fifteen minutes early to have a private word with his host. He indicated that what he had to say "was very secret and asked me if there was anyone listening. I told him no." MacDonald then announced that he planned to marry Mrs. John Rowley, an Ottawa woman whose husband had been killed during the war. The Prime Minister was delighted. "It was plain that Malcolm was completely happy and more delighted about this than anything. His plan is to go to Malaya, open up the Government House there, get settled, then fly back to England. On his way back to Malaya come and be married in Ottawa in September. He said he would want me here at that time. I am really very happy about this as I think it is very wise. Malcolm would have found life in Malaya very lonely. It will now be a glorious adventure."

Mackenzie King enjoyed the party immensely. Before his guests left, he "read aloud the little passage from Ramsay MacDonald's speech when he was here in Ottawa, referring to the homes that we make for ourselves. Showed Malcolm the inscriptions reminiscent of the long friendship I had enjoyed with his father. An interesting fact which Malcolm reminded us all at the table was that it was just five years ago today that I met him at the station on his arrival at Ottawa as High Commissioner. Brought him to Laurier House to lunch and then took him to Earnscliffe. That circle is complete."

One of the most welcome foreign visitors to Ottawa in 1946 was Léon Blum who arrived on April 4 and came to Laurier House that afternoon accompanied by the French Ambassador. Blum, a prewar socialist premier of France who had been interned by the Germans during the war, was on a special mission to Washington for General de Gaulle. Ernest

Post-War Economic Problems   197

Bertrand, at Mackenzie King's request, came "to help in translation. Blum was much touched when we met at the door. He told me during the evening that mine was the first telegram he received after the German defeat. It was followed by one from Attlee and Churchill. He has a fine appearance – is a very handsome man. He gave me a lengthy account of his experiences. Said he had found fighting against his own men much worse than being in prison in Germany. . . .

"Blum spoke nicely of de Gaulle. Seemed to have a pretty strong feeling against Pétain still. Said France has suffered very much, particularly through destruction of bridges and the like, done by the Allies, to prevent the Germans coming in at the end. He spoke of the distress generally but I felt he did not emphasize unduly the problem of starvation. I was very much moved by his whole account and fine noble appearance of the man himself. I was very proud to have him in my house and as a friend."

The Prime Minister and Blum had another talk at the House of Commons on April 8. Blum "said he had nothing to add to what he had told a group of Ministers the other day, except he wished to say to me he could not exaggerate the need there was for wheat and meat. That the conditions were very grave in the matter of food. He asked about the statistics that he had brought and said he would be pleased after we had looked them over, if we could arrange at our convenience to have French experts come over and work out the best arrangements for exports and imports under our credit for the period of the next five years. I was to send him word to Washington. Later I let Robertson know and he is looking into the matter. M. Blum then spoke quite earnestly about himself. He said that he wanted me to know that he and I held the same views; that his aim and purpose was the same as mine. He did not intend however to have anything more to do with party politics as such. What time was left to him he wished to devote to furthering friendship and good-will between nations; above party and above class. I thanked him for even remotely mentioning my name in association with his own and spoke again of how greatly I admired his life and work and the service he had rendered the world. As I looked at him intently I felt he was none too strong; that the years of imprisonment had told on him. There is too a fine refinement in his countenance. He is one of the great company of martyrs and saints."

That evening there was a dinner for Blum at the French Embassy. Mr. Speaker Fauteux "presented Blum with a number of books. I got Bracken, Coldwell and myself together and thanked Fauteux for presenting these books on our behalf. I then got all present to join in a circle and sing 'Happy Birthday,' 'For He's a Jolly Good Fellow.' M. Blum looked very happy. In saying goodbye to him he spoke with deep feeling to me about his visit and then kissed me on both cheeks. It was really very touching to see the warmth of his feeling. He said he thanked me du fond du cœur. Words cannot begin to express the feeling I have of admiration and friendship for him. He represents to me the very pinnacle of statesmanship; an honourable, true, fearless man, defender of the rights of the people. One who has fought their battles in the truest sense of the word; gifted, highly cultured, very learned and skilful." Mackenzie King's somewhat emotional friendship with Léon Blum was renewed later in the year in Paris.

The new Governor-General of Canada, Viscount Alexander, arrived in Ottawa on April 12. Characteristically, the Prime Minister described the event in great detail in his diary. Except for one or two minor slips, which irritated Mackenzie King, the welcoming ceremonies went well. In his judgment, Alexander "made a fine impression. He really is a remarkably fine type. Very modest, very firm, and self contained, and alert. He looked exceedingly well. His arrival was greeted with enthusiasm. I felt very proud of the way in which the whole ceremony went. . . ."

The Prime Minister called at Government House later in the afternoon. He told Alexander he "had come to say how pleased I was he had arrived. I asked if everything was all right, if there was anything I could do. I then spoke about Montgomery's visit. Showed him the communication from Montgomery and my reply. It is plain to me from the way he received the communications that he is not any too fond of Montgomery. He said that it would be all right so far as he was concerned if he came in September, but he could not feel that he would have to alter his plans in any way himself. He had not arranged his tour of Canada as yet. The only thing that will have to be watched would be to see that Montgomery and he did not clash at any place, both being, for example, at Kingston's military college at the same time. When I said that Montgomery had wanted to come some time before, he said he knew that, but he knew also that they were opposed in England to his coming before he himself came out. I said that that was also our view. He mentioned that Montgomery's visit would be partly in official duty, as he would want to see our C.G.S. He is now Chief of Staff and would have much work to do. I explained about there being little chance in shipping matter to fix a definite date.

"I gave the Governor extra copies of the Address of Welcome. He said he was glad to have them as he would like to send one to the King. He knew that the King would be much interested. I told him I had sent a cable earlier in the day to Lascelles to transmit to the King. He then said to me: 'This is a very nice place.' He said he had been out exploring and he thought it was delightful. I said I feared he might find it a bit lonely. He said more than that, he was glad to have a chance to see something of his own family.

"I spoke to him about an invitation to dinner and said I hoped he would come to Laurier House one evening. This was left to be arranged. I told him about Laurier House and Kingsmere and of my spending Sundays out there. He said Churchill always went to Chequers for the week-end."

Mackenzie King was convinced that "Alexander will not tolerate anything that is not strictly correct. That he is right in that. I told H.E. that I thought perhaps I had been a bit spoiled at G.H. and of the close friendship I had with the different Governors and may have left most things assumed or undone that otherwise I should pay attention to. I hoped he would let me know at any moment that he wished to see me; I would be available at any time. I then spoke to him about touring the West. I said I thought his presence there at this time would be particularly helpful. I would like him to go out to the West right up to the new highway – into the Alaska zone and see a little for himself about the whole lay of the land there. I said I did not know what future might bring but that we would have to have regard for any situation that might arise. This caused the Governor to say: I was very glad to see how you dealt with the situation that has arisen here. He said: I know the Russians. They will respect you greatly for that. One thing they have contempt for is anyone who is afraid of them or of standing up for his right. I said we would talk over that situation some time at his pleasure but that the whole situation was something we would have to face. We had to look at it in a realistic way. He said: my sword is at your disposal if you ever need it." The Prime Minister dined alone with the Alexanders at Government House on April 15 and again was favourably impressed.

With a small majority in the House of Commons, the relationship between the Liberal cabinet and caucus became even more critical than usual. Caucus was restive and on April 12 the Prime Minister met the Liberal whips who wanted to talk about "the lack of contact of Ministers with Members, Ministers not assisting each other in debate, absence of our Members from the House while others stayed in; no attention paid to forming study groups, and ending up finally with not enough entertainment for Members, etc. I spoke to them quietly and sympathetically for about an hour, giving them my own position, my inability to arrange for organization of office, etc., and my views of what would become of the party if the Members themselves did not take on these tasks. I said that Canada's Liberal party would suffer a fate similar to that of the Liberal party in England. . . . I spoke of the limitations of my strength."

One of the key areas where communication between members of the caucus and the cabinet seemed particularly weak was the question of price control policy. The need for controls had not ceased with the end of the war. Serious shortages of many types of commodities persisted and, in the face of rising production costs, inflated war-time incomes, and high prices in other countries, controls were needed to prevent a sudden inflationary spiral of prices and costs in Canada. An important first step in the dismantling of controls occurred in February 1946 when price controls were suspended on a number of goods and services, principally non-staple commodities relatively unimportant in the average family budget. Reflecting increased production costs, maximum prices of iron and steel products and pulp and paper products were allowed to rise on April 1, 1946. Price increases were also authorized for furniture and for butter, pork and certain other food products. It was emphasized that these steps did not represent a weakening of the government's anti-inflationary policies but, instead, a planned policy of adjustment to peace-time conditions. When Mackenzie King returned to Laurier House late in the evening on April 12, the policeman on duty told him that the Minister of Agriculture had telephoned to say he had heard on the radio that the price ceiling on agricultural implements would be lifted as a consequence of the increase in steel prices already authorized by the Wartime Prices and Trade Board. Gardiner, the Prime Minister reported, "was in quite a state about it. I could not believe my ears. Not a word had been said of it in Council to anyone. Announcement had been made by [Donald] Gordon [the chairman of the Board]. I decided to call the Cabinet together in the morning at 10.00 A.M. if morning press confirmed the statement."

The following morning (Saturday, April 13) Mackenzie King discovered that the report was correct and called a meeting of the Cabinet for 10.30 A.M. When the meeting was over, he was convinced that he had "saved, or partially saved, a situation that might easily have split the whole Liberal party. Ilsley admitted to Council that he was to blame; he and Gordon had had a talk together, very rushed. Gordon had said he agreed there had to be either more subsidies or allow the price to rise, on account of the price of steel. He had left Gordon under the impression there would be a further consideration of the matter, but they had not seen each other since. Ilsley himself had not known that the announcement had been made.

"I pointed out that on Monday, we would be accused of letting this announcement be released late Friday night as the House would not be sitting on Saturday and Sunday. Our own people would be very concerned and opposition would give us severe chastising. They would all be arrayed against us. Gardiner stressed about the need of putting out some statement about increase of prices. Everyone felt much strained. One recognized

Ilsley had been overworking. That it was difficult to say much. I did what I could to ease the situation."

The Minister of Finance prepared a statement over the weekend and, after securing Cabinet approval, read it in the House of Commons on April 15. "I felt we were certain to be in for a time and we were when the House opened at 3," Mackenzie King wrote. "Ilsley fortunately had his statement, was able to get it in before other leaders. Each of the three was ready and moved to adjourn the House to discuss a matter of urgent public importance. There was some confusion through the Speaker seeking to prevent the discussion. I was able I think to save an appeal from the Speaker's ruling which I feel sure would have carried had he not permitted at the right stage a free discussion of the whole matter. Throughout the afternoon and evening, the Government was attacked by all opposition groups and some of our own members. Ilsley made a good defence late at night. Also Gardiner played the game very well. I thought Bracken showed up well at the end in making clear that all the opposition were after was to protest against the action that had been taken and more particularly its timing and lack of relationship with wages and prices. The Government had certainly been placed wholly in the wrong. First by the Prices Board in issuing the statement when it did and secondly, by Ilsley in not having the whole matter considered, as it should have been, in the light of political significance. We deserved all we got, and for that reason I did not try to do other than see that there was fair play in the House. I am not at all sure, however, that this particular happening is not the beginning of a little breach – of a crack in the Government's position which will widen steadily as we seek to deal with the matter of removing controls and the position that will arise therewith. The truth is these are inevitable consequences of what was done in the war.

"I thought all the Members showed great consideration for Ilsley as indeed they ought. It is apparent, however, that he lacks political judgment. The discussion in Council was worth while. If we had not had the meeting on Saturday, I do not know where we would have been."

At the Cabinet meeting on April 17 the elimination of the two cents per quart consumer subsidy on milk was discussed. It was "decided to leave over until after Easter recess announcement regarding removal of subsidy on milk which may mean a few cents' increase a quart. The whole thing is bound up with wage contracts, etc. We concluded it was the right thing to let labour know in advance of this increase rather than have it come in the autumn, particularly as the increased milk flow comes in the months of May and June. Ilsley confessed he was a bit timorous about making the announcement today. We shall have to take a lot of grief on decontrols.

There must be decontrols if there is to be relief in taxation." The subsidy was cancelled on June 1, 1946, and control over milk prices was returned to the provincial governments.

Reflecting on his colleagues in his diary for April 19, the Prime Minister wrote: "Claxton is the most thorough, useful and promising of the young men. I shall not be surprised if he becomes the choice of the party as my successor. Abbott would be a contender, and has some gifts which are not as apparent at first glance as those possessed by Claxton. The latter, however, has a wider knowledge, and I think sounder judgment."

Three days later Mackenzie King received a long telegram from the British Prime Minister urging him "very strongly" to come to Britain before May 12 to participate in the closing sessions of the meeting of Commonwealth Prime Ministers. Earlier he had told Attlee that the pressure of domestic business would prevent him from attending the opening of the conference. "I felt quite annoyed when I read in it reference to public opinion in Britain being disappointed if I were not present," Mackenzie King wrote. "The public opinion I have to consider is that of Canada. It annoys me beyond words to have this effort made, which is very largely one of appearance, but mostly to commit the Dominions if possible in Imperial affairs, to have pressure put on from a Government in Britain as though our Government were in some way subordinate to it. I told Robertson this afternoon we would hold to our original decision and to have a message drafted on that line. The British loan has still to go through. The Dominion-Provincial Conference and its findings have to be reckoned with. The Budget to be settled, and my External Affairs estimates to be dealt with. These are matters to which our Parliament attaches real importance and which concern in no uncertain way the future of the Party itself. It is the height of folly that I should be expected, as Prime Minister, to leave Parliament, to go and meet Evatt, of Australia, and Nash, of New Zealand, their Premiers being in their own countries, and only Smuts, who has come to Britain much as I have under a good deal of protest. He no doubt is glad to be in England and away from Africa. His associations are so largely with friends and public men in Britain."

The next day (April 23) the Prime Minister replied that he could not possibly arrive in the United Kingdom before May 18. The Cabinet was consulted on the matter and he noted that "Ilsley openly expressed the wish that I would stay, and all others agreed that if at all possible I should not go. I told them I did not want to go at all, but they must expect to find some criticism in Parliament for refusal."

At this time, the third meeting of the Dominion-Provincial Co-ordinating Committee was imminent. At the second meeting, which had concluded on February 1, the federal and provincial governments had agreed to meet again on April 25. In the interval, there had been no evidence of a softening of the views of Ontario and Quebec on the federal government's proposals and, in Ottawa, insistence on the need for centralization of taxing authority had not diminished even though Mackenzie King really was no closer to an acceptance or understanding of the Keynesian arguments for the use of central fiscal and monetary policies as economic stabilizers. Parliament adjourned on April 12 to make room for the meeting and this prompted the Prime Minister to note that Ilsley "stated seriously a day or two ago he saw no hope of our reaching agreement on financial matters with the Provinces and had come to the conclusion we were giving far too much money to them. He used the expression in dealing with this situation of increasing expenditures and trying to reduce taxation, he was like a man in a fog; did not know just where he was at at all. This is about the position he is in with the financial worries he has now to contend with. I am pleased there is not going to be an attempt to go on increasing subsidies to the Provinces. I think that is a wrong method to pursue."

The Cabinet as a whole began serious preparations for the meeting on April 23. "Ilsley said quite frankly he could not see where things were getting to," Mackenzie King wrote. "As far as he could tell, budgets would have to be from now on for some time to the extent of two billion dollars. He did not see how it was going to be possible to balance these budgets and at the same time make any reduction in taxation; also keep up vast expenditures on social services, war veterans outlays, which have gone up by leaps and bounds. Family allowances were also taking large amounts. He and other members of Council were doubtful if we would reach a settlement at the forthcoming Conference. I myself think a great mistake has been made by taking vast sums from the federal treasury and giving them to provinces by way of subsidies. Much better for everyone [to have] the body spending the money, the body required to raise the necessary taxation. However, we have all been pushed into this new method of financing for which I think Keynes perhaps has been mainly responsible in influencing governments of the U.S. and Canada, etc. Certainly the policy that Clark has advocated. I personally doubt very much if a serious situation does not come within a very few years. It may be that a period of prosperity will carry the situation for a couple of years, but a high level of employment, adequate to our needs, to prevent reduction of taxation, is not something that I believe any country can keep up."

At the Cabinet meeting the next day, with Clark and Skelton in attendance, another five hours were spent preparing for the conference. Mackenzie King reported that his "colleagues [were] much concerned over questions of taxation of corporations – on the one hand, danger of driving provinces into nationalization and socialization of industry, and on the other, if Federal Government tries to do too much from that source, the inability of getting revenue unless that source tapped. Also a difficult problem in that Ontario Hydro gets away from taxation whereas Light, Heat and Power Co. of Quebec would be taxed. Clark advanced the idea that where Federal Government and Provinces were both doing taxing, lumping sums together and splitting in half – crediting the Provinces with their share. This may help to keep things where they are."

"We continued going over the whole document clause by clause. I felt very tired and during part of the afternoon, could hardly keep awake, partly I think to having changed my clothes and put on lighter shoes, day being very warm. Ilsley seemed quite baffled by the situation confronting him. After the meeting he came to my room and told me he really did not know whether he could hold out. He had gotten out of going to G.H. [Government House] tonight but said there was little use of his trying to rest. He would wake at 4 o'clock in the morning and would be going over what could be done, his budget, also what would take place at the Conference – too many things coming together. He wanted to get out of the Finance Department altogether. He spoke of the possibility of Clark taking this on. I spoke about the Prices Board going to one of the others. He said he could deal with that, he knew Gordon and they worked together. There was little difficulty there. It was the budget that was worrying him. He said he certainly would have to leave the Government in August, if he could hold out that long. He would try to do the best he can.

"I said I would have a talk with St. Laurent and Abbott about the whole situation. He thanked me for not going to England sooner than I am. Said he would have found it very hard to be left alone. It just would not be possible for me to go any sooner as I see it.

"MacKinnon told me tonight that Ilsley had said to him he wished he might break down so that he would not have to tackle the job of the budget."

With an exhausted Minister of Finance and no great hope of success, the federal delegates met their provincial colleagues at 10.30 A.M. on Thursday, April 25. The Co-ordinating Committee met in camera and, according to the Prime Minister, "all settled down as if we had just left the proceedings a few hours before." Mackenzie King "did not attempt any formal speech but made a few introductory remarks.... Outlined the procedure, etc." Duplessis was the first of the provincial premiers to speak. "He made it clear he did not like proceedings on the basis of subsidies. I thought he went so far as to say he would not agree to that."

Premier Drew spoke next and concentrated on procedural matters. He demanded "an open session as soon as possible. He did not want to make any statement except before the public so that his position could not be misrepresented. He claimed that other points of view had been put out to the public since the last meeting. He rather left the impression he wanted the Conference to succeed but I gathered that what was in his mind [was] to come to some agreement [for] the next three years, but that sooner or later the whole issue would have to go before the public. My guess is he and Duplessis have framed up an issue for the next general elections: Provincial rights versus centralization and are preparing for that. I doubt if he will let the present Conference fall entirely through, but will probably make a strong plea for certain principles being adopted. He sort of pressed for the open Conference at once. Other Prime Ministers were opposed to that. Wanted more in the way of discussion.

"The day was taken up first by the reading of the questions and the answers by St. Laurent and later taking them up one by one with Ilsley setting forth the Government's position in more detail. It was clear he was very tired. He spoke very quietly and quite low through the whole proceedings. Almost a note of despair in his voice.

"Tonight, before adjournment, Drew presented his motion for an open session tomorrow. I kept holding the motion before the Committee, allowing them pretty wide latitude in discussion. Largely as a result of John Hart's representations, it was agreed an open session should be left over until Monday morning at 10.30. The Co-ordinating Committee should meet again tomorrow to continue discussion re pros and cons. The additional questions taken up were Duplessis' brief and a supplementary brief presented by Douglas of Saskatchewan. We were ready to go on in the afternoon but not in the morning. However, the way things came out in the end was all to the good so far as the Federal Government is concerned. It gives us Saturday to meet in Council again and to get out a statement of our position clearly before the public, at the same time with others presenting theirs anew.

"Drew kept insisting that after the discussion in plenary session, the Co-ordinating Committee might come back into a secret session to work out details on the basis of the principles accepted and adopted. I feel in a way that the Premiers are rather determined not to let this Conference fail, but to come to some agreement on a temporary basis; to arrange something for 3 years with the proviso that, in the interval, we will try to really work out a better system of allocation of taxes, giving greater rights to the Provinces. Claxton and Pickersgill seemed to think that Drew and Duplessis wanted the Conference to fail but wanted it to appear that nobody was satisfied with the Dominion proposals and that they will be relieved therefore of having the Conference break up.

"Ilsley himself has come now where he will not be sorry if the Conference did not succeed. Personally I have myself never liked the subsidy business. I fought it years ago and the whole line taken by the Finance Department from the start which leads to centralization which I think is a mistake."

The next day (April 26) the Prime Minister presided at the committee's meeting from 11.30 until 1.00 P.M. "General discussion, but not much headway made. . . . Back for luncheon and a short rest. Again, to the House of Commons to a meeting of the . . . Committee. Got agreement on adjournment at 5, with right of the Federal Government to present its case first, at the sittings on Monday, and Drew to follow. I was able, during the day, to get the several Provinces with the exception of Quebec and Ontario, duly committed on their attitude toward the Government taking over the personal income tax, also the corporation . . . tax and the succession duty tax, and the right of the Provinces to share in the latter. Duplessis agreed he was ready to concede the principle of the income tax and the corporation tax. Drew would not say where he stood on anything till he had a chance to make his statement in public himself. All the statements were conditional on getting proper compensation. This has brought us along further than we have been at any time.

"I confess I was impressed by Macdonald's statements as to the impotent position in which the Premier of a Province would be placed without any field of taxation left to himself. He was urging that several fields of taxation be left to the Provinces. With this I am in sympathy. . . . I have never agreed with what was done by a group of the Cabinet working in close association with the Finance Department at a time when I was either away or not in a position to give much attention to the Dominion's financial proposals. Still the Cabinet having reached agreement I have held with them ever since but I think the really sound position is along lines that would reserve definite fields of taxation to the Dominion and Provincial Governments respectively, avoiding double taxation and causing the Government which has to do with the spending of public money to be obliged for the raising of the necessary revenues."

The Committee adjourned for the weekend but the federal Cabinet met on Saturday, April 27. Mackenzie King "spoke quite strongly about the situation. Said I thought we were incurring a greater responsibility than ever now that we had a chance to get the income, corporation and succession duty tax; that I felt to secure that ground for the Dominion for practically all the time to come was something very much worth while along with the power of indirect taxation. Then I said the Provinces ought to be given some fields of taxation for themselves. That we should lessen the amounts we were giving to them in payments for the fields they had surrendered or cause them to give us an amount of payment for the fields of taxation we were allowing them to take and work out a settlement on that basis. I knew that some of the others did not have that view but I thought it was my duty to express it. I said I felt all my Liberal training in the past as well as what I had said caused me to feel the wisdom of not allowing an issue to be raised on the endeavour on the part of the Federal Government to centralize everything in Ottawa but to keep to certain measures of Provincial autonomy. That the Liberal background was all in that direction and that we were going far too rapidly with some of our social legislation. I mentioned that I thought the family allowances tax was right but all these grants to the Provinces for different health measures, etc., were simply handing from the Federal Treasury so much money to Provinces to spend in ways which were helping them to fight us politically and were not economical.

"Howe made a very good proposal that the amusement tax should be left to the Provinces. They, to surrender the health grants. I favoured that. Also spoke strongly of giving them the gasoline tax on surrendering something else. The suggestion was made for them to take over the old age pensions under 70 in exchange. I favoured that. We got some modifications but only in the form of alternative proposals, not a raising of the total amount but getting what we call a financial equivalent.

"Dr. Clark is really the one who is responsible for members of Government not doing what I think the judgment of most of them inclines them to do. Ilsley feels helpless without him. Does not favour I know some of his views, but yields to them as he cannot himself handle things without him. In Cabinet today he said he felt terrible to think he would be leaving to his successor a position that was impossible to meet and that that represented all he had done as Minister of Finance. I was deeply depressed. I could see he is almost ready for the breaking point. Indeed, I feel terribly sorry for him. He is just like a lamb being slaughtered, with the things he has to do and he had come to the point where some of the bills of the past have to be paid. I felt I owed it to myself to speak out very strongly and put my position on record.

"I said to them I thought it might cost the Liberal Party power. We were simply allowing Drew to take the Liberal position and to get the support of Macdonald and others and that we could not hope to win with Provinces against us one after the other. I spoke of the advantages of the Family Allowances legislation in that people who received their cheques got them from the Federal Government and not from the Provincial Government. They knew we were responsible and were carrying out our responsibility."

It had been agreed that the Prime Minister would make the first speech at the plenary session of the Dominion-Provincial Conference on April 29 and he worked on revisions of the text all day Sunday. In the sessions of the Co-ordinating Committee, all the provinces except Quebec and Ontario had accepted the federal government's proposals in principle but some, led by Angus Macdonald, the Premier of Nova Scotia, continued to urge that some minor tax fields should remain within exclusive provincial jurisdiction. The Quebec government seemed to have conceded the personal and corporate income tax fields to the federal government but was not prepared to give up the right to levy succession duties. Premier Drew's position was unclear since he had refused to outline his government's proposals in closed session. In an effort to salvage something from the negotiations, the federal government was now prepared to increase the guaranteed minimum annual subsidy from $12 to $15 per capita and to permit provinces that wished to continue levying succession duties to do so subject to an adjustment in their annual subsidies and with some provision for offsetting credits to the taxpayer. In addition, the federal government agreed to withdraw from the amusement and gasoline tax fields in return for an adequate financial equivalent. A few days later Ilsley also conceded the tax on parimutuel betting.

At 10.30 A.M. on April 29, Mackenzie King opened the Conference proceedings in the Senate Chamber. He read "through the speech which we prepared last night. was followed by Drew who had a little of ground cut out from under his feet by some of the changes the Government had made since Friday." Ontario's submission suggested an alternative approach to tax-sharing and differed in principle from the federal proposals on some important issues. Rejecting the three-year moving average, Premier Drew suggested that, in return for exclusive federal jurisdiction in the personal and corporate income tax fields, each province should receive an unspecified annual subsidy per capita (the "X" factor) augmented by the ratio of gross national product per capita in each of the three years of the agreement to gross national product per capita in the base year, 1941. In addition, the federal government would vacate the succession duty field and concede the gasoline, amusement, parimutuel,

Post-War Economic Problems 209

security transfer, and electricity tax fields to the provinces. Mackenzie King was impressed. Drew "made what I thought was a very good speech, but too long. He repeated himself, but on the whole I confess I was more sympathetic with his point of view than I was with our own. Except as a temporary measure to meet the situation in this transitional period, and as it has grown out of the war, I would not try to defend our position for a moment. Drew concluded about a quarter to 1; we then adjourned.

"St. Laurent, Ilsley, Clark, Howe and Skelton came to my office where we had a short talk, Ilsley seemed to feel that there was no longer any hope of any agreement being reached. He seemed to be quite anxious as to how Angus Macdonald would act. I told him I thought Angus would follow the line he had taken in the secret session. I suggested again that we consider trying to secure from the Provinces payment for letting them have the smaller revenue fields themselves and reducing correspondingly the payments we are making for the fields they had sold to us. Clark, however, always raises objections to this on the score that we must have all the fields to be able to meet what will be required in the way of taxes. The truth is the Finance Department has allowed such tremendous expenditures, and made so many commitments that it finds itself in the position that it is going to be very difficult to work out. Ilsley is too worn and tired and sensitive to expect anything from him in the way of seeing other sides of the situation at this time. St. Laurent I think shares my view in large part."

The Conference resumed at 3.45 P.M. In Mackenzie King's judgment, Duplessis "made a fool speech; absolutely nothing to it but demagogic platitudes. It was in the nature of an appeal to the masses; thought of centralization and comparing the Government with Hitler, gangsters, etc. Was really very awful for the head of a great Province.

"I was greatly disappointed in Macdonald. He did not go as far as he had gone in trying to help but went to other extremes. Almost to an insulting degree in his reference to the position in which the Provinces were being placed under Dominion proposals. I thought he might well have had a little more regard for Ilsley who is from his own Province and who was ready to help him when he was seeking to break up the Government over the conscription issue. I do not trust him at all. Had he repeated what he had said in camera I would have been quite content; but he went far beyond that in seeking to side with Drew against the Government.

"McNair, I thought, was on the whole helpful in saying wherein he was prepared to accept the Dominion's proposals.

"I was glad Garson spoke for half an hour before 6 as he supported the Government proposals very strongly. He made out a good case for the Dominion taking over the succession duties. It helped to balance the day's proceedings. He will continue tomorrow."

When the Conference resumed on the morning of April 30, "Drew started to raise a question with Claxton over some article in the Toronto Star. All cheap politician's stage play. I thought Claxton in his quiet way got quite the better of Drew. The several Premiers began then to continue the discussion on my statement of Monday.

"Garson was first, continuing from last night. He made I thought a most effective speech – very telling. He was followed by Hart of B.C. who was disappointing in not giving much help to the Federal Government. In fact if anything he made the situation a little more difficult.

"Jones, of P.E.I., was just impossible. It was childish to listen to his talk of the Island in pre-Confederation days.

"After Mr. Hart had finished we met in my office. There was a short meeting with Ilsley, St. Laurent, Howe, Claxton, Clark and myself at which we reviewed the situation. Once again, I stressed the desirability of considering giving the Provinces a couple of smaller yielding taxes. Clark holds out very strongly against anything of the kind and Ilsley follows suit. I said to someone, I think it was Pickersgill, I feared the Finance Department's attitude was too much that of a small boy trying to take nuts out of a jar and in the end endeavouring to take them all he will lose them all. We did outline in a way the speech that Ilsley should make tomorrow in reviewing the Dominion situation. I kept stressing to him to emphasize the financial equivalent idea. I confess however I did not feel any too secure in the Government's position. As a matter of fact there have not been the right people, or enough of them, handling this business from the start. Had Norman Rogers been alive, and we had had the benefit of him and a few other men of broader vision the Government would probably not have got into so many commitments before we could see our way of meeting them."

In the afternoon session, Mackenzie King felt that Premier Douglas made "a very good speech on distinctly helpful lines. Helpful to the Government. Manning from Alberta followed also with a good speech, but I thought [there] was too much high-faluting admonition of what should be done without quite enough appreciation of what was involved. Still, it caused the day to end with at least another Province on our side."

The Minister of Finance replied for the federal government on May 1 with what Mackenzie King thought was "an exceptionally fine speech. Indeed, I have heard him make no better speech. It is something that I think all Finance Ministers will in years to come have to take account of. I told him afterwards that I never heard him speak as well. He spoke largely without notes, very carefully, discreetly, and persuasively. I felt, when he was through, I did not care how the Conference went – that our position had been correctly placed on record. He was followed by Drew who made, I thought, a very brutal kind of attack upon him. He was very arrogant in speaking – most unfair in imputing feelings to Ilsley while he spoke. He clearly kept talking for a time so as to get on again in the afternoon. I thought he had really done his cause an injury.

"We had a meeting in my office afterwards. Ilsley said he had worked until two last night. He had felt, before going to bed, like a man who was nearly beside himself, and that the best he would do was to shoot himself. He was terribly depressed. I told him to go and read Lincoln's speech at Gettysburg, where he thought he had made such a terrible failure and found out afterward it was the speech of his life. All were agreed that he had made a fine presentation of the Dominion's position. I was glad that he went so far as adding pari-mutuel to amusement and gasoline taxes as among the number he was prepared to consider for financial equivalents."

During the afternoon, Drew "continued his speech more effectively than in the morning. He was followed by Duplessis, whose name ought to be Duplicity. A most asinine kind of speech – all attempt to have it appear that the Dominion was for centralization, etc. Nothing said to help an agreement one way or the other. Macdonald was very different from what he was yesterday. He evidently saw he was going to lose what the agreement would bring to Nova Scotia and rather work toward bringing the party together. Manning followed, [and], to the surprise of everyone, made a very bitter attack on the Government. He said he had spoken last night about the Conference hanging in the balance. He thought it was more so now. If there was a failure it would be because of Ilsley's rigidity. He was prepared to accept the agreement but he certainly lent ammunition to Drew.

"Douglas followed and was very sensible and helpful really.

"When we came back to my room at six, Ilsley was feeling pretty depressed. I think he saw that what I had been telling him right along was only too true. That it was a mistake to hold on to all these little taxes; that we should have come out and tried to give the Provinces at least two or three small fields of their own. It was exactly the same kind of mistake that he made over the Members' salaries. He would not yield a little at the start and had to pay treble later on. He himself began to wonder if he could now give something.

"St. Laurent sees the situation very clearly himself. He and I have done what we could to influence Ilsley. Claxton was too much wrapped up in social security expenditures and too bitter in his feelings against Drew, and perhaps too inexperienced as yet; does not throw his influence the right way. I am perfectly sure that from the beginning I have taken the position that public feeling in all Provinces would be against centralization. That is how they would try to focus up the issue on what we were proposing. I have been equally strong, from the beginning of the Conference, though I have been hoping the Provinces would give us a quid pro quo for letting us have the income tax, corporation tax, and succession duty. These are the broad outlines as the public will see them. But you cannot get Clark, whose mind is wholly academic, to realize that no matter how theoretically accurate you may be or in accord with strict financial rules that what you are doing is no good unless you can get the public to understand and support it. I am really afraid that the situation we are now in will, by tomorrow night, have cost us the success of the Conference and may all too soon cost Ilsley what reserve and strength he may have left."

Mackenzie King added that he "would like to see us succeed, because I think if we do not reach an agreement, conditions are going to be unsettled and become increasingly so in Canada. I wish I were not so fatigued and felt in a position to take part in speaking in the Conference itself. As things stand, I feel that all I am good for is to exert what influence I have towards keeping matters on as even a keel as possible."

On May 2, St. Laurent spoke for the federal government at the opening of the Conference proceedings. St. Laurent "brought out what I have all along stressed most strongly, namely, that our position was being misrepresented as being that of the Provinces having given the large tax fields in exchange for a series of minor tax fields, instead of being represented as the Dominion giving payment or rent for exclusive right in three large tax fields and the Provinces were unwilling to give any payment or rent to the Dominion for being given an exclusive right in the minor fields of gasoline, amusements, and pari-mutuels taxes.

"When I met my colleagues in my office at 10.15 I urged very strongly that this should be brought out clearly and that above all we should not hesitate to make clear our readiness to give some of the local fields exclusively to the Provinces if we got financial outlay where it is now fixed. As St. Laurent has pointed out none of the Provinces have challenged our taking the position that we cannot, in total expenditures, go further than we have. What St. Laurent himself brought out most strongly, both before going into the Conference and at the Conference, was that neither Ontario nor Quebec had made clear yet what they would regard as an adequate payment for giving the Dominion exclusive rights in fields of personal income tax and corporation tax and right of continuing in inheritance tax field."

Mackenzie King added that St. Laurent "made a very sound, solid, logical speech. I felt that with what Ilsley had said on the one side and St. Laurent on the other, that our position was one that would stand the tests of whatever might come either from proceedings at the Conference, or in the years hereafter. Once he had made clear that the question was one of the rent to be paid by the Provinces on the one hand to the Dominion, and the rent to be paid by the Dominion to the Provinces on the other, for the exclusive use of certain fields of taxation, and that all that was left was to come to a decision as to what within that area would be fair, as between the Dominion and the Provinces, I felt that we had really got into our right position before the public. Even at the Conference itself we would not be as we were, yesterday afternoon, after Manning spoke, in a wholly false light but rather in a true light with public approval of our position insured.

"Hart introduced a motion about adjourning to private session. He had spoken to me of this before the meeting. I told him not to move it until everyone had spoken. When he put it forward he made it clear others were to have a chance to speak first. The motion was seconded by Jones, before luncheon.

"After luncheon I asked Hart for it. He had framed it differently than he had worded it, by suggesting that not only should we return to the private sessions, but come back again to the report of the plenary committee. I drew his attention to this and told him I thought he should hold it as originally made, simply to adjourn Conference proceedings and to return to co-ordinating committee for discussion. We could there decide what we would do and whether we would leave matters there or come back.

"Before the motion was put forward in the afternoon, Duplessis had indicated he was going back home. Drew had made even a stronger protest about returning to closed sessions. I felt the time had come where I should get in and make it clear we were prepared to do whatever the Provinces would agree upon in the matter of open session or closed session. That that had been our attitude from the start. It gave me a chance to explain my acting in two capacities of member of the Federal Government and also Chairman of the Conference, thereby making clear that I took full responsibility for our policies, but kept free from participating in the discussion, so as to be impartial. I then came out strongly with the statement that whereas we as a Government representing all Provinces had come to an agreement on our proposals, we had not yet received any proposals from the Provinces to which they could agree. I stated I thought they should meet themselves and we would be prepared to consider any proposals which they might make, vis-à-vis those we had put forward. From this time on the Conference took a bit of a different turn. Drew came out finally with a statement as to what his mysterious "X" in an algebraic formula meant – namely $12. We got the discussion to turn on his proposal and what it meant. This brings us at last where there is a real chance of the Conference working out something which will be accepted. Ilsley has been most anxious from day to day to end everything. This I think is due to great physical exhaustion. Howe would agree to it in a moment. St. Laurent has been with me when I have sought to have the Conference continued, and in no event allowing it to terminate at our instance. I am quite sure that but for my determination on this latter point, all would have been over today. I now have a feeling that it may run over until Saturday and that by that time some kind of an agreement will be reached. My disgust for Duplessis grows greater every hour."

When the Conference met on May 3, Ilsley explained the implications of the Ontario proposal and "what it involved over and above the Dominion proposals.

"Drew followed and was followed by Duplessis. It was apparent that the two of them had made up their mind not to continue. Drew made an arrogant sort of speech, quite misrepresenting the Federal Government's position and placing his unwillingness to continue on the score that the Dominion was rigid in its many demands. Duplessis was not going to continue on the principle that the Dominion proposals meant one authority raising taxes and the other authority spending it. He brought into his speech reference to previous speeches of my own which I have wondered had not been quoted before and which I described as a process of a vicious system which it certainly is. Duplessis has never said the Government of Quebec would accept the Ontario terms for the personal and income taxes. He threatened to leave and did leave after lunch to return to Quebec. I understand he had previously arranged to have some reception there on his arrival tonight, as a great champion of autonomy for Quebec opposition to centralization.

"It was apparent when we broke up for luncheon that the Conference was practically over. Our group came to my office to talk over the course to be adopted. We all agreed that it would be unwise to have the Conference adjourn until any particular date. It was better for Ilsley to go ahead with preparation of his budget, and in his budget statement declare what he might find it necessary to do. That he should say we would take into consideration the representations that had been made at the Conference and would not go further than that.

"Angus Macdonald had suggested a meeting on June the 10th. He sent me a note this afternoon to ask what I thought of that. I told him there were too many factors involved to fix any definite date."

The Prime Minister added that "when the sessions opened this afternoon, speeches were made by Garson who was quite outspoken against Drew. McNair also spoke and Douglas. Manning said nothing. Duplessis was not present. Claxton made a speech of some length presenting the social legislation side of which earlier mention had been made by those who had spoken and which is now in a way being cast to the winds.

"Adjournment came around five. I saw that the motion was granted and there was adjournment sine die. Also a motion was put and the ayes and nays called for and the result registered as unanimous in favour of adjournment sine die. Ilsley can now go on with the preparation of his budget.

"The more I think over the whole situation the more I think that it owed its genesis to the Bank of Canada – a desire on the part of the Bank to get funds centralized in Dominion hands so that the Provinces can be controlled in the matter of their financial expenditures on social legislation by a certain Dominion control. I really feel that while, in years to come, we will have to have more and more of single government, and that the Provinces would become less important relatively, that is still a long way off. It would be much better to hold for some years to come to giving Provinces certain fields of taxation and charge them more and more with the business of raising taxes for essential services, the Dominion keeping out of these fields altogether except by seeking to maintain certain standards. Claxton being on one of the Committees has pushed the social legislation to make too many commitments in the matter of social reform, particularly any commitments for legislation involving more in the way of taxation by a levy on all classes. I am going to advise Ilsley against doing anything in the budget which means the imposition of further taxes.

"The public simply will not stand for it at this time and it is not right. We have done enough. We can meet what we are pledged to do for the veterans, in that way, but our attention must otherwise be given to the immediate needs of the people, housing, etc., and allow these social measures to follow on later.

"I was not sorry when the Conference was over. Experienced neither elation nor depression but was glad to be able now to get down to some of our own business. I do feel a real concern, however, in leaving the Government and Parliament for another six weeks at this particular time."

At the Cabinet meeting on May 6, the implications of and reasons for the Conference's failure were reviewed. Mackenzie King "spoke out very plainly. . . . I reminded my colleagues that I had said all along we were taking the wrong course in handing to the Provinces an excuse for an attack on us on the score of centralization and not allowing certain tax fields to the Provinces. I said we had a greater responsibility than ever; to consider their responsibilities once they yielded big sources of revenue for a consideration.

"I did not want to attack Ilsley too directly but it is perfectly true what Manning has said that his rigidity which is really the rigidity of Clark and Towers was what had turned some of the Provinces against us, giving Drew and Duplessis a real chance. They had not intended to meet us but as a consequence they were able to say all the Provinces to some extent were against us. I also spoke of feeling sure that what the people wanted was a reduction in taxation rather than more taxes added, and that commitments had been made with regard to what we were prepared to do in old age pensions and the like. I did not think these matters had ever been discussed in the Cabinet. I spoke particularly of the direct tax on everybody to meet old age pensions for those over 70. Until the Conference was held, I never heard mention of the poll tax or of the amount that was suggested nor did other members of the Council. Claxton has pushed these things much too far.

"In Council, Claxton was urging that he had not gone further than I had in what we had promised, in speeches from the Throne, and what I had said in my own speeches and what Ilsley had said. I sent for the speech from the Throne on the eve of elections and read it through pointing out there was not one single clause in it which did not refer to what had been done and made no promise in regard to the future except on the basis of an agreement reached with the Provinces. Everyone there was impressed by the clearness of the statement. I challenged Claxton to find any of my speeches which had gone further. I said I had been careful not to make any promises but to speak solely of our record and the ground on which we should be returned. I had never dreamt of a health programme and the like to be a matter of a year or so but that it would take years to work out an agreement with the Provinces which would help to establish a national minimum. All of this is very true but the way in which the thing has been misrepresented in the public mind is deplorable. We have gotten in far too deeply in the matter of possible outlays. . . .

"I said we were really trying to do in a year and that even before the year was up, what ought to be extended over five or ten years. I mentioned to the Cabinet the time it had taken to get old age pensions, unemployment insurance, etc. We had made the former an issue at an election. We had timed correctly the measure re family allowances and that was as far as we should have thought of going into that class of expenditure until the end of another four or five years. Cabinet agreed Ilsley should not attempt in his budget to supplement this social legislation programme by additional expenditures at the present time. We would hold to our foundational statement that what we did in those fields would be based on agreement with the Provinces. I did tell Cabinet quite frankly that the main source of difficulty had been we were acting at the instance of the Bank of Canada and through Clark who was closely associated with others in the Bank. It might be an admirable financial plan to control expenditures for the Provinces and the Dominion alike from headquarters here but that the people would never stand for it politically. It makes me really very sad to see how this whole ground has been turned out from under us and the position which was sound. The Liberal position which we had held for years is being now turned against us. Ilsley reminded me that I had approved the brief which was presented at the start. I told him I had but he would notice on reading it, how completely conditional it was. How little there was in the way of actual commitment and he would recall I had always been opposed to centralizing aspects. I had said I believed we would have to change them before getting final settlement. The proposals were only a basis. They had been changed since and gone much further since. I had never liked the subsidies and had told my colleagues so."

During the Dominion-Provincial Conference the Prime Minister received a second appeal from Attlee, strongly urging him to come to the United Kingdom as soon as possible or to send a representative who could participate in the discussions with the other Commonwealth countries. Attlee's message was delivered by the Deputy British High Commissioner on April 27. Mackenzie King was, if anything, less enthusiastic about the trip than before. He could see little point in the Commonwealth countries meeting while the British government was preoccupied with problems in India, Palestine and Ireland, the first session of the United Nations General Assembly had only recently concluded, the Security Council was debating the problem of Iran, and the Council of Foreign Ministers was deadlocked over the details of the minor peace treaties. He recalled that he had "told Attlee long ago what he could expect in the way of my coming over. That a substitute would not do. They were claiming they were wanting me for my experience and I alone could fill that role. Besides, I did not like the idea of our Government assuming responsibility without any power – for us simply to be over there to meet with a foreign minister who was a member of the Foreign Minister's Council, but not being on the Council ourselves, was to be made use of. It was repeating what was suggested last autumn. Holmes [the Deputy High Commissioner] spoke about many minor papers [in the United Kingdom] commenting against the Government for not having all the Governments represented in the picture. I told him I was sick of façades. I thought it was time we thought of reality. I thought it was a shame Churchill, Roosevelt and Stalin could have made commitments as to the whole future of Europe, as well as other parts of the world, without even consulting any government in advance. Holmes said the British Government would take the same view. I said I intend to fight against a one-man authority for all I was worth. During six years of war we had managed to settle all questions by communication or by cable. I thought in this time of peace we would do the same. However I was only too ready to help Attlee and others if circumstances permitted, but I told him confidentially of Ilsley's condition. Mentioned the impossibility of being away while the Dominion-Provincial Conference was on or for some days thereafter, while we were settling policies arriving out of the conference.

"There was also a telegram regarding the significance of the agreement signed by Attlee, President Truman and myself, regarding co-operation in the knowledge of atomic energy. The United States are refusing to give the British the information they have about the manufacturing end of the bomb. I do not like this at all. It is not square-dealing. If they had a thought of the kind in mind they should have brought it to the surface when we were being asked to sign an agreement on co-operation. It is most unfortunate the British have not the knowledge. It would take them a year or two to work it out. Meanwhile, the Americans are manufacturing bombs for all they are worth, having the secret themselves. After all England is getting in this what Russia got through Churchill's decision not to share any information. What a world this is!

"Churchill's address at Aberdeen that this is a sick world, all based on hate, is true. That is an inevitable legacy of war. There is nothing about war that is helpful in the end."

At the Liberal caucus on May 8, the Prime Minister "spoke at some little length of circumstances which made it necessary for me to go overseas, to the Conference in London. Outlined the communications that had taken place. Spoke quite strongly of my own feelings, of the care which had to be taken to see that we were not committed – either in appearance or reality, to matters that were intended to help the British Government out of difficult positions but might end us in situations that would be extremely difficult. I spoke about the work to be done in the House and the necessity for the party loyally supporting others who might be in charge during my absence. I said to them quite frankly it was well they should recognize that it might not be long before some of the present Members of the Ministry would be giving up their positions for others and younger men in the Cabinet must be prepared to take on new responsibilities and duties. I let them see plainly I myself was prepared to do what I could for a while but they must be prepared for emergent situations arising."

In his diary for May 9, Mackenzie King wrote that he felt "deeply concerned because of a letter from Attlee received yesterday making suggestions as to the kind of conference to take place when I get over to England. Many things seemed to focus today in a manner which brought many feelings to the top and caused me to speak out more emphatically than I otherwise would. First of all, we had a long meeting of the Cabinet at which many questions were discussed.... Most important of all were matters connected with increased expenditures for the maintenance of bases and ports on our Northern coasts; keeping the Alaska Highway, the Western staging route and other things in shape and in much that grew out of the last report of the Joint Board on Defence. I spoke to the Cabinet very plainly as to my convictions. I said I believed the long range policy of the Americans was to absorb Canada. They would seek to get this hemisphere as completely one as possible. They are already in one way or another building up military strength in the North of Canada. It was inevitable that for their own protection, they would have to do that. We should not shut our eyes to the fact that this was going on consciously as part of the American policy. It might be inevitable for us to have to submit to it – being so few in numbers and no longer able to look to British power for protection. I thought we should see to it that whatever was permitted was done with the full knowledge of the British and that we should aim at everything to further co-operation between all three countries.

"I declined to let Council accept recommendations of the Joint Board until after I had a chance to dicuss aspects of them with the British. I found younger members of the Cabinet seemed surprised at the vision of things as I presented them but no one was able to take exception, to what was said. I stressed the view that some others had taken in the past to geography in the end being the strongest of the determining factors in matters of the kind."

Later that afternoon Mackenzie King outlined the discussion in Cabinet for the Governor-General. "He said to me the war has changed the whole problem of strategy. So far as this continent is concerned, the strategy must necessarily be one. The United States inevitably to protect itself must take many measures in Canada which Canada herself would not be able to take. This will go on but, in the meantime, there will be developments in the world which perhaps before it is too late will result in a sort of U.S.-U.K.-Canada federation or alliance. Each maintaining our own but working co-operatively and effectively together. The atomic bomb has changed everything. It has made the north of Canada the vulnerable area of attack of this continent; even the industries of Pittsburgh, etc. I was struck by the clear vision which he seemed to have of the whole situation."

An incident in the House of Commons on May 8 only increased Mackenzie King's doubts about the meeting in London. Quite unexpectedly, Bracken asked the Prime Minister whether it was correct, as Attlee had stated in the British House of Commons, that the Dominions had been consulted on and agreed with the British government's decision to propose a staged withdrawal of their troops from Egyptian territory as part of a revision of the Anglo-Egyptian treaty of 1936. Mackenzie King, who had not seen press reports of the statement, "made it clear I was not sure that the report was correct but if it was, it could not have meant Canada. We had neither been asked for nor given advice. It irritates me beyond words to see the British try to bring all the self-governing nations into one bag, as it were, labelled 'The Dominions' as if we had a common policy on everything and seeking to make us the screen for their own inadequacies and the reason for their policies, etc. I felt strongly what the battle was likely to be in England when I go across."

In the House on May 9 several questions were asked about the London conference and Canada's part in it. Mackenzie King admitted frankly that if he "had consulted my own feelings at this time," he would have remained in Ottawa and he undertook to "be careful to refrain from committing anyone in a manner that is likely to occasion embarrassment." In writing his diary for the day, the Prime Minister realized that, since he "was very tired," he might have said "much more than I would otherwise have said. I had on my mind what I had said in Council and gave a freer expression to it in the House than I would have given, had I been more guarded. I know what I have said will excite a good deal of comment but after all Canada has done and is doing, I can afford to speak out specially as other Dominions in London have found it necessary to do so to save themselves in their own country.

"I was able to give Graydon a mild form of rebuke for an asinine question he had put on the paper. I had outlined to Robertson what I thought should be said in a message to Attlee; when, however, I came to my room at night, and found the papers which had come from England all a record of proceedings labelled 'Meeting of Prime Ministers' and all in form and substance akin to a full fledged Imperial Conference, I felt the time had come when I should speak out to save a perfectly exasperating situation once I get to London. As a result, I spent the latter part of the evening dictating what I thought should go. I confess to feeling considerably upset in having to make this protest. It has been a fight that I have had to make ever since the first Conference I attended in London in 1923. What I said in London in 1944 and by the way, it was this time two years ago, almost to the day, I shall have to repeat I think again when I go to London this time. I said the same thing at a dinner which the British gave me when I was last there."

During the morning of May 10 the Prime Minister spent some time revising his letter to Attlee. "It is much longer than I would care to have it and in some ways a little more emphatic to one who I know is having his problems and is a true friend. At the same time, I know it is not Attlee who writes the letters or who is controlling the situation. I certainly am not going to have Canada made a puppet of any official in the Dominions [Office] or any other official of the British Government. I believe that getting the position registered in Parliament yesterday and in the letter which I have sent off today, I might find the atmosphere one in which I can live in London. As Prime Minister of Canada, I do not need to be at the beck and nod of any man on earth with my nineteen years of experience in the office of Prime Minister.

"To my great surprise, this morning, I found the despatches from Britain, for the first time, were of a wholly satisfying and realistic character. It made clear that the 'Dominions' were asserting their position along lines that I have been striving for right along."

That day he completed preparations for his trip. Word came in the morning of the death of Harry Leader, the Liberal M.P. for Portage la Prairie, and the Prime Minister toyed briefly with the idea of encouraging Lester Pearson to run in the constituency. "It would be worthwhile bringing him into the Ministry at once as Minister of External Affairs. Claxton suggested getting in touch with Garson of Manitoba and getting him into the House. Either of these would be important. It is absolutely essential if Canada's future is to be saved that we should get the ablest men we possibly can into the House of Commons. That is almost the greatest service I believe I could render if it were possible in the time that remains to me."

In the afternoon he informed the Cabinet that Ilsley would be acting Prime Minister during his absence. "Ilsley then said he would like to know what procedure should be followed if the Government were defeated. That he, himself, felt that was a real possibility. The pressure would become such on the budget that he could not meet it. Members were becoming too aggressive, etc. I said that I, too, had shared the view that there was a possibility of the collapse of the party in the mood in which men were getting today. It was all part of the order of things – tension and excitement, and trying to create difficulties, to be assertive and use a kind of force drawing everything.

"We, however, must keep close together. If the Government disintegrated in any way, the party would go for good. I then told my colleagues I had spoken to Ilsley about taking on the acting Prime Ministership. He had asked whether I really thought he should; whether someone else should not take it on. He had such a load. I then spoke very feelingly of the load he had carried and what we all owed to him, and how essential it was that members should be loyal to him in my absence. Gardiner had spoken about all being united. That he wanted to have unity on Liberal principles. Made some reference to what had happened when I was away the last time. I said I thought they should have cabled me about the situation and that I would have stood firm against any action of the kind. Certainly was not in accord with Liberal principles. Ilsley wanted to know about who would have the final say. I told him he must take that responsibility as I had taken it.

"In reply to what was to be done in case of a crisis, I said that Parliament should be adjourned immediately until I got back. Ilsley said there would be all kinds of speculation as to what was going to happen. I said it was much better that that course should be taken than that he should follow the procedure of going immediately to the Governor General and tendering the resignation of the Ministry. He could assert that I was absent and let matters stand over until I returned. I was not sorry that he mentioned the possibility of such a situation arising as I know there is far too loose a feeling about what can and cannot be done with the majority we have and the situation we have to meet. In concluding my remarks, I turned to Ilsley and said not to be concerned. He would come on top in the end. That was my parting word with my colleagues. I did not wait to shake hands. . . ."

Mackenzie King left Ottawa on May 12, accompanied by Norman Robertson and a secretary, and sailed from New York on the *Queen Mary* on Monday, May 13.

CHAPTER SEVEN

The Heart of Empire

THE PRIME MINISTER and his party arrived in England on Sunday, May 19, and immediately left for London by special train. Mackenzie King spent most of the trip talking with Vincent Massey and Norman Robertson. "Vincent very reserved and proper in everything. Alice was at Waterloo Station. I greeted her very cordially and asked her and Vincent to drive with me to the hotel. It was lucky I did as I did not really recognize whether it was for me to do this, not knowing about their own plans.

"At the hotel, Alice had in the room a large bowl of flowers with a note extending an affectionate welcome. I sat down immediately and wrote a note of thanks to her." Rather than accepting Attlee's invitation to come out to Chequers, the Prime Minister decided to stay in London and dined with the Salisburys.

By the time Mackenzie King arrived, the conference was virtually over. J. B. Chifley, the Prime Minister of Australia, had already returned home but Dr. Evatt, the Australian Minister for External Affairs, was still in London. New Zealand was represented by Walter Nash, the Deputy Prime Minister, and South Africa by General Smuts who had arrived in the United Kingdom a week after the conference had begun. In many respects, the conference had become a series of bilateral discussions between the British and Commonwealth governments although Australia and New Zealand had a joint interest in discussing security and defence arrangements in the South Pacific and Southeast Asia. A subject of particular interest to the British government was the improvement of liaison on military affairs between the Commonwealth governments.

During the morning of May 20, Smuts came to call on Mackenzie King. "He said that there were far too many conferences. He felt this one had been badly arranged. He told me that he had rejected a proposal that came from the Chiefs of Staff here for a military mission from each Dominion to the U.K. and a mission from the U.K. to each of the Dominions. He has asked why, in each Dominion, some one member of the Embassy could not do all that was necessary in securing and giving the necessary information. I said to him I had a strong feeling that the military, air and navy attaché business ought to be done away with altogether and embassies should be left free to discharge what are obviously their right duties. Smuts said the trouble was the European system was based on Embassies and their Attachés, etc. Doubted if it would be changed. I said that the present arrangement seemed to recognize war as an institution and to make it a business of all governments to have to do with it. He seemed to think that it might be November before the Paris Conference would be called. He has arranged to stay for Victory Day and will return to Africa the following week."

Lord Addison joined the Prime Minister for lunch but, before briefing him on developments at the conference, indulged in some discreet flattery. "He spoke about the length of time I had been P.M.," Mackenzie King wrote. "Said his son had been figuring out the years. It was apparent he must have got the particulars from something that came from my office or Malcolm MacDonald or in some other way, for he spoke of Pitt, Walpole, etc. It may be that the press have carried something. . . .

"He went over what had been done at the Conference thus far giving me the outline. Indicated that Evatt had been on the whole helpful but was pretty persistent about having a Conference of all the nations called soon and that he had indicated if I were here, he thought that would be my view also. I told Lord Addison that I agreed with the view that some way would have to be found of getting the Big Four to work together. If they could not do that by themselves, putting a lot of nations around them would not make the situation any easier but more difficult. Felt we had to be very patient with the Russians. It was better to take longer and get agreement than a situation which might mean the lining up of certain nations – large number of the United Nations against Russia. That apparently is strongly the view which the British Government hold.

"Addison made it clear in reply to a remark of mine that Attlee had been a little concerned when they got my long wire, and I can see that the whole programme has been modified in the light of it. I recalled our conversations last autumn which he remembered. He was very tactful in not pressing any point but rather making clear to me what danger there was of any question being raised which might be embarrassing.

"When he told me the Conference would end Thursday, I spoke about going to Europe. Had decided on this with Robertson after my talk with Smuts. Lord Addison had said the government would like me to stay on here a little to discuss matters with them. Naturally they would suit my convenience on that. I told him quite the contrary. I would stay in accordance with what would best suit their plans. That matter was left open. However it means, according to sailings, that instead of going back on the

Queen Mary on the 10th, we shall go on the *Ile de France* or the *Aquitania* about the 18th or the 20th, direct to Halifax, which means Ottawa before the end of June...."

At the session of the conference that afternoon, "Attlee made a reference to my presence," Mackenzie King reported. "I said I was sorry not to have been present at other meetings but it was unavoidable.

"Bevin then gave an interesting account of the negotiations of the Foreign Ministers at their meeting in Paris. The impression one receives was he had made the same statement, I think, with perhaps additional information, to the Cabinet in the morning. The impression one got, as Addison told me, was that they had made some headway. That the matter had got down pretty much to a question of the Danube and Trieste. If the Russians got their way in that particular, everything could be settled.

"When Bevin had finished, Attlee looked to me and I simply said I had no comment to make but wished to express appreciation of the review which the Foreign Minister had made and left it at that.

"Evatt reviewed some ground. Made his protest as he had previously. Made some suggestions.

"Smuts spoke of what he thought might be considered in the way of some concessions. Evatt repeated his protest about the Dominions not being called in just as rubber stamps. Thought they should participate in the settlement. Nash made a protest about our all being brought here unfairly. We should have come only when the Paris Conference was definitely decided on. I felt more satisfied than ever that I had adopted the right course."

The Prime Minister reported on May 21 that the meeting that morning was "an exceedingly interesting one. Bevin spoke on the situation in Germany in a deeply impressive way. He regards the world situation as extremely critical. Says he has not yet made up his mind whether the Russians intend to live with other people or not. What he regards as most dangerous of all is whether with the bureaucratic machine that they have built up in Russia, it is possible for them to lessen its momentum in any way. He points out it has really developed further than Hitler's machine had. They have isolated themselves so completely. No one knows, even as respects the Russian zone in Germany, what is going on there in detail. Generally it is known they are doing all they can to cause Eastern Germany to become a part of the Russian system, spreading Communism, etc. He stressed the importance of the policy of settling matters from now on on the basis of dealing with Germany as a whole and with the Russians in the matter of knowledge and settlement on a basis of reciprocity. He says their policy clearly is to try and consolidate the whole of Eastern Germany in their regime and when they have that consolidated, then to begin to deal with the question of the rest of Germany as though it were a problem quite apart. Bevin said that was their method, to keep pressing on consolidating a position; not letting anyone interfere with them, know anything about what they were doing. Draw an iron curtain there and go and demand equal rights with others with respect to what remained.

"He said that Stalin was the only one in the Russian regime that he felt could be relied upon to keep his word; part of their method was to give directions for certain policy to be followed and then, at the moment that suited them, to give exactly the reverse. He could count on nothing that they represented as their procedure, being continued. (Just as I looked at the clock, hands are in a straight line at 16 to 3 P.M.)

"He said that in negotiations, he would put forward an idea which obviously Molotov was attracted by, and if left to himself, might accept but the next morning or next afternoon, a statement would come in the interval from Moscow and he would argue entirely against the idea. It was almost impossible to negotiate with people who negotiated in that way."

When the British Foreign Secretary had concluded, Attlee asked Mackenzie King for his views. "I spoke about how impressive Bevin's statement had been. Said I spoke with diffidence not having been at other conferences and knowing perhaps less than others at the table about the whole situation but that I would say that I did agree with the main outline of all that the Foreign Secretary had said. That I thought he was right in saying we should deal with Germany as a whole in reaching any settlement. Also that I thought he was very wise in aiming at getting production started and taking a policy that would lead to the development of industry, getting people employed and goods produced so that they could arrange for exchange with other parts of the world and commodities. The sooner that was done, the better. And further that I felt he was right in regarding reciprocity as the line on which information should be given and concessions and agreements reached. That co-operation was the word that would have to govern if the world was to be at peace, and that we must now realize we had come to a point where the big issue was either one world living together or a world divided in itself against itself into two great forces. Russia with its philosophy of Communism controlling or all co-operating in a world in which views were shared. I spoke of agreeing with Evatt as to the smaller nations not liking to have everything settled by the Big Four or being regarded as rubber stamps or regretting that we had been committed in so many particulars by what had been done at Teheran and Potsdam, but that the present government or ourselves were not responsible; also that it was to be remembered situations had to be dealt with in the light of what seemed best at the moment. I thought I would not even be critical of the past in that way. I felt, however, that conferences such as we were now having – and I thought this was a good conference – was giving information which those present could give to their colleagues and to other governments. We would not be facing a decision made without a voice but were able to make our representations and have British policy take them into account. That I did not agree that it was wise to hurry final settlement. That the issues to be settled were very large and time was a great factor. That, of course, one did not wish to allow the Russians to consolidate their position too much or stir up strife elsewhere but I thought, however, that the thing to do if they were in the wrong was to make that so apparent that other nations would change their views toward them. They could not go on ceasing to co-operate without different free countries getting a strong public opinion against them and equally against the spread of Communism. On the other hand, if we let them get into the position before the world where they could say they were being crowded and that the other powers were ganging up against them, etc., we would find that within many countries there was, to our amazement, communistic sympathy in quarters we had never anticipated or expected.

"At one stage, Bevin said he would not wish the remark to be repeated but he felt in beginning in negotiations with the Russians, they had been proceeding on the idea of an understanding between Russia and the U.S. That they would manage the world between them, so much so that he, Bevin, had finally said that as a junior partner, he would like to have a chance to say a word on such and such a question. He said subsequently the Americans had a little falling out with Russians and had swung now more the other way. I spoke about being sympathetic with Nash as to the way we had been brought here to attend conferences before dates were definitely settled. That that was not the fault of the present government but some things would have to be watched as all P.M.s had their problems at home, and the date such as the Paris Conference when it came, would have been better for a meeting immediately before or immediately after or while the Conference itself was on, for a discussion of many things. I said from what we had learned in Canada I had been amazed at the penetration of communistic activities and even more of communistic sympathies in ways and places that we had not dreamt of. It was for this reason that I felt it undesirable to try and bring many more nations in to settle difficulties, to try and arrange to reach an agreement where the Big Four themselves had found it impossible to do so, specially as the Big Four would be a main portion of the larger number that would come together. I was afraid that would lead to a lining up in public with recriminations, positions taken, etc., which would make the last stage worse than the first.

"When I had finished, Attlee asked me a specific question if he understood that I was against carving Germany up to pieces, etc. I said: certainly I was. You could not change the love of man for his own country. If the Russians were to begin to carve up the East of Germany, take away part of their territory, this would only cause people living there to be sympathetic with the Russian absorption on the East and central Germany would be feeling that they had no better friends in the British themselves than they had in the Russians. It would all lead to communistic Germany and to a Germany determined to again unite as one. I said if they thought they could get industry going and definite order established, a great body of German people, once they felt a sense of security and had work, would be no more anxious for another war than any other of the great bodies of the people.

"Evatt had no fears of Communism. Spoke about not having any Communist elected in Australia. Pressed again for early conference bringing in other countries. Seemed surprised that I had taken the position I did. It was explained to him afterwards that what I had said and others related to the conference respecting Germany itself and related to conferences as such, as respects the effect of publicity and the like. Once the Big Four saw it was possible to get agreement in regard to the immediate conference they had in mind, the sooner the different nations were brought together, the better. My point was not to bring them together where there was disagreement with a view to trying to remedy the situation by increasing the numbers and having public discussion. Evatt thought public discussion had done great good. I said I was against old, secret methods of treaties, etc., but thought we had swung now again to the other extreme and going too far in stating positions before there had been reasonable thought and argument."

Smuts made a very good statement, Mackenzie King thought. "He spoke of being really very deeply concerned about the present situation which he regarded as extremely critical. He could not say whether we had really won or lost the war in the light of the way matters were developing. He was very strong for dealing with Germany as one and supported Bevin's position throughout. He stressed, however, an immediate as well as long run policy and said that having just visited Germany, he had been terribly impressed with how bad conditions in the British occupation zones were getting. Industries stopped. There was not food enough. He was afraid comparison would begin to be made between the state of the

Germans in the British occupation zones and the Russian, much to the disadvantage of the British. He fell into the old method of speaking of 'our' zone as in the days of the War Cabinet. Seeing that Smuts had no troops there, as Robertson pointed out, was a reversion back.

"He agreed entirely with my point of view about the wisdom of not hastening a settlement unduly, taking time, not being afraid of views getting worked out. He, himself, and others at the moment were not clear in their own minds what the intention of Russia was, whether this was a passing phase or a method of bargaining. How far she would have problems with her own people, etc. He thought that while it was a very hard job for the Foreign Secretary, it was better to have him rested up, getting a little ground bit by bit than by bringing others in that did not have the same sense of responsibility and getting the issue even more confused in the public mind.

"Lord Addison took much the same position when he spoke.

"Nash, I thought, spoke nicely. Agreed with the Foreign Secretary as, in fact, all did, treating Germany as a whole, but Nash stressed the importance of getting other nations in and also publicity. He was not very much afraid of Communism though he admitted that the whole Russian movement had taken a different trend than he had hoped it might or expected it would."

The meetings on May 22 did not greatly interest Mackenzie King. The concluding meeting was held on May 23 in Attlee's office in the House of Commons. According to the Prime Minister, "the discussion had to do with preferences, conferences, and a few concluding remarks. I found everyone more or less in agreement about the mad manner in which Ministers, officials and all were being scattered over all the countries. Nobody able to get on with their own work."

The fact that the conference was inconclusive and that no real commitments had been given or asked for made it a success from Mackenzie King's point of view. In the final communiqué issued on May 23, what had taken place was described as an informal exchange of views on a variety of subjects including the draft peace treaties with Germany and other belligerent states, "security responsibilities," and arrangements for liaison on military matters between the Commonwealth countries. As could be expected, a preference was expressed for flexible methods of consultation over "any rigid centralized machinery," a view to which even the Australian government now enthusiastically subscribed.

At this time, the Masseys were just about to leave for Canada. On May 21 Mackenzie King, on his way to a meeting at Attlee's residence, picked up the High Commissioner at Canada House. According to the

Prime Minister, Massey was "very silent – uncommunicative. Looks as though he had the burden of the world on his shoulders. Hardly had a word of greeting or a pleasant word to say to any of us on the way to Downing Street."

Relations between Mackenzie King and Vincent Massey had always been somewhat ambivalent and often strained and, that afternoon at tea with Attlee, the Prime Minister was forced to return to the distasteful subject of honours and titles which had plagued him earlier in the year, this time in the context of his personal relationship with Massey. Attlee informed him that the King wished "to have some recognition given Massey's services in England during the time that he had been High Commissioner here and especially in connection with the war. He said he understood that titles were not permissible under a Canadian resolution but wondered whether there would be any objection to a 'Companion of Honour' being bestowed. Whether it came within the restricted list. I replied that General Crerar had been made a 'C.H.' That we had ourselves put forward that recommendation. I said that I had had a very difficult time with my colleagues and others over the appointment of Ilsley and St. Laurent as Privy Councillors. That I thought it would be better not to risk raising a further question as some others were not included.

"I was afraid if recognition for Massey was arranged at this time from here, it might give rise to feelings anew on the part of some of my colleagues who were equally entitled to recognition.

"Attlee said he learned that Howe and Mackenzie had felt hurt. Said something about Howe. I said I would have been glad if his name had been included. That I did not feel the same way about Mackenzie. I said the whole question of honours had become a most embarrassing one to myself and the Government. That, in fact, so far as the Department of External Affairs, Prime Minister's Office and Privy Council were concerned, we had decided not to make any recommendations for inclusion in the list that is being prepared in Canada. I did not make an out and out refusal but simply stated the embarrassment and the unwisdom of raising the question at the moment. I left matters there."

The Prime Minister saw the Masseys that evening but the matter was not discussed. "When I came back to my room, I sent at once for Robertson. I had been told he had been in to see Vincent. I asked him if Massey had said anything to him. Apparently he had not been in to see him at all but Hudd [the Deputy High Commissioner in London] had seen him, Robertson. He then told me Hudd had mentioned to him that Lascelles [the King's private secretary] had told him that the Palace was anxious to have Massey given some recognition. I said at once: what business has

Lascelles to be talking to Hudd on these matters, and Hudd to be running back and forth between Massey and the Palace? I said to Robertson that I was sure that my talk with Attlee had already been reported to the Palace and that Massey had been told I was against doing anything and that accounted for his manner being what it was when I saw him tonight and what he said of the desire of the people here to mark his services. I felt incensed about having matters arranged between Lascelles and Massey before a word had been said to me when I was in the city as Prime Minister. I said to Robertson that we ought to get some kind of decision before we left.

"I then said to Robertson I thought I should cable St. Laurent instead of Ilsley. Tell him of the talk with Attlee and then have St. Laurent see the Cabinet and tell them that if they were agreeable, I would agree to the 'C.H.' I did not wish to take sole responsibility of either approving or disapproving. Robertson raised the question about our having to make the recommendation. I told him that I understood that, but had gathered already we had agreed to letting the British Government make certain nominations for services being rendered here and we had held them over for our July 1st. I assumed this would be on all fours – would be a recommendation that had come from the King here to be approved by us. I then dictated a cable to St. Laurent in Robertson's presence. After it was drafted, I thought at once of how it could be sent without Massey's office getting full particulars. Decided later as it was 1st of July matter, we could send message by airmail and left the question there. I expressed in the message desire to see McNaughton honoured at the same time on our recommendation. I then went to bed."

The next morning (May 22) Mackenzie King's thoughts were still focussed on "the Massey matter." He "felt very strongly that what was really wanted was a decision before Massey left so that his last moments could be spent at the Court. I said to Robertson he would rather get a recognition from the British Government than from the Canadian government. He had become an Imperialist, and would be such from now on. Feeling it was an immediate thing, I then put in a call for St. Laurent to be prepared for a message from me at 2 o'clock. I told Gordon Robertson [of the Prime Minister's office] to make arrangements accordingly.

"Discussed the matter further with N.A.R. but before seeing him, I had noticed that Attlee had been at the Palace last night; received by the King. I said to Robertson: that discloses the whole business. Lascelles has told Hudd of my view of what has transpired between Attlee and myself. . . . Norman said Massey wanted to see him this morning. Norman was then prepared to go in and explain just exactly the line I had taken by telegraph;

message I had under way, etc., making it a matter of collective responsibility but of my readiness to acquiesce in his receiving this honour.

"He did see Massey but Massey did not bring up the subject. Robertson told me he was quite tense in his manner. When I got to Downing St. at 11, I spoke before the meeting to Attlee and told him what I was planning to do. I then asked him the question: was it proposed that the name should be given to us to be included in our list, or was it feeling that this was a decoration which was to be bestowed here; the act being performed with my approval though not at my instance. He said he was quite sure it was the latter. That it was something that would be done here.

"After the meeting of the Cabinet, Attlee asked me to wait a moment – this was at 1 – and then read from a memo which he said he had got his boy to look into since I had spoken to him. The memo was to the effect that the King himself was anxious to confer this decoration on Massey before he left and that the practice was that the King himself on occasions could put forth names that he might wish to have honoured and that this honour would be one which would be given at the instance of the British Government rather than at the instance of our own Government. I shall ask Attlee for a copy of that memo, as to procedure. I then told Attlee what I had planned to do. That I was getting in touch with St. Laurent at 2 o'clock. As he knew, I did not want, as Prime Minister, to take these matters as matters which I would deal with alone but wished to have the Cabinet know of them and share the responsibility. I would tell the Cabinet of the situation through St. Laurent, as it now exists, and would say that I would be prepared to approve what the King wished to do if my colleagues were in agreement with me. If they were not, I would just have to say so but that I had a feeling if they were told by myself that it was the King's wish and that I had to either disapprove or approve, they would feel in the circumstances I was adopting the right course in approving. Attlee thanked me and said that he thought that would be all right. He then said to me: would you like *Howe* to be appointed a P.C.?

"I said, as he knew, I would be glad were Howe appointed but I left the inference that I was not making any recommendation myself. This, of course, will raise a big question with Mackenzie and perhaps lead to his resignation from the government but again it was a question of my having to say that I would not approve Howe being made a P.C. which, once again, would have put me quite in the wrong."

Before leaving Downing Street, the Prime Minister told Robertson the substance of his conversation with Attlee. "He thought that the decoration being given at once in the manner described would make it obviously an exception to a rule. I said it would open up the whole question as to what was to be done in the future and it was just as well to have it raised in regard to Massey. That certainly I confess . . . makes me despise Massey more than ever. It shows all of what is back of his public service – vain glory; desire for Royal recognition; preferring another country, as Bennett did, to his own instead of remaining with the country that had honoured him with the position of High Commissioner."

The call to St. Laurent was put through about 2.30 P.M. and Mackenzie King reported that "he got my message quite clearly. An answer had not come during the meeting of the Conference in the afternoon but when I got back to the Dorchester, an answer came saying the Cabinet had been pleased to accept the recommendation – to meet the request that I had made. Through Rowan, I let Attlee know at once."

The Prime Minister then took St. Laurent's telegram to Massey's room. "He was there alone. I said to him: Vincent, I think you will be interested in reading this telegram, which I then showed him. He read it over and I could see he had great difficulty restraining himself. He said to me: O Rex, this means so much. There is nothing in the world I would rather have than this. I cannot tell you how deeply I feel or how grateful I am to you. I said: You have nothing to thank me for, Vincent. You have had a great record here; done a great work and I am pleased it has been recognized. It has given me pleasure to have to do with its recognition. I said: You will be glad at this, I am sure, as having been approved by the entire Cabinet. You will know from this that they have wished to share in the recognition of your work. I found it pretty hard to restrain my own feelings. It was such a complete overcoming of one's own personal feelings and forgiving very much on both Vincent's part and Alice's but seeking to not let prejudice in my case stand in the way of recognition of another. He was clearly quite deeply moved and walked back with me to my own suite. Vincent had not heard from the Palace. I said to him a word about Attlee having spoken to me. He had had the impression at the time and I had, that the matter related to birthday honours. I had expressed to him the hope he would not raise that question just now. I had had great difficulty and embarrassment over the Privy Councillorships and did not wish to be further embarrassed with my colleagues at the moment. I then said, however, during the night, I thought probably it was desire on the King's part to have some recognition given before he left and, as a result, in the morning, I had telephoned to St. Laurent and had made the suggestion I did. I shall always believe that in every move, I was directed – that in this connection, I had received some direction from Beyond. Having gone in Massey's room at the time I did the night before, his mentioning of their wishing to give a mark, etc., – all led to my communicating with Ottawa, etc. I confess it made me feel very happy to have felt that I had submerged all my own feelings and to see the complete change in Vincent's mind and nature as a consequence. It will mean when he goes back to Canada, he will return with kindly feelings toward myself and the Government whereas during the last year or two, he and Alice have been rather embittered and a relationship between us purely formal.

"I have been prepared to make great allowances for Alice in the anxiety and strain she has had. What I do feel about the Masseys is that vain glory helps to destroy the virtue of service, no matter and to what degree it may have been rendered.

"Later in the evening, when I got back from being with Churchill, I went down to congratulate Vincent and Alice. The order of the Companion of Honour was on the arm of a chair. Vincent had been looking at it, if not worshipping it. I said I had come in to congratulate him. He then again spoke of how grateful he was. I had learned that in the interval, he and Alice had been at the Palace and that the King had personally bestowed the honour in the presence of the Queen and the Princesses. This was, of course, the apex of Vincent's ambitions and career. It was really amazing to see the change."

Mackenzie King had dined with Churchill that evening and enjoyed himself immensely. He reported that Churchill first "spoke about his speech at Fulton. Told me of the President having read it on the train on the way there and its being given to the press before it was delivered. After the President had seen it. Also that Byrnes had seen the address earlier and Admiral Leahy who was on the train with Churchill. Churchill seemed to feel that the net result would be all to the good. He feels very keenly his defeat. One of the first things he spoke of. Also feels very strongly that the present government are taking measures which are leading to the break up of the Empire.

"During the evening, he spoke two or three times very earnestly to me about when it was possible to encourage the present government to feel that the Empire Commonwealth was something they should feel a pride in seeking to preserve. Having them feel that we all had a measure of pride in it. He said: You can do more with them than anyone else. A word or two from you, spoken individually or publicly, will go very far. He said: They were all very crowded in events and everyone was more or less tired. He thought a word of encouragement would be all to the good. He mentioned that Attlee had asked him to drive with him on the day of the Victory procession. He had not known whether he should. Some of his following thought he should not. He had decided to do so. I told him I thought he was right in that. He spoke of intending to go after

The Heart of Empire 235

the government pretty strongly on the Egyptian affair – over the troops from Egypt. Also he spoke about India, regretting the way in which it was being allowed to pull out. He said if I had been again in office, I would have dealt with the situation in a very different way. I said to him I thought in many ways, he should be thankful he was not in at this time. He might have found there would have been very difficult situations – industrial strife. He would have had a hard time meeting it. He agreed with this. Said that of course the Labour fellows had put in this government and they felt obliged not to embarrass them too much for he thought that the government itself, in its legislation, was going far too far. He thought the extent to which private industry was being destroyed would militate greatly against the position of the U.K. He had had in mind before dinner showing me different despatches which he published during the war. He had them all printed together and bound in special volumes while he was still in office. He wanted to read some of the communications he had sent to me in Canada and also some of the earlier communications to show how true his vision had been at the beginning of the war.

"He read over the communications within the day after he had taken office and the days immediately following. Some to the President; some to myself and Smuts and others. He went on to speak of how nearly defeat came at that time and referred to the very heroic manner in which Canadians had moved over to the main land. How near everything was to extinction. I said to him I thought McNaughton had never received the recognition he should. That something should be done for him. Churchill agreed that his service had been a very great one; but for the Canadians, at the beginning, under him, the whole situation might have been vastly different. He said: You have only to say a word to Attlee and he will do whatever you like for him. What I was after was really making sure that Churchill felt that McNaughton was deserving of recognition similar to that given Crerar. I put it in those terms – that each of them had to do with the command of the Army. I saw that Churchill was wholly friendly to this idea. He has a fine sense of justice.

"He took up the early part of the war and also some of the communications regarding D-day and the situation there. Said he would like to have these published but added something about perhaps both he and I would be gone or too old and feeble by the time they would be made public. I said I could not understand why they should not be made public immediately. He said he would like that but did not know whether the government here would agree to it."

The most interesting part of the evening for Mackenzie King was "when we began to speak of the present life and the life hereafter. This grew out of his speaking of the decision that had to be made in regard to the use of the atom bomb. He said he was surprised that the second attack came so soon after the first. They had, however, given very ample warning. The way Churchill put it when discussing it with me was he expected that he would have to account to God as he had to his own conscience for the decision made which involved killing women and children and in such numbers. That God would ask him why he had done this and that he would reply he had seen the terrors of war. He knew something of what the Japanese method of warfare was like. That there were these thousands of lives – fine American soldiers – all of which would likely be destroyed or tortured. War might go on for another year or two with cities destroyed and numbers so much greater than could possibly be foreseen and with a breaking down of civilization bit by bit. He had had to decide what in the end would be best for mankind and felt that he, regardless of what the consequences might be, had done what was right. He said something to the equivalent of welcoming a chance to be judged in the light of omnipotent knowledge.

"I spoke to him about personal survival after death. He said he did not know – could not say whether that would be so. That he felt one might lie down – he used some expression which sounded to me like a black velvet pillow, and that would be all. On the other hand, he felt there was reason to believe that life would go on. But he said of one thing he was perfectly certain: that the order of the world was a moral order. That this was a universe governed by moral laws of justice and right.

"We spoke about Stalin. He said he would trust him further than any other Russian leader. He felt Stalin's word could be relied upon. He was the one man in Russia today who could save a situation and might save it. That the only question in dealing with the Russians was to let them see we were in earnest and to have no fear of them. He asked me if he had not told me about his agreement with Stalin to let Stalin look after Roumania, etc., while he would be busy getting peace restored in Greece. This involved killing of large numbers of Communists in Greece. Stalin knew that. It went on for a month. Never once said a word. He held to the undertaking he had given.

"The most important of all the utterances of the evening – something I shall never forget – was when I asked him what he thought of the future. He said: You ask me what I believe may develop in the next few years. He looked at me very intently and said: in another eight years, the war. The greatest war – the most terrible war which may mean the end of our civilization. Then he recovered himself a bit and said: It can still be prevented. We are in the same position as we were with Hitler. This last war might have been prevented if we had dealt with Hitler at once and in the right way. Did not allow him to go the lengths that he should never have been permitted to go. It is the same with the Russians. If we let them have their way and bit by bit crush on the free world as they are doing, there is no doubt we will pay a greater penalty than any that the world has thus far paid to dictators. He spoke of the regime of Russia as being a terrible regime – a regime of terror.

"We talked at some length of the Ottawa espionage enquiry. He said that had been handled in a magnificent way. Spoke of the courage I had in bringing the matter out and said that what we had done would be a factor that might help to save a situation, while letting other countries see what the Russians were really doing. Something of the menace of their fifth column. He repeated again what he told me before, about Stalin showing no surprise at the use of the atomic bomb. That Truman had asked him, Churchill, had he better not tell Stalin about its intended use within a few days. Churchill said he saw with his own eyes the conversation between Truman and Stalin. Truman was talking to Stalin in a corner and he seemed very pleased. His words were to the effect he was glad to know they had a more powerful weapon. Said something about the Japanese; that he was contemptuous of them. It was fortunate if they could destroy them more rapidly but there was nothing that indicated either that Stalin realized or even believed how effective the weapon would be. Nothing that indicated that he should have been told of it as matters progressed until it had been used. Churchill said we could not have told him of it until we had tested it out in the New Mexican desert. That it might not have worked. It would have been a mistake to have spoken of it until we were sure it was going to effect the results that it did.

"When I came away, I thanked him for the great pleasure of the evening and having given me so much of his confidence. His reply was I was the one to be thanked. I had said to him at dinner that I could not recall any point where we had failed him during the war and any difference save the matter that came up over our troops landing in Sicily. He waved the last one aside by some word that was something related to not wanting the enemy to know what forces we had or where they were but said that was nothing. Said that was nothing, and replied: Indeed you have never once failed in anything. Went on to say it is marvellous what you have done. What you have done in every way. His last words when we came out on to the sidewalk and I was getting into my car, and was thanking him, were: I thank you."

The Prime Minister added that "in speaking with Churchill, in reference to the atomic bomb, he said for me not to forget it was not true that the one who got the first shot in would win. It was not true that a bomb could be constructed which would blow a whole part of a nation to pieces. A bomb might destroy the city of New York in one blow; another, the city of Pittsburgh, but it would take a large number of bombs to destroy America. He hoped with America having a much larger supply, a reply could be made from some other part of the continent which would soon begin to destroy cities in other parts of the world. He hoped I would not object to having bombs planted in different parts of the world, for example, different places in the British Isles and in friendly countries, etc., so that if enemy country began using them against any one place, replies could be made from others. He felt sure that one of the greatest protections against the bomb would be the knowledge of the quantities that might be held by the United States."

It took over a week to settle the question of a United Kingdom Privy Councillorship for C. D. Howe. On May 24 the Prime Minister sent a long telegram to St. Laurent framed "in such a way that responsibility would rest on Mackenzie and Gardiner if they were unwilling to concede to Howe this honour, and thereby let Howe see where the matter rested. I made it clear I wished the Cabinet as a whole to understand the situation if Gardiner and Mackenzie raised any real objection. I feel pretty sure that everything will come through all right. When it comes to preventing Howe, Gardiner, at least, will not be troublesome. If Mackenzie is, I think Council will overrule him. They will probably wish to leave it in my hands. If they do, I shall agree to Howe being appointed."

On May 29 Mackenzie King received a reply from St. Laurent "indicating that Mackenzie and Gardiner between them were trying to hold out for Mackenzie's appointment as a P.C. Gardiner saying he would be hurt if Howe alone was appointed.

"Part of the morning was taken up with the drafting of a reply to St. Laurent in which I made clear that Gardiner and Mackenzie would have wholeheartedly to agree to Howe's appointment or I would withhold approval of the latter. That this would have to be done with Howe's knowledge. It is perfectly ridiculous Gardiner trying to put on me the onus of Mackenzie not being appointed. I shall be glad to see Howe appointed. I really do not care very much for what either Gardiner or Mackenzie feel. Mackenzie certainly is not worthy of appointment and Gardiner has no special claim, except for support which he is looking for for himself in case of some future nomination. I cannot see why Gardiner should raise any question at all. I might have replied sharply but I tried to do so in terms that were explanatory."

The next day the Prime Minister "was surprised and a little perturbed today not having heard from St. Laurent about Howe's honour. No doubt in the morning, I should hear all are agreed. If they are not, I am inclined to acquiesce in Howe's appointment whether Mackenzie and Gardiner like it or not. It is a contemptible thing that they should embarrass a colleague from receiving recognition or try to gain places of prominence themselves. Gardiner is hoping to get the leadership of the party and wants Mackenzie's support but he will never be Prime Minister. I should be surprised if Mackenzie lasts out very long. Howe deserves the recognition. He will see I have really been his friend. What I need to do from now on is to be a little more firm with the Ministers and master of the administration regardless of views of individual colleagues. All I pray for is strength and ability to hold on for some time longer and to guide the party right." The next morning (May 31) Mackenzie King "received word the Ministers were agreeable to Howe's recognition. So informed Rowan and telegraphed reply of appreciation to St. Laurent."

Meanwhile, on May 30 the Prime Minister had received a message from Ilsley and Arnold Heeney urging that he return on the *Queen Mary*, sailing on June 10. "I was not surprised and indeed I feel somewhat relieved at not going to the Continent at this time though I should much like to have seen the battlefields and also Berlin. However, I am sure that from the party's point of view, I should be at home while Parliament is in session. I think Ilsley is right in saying it is necessary. I should give the final word as to what should be done in relations with the Provinces; also as to budget resolutions. It is a tremendous compliment that the Cabinet as a whole wanted me back to give final decision. It shows how dependent the Ministers are on my judgment on these matters. I cabled immediately I would leave on the 10th."

A high spot of this visit to London was lunch with the King and Queen at Buckingham Palace on May 24. Mackenzie King found conversation "very easy and pleasant." "The King was specially interested in getting particulars of the Russian espionage matter. He had followed it pretty closely and seemed to be remarkably familiar with details. He told me that he thought what we had done might be a very helpful *exposé* in regard to similar situations in different countries. He spoke of feeling very greatly concerned about Russian attitude and behaviour. Their establishment of the 5th column and the like. Later in the afternoon, I sent to H.M. a copy of Gouzenko's confession.

"The King spoke about their forthcoming trip to South Africa; referred to it as looking forward to it particularly as a chance to get a rest and change. They have had no real change of the kind. He saw no reason why, if any important matters came up and his signature was required, he should not fly back at some moment's notice or have someone bring papers to him. He told me he found it very difficult to have anyone to talk with. He missed Churchill very much. Attlee, when he came to the Palace, never talked at all. In fact, he said speaking humorously and quite confidentially he referred to him as 'Clem the Clam' because he said nothing.

"When I want to talk with Bevin, he said, he is either in Paris or going away somewhere or there is some conference and I get very little chance for a word with him. His whole attitude was that of being quite alone in having to make up his mind and keep informed on important State matters. I can see that the government here is in the same situation we are. It is getting to be impossible for Ministers, particularly the Prime Minister or Foreign Minister, to see much of the Sovereign. His position must become increasingly a representative one rather than in any sense administrative.

"We talked a little of Lord Alexander whom he said was a great friend of his. I spoke also of Athlone and how helpful he and Princess Alice had been. I was quite struck by the appearance of the King when I first saw him. He looks much more alert and keen. His face seems to me to be much more robust than it was. He has a touch of silver in his hair which is rather becoming. Also I noticed in speaking he hardly stammered at all. Only on one or two occasions, he had difficulty in uttering a word. He was much at his ease in talking with me and I felt much at ease in talking with him.

"The Queen was just the same as ever, very natural; very unassuming; very sweet and pleasant. She seems to be a little slighter than she was. Princess Elizabeth is developing into a fine young woman. The Queen and the Princesses waited in the adjoining room until the King and I came out. I then shook hands with all and said good-bye. The King mentioned that they were expecting to see me on Thursday night at dinner."

The dinner at the Palace on May 30 was, the Prime Minister wrote, "a very memorable" occasion. During dinner he chatted with the Queen and Queen Mary, mainly recalling incidents from their visits to Canada. After the ladies withdrew, "the King invited me to sit between him and Attlee. Churchill was on the other side of Attlee. I first talked with the King at some length on the situation in Russia. He asked me to see particularly the despatch from Peterson [the British Ambassador in Moscow] to him. He thought it was straight from the shoulder. I listened for a while. We also spoke of the situation in America. I found the King much keener and better informed.

"In the latter part of the dinner, I listened to Attlee and Churchill exchange views, first in regard to elections in Italy and then in regard to present conditions of Europe and of England. It was really very fine to hear each of them run over parts of the British history in relation to the present. . . ."

During the conversation, Churchill "made no bones about his view about the break up of the Empire. He thought the Empire today was split in two. India was disappearing. Egypt had been cleft in two. Inside of a few years, we would find that the British Empire as such had disappeared. That we were today witnessing the moment of breakup. He spoke with great fervour and eloquence and earnestness. His eyes protruding from their sockets, not sparing any feeling that he had.

"He recalled how he had told me what would happen as to the invasion of Germany and asked me to remember what he was saying now. He said he might die at any moment. Was very sad at heart at seeing this great Empire which we sought to preserve being destroyed by the party which is in power today.

"I sought to have him feel that he was mistaken. That, at heart, he was for self-government and self-government would work out in the case of India all to the good. I also told him that I thought he should be out of party politics and to take a world outlook of affairs. He said he was going to stay in and fight to the end.

"Later in the evening, he had quite a talk with Attlee, both setting forth in a very friendly way their opposing views. I had a very good talk with Attlee. Told him I found many people feeling confidence in him and his judgment. Mentioned particularly Peacock of the Bank of England who told me yesterday that he had been quite reconciled to the government taking over the Bank of England. That was something they had fought for in elections. Also it was perhaps wise to take over the coal industry but they had made a great mistake in iron and steel. Attlee mentioned to me later that was part of a cartel. Admitted it was a difficult thing to decide and agreed caution was desirable. . . . Mrs. Attlee could not have been sweeter than she was. She is a lovely woman.

"It was exactly midnight when I looked at my watch when we left the Palace."

Three days earlier, on May 27, Lord Addison had dined with the Prime Minister. They talked for three hours and "went over a number of subjects, first the question of the dinner to myself. I told him I thought I ought to leave on the Queen Mary. He seemed quite regretful of this; said the government were really hoping to give me an important dinner at Downing Street in Walpole's rooms. It was an event of British history. When I suggested the Friday, he said he would see what his colleagues might think possible. After he had talked at some length, I agreed I would telegraph my colleagues tomorrow letting them know exactly the situation. I felt torn between the two duties of being back with them and also the importance of seeing Europe at this time. If they thought it would be all right for me to remain, I would consider going to the continent and having the dinner when I returned and before I left for Canada. He spoke next of the Governor of Newfoundland visiting Ottawa – Gordon Macdonald. Thought it was best he should come after their elections in Newfoundland. I said he should be a guest at Government House. This was agreed and it was decided we would arrange it. . . .

"Finally we spoke of the important meeting of the Cabinet they had had this morning in which the Chiefs of Staff had presented arguments for headquarter staff on frontiers of Suez Canal. The government thought they had not made up their case and suggested they should reconsider further. He wanted to know whether I would object to having one of the Canadian military authorities at H.Q. staff present to listen to the discussion for the sake of getting information. Canada being informed of the situation. I said I might as well be blunt and tell him how we viewed these matters. I said Canada was not in favour of a Commonwealth policy. In other words, a single foreign policy for the Empire. That we felt Australia might have one foreign policy; S.A., another; and ours would necessarily be based on our immediate neighbours, the Americans, for questions of Defence and the like. Also association with other nations of the Empire – it would not necessarily be identical with that of any other part of the Empire. Naturally we would all wish to harmonize our policies to the greatest degree possible. Addison said he understood this thoroughly. He then used the words: would we agree to someone coming in as an observer – give no expression of opinion – but simply to report the situation to the government. I said that I thought as long as it was understood it was simply for the sake of information and that no commitments were to arise nor were we to be regarded thereby as being consulted as distinguished from being informed, I would be agreeable to someone being present. I could not say we were unwilling to have information on a matter which affected the world at a time like this. It was obvious that whatever was done by way of protecting the Suez would have relation to a certain country – no name being mentioned.

"This brought up question of espionage and I read to him Gouzenko's statement. He felt unfortunately it was only too true. A letter received from Lascelles mentioned that the King was pleased to have the statement and he, Lascelles, for one believed every line of it was true.

"Lord Addison said he did not know what might be going on behind the iron curtain, whether Stalin really controlled the situation or whether the machine controlled Stalin. Also whether Russia might not come to

The Heart of Empire 243

have many problems of her own. Whether over the years, in some way, our standards – in democracies – might not become known to the Russian people. I asked if he felt the situation was very dangerous. He had been talking to some foreign person of importance who had been spending time in Russia and who thought that in a few years, Russia would want two things: (1) religion; the other, I think it was something equivalent to co-operation with the rest of the world. This might well help to save the situation."

Mackenzie King had Field Marshal Montgomery to lunch on May 30. Montgomery "could not have been pleasanter. He is really a fine character despite all the little vanities which he is supposed to possess. I do not wonder he is the man he is, when he is the grandson of Farrer who wrote the Life of Christ. He told me about his boyhood at Canterbury; of remembering Dean Farrer though he was only three and of his being present when he was buried in cloister grounds at Canterbury. We talked of his trip to Canada. He told me the line he would take at McGill and at Toronto. He will speak on leadership and the Canadian soldiers. . . . He will spend his time largely speaking to veterans. Told me he did not want to stay at Government Houses. Not even at Government House at Ottawa. He had told Alexander he would be pleased to dine with him but he would like to stay at a hotel where he would be by himself. He said if he stayed at Government Houses, he would have to speak all evening. He, himself, is a complete teetotaler; does not smoke and I am quite sure is a man whose whole life is deeply religious and who realizes that he is being guided by powers from Beyond. I spoke to him quite frankly about the talk about the Dominions as though they were a group in a bag; making sure each unit has complete independence.

"He spoke about having Simonds [Lt.-General Guy G. Simonds] become a member of his staff here. I told him I would have to take the matter up with the Minister of Defence on return. He spoke about liaisons; also asked if some members could attend the conference he was having of the Generals of all parts of the Commonwealth with which he wished to speak of military tactics; about uniformity of organization, equipment, etc. I asked if he did not favour something with the U.S. He said indeed he did, very strongly. He regretted that Ike Eisenhower would not be here for the Victory Parade but he is looking forward to spending a week with him in America. . . .

"In the course of the conversation, he spoke of Andy McNaughton. Said he would like to have him come and lunch with him in Ottawa, New York or elsewhere. He really loved Andy and felt sorry for how he had felt. I told him McNaughton was still pretty bitter. Felt he should have had the command. He said but for McNaughton's cleverness in organizing the army and training them, the results that were achieved could not have been achieved. He favoured his getting the same recognition as Crerar. Suggested I speak to the Prime Minister here to obtain it. I told him, however, we could give him the appointment ourselves.

"I have now both Montgomery's approval and Churchill's of McNaughton being given the same honour as was given to Crerar. Though I was very tired at the time of the luncheon, I very much enjoyed the talk we had together."

On May 31 the Prime Minister had lunch at Claridge's with Averill Harriman, the United States Ambassador. "Harriman gave me a very full account of his impressions of the Russian situation," Mackenzie King wrote. "In a word, he feels that what we have unearthed at Ottawa is of the greatest significance and represents what is going on throughout the world from Moscow. He says there is no doubt at all about an effort being made to spread Communism over the world and to do so by all means possible. He described how circumscribed the opportunities were in Russia to have democratic ideas spread in any way but he wisely takes the view we must be very patient with the Russians. Remember it was only since Theodore Roosevelt's time that new ideas of relations between classes have developed in America. The new deal is not yet accepted generally and that Russia is far from prepared for anything of the kind.

"I reminded him of the fact that five of us at the table on Tuesday night [at the Pilgrims dinner in honour of Halifax and Harriman on May 28 which Mackenzie King had attended as a guest of Viscount Greenwood] had all at one time represented peoples who were bitterly opposed to England – except Halifax. Could not say enough against her. The United States broke off; the Canadians had a rebellion; Smuts was a foe, but there we all [were] preaching a gospel of unity between English-speaking nations. We would have to judge the Russian people by the centuries it had taken Britain to reach the stage she has today. . . .

"Harriman said something happened at Yalta which had changed the whole situation between the United States and Russia. That Stalin somehow got the impression that a separate peace was going to be made with Italy. He said it nearly broke President Roosevelt's heart to think that Stalin would feel he could act in that way and betray an agreement which they had reached.

"Harriman said he did not think signed agreements with Russia were worth anything. He thought Stalin was the best of all to deal with, but he changed his views when it suited him – whenever it suited his purpose. He thought Molotov thoroughly unreliable and one who represented a type who was very dangerous. He did not fear war immediately but felt it would require great restraint over the years to prevent it. . . .

"Harriman was quite strongly in favour of what Byrnes had done in standing up to the Russians as he has recently. Wished that the United States could do a little more in disclosing the kind of thing that we have so, as he said, courageously disclosed. . . ."

The Prime Minister spent the weekend of June 1–2 at Chequers. After breakfast on June 2, he and Attlee had a talk in the library. Attlee "spoke about the honour for Mr. Howe. He asked me whether I would prefer to have him informed about it through myself or to have him, Mr. Attlee, communicate direct. I replied that I thought it would be preferable in every way for him to reply direct. I subsequently saw that he already had a message prepared to send himself. I again spoke about the manner in which understanding in regard to these appointments, as to recommendations, etc., had been reached.

"Attlee next spoke about the dinner to be given myself at Downing Street. Said that he and Lord Addison had both had it much in mind and were delighted to be able to arrange it for Friday night. I said that as he was giving a luncheon on Saturday, I thought that was rather too much. He said: no. This was historic and a separate occasion for myself. The luncheon was simply for those who might be present with the King in the morning at the march past. He then said they were considering whether to make it a very large affair or one restricted in numbers. Referred to having Lord Mayor present and others. I replied I would infinitely prefer a small dinner and the more private it could be, the better. I asked him about speeches – whether an important speech would be expected. What would be expected in that way. He said of course he would propose my health and would be pleased if I would reply. I asked if it was intended it should be an important speech on some matter to be reported. He said he thought if it were a small dinner, it would be preferable to have a write-up of the occasion itself which they would arrange to have done giving the historic significance, etc., and leave a little more freedom for those men to have a meeting with myself, etc. I said that was exactly the kind of evening I would prefer. . . .

"Later in the day, Lord Addison told me it had been arranged to have about thirty present. Invitations are being extended to the former Prime Minister and Secretary of State for the Dominions and Smuts, Nash and Beasley [a Minister in the Australian Cabinet]. Lord Athlone and Lord Alexander, etc., and several members of the British Cabinet."

When he returned to the Dorchester that evening, Mackenzie King received a cable from St. Laurent informing him that Ian Mackenzie had tendered his resignation again. "He told St. Laurent he had resigned following the message sent me about Gardiner. I do not want to have any difficulty with Mackenzie. It is his Highland pride on the one side and his unfortunate habits on the other. It may well be that he will not take that step at present. He resigned before and withdrew. I have quite enough in his previous telegram to make wholly apparent to everyone wherein with his action at this time, it would have been impossible to recognize him at this time when Howe is being recognized. He could not put himself in a more unfortunate light. There is more behind the whole business than appears on the surface. On the other hand, he has been a loyal colleague and has done good work but it would be a great mistake to end a career of twenty-five years with resignation on the ground he was not made a member of the Imperial Privy Council. I shall know better after reading his wire whether he is resigning before Howe's appointment or whether he will wait until after my return. It may be a means of trying to force some appointment."

Next morning (June 3) the Prime Minister received a message directly from Mackenzie "tendering his resignation; saying he intended to have announcement made in the house on Tuesday. This was disconcerting. I at once drafted a telegram to him and then decided to 'phone him as well, and also to 'phone St. Laurent. This I did in the afternoon around 3 P.M.

"I could hear St. Laurent quite distinctly and he I think could hear me. I gave him the substance of the wire I drafted. When I spoke to Mackenzie, he at once said he recognized the truth of what I was saying about not making any statement in the House; that he owed his appointment to the Crown and it would be for the Crown through the Prime Minister to make any announcement of his resignation, not for him. He said that was quite right. He understood that. I then spoke to him about giving me assurance he would do nothing until I got back and he gave me that assurance. I think he was perhaps relieved at my 'phoning him. There was no arrogance in his manner or voice. He is really breaking up. He still believes I am sure that I can get him the position if I wished to; even if I could, I would be doing the U.K. an injustice knowing what I do and with his present condition of health and matters connected with his life. However, this difficulty is now bridged over. Both St. Laurent and Mackenzie say progress has been exceedingly slow in the House."

To some extent the Prime Minister's last week in London was spoiled by depression and nervousness induced by the necessity of preparing a speech for the dinner in his honour on June 7. As a result, he did not go to the House of Commons to hear Bevin and Churchill speak on foreign affairs. On June 6 he was upset by reports in the morning papers "that Churchill had delivered one of his greatest speeches yesterday afternoon, and that Smuts among others had been present. I felt a sense of real anguish at not having heard Bevin on Tuesday and missing Churchill yesterday. On every count, I should have been there on both occasions. First because of the subject matter as it was related to the greatest problem at the moment, the debate related to the greatest issue, and a guest of the government, I should have been on hand to represent Canada on an outstanding occasion thereby showing my support of the British cause. On Canada's account, I should have been there. I felt terribly depressed and chagrined. This trip has been a great disappointment in many ways. I seem to have gotten off on the wrong foot at the start and never to have regained the ground. However, I resolved not to become too depressed but to make a valiant effort at meeting what I have in mind saying tomorrow night.

"I now begin to wonder if I have not helped to spoil that occasion by not having the inspiration which the debate would have brought and the good-will which I would have experienced from the members of both parties at my being present. It is really almost beyond my belief that I could have erred as I have in not giving this debate preference over everything else. It was a brainstorm on Tuesday occasioned by the confusion and the like that made me make the decision I did. I hope I may regain what has been lost."

On June 7 Mackenzie King exceeded Sir John A. Macdonald's record for years of service as Prime Minister of Canada. In the morning, Norman Robertson, Gordon Robertson, Gibson and Handy "came in to extend congratulations and presented me with three volumes of Oliver's Life of Walpole – entitled 'The Endless Adventure' – inscribed by all four and P [Pickersgill]. 'On a memorable day from members of the staff in London.' I felt deeply touched by this exceptionally appropriate gift in its association with the day."

The King also sent a letter of congratulations "in the following words: 'I send you my hearty congratulations on the remarkable record of distinguished service that you have established as first Minister of the Crown of Canada – Signed: George R.I..' I wrote a letter by hand in reply."

The Prime Minister went to Downing Street at 3.00 P.M. to keep an appointment with Attlee and Lord Addison. General Ismay [Military Secretary to the U.K. Cabinet] was also present. "What they had wished to discuss was the question of possible liaison in connection with the different staffs. It was represented that during the war, the British Govt. had had representatives of the three services on the staff of the High Commissioner. I said they had fortunately kept in the background and had not figured prominently. They wanted to know if I would object to this becoming part of a continuing order of things, the purpose being simply that of helping to keep British Headquarters staff in touch with our staff. I said that so long as the matter was one of exchanging information, I could see no objection to it and many advantages.

"They wanted to know if I would agree to our having representatives of our defence staffs here in a purely liaison capacity, to be present at meetings of the general staff and to listen to discussions to keep us informed and to give information to them. I asked if what they meant was something similar to Pope's representation of Canada at the Joint Board in Washington. They intimated it was exactly that. They expect that the U.S. may wish to have a Joint Board here in case a proposal should be put forward. They have a paper all ready in which to answer them and agree to an arrangement. I said I thought it was most advisable that the staffs of the U.S., U.K. should keep in close touch with each other and it would be helpful for us to have that information re matters discussed, etc. I made clear that I would not give any final reply myself at the moment. I would wish to discuss the matter not only with Ministers of Defence but my colleagues in the Cabinet as well. Attlee asked me whether the Chiefs of Staff were so to speak a projection of myself. I replied: no, they were under Ministers of Defence; explained that we had had only one Minister at the start and expanded to three and now were back to two and might get back to one. That Ministers of Defence were administrative heads of departments. They [the Chiefs of Staff] reported to him. They also came to Cabinet meetings during the war as they did here but that the decisions were reached as a result of Cabinet discussion on matters of policy and I, as Prime Minister, had the final decision.

"I made it quite clear that whatever was done should be done quietly. That there should be no making of a formal body or council or anything of that kind. I then said I would like to tell them of the work of the Permanent Joint Board and described how it had been formed; its power to make recommendations but not to determine policy. I said we had now reached very important stage where we would have to consider all questions of American relations with ourselves with regard to northern parts of Canada. I told him how they had built the Alaska Highway and spoke of the staging routes connecting the airports. Also airports established in Labrador during the war. We had bought these properties back and they were in our possession but there were still American soldiers and airmen stationed there. That one of the problems we would have now would be the desire of the Americans to protect themselves by having forces kept in the North. They would say to us if we could not keep them, they would pay expenses. We had to consider what we would have to do in matters of farming. I thought it would be well to have the British govt. informed of all developments. . . .

"I said we, of course, would have to make some joint arrangement for the defence of our coasts on the Atlantic and the Pacific with the Americans. It was much better we should. Our people could not look to other parts of the Empire for that protection. Also that it would be a helpful liaison with the British Commonwealth.

"All of this was met with approval so far as I could see from all three. I promised to take up the matter further on my return."

Mackenzie King returned to 10 Downing Street that evening at 8.00 P.M. for the dinner in his honour. "We were received by Attlee very kindly in the large rooms of Downing Street.... The table filled the entire room and had the appearance of a distinguished banqueting hall. I met the guests as they arrived. They included Churchill . . ., Lord Addison, leader of the House of Lords; Cranborne, leader of the opposition, House of Lords; Smuts of S.A., Nash of N.Z., and Beasley of Australia, the Speaker of the House of Commons – Brown – and the Lord Chancellor, Jowitt. Sir Eric Crankshaw [a senior civil servant], Machtig [Permanent Undersecretary of the Dominions Office], and Sir Alan Lascelles. Herbert Morrison, Greenwood with others as well as Robertson and Hudd. At the table, I was to Attlee's right with Greenwood to my right . . . Smuts and Churchill were to his left. Lord Alexander was immediately opposite with Morrison to his right and Lord Athlone to Morrison's right.

"I feared part of the evening that I might find it difficult to speak, being tired and really my mind not too clear. However, when the time came, and Attlee proposed my health, I began to get over what nervousness I felt.

"Attlee made a very nice speech. He spoke of the long record I had had comparing it with that of other P.M.s. He had discovered today or rather the Daily Mail had, that Lord Craigavon of Northern Ireland had held the office of P.M. about five months longer. However, Northern Ireland is in a very different position. Is represented in the British Parliament as well as having its own sort of provincial affair. Attlee spoke of the length of office of some P.M.s. Spoke of what a novice he was compared to Smuts, Churchill and one or two others he named. He was very modest as he always is. Referred to my career as Deputy Minister and as Minister and spoke particularly of Canada's service during the war. When I came to reply, I found it quite easy to speak though I was a little tired and on dates, could not quite recall them all. Got mixed up on Sir John's tenure of office – 1867 to 1891. I used the expression 1901 I think. However that soon was corrected. All were most attentive throughout. . . . I used all the notes I had prepared and got through all the points of what was written out in my speech – much in the order in which they appeared.

After the dinner, I received no end of congratulations from those present. Churchill [said] that what I had said was just right; that I could do more here than anyone else. He spoke of Canada amazing him again in what we had done on many matters as well as having a navy of our own.... The Lord Chancellor, Jowitt, said a couple of times that it was not only an honour to me but it had been an honour to all present to hear what I had said. Lascelles thought it was the best speech he had heard me make and Clarendon [the Earl of Clarendon, a long-time personal friend of Mackenzie King] too was most complimentary. Spoke of how well I had understood our own people....

"I shall never forget Attlee's kindness in giving this dinner on one which of all nights must have meant very much to him; also of all present to have spared the time. Also Lord Addison's part. Morrison and Addison were most appreciative in their comments of what I had said....

"Shortly after 10, I said goodnight and came away feeling that the evening had marked the summit of the long road which as I have said began with grandfather's visit to Downing Street in 1832. So many remarked on the dramatic story that it all presented. Both Robertson and Hudd thought the address most appropriate.

"We drove back together. Coming out of Downing Street, I was given many cheers by the large crowd that were assembled. What a story! What my grandparents and father and mother must be feeling tonight! What I feel in my heart of thanks to God, no words can begin to express."

On June 8, the day after his dinner at Downing Street, Mackenzie King participated in the massive Victory Day celebrations in London, a pageant he described with his usual care for detail in his diary.

He left the hotel for 10 Downing Street at 9.15 A.M. "We came in through the garden and through the back entrance. Were shown into the reception rooms upstairs. There had talks among others with Mrs. Attlee, Mrs. Neville Chamberlain and a talk of some length with Winston Churchill. We sat on a sofa together. I asked him if he did not feel that he ought to be devoting time to writing. He told me that he was doing some of that. As a matter of fact, he had everything in the form of documents carefully together, documented, etc. All important despatches, etc. He said: You saw what a number of communications there were between you and me. He then went on to say that he was doing a certain amount of dictating each day. He said: I do it sometimes when I am travelling in a car, to one of my secretaries: also at odd moments back and forth. He then said he felt there were things he wished to record that he alone knew. He began to speak about the planning for the campaign in the matter of crossing the channel. How he had held back for some time

The Heart of Empire   251

against the invasion.... He said at the start Gort [then Chief of Imperial General Staff] had wanted to remain to the last man on the beaches after Dunkirk. He knew that Gort would wish to wait but he would not allow that. Alexander came to be the last. He said Gort would have allowed himself to be killed and if that had happened, anything might have followed. He had absolutely prohibited his remaining beyond a certain time. He spoke about his talks with Marshall of the U.S. Army and pointed out where he thought his action here had saved McArthur in similar ways in Japan.

"He spoke at some length of the arrangements respecting the plan of campaign as related to the Mediterranean. What he wished to do there and what was subsequently effected in the crossing. I said to him that I thought that what was prevented was often more important than what was achieved. I felt one of the greatest things he had ever done was the way he had held out against too early a crossing of the channel despite Stalin's continued protest. He agreed that was one of the hardest things he had to do. I asked him if Beaverbrook was trying to help him by his opposition so as to keep two different opinions facing each other as it were in this country. He said he really had been troublesome at times. He was a sick man. Went on to say that whenever he really asked him anything important, Beaverbrook helped to meet the situation. I spoke too of some of his talks with Roosevelt. He referred particularly to how completely he had changed at Yalta. He said: I can close my eyes and see him very clearly. Some remark was made by someone of a Prime Minister in England who had won an election in an advanced age. Churchill said there was time yet.

"Last night, after dinner, I had talked to him about devoting his time to writing, etc., instead of continuing on in party strife. He, Smuts and I were talking together along with General Ismay and one or two others. They all left to allow me to have a word with Churchill himself. He said that he would not give up the fight with this crowd. That he intended to defeat them and would win in the next elections or something to that effect. He keeps coming back to deploring what he refers to as the loss of India. He said these people have just given India away. He said that grieves me more than anything else. Also refers to Egypt. He said so much might have been done with India but in a different way – done by degrees. Let them have their differences between themselves and show the world their divided opinion but these men had just handed the whole thing over. I felt that my talk with him there at Downing Street that night which really basically was an effort at preventing political controversy and helping Churchill thereby to rise to fuller stature, would be helpful. He will go down in the public estimation if he keeps on party strife. It was one of the significant circumstances of the evening."

The Prime Minister's account of the celebrations continued: "On leaving Downing Street, came the most amazing surprise of all. The King had offered three of the Royal coaches – open, for the procession from Downing Street to the Saluting Base on the Mall. Churchill and Attlee and the Minister of Public Works drove in the first carriage. Then General Smuts and myself with Walter Nash and Beasley immediately opposite. Poor Nash was much embarrassed throughout by Beasley not having a silk hat or a black coat. I think Beasley must have been even more embarrassed. It meant that Nash had to go bareheaded through the procession all morning and at the saluting base so as not to embarrass Beasley. He was very fine about it.

"To be driving in a Royal coach from Downing Street and having precedence over Field Marshal Smuts, to be receiving the cheers of the people of London all the way from Downing Street to the saluting base where we were to greet the King and Queen, Queen Mary and others of the Royal family on their arrival, and witness the march past of the different defence forces, was indeed beyond anything one could have imagined. Something again completely unsought and unthought of. Very significant in its relation with Downing Street.

"At the saluting base, I was amazed to find how many of those who occupied the seats were persons that I knew. Even more particularly were how many I had entertained either at Laurier House or in the country. Among the number were Princess Juliana and Prince Bernhard. The guardian of the King of Iraq – a little chap of 10 years of age whom his guardian prince introduced to me. I did think how strange it was to have a little child like that kept for a position of ruler. There is something about heredity in Royalty that will vanish and must vanish. It is a survival of the old Divine Right of Kings. It cannot endure as each individual from the masses of the people is entitled to the dignity of manhood and equality based on character and true worth. That is going to be the greatest of all the troubles. I do not know that it will serve to improve conditions. What took place in America at the time of the revolution will take place I believe wherever, in the course of years, a monarch continues to reign in virtue of his gallant birth.

"There were many members of the present Ministry and of other Ministries. Also representatives of other countries. Among the number I saw Bruce, of Australia. I remarked to someone that he was looking very much older. The person to whom I spoke (it may have been Smuts) said he was looking fierce and he certainly did. It is interesting to note the change which time brings in the countenances of men – life's ambitions showing in their faces.

"When Queen Mary arrived at the saluting base and stepped out of her car, I happened to be immediately opposite. She came forward and shook hands with me first of all and then with Attlee and Churchill and later with Smuts.

"Later when the King and Queen arrived and the Princesses, Their Majesties and Their Royal Highnesses shook hands with Attlee, Churchill, myself and Smuts in that order before taking their position on the saluting base. The Queen stopped to ask about my going back and extended good wishes. The King spoke about the dinner last night and having heard that I had made a very good speech. Later the Princess Royal came and shook hands. Also introduced her little son. She was particularly happy and pleasant in the way she spoke. Later from the saluting base itself, the Queen looked down and smiled on one or two occasions in a very kind manner. I could tell that it had reference to the visit to Canada and the feeling they have in that regard."

"To me," the Prime Minister continued, "the people seated in the stand at the saluting base were much more representative of privilege and interest than really of the people. Attlee is not to be included in this thought. It has not been the love of power that has brought him in power but the love of service. He looked the humblest and the meekest of all present. He felt his position very similar to what my own has been all the way through in its relation to the Tories and their attitude toward me in Canada. The kind of thing I have suffered under Meighen and Bennett. However he has the people behind him. There it seems to me is the great struggle that has yet to come in an endeavour to overthrow privilege. Power based on privilege and possessions. I felt more deeply stirred by the march past of the various defence forces [including several Canadian units] than by the mechanized groups. The men that have been fighting. There again one's thoughts came to the multitudes that have been slain. Churchill spoke to me of that himself; of the numbers that have been killed right from this city alone. It was a fine pageant of Empire but looking through the iron and steel and the universe behind all is a terrible story of the failure of our civilization. That is where civilization has failed; not in the destruction of property."

That evening Mackenzie King had an audience with the King. "By almost a miracle," he wrote, "a cable came in the morning from Paul Martin saying he assumed that McNaughton's matter was being followed up here. . . . Luckily I recalled it on the way to the Palace. As soon as I reached there, I had a word with Lascelles concerning it. By great good fortune, Lord Alexander was in the room with Lascelles. I told Lascelles what I had in mind, saying that I had been in touch with my colleagues at Ottawa about having Andy McNaughton given the same honour that had been given to Crerar, he having had to do with the organization of the Canadian Army and its command at the beginning. I have just found that my colleagues expected me to take up the question of a submission with the King and the G.G. while in London. I wondered whether it would be possible to have McNaughton's name appear in our military birthday list which comes out about the same time as the list of the U.K. I said I had known of the difficulties there had been in the situation here and had talked privately with both Churchill and Montgomery, each of whom felt that McNaughton should receive the recognition suggested. Alexander at once broke in and said: I do think that this should be done. He volunteered it himself adding Andy has had a difficult time but he certainly merits this recognition. His organization of the Canadian army, command and service entitles him to this recognition. I said I felt sure that knowing how Lord Alexander felt toward McNaughton, that he would be wholly agreeable. Lascelles at once said that he was quite certain if I mentioned the matter to the King when I saw him, the King would at once approve. Lascelles also asked me if I had had a word with the P.M. whom he said he was sure would be glad to make the recommendation. I said that I thought Crerar's recommendation had been made by the Canadian Govt. and that what I was seeking was a similar procedure. I recall the matter having come before our Cabinet and our Cabinet having approved Crerar receiving this recognition. Lascelles said he felt pretty sure that the appointment must have been at the instance of the U.K. Govt. as Canada had refused to take any allotment of C.H. and there was no allotment to Canada from which the honour could be taken. However he said that was a technicality. Some way could be found to get things over. I then was shown upstairs to the room in which the King received me."

"The King himself was quite obviously tired," he wrote, "and I found myself, to my amazement, more tired than I could imagine. I could hardly remember McNaughton's name. The King took an arm chair in front of the fireplace and gave me a seat just facing his. He spoke about the morning's parade and I remarked how impressive it was. How much I wished that all parts of the British Commonwealth could have seen what had been the privilege of those present to witness this morning. I spoke, too, of the conference, and said I had been much pleased with its proceedings. The King then spoke to me again of the dinner last night and said he had heard I had made a fine speech. Lascelles downstairs repeated he had heard me speak several times but thought last night was the best of all.

He would always remember what I had said. The King spoke of having heard what I had said of his uncle Lord Athlone and of Alexander and was much pleased at that. I said how very sincerely I had meant every word I had said.

"I then said I would like to speak to H.M. about the possibility of having the honour of C.H. conferred upon General Andy McNaughton. That his services had been very similar to those of General Crerar and that I had been in touch with my colleagues who felt that they would like it very much if McNaughton's services could be similarly recognized. I felt sure that the Canadian people too would appreciate it. The King immediately said he would be very pleased to bestow the honour on McNaughton. He went on at once to say I could give it – referring to the insignia – to Alec, meaning Alexander, to take back with him on Monday to bestow it on McNaughton on my behalf. I said that would be deeply appreciated and then thanked the King. I spoke again of McNaughton's services and the King also spoke appreciatively of what the presence of the Canadian army had meant, under McNaughton's control at the outbreak of war. . . .

"The King spoke about how during the war, one evening, he and Churchill and Smuts had talked until 3 or 4 in the morning. I had been speaking to him about Smuts. He had in mind what it meant to him to see all sides of a situation. I confess I felt an inward pang at not having been myself a little more helpful in these ways. Too much of my time has been given to personal correspondence and the like and not enough to the study of these all important questions and more active participation with other leaders."

After leaving the King, the Prime Minister had another talk with Lascelles about protocol arrangements for McNaughton's decoration. Next day he received word that Attlee had made the appropriate recommendation to the King. "Last night, in the Chancellor's rooms, I had spoken to Attlee just to have him informed but had not thought that he would immediately make the submission that he had. On thinking everything over, it seemed to me that it would be ungracious toward the King, Attlee, Lascelles and all, if in the light of the matter having been discussed with Alexander as well while he was here, if I did not at once express deep appreciation of what had been proposed and agree to it. The fundamental point is that my own colleagues have already agreed to my making the recommendation. I have already made the recommendation to the King and got his approval. Unfortunately there is no C.H. allotted to Canada. The matter would be arranged by taking one from the British quota (whether on loan or not, I don't know) and allotting it to Canada because of the exceptional nature of the circumstances. It seems to me in all this I have protected the position of the appointment being made only on the recommendation of the Canadian P.M. with the approval of the King. This was done but for technical reasons, it required the recommendation of the British P.M. to secure the honour from the list recognized by law. What was at the basis of all was that it should be the same in McNaughton's case as was done for Crerar.

"I was left then with the sole matter of getting McNaughton's consent and clearing the simultaneous announcement in Canada and England."

The Prime Minister immediately placed a long distance call to McNaughton but was unable to get through. However, on June 10 Pickersgill telephoned to say that the General "was greatly pleased at the thought of his receiving the recognition mentioned."

Thoroughly exhausted by the social and political rigours of London and the intricacies of royal protocol, Mackenzie King boarded the *Queen Mary* at Southampton on June 10. The ship sailed the next morning. If anything, the Prime Minister's forebodings about the international situation, more particularly relations between the Western nations and the Soviet Union, had been increased by the talks he had had and that afternoon he "got down to work on Commonwealth defence policy. Several papers presented at the Conference which I found intensely interesting, doubly so in the light of the experience of the war. I am beginning to feel that the time has come to change the orientation of our whole policy with regard to defence. Even the reading of these papers discloses that Britain herself recognizes that she is helpless in the world to defend herself as it is now and will continue increasingly to be. That it will require the U.S. and the aid of all the Dominions. I am equally sure the next war, if there will be war, will be with Russia and that Canada more than any country in any part of the world will require all in the way of defence that it may be possible for her to possess. This means that we must not so much as spend money on the material side of defence as nothing we can do in that direction would save us. While not neglecting the preparing of strategic areas, etc., do all we possibly can to make war altogether impossible. As a single nation, we are perhaps the most vulnerable in the world. As a part of the British Commonwealth and continent of North America, we are perhaps the most fortunate that policies will have to be based on this geographical fact. I think, too, we must seek to get more people and develop our industries and resources."

CHAPTER EIGHT

An Ottawa Interlude

THE PRIME MINISTER and his party landed at Halifax on June 15 and the next evening arrived back in Ottawa. Mackenzie King was surprised to be met by a large crowd of ministers, members and newspapermen, including his wayward colleague, Ian Mackenzie, who was the first to greet him when he stepped off the train. On the afternoon of June 17 he was in his seat in the House of Commons and received a warm welcome from his own supporters and the opposition. "As soon as prayers were over, Bracken at once extended a welcome back. Was joined by Coldwell and Low in a few words. I thought it best to leave to my feelings at the time what it might be best to say. How far to go. With the exception of one or two rather badly expressed phrases, I managed to place on record what I think were suitable words for the occasion. I was given a great ovation by our men and indeed members on all sides of the House applauded quite generously."

That evening the House adjourned until 9.00 P.M. to allow the members to attend a testimonial dinner for Mackenzie King organized by the press gallery. After a long series of tributes from spokesmen for all parties, the Prime Minister was called upon to speak. Though very tired he "did bring in the main features that I had had in mind, namely, the significance of the journey to London; the gathering there; also the fact, the truth being stranger than fiction, for example, in contemplating a long political derby with Sir John Macdonald and Sir Wilfrid Laurier. . . . Said these milestones made clear how near one was to the wings of the political stage. I made clear my intention not to run again and while I had not intended to say anything about writing memoirs, as reference had been made by some of the speakers to the book that I would write, I thought it well to indicate that I had in mind leaving an inside history along political lines. I did speak of the Rebellion of '37 and of the selection of G.G.'s etc., but was not as happy in the shaping of what I had to say as I would like to have been.

"I was given a very warm reception when I was through but I felt I had not done myself justice or the occasion justice in the manner and substance of what I had said. One terrible handicap I am feeling is the fatigue of my eyes which prevents me from seeing an audience without my glasses and occasions a certain pain that I otherwise would not have in my head."

On the way home from the House that evening, Mackenzie King worried that he might have been indiscreet in his remarks. He "had a feeling of appalling sensitiveness to what the press might have in the morning which would touch on what I had said about the motive that I had had in public life being one, continuation of Mackenzie's work and bringing Canada to full status of a nation – of working toward that goal. No personal ambition, and also of writing of some political volume which I have kept much to myself thus far. . . . I wondered too if I had done the right thing by my party in again stressing my intention not to run in another election.

"I went to bed quite depressed but feeling that it was a chastisement in a way for having left undone some of the things in England that I should have done, and having done others which should have been left undone. I was determined to take what would come, in that spirit."

By the next day, he was more cheerful. "I ought to be very happy and proud. I confess the feeling that has been expressed toward myself both in England and here, in the U.S. and elsewhere, has made me desirous of staying in public life a time longer and seek to redeem the wish there has been through the years by getting a more adequate knowledge of affairs and being more active in the work of Parliament itself. Trying to give it priority over everything. I would like if it should be within the Providence of God to have strength sufficient to outdistance Walpole's record [for years of service as Prime Minister] if only for the sake of helping to fulfil the purposes of my life and doing honour to the names I bear in the manner which would fix for all time in the public mind the real service that Mackenzie had rendered freedom in his day.

"I have felt more rested in my mind at the thought of having told the Members of Parliament the real secret of the effort of my public life and have made clear the purpose of my desire to retire – a highly honourable purpose and [one] which the country itself would approve. I think, too, I am doing what public men should do who, after strenuous years such as those we have gone through, have taken that course. How I wish I had paid more attention to literature, to history, public speaking, been more thorough in my reading and understanding of affairs! I might have accomplished a great deal."

On June 21 the Prime Minister attended the first party caucus after his return from the United Kingdom. "The caucus was one I shall never forget," he wrote. "It was a deeply impressive affair. The Members had evidently been considerably perturbed or stirred at my reference at the testimonial dinner to my intention not to contest another election and had, I imagine, gathered I might be retiring at any time. They showed in the clearest manner possible how greatly they would deplore anything of the kind."

Mackenzie King "spoke for a little over half an hour, referring first of all to the message I had received from the previous Caucus and what it meant to me; also to the dinner, thanking Golding [M.P. for Huron-Perth], the Whips, and Mackenzie for their part and all present for their presence at the dinner and reception of what had been said there. I then said that perhaps I had spoken a little more in a personal way than I should have and had been regretting since that perhaps I had gone too far in disclosing what was nearest to my heart. The Caucus immediately indicated that this was not so.

"I then referred to the matter of retirement, pointing out that we had until 1950 to run. I would then be 76, if spared, and asked what use a man of 76 would be to a political party in times like the present. Also that I thought it most important that there should be no misunderstanding on the part of either the Members or the public of the reasons of my retirement when the time came, etc."

The Prime Minister then reviewed his impressions of conditions in Britain and Europe. "I gave as my belief that the next war would be a war of world conquest and stressed the necessity of our keeping close friendship with the U.S. I told them that we were in a position at the moment not unlike the world situation at Munich, only something that would go much further through the spread of Communistic, materialistic thought. I think I made a powerful appeal as to the necessity of Canada keeping well within the community of British nations and preserving close friendship with the U.S.

"I spoke for half an hour. It was exactly twelve when I looked at the clock. When I finished there was loud applause and then a series of speeches. First, by Pouliot [M.P. for Témiscouata], who spoke very feelingly of the long friendship he had had with me and my patience with him and what it meant to have me as leader. Tucker [M.P. for Rosthern] then followed on it being my duty to stay and that Providence had given me to the party and to the country at this time. McIvor [M.P. for Fort William] followed on similar lines, Then Lapointe [M.P. for Lotbinière] spoke. He said I should know that it was not Lalonde [M.P. for Labelle] that carried his constituency but Mackenzie King and that that was true of the constituencies generally in Quebec. There was real applause by the French Members at that statement. There were other speeches which were all a strong appeal that I should reconsider my decision to retire, etc.

"In reply I made it clear that I had not thought of retiring soon. That met with loud applause. But I pointed out that I had always tried to look far ahead and picture the decision that might be made when a certain situation had to be met. I thought it was wiser to build up the party meanwhile and have things in readiness for the next campaign. I spoke of the condition of the party, of the present situation, and of the necessity above everything else of winning by-elections.

"Mackenzie made a nice little speech, in which he spoke of Ilsley and Howe. How Ilsley had managed during my absence and congratulated Howe on his honour. Made other references which brought considerable applause. It was really splendid the way in which he rose above his own feelings."

The Cabinet had met on June 18 and Mackenzie King was immediately embroiled in the preparation of the budget. The most serious problem the Minister of Finance faced was to devise a tax-rental formula which would be acceptable to the provinces. The Prime Minister "made a strong plea for keeping to the fore the programme of social legislation which we have foreshadowed in speeches from the Throne while making clear that most of it has been conditional on agreement with the provinces." He urged less rigidity "in adhering to certain forms of expression; for example, an argument took place whether the speech contained the words: agreement of all the provinces, or agreement by the provinces – the two meaning the same thing – but the 'all' in one case standing out, so as to avoid comment that . . . P.E.I. for example could destroy the whole scheme of social legislation. The other leaving a broad interpretation to allow an appeal at a general election to more or less decide matters to whether all the provinces were in favour. I said quite openly that I thought it was the extreme rigidity that cost us the success of the Dominion-Provincial Conference. Had we conceded at the outset some sources of revenue to the provinces, we would have got through. Howe, Ilsley and to some extent St. Laurent, on account of the constitutional and judicial aspects, seemed to have one point of view. Gardiner, Claxton and myself, much more the other. St. Laurent could, of course, meet the situation in a final discussion.

"I spoke to Ilsley, this afternoon, about letting me look over his material. I could see he seemed afraid of that and averse to it. He is ready to let me see one page when it was revised. He does, however, try to hang on to the whole material. The truth is he does not, in his own mind, understand some of these problems and feels he must adhere rigidly to anything that Clark proposes. I suggested he have Clark bring the material and let us go over it together as to the wording.

"He then brought up the question again of thinking of a successor for him. Said he must get out after this session. He could not stand the terror of this kind any longer. This is the explanation and describes his real condition. It is not one which permits a man to give his best judgment to a matter.

"I was surprised at the extent to which there will be a reduction in the tax rate; also the extent of exemptions having regard to the total amount that has to be raised. On the other hand, I was greatly pleased to see what has been done in the way of simplifying returns to be made. Ilsley as Minister of Finance found it impossible himself to explain some phases of the taxation question, and had to rely on Clark and his other officials to explain the matter to Council. It has all become highly technical and involved."

On Saturday morning, June 22, the Prime Minister got to work on the draft budget speech. "Made quite a number of revisions and one or two additions. The most important of all was striking out anything which indicated that the Conference was a failure, but stating explicitly in another place that the Conference had served a particularly useful purpose in enabling the provinces and the Dominion to understand each other's position and the difficult problems and situations which had to be faced; that it was as a result of the representations made at the Conference, and what had been learned in the course of the discussions, that the budget proposals in reference to the provinces had been framed and were being made in the budget. This, I think, is the correct and true line.

"When I read this portion over to Clark he was inclined at first to take exception to it. He said that Drew's conscience had been troubling him, and he had been making speeches trying to excuse himself. He thought he ought to be left to carry the blame of the failure of the conference. I reminded Clark that Manning of Alberta had stated the conference had failed because of the rigid views taken by the Department of Finance. That I thought it was better not to admit failure at all but rather an adjournment sine die which leaves the door open for taking up those portions of the matters presented to the conference which lie outside the immediate tax agreement. Clark did not press his point, but said I would perhaps be a better political judge than him. He kept stressing that Ilsley did not want any further conferences. I am sure that if we shut the door against any further conferences we would have a position that we could not maintain as further conferences will have to be held in reference to health, old age pensions, etc."

The budget speech was delivered on the evening of June 27. In it Ilsley outlined proposals for a tax agreement which could be entered into by any individual province. In compliance with the war-time tax agreements, the federal government undertook to reduce the standard corporation income tax from 40 per cent to 30 per cent effective January 1, 1947.

Personal income taxes were also cut. Federal succession duties were doubled but any province was allowed to impose duties up to 50 per cent of the federal total which could be deducted from the federal tax. If a province agreed to withdraw from the personal and corporate income tax and succession duty fields for a five-year period, the Minister of Finance proposed that it would receive an annual per capita subsidy under the terms presented by the federal government at the conference. Provinces which accepted these terms would be required to levy a 5 per cent tax on net corporate income within the province to be collected by the federal government and deducted from the annual subsidy.

Provincial reaction to the specific proposals was generally hostile and, during detailed negotiations early in 1947, the federal formula was significantly altered. However, the Prime Minister was reasonably pleased by the budget's reception in the House. "The part relating to the government's decisions respecting the provinces was loudly applauded by our Members and all groups opposite excepting the Conservatives. Also the portion of the budget dealing with reduction of taxation. Treatment of co-operatives. I think we were wise in not touching tariffs and also wise in not going ahead with increased outlays on health and social security matters at present.

"I was glad I had been present in regard to the budget and particularly to change the emphasis on the conference, pointing out that it had helped us to reach decisions on the budget, not taking the attitude that it had been a failure which I do not think it was. It seems to me we have done the logical and right thing."

Another urgent question facing Mackenzie King when he returned from London was wheat policy, particularly the conclusion of a long-term sales contract with the United Kingdom. In January 1946 Gardiner and MacKinnon had visited London to open the negotiations and talks had continued during the intervening months, complicated by suspicions in the United States that Britain and Canada were attempting to conclude an agreement which might discriminate against non-Canadian supplies and run counter to the American government's strong preference for multilateral rather than bilateral trade arrangements. A draft contract, which the British Minister of Food, Strachey, was in Ottawa to sign, was considered at the Cabinet meeting on June 19. "The contract itself, while it has advantages with regard to stabilization for the farmers, has nevertheless elements which are in the nature of a great gamble, as, for example, the certainty that the British Government will pay a higher rate than may be the current rate in a couple of years hence, to make up for their getting wheat at the present time at less than the current rate. Also whether we would not be blamed for entering into a bilateral agreement that destroys the multilateral plan which lies at the basis of the U.S. commercial policy for freer trade among nations and an ultimate world price for wheat. Still further whether it may not cost us some of the markets we should be able to have with other nations.

"Robertson had spoken to me about this over the 'phone at some length. I brought the matter up yesterday but brought it up anew today in considerable detail. I had Robertson come in to the Cabinet along with McIvor of the Wheat Board. Robertson outlined the dangerous position in which we might get Canada vis-à-vis the U.S. in negotiations. Looked very tired and it was embarrassing for him with Gardiner more or less abrupt in his way of meeting statements.

"The trouble is no one knows whether what he [Gardiner] is saying is altogether in accord with the facts or whether, what is perhaps more to the point, he may be on true ground as regards purely departmental arrangements and negotiations with some Board but quite wrong when he assumes that the U.S. Govt. etc., in relation to making a world peace have been kept informed as they should. The real truth is that enough people have not been safeguarding the situation in any of the countries and that transactions in any large order are left to the last moment and then put through as the result of pressure in one direction or another without the knowledge of more than a very few persons.

"While I was very tired, I managed to keep my mind and the mind of Council concentrated on this problem for a couple of hours and ultimately get agreement in a position from which there was no satisfactory solution. It was the choice of a lesser of two evils. We had a certainty in the matter of agreement against an uncertainty as to what American negotiations might come to. What I stressed, however, was we must let the Americans know our position before we sign any contract so that they could not say they would have objected had they known and wished we would have told them in advance, etc. It was agreed Pearson should tell them the situation.

"Strachey was to go to New York and contract was not to be signed until after his return, nothing to be said of it meanwhile. If agreement was reached while he was there, with approval by the Americans, well and good. Gardiner had insisted that Clayton of the [American] Secretary of State's Department had been present at negotiations . . . at which he, Gardiner, had explained the situation. Ilsley is very fearful of all these things but seems unable to suggest alternatives. The Cabinet, however, were unanimous as to what seemed possible to do in the light of the circumstances as they existed. I felt I had helped to save a very serious situation by keeping the discussion on the level it was at this morning and getting the E.A. [External Affairs] position properly registered."

The proposed agreement was considered again in Cabinet on June 20.

The Prime Minister "read a long despatch from Pearson which brought up the feelings of Americans now that they knew what was being arranged; a letter from Parker, of the Winnipeg Grain Pool, and a statement sent in by Lambert [Senator N. P. Lambert] and Senator Paterson which dealt with the dangers of the contract itself as Gardiner was seeking to have it arranged. After a very full discussion, it was agreed that Strachey who was now in Washington should go to see the State Department and explain the whole situation and get something worked out with them which would be satisfactory to Britain and the U.S. Word was to be sent to Pearson to let the Americans know the whole situation. Tell them we were prepared to hold up the signing of the agreement to see if they could work out something that would be satisfactory to both; if they could not, then we might have to sign when Strachey returned. . . ."

On June 25 Mackenzie King had a talk with Strachey who had just arrived back in Ottawa. "He admitted it was fortunate he had been there and that no statement had been made of our agreement prior to the settlement of the loan question," Mackenzie King wrote. "He admitted it might have prejudiced the loan," which had finally received President Truman's signature. Strachey "was entirely agreeable to have the agreement wait but felt it would be doubtful if we could do anything better in the end. Said the Americans had nothing constructive to offer."

Mackenzie King's next reference to the British agreement was on July 16 when he "talked with Robertson about wheat contract which was taken up later in Council. Apparently matters have gone so far that a contract will have to be carried out with Britain. . . . Gardiner has taken matters rather too much into his own hands. Fault not wholly his since matter discussed several times. However, it brings quite a conflict between the Departments of Agriculture and External Affairs." At the Cabinet meeting on July 17 there was another "long discussion on the wheat contract for Britain. Insisted no signature till British reply to U.S. received; also insertion of clauses prepared by Robertson in preamble and text to make clear Canada's position in not wishing to embarrass negotiations re U.S. commercial policy for freer world trade." The remaining difficulties were cleared away and the wheat agreement was signed on July 24. The United Kingdom agreed to purchase 160 million bushels of Canadian wheat in each of the next two crop years beginning August 1, 1946, and 140 million bushels annually in the third and fourth years of the agreement. A price of $1.55 a bushel was fixed for the first two crop years, declining to $1.25 a bushel in the third year and $1.00 a bushel in the fourth year.

Another major issue considered in the Cabinet was national defence policy. For some time the strategic importance of the Canadian north had been a matter of concern in both Ottawa and Washington and Mackenzie King had discussed some aspects of the problem with the British authorities during his visit to London. On April 1, 1946, the Canadian army had taken over the maintenance of the Canadian section of the Alaska Highway. Two months later the RCAF assumed charge of all facilities on the North West Staging Route, as American personnel were withdrawn, and also took over operation of the telegraph system from Edmonton to the Alaska border. "Exercise Muskox," which had been organized by the Department of National Defence earlier in the year, had yielded a good deal of useful information on logistical problems in a low-temperature climate but had also attracted an embarrassing amount of publicity, particularly since a few American civilian scientists and technicians had taken part. In the United States, the exercise seemed to be regarded as an initial step in a common plan of Arctic defence and rumours had circulated for some time that Canada had been asked to consider a full-scale plan for mutual defence in the region. At the Cabinet meeting on June 20, the Prime Minister reported, "the question was brought up of the U.S. seeking to get certain weather stations established in our territory and reference was made to a discussion of Council during my absence as to not allowing the Americans the use of Canadian territory for the protection of their own country. Gardiner had suggested that the exchange be made of the Pan-handle on the Pacific Coast for certain islands in the north. I am not at all sure that the Pan-handle is not in many respects a very strong protection to our own country. However, apart from this, I told Council what I had said in conference with Attlee, Lord Addison and Ismay with respect to the arrangements that would have to be made on this continent between the Americans and ourselves for the protection of North America; that the British admitted they could not hope to hold their own against Russia without the aid of the U.S. Also the belief . . . that the only war that was likely to come in the future would be a war with Russia and would be a war for world conquest.

"In overtaking the U.S., the Russians would make the base of operations – Canada, and on the whole we had to re-orient all our ideas about protection. I insisted there should be the fullest discussion with the British before we made any agreement with the U.S. which might affect the general plan, and also that we were not to be rushed in settlement on what was to be done. I said this whole matter needed the fullest possible discussion."

The *Financial Post* for June 29 carried a sensational article which charged that the United States, through its members on the Permanent Joint Board on Defence, had issued a virtual ultimatum to Canada on northern defence and had offered to build a series of air bases in the Arctic region to be equipped and operated by American personnel. In the House on June 28 Mackenzie King denied the charges and described the article as "wholly misleading and containing many inaccuracies," though he did admit that the Board was studying the question of Arctic defence, adding that it "would be remiss in its duties if it did not." The following day it was announced that a small group of American coast guard ships were scheduled for a training cruise in the north "to amplify existing knowledge of navigational and weather conditions," with the participation of Canadian navy, army and air force personnel. The expedition, which returned in October 1946, did establish a weather station in northern Greenland.

On July 9 Mackenzie King met with several of the Ministers "to enable the Chiefs of Staff and the members of the Intelligence Service [to] give us a presentation of the problem for the defence of Canada. I thought the whole business was well done. The subject was presented on the basis of the polar map instead of using mercator's projection. By the polar map, a clear picture was given of how this continent could be attacked from the North, from parts of both Europe and Asia and how it could be attacked also from Siberia. The purpose was to show the need of developing protection of the North by air. Something, too, of the protection of the seas and the whole involving a fantastic expenditure. It became perfectly apparent, I think, to all as we listened that Canada simply could not do what was necessary to protect itself. Our country would be a mere pawn in the world conflict.

"I drew out how the whole business had been worked out between the planning committee here and opposite numbers in Washington. That up to the present, the British had not been brought into the matter excepting being told something of the kind was under way. I said there must be the fullest exchange of views with the British on the whole question of defence. It was perfectly clear that the U.K., the U.S. and Canada must all work together and have their plans made complementarily as well as supplementarily – [plans] that are made relevant to each other and made in relation to those of other countries as well.

"The great thing was for Canada to be the link that would keep the other two great powers united. The whole story was very revealing but appalling particularly when it was pointed out that within five years' time, Russia might be in a position to deal with the atomic bomb. Her own power today being vastly greater than most countries conceived, and that the possibility of war might come at any time thereafter and it was almost certain to come within the next fifty years, perhaps very much sooner if there was not a complete change of attitude between Russia and other countries.

"The disclosures of this morning made clearer than ever the wisdom of my going to Europe and seeing while there as much as I can of the real situation; having as many interviews as possible with those who are really in the know." The implication was that no firm decisions would be made on this matter until after the Prime Minister had returned from Europe, if then.

Anthony Eden visited Ottawa late in June as a member of an Empire Parliamentary Association delegation and met the Prime Minister at Kingsmere on Sunday, June 23. Mackenzie King found him "a most delightful and companionable person." They talked "a good deal about Churchill. He told me, in confidence, that when Churchill came back from the States he had told Eden he would chuck the job, and he, Eden, would have to take on the leadership. However, after some weeks he decided he would keep on. Eden thought he would have to change and that the younger men in the Party did not like his getting into wrangles with the Government, and felt in some things he was too Conservative. He had been there long enough. Eden thought that perhaps when he went back this time it might be necessary to come to some arrangement. He, Eden himself, had thought it best for him not to continue. I told him what I had said. Smuts had said practically the same. He said Winston was wrong in thinking he could keep up the party fight. We both agreed he was not as strong as he had been, and it would be wiser for him to take the larger role of, if he likes, heading the party, but not leading in the House – even better, quitting party politics altogether.

"We talked considerably about the Russians. Eden was interested in what had taken place here. Thought it was an intensely interesting story. Said we had handled the whole matter superbly. He felt sure Churchill would much have appreciated our talks together. He told me Baldwin had always said to him that I was a very wise man. He himself spoke several times about the wisdom I had shown in different directions. He said at the time of the elections he had urged Churchill to stay on until the war with Japan was over, and keep the coalition together. They could then have broken up naturally, and if the Conservatives had lost then, well and good – if they had won, well and good. But Winston had persisted on going ahead at the time he did. He thought the most unfortunate thing was the break that had come between W. and Stalin. He did not know what could account for it, but said something he thought had happened at Potsdam, which caused them to become estranged. He thought that the speech made at Fulton went too far in getting directly at Stalin. Said that he, Eden, had cabled him in regard to the N.Y. speech not to say anything further on those lines, but to be very guarded. Eden feels deeply concerned about the whole situation in Europe and Russia's attitude in particular. Agrees we must be most patient. We had tea together after coming back [from a walk], and he left at a quarter to six for Government House."

Another visitor to Ottawa was Herbert Hoover, the former President of the United States. He had been commissioned by the American Famine Emergency Committee, appointed by President Truman, to make a survey of world food conditions and, as a gesture of appreciation for Canada's relief contributions, made a nation-wide broadcast outlining his findings on June 28. Mackenzie King had lunch with him at the American Embassy and "was much surprised to see how changed he had become in a few years, since I had last met him. He looked to me quite like Churchill. Admitted that had been quite frequently remarked. His voice was not prepossessing. However, once he began speaking of his recent tour, and narrated the chief incidents of it, I was agreeably surprised and impressed by the amount of information he gave in a precise and most interesting way. He told the Ambassador and myself that he had found the reports about starvation much exaggerated. When he got down to discuss with technical officers the actual situation, he found it, in many countries, quite different from that which the politicians had been stating it was. Later in the afternoon, he spoke at considerable length about Communism. Mentioned that in practically all the countries he visited, he found evidence of Communist propaganda which must have been paid for by Russia. Could not possibly have been met out of advertising or subscriptions for the papers that were using it. He feels it is a real menace to the world. He was critical of both Churchill and Roosevelt, having given Russia so much at some of the conferences. Also he is critical of the U.S. administration in yielding so completely to Labour. He says matters have come now to where some 8 or 10 men wield enough power through trade unions to control the business of the U.S.. . . I felt when he began to read his address over the radio, he was not doing himself justice. Atherton says this is the tragedy of his whole career. That when he is alone with 2 or 3, it is apparent how brilliant and well informed he is but once it becomes a matter of meeting numbers, he ceases to be able to express himself and becomes very silent.

"I was glad to have the conversation I had with him as it left a much more favourable impression than I had previously had. Indeed one felt there was wide knowledge and much in the way of sound judgment in his make-up."

With Vincent Massey's retirement as High Commissioner in London, Mackenzie King was faced with the problem of finding a successor among the senior officers of the Department of External Affairs. He had discussed the question with Norman Robertson on June 12. "Told him I thought Pearson would be the best man for London unless he wished to go there himself. He said that would raise the question of Wrong's going to Washington and that he did not feel equal to managing without Wrong. He himself would like to go to some small place like Switzerland or Dublin. I told him that would be quite wrong; in his present position he would have to take one of the larger posts if he left Ottawa but would not find that difficult seeing that the main problem was to have to do so many different things and not concentrate on any one. He would find Washington quite simple but would be nearer to Ottawa. I said that would leave Wrong in charge at Ottawa.

"Later I thought of Wilgress as another possibility for London. He thought of Tommy Davis for Moscow; changing Turgeon from Belgium to some other place and having Désy perhaps go back to Belgium as Ambassador. We left the matter for further consideration."

The Prime Minister had Pearson to dinner at Kingsmere on June 29 to discuss the London post. "Pearson is quite prepared to do whatever I may think best," Mackenzie King wrote, "either to stay at Washington, come to Ottawa, go to London, or elsewhere. He admits that, for him, London would represent the highest post of all and he would greatly welcome going there. He is concerned, however, about Robertson. He realizes that he is very tired and a little at a loss to know what decision to make respecting himself. He thought Wilgress would be a good person to bring to Ottawa, and let Wrong go to Washington. He believes Wrong has many friends in the State Department and would work well there. Pearson left about 9. I spoke to him of keeping in mind a possible future for himself in Canadian public life, stressing the need of leadership by those who have an understanding of world affairs."

Complicating this problem was the announcement on July 4 that the Council of Foreign Ministers had finally been able to agree on issuing invitations to a general conference of the twenty-one states, other than the great powers, who had participated in the war against Germany and its allies. The conference was scheduled to convene in Paris on July 29 to consider the minor draft peace treaties prepared by the Foreign Ministers. This development, Mackenzie King noted on July 5, "opened up an entirely new vista for the next few months. . . . Bracken asked me when the House opened whether I had received an invitation and whether I intended to represent Canada at the conference. He said he thought both the country and the Parliament would expect this and the official Opposition would help to make my going possible. I simply stated that no invitation had been yet received but I would make known the intention as soon as possible thereafter.

"I sent for Robertson and spoke to him at once about what might be necessary in the way of plans. I said I personally would like to stay on in Ottawa for the summer. That I was getting older; that I measured time in terms of the time I could have quietly in the country each year and that if I consulted my wishes, and feelings, I would definitely have St. Laurent go instead of myself. On the other hand, I said I thought Bracken was quite right when he said the country and Parliament would expect me to represent Canada at the Peace Conference. That had been one of the grounds on which the party had been returned to power. Also that among the public men of the world today, I was one of the few that had led his country through the war and was in the position now of the one who had held office longer than any living man. I thought Canada would expect me to go. I therefore said we should decide at once and seek to arrange accordingly. I told him to find out at once about ships. I would of course expect him to come with me.

"He spoke of Heeney. I said, yes, I had promised Heeney he would go to the conference but I would not wish to take many others. Heeney will have to take on some of the duties the others had taken on who were with me in London."

The Prime Minister then told Robertson about his talk with Pearson. "Asked him if he had seen Pearson since and how he felt about it. To my amazement, he said he had felt disappointed. I asked what had occasioned his disappointment. He said that he himself would have liked London. I said immediately to him that I had from the beginning told him that whatever post he wanted, he could have, mentioning London specifically. That I had gathered from Pearson when he was out the other night that he Robertson had talked the matter over with him before he came to see me. That they had talked on the lines on which we had talked on board the ship while on the ocean, at which time he, Robertson, had given me a little outline himself of what he thought the arrangements should be. That I had gathered from him that while he would have liked London for some reasons, he would not care for public appearances and public speaking which would be expected in London, but even more he would not like to give up the power of the great position which he now held for something that could not equal in influence what it amounts to. I said to him I had a distinct understanding with Pearson that there was no commitment. If in any way, Robertson preferred London, he should have it. Pearson thoroughly understood this and had taken the same view. Robertson said, yes, Pearson told me you had said that and that was how he felt. I then said to him would he say definitely that he wanted London, and he would have it. He fell back again in a chair and mentioned Dublin or Geneva; if he could be there for two or three years. I said that to me would be an indignity so far as he was concerned; also to the office, his position and Canada. These were trivial posts and he had a great position which should be maintained. I knew how he felt; that was due to fatigue; like the rest of us; he would like something easy for a while. That could be worked out right away. I said to him what I thought would influence him and what my own view would be was that in the position he now held, he exercised a great influence, not only in Canadian affairs and in Continental affairs but in world affairs. He was helping in the shaping of policy for Canada. He admitted he liked politics and liked to have to do with that side of things and would hate to give it up. Admitted that that was so. I said I thought that probably after he had been in London for a short time, he would realize the power he had exercised had passed into other hands. He would begin perhaps to regret that he had given up the most influential post in the service of the country (excepting possibly that of the Deputy Minister of Finance). I said it was for him to say he wanted London and that would then be decided. I think we must let Parliament know who is going to London, settle the matter definitely and plan accordingly.

"As a matter of fact, while in London, I told both Attlee and Addison I thought I would have Robertson come to London. I also told the King when he was asking me; that he was the one that I had in mind, but that I was not at all sure that he would be willing to take the post. I told Robertson that I intended myself to get rid of External Affairs between now and the end of the year. I said to him again not to make [up] his mind while he was tired. I would not press him in making up his mind but to be assured that whatever he wanted, whatever he wished was what I most wished, and also that I would feel perfect confidence of his handling of situations in London. I notice he is very tired and that there is no doubt he has very decidedly lost his grip on administrative end of departmental affairs."

Their discussion was resumed on July 6 and covered much the same ground. On July 9 the Prime Minister received a letter from Robertson stating that he would accept the London post. Arrangements for the trip to Europe were completed the same day. "Decided to give A.H. [Arnold Heeney] a chance. He spoke to me about taking a few days off for a holiday. Seemed surprised when I mentioned to him I thought of carrying out the promise I had made about his coming over to the Peace Conference. Said he would like that very much. I told him he would have to take on the duties that Gordon Robertson had taken on the last trip. Also the kind of thing that Vanier had done for me in London in looking after invitations and important correspondence, making plans for trips, etc. He said that he would not want to come unless he could be really useful. Naturally he would want to do all he could to help.

"With Robertson, I said we must decide at once on his successor. Thought that perhaps it would be best to have Pearson come to Ottawa and have Wrong go to Washington. Robertson had 'phoned Pearson on Sunday. He was quite agreeable to taking the new post. I mentioned Pearson being near at hand where he might be taken into the Ministry as Minister for External Affairs.

"Robertson spoke of taking [Charles] Ritchie who has been dealing with the [peace] treaties. I also said I would take [James] Gibson. Spoke to him in the afternoon. He seemed greatly pleased. He mentioned I had said a couple of years ago when the war was on, he might get that chance when the peace came. I wish he had measured up a little more in the interval. However, he is now seeking to do his best. . . .

"Robertson suggested Pearson might come over to UNRRA meeting in Switzerland, where he is much needed. We could talk over some matters in Paris. He also said Wilgress will be on a holiday in Geneva. He would come to Paris to help us there. With this group, I should have all the assistance necessary."

Mackenzie King telephoned Pearson on July 10 to tell him about Robertson's decision to go to London. "Also spoke to him about coming to Geneva to join LaGuardia on UNRRA matters. He quite understood Robertson's decision. Will also agree to go to Geneva. Said he would be prepared to do whatever was wished here between Washington and coming back to Ottawa. Reminded him it might be well to keep closely in touch with Canada with a view to getting into public life here. He would like an extra year in Washington. I think that is what Robertson and he have been hoping for. That I would hold on that time and then get out. I have felt we must make the decision now and not wait longer."

A number of major problems had to be either solved or aired before Mackenzie King left for Paris. Among the more important issues was further elimination of price controls. On the evening of July 3 he met at Laurier House with Ilsley, Towers, Gordon and Clark to discuss "taking the controls off a vast number of small commodities – having a list given of categories on which controls were being retained, but having it understood that on all of the commodities the price ceiling would be removed.

An Ottawa Interlude 273

I had said some days ago I thought this was wise. Gordon pointed out that people get terribly irritated when they read lists of [controls on] small commodities being removed. They get the idea the whole structure is going, whereas the real situation is not affected one way or the other. Ilsley was fearful lest some category might be omitted of significance. It was felt this could be covered at any time. We were all agreed on this."

The question of restoring the Canadian dollar to parity with the American, while maintaining the war-time system of foreign exchange control, was also discussed. Revaluation of the dollar represented an attempt to reduce the impact on the Canadian economy of rapid price inflation in the United States which resulted from the abolition of price controls in that country. Events were to show that the two assumptions on which the decision was based were unwarranted. Deflationary forces in the economy did not strengthen and Canada's foreign exchange reserves did not prove adequate to meet balance of payments problems which gradually emerged. In Mackenzie King's judgment, parity of the Canadian and American dollars would "be helpful to the masses of the people, particularly to farming communities. The manufacturers of implements may not like it; the gold mining people will certainly not like it and will raise good deal of a howl. I asked how the department justified keeping the Canadian dollar at a discount. Towers mentioned that there was always the objection at changing a rate because matters get settled around a certain ratio. Ilsley felt he would be asked why he had not done so a year ago. The answer of course is that matters at that time were very unsettled. The reason for doing it at the present time is the turn the crisis is taking in the U.S. with the removal of the Office of Prices Administration. That makes the present time opportune. Gordon says we cannot hold the price ceiling against what is happening in the U.S. without some change. The getting back to parity of currencies would help to steady the situation here a bit. I listened to all the arguments and felt what was being suggested was the wisest course. I strongly advised taking Parliament into confidence on Friday night and not to have the matter done by radio on Saturday or Sunday when the House was not in session. Ilsley stressed that great secrecy [was] essential. I suggested discussing the matter with St. Laurent and Howe before Council in the morning and with the balance of Council before six o'clock in the evening, making the announcement at 8. The announcement has to wait until 8 because of the difference of time in Vancouver. It would be a terrible scandal if any publicity was given to the announcement in advance."

At 6.00 P.M. on July 5 the Prime Minister met the entire Cabinet in his office and Ilsley "brought forward the statement of the financial measures deemed necessary to keep control of price ceiling, among others including having Canadian dollar again at par. Towers and Gordon and Clark were present. Dr. McCann was the one who questioned most the wisdom of the change because of the effect it would have on gold mining. Another reaction was from Fournier and other Quebec Liberals of the effect this would necessarily have on our chances in a by-election in Pontiac.

"I had written from N.Y. [in May] to bring on the election at once fearing just this sort of thing. That is the way by-elections are lost and governments defeated. I think we will have hard runs in all three by-elections. It will be lucky if we win Pontiac. We will not win Ontario and will probably lose Kenora-Rainy River. That meeting reminded me of the time when I returned from my talk with Byng after having resigned, and told the Cabinet they no longer existed. I think they all wondered whether we were defeating ourselves by the measures that were being introduced. I am personally wholly favourable to the step taken today which Ilsley announced at 8 in the House tonight."

At the Cabinet meeting on July 4 there was some discussion of the flag issue. Mackenzie King "urged strongly that we should press on and get a decision by Parliament on the flag. Cabinet were all favourable but seemed fearful of the opposition that the younger element in Quebec might raise. Also in some quarters there still continues to be a demand for a distinctive flag without people realizing how impossible it will be to get any agreement on a distinctive flag. I have no doubt myself that the Committee [of the House] will recommend the Ensign with a maple leaf in gold instead of a shield." The next day the Prime Minister gave the committee's chairman, Walter Harris, "painted maple leaf from Canada House as a symbol of the kind I thought should go on the Canadian flag."

During the meeting of caucus on July 10 Mackenzie King spoke at some length on the subject. "Went through the various steps taken to reach the point that we had now arrived at. Began with the McIntosh resolutions which had asked for a distinctive flag but one to retain the Union Jack and which our party had supported in the House. Made clear a distinctive flag did not necessarily mean a flag without the Union Jack. It meant something distinctive from the Union Jack itself. Told how gradually we had introduced the Red Ensign at Legations and conferences abroad. Of my promise at the Winnipeg meeting to have Parliament consider a national flag. Had used the Red Ensign for the Army in going into battle. Had the Red Ensign put up at Quebec when Roosevelt and Churchill were there. Had sent word from San Francisco to hoist the Red Ensign from the Tower; to keep it there V-E Day, and Remembrance Day. That was for a week and then again when Parliament met, passed the Order to place it there. Everyone rejoicing up to that point.

"We had then appointed a committee of the House; also incorporated in our Speeches from the Throne the satisfaction that Parliament had in endorsing the idea of a national flag, and has now appointed another committee to deal simply with the design. Made clear that members of the committee themselves could not agree on a design without the Jack. That the choice lay between the Union Jack as such and the Red Ensign with the maple leaf in autumnal colours. I strongly advocated the latter. Spoke too of the Jack not standing for subjugation. The Jack itself had not come into being until 1801. Also that it was under the British flag that Quebec was given her freedom of religion. She would not have had it under the Stars and Stripes and would not have had it under any other flag. Spoke very firmly about the day of nationalism being passed and the need of all countries sharing common ideas of freedom, to keep as close together as they can.

"I was given a fine reception immediately after. However, Arsenault [M.P. for Bonaventure] who had been a former Tory made a long speech which he read, arguing for a separate flag and wanting a further Caucus. He was listened to quietly but I made no reply and the Caucus broke up. I had told Caucus earlier I would be leaving for Europe and said I wanted to bring up these questions now before starting off."

On July 11 Mackenzie King talked again with Harris about proceedings in the committee. "I gather that at yesterday's meeting several of our Members were not present. They were at other meetings. However by a vote of 15 to 8, the flag proposed by the French Members was defeated in committee and sub-committee appointed to consider further the design of the flag with the Maple Leaf. [The sub-committee] met today and tonight radio announced there was only one against on the vote – LaCroix [who] ... opposed the design which all are agreed upon. It is the one that I have worked for from the start – substitution of the golden maple leaf for the Canadian coat of arms. And later the autumnal colours. The only point that I am doubtful about is the wisdom of having a white background to the maple leaf which the committee have put in as a means of satisfying Quebec but how and why it should be done for that reason, I do not understand. I think they have been led into errors through looking at the design that is before the committee – which is a flag being pasted on a white baseboard with a little margin around it. That seemed to call for a white border around the flag. However that can be made so small as to simply help to outline the leaf itself. I am glad the particular leaf I chose and which is based on the one taken from Canada House was used. It is the one I selected the last day I was in London. That is the one that has been agreed upon. It looks very beautiful. Its association with Canada

House in London is significant. I had to do with establishing Canada House. Canada House means its name in London itself and our flag comes to have the leaf which appeared there at the time of the Victory celebrations.

"St. Laurent spoke to me today about the government simply passing an order-in-council based on the resolution of the committee. If that were done, the French Members would probably let the whole matter drop. We would not need a debate in the House. I am inclined to think that is perhaps the best course to pursue. There will be no speeches made of an extremist character. Unless something is said which commits me to a formal resolution in the House I would think this course was correct. We did get a resolution favouring a distinct national flag at the first session of this Parliament.... The Committee having selected the design, the Cabinet can now proceed by order-in-council and accept it."

The committee's report was discussed in the Cabinet on July 12 and tabled in the House that afternoon. "It may well be that we can get through without a division," Mackenzie King wrote. "At any rate, the design is now agreed upon and it is the one toward which I have worked from the outset."

Angus Macdonald was the first provincial premier to respond to the federal government's new tax rental proposals. The matter was discussed in Cabinet on July 5. "I found Clark and Ilsley reverting back to the old order of having to refrain from giving the provinces any tax field of their own. I said quite openly that I thought holding to that attitude was only delivering the party over to the parties in power in Ontario and Quebec and in other provinces.... I thought the attitude we had taken, as I had said at the time, would cost us making an agreement then. We would have to yield in the end and it was only perpetuating a mistake to go on in that way. It was apparent that Council was with me and the telegraph reply was considerably modified. I feel very strongly we have been put in an entirely false position as a Liberal party by the way things have been handled by the Finance Department in regard to Federal-Provincial relations. Indeed it has been a great mistake leaving matters of this kind to the Bank of Canada and to Sandy Skelton and others who really had not the knowledge required. I am far from being sure that the party may not suffer heavily for the mistaken course it has taken in these matters. Manning of Alberta was prepared to sign and had most of the other provinces with him when Ilsley's rigidity, as he said, caused him to change. The unfortunate part of it all is that Duplessis is winning by pure demagoguery in Quebec. It will be a crime to allow him to run ahead of St. Laurent in the popular esteem. That is where this kind of thing leads to. I think I was helpful in Council in getting some things modified and other things left alone."

On July 15 the Cabinet discussed a draft reply to T. C. Douglas, the Premier of Saskatchewan, who was pressing for another full-scale conference with the provincial governments. "Ilsley was determined there would be no more conferences. I said I would never allow Government of Canada to say it would not confer with the provinces. We had made it clear we intended to confer on our welfare programme. The financial things were settled definitely in the budget. The others would come up in due course. Ilsley wanted Clark in. He wanted him to do the talking. Clark was very insistent on keeping in paragraphs to the effect that we could not hope for any settlement with the provinces and drawing attention to attitude of Ontario and Quebec, etc. I objected strongly to this. I said it was re-hashing, and reviving old grievances. What they wanted to know was for the future, not the past.

"Later I left it to Abbott as the one who would be acting Minister of Finance to work out with Clark a revised statement. I handed him in writing the paragraph that I thought should go in which was that we would meet with the provinces to discuss welfare matters in due course, and that this should go near the front. This was arranged during the day and several objectionable parts taken out but one or two others remained. I refused to sign with those parts in which had the effect of our Government pronouncing judgment as to certain failure of a conference if called.

"Left this to P. [Pickersgill] to take back to Clark. Later on, he said Clark had reluctantly agreed to cut them out. A telegram was sent with these further revisions."

Some days before it had been decided that Ilsley would leave Ottawa for a long overdue rest. On July 5 he had come to see Mackenzie King in his office. "He said I think I ought to quit right now. Everything is getting beyond me. I suffer terribly from depression in the mornings. Also my stomach is reacting against me. I cannot keep food on my stomach. But what is worse, I have this obsession as to whether I should have done this or that. It is just bordering on insanity and I think I ought to go out, to leave at once. I have been talking matters over with Abbott and he is ready to take on the budget. I will get out today or tomorrow if you think best. I said to him that I thought the symptoms he was exhibiting were those of race horses, actors and others before entering upon an immediate task. That once he had made his statement tonight, he would feel a great sense of relief. Also once the debate on the budget was under way. I said, however, if you feel that way, don't be concerned at all. We will manage all right. The budget is down now; what I think would be best is that you should stick it out over Monday and Tuesday. When we get to the resolution stage, let Abbott take over and handle the resolutions. He kept speaking about not wanting it to look as though he was running away. I said the public had too high regard for his character to think of anything of the sort. Apparently what had moved him was Bracken's statement, for he said: You of course will be going to the peace treaty. I could not act as Prime Minister. I could not stand the strain. I could not be making decisions; I could not stand the fight with Gardiner; I could not do it. In reply, I said to him not to be concerned about that. What I would like to do if he was away would be to make St. Laurent acting Prime Minister. St. Laurent would get along all right. This, of course, would bring another complication with Mackenzie. I had once thought of having St. Laurent come with me but the moment Ilsley spoke as he did, I thought the way was clear to have St. Laurent act as long as the House continues and perhaps come over later. He, I think, would feel honoured having the post of Acting Prime Minister. Ilsley then said he would let me know tomorrow."

The Prime Minister sent for Abbott and told him "to speak to Ilsley along lines I had indicated which he agreed were the best.

"I think the thing that worried Ilsley was the thought of the different provincial premiers coming to bargain with him about further agreements. The truth is that so far as Finance Department with their policies is concerned, he sees no way out of meeting a situation that is greater than he is capable of meeting. I do not wonder he feels concerned. The expenditures should never have reached the proportions they have. I myself have quite made up my mind after the talk with Ilsley to follow the course that I had been thinking over, namely, definitely decide to go and reach Paris in time for the opening. Make St. Laurent Acting Prime Minister and let Ilsley get away."

Mackenzie King discussed the matter with St. Laurent on July 9. St. Laurent "agrees I ought to go as P.M. and because of what was promised in the campaign," he wrote. "Also he thinks there might be a real chance for me to do something to help avoid the terrible situation that the world seems to be heading into. He spoke of the possibility of talks with Stalin. He, St. Laurent, is prepared to act as P.M. while I am away. Ilsley will be leaving as soon as the main votes on the budget are over. Abbott will be taking on that work. The problem of Mackenzie comes up anew but I think I can perhaps get him to accept the situation by intimating I may see whether I cannot arrange to have him made an Imperial P.C. After all, he is the oldest colleague I have and has perhaps done more than the others toward furthering social programme that has helped us to carry the elections. He has certainly shown a very fine spirit since my return. Quite a different man."

At next day's Cabinet meeting the Prime Minister raised the question of representation at the Paris conference. "St. Laurent and Mackenzie advocated having the Opposition represented. St. Laurent took the view that the people at large would like that attitude. I strongly opposed it myself on the score that Canada's interests in the Conference itself would not justify that and found all the other Members of the Cabinet with me. I said I felt rather strongly about not being the sole representative of the Government. I thought there should be a Minister with me. Cabinet were quite prepared to leave that to me to decide."

In conversation with St. Laurent on July 11, the Prime Minister asked him about the advisability of inviting Claxton to come to Paris. "I could see St. Laurent was a little embarrassed about anything being said until I spoke of the whole plan of his becoming Acting P.M., etc. I myself see as I thought it over during the night and morning and felt it would be well to have a colleague with me, not to take the sole responsibility for the Conference. It would be helpful to have some one to confer with; also to travel with in seeing battlefields, etc. I almost feel that members of the staff want to separate themselves, travel by themselves. Talk by themselves. They do not really share general things with me. With Claxton, it would be different. He, too, has a knowledge of French; is from Quebec; having been in the last war would be useful to travel with; also would debate questions in the House later. I would not have to defend everything myself should a difficult situation arise. I feel very strongly it is wise to have him come and have this known at once."

Everything was finally settled on July 12. Instead of attending the Cabinet meeting, Mackenzie King "had different Ministers come and talk over the situation with me. First of all, Mackenzie. Went over with him briefly again the circumstances of Privy Councillorships. Told him I could appreciate his disappointment and was prepared to make all allowances for his resentments, etc. That as a matter of fact, if I could do so in a way that would not be embarrassing to the British Government, I would still try to have his name considered. I felt he was my oldest colleague and had done great service in connection with war veterans and social legislation and also had been for over a quarter of a century in public life. He seemed to appreciate this very much. I then spoke about Ilsley's absence which brought up the question of who should act as P.M. I said I wanted him to know that in making a selection for this purpose, I had the responsibility of doing what I thought should be done in the interests of Canada and that with the knowledge I had of his physical condition and the documents which he himself had given me that I did not think I would be justified in having him in that position during my absence. I felt that the House and our colleagues would probably expect St. Laurent to assume this obligation. He said at once that St. Laurent was one of the finest of men; that that would suit him all right. He would be very happy. I said: You will continue as President of the Council and act as House leader. I told him also what I had in mind for Ilsley. He was quite pleased and I am sure the talk has helped to remove all feeling. His manner throughout the day made it clear he was really relieved in feeling.

"I then had St. Laurent come in and told him of my talk with Mackenzie and that I had felt I should take another Minister with me and that I thought Claxton was the one to take. That I had in mind the possibility of having Claxton succeed me in External Affairs and this would be the best way to make him obviously the choice for that position. I did not want any of the Ministers to feel that they had a prescriptive right to any of the posts of the Government. St. Laurent admitted Claxton was one of the most helpful men in the Government and it might be a little hard for him in his dealings with Howe and others if Claxton were away, but he thought he would be the right choice and I would be wise to take him.

"I then sent for Claxton himself. Told him what I had in mind and asked if he would arrange to come. He said it would be a great honour. He would be greatly pleased but would prefer to fly and spend the intervening ten days assisting in the Government.

"I then got something prepared on Ilsley – an order-in-council appointing him to UNRRA Council in Geneva and went into the Cabinet with my statement as finally revised. I read it aloud. When I came to the part about a Minister accompanying me, I said I had felt definitely that I should have someone with me and if anything happened to prevent my being in the next House, someone should have a first-hand knowledge of the Paris Conference and be in a position to report upon it. That was only one reason. Others were I felt the desirability of having a colleague to counsel with myself and I ought to have someone from the Province of Quebec – someone who would be helpful too in the French language and useful in proceedings of the Conference itself. I then said I had decided to ask Mr. Claxton to come.

"I had earlier explained the position about Ilsley. We had all recognized he was tired and should go away. I felt it would be much better for him if he would go to Switzerland instead of to California. I read the letters that had come from LaGuardia and said it seemed to me this was a mission he could well undertake; one which was an important one and that it could be made quite plain he was combining the work with rest and change. I asked Ilsley if that would suit him. He said nothing would suit him better. He seemed greatly pleased and all colleagues seemed pleased. I then said that raised the question of the Acting Prime Minister. That I had thought we would all agree Mr. St. Laurent should certainly act in that capacity.

An Ottawa Interlude

It was putting a heavy load on him with other matters but we knew he would be equal to anything of the kind. Colleagues also seemed quite pleased at this."

In the House of Commons that afternoon the Prime Minister announced that he would lead the Canadian delegation to Paris and would be assisted by Claxton. The alternate delegates were Robertson, Heeney, Wilgress, Vanier and Lieut.-General Maurice Pope, head of the Canadian Military Mission to the Allied Control Council in Germany. Mackenzie King made it clear that the Canadian delegation would take an interest only in the general nature of the peace treaties and not in the specific issues such as boundaries, population transfers, war damage and indemnities which were of direct concern to the European states. Canada's role, he suggested, would "lie in helping the countries more directly concerned to work out agreed solutions which are fair and will be likely to endure."

Earlier in the day the Prime Minister had received an advance copy of the final report of the Royal Commission on Espionage, and had made arrangements to see the Soviet Chargé d'Affaires at his office in the afternoon. The report "is a huge volume," he wrote. "I am sorry for this. I am afraid it will be made use of by Russia as an effort on the part of Canada to destroy Communism and may hinder rather than further the object we have in mind. However, as the report names additional persons of the Embassy involved, Robertson and I felt it desirable to tell them in advance who these persons were and to say that the Government thought they might wish to have these people return themselves of their own accord instead of having the Government make a formal request.

"I had a memo before me of the numbers involved in the Embassy – some seventeen in all, with some six new names. Belokhvostikov came as Chargé d'Affaires. He had with him a lady member of the Embassy whom I met with Mrs. Zaroubin and who acted as interpreter. The Chargé d'Affaires coloured up quite a bit as additional names were mentioned. They were relieved when I said I hoped they would let Mrs. Zaroubin know for me that the Commission had directly stated that the Ambassador was not involved.

"I gave him a list of the names as given in the report and a memo of particulars I had stated orally. He said he could see that the matter was one the Government at Moscow would have to deal with and he would advise them at once. He said the attitude of the Moscow Government had been set out in a communication received in February and then later he spoke of a communication in April. I said nothing about those excepting to identify the one of February which made use of the expression that the same things that were inadmissible had been done by the Embassy officials here.

"It was the second communication that the Chargé d'Affaires evidently wanted to make particular reference to.

"Robertson at the outset had intended to give a copy of the report to the Chargé d'Affaires. I was amazed at this. It shows how tired he is or he could never have thought of letting a document of the kind get into the hands of the enemy before it was even presented to Parliament. One could be assured that between now and Monday next, the whole business would have been gone over by Russian Embassy lawyers and others, and probably given in part to the public before our own press and Parliament and people had any knowledge of it.

"Robertson of course agreed it was better to follow the course I was taking and cancel the report itself entirely until it is tabled. I had hoped to be able to make the statement in the House on this report this afternoon but though some of the staff had worked all night getting matters in readiness, they had only been able to make out an index with important quotations. Robertson undertook to have something prepared over the week-end."

The report, which was dated June 27, 1946, was tabled in the House on July 15 and, the following day, Mackenzie King met Igor Gouzenko for the first time. "I had the police bring Gouzenko to my office and . . . Robertson and I had a talk with him in their presence. I told him I was very pleased at the way in which he had conducted himself throughout the period of great anxiety. I thought he had done a great service and wanted him to know that I appreciated his manliness, his courage and standing for the right, etc. I asked him if he had read the book 'I Chose Freedom.' He said he had. I asked him if he had thought of writing himself. He said that he was writing something, bit by bit. I said to him I thought he ought to have in mind not to do it too quickly but to begin with his own life; his ancestors and early bringing up. His ideas; his training; what caused him to change his views, etc. He told me afterwards he was very pleased to know I had thought well of his writing his life. I asked him a number of pointed questions, among the number as to whether the atomic bomb had made any difference in the espionage business, so far as Canada was concerned, or a difference between America and Russia. He said he did not think so. That the espionage had been on for years. It began immediately after the Russian revolution. Plans were made then for training men. That the Russians were imbued with the Marxian doctrines. So far as the bomb was concerned, it was just one more weapon that had to be considered. They believed that Communism would have to conquer the world. That they would not let any information in to Russia but would [not] give the Russians much information about the outside world. They did not want our ideas of democracy to develop there. I

An Ottawa Interlude 283

said I had thought of going to Russia; asked him what he thought of it. He said Stalin would receive me nicely. Would tell me he knew nothing about these inadmissible things; was sorry but they did not represent the Government's attitude toward Canada. I asked if it [a visit] would be looked upon as an effort at appeasement. He said the Russians always advertise any distinguished visitor as an evidence of the great respect the rest of the world had for Russia.

"Gouzenko said you would not get carried away by banquets and the attentions they would show you. You would talk to Stalin frankly. He would be equally frank in talking with you because it would not make any difference in what they would do. They would go on in the same way. He thought writers in America made a mistake in not distinguishing between the Soviet Govt. and the Russian people. It was a trained minority that really governed. It was a tyranny. I asked him if he thought the Ambassador was really without knowledge of what was going on. He said that Russia's policy was to choose as Ambassadors men who were either very innocent or were nonentities, depending on the place to which they were going. They were chosen so as to keep them out of being in the 'know' of things. He felt, however, that the present Ambassador had had a wider knowledge than the Commission had assumed; for example, when the two Generals came over from Russia, went through Canada, the U.S. and Mexico and returned to Canada, the Ambassador had promised to help them on their mission in any way he could. He said sometimes the real Ambassador was the chauffeur. An Ambassador would have to report to the chauffeur at the end of the day's proceedings if the chauffeur happened to be a General or whoever was in charge. He made a fine impression on Robertson and myself.

"Gouzenko is a young man of about 27 – youthful in appearance. . . . Clean cut. Steady eyes. Keen intellect. Spoke well of the support his wife had given him. I spoke nicely about her and the children. Told him the Government would keep an eye on them all and to keep his faith strong. He said he would certainly do that.

"I spoke to him about his paintings. He said: Yes, he had some paintings; his wife also. He would like to have brought some along. I noticed when I shook hands with him as he was going away that he had apparently been under a strain in talking with me. His hand was warm, perspiring a little. He showed no sign of it as he conversed. I let him see that I believed in him as I do and felt him to be a real person with a mission. I would have liked to have had an afternoon instead of an hour with him. May do so after returning from the Conference. He certainly reveals a condition of things that is alarming."

On the basis of the information in the reports of the Royal Commission, eighteen persons were brought to trial. Eight were found guilty and served a prison sentence, one was fined, and the rest were acquitted either in the first instance or on appeal. Fred Rose was convicted on June 20 and received a six-year sentence; Sam Carr, who had disappeared after Gouzenko's disclosures, was arrested in New York on January 28, 1949, and sentenced to six years in prison on April 8, 1949. Allan Nunn May, "Primrose," was convicted in London on May 1, 1946, for violations of the Official Secrets Act and sentenced to ten years imprisonment. Kathleen Willsher, the Deputy Registrar in the United Kingdom High Commissioner's office, received a three-year sentence and Emma Woikin was sentenced to serve two and a half years on April 15, 1946.

On July 15, just before the Prime Minister left for Paris, the Steel Workers Organizing Committee of the Canadian Congress of Labour called a strike against the Steel Company of Canada, Algoma Steel Corporation, and Dominion Steel and Coal Corporation, Sydney, Nova Scotia, the most spectacular of a long series of work stoppages during 1946. At both Sydney and Algoma the plants were closed completely but in Hamilton the Steel Company had made arrangements to house and feed a portion of the work force and the plant continued to operate at about half capacity. The union demanded a return to the 40-hour week in the industry and, noting the $5.00 per ton increase in the price of steel authorized earlier by the Wartime Prices and Trade Board, a wage increase of 19 1/2 cents an hour. With war-time regulations still in effect, the strike was technically illegal since the union had made no attempt to carry the case for a wage increase to either the national or regional War Labour Boards. Anticipating strike action on July 10, the federal government had taken control of the three plants and the Minister of Labour announced the appointment of F. B. Kilbourn as Controller.

The strike was discussed in Cabinet on July 15 and Mackenzie King "strongly counselled avoidance of any use of force; to let the provincial government ask for assistance of the civil authorities but to be very careful not to interfere. To use police rather than armed soldiers if matters demanded that. But at all costs to keep on with conciliation. Suggested some form of enquiry to be going on publicly while the strike is continuing and which would help to disclose who is at the bottom of violating the law; not to attempt any imprisonment at present.

"Ilsley said this would be letting Labour defy the Government – something that the Government should not stand for. I asked him how he could succeed. I pointed out that if the Government today would make labour work by force, it would create a civil war if anything of the kind were attempted. Howe who had been brave on these lines some time ago was pretty silent."

An Ottawa Interlude   285

By next day, Mackenzie King was even more convinced that some sort of inquiry should be begun, preferably by the Industrial Relations Committee of the House of Commons. At the Cabinet meeting he told his colleagues that he "had been thinking matters over very carefully and wished to say that I thought the utmost caution should be taken against trying to enforce penalties or coping with the situation by force. That I would like to repeat what I had said yesterday about appointing some body that could bring out the facts authoritatively and keep feeding them to the public so as to help to create public opinion that would on one hand bring the parties in dispute together, and on the other, give the Government reason for not taking immediate action with respect to penalties, but which would justify them in enforcing the penalties where investigation showed that certain persons were responsible for continuing the strike unnecessarily. Howe later agreed with this. Mitchell was a little slow about agreeing with it.

"After discussion of the matter for a time, I left it with a final word to colleagues during my absence. Singularly enough, when the House opened this afternoon, the debate began on the budget, Smith, of Calgary, intervened in the debate to suggest that a committee of industrial relations be called together at once and that the parties be made to appear before them. I thought his suggestion a very wise one and right along the lines of what I had been discussing in Council. Only he got the question before the House of Commons. I had not intended to speak in the budget debate but fortunately I had remained in when I saw Smith was speaking on the strike. I said to Mackenzie and St. Laurent I thought he was right in his suggestion. Mackenzie agreed and said why don't you follow him at once. I told Mackenzie to ask Howe and Mitchell what they thought of my doing that. Howe said he agreed. Mitchell also. I did not wait to speak to anyone else but the minute Smith concluded I rose in my place and said I thought he was right in his suggestion and I would be prepared to second it. I spoke for a few minutes on the importance of the community as the third party to industry. I noticed the House seemed quite pleased at the attitude I took. Tories applauded and other parties as well. Our own men were much relieved. Chevrier said he thought it was a ten-strike.

"I was particularly pleased to be able to have a word on the strike before leaving, to participate in this debate offhand without any notes and to really give in a few words the substance of what appears in my Industry and Humanity. I am hopeful that good may come of this. I think Howe and Mitchell are for fighting the issue out. I do not believe they can succeed. I think the plans the Hamilton Company are adopting of bringing in food by aeroplane to men and the like is all nonsense. What I do hope is that the enquiry before the industrial commission will bring out the facts, and the mere fact that they are being investigated publicly will make the party in the wrong come to time. I am far from believing that the wrong is all on one side."

At the Cabinet meeting on July 17, the Prime Minister again counselled "great moderation" in the handling of the dispute, an attitude he carried with him to the deliberations in Paris.

CHAPTER NINE

The Paris Conference

THE PRIME MINISTER, accompanied by Robertson, Heeney, Gibson, Handy and Nicol, left Ottawa for Halifax on July 18 and sailed for Liverpool on the *Georgic* the following day. The voyage was uneventful. They docked on the morning of July 26 and arrived in London about 3.30 P.M. Among others who met them at the station was Claxton who had arrived by plane earlier in the day.

Mackenzie King's first caller was Lord Addison and then Attlee. The former "was exceedingly pleasant and is much looking forward to visiting Canada. . . . Attlee, I found, also very pleasant but I could see was quite tired. He kept rubbing the top of his head with his fingers, twirling his hair most of the time that he talked. I could see that he was experiencing considerable nervous strain but said nothing about it. He had given up the thought of going to Australia. I gathered from him and Lord Addison that Bevin was rather hopeful of things going well at the Conference. Also that the Russians had been less difficult toward the end [of the meetings of the Council of Foreign Ministers] and it was quite clear they did not intend to let things come to a break. They had found a good deal of difficulty with America in connection with the Jewish situation in Palestine through America not understanding the implications. Again Attlee thought that there was some improvement in the situation there but admitted it was very grave.

"Lord Addison spoke of an Indian visitor who had been a long time in Russia and had said that even now the Russian people did not realize they were still slaves. He thought the country would wake up to the need of two things: freedom and religion. He believed that would help to solve their problem vis-à-vis the rest of the world.

"Both Addison and Attlee spoke most appreciatively of the wheat agreement. Addison said he did not think the Americans should complain about the purchase. They had already bought the entire Cuban output of sugar."

The Prime Minister had noted in the House of Lords Hansard that R. B. Bennett's speech on the amendment to the British North America Act on redistribution had been helpful and constructive. Reporting on his first evening in London, which was spent with the Salisburys, he wrote that "Frank spoke with deep feeling about the way in which Bennett had referred to the painting [of Mackenzie King]. Said he did not think Salisbury could ever do anything finer. Also that he had spoken very nicely about myself. He said Bennett does not look well. He himself suggested the possibility of our going to see Bennett. I told him of what I had been thinking over and I am to let him know in the morning." Mackenzie King did decide to call on his old political enemy the next day, only to find that he was not in London.

The great event of the Prime Minister's brief stay in London was receiving a letter, which had gone to Ottawa and been returned to London, inviting him to become a Bencher of Gray's Inn. "I do not know of anything that my father could have believed to be a higher honour nor can I begin to say what I feel in my soul about this link with the legal profession. To be made a Bencher of any of the Inns of Court of London, England, was a higher honour than can be given by the legal profession in Canada to anyone. My own country has not thought it well to make me an honorary member of the legal profession though [it] has been known to the Chief Justice and others that this is something I would have really appreciated beyond words. However, this higher honour has come which brings me into the profession to which my father did great honour in his day. I am happy beyond words about it. That this honour should come in the first night in London is something I am profoundly grateful for.

"I rang up [Viscount] Greenwood in the morning to let him know about it and to answer a couple of letters I had received from him. He told me that Churchill and others had been most enthusiastic about my being invited to become a Bencher. Churchill himself is a Bencher of Gray's Inn."

On Sunday, July 28, Mackenzie King and his party took the morning boat train to Paris. They arrived at 6.30 P.M. and the Prime Minister drove with Georges and Pauline Vanier to the Hôtel Crillon, the headquarters of the Canadian delegation. "Nothing in this world could be lovelier than the rooms that have been assigned to us. I have a suite corresponding to that which I had when here before, looking out on to the Place de la Concorde and overlooking the U.S. Embassy – only it is on the third floor instead of the first. The sunlight was shining in the window when we came in. There were flowers in the room. Walls freshly painted. Furnishings and all just as lovely as they could possibly be. Looking out across the Place de la Concorde was a sight which it was beautiful to behold.

The Paris Conference

"Claxton had been given a suite next to mine, overlooking the Place de la Concorde. Robertson and Heeney have suites immediately adjoining and facing the front. Handy's room, just immediately adjoining mine, looking out across the Place de la Concorde."

The following morning (July 29) the Prime Minister went to the Ministry of Foreign Affairs to be received by M. Bidault, the provisional President of France. "M. Bidault looked splendidly groomed, very alert. He is most active. Has a tremendously difficult post. Is provisional President of the Republic; also President of the Council and Minister of Foreign Affairs.

"As, at the present time, there is no second Chamber, the people will be having a referendum on the new Constitution which likely will provide one. One could not have been received with greater dignity and formality. Officials everywhere punctilious in their respective duties. The office in which M. Bidault received Vanier, Claxton and myself was one in which I was received by Briand at the time of the Briand-Kellog Pact after the last war.

"I recalled witnessing there the reception of Stresemann, of Germany, by Briand – the first time the Foreign Minister had been received in that office after the Franco-Prussian war. Mr. Bidault extended a very cordial welcome to France. Spoke of his visit to Canada. Our meeting in Geneva, and of the Conference. He said about the Conference, it might last a long time – possibly seven weeks. There were lots of people that liked to talk. Others that liked to stay in Paris. It was time to think that the date fixed for the opening of the United Nations in New York – the 23rd of September – might hasten the conclusion. I said to him I doubted if I could stay beyond August. Wondered if it would be necessary. He said he thought that by that time, some of the more important members might be taking their departure leaving others to follow up. He seemed quite certain that the Conference would run on for about two months altogether. Spoke particularly of the translation of speeches into Russian as well as French and English.

"He said when I referred to his heavy responsibilities, wishing him well etc., that he hoped we would have compassion on him. I said we would give immediate evidence of that by not taking up his time. Expressed appreciation of the honour he had done Canada in receiving myself and colleagues, the first of any of the delegations. It was arranged that Mr. Attlee was to be received at half past twelve."

From the Quai d'Orsay, Mackenzie King and Claxton went to the Hotel George V where Attlee and other members of the British delegation were meeting with representatives of the Dominions and their advisers. Most of the discussion at the meeting concerned the thorny question of voting procedure. Of course, the conference as such had no power to *draft* the peace treaties because it had been called merely to examine the material prepared by the Council of Foreign Ministers and to make observations and recommendations. The issue was whether these recommendations should be adopted by a two-thirds majority, the system preferred by the Soviet bloc, or by a simple majority. The great powers, including the United Kingdom, had agreed to act together in upholding clauses of the treaties upon which agreement had already been reached and simple mechanics dictated that it would be impossible to secure a recommendation for modification of these clauses with a two-thirds majority because the great power votes, with those of the Soviet bloc, could prevent such a result. The Prime Minister reported that the morning "was taken up pretty much with Evatt monopolizing the entire proceedings and in a manner which was distinctly rude and unpleasant. I thought Attlee was wonderfully patient with him though I did notice that, on a couple of occasions, he spoke most forcibly and I was afraid was going to lose his temper in replying to Evatt.

"Evatt's line was all in the way of objection to the Big Four having taken matters into their own hands; that the other nations really had little to do with the making of the peace. He opposed the idea of two-thirds majority rule for amendments, etc.

"I had just been seated when I was asked my views on the latter question. I said I thought on important matters, two-thirds majority was all right as against a bare majority in that I doubted if the Big Four would pay any attention to a bare majority. Two-thirds majority would be impressive.

"During the discussion later, after finding most of the other Dominions including India siding pretty much almost altogether with Evatt and ending up each time by saying the whole thing would be a farce; an upset; nothing would be done and so forth, I stressed the work that had already been done. Emphasized taking the long view; making this Conference succeed; protesting, if they liked, against the extent to which we had been circumscribed and not making certain things precedents but at all costs keeping Russia in the Conference, not allowing her to bring forward fresh difficulties each time fresh difficulties were raised by our own people.

"Attlee spoke with warm feeling about the necessity of viewing the results as a whole and in considering amendments, having regard to the composition as well as numbers in the votes taken.

"I must say I was altogether with Attlee . . . not only in sympathy but as to the wisdom of the procedure in the light of circumstances as they are.

The whole business was more like a family quarrel than anything else. It was arranged to continue discussion later in the evening."

After dinner, Mackenzie King returned to the British Prime Minister's suite where the morning's discussions were continued in "a somewhat better mood. The British took the position which in the morning I said I thought they would surely be able to take which was they must support what the Big Four did on matters on which they were agreed but that they would be free to consider further representations among the Big Four on all matters other than those on which the Four were actually agreed, and there to consider matters in the light of fresh arguments presented.

"What Attlee kept emphasizing and rightly so was the encompassing nature of what had been achieved – some things Russia had given up which Britain was most anxious she should, and the yielding on one or two things by Britain to make this more important step possible. He felt if these things were all re-opened, the whole business would go to pieces. Also I felt the last thing we would wish is to have the subject matter of this conference thrown into a United Nations as a whole. There would be no peace settlement if it ever reaches that stage.

"Tonight I stated that I would modify my position on the simple majority rule as against two-thirds and would support those with a bare majority seeing that the wording of one of the agreements provided that recommendations would be considered by the Big Four. The British will support that position after having taken the other in the first instance but finding too strong support for it. I pointed out to Evatt during the night that at the Prime Ministers' Conference in London, we had all agreed that Bevin had taken great care of the Dominions position and that we had all been making representations right along and things were being carefully watched.

"Attlee said to me I had been most helpful and I think I was. Claxton also brought forward and I supported him, the view that the Big Four should consider recommendations as we went along, as was done at San Francisco; not leave everything to the end to be gone over before the signing but rather to clean up as we went along. That seemed to impress the British and they are going to try to have that followed." Mackenzie King made this suggestion at the first plenary session of the conference and, in fact, the foreign ministers of the great powers did meet periodically to review and discuss proposals which emerged during the conference's proceedings.

At the end of the meeting, one of the British delegates speculated that the Soviet Union would oppose any recommendations for alterations in the draft treaties. Mackenzie King "said if they did, mounting public opinion would rise against them, and that publicly it would lead in the end to their accepting enough to make sure that the Conference did not break up just as they had done at the gathering of Foreign Ministers."

That afternoon, the formal opening of the conference had taken place at the Luxembourg Palace. "Among others whom I recognized," the Prime Minister wrote, "was my little friend from Ethiopia who had been at Geneva. He was quick in returning my smile toward him. I began to notice how tired I was when I could not think of the title or name of Haile Selassie; also I found other names difficult to recall. I enjoyed the few formal proceedings though again was somewhat disgusted at Evatt leaping into the arena at the start and making a somewhat immoderate speech in relation to procedure in respect to which, in itself, he was technically in the right. He seemed, however, to want to get on record he was fighting for the small powers as against the Big Four Powers. It is really unfortunate a man of his temperament and character should be taking the prominent place he is everywhere. It is equivalent almost to an abdication on the part of Britain of her position. I personally feel it is much better to maintain a dignified silence."

The plenary session on July 30 was again concerned with procedure. Mackenzie King was asked if he would nominate M. Spaak of Belgium as chairman of the committee on procedure. "Not knowing anything about what the attitude of the delegates generally might be, I felt it wiser to decline. To my amazement, when the proceedings opened, Evatt jumped in and proposed Spaak. Immediately after, Molotov proposed a delegate of Yugoslavia. It would have been most unfortunate if the proceedings had opened by Molotov apparently taking some exception and a nomination made by myself at the opening. This of itself would have made a sensational feature. As it was I thought it was a great pity that there had not been some arrangement in advance. It would have prevented the nomination of two candidates which gave the appearances of Russian and anti-Russian forces, thereby defeating the Conference in this way at the very beginning.

"Later it was moved by Mazaryk of Czechoslovakia that they should hold office alternately, a day at a time. The British opposed this; also the U.S. Molotov favoured it. I favoured it. Glad to have a chance at the outset to cast a first vote which showed no antagonism toward anyone. The motion was lost by 12 to 8 and one abstaining. In voting for the Chairman, I voted for Spaak. The ballot was secret. 13 to 7 – one abstaining. It was a pity that those favourable to Spaak were forced to appear to support Evatt's nomination. The greater part of the morning was taken up by proposals and counter-proposals by him [Evatt] and Molotov over the smallest kinds of point. I was surprised at the British attitude. Indeed the Big Four had not themselves taken care to see that this nomination was properly arranged without any division. It just seemed to me that everything that was done this morning seemed, if not to have been wrong in itself, to have been done in the wrong way and most unfortunate in serving to divide forces rather than to unite them. One feels there is no guiding spirit or direction at the Conference. That the Big Four have evidently decided to let things take pretty much their course. One senses the feeling of fatigue on all sides."

Another strike against the conference's potential success, in Mackenzie King's judgment, was the decision that morning "that the press should be admitted not only to plenary sessions but also to proceedings of the procedure committee and of the several commissions. This means that many more speeches will be made than would otherwise be the case and the playing up to the susceptibilities of the different countries and peoples. I believe an almost impossible way to secure agreement. Another way of widening the breach between those countries already more or less opposed."

The Prime Minister spent most of August 1 working on his own speech for the fifth plenary session. In the list of speakers the next day, he followed Masaryk and, repeating the substance of his remarks in the House on July 12, indicated that Canada's role in the conference would be a modest but constructive one. "Canada's interest in the successful outcome of the deliberations of this Conference is obviously less immediate and direct than that of some of the participating countries," he asserted. "Our concern as a nation is to see that, as far as we can help to make them so, the peace treaties will be based upon broad and enduring principles of justice and equity." He "found no difficulty in reading the material I had. There seemed to be an astonishing silence while I was speaking and my voice sounded to me much stronger than I had expected it would be. Here and there, I made a slip or two which I corrected in a natural way and altogether got through without any mishap, and I think, on the whole, with good effect.

"At any rate, I was given a very cordial reception at the close. Attlee shook hands quite warmly when I resumed my seat and later Byrnes who had been out when I was speaking, had the new [American] Ambassador to Italy come to my seat to ask if I had a copy of the manuscript that he might read. Later he brought it back to me himself and spoke most appreciatively of it.

"One member of the Australian delegation . . . came from his seat and said to me he thought it was the best delivered speech and the best speech which he had heard at the Conference. My own little group seemed to feel that all had gone well."

"Through the day," he added, "my thoughts have been much of Pasteur and how remarkable it is that it should fall into my lot to speak of him in the heart of Paris and to bring to the attention of the world anew his great contribution as one of the saviours of mankind. I have recalled how my brother Max was the first to draw my attention to him when he sent to me Vallery Renaud's LIFE OF PASTEUR and drew my attention to the paragraph which inspired my INDUSTRY AND HUMANITY. I have since placed a replica of the slab over Pasteur's grave, over my brother's grave, at Mount Pleasant.

"What I was saying today brings before the world anew what I wrote in my Industry and Humanity. It all helps to complete the circle which began with my care of my brother in his illness; of his being the one responsible for the theme which I developed in INDUSTRY AND HUMANITY; of writing the book 'a Study in the Principles Underlying Industrial Reconstruction' at the end of the last war and now bringing them to the attention of the world anew after the last war and at this time of the first Treaty of Peace."

On the evening of August 3 Mackenzie King had a talk with Pearson who had just arrived from Geneva and who reported that Ilsley was "in much better shape and enjoyed the trip across. Believes he will be all right after a little time in Switzerland. I opened up with Pearson the question of his coming to Ottawa as Under-Secretary of State for External Affairs. He is of the same opinion as myself that Robertson had really not known his own mind and had changed it at the last. He, Pearson, had had the distinct impression from him that he was to stay on in Ottawa. However this is now definitely decided and also that Wrong will go to Washington. Pearson was troubled about two things: (1) the problem of getting a house in Ottawa, time, etc. I said I thought we must make an announcement at once and have all the changes arranged during the autumn. The other (2) was the expenses of living and the need of some allowance to enable him to entertain persons from foreign departments of government who would be coming from time to time to the city. He explains that he has become used to a certain scale of living which he finds essential for carrying on the business of representation of Canada and feels that the situation would be more difficult at Ottawa. He knows Robertson has found it such. I agreed it was necessary to have a fund which could be used for entertaining foreign guests. I, myself, had felt the need of it. Could not have thought of doing the entertaining I had done without it. I told him this would be managed somehow. Robertson has since suggested that the salary of the Under-Secretary of State of External Affairs should be that recommended by the Commission on Salaries – $15,000. I imagine Ministers will not altogether like this but I, myself, feel it will be necessary to have something done along that line.

"I spoke to Pearson about the possibilities the post might offer of his entering politics which I think he would like to do, but he wisely states that he is not letting that enter his mind at all. Will concentrate wholly on External Affairs regardless of party altogether and will be quite happy to stay on in that field and later perhaps return to some post of representation abroad. I could see that for him as well as for Robertson, the whole situation has occasioned a good deal of concern."

The next day (August 4) the Prime Minister talked to Robertson about the impending changes. Robertson "was worrying considerably about them. Did not feel too sure he had done the right thing. I can understand this. As other men begin to take on one's place, one realizes what one's particular position means. If I had been Robertson, I would never have changed. I can see that one of the great problems ahead of External Affairs is the provision of residences; the cost of living, etc. In all these Capitals, there will be vast expenditures. A scale of living that our people are in no way accustomed to and the moment will come when there will be great difficulty getting from Parliament the support that is needed to maintain Embassies, etc. In addition, there is a danger of a government growing up which is not a government. A bureaucracy which will try to control things from Embassies rather than having Embassies the agents of government. It is all a very difficult and dangerous business. I am quite determined, in my own mind, to give up the post of External Affairs and arrange for a separate Minister at the time of announcing the changes that will be made. I must hold to reserving these until after getting back to Canada."

That afternoon the Vaniers took Mackenzie King to call on Léon Blum at his country residence. Part of the time they talked of Blum's period in a German concentration camp. "For two years, he had lived there, fully expecting that both he and his wife would be executed at some time. Did not feel the strain as much as when, toward the very last, there seemed a prospect of their being released. That, he found most trying of all. He said he learned that a man could not work mentally or physically when he was hungry or starving. He did not live under a sense of fear. Was reconciled to death.

"He spoke of how happy he was now to have made the fight he did before the war for the masses of the people. Both he and his wife spoke with great feeling of the horrible tortures and atrocities of the Germans.

Of their having a certain love for beauty, children and the like, but this so long as it was their own. What they seemed to lack was a sense of justice and brotherhood with others. As he talked, I pictured to myself vividly the suffering which Mackenzie endured when in prison in Rochester – all the same as what Mr. Blum had gone through.

"It was a moving experience and beautiful sight to be there to spend a couple of hours with this great man, and his wife, a truly noble person, who had gone through all the strain and stress of the period. Blum could not have given a more beautiful expression of his friendship. I felt the kind of life that he is living there is what I want to live at Kingsmere: quiet of the country and the influence of the 'res eternitatis' – things eternal."

Perhaps it was this conversation with Blum which caused the Prime Minister on August 5 to think "carefully over plan for next few weeks. Having decided to leave on the 27th, have concluded I must either visit battlefields and Berlin while Conference is sitting or give up the idea of seeing them altogether. With the men I have here, the Conference can well take care of itself. I have a feeling that those around me would as soon have me avoid taking too active a part. Whether this is that they feel they are more competent or are considerate in a way, I cannot say. I have felt that Claxton was anxious to figure prominently himself in the debate. He knows the Conference personnel and general strategy. I do not know the personages and find the whole system of amendments and amendments quite wearisome. With my terrible feeling of fatigue, I realize I am not quick witted in some things and feel that it may be just as well not to get unnecessarily involved in international entanglements. With this in mind, I desire to get plans worked out a little.

"I did not go to the first part of the meeting this morning until I had talked over matters with Robertson. However, I was glad I did later as Byrnes referred to my suggestion of the other day [concerning periodic meetings of the foreign ministers], approving it. I also told Claxton I felt British amendment which is being supported by the U.S. should be supported by us. It should be made clear we would support a bare majority if that amendment came first, but we felt the British amendment was eminently fair. Claxton, this afternoon, took that position. To my surprise, I learned that Molotov had agreed to the procedure I had suggested but claimed that he had made it himself at an earlier stage and that the U.S. had turned it down. However, there is now agreement between Molotov, U.S. and I should think the U.K. There ought to be and will be agreement of the Conference; that that is one important point in the whole procedure that has been gained by Canada." The conference, after further debate, did agree that recommendations to the Council of Foreign Ministers could be adopted either by a two-thirds majority or a simple majority, the implication being that those in the first category would carry greater weight.

Depressed as he was, Mackenzie King found the day "intolerably hot" and experienced difficulty in getting "the energy to work. The truth is I am really very tired. When I waken in the morning, my back pains me and I have had to get in and out of the bath with great care. I am really not at all fit for any kind of discussion."

That evening he decided "not to go to the meeting at which the debate on procedure will be continuing though my conscience rebukes me a little for not doing so. I feel, perhaps, I should be asserting myself and my beliefs more. However, the Conference is not one at which I intend to participate to any extent and I feel I shall make a greater headway in the end by beginning to get a really good sleep."

After a good night's rest and in much better humour, Mackenzie King was on hand for the convening of the committee on procedure on the morning of August 6. "Byrnes made a very telling speech," he reported, "but did not stir Molotov. I think he showed conclusively that Molotov is a man wholly without principle – indeed his whole performance throughout the day was one akin to that of Duplessis; no sincerity in it at all. I am really amazed that a man of Molotov's position should lend himself to such downright deception in dealing with world affairs. The forenoon's proceedings were very tiresome."

Later in the day, Byrnes told the Prime Minister that "he and Bevin had had to stand, over several months, from Molotov, the kind of thing we were all witnessing. Molotov barely tolerated Bevin and was always trying with him, Byrnes, to have it understood that Russia and the U.S. would settle the affairs of the world. This was very like Hitler's tactics in wishing to have Britain and Germany settle the world's affairs."

The longer he stayed in Paris, the more oppressive the atmosphere became for Mackenzie King. On August 9 he wrote that "social life of the kind one sees in a great capital is something which terrifies me. I thank God for not having been drawn into that whirlpool of suspicion, vanity, deception, and what not. I am beginning to wonder more and more if the world would not be better off without any Ambassadors or Legations at all. Certainly it will be a blessing when the time comes and they become straight business institutions and social business is all but eliminated. It is really terrible how the thoughts of so many of those in diplomatic life are centred on use of words, expressions, attitudes, positions, calls, dinner jackets, dress and Heaven knows what not. I was interested in noticing that Molotov was among the few who did not wear any evening dress. Not even a dinner jacket. He wore simply an ordinary every day suit.

"I had a very pleasant talk with Byrnes and his wife last night during which time I told them that Blair House had given me the thought of leaving Laurier House to the nation, to be used for distinguished visitors. Byrnes is very strong in his expression of the hope that I would do that very thing. He urged, however, I should do it while I am living to make sure that arrangements will be properly made. He suggested making everything subject to remaining there as long as I lived and thereafter passing it over to the nation for that purpose. It is something to which I will continue to give careful thought."

That evening the Prime Minister attended a reception at the Russian Embassy and was curious to see how he would be received. "The Ambassador and his wife received. They shook hands in a polite, formal manner but there was nothing expressive of a welcome. Fairly early in the evening, the Bielorussian Delegation came. We had met at San Francisco. They were quite pleasant and ready to talk. Wanted me to drink vodka with them but I simply took a glass and later put it on the table.

"I was most of all interested in making sure of meeting Molotov in his own house. I came along to the group of people with whom he was shaking hands. Got on his line of approach, as he went by, and shook hands. I said the last time we had met he was leaving for Russia by Edmonton. That I hoped he had found arrangements satisfactory and everything pleasant when he went through at Edmonton on his way through Canada to Russia. He replied that everything seemed to be quite satisfactory at that time, smiled a little and went on. I did not catch all he had said but the translator gave me enough to make out the substance of it. There was a smile on his face as he said 'about that time.' Carefully avoided any reference to the present owing to present relations.

"After this contact, I felt we had been there long enough and left shortly after 11. What I noticed in particular was the complete change of atmosphere from that of other Embassies, more of a certain type of people that seemed to be present. Some pretty ordinary and rough looking characters without any evening dress or even black clothes. Also the almost savage way in which numbers of people were stacking up around the tables where I could see there was plenty of caviar and other foods and vodka. Gave one a feeling of pain to see some young women drinking vodka. I am afraid many of these social events are the path on the road to destruction of many of the young lives. One observes that the Russian Government seeks to impress others with the grandeur of social occasions. The power they represent. Around the doors of the Embassy, there were gatherings of people held back, peering into carriage windows and the like. I felt one was walking about in a nest of spies. Wondered what there was that could be gained from anything they could see on such an occasion. It was quite clear that the atmosphere so far as Canada was concerned was not a cordial one. I had debated much as to whether I should go or not. I think it was perhaps the right decision to go. Had I stayed away, this of itself might have been used as an evidence of Canada wishing to do other than further friendly relations."

Early Saturday morning (August 10) the Prime Minister and his party left Paris for a visit to the battlefields of Normandy. "I shall not attempt now to record the incidents of the day in any order of sequence," he wrote. "They will have to be brought together in a separate memorandum. There were a succession of communities visited; a succession of speeches made. A good many miles to be covered, driving, and a very late return to the Hotel.

"What is outstanding in my mind as I write, above all else, is the spontaneous, very sincere and very hearty welcome given by the people everywhere. Addresses of welcome by the Mayors – all speaking in terms of profound gratitude to Canada for the liberation. The children came forward with many bouquets of beautiful flowers – women as well as men cheering 'Vive le Canada.' Little scenes of groups of children having learned by heart the Canadian National Anthem – also God Save the King in English and singing by all of La Marseillaise with great fervour. Some of the little cottages were decorated with arches which had been made for the occasion – with banners 'Honneur aux Canadiens.' Flags displayed on the buildings on the streets. Reception carefully organized. I was much impressed with the character of the men who hold the office of Mayors. They were persons of character and who, for the most part, were prominent in their respective callings, positions, etc. – some of whom were leading physicians.

"At Caen itself, we were received first by the Mayor who read an address of welcome to which I replied in part in French and in considerable length in English in the presence of the City Council and others.

"We then walked through the streets to the Prefecture where a sumptuous and most delicious meal was served. Another address of welcome by M. Pasquier, Secretary General of the Prefecture. We had been met by Pasquier on the way. He has strong resemblance to Bidault. Nothing could have been kinder than his attention throughout.

"In going about from place to place, he sat with me and we were accompanied by [Charles] Stacey, the historian, who gave interesting accounts of the places of interest and of the positions of troops, etc. on the battlefields. While going through the streets, crowds were loud in their acclaim of Canada. It really was a remarkable sight; even the little dogs in the streets seemed to join in what appeared to be an expression of thanksgiving.

"We went over the fields on which our army had fought, stopping at one point where a wide stretch of open land afforded a splendid view of the battlefields. One wondered how our men were able to make the progress they did and enable the American troops to get in at another side. One felt that the Canadians were, without question, around each occasion, in difficult and critical positions.

"We had with us Ross Munro, [Matthew] Halton, [Marcel] Ouimet – all of whom were correspondents in the war. It happened to be the second anniversary of where they had been at the time of the fighting – August 10, 1944. I crossed from the roadside to the field and gathered a little poppy. I was told to be careful as there were still mines in that area.

"Today the grain is just about ready to be harvested. The sheaves looked very full. The landscape beautiful with their brown gold. Fortunately there is exceptionally good harvest. It interested me to see how Stacey, the historian, seemed to pick out each particular class of tank by name. One felt it was almost a sort of worship of these various instruments of destruction. Horrible looking things. All rusted. Piled up. In some places gathered together in what is termed 'tank cemeteries.' One of the last places visited in the afternoon was one of our Canadian cemeteries at Bretteville-sur-Laize. It lies peacefully under the open sky in the centre of a wide stretch of open country. In part of it, the grass has grown between the graves; in other parts, grass has still to be sown. Each little grave had its separate mound, all uniform in shape. It touched me deeply to see between the graves that were named, here and there, one simply classified as an 'unknown soldier.' We took the flowers that had been given us at other centres and placed them before the cross of sacrifice which is in the middle of the cemetery. The sun was shining brightly. Looking at the crosses one way, they were in shadow. The other, very white against the sun. I found it quite impossible to give any expression to my feelings. Indeed, as I said, I felt silence was the only language in such a place.

"As we went about, I endeavoured to single out the persons that looked to me most deeply distressed. Many women up in years wearing black mourning; some of the older men. I also made it a point of shaking hands with little children and kissing some of them as they brought their little arms full of flowers, all beautifully arranged with ribbons of French tricolour, to present them.

"Particularly moving were the last two places visited. People had been waiting for an hour or two. I was glad we decided not to disappoint them. There seemed to be nothing left of their little villages, of their communities.

"As we stood in front of the municipal building, the moon was shining quite brightly. Across the way, in another direction, church bells were being rung specially as a welcome. We were greeted by the municipal head of the community and also by the Curé.

"I also asked Claxton to speak in French at one or two places. He was well received. At most places, I spoke in English and asked Vanier to translate. His translation was quite beautiful to listen to. His whole manner, quite impressive. One could feel he was deeply loved by the people. Indeed he looked like a patriarch himself as he went quietly from place to place. To me, he was everything one could wish for as a guide, philosopher and friend."

His visit to Falaise particularly interested Mackenzie King. He was met "on the steps of the municipal buildings by the Mayor and people gathered in large numbers on either side of the statue of William the Conqueror which faces the building and which escaped damage. The whole city, however, is a mass of ruins. Beautiful ecclesiastical buildings. Other public and private buildings all destroyed. The place brought back to my mind recollections of the ruins of Pompeii. To me the Falaise is even more of a tragedy than Caen. One feels about these communities that they are so isolated. In Falaise, there is very little of the town itself left so the people have not even neighbours to help them. In Caen, there is still a big part of the population to help to look after the other but one feels that the ruins about these places are even worse than around St. Paul's because there the city remains to help those that have suffered. It really touches one's heart deeply to see the state of the ruins there.

"I was immensely surprised as we drove into Falaise to get a view of the Castle which belonged to William the Conqueror and in which he was born. It is a thousand years old: is on a commanding height. An enormous building in itself. We had not unfortunately planned to visit the Castle but it was something just to have seen it as it commands a city that is all but completely destroyed.

"At Falaise, I had to make a short speech in reply to a couple of addresses. I re-echoed the note expressed by one that we wish they would drop discussion on procedure at the Conference and get on with the making of peace. I also remarked that, at times during the years of war, I had wondered whether Canada was able to take on the burdens she had in the army, navy and air, etc. From hereafter, I would never have any doubt. With what I had seen, I had felt that more if possible might well have been done, considering what they have suffered and what we have been told. This I now feel very strongly. During the day, I referred repeatedly to the historic associations of Normandy and Canada; farmers leaving and settling parts of Canada and laying foundations of a country there. The descendants returning after the years to help to liberate those who were of the same stock. Spoke of the friendship between French and English. It is really deeply moving to think of this historic association."

It was 3.00 A.M. on August 11 when the Prime Minister finally retired, sleeping in the bed which General de Gaulle had used on his last visit to Caen. At 9.30 A.M. he left his hotel "to visit the beaches and the communities en route. A guard of honour was drawn up in front of the hotel. Numerous people were gathered on opposite sides of the entrance and cheered when we started off.

"Our first stop on the way was at a high point overlooking the city of Caen which General Crerar used as his observation point. While there we were much amused to see a man and his wife on a bicycle and pulling a little cart behind carrying a black dog; it was one of the most amusing sights I have seen. I got particular pleasure out of the little dogs I met on the way.

"From Crerar's observation point, one saw what a vast area our men had fought over and how exposed they were to dangers while they sought to relieve the city of Caen.

"We arrived at the Channel shortly after 10. I was amazed at the large gathering of people assembled there. The Mayor, leading members of the clergy received us on a platform which was erected near a spot at which a plaque was being raised to commemorate the landing of troops at that point. Speeches of welcome were delivered. Little girls presented bouquets of flowers and a great reception was given by the people. I had to make an impromptu address but found it a little less difficult than yesterday. Felt more like speaking today, particularly this morning, after the night's rest and reception of the day before. Invited Claxton to speak. Was astonished at the crowds and their enthusiasm. This was at St. Aubin.

"From there we went on to Bernières and Courseulles where the Regiment de la Chaudière had landed and relieved the town. Here again very large numbers were gathered together. Addresses were given by the Mayor and by the head of the Normandy-Canadian organization newly formed. Particular enthusiasm seemed to be felt from the fact that the French soldiers had landed at this point. We visited the building which the journalists had used for the first time when their troops landed. It was at these points along the beach that the soldiers came ashore under the guns of the *Rodney, Nelson* and other ships. Further along we stopped at a sort of summer resort at which a number of people were bathing on the beaches. I went aboard one of the ships from which our men had landed. It is now old and rusty and lying on the beach. At this particular place, there was a merry-go-round; also a monument which had been erected to the dead of the previous war. I placed a wreath on this particular memorial and stood in silence before it while the band played 'O Canada.' No special meeting had been arranged for this locality. . . .

"I did not realize until yesterday that our troops had to land on shores, to clear the beaches and make it possible to have ships sunk which constituted a harbour for the landing craft and the landing of large numbers, etc. It was nearly half past one when we left for Bayeux.

"Unfortunately we were over an hour or two late in arriving at Bayeux. The Mayor was waiting in front of the City Hall with quite a considerable gathering present. The Mayor said there had been some 2,000 people assembled there earlier in the day but he did not try to keep them on account of the mid-day hour.

"A civic reception was tendered in the City Hall. . . . At the luncheon, the Mayor made a speech of welcome most cordially expressed. He had invited four of the Canadian Red Cross nurses who are distributing clothing in the Normandy area to be present, along with members of the Council and our party. Also some of the journalists. In replying, I made an impromptu speech which those present seemed to think was effective. But to tell the truth, it cost me less in the way of thought than any of the others as I took advantage of what had been said by the Mayor to respond spontaneously. This was the original home of General de Gaulle. I took occasion to tell the incident of de Gaulle's presence in my library when I showed him the book on Mackenzie's Life and Times, and copy of the money issued by my grandfather, as provisional president of the Republic of Canada, which had been set up at Navy Island in 1838, and when I told de Gaulle France would be certain to have a provisional government before long. I asked that this incident be not referred to in what I was saying. However it was another rounding out of the circle in much that relates to my life and its relationship to my grandfather's. . . . The Mayor gave me an opportunity in referring to de Gaulle's association with the locality. I stressed at this gathering particularly the impressions that the trip had left.

"Between two of the earlier visits, we had visited the Canadian cemetery at Beny-sur-Mer where a ceremony had been arranged in the nature of a service. We were met at the entrance by the Mayor, priests, and others and proceeded first to the circle where the Canadian flag was flying and then on to the cross of sacrifice where a service was held. I asked that the service should be held first and said a few words standing at the side of the cross of sacrifice. Thanked the clergy for the service. Spoke of the losses which the population had sustained; of their lost ones and of those of other countries, and then referred to the quiet beauty of the resting place of our dead – sky overhead to the sea beyond which provided an open area surrounding the cemetery itself. Spoke of our being present there as evidence that those who had died had not died in vain but had given us liberty. Said we were but a little circle there but symbolic of the larger world which had regained its freedom, and then referred to our own dead, quoting the little poem 'O Valiant Hearts.'

"I sought to convey the thought that their spirit continued to exist in the life hereafter and that we had evidence that the spiritual things were eternal. That materialism had not triumphed but that freedom had been the gift of those who had given their lives. We believed they received their reward beyond. I would have given very much if my mind and body had not been so fatigued. It was one occasion when one really should have delivered a great oration. However, I had no knowledge when we started that anything at all would be expected in the way of speaking. Everything had to be impromptu – without any preparation – and I might add, without any slip, and with the fatigue of much motoring.

"There were many touching scenes at this service. Choirs of little boys who sang God Save the King in English, many of whom were orphans. One little fellow lost both his father and mother and one of his arms. The priest who had the mission teaching them had himself been in a German concentration camp for nearly three years. I was tremendously interested in seeing how all the people sang La Marseillaise, and how the priests seemed to emphasize the singing with the movements of their hands. One could see their whole feelings were stirred. It interested me to be participating in a service at a Roman Catholic altar. It seemed to be a sign of the toleration that the Catholic Church should have permitted this, and I am sure they would feel it equally an evidence of toleration that a Protestant should speak from what seemed to be a Catholic pulpit. Nothing could have been more appropriate in the existing circumstances. I am sorry, however, I did not make more of what it signified of our worshipping from different altars but the one God; different languages but the one voice of Humanity in our hearts. Different races but all one brotherhood. I can perhaps bring in that thought at Dieppe.

"It was a day one will always remember. Particularly impressive were the sheaves of flowers which little children and others brought and which we left around the cross of sacrifice. . . .

"After the luncheon, we were taken to see the Bayeux tapestry – story of the conquest of England by William the Norman. At Bayeux, we also saw the tree of liberty – one was impressed with its personality. It is a tree that was planted at the time of the revolution and stood there in majesty, in full leaf. Bayeux itself seems to have been saved much destruction. . . .

"We then visited the graves of our Canadian men and placed wreaths of flowers upon them. I confess it seemed to me one of the saddest moments I have known. Our young men from the Winnipeg Rifles in most part had been murdered there. What a terrible thing! How appalling the cruelty of war! . . .

"From there, we went back to Caen and visited the Cathedral. We were received by the prelate. A fine looking old gentleman who personally conducted us through the Cathedral. It was built at the time of William the Conqueror. Looks inside as though it had been built yesterday, so fresh and clean and beautiful does it appear. We saw there the place in front of the altar where the remains of William the Conqueror had been placed for a time. The tablet bears the title of him as King of England. It seemed quite strange to see this particular description. On reading British history, one had seldom thought of him as a Norman who continued on in the line of Kings of Britain. I felt an immense interest in being in the environment in which William the Conqueror lived. The Cathedral we were in had been erected by his wife. We were told by the Canon that one of the Canadian soldiers had died in the Cathedral; another had come to tell him of the liberation of Caen. I felt I should like to go back to Falaise for two reasons: (1) because it seemed to me the scene of destruction was greater there than any other spot and (2) to visit the Castle in which William was born. It was well worth the extra time it took for the journey and the lateness of the hour which it would mean before we reached Paris.

"Falaise itself is a scene of all but total destruction. We walked up the long stretch to the Castle and through the Castle to the top of the Tower. Went into the little circular room in which William the Conqueror was born. From the window of the Tower nearby, we saw beneath the place of a fountain on a street below where his mother had been seen by his father while she was getting water at the fountain. William himself was an illegitimate child. The Castle itself is a tremendous building; an enormous and powerful sort of place. It must have taken many many years to build. It has a commanding height, and at the hour we were visiting, the crows were crowing in and about the ruins. They are marvellous ruins, indicative of power and vanity of the day. One gets a new vision of war as one visits these older countries and realizes how it seemed to be an inevitable part of the life of nations. We have witnessed what is worse than anything the world has known and it is strange to think that one oneself has been a participant in it all. There is certainly a destiny that shapes our ends, otherwise how could anyone have ever believed that I would have been spending a day such as today among other places at the birthplace of William the Conqueror. In the very room in which he was born, and also visited the place of his remains. Received honours from the city of which he was a founder, and the gratitude of the people of Normandy to the Canadian nation for their services in the war. I began to feel how, in the end, despite all else, my own endeavours in the war were receiving some of the reward which they perhaps merited because of the single-mindedness of my effort through that appalling period of time and the terrible responsibility of having had to bring a nation into war and to guide its course throughout.

"After Falaise, we came by a different route back to Paris, arriving shortly after 11 tonight. . . .

"The experience of the last two days has been as great as any I have known in the course of my life. Deeply moving and very solemn experience from active direct contact with life and death and all that they speak of human relations on this globe."

"The trip of the last two days made me feel much happier," Mackenzie King reflected on August 12. "I have felt about it it was a reward of the past few years and was giving me anew my rightful place among the representatives of the different nations. I have been far too much a permanent civil servant and far too little, Prime Minister, either in my own interest or in the interests of the country.

"The last two days have helped to restore the balance. It makes me very happy to think that Canada holds the place which she evidently does in the hearts of the people of France and indeed also of other countries."

That day the Prime Minister gave a reception at the Canadian Embassy which he regarded as a success. Next day, General Pope arrived from Allied headquarters in Berlin and Mackenzie King arranged the details of his visit to Berlin and Nuremberg later in the month.

After dinner on August 14 the Prime Minister had a talk with Ernest Bevin. "I confess I was a bit relieved in my mind by the talk I had with him. He thinks the Russian attitude is very largely due to fear. They seem to be afraid that they may be attacked. Also that, but for purposes of internal cohesion, they must have some outside foe. He is not sure that the Conference will last too long. Says that it will not. He thinks it possible to change any of the parts that have already been agreed to in the treaties. What he would like to do is get technical state of war at an end so that he could begin to deal with Italy and other countries on his own. He does not want to yield in a treaty matter under Russian pressure, but once a treaty has been signed, he will be prepared then and would like the Dominions to join with him in helping to build up Italy in whatever way is possible to restore a close friendship. He feels that to yield to a Russian pressure would be a great mistake. He believes the Palestine question will be settled all right on the basis of having two zones but not having partition at the instance of Britain but rather by request of the Jews themselves and Palestine made into a narrow federation rather than into a Jewish colony of the British Commonwealth.

"Bevin has in mind building up a sort of new federation out in the far east, around Malaya – a sort of trading centre there which would have America at one side and Russia on the other so that, as he said, if America and Russia should ever come to blows, they would be kept at arms' length around this centre rather than where they could strike at each other. I was particularly struck by a statement that Bevin made which was to the effect that Russia had been given the Kuriles and other properties which brought her much nearer to Canada without the knowledge of Churchill or the British. That this business had been worked out by Roosevelt. I said to Bevin I had no faith whatever in the arrangement between China and Russia as being other than subjugating China gradually to Russia. He thinks the English will be back in pretty good shape by November. Says that the way the British people have tightened up everything to the present, has shown their fine spirit. He is really surprised that their position has developed to the point it has. I confess I feel we have been pretty easy in the extent to which we have been taxing our own people for what Britain herself is being able to do and which we might well have had in mind for ourselves. Bevin spoke of the possibility of his going out to the U.N. Assembly and of paying Canada a visit if he did.

"I spoke about our espionage report which he had seen. An awful affair or words to that effect. What he wishes to do is to get quantities of the report and send them to every trade union in England. He said he has had to fight that Communist business from the days before he was Minister of Labour in the trade unions. That that report would do more to help to save the situation among the labour element in Britain than anything he can think of. He said that that is the kind of thing that Russia has been doing right along. He asked me if I had read 'I Chose Freedom' and another book which he thought was just a parallel to what this report had disclosed. He did not seem to be too greatly concerned about Europe. I can see from the talk I had with Bevin what folly it would be for any of our people to go poking their fingers into the European pie too deeply. There is a mass of intrigue, grievance, etc., which none but those who are parties to them will ever be able to know or understand."

By this time Mackenzie King was in a characteristic dither about preparing a major speech for his visit to Dieppe and was devoting no time to the proceedings of the conference. "It was really sort of tragic that my time should be taken up in preparation of speeches while at this Conference," he wrote on August 14. "I realize, however, that so far as Canada is concerned, an effective speech at Dieppe will mean more in the eyes of our people than a month's effort at the Conference. I must do my utmost to make it worthy of the occasion. God knows, as I dictate, I feel more deeply than ever what an appalling curse the war mind is."

The following day he was "shown an itinerary of the meetings for Saturday evening, Sunday and Monday. It is an appalling itinerary. More than would be expected in the way of speaking in any political campaign. I am not sure that the thing is not being overdone. I have no doubt, however, that the impression the tour will make is something that will be much appreciated in Canada and without question will be remembered as a bond between our two countries."

Most of August 17 was devoted to the revision of the last part of his speech for the ceremony. The Prime Minister showed the draft to Claxton who "suggested the omission of a part which dealt with the significance of Dieppe, in it being the first of the combined operations and also what that meant for subsequent landings in other parts of Europe and on D-Day. Also what it signifies in the way of relieving Russian forces at the time when they were being hard pressed. Claxton was suggesting that that might raise discussion which had already taken place and died down. I was very loath to delete this part of the speech but, on reflection, felt he was right. Also felt the speech was too long, so I sacrificed about three pages in all. It was not a pleasant business but I am sure that his advice in the matter was right. I was not able to bring what I had to say to the kind of conclusion I should like to have been able to make but I think I have something which is fitting for the occasion, more or less complete and appropriate. It brings out the thought of Dieppe being a beacon light, prophetic of victory. I was able to bring out the thought that Canada may also be a beacon light in the example of national unity based on the difference of race, religion, etc., to other nations and then express the hope that the present Conference in Paris might prove a beacon light to the world in showing the way from conflict to co-operation. It is quite a job making revisions, getting copy to Vanier for translation; other copies to the press, etc. I had to give up all thought of the conference."

That afternoon Mackenzie King left for Dieppe at 4.30. "We had met Gardiner en route. He had left Montreal yesterday at noon with his bride. They had arrived only an hour before. Mrs. Gardiner came to the dinner tonight. An amazing achievement for a woman of her years. I hope not too much in the way of effort as she does not herself look any too strong. There was a large gathering in front of the Mayor's residence. The people cheered lustily for Canada both as we went into the Mayor's house and on coming out. It was quite stirring to see the great spontaneous reception given."

The Paris Conference 309

August 18 was a Sunday and, immediately after breakfast, the Prime Minister was taken to "Puys which is the spot at which the Royal Regiment of Canada landed.

"There we attended a morning service. The English-speaking Minister talked at length about himself, giving reasons why he was not on the beach at the time of the raid and ended up by saying he had studied maps and knew exactly where he would go if he had to escape and ended up by saying he thought the lesson of life was to be thinking of others. The most self satisfied type of man I have seen for a long time. It made me indignant to hear that sort of service. The Roman Catholic service which followed was a very beautiful and dignified one. The Cardinal was present – a very fine, dignified old gentleman who spoke beautifully in an address of some considerable length. He is very feeble. I admired immensely his whole attitude and I was greatly impressed by what he said. I shall never forget the scene as we approached Puys and proceeded to the morning service. The hillsides were crowded with people. The place itself where the Royal Regiment landed seemed to be of the most difficult for a landing it would be possible to find anywhere. One sees cliffs rising steeply out of the sea; then there was a narrow sort of valley which led into the town, and then on the other side a very high hill on top of which was a gun emplacement which was occupied at the time by German soldiers and guns. The gun emplacement commands a complete view of the beach and one man with the help of the gun, it seemed to me, could destroy men as rapidly as they would land. It was a steep ascent everywhere. What would have been done once the heights were gained, I don't understand, as it would have been as difficult again getting into town as getting up. I really felt as though the men who had planned that raid ought to have been cashiered. . . . It was sending men to certain death without a ghost of a chance. Apparently it was thought they might effect a surprise landing in the dark. I was told today the ships of the navy were an hour late in arriving so that the men were exposed in the light when they landed. I felt a hatred of war greater than I have experienced at any time as the names of a fine lot of young Canadians were read out. Men who were killed and one thought of many others. It just made one indignant beyond words. The people themselves were full of cheering for Canada. Fortunately there was no speaking at the service but during the day, there were large numbers of gatherings.

"Tonight, as I dictate this diary, I am far too fatigued to run over the list of places. I cannot even recall the number of speeches I made but will secure the record somewhere else. I was really quite done out and tired in the morning but seemed to revive with the enthusiasm of the people during the day. I feel quite sensitive about receiving all the acclaim, especially in the presence of other Ministers and more particularly members of the Defence forces. However, I feel that the situation was understood and besides it was all for Canada. . . .

"In different speeches, I tried to express thanks to the people for the care they had given our dead and the way in which the graves were being cared for. Also sympathy of the people of Canada for their sufferings and a word about closer friendship between our countries which the associations of the past and which the war had brought about; speaking more particularly of the feelings of today. Addresses were read at different places. . . .

"I did not feel up to the mark in speaking in any of the places though there were times when the inspiration of the moment gave me sufficient words to make a short address. I believe some of the addresses were broadcast including the whole impromptu one at luncheon, part of which was in French, but mostly in English. As a gentleman said to me tonight, the French would, of course, have liked their own troops to have relieved their cities along the coast but the French troops were mostly in the south and fighting against Germany. Next to their own troops, they had hoped the Canadians would be sent. The joy that they had when the Canadians came knew no bounds.

"We met a few of the officers and men who had been through a terrible battle at Puys. The faces of the people were quite a study. Most of them bore the signs of fright. However, there can be no question about the feelings in their hearts for Canada. One almost felt while here that we were in a part of our own country, more so than even in England. I felt more at home myself with the people here than I do with the English people though I confess I have not made any effort of touring the cities and towns there. I doubt if I could have been persuaded to make this tour if it had not been all prepared and arranged without my knowledge.

"When we came back through Dieppe, on the way to one of the other communities, both sides of the streets were lined with people; in some places, several deep. They cheered and cheered. Part of the way we walked on the streets. When we returned from the little churchyard service and came again to Dieppe, there was a tremendous gathering in front of the hotel where we went in for evening's refreshments."

The next morning (August 19) Mackenzie King was up early and felt "much rested and in better shape for the day. I got through breakfast in plenty of time and then went to the City Hall where a very large gathering were assembled as well as crowds all along the streets. There was great cheering of 'Vive le Canada.' No end of clapping, flags out from all the streets. Was met there by the Mayor . . . who escorted me up and down the main street. Met members of Council. We then drove some distance

The Paris Conference

to a cemetery.... There there was a service first by the R.C. Church and later the Protestant Church. Little children sang hymns in French, quite beautiful. There was an enormous gathering of people there. The approach was by driving along fields of grain which had been piled, etc. Troops were drawn up. Guards of Honour, etc.

"The service was held in the open. I was greatly moved to see the scene, location of cemetery and all. Enjoyed the quiet service. Here again I did not like the Anglican Protestant Minister – kind of talk not at all suited for the occasion. I felt during the service that I would like to say a word about what I felt; about bodies of men returned to mother earth while their souls were in the keeping of a common Father. I felt very strongly the rational, common sense of the earth getting back what belonged to it and freeing the soul for a larger freedom. I also felt I should say something about the men behind them having done their duty; also a word about the Conference, as to their voice being one which was the voice of the people today. That no time should be lost in the making of peace. That we should end the control and try and get an enduring peace. This was one occasion when it had been understood I should not speak. I felt I should insist on saying something once morning programme was over. This I did by moving out into an open space and saying what had been in my thoughts during the service. I think I was able to express my thoughts in a clear way and that I said the right thing. At all events, afterwards, many spoke appreciatively of it. There were many demonstrations of the people along the roadside on the way back into the city....

"We then moved indoors, and in the Council Chamber were informal proceedings and I was presented with the freedom of the city or, in much better words, was made 'citoyen d'honneur of Dieppe.' Georges Vanier also received the same honour. I had had no preparation but felt that this being the day of the anniversary, I should say something about the significance of the anniversary. Referred to the landing on August the 19th, 1942 as giving Hitler what he most dreaded. Also that it showed the strength and weakness of those who attacked and who were attacked. Was helpful in consideration of further landings in North Africa, Sicily and Italy; also on D-Day as it led to diversionary movement of Germans who were hard pressing against the Russians at Stalingrad at the time. I made it clear that in the sum total of things, it had been of some real contribution. I confess in my heart I felt that it had been a terrible thing to send men into that area to discharge a mission that could only end in death to large numbers. I spoke of Canada having given an example to the world of today. The United Nations, partnership of peoples of different religions, etc., inheriting the common love of liberty. On the one hand, a country which was part of the larger commonwealth of brotherhood, etc. On the other, a good neighbour policy, and where over a century, there had been no force on a boundary of about 3,000 miles. No doubt we have much to teach this old world.

"I felt that Claxton would be a little critical of what I had been saying as he had not wanted me to speak on this suggestion at all. Vanier agreed I was right and I was quite sure I was. I am glad I ruled it out of my main speech for today. There was tremendous cheering and I was then presented with an ivory medal bearing the crest of the city. It is astonishing how it as well as the diploma have been carefully worded.

"Again there was great applause in the streets as we drove off to visit the city hospital. There I shook hands with a great many persons, soldiers, and old women. Visited some of the wards."

After lunch, the Prime Minister and his party attended the unveiling of a memorial to the Canadians who had lost their lives at Dieppe. "There a tremendous crowd was assembled. I shall never forget the beauty of the scene – the place where a monument was being erected. It was beneath the walls of a huge castle. View of the beaches in one direction and out over the channel on the other while we were standing up on a hill near the wall, and among ruins.

"The Mayor made one address. M. Colin, Minister of State, another. My speech came at the end. Was in English, rather long. Did not produce much effect on the gathering but when translated by Vanier, was well received. There was great applause as we moved about a little and witnessed a march past of Canadian soldiers. I was very much struck with the monument which is already in that spot recording the relations of Dieppe and Canada going back to the foundations of the Dominion. I think the speech will make a good impression in Canada. I did a lot of work on this. So far as local effect was concerned, I think all the other speeches were preferable to this one but this is an enduring one which will be remembered.

"After this ceremony, we followed the soldiers, General Roberts and I walking together with the Secretary of State and the Mayor, four abreast. We must have walked for a mile. There were crowds cheering on both sides of the street all the way. From windows, they began throwing flowers. Little children clapping their hands; dogs barking; old soldiers wearing medals. All happy and rejoicing, singing 'Vive le Canada.' In reply, we said: 'Vive la France.' There were tremendous cheers. No expression of rejoicing could be more touching than this expression of love and rejoicing, this afternoon.

"We ended up at the Chamber of Commerce where M. Mouquet made a little speech and extending a welcome and presenting me with a gold medallion symbolical of France and freedom. He will get it engraved and bring it to Ottawa later.

"We then went back to the City Hall where a Vin d'Honneur was served to the soldiers. That gave me a chance to end the day's celebration by saying that while we had been the recipients, it was only in our representative capacity of the people of Canada and more particularly of the soldiers, sailors and airmen. It was meant for those who had saved Dieppe; freed the city. I was glad that the celebrations should have ended on this particular note."

The Prime Minister returned to Paris late that evening. During his final week on the Continent, Mackenzie King devoted almost no time to the conference which was still bogged down in procedural tangles. On August 20, the day after he returned from Dieppe, he flew to Berlin with General Pope. They were met by Ilsley and Pearson, who had come from Geneva, and drove at once to Pope's residence for dinner. Next morning they toured Berlin. "It was all very familiar but an appalling sight. Tiergarten, one waste of ground. Beautiful buildings demolished beyond recognition. The whole centre of the city all but totally destroyed. I recognized building after building – a complete destruction. So strange to pass the Adlon Hotel where I stayed when I met Hitler. After covering a part of the city and seeing particularly the Reichstag which Goering had set on fire, and other well-known buildings, we were taken to the Chancellery buildings. I doubt if that building was finished when I was last in Berlin – enormous place. We went through the large hall where treaties were signed, on through the dining room quarters and were shown where Hitler's living quarters were, etc. What was interesting about the building was how everything appeared to be shoddy. Compressed stone and pressed wood – nothing genuine. Walls made to represent marble – walls to represent Germany under Naziism. The immensity of the place, however, was what interested one.

"Most interesting of all was being taken down to the bunker which Hitler had had constructed during the war as a place of final refuge. We went down three or four flights of stone stairs. Came to a series of rooms – one dark room in which he did a certain amount of his work. Shown from there into his own bedroom which adjoined the room that Eva Braun had. There was a toilet room in between. Beyond was a telephone room – complete equipment. We also saw the room that Goebbels occupied. Beds still there. The bed that Goebbels had used seemed to be furnished better than others but nothing elaborate. People had torn away tops of sofas and chairs and the like as souvenirs.

"While passing through the large hall, I picked up a piece of a bit from the wall which I thought was an interesting souvenir. Was also given a tile from Hitler's bathroom, off from the main hall. I felt a sort of feeling of appalling disgust as I went through these lower rooms constructed as a sort of hide-out. Final retreat and hide-out. At the top of the steps were two heaps. There is a debate whether the two bodies were thrown and burnt up with oil on one heap or the other. In one room we were shown the sofa that had a lot of blood on, where it was thought Eva Braun had committed suicide. The thought went through my mind as I went into the basement how these men had degraded themselves, so completely had they reverted to animal form of lower life – something that corresponds to vermin and rats and the like, with holes in the ground, etc. The idea of men supposed to be carrying on government seeking a place like that to govern.

"When I came up from these lower regions to the top of the stairs, I could not help repeating to the journalists, especially to Ross Munro, that I thought of the time Ramsay MacDonald at Ottawa spoke of the days he and I had lived in London, interested in social settlements and the like. We had come into the positions we had through that class of effort. He had said it all went to show we make our own homes; also our homes at the end of the road. He had become P.M. and I had become P.M. Also spoke of Sidney Webb, member of the House of Lords. I thought of how true that statement was. Hitler and his gang had begun the wrong way at the start. They had made their homes at the end of the road which was this degraded cellar they were living in, where ultimately Hitler and his consort were burnt to death with oil.

"I thought of the talks I had with him and of my feelings that the time would show which was the right course and which was the wrong one. There came also to my mind the thought as expressed by Tennyson of man becoming the loathsome opposite of all he was meant to be. Also thought of the Frankenstein monster. How completely the whole idea had been fulfilled there."

After leaving the Chancellery, the party went to the Hindenburg Palace where Mackenzie King had been received by Hitler. "I recalled the guard of honour that was in front of the door steps and also being photographed as I came out of the building. I went inside the building and one could see through places upstairs, the staircase running up into something that was completely blasted I could see the rooms where we had had our conversation together. Then we passed the British Embassy where I had lunch with Goering and others. Came back to try and find the corner in which I lived – a block of the Tiergarten, with the Webers in 1900. The name of the street has been changed and we came within a few yards of the place though the police ran way past it at the start.

"We then drove to Pope's residence where he had an interesting luncheon party. Sir Sholto Douglas, Commander of the British region, the

The Paris Conference 315

Deputy Commander, Sir Brian Robertson, Mr. Murphy whom I had met along with President Roosevelt, when Murphy was getting instructions to proceed to Africa to prepare for the war. This was in Roosevelt's circular room. General and Mrs. Clay, the latter from Georgia. We talked together of Leniar who by the way went to a lot of trouble in regard to my visit to Nuremberg.

"Sir William Strang who sat to my left at lunch and who remembered my despatch to Chamberlain after my visit to Germany, and one or two others.

"I had interesting talks with these men before luncheon and at luncheon. I got the impression that conditions so far as food is concerned are much improved. They will be given more food a little later. The transportation is the brightest aspect of all. That is all now in very good shape. The really very difficult spot is coal which is needed for factories and homes. Also housing very bad. It will take some time to get housing or any kind of accommodation for housing of people. Many thousands are returning which keeps the problems to the fore.

"I gather this is where the French, British and Americans have their difference. The French do not like to have coal mines developed to have the Germans get on their feet, while they cannot get enough themselves. The view held by the Americans is once they get Germany on her feet, she will be able to pay for things and produce more coal and light in the end.

"There is nothing to the question of possible unrest and uprising. Only a few lads who get together and make trouble but all of that is well in hand. The complete separation of Russian zone from the rest is one of the most embarrassing of all the features. There is nothing in the idea they need more troops to keep order and discipline. That is only an excuse for keeping soldiers here. I have it from Sholto Douglas himself that there is no real difficulty in handling the discipline side of things. I gave them my point of view which accords with Ludwig's. They indicated their difficulty was with the British Government and Parliament. They were sentimental in a way and were inclined not to let the army people be as stern as they otherwise would. (It is an interesting glimpse that today's paper revealed for the first time very serious riots in Calcutta – some 2,000 people killed, arising out of the Moslem and Hindu attitude of self-government.)

"I felt sorry for the people on the streets. Their faces looked very weary and frightened and surly and sad. Very different from the expression we encountered in Normandy; also women working in piles of bricks, ruined buildings, cleaning them up, etc. There did not seem to be very large numbers of people anywhere."

After lunch, the Prime Minister and his party drove to the airport for the flight to Nuremberg. "I was told that the Russians had been practising in their region some little distance off. Just shortly after we arrived, large pieces of shrapnel fell near our plane. There could not be anything intentional about it but it was a curious sort of incident. There had been many protests about their doing this kind of thing but they don't stop.

"The journey from Berlin to Nuremberg was very easy and very pleasant. Hardly any motion all the way in the plane, either on leaving the ground or alighting. I read the *Times*. Some account of Dieppe and speeches there. Badly reported. Got a great view of Berlin from the air. One sees there how completely different buildings had been bombed from the air. There were some beautiful bits, in addition to enjoying glimpses of the country, wherever the ground looked green and fresh. There were also some beautiful cloud effects as the sun shone on the clouds. To avert a storm, we went up some 10,000 feet but I did not notice the effect at all. Enjoyed reading on the way.

"Reached Nuremberg exactly at 6 o'clock, Nuremberg time. Was met by Major Hodges who said he had come with a personal message of welcome and greeting from Mr. Justice Biddle. Invited me to dine with him in the evening. He had arranged that a guard of honour of a couple of companies be on hand. I was met then by Colonel Williams with whom I inspected the guard and then addressed them briefly. Thanked them for the courtesy extended Canada through myself. Hoped for pleasure of being on what seemed to be American soil.

"I then was driven through the village to a residence of a former millionaire banker of Nuremberg where we were put up for the night. Quite a delightful spot."

The Nuremberg trials of twenty prominent Nazi leaders had commenced in November 1945 and ended, shortly after Mackenzie King's visit, on August 31, 1946. At dinner that evening at Justice Biddle's home, the Prime Minister met most of the judges and found their accounts of the trials fascinating. Biddle "could not have been friendlier. Asked me if I would not stay the night at his house. Also arranged that I will lunch with the Judges tomorrow after the trial. He had given instructions about my being shown everything that is to be seen. The main thing I am told is to maintain an attitude of complete passivity, not even recognizing one has ever known anyone. If Ribbentrop would look at me, it is best not to let on one has ever known him. It will be interesting to see them. We talked until about half past ten and I then drove back to the city to the residence where we had been put for the night."

To Mackenzie King the day had been "one of the most interesting in my life, particularly in what it represents of the rounding out of another circle, which links up the very beginning of my life with today. Links up my university and post-graduate days, beginning of constructive work and social problems, with today. Links up visit to Berlin at the time of the Coronation; talks with Hitler and other men then in their power and glory, in their palaces. My sleeping within a block or two of where that was in the city. Today their city destroyed and tonight they lie in cells of criminals waiting to be hanged. I gather that Goering and Hess and Ribbentrop, Kaltenbrunner and Streicher and certain others are certain to be hanged. But a number will receive life sentences or heavy sentences.

"Today Goering was interesting as a witness. Tomorrow may not be so interesting, simply approving of documents and the like but it will be a great chance to see these men and also visiting the cells where they are confined."

Next morning (August 22), the Prime Minister left for the trials shortly after 9.00. "The motor cycle police on ahead tearing through the streets of Nuremberg as if they were a Prussian force. Much the same thing in Berlin by the British police there. All part of the war mentality.

"When we arrived at the Court House, we had to go through a good deal of signing passes; having them countersigned. Were given a booklet which contained the charges against the criminals. Brief statement of their careers and what was extraordinarily valuable, a plan of the Court room, etc.

"We were taken upstairs to the gallery overlooking the court room, given a front seat in the centre of the front row. Most of the prisoners were already in the dock – Ribbentrop, Goering were the last two to come in. Hess was not there. They seemed to chat with each other to a certain extent. They are allowed to do that in the dock, though not allowed to talk anywhere else. It really was a horrible and pathetic, tragic sight to see the men and to think that that particular group of men under one leader – a maniac – a devil incarnate – had been able to bring destruction upon themselves, their country and the world to the extent they have and, worst of all, destruction to moral standards.

"Soon the Judges filed into the Court. It was quite a satisfaction to feel one knew each of them individually and one had met them all at the same level the night before. I thought Judge Biddle looked a little tired and a little sad. He admitted to me he was quite lonely. It had been quite a long siege.

"The morning proceedings were the last of the taking of evidence which related to Nazi organizations. German lawyer was particularly stupid and seemed to me to be doing his own cause endless harm by wanting to read long affidavits, etc. . . . The figure that impressed me more was von

Neurath. He has got much older. He sat with his hands folded across his lap; hardly turning his head, looking straight ahead. A very pathetic, solitary figure. When one thinks of how pleasant he was as a gentleman in a high position, honourable, graduate of Oxford, etc., it seemed an appalling fate – an example of a man who had got in with the wrong gang – got to where finally he could not get out of situation he found himself in.

"Goering had shrunk to almost half the size as I remember him. Von Ribbentrop looked a mere shadow of himself. An old, weary looking man, taking voluminous notes. Schacht is a good business looking man. I thought too the Generals Doenitz, Raeder and Keitel looked like military men of high intelligence. Some of the others, particularly Streicher and a few others, looked more like real criminals. It was a terrible thing to think that that particular group of men were seeking to exterminate groups of men, women and children – burn bodies and the like. The world had known nothing like it in all of its history. If there ever was a real exhibition of what hell can be and must be, it must be what was exemplified by what one saw and thought of these men. I was fortunate in not having to meet the eyes of any of those whom I knew."

After the court proceedings in the morning, the Canadian party was taken into the prison and shown the cells. "This was really a heart-rending sight. A bed, a few blankets, table rather flimsy; little place for a few papers and books and very little else. In some of the rooms, the Bible was conspicuous. One felt it would be really an instrument of torment when they read of what law and righteousness was like, meaning of the Divine law, inevitable retribution following wrong. Each cell had its little closet in the corner and they have to look after these things themselves. One saw how Ley had hanged himself by tying a bit of curtain around the handle near the top of the toilet and stuffed his sock in his mouth and choked himself hanging over the toilet receptacle. That was his end. Anything more ignominious could not be imagined. . . .

"The cell we went through was one occupied by Seyss-Inquart. What interested me particularly was the sight of Hess. He had not come into the Court, pretending he was sick. They paid little attention to him. He was sitting up. Looked through his little cell aperture. Was sitting up eating his food, his back to the door. It recalled in a singular way how he had been sitting opposite me when we had our talk together in Berlin, in 1937. When we came back to the cell, a second time, he was lying on his back, and looking toward the opening. When I looked in, his eyes suddenly blazed up as though he recognized me in a moment. They were like coals of fire. He himself is like a man dying of consumption. A hideous, pathetic figure. I shall never forget the look in his face. I took care not to wait a second but to move right on.

"We were shown where prisoners were exercised. Told of how they were exercised. There they had been for nearly ten months; been led out of these cells day by day. Always, for some of them, the certainty of death by hanging ahead. I could think of no torture comparable. How right it is to what they have given others to endure. As we were going about, I thought of the choice that was given to David and his decision. One thing he did not want was to fall into the hands of his enemies. I thought, too, as I was looking around of the yard where Hitler's remains were burnt up; of the lines 'sic gloria mundi transit' – 'Thus passeth the glory of the world.' This experience in Europe has brought home as nothing else could, the fullness of the meaning that one reads in the Scriptures. There was a nauseating kind of odour in some of the rooms. I noticed in the storeroom which contained the supplies of the prisoners, about all Goering had to his credit were two neckties; pictures of their wives and members of their family that were visible in one or two cells. I find it hard to get the odour out of my nostrils and the feeling left on me throughout the day was one of having been in some unclean and unwholesome place. Like sharing the habitation of rats and vermin though the cells themselves were clean.

"The man who took us about, Colonel Andrus, seemed to me to have the mentality, manner and appearance very much of a Prussian himself but no doubt the necessary type for that particular job. He seemed to get a satisfaction in talking about his different prisoners that he had to look after."

Following lunch, Mackenzie King and his colleagues drove to the airport for the flight to Paris. "A wonderful trip. Smooth and gentle as if one were just sailing through the air. We hardly knew we rose from the ground; hardly knew when we touched it."

On the morning of August 24 the Prime Minister attended a meeting with Bevin and the heads of the other Commonwealth delegations to discuss one or two of the substantive issues which had emerged at the conference. "Smuts was present," he reported, "looking much the same but if anything a little thinner. The discussion was on the Mediterranean and Africa. The New Zealanders and the Indians were in favour of allowing the questions to go beyond this Conference to the U.N. saying this was after all to form world opinion. I expressed myself as believing the U.N.O. was just coming into being and it was the last thing that should be done to let forty or fifty nations [discuss] these questions. I really feel the U.N. threatens to become as great a menace as the League of Nations – a lot of immature, untrained minds, wishing to register their positions, etc. I agreed entirely with Bevin's point of view as against Smuts, that an effort to open any question at once with the Big Four was not likely to succeed.

That time would give a better chance. Smuts seemed to trust Yugoslavia. I would not trust them at all, nor any of the countries that are satellites of Russia. Bevin used the expression today that a man who would take the office of Foreign Minister for improving his position would be much better to go to hell for his pleasure. It really is a terrible job. I find Bevin remarkably sensible. He has such a gentle way of speaking and a very shrewd, clear mind. He told me very confidentially that in a talk with Byrnes a day or two ago, he thought he, Byrnes, would be able to arrange for reciprocal use of airports and bases between U.S. and Britain. There would not be any treaty but just some arrangement in which each would be guaranteed the use of the other's ports. I spoke to him about the northern regions of Canada; how impossible it would be for us to finance defence there. He felt anything we could do to follow along the same line, in a reciprocal way, allowing the U.S. rights for those areas for anything we might take for them, might be a good way of adjusting that matter. He told me he had no concern about unrest in Germany. That France was diffident about coal. He was going to control the coal in those areas for some little time and then would be able to give France a larger percentage than ever.

"Bevin had no confidence whatever in Russia. Is getting a condensed copy of the Canadian report on the spy question printed for wide distribution through England.

"I heard Smuts say he understood it was a tremendously important document.

"I spoke to Bevin about my thought of having a word with Molotov but had mentioned it was perhaps better not to run the risk of being insulted by him, if I should bring up the subject of relations with Russia. He told me if he were me, he would not want a word with Molotov. He is a wicked man; bad; has the whole mentality of a common mind. Stalin, he thought, would be different if I wanted to see him at any time. I am glad for Bevin's counsel and advice on this. I had said this very thing to Robertson this morning and he has agreed to it. . . .

"Bevin had invited me along with Smuts and one or two others to lunch with his party in his suite. The British Ambassador was also there. Some questions came up about Munich. Duff Cooper was very strong about it being a mistake. I might well have realized he would have Churchill's point of view. Bevin agreed that England would not have gone into war and I said certainly Canada would not have at the time of Munich. Someone asked: Would not have come in when they saw Czechoslovakia fighting and lives being lost? I replied I did not think any of our people knew where Czechoslovakia was. They would have found it almost impossible to come in. I think the most that could have been expected at that time was that Russia might have joined with Czechoslovakia but knowing the strength of Germany and the plans that were made, Russia might not have made out as well in the end.

"After the luncheon, Bevin spent some time telling us what the policy was in Palestine. He thinks it is going to be possible to have that question settled by the establishment of a Federation. Individual talks have gone pretty well.

"At the end of the luncheon, I said a few words of thanks for his great courtesy and that we all wished to have him feel he had our strength behind him. We must keep the English-speaking people together, etc. I told him to cling strongly to Byrnes, not to let any break come between Britain and the U.S. I am afraid there is an inevitable fight between materialistic and Christian forces."

Later he added: "In talking with Bevin and others, Bevin said to me he did not think anything could be done in next few weeks. He was going back to England tomorrow. Did not think the Conference should adjourn. They might be able to fix a definite time for the U.N. Conference in N.Y. to last. He felt sure the Russians would oppose any adjournment here.

"After the talk with him, and what I learned in other ways, I feel wholly justified in returning to Canada at this time. Indeed if I stayed on for another fortnight, it would be more for the opportunity of visiting Holland and Belgium; meeting others, more for my own enjoyment than from a sense of fulfilling a duty to the country."

Mackenzie King's last day in Paris (August 24) was not a happy one. He began the day by talking to Robertson about a building Georges Vanier wished to acquire as a Canadian embassy. The whole proposal struck him as far too extravagant. "I felt the time had come when I should speak out plainly as to where we were getting and said to R. I had become very deeply concerned about expenditures in connection with External Affairs. That the bill that had been sent for San Francisco – over $100,000 – was a thing which I thought might bring on an enquiry by Parliament – the public accounts committee. I was deeply concerned about expenditures though he keeps emphasizing that our delegation is one of the smallest. Also that I felt we had to consider together various suggestions that had been made. In Washington, we had gone from one to the other and were now considering another very expensive property – Stimson's building, which had associations, and many acres of land about it. Also would have to consider some place of residence in London for the High Commissioner there. We were being pressed for extra quarters for other Embassies. I did not think our people would understand it. I did not want the last of my associations with External Affairs to be one concerning which there might be great public discussion in Canada as to questionable expenditures, etc. I reminded him of the tremendous outcry there was when Thornton purchased the Scribe Hotel in Paris for Canadian National Headquarters, – an excellent investment commercially and location splendid. It had been made an issue in a general election. That I believed the two oppositions were lying low and were watching Minister after Minister coming to the Continent, staying considerable length of time and that with the talk of need of money for UNRRA, devastated areas, etc., to feed the people in England, etc., I did not see how we could very well defend these expenses. At any rate, I was not prepared to take them on myself without going over the whole situation very fully with the Cabinet and having them share responsibility. I added that I might leave all that business to whoever I shall appoint as a successor. Let him take responsibility as he would be the one who would have to continue to face it in Parliament. I then said that I thought what would be the best plan, was to have the committee on External Affairs go into the whole question of outlays for conferences, buildings, etc. Robertson saw pretty quickly that I thought things were going too far. Did not press very much. I told him I would do nothing while on this side at all until I had a chance for a conference with colleagues."

However, the Prime Minister did agree to see the property that morning. "On the way, Georges kept speaking about how ideal this property was. Exceptional in every way. Mentioned that the locality it was in was on the other side of the Seine – different direction from the Arc de Triomphe. Just the place for an Embassy, etc. We stopped in front of the building. It was like some of the older Embassies where there are stone walls, entrance locked; all as forbidding . . . as could be. The gates were opened. There was a large courtyard and I saw at once that the building was quite the same in style, appearance, as the British Embassy – not one bit smaller – if anything, larger. The Count who owns the property was there to show us over it, and a lady from the Argentine – some millionaire lady, who allowed us to see the different rooms. There were exceptionally beautiful tapestries; paintings of the lady herself, etc. Windows looking out onto a very beautiful garden. All enclosed with trees. Fountain in the centre. Georges kept emphasizing how peaceful and quiet and wonderful it all was. He then took me over to see the façade as seen from the other side. As I looked at it, I thought that to any Canadian, it would look like Buckingham Palace. When we came away, I agreed with Vanier about the beauty of the building, etc. Thought it well to come out at once and say that I would want to consider very carefully any purchase of the kind not being made without the approval of all political parties, in the House. I thought what I should do was to appoint a delegation from our party, the Conservative and C.C.F. parties and allow them to go over the plans and if necessary come and see the building; see styles of others. See how other countries were housed, etc. . . . Spoke about the building becoming a factor in a general election; photos taken, exhibited in different parts of Canada; relation to high cost of living; moneys we were loaning to feed people elsewhere, etc. Said I saw in it great dangers. It was a matter that would have to be carefully weighed. Vanier said at once these were things I would have to consider very naturally, very carefully. . . ."

Still in his economy mood, Mackenzie King returned to the hotel, called in Heeney "and spoke to him about the expenditures in connection with the Conference. Said I would like to have a breakdown as much as possible of the amounts chargeable to different persons. I was particularly anxious to have my own accounts as near as possible segregated from the others. There was the expenditure for the reception at the Embassy. There was, of course, my rooms and shares of meals, etc. A.H. then said all accounts would be put down to the delegation expenses. I said that is what I do not want. I want to have separate accounts as far as possible and the accounting to end tomorrow in relation to myself; from then on, Claxton would have to take full responsibility for expenses during the time he was there. Of course, accounts would show a diminution, H. said. I answered I hoped that would be the case but I wanted them separated. He then spoke about Ilsley coming to Paris and said they had been planning to let Ilsley have the suite I was occupying for a week. I said I wished nothing of the kind. Ilsley was Minister of Finance. He was on his own and his account should be kept separately. There was, of course, no objection to his having the suite reserved for him but it should not be charged up to the delegation to the Conference with which he was in no way associated. It would be a part of his own expenses of his European trip. I told both Vanier and Norman I hoped if Ilsley came, they would show him the properties they had shown to me, particularly the last one, so that he might be able to judge for himself what would be involved in expenditure. I said to A.H. I thought some arrangements would have to be made to control outlays at these gatherings. He said he thought we had done very little. Mentioned the reception that Claxton had given on his birthday, as he thought being very nice and necessary, adding there were representatives of other nations present. I did not say though I was inclined to say that all that had been after the reception I had given at the Embassy. Nothing was said about the smaller receptions that had taken place in different places."

At 1.00 P.M. the Prime Minister met the press and told them of his intention to return to Canada. "That I thought the Conference was at the committee stage. Treaties being considered clause by clause. Period of Conference indefinite. Had been away since middle of July, not getting back until September; Parliament proroguing; Ministers likely to scatter. Social security meeting on the 11th of September. U.N. meeting in N.Y. on the 23rd, and matters connected with them. Important I should not be away longer. Said Claxton would stay on and keep in touch. Cabinet will wish to consider matters; would be in touch by cable. If situation demanded it, I might return later but I could not be sure of that. Added that Attlee had been here only for a short time. Smuts would be here for only a week or two. Then said mistake I thought had been made in having publicity for the commissions; also it would have been better if we had a system of translation such as was adopted at Nuremberg. Was careful not to criticize the Conference except in these particulars. Indicated that perhaps in the long run discussion which had been to this time long on some matters, would be shorter on others later on.

"I felt it my duty to be back particularly as this was my third absence from Canada within a year."

After attending a series of receptions in the afternoon, the Prime Minister returned to the Crillon and dined with the Vaniers. "We had a very pleasant talk together but it was evident they were both pretty tired. I imagine they certainly have had a strenuous time. Pauline brought up the question of the house which we had seen. I felt that while it might be difficult to speak out, while they were my guests, that nevertheless it was the thing I should do so that there would be no misunderstanding later on. I repeated more or less what I had said to Georges in the morning about political dangers there were in large expenditures of the kind. Georges began saying something about Lybia, Roumania, and other small countries having very large legations . . . Poland, the Embassy which we had seen the other night, and rather indicating having to keep up to a certain standard with these countries. I said after what I had seen of this kind of thing, I was going to revise my views as to all further contributions Canada should make to these countries to aid them finding food and the like. To my mind, there was something scandalous about these countries having great buildings of the kind, spending millions of dollars while the money was being drawn from the people who were starving. Instead of imitating them, we should get away from it. It was that kind of thing feeding the unrest of today – people who saw plutocrats entertaining and being entertained. I felt there was a real menace in the whole thing.

"Georges himself said it was quite right to feel that way. One could not help feeling at the same time a little disappointed in both Georges and his wife having at the back of their minds letting Canada in for wild extravagances of the kind. It was the one shadow over the visit. I began to see clearly how step after step, attention after attention, etc., had all had as an ulterior motive, acquisition of these properties at the end. If there were such a motive, a more effective means of defeating this objective could not be adopted. I came over prepared to having the government purchase a large house for the government in England and other purchases here. I have now decided to see that henceforth, there will have to be approval of a committee of the House of Commons which will have on it members of all parties and not a result of any combination or of officials coming to be more powerful than the government itself.

"I drove Georges and Pauline Vanier home about 11.30. We had a very nice little talk in the last half hour. I am sure it was the pleasantest way of ending my association with both of them. They certainly could not have been more considerate and helpful than they have been. Canada has great reason to be proud of Vanier as our representative."

Before leaving Paris on August 25, Mackenzie King made an emotional pilgrimage to Pasteur's tomb. "I was so delighted that it was a quiet Sunday morning," he wrote. "It happened to be the second anniversary of the day on which Paris was freed of the enemy. Mr. Bidault had invited the heads of delegations to come to luncheon; also extended invitations to Ambassadors. Was to speak himself. . . . The anniversary is to be celebrated in the city by a march past of troops. Flags are appearing on the streets in front of the Chamber of Deputies, Foreign Office and elsewhere. It will be a day of great rejoicing and celebration.

"Vanier came in to tell me he had just received an invitation and thought that it would be well for him to be present, and not to attempt to come to the station. That Canada should be represented. That was right and I told him I was so glad he took that view. He said that Pauline would represent him at the station. He seemed much filled with the thought of being present at that gathering. A little preoccupied in his mind. I think perhaps my attitude toward the purchase of a house has taken just a little of the sugar off the gingerbread but that is natural. I thanked him for all his kindness. He said that was just his duty. He certainly has performed his duty to perfection. One likes to feel that there is something even more than the performance of duty. I was glad that, in this way, it had become possible for me to go to Pasteur's Tomb accompanied by Handy quite alone. I might easily have decided to go to the great ceremony today; figure in public prints in very foreground of those who had helped to relieve Paris. Receive a welcome perhaps greater than that which might have been given to other nations, simply as representing Canada, but to me this was as nothing compared to the reality of the experience in visiting Pasteur's Tomb and paying that tribute privately to him in the eyes of the nation and of the world. We drove through the silent streets. People had not yet begun to assemble for the parade except at the Champs Elysées and the Foreign Office.

"We were met at the entrance of the Institute by a member of the staff who was distressed that word had not been given in advance and other gentlemen had not been there. They apparently had planned to give me a public reception instead of my visiting the Tomb in a quiet way. I was presented with a volume bearing inscription of the tomb and relating incidents connected with Pasteur's Life. . . . I felt a great sense of peace and happiness in that little sepulchre. The stone of Pasteur's tomb is so simple – just his name at one end and place of birth at the other. It has been erected by his wife and a few friends. Words symbolical of his work; pictures and scenes illustrative of his studies – rabies and the like. One felt how truly it pictured, by contrast, the world in which men in Nuremberg and others who were allowing their lives to be destroyed by their own folly. Over the entrance of the Tomb are the words which Handy noted in his little book: 'Heureux celui qui porte en soi un Dieu, un idéal de beauté et qui lui obéit. Idéal de l'art; idéal de la science; idéal de la patrie. Idéal des vertus de l'Evangile.'

"To me they express all that I value the most. I was particularly impressed with the death mask of the face of Pasteur – a very noble face. Revealing infinite sympathy and tenderness; research. I contrasted it in my mind with the death mask of Napoleon which we saw yesterday – brutality manifested by his lower jaw. Nothing of the spirit or quality of Pasteur's face."

The Prime Minister left Paris by train later in the morning. Claxton took over as head of the Canadian delegation at the conference which, in the event, did not adjourn until October 15 thus delaying the opening of the second part of the first UN General Assembly meeting in New York until October 23. Claxton acted as chairman of the important Legal and Drafting Commission and General Pope, in a unique recognition of Canada's disinterested position in such matters, was asked by the parties to chair a special meeting to discuss the delimitation of the frontier between Hungary and Czechoslovakia. Wilgress and his advisers were active in the various economic commissions. However, following Mackenzie King's general conception of Canada's role at the conference, members of the Canadian delegation made only eleven speeches, three in plenary sessions and eight on major issues discussed in commissions. The conference approved fifty-three recommendations for changes in the draft treaties by a two-thirds majority, forty-one by a simple majority, and all went forward to the Council of Foreign Ministers which met in New York on November 4. Suspicion between the Western nations and the Soviet Union was only highlighted and accentuated by the tediousness and wrangling which featured the Paris conference and, henceforth, great power tension and conflict became the major factors conditioning the development of Canadian foreign policy.

CHAPTER TEN

The Shift in External Affairs

GRATEFULLY ESCAPING the rigours of Paris, Mackenzie King arrived in London during the evening of August 25 and next day attended a luncheon at Downing Street. He told Attlee "of my thought of appointing Robertson [as High Commissioner]. He said Robertson would be most acceptable to their government. Seemed greatly pleased at the thought of his coming to London. Attlee made a nice little informal speech. Among other things, he made a kindly reference to my wise counsel in many matters. He is strongly agreed with what I said about publicity of negotiations. Spoke about Russia's position being an extraordinarily difficult one, etc.

"I said a few words in reply, among other things saying I thought he might perhaps be able to hold a cabinet meeting in Canada. Dalton was coming over as well as the Minister of Pensions. The Minister of Agriculture had just been over; and also Lord Addison was coming over next week. I said I could hold a better meeting in London or Paris than at Ottawa. While all this was said jocularly, there was a good deal of truth beneath it. Mackenzie is leaving today by the Mauretania. Gardiner was at the luncheon. Claxton is in Paris. Ilsley in Austria or Warsaw. I myself away. I really felt that the situation at Ottawa was pretty dangerous. Fortunately, I trust St. Laurent's judgment very well but Howe, Mitchell, and others are not the men to be trusted with direction of government."

Increasingly preoccupied as he was by the situation in Ottawa, the Prime Minister was convinced that "there was great danger at the close of the session that the Conservatives and other parties might combine to make things very difficult with a view of demonstrating the weakness of the Cabinet without myself and certain others present. My worst fears in this particular were confirmed before the day was over. A very strong message came saying that the House would not end before Wednesday or Thursday." He was also informed that the Senate was being uncooperative on some government measures and that the steel strike situation was deteriorating with no immediate prospect of settlement. "There was also mention of newspapers and C.C.F. saying that the House should be kept sitting until I returned home. I should not be surprised if this happened although I do not actually believe it will. I think Members find if I do not get back this week, they will not run over into another week-end in September. It is quite conceivable the Government may come within an ace of being defeated. All of this is making very difficult and next to impossible our winning by-elections outside of Quebec. It certainly justified my not waiting longer in Paris."

During the evening the Prime Minister went to Southampton by train and boarded the *Queen Mary* at 10.00 P.M. His friends, the Salisburys, were also on board. Mackenzie King continued to be concerned that the session would not be over when he returned to Ottawa. On August 29 he was somewhat relieved to receive word "that better progress was being made . . . but also a cable from Carnegie [head of the Canadian Press Ottawa Bureau] asking if I would comment on intention to address Parliament on world situation before prorogation. I sent a reply to P. to give to St. Laurent saying that, if necessary, to inform the House I did not feel I would care to make any statement to Parliament without opportunity for careful reflection. I doubt if Parliament will sit beyond this week. Certainly I will not attempt anything which cannot do other than create embarrassment to an already embarrassing situation by attempting observations on conditions in Europe until it becomes absolutely necessary to make some statement which I can carefully prepare.

"Received from Mackenzie in mid-ocean a telegram of greetings. I greatly fear this exit of Ministers from so many sides will itself become a matter of adverse comment in the country. One thing that has given me some satisfaction is that Howe, Ilsley and several others have found out that strikes cannot be handled by a mere fixing of penalties by government action. They may perhaps now see what I saved the Government at a time of war by taking the action I did to avert a strike in the steel industry for which I got no end of criticism and adverse comment. I have a feeling that the steel strike may end soon. It may be I may yet be fortunate enough to make a settlement myself. For this, I am not too sanguine."

That evening while the Prime Minister was finishing dinner, "Robertson came along with Heeney and Pearson with a brown envelope containing papers in his hand, saying they had been working over some matters that they would like to take up with me in the morning and asked what hour they could come. He was going to leave the papers with me but I was rather silent and then said he would leave them in my room. I replied that I was speaking to the [war] brides in the morning but would see what arrangements could be made.

"Until I have completed letters growing out of the Conference meetings, prepared my statements for the press and have something in readiness for the House, should it still be meeting on Monday, I do not think I will try to take up with Robertson or Pearson any matters pertaining to External Affairs. Indeed I shall take the position that I wish to talk over the whole situation with my colleagues before making any appointments or reaching any decision with respect to purchases of houses and the like."

As soon as he came on deck the next morning (August 30), Mackenzie King was met by Robertson, Pearson and Heeney. His mood was no better than it had been the night before. "The first question was would I now come in and talk over the matters that had been prepared. I said I thought I would take a little walk first. I kept debating in my mind just what the next step should be. As Pearson and Robertson had gone off by themselves, Arnold remained talking to Mrs. Salisbury and Frank, I finally said to Arnold I wished he would come over, that I wanted to have a word with him. I then said to him, as nearly as I recall, something as follows: Arnold, I do not wish to take up the questions of staffs, changes, etc. at this time, feeling as I do. I wish you would tell Robertson and Pearson that I would prefer to leave over these matters until we are at Ottawa and I have an opportunity to take them up in my own office. I would wish to have some talks with my colleagues in the first instance about many considerations of which account will have to be taken.

"I then went on to say that I had gone over hoping to be able to further the interests of all concerned and prepared to consider what would be done in the way of obtaining new premises and the like. That I felt in regard to proposals that were being made for palatial quarters in Paris, new buildings in London and Washington, that I would have to be very careful about what I should recommend and would have to discuss that situation very carefully with my colleagues.... I had to remember that I was responsible to the Cabinet, the Cabinet to Parliament, and Parliament to the people. That I thought before any of these purchases would be made, they would have to be considered by a joint committee of Parliament composed of members of different parties so that there would be no charge that I had been reckless in expenditures of public money.

"I then said that I had never felt so let down in all my life as I had been by some of those around me in the last couple of weeks. That except where there was something that they wanted for themselves, there had not been even a question as to whether there was anything they could do in furthering my interests or wishes. That I had spent this entire week for the most part writing communications which I had expected would be prepared for me. That I had still more to write. I mentioned about being made a Bencher of Gray's Inn but that I had not had time to even acknowledge that communication since leaving for Paris though it meant a very high honour to myself. I had been giving my time to work that I had hoped members of the staff who had come with me might be able to relieve me of entirely. I thought I would require the rest of the week to conclude the correspondence that I have and yet to be covered. Have to be prepared for press interview tomorrow, and also for speaking in Parliament next week on External Affairs should Parliament still be sitting as I began to feel it might be. I said these were my first duties as Prime Minister and would have to demand my first attention.

"Arnold said he felt so sorry. He would speak to the others. Said if I liked, he would speak to the others about the buildings. I told him that was a matter I would deal with myself. All I wanted him to speak of was the necessity of myself having the remainder of the trip to devote to public business which I had not overtaken and which related to the staff. I preferred to take up other matters in my own office after I had been in touch with my colleagues.

"I again repeated I had never felt so let down in my life nor had I suffered as much in mind and heart as I had in the last little while; that I was returning to Ottawa a much sadder but a much wiser man. That the experience had been dearly bought but it might help to save a much more deplorable situation.

"Arnold said he himself had asked if there was anything he could do in the way of helping. I said I thought most of what he might have done had been accomplished. That I thought I could manage the rest.

"He then said he had spoken frequently to Handy to let him know if there was anything he could do, and to tell me he was ready at any time. I did not answer that but was sorry I did not. I saw no reason why he should necessarily avoid me all the time. However he did say he had come on at London to see if there was anything he could do. I then said flatly to him: Arnold, you did not. You did not come to see what you could do for me. You came to tell me what you and Pearson would do in the morning and through the day. I was not asked if there was anything you could do or which required to be done by others for me. I said, however, that is past and I shall say no more about it. Each man can look into his own conscience for himself. I want to repeat again I have never in my life felt more hurt. I also stated that I had begun over twenty years ago to build up the Department of External Affairs, that I had sought to develop it, meet the wishes of those who were working so splendidly in it, and did not want my connection with the Department to end in any questionable way as to my care of the people's rights in the matter of their taxation. That I had given my life not for position or pleasure but to serve the people, to safeguard their taxes and their homes. I did not intend to give up office by any acts that would undo all the good that might have been accomplished in the years of my association with the Department.

"I also indicated at another point that I had much in mind that I would reconsider just who I might wish to have take over the office when I dropped out. It was something to which I had come to see I would have to give more serious thought than I had previously believed."

Pearson seemed to escape the prime ministerial wrath and joined Mackenzie King for a movie after dinner. "I like Pearson exceedingly," he wrote. "I feel sure his judgment will be helpful in the working out of what is best for all concerned."

The *Queen Mary* arrived at Halifax on August 31 and the Prime Minister was delighted to get word that the session had been prorogued that afternoon. On the train the next day Mackenzie King reported that "Heeney came in to bring me some papers this morning. He was in an entirely different mood than I had seen him for some time. Seemed to be thoroughly understanding about the relationship which should be maintained. I think letting Robertson and Pearson themselves see that I intended to maintain my own position and that I had a position that had to be maintained has become pretty evident and has been in the nature of a very wholesome lesson. As I said to A.H. the other day, I am going back a sadder but a much wiser man. I can see that, from now, the one thing for me to do is to assert my own position and my own views and make clear to others where the course of power lies in government. If I did not feel that my whole life had been given to protect the interests of the people by being careful of the trust that they have placed in me through position and power, I might feel differently. I am satisfied, however, that I am right and that the thing now is to be careful not to lose the pearl of public confidence which has been mine over many years but to maintain it to the end."

Just after dinner, St. Laurent boarded the train at St. Henri. "He gave me a very full account of all that had taken place," Mackenzie King wrote. "My admiration for his ability, [and] integrity surpassed all words. I told him that I wished above everything else he would continue in public life. If he would, I believe he would be chosen Leader of the Party and would do all in my power to have him gain that position. He told me that that was something he could not think of. He could not stand the strain. He had seen by what he has already experienced, how great the strain was. At his age, it would break him down. I said next to that, I would like to see him on the Supreme Court Bench as Chief Justice. He said the present Chief Justice was there and doing exceedingly well. I said I doubted if his health would hold out very long though, of course, no one could say. At any rate, if not Chief Justice, one of the Judges. He said he would rather be at his practice with his son coming on. If he got past 65, it would be hard to regain his practice. I then said I wished he would take on External Affairs. He said he feared if he did, his Quebec followers would think he was going to stay on permanently. He thought he ought to drop out at the end of the year. He thought Ilsley might perhaps be willing to take the Justice Department. I said I wished he himself would take Finance. All of this would be followed up with a further discussion later on.

"I gathered he was not too enamoured of Mackenzie's actions in the House or leaving when he did to go abroad. St. Laurent made no complaint about the load though he admitted it was pretty heavy."

It was after midnight when the train finally reached Ottawa. "It was raining but there was quite a gathering at the station. . . . I declined giving any press interviews in the rain. Also present were wives of members of the staff. I noticed as I was leaving that members of my party all came up to say good-bye.

"I was pleased to see Pickersgill; sorry, however, to see him getting so heavy. Thanked him for the splendid way he had managed. St. Laurent said he had been most helpful."

By the next morning (September 2), Mackenzie King had concluded that he "should try and get St. Laurent to take on External Affairs at least until the end of the year, with the knowledge that he would not retain the position indefinitely, so as to get rid of External Affairs altogether and then give my time wholeheartedly to the work of the Prime Minister's Office. I really believe that will make a tremendous difference. The mere thought of it took a tremendous load off my mind." The following morning he wrote: "When I got up, my mind was quite clear as to what it was advisable to do. I decided I would see if I could not persuade Mr. St. Laurent to take on immediately the portfolio of Secretary of State for External Affairs on the ground that he was heading the delegation to [the UN General Assembly in Flushing Meadow] New York. Had been Acting Minister and was familiar with the problems; also that I would make it clear this was only a temporary arrangement and that the portfolio would go to a Minister who would give his exclusive time to it before Parliament reassembled. That will give me a chance to make readjustments that are necessary and will get over Mr. St. Laurent's difficulty of having it appear that he is staying on permanently. I decided that I might talk over the whole External Affairs situation with him."

At 4.30 that afternoon, St. Laurent came to Kingsmere and the Prime Minister wasted no time in putting the proposal to him. "St. Laurent responded very nicely. He said immediately as it was only for a time it might be of assistance to me. If he could assist in any way, he would be only too ready to comply. I said to him then I thought I would like to put the order through tomorrow and also the order appointing Robertson, to London; Wrong, to Washington; and Pearson, to Ottawa. Would discuss matters in Council and have a meeting of the press later in the day, thereby making clear I had taken the earliest opportunity to give my exclusive time to the work of the office of the Prime Minister and President of the Council.

"I then told him of the situation I had encountered while I was abroad. Discussed the matter of the proposed expenditure on elaborate houses. . . . I then read over to him a memorandum Robertson had prepared about different appointments, telling him what I thought of certain of the suggestions and where I concurred in others. He and I shared, as I thought we would, exactly the same view. I told him I would leave all these problems for him to work out. He could bring them to the Cabinet. We must keep Cabinet responsibility in these matters and not let a bureaucracy be built which is made up of intimate friends to the exclusion of others. Robertson has been trying to work in Brockington, [Fred] Bronson, Ken Greene [leading businessmen in Ottawa] – all three from Ottawa, of which they already have drafted far too many. He also suggested Hudd as the Deputy High Commissioner [in London]. St. Laurent and I both laughed at the idea of having any Deputy to the High Commissioner; that was not the kind of role we proposed establishing overseas in our representation, etc., in the different Capitals.

"The talk with St. Laurent was most satisfactory in every way. It will enable me to decide between now and the end of the year who I will make the permanent Secretary of State for External Affairs, and things not going just as everyone had taken for granted will perhaps bring a number of persons to their senses and full appreciation of the fact that there is a government that, after all, has a responsibility to the people and has to do with the shaping of policy and determining of appointments, etc. I feel very strongly that bringing the Prime Minister's office now exclusively into association with Privy Council in all matters will make a tremendous difference and will make for much greater efficiency. Instead of Pickersgill and Heeney taking their direction from Robertson and often ignoring myself, there will now be immediate relationships with the Prime Minister and such additions to his staff as may be necessary to bring about the needed efficiency."

"Today has been one of the most significant days of my life," Mackenzie King wrote on September 4, "marking as it does the termination of a long association of on into 20 years with the Department of External Affairs,

The Shift in External Affairs 335

and more in the way of freedom for my duty in the office of Prime Minister, with the possible longer lease of office as a consequence thereof. I have taken tremendous satisfaction out of reaching the decision that I have myself without counsel from any source save the conversation I had with St. Laurent."

When he reached the East Block that morning, the Prime Minister informed Pickersgill of his decision and then sent for Robertson. "It was the first time I had had a word with him in several days," he wrote. "He came into the office with a number of papers in his hands, intending apparently to take up some matters. I said to him that I thought before taking up any matters I should let him know I had decided to give up the Department of External Affairs immediately and to telephone the Governor General this morning asking him to accept my resignation. I also said it was my intention to recommend Mr. St. Laurent as my successor; that I talked with him of the matter and he had agreed to accept the position and to carry on at least until the end of the year. I thought it was better some of the matters to be dealt with in External Affairs should be taken up quite independently of myself, at least in the first instance.

"Robertson was visibly surprised. I think he had counted on our having further talks. Also upon the possibility of Claxton succeeding. He said to me that he was sorry I was severing associations with the Department of External Affairs but he knew what the burden had been and thought it would be best for me in the end. He then said that I had really brought Canada into the world arena in the 20 years that I had been at the head of the Department; had created all its missions. It was a wonderful record.

"I said to him I wished he would have drafted at once the recommendations for himself as High Commissioner to London; Pearson to succeed him in Ottawa, and Wrong to go to Washington. The orders to be passed today. Robertson said there was a technical difficulty which might prevent this, which was that there would have to be an agreement on the part of the United States to accept Wrong as Minister. I said to him I did not care what the technical difficulties were. They would be gotten over somehow. I intended to make public today in one form or another my termination with the Department and the appointments that were to be made. He said he would take up the matter of agreement with Atherton at once and perhaps would get a special message to the President. I said I was sure the President would understand if I found it necessary to make a statement even in advance of his approval. That I felt the circumstances were such that I did not wish to delay an hour. He then said he wanted to thank me for what I had done for him and as he was about to leave, said he feared he had failed off and on but that he had tried to do his best. I said I had appreciated all he had done over the years and wished him all that was best in the new position."

The Prime Minister then saw Wrong and informed him of his appointment to Washington. "He was exceedingly pleasant in his manner. . . . He said he would enjoy Washington. Felt he had been getting stale in the work of the office here. That he was sure Robertson had felt the same and he believed Pearson would bring a fresh mind and direction to affairs. That the changes all round would be for the best. He expressed appreciation of our relations in the Department and thanked me for the appointment anew."

Earlier Mackenzie King had placed a call to the Governor-General, who was in residence at the Citadel. The call came through while Wrong was in the office and the Prime Minister invited him to stay as he informed Alexander of his decision to appoint St. Laurent as his successor in External Affairs. When Wrong left, he sent for Pearson. "As Pearson came into the office, I was struck by his fine face and appearance. There was a light from within which shone through his countenance." After Mackenzie King had outlined the changes in the Department, "Pearson at once said he was sorry to begin his work in the Department of External Affairs without me at the head; that he had begun his work in the Department under myself as Secretary of the Department, and had learned a great deal from me, and had hoped to have had that further opportunity in a relationship of Under-Secretary. . . . I [said I] hoped he would realize that what he was he owed to himself. . . . I know what this sort of thing was from my own life which so often was attributed to Sir Wilfrid's, or Mulock's, or others – that they had furnished the opportunity, but I thought the development had been due to my own home and ancestry, etc. I hoped he would feel the same way about our relationship. I said of course I would be here in the office of Prime Minister. He said I would still be here in any event and he would look to me for guidance. I said that I would look to him to help me and would probably need help in my present position. I was immensely taken with his whole manner, which is very natural – a self-effacing one. I told him I felt he had a great career before him and wished him all that was best."

St. Laurent was sworn in as Secretary of State for External Affairs by the Chief Justice just before 5.30 P.M. and, immediately after the ceremony, the Prime Minister returned to his office to meet the press. "Arnold was most anxious to know if I desired him at the conference. I told him to do entirely as he wished; if he would like to come, he would be welcome. He came as I expected he would. Robertson had asked if on account of

The Shift in External Affairs 337

appointments, I would wish him there. I suggested he might come. However I said nothing to anyone as to what I would say.

"Robertson had prepared a note for use in the House in case we arrived before the session was over, but I made no reference to it. There was a large attendance of the press.

"I began by stating that as they were aware I had been anxious to give up External Affairs for some time past. That I had asked this morning the Governor General to accept my resignation, and that St. Laurent had been not only appointed but sworn in. I referred then to other appointments, saying a kindly word in reference to each in turn. Of Robertson that no Prime Minister could have been served better than I was during the years by his wise counsel, etc., and as a friend, referred to the reputation he had gained, and referred to Wrong's service and of his appointment as Ambassador. I then spoke about the Paris Conference. I said I thought they would succeed in time. Must have faith and make allowances. I spoke then of my association with the Department for twenty years, saying I could not sever without some regret, but had the satisfaction of seeing all missions created in that time, and leaving the Department in a fine position in the world. I hoped that giving up the Department would enable me to have a longer time in the office of Prime Minister than would otherwise have been possible. I mentioned the speculation there was as to a successor, reminded them that, while I had said I would not contest another general election, I had not said I would not continue on as long as the party in Parliament supported me. For them to please remember this Parliament could run until August, 1950. Then regarding the flag I mentioned nothing would be done by Order in Council.

"The conference lasted for three quarters of an hour. I paid a deserved tribute to St. Laurent, had no notes. Members seemed well satisfied."

At the end of the day, Mackenzie King "felt a tremendous sense of relief at having done a good and important day's work. I think it let everyone see where I was quite capable of taking care of myself and of making my own decisions, the fact that I consulted no one and went ahead as I did, I think will have a wholesome effect on letting others see just where the authority and power of government rests. I am convinced that no better moment could have been selected for the decision I had made, and given effect to. I shall now have time between the present and the beginning of the new session to reconstruct the Ministry. This is a considerable task, but if I am spared in health and strength it will bring me at least in office into the year 1947. I must try now to get everything as much in order . . . as possible in connection with my own affairs."

The most urgent problem facing the Prime Minister when he returned was the steel strike which had been dragging on since July 15, marked by several serious outbreaks of picket line violence in Hamilton and Toronto. During Mackenzie King's absence, both the Minister of Labour and the chairman of the Wartime Prices and Trade Board had projected the federal government into the middle of the dispute by publicly declaring that the government could not accept a wage increase of more than 10 cents an hour, well below the union demand for 19½ cents an hour. Their intervention made the relationship between wage increases and inflationary pressures in the economy a key issue in public debate about the strike. During the morning of September 3, the Prime Minister had a long telephone conversation with the Minister of Labour and then sent a message to Charles Millard, the director of the Steel Workers Organizing Committee, suggesting that they meet on September 5 following an already scheduled meeting the next day between officials of the Department of Labour and representatives of the union. "I am inclined to believe the settlement is now in sight," Mackenzie King wrote. "I told Mitchell I would be prepared to help or to keep out as he might think best. Would lend him the strength of my backing."

He met Mitchell and his Deputy Minister at his office on September 5. They told him "of their conversations with the committee of strikers this morning. They seemed to be somewhat of a queer pair. Neither too direct in their statements, not too sure of either the stand the men were taking or of their own position. They indicated that in the morning the men seemed a little less defiant than yesterday, and they were prepared to suggest one or two small additional concessions. . . . Stated the Hamilton people did not want the arbitration of certain matters and would not yield to it. I was myself unwilling to impose arbitration on both parties if they were unwilling to accept, but I was quite ready to have the Company and the men agree to arbitrate certain questions of union security, etc., and to urge that they should do this. I made it clear that I did not want to put forward any suggestions of my own, which would be in the nature of a further concession, but would be glad to support in Council what they would think best."

Before seeing Millard and his colleagues, Mackenzie King had a private talk with A. R. Mosher, the President of the Canadian Congress of Labour, and Pat Conroy, the Secretary-Treasurer. "When they came in I spoke of the meeting of last year [the presentation of the CCL's annual brief to the Cabinet], and had before me the printed representations they had made. Said I had hoped to see both of them since to let them know I had no feeling toward either of them, but that I had been amazed at what they had said, and had always thought that we were friends, and meant to keep them as friends, that my statements were natural reactions of a man who felt no friend could speak to another in that way. They knew better.

"Mosher said the statement was too strong. They put down that which suited those around them – it was not what they themselves believed. Conroy said he had not meant to say what had been said, or words to that effect. I did everything I could to make them feel reassured of my good will. I said to each of them they had great responsibilities. I wanted to see them exercise them in the best possible way, – that I would work with them as far as I could. Conroy gave me a little statement of the background of the strike, saying it might have been avoided had the Government accepted their offer many months ago, – to anticipate the strikes that might come on later, but no heed had been paid to what they had said."

At this point, the Minister and Deputy Minister of Labour joined the three men and Millard and two of his colleagues were invited in. "I let Millard go over the ground, and then began to take up different points with him. What I told them was that the Government had gone just as far as we felt we could go. They must remember we were imposing conditions on private employers, and we felt we had gone as far as it was possible for the Government to go, and would have to withdraw altogether unless some settlements were speedily made. I drew their attention to what was said in the Industrial Relations Commission in relation to picketing and said as a Government we would want to keep the freedom of the individual uppermost. I also pointed out that as long as there was machinery the state had created, and they were not taking advantage of it, I could not see how we could deal with them. I suggested, however, they might express their readiness to accept the good offices of the Regional Labour Board in regard to three or four things they might be ready to refer to it. Millard said he would not expect the Labour part to go as far as was gone in the Windsor case by Judge Rand [a reference to the 'Rand formula' on union security arrangements which had been part of the arbitration judgment on the Ford Motors strike earlier in the year]. Was not altogether particular as to what their findings might be, but was opposed to accepting a formula for final settlement fearing the men would not accept it, even if the Company would. I kept sensing as they talked a readiness on their part to bring the strike to a close if they could, under the guise of having been here in Ottawa for some days, and discussing it with the Government, and among others with myself.

"In opening with Millard I said he had written me nice letters, and I had agreed to see him for that reason. I assume that Mitchell was a party to my seeing him. The real stumbling block seems to have been the granting of 16 cents to the lumber industry in the west, under the men who were

Communist leaders. They themselves as representing the C.C.L. are fighting the Communists in part.

"I talked quietly with them for quite a long time. I drew attention amongst other things to the seriousness of the world situation, and to the injury [that] was being done their own people by the continual stoppages of labour, increased cost of living, etc. Millard then suggested that I should myself bring their representations to the attention of the Government. I agreed to do this, said the Cabinet was meeting. I would go in at once, but that they must realize that what we might decide now would be as far as we as a government could go, – that I hoped they would feel this was a moment to bring matters to a close. As they went out I said to Millard that while he and I wrote each other pretty sharp letters at times, we were both good friends, and I hoped always would be. All of the men were quite happy in the way they said good-bye and seemed to recognize a real friend in myself. I made it clear to them I had no political interest to serve, but was seeking from now on to serve alone the interests of the country."

In Cabinet the Prime Minister found, to his surprise, "that all seemed to be in agreement on what had been proposed by Mitchell and myself. McCann summed up the whole business in very clear and concise language and was definitely for a settlement. Chevrier, who had come in, was equally strong for the terms. Said he thought Mr. Howe would approve. I said to Council I wanted them to keep in mind many things that had been expressed by other members of the Cabinet not present today. There was some discussion of how Mr. Howe might view some things. Those present seemed prepared to accept what had been done, though he, Howe, had left town saying to Mitchell that he would not go a step farther. Baldwin had told the Cabinet that Howe would accept what had been agreed to by Mitchell a day or two before. The truth is they are all afraid of Howe who adopts very arbitrary methods and is rough in the manner in which he speaks. I reviewed the situation to which Council agreed unanimously."

Despite this unanimous agreement in the Cabinet, the strike was still not settled on September 26 when Mackenzie King "spent some time with Mitchell and his Deputy, Macnamara, drafting a reply to a telegram received from Pat Conroy, sent on behalf of the Canadian Congress of Labour, asking me to direct the Minister to request the Steel Company to arbitrate certain matters. I had spent some little time in drafting a statement myself, and, after discussing matters fully with Mitchell, continued to draft the statement. Meanwhile, I had Macnamara prepare something of his own which I could weld in with mine.

"I had lunch sent up to the office and at 2.30 Mitchell and Macnamara returned. We agreed on the final terms of the message, which included a statement by myself that I would not direct Ministers myself as they had their own responsibilities to Parliament, but would confer with Cabinet as a whole, as to the action to be taken on the request contained in the telegram. I indicated the Government would recommend arbitration, and should there be any failure in arbitration, I would send a series of questions to both parties in order that the public would know who were right and who were wrong. I also stated we would withdraw the Order in Council appointing a Controller so that the parties might be free to negotiate voluntarily.

"Blackwell, the Attorney-General of Ontario, had issued a statement that, as we had appointed a Controller, it was the Government and not the company who had the say in the matter of negotiations. I decided to put the responsibility right back on his own doorstep, and off ours. The statement, a fairly lengthy one, was ready at 3.30. I took it into Council and obtained the consent of Cabinet to all it expressed. Howe had been doubtful about our withdrawing, and in passing the Order getting rid of the Controller, but both he and Mitchell had come round to see that it was wise. Howe did not like the idea of compelling the Company to say whether they would arbitrate Union security. I took the position that we were not interested in the Company or the men, but that it was in public interest that disputes which could not be settled voluntarily should be settled by arbitration, but we must put this request to both parties. Cabinet agreed ultimately with the communication I had proposed sending and I left for my office to have the final draft carefully prepared and checked. Mitchell and Macnamara came to the office for this final check and we had just completed the revisions about five when Howe came in to say that there had been a later development. Millard had been in Montreal today negotiating with the Controller for final settlement; had agreed that if the Company would give an extra half a cent an hour and would arbitrate other questions, he would be prepared to see that the men were ordered back to work on Monday morning next. Whether Howe had 'phoned to the Company meanwhile, letting them know my determination to put both parties on the spot or not I cannot say. He seemed a little indefinite about who had 'phoned the other first. I decided not to embarrass the situation by sending the messages, but to hold them for the present and dictated a telegram to be sent to Conroy at 6.00 o'clock saying that I had learned of the negotiations taking place today and was withholding my answer to his message for the present.

"Meanwhile, recommendation had gone to the Council cancelling as of six tonight the Order in Council. I had not signed the Order and requested it should be held until receiving authority from Council whatever they might deem best tomorrow, should an agreement not be reached at that time. I am not too sure that an agreement will be reached. I am inclined to think that the parties have now come to realize that the Government has gone as far as it intends to go. The weakness of each will be shown by the questions as put to them for reply in public, unless the settlement takes place at once."

The next day (September 27) the Prime Minister did not release the statement because he received word that progress was being made towards a settlement. "It now looks as if men might be back at work next week. Was glad to know that Pat Conroy thought my message to the Congress the right one and said so by telephoning down to the office."

A few days later the strike was settled on the basis of a 13½ cents an hour increase and a uniform wage scale for all three major firms in the industry. The union agreed to drop its demand for a 40-hour week.

During much of September and early October, the Prime Minister spent a good deal of his time at Kingsmere in relative tranquillity. Both Lord Addison and Field Marshal Montgomery were in Ottawa on September 9. Mackenzie King was at the Canadian Club luncheon to hear Addison speak and then returned to Laurier House to receive Montgomery at 3.00 P.M. "Abbott came just a few minutes before Montgomery arrived. Montgomery was accompanied by General Foulkes. I met him on the front steps. He was very cheerful. Spoke at once when he came into the house of the beauty of the house.

"We went up to the library together. I left the others downstairs. The first thing he spoke of was my mother's picture. He remembers having seen the copy at Salisbury's studio. I had shown it to him. I spoke to him about his own mother who is quite ill. He said it is the third stroke she has had. He thought she would get on all right for a time. I showed him the little pamphlet by Mackenzie on the Lives of a Thousand Irishmen including one on Montgomery who came out with Wolfe and subsequently led the continental army of the United States against Quebec. I asked if he was a relative. Montgomery said he had relations in Ireland but did not know whether this one was or not. It is curious he did not seem to know much about this particular Montgomery. I gave him a copy of the article and he is to let me have particulars."

Discussion then turned to the matters which Montgomery was particularly interested in, defence co-ordination and liaison. "After he had dealt with them, he suggested we might have Abbott and Foulkes come up and we would go over with them the conversation we had had together. This was arranged and after a further talk in the library we then went down to the drawing room where we had tea together. I was surprised during the conversation in the library to see a photographer come in unannounced and take a picture. I did not know whether he was from the Department of Defence, Montgomery's man or who he was. However, I let him go ahead.

"Was somewhat sorry afterwards when I saw the picture, in one of the evening papers, of us all at tea. A poor looking affair.

"After a pleasant talk at the tea table, Montgomery left shortly after 4.30 to take his plane on to Quebec. He could not have been pleasanter than he was. Spoke very appreciatively of his trip. I found him exceedingly pleasant."

After Montgomery left, Mackenzie King went to Earnscliffe to pick up Lord Addison. They returned to Laurier House "for a short talk together. We had a cup of tea in the drawing room. He was immensely interested in its appearance. I then took him over the house. The different rooms and up to the library where we had a very happy talk together [trading stories about British politics in the 1920s]. He seemed most anxious that his wife should see Laurier House. To him it was quite a revelation to find what had been done for me by Lady Laurier, Mr. Larkin and other friends. Montgomery told me that all that he possessed had been destroyed in the war. He hoped when he was through with being Chief of Staff, he might have a little house he could retire to with his books and papers but said he had nothing at all at the present time. I said the nation was sure to make some provision for him in that regard. He thought a man should have the last of his life to devote to his books and papers. Addison, too, spoke of what it meant to have a provision of the kind made for one's future."

Another distinguished visitor to Ottawa in the fall of 1946 was Dean Acheson, the American Under-Secretary of State. The Prime Minister dined with him at the American Embassy on September 17 and "enjoyed the evening exceedingly. Acheson told me of the Cabinet crisis which would be disclosed in tomorrow's papers, referring to it as a first-class crisis [Henry Wallace's resignation from the Truman Cabinet]. I expressed strong admiration of and sympathy with Byrnes. It seems to me that Wallace is playing a very dangerous game and really very unpatriotic, when one considers that Byrnes is seeking to keep the English-speaking people united against might and aggression. I shall be amazed if public opinion does not go strongly against him. He is counting on leading a democratic party of an extreme left position and becoming its candidate [in 1948]."

By September 21 Mackenzie King had changed his mind. "I feel that Wallace has the popular end of the present controversy so far as the U.S. is concerned, 'fight for peace' – and will bring the Democratic Party to his side – the other wing Truman and Byrnes may become more and more Republican. The 'one world' concept is the only one to prevent war – one world achieved not by conquest of arms that level but by conquest of ideas." Next day he was "glad to hear Harriman had been appointed Secretary of Commerce. I still think Wallace will be a formidable opponent of 'the interests' and may be responsible for making national unity increasingly difficult. He will get the numbers."

The Prime Minister became preoccupied at this time with plans for the disposition of Laurier House, Kingsmere, and his personal and state papers. On September 10 he had a talk with a young graduate student in history, "F. W. Gibson of Kingston, Ont., who had learned I was looking for someone to go through my papers and who had made it known that he would be prepared to give up a year or two of study in order to have the opportunity of gaining a wider knowledge of Canadian history if he could undertake sorting of the papers. . . . Prof. Elliott of Harvard had written Robertson that he would recommend Gibson very highly for work of the kind. Pickersgill had had Gibson come down from Kingston. He had had a talk with him and felt impressed at once with the clarity with which he explained his method of classifying documents. . . . I could see he was really very keen. He hopes to be a professor of Canadian history. . . . When I asked about his politics he said his father had been a strong follower of Sir John Macdonald. They were Irish Catholics. He himself had always been sympathetic to our administration and he himself an admirer of myself.

"When I spoke to Pickersgill he reminded me that both [Norman] Rogers and himself had been Tory fostered and had become Liberals and at some times a convert is more enthusiastic than one who held to his old faith. At any rate it was apparent to me that Gibson was interested in facts – in what he could gain from reading and classifying facts. I spoke to him particularly about not having more done to my papers than classifying them. Said I wished to write my own memoirs or might wish to get others to write them for me. Ludwig had spoken of undertaking this task. He told me he would in no way expect to have any right to writing the life. All he wanted was the knowledge gained and all he would undertake to do was classify. He thought if he could get a room at the Archives and an assistant there, that would be the best way to proceed. Pickersgill had taken up the matter with Bland [the Chairman, Civil Service Commission]. He also had spoken to Paul Martin and I myself took up the question with Lanctot [the Dominion Archivist]. I made clear that what I am anxious to do is to have papers so arranged that I could give the majority of them to the Archives or External Affairs or to the P.M.'s office; that I have no descendants to whom I wish to leave any of this material and that, therefore, it was really in the public interest that the papers should be gone through – if possible, as Gibson remarked apologetically, while I was still alive, and able to give directions, answer questions, etc. All are agreed that it is quite the right thing to have this work undertaken through the public offices, as described. I did the same thing for Sir Robert Borden. . . . I therefore feel that in making this arrangement I am doing what is in the public interest. Gibson seemed to think and said that the Harvard authorities believed more of the inside of Canadian politics could be secured from my papers than from any other source covering the last twenty or thirty years. That undoubtedly is true. When I asked about where he would like to begin and mentioned the possibility of starting with 1900, at the time of the beginning of the Department of Labour, or beginning with the war or some other period, I was pleased to see at once that he would like to begin in 1900 with my coming to Ottawa.

"Later I had him visit Laurier House. Still later I talked with Lanctot myself who said he would arrange for a room. He is known at the Archives. Lanctot thought he was just the person to do the work there, and promised to give him any assistance possible. Altogether I think this arrangement is a very happy one and seems to me almost a providential one. If I can have that work begun at once it would be a great stroke."

The monumental job began shortly afterwards. On October 4 Mackenzie King himself began to look over files stored in the basement of Laurier House. He "was amazed at the amount of material that has already been indexed and was surprised to find that what had gone to the Archives had already been classified and was material that I would have preferred myself to go through in the first instance. Had Gibson and Deacey [a clerk], along with Handy and Miss Z. [Zavitske] with me and tried to explain to the four the order in which I wish material classified, beginning with the early part of my life and taking the main divisions. Decided to send to Archives the material from the office from the time that I became Prime Minister, to have Gibson at the Archives go on with the earlier material. Telephoned to him and explained the situation which he wholly approved. He says that in the material he has already started on he found some excellent material related to personal biography, showing interest in social problems, etc., at Chicago University. What I feel is necessary is to get the basement into proper working shape. It was discouraging to see material in masses here, there and everywhere, instead of in chronological sequence. What is needed in particular is an index of the indexes already made."

Undaunted, he returned to the basement the next day and "was surprised to find that Deacey and Roger [Frankham] had already carried huge boxes into the yard and were sending down all cases of the card index, as well as correspondence. However, the thing being under way I decided to press on with it. Later I 'phoned Lanctot. I secured his undertaking to give additional space if necessary and told him I was prepared to have the material, as sorted, kept on in the Archives, to be placed in vaults in other parts of the building. This ought to avoid any question about the services being performed at present being wholly for the state."

A few days earlier, on September 28, the Salisburys had arrived in Ottawa and a great deal of Mackenzie King's time for the next week was devoted to them. The first day they visited the National Gallery where the Prime Minister's portrait was hanging. They "were both more pleased than ever with my portrait. Maude said the two pictures marked the high water mark in Frank's painting. That of the Coronation picture, in his ceremonial paintings, and in the portraits, one of myself."

On October 1 Mackenzie King discussed the future disposition of Laurier House and Kingsmere with his visitors who, he reported, "were both strong for making Laurier House the centre of what would be the Memorial that should be preserved. We talked of having it left as it is to be used for distinguished guests coming to the Capital. The more, however, we went over the different considerations which weigh in a decision of the kind, the more strongly they both felt that it would be wiser to take all the treasures that I have and have them exhibited in Laurier House itself rather than put into the Archives or alter the internal arrangement. They thought I might change some of the pictures. Substitute others. Arrange books, photographs, etc., as I might think best. Gradually catalogue everything and then have the rooms so arranged as to enable the public to be admitted. Certain days in the week, and the house available for certain occasions. They both agreed with me that this would have the advantage of preserving a house that had belonged to Sir Wilfrid as well as to myself and had an association with both our names and lives. One thing Frank felt very strongly about and it causes me some concern. It is that the house should carry the name of Laurier House. He thinks that in future generations, that would be difficult to understand and that some name should be thought of which would avoid the misunderstanding and leave the association of both names. There are distinct advantages at 'Earnscliffe' in having the house so named there but carrying with it the association of Sir John Macdonald. Had Laurier House been carrying a natural name, it would have had the association of both Sir Wilfrid and myself. However having been given by Lady Laurier to me, I am myself indifferent and would not like to make a change. I need not fear the future not doing full justice to both Sir Wilfrid and myself in the relation of our lives and work. I think it might be helpful to others to see our names associated in that way. A great chapter of Liberalism it will represent in years to come.

"As for Kingsmere, they would like my idea of having it given to the nation as a park. Frank advises against attempting any building out there or improvements other than in the open. Indeed, he thinks I should not be too generous about giving the whole of it to the State. If I do, it would be a noble gift."

The Prime Minister was very anxious to have his Salisbury portrait hung in the Parliament Buildings but was well aware of possible difficulties. "Except for fact that I, myself, would feel some embarrassment in seeing my own painting in a conspicuous place in the Parliament Buildings and the kind of references that I know may be made by a Tory press," he wrote on October 2, "I would, for reasons of security and final and definite settlement, like to see it hung from now on in the Buildings before the opening of the next session. I may take the subject up with the Cabinet and the Speaker. I may be super-sensitive but having regard to the kind of painting it is and the years of my public service, I do not think that much exception could be taken to it being hung at any time from now on. Pictures of the Speakers are there while they are still alive and in office. They are painted at public expense. Mine is a gift at my own expense." Some months were to pass before the portrait was finally hung.

October 2 was the last full day of the Salisburys' visit. At the end of the day, Mackenzie King wrote: "One has the feeling with them that they are two very precious persons and their devotion and friendship is so great and so evident that one feels a delight to talk over with them the problems of one's life. I fear that I have talked too much of myself in the time that they have been here." After his visitors left on the afternoon train on October 3, he was sorry that he had not accompanied them to Toronto in his private car. "I tried to console myself a little by getting off a wire to Frank which he would receive on the train as he leaves for Chicago. What a pity I could not go with him so he would have only the night journey alone. I said to H. we must without fail go to N.Y. before he and Maude leave. It would not do to let an ocean come between us with the feeling that I have in my heart tonight.

"One of the effects of sharing the week together has been to realize, as I have never realized before, what a mass of material has to be gone through ... and arranged if my papers are to be in any sort of order before the end comes. How much has to be done in Laurier House itself to have it made the temple of peace that I should like to have it become. Above all how much in my own nature I must learn to control so that my time and thought can be given not only day by day but hour by hour to what has to be accomplished. I can only pray that God may give me the strength and power out of this little visit to begin anew and once more try to fill the purpose of my life."

Mackenzie King's preoccupation with personal matters may have been, in part, a reaction to the discouraging political prospects of the Liberal party in the fall of 1946. Although evening radio reports about the Pontiac by-election on September 16 indicated a Social Credit victory, the first news the Prime Minister received from Fournier was favourable. However, at 11.30 P.M., Ross Martin telephoned and gave him "the latest news which puts the Social Credit candidate at the head in Pontiac, and means we have lost the by-election. With Fournier, the wish was father to the thought. It is a clear case of the party losing because of not having brought on the by-election at once, as I strongly urged should be done, and made my urging of record in a letter from New York before leaving for England [in May]. It is the beginning of the end of Liberal rule in Canada – for how long who can say. I doubt if we shall win either Portage la Prairie or Toronto-Parkdale [by-elections scheduled for October 21] – the loss of three by-elections – and these the first three in a new parliament is a sure sign of loss in the General Elections. It looks as if a party further to the left than even the Liberals will come into power. It makes me sad to sense the situation in this way, but I certainly have warned the party both in caucus and by letter and if they have been indifferent to my counsel and direction at least I am free from blame. My absences abroad have not helped any; neither have the many absences at the present time. The times change and we change with them. The one thing to do is to hold firm to the eternal principles which never change."

The next day, Mackenzie King met the Quebec Liberal leader at his office. According to Godbout, "yesterday's defeat in Pontiac was due to personal jealousies in our own party. The Mayor of Rouyn was disgruntled because he had not been chosen as candidate, and there were divided factions there. It is quite clear that we have not had any proper organization. Godbout felt that the Social Credit people had been working secretly and that henceforth they would join with the Bloc Populaire. They were really an extreme nationalist party and under the influence of the mining people in these northern parts." After this conversation, the Prime Minister went to a meeting of the Cabinet. Only Chevrier, Fournier, Jean, McCann, Gibson, St. Laurent and Robertson were present. "I spoke out very strongly about the results in Pontiac and of our defeat being due to the election not being brought on promptly – that it could have been won but for the postponements. Chevrier thought that our defeat was due to the general wave of unrest, being the first by-election in which the unrest after the war was asserting itself. I predicted a hopeless outlook for the future of Liberalism if we view these situations in that light. I read the letters which I had written to Gardiner, Howe and Claxton in May, asking that the election be brought on right away. I also spoke of the lack of organization being the cause of losing the by-election."

The Prime Minister's gloom was intensified on October 21 when he received the returns from by-elections in Toronto-Parkdale, a Progressive Conservative seat, and Portage la Prairie, held for the Liberals until his death by Harry Leader. In his diary he noted that early returns from Parkdale "gave Hunter, Liberal candidate, a lead in the first thirteen polls. He maintained a good position to the end, but his opponent won by some 500; the C.C.F. coming later with a considerable vote. It is the old story of the Tory party winning through Liberal forces being divided. Had the C.C.F. kept out in Toronto, I believe we would have won, as the C.C.F. did when we kept out at the time of Meighen's by-election. In Portage la Prairie the results were not encouraging from the start. The final results showed again that the Liberal candidate was only some 500 behind. The C.C.F. also a fairly good vote. The Tory won again by a minority vote. I had said right along that I did not believe we would win either by-election tonight. Indeed, we did much better in Toronto than I had expected, and better also in Portage.... The Tories have a first-class organization and began early to win the seat. The loss of Pontiac was a further factor which operated against us. Having no organization, excepting what was arranged in the constituencies at the last moment, was of course a major factor. I do not see how the latter is to be overcome because none of the young Liberals are prepared to put time or money into an organization or to seek to find the latter. The older Liberals have lost or are losing their interest in the future of the party. Had Portage la Prairie been won, Gardiner's chances for leadership would have been substantially increased. I think the defeat ends his chance of recognition from the party as a whole."

In the Cabinet meeting next day, Mackenzie King argued that the by-election defeats were "certain to cost the party heavily. Felt they were due to delay in bringing on the by-elections; to the loss of Pontiac, and to the absence of any federal organization. I had spoken often in Caucus and in the Council about Tory organization and Bracken House which was a centre for organization activities, propaganda, election funds, etc.... Gardiner tries to have it appear that the announcement that the railways were applying for increase in freight rates had had an influence on the election and that Ottawa was to blame along with the railways for allowing this announcement to be made while the election was on. I took that, as I believe other Ministers did, as a mere excuse. It is without any substance in fact."

Two days before another by-election had become necessary with the death of P. J. A. Cardin. The Prime Minister faced it without confidence or, indeed, much hope of winning. He had received word on October 3 that Cardin had had a stroke and had received the last rites of the Roman Catholic church. "Cardin was the veteran member of the House," Mackenzie King wrote on October 20. "In his passing, I took that place and am now in point of service in the House of Commons the oldest member of that House; a Member for thirty years, two-thirds of which time has been in the office of Prime Minister. That is truly a remarkable record and one which brings with it great responsibilities as well as great honour. It is no wonder that I find that I am not equal today to what I was in earlier years and also have felt so keenly at times some of the indifference of some of those around me."

At breakfast the next morning, Mackenzie King telephoned Simard. "I had a most interesting conversation with him. He told me that he was present with Mr. Cardin when he died at 8.15 last night, and that I was the first person to be 'phoned to concerning his death.... Simard then said to me he [Cardin] had at the time of his death under his pillow the telegram that I had sent to him [when the Prime Minister learned of his illness]. It had been there from the time it was received to the time of his death. He had shown it to different friends who had come to see him. He said there was no doubt that Cardin had a great affection for me and had told him, Simard, that they might say what they liked about Sir John Macdonald and Sir Wilfrid Laurier in maintaining Canadian unity but that I had had [a] much more difficult task than either. That he had known what I had gone through and, while he had taken the position he did, he quite understood my whole position [on conscription]....

"After writing a short appreciation for the press, just a few lines, in which I made clear that our political differences had not affected our personal friendship, also that I would have liked to attend the funeral on Thursday, I dictated the diary to date feeling that the thoughts and events of the past twenty-four hours have a real significance in one's life."

One political bright spot in the fall was St. Laurent's decision to remain in the Cabinet until the end of the next session. In a conversation with him on September 27, Mackenzie King was "immensely relieved and delighted when he said to me at the end of our talk, and as he was leaving the room, that he supposed all of us would be perhaps better pleased if he stayed on through the session and did not leave till it was over. I told him that I could not begin to thank him for undertaking to do this; that it took a tremendous load from my mind and would make possible my having the courage to stay on. He said he would tell his firm confidentially what they might expect; that he would definitely be out of public life after the next session.

I cannot begin to say what this means to me. I stressed that strongly to him, and as I spoke he reached forth his hand and shook hands with me. It is as noble a sacrifice as one can make. It reminded me of the staunchness of Ernest Lapointe and his friendship."

The two by-election defeats had been a particularly bitter blow to Mackenzie King because his spirits had been considerably buoyed several days before by an overnight visit with J. W. McConnell, the publisher of the *Montreal Star*. He had reached Montreal late in the afternoon on October 18 during a blinding rainstorm and a power failure. "The electricity was off through the town and when we reached McConnell's residence, the house had to be lighted by candle light. Was met at the door by a man servant who took everything in hand. McConnell showed me my room. Quite a delightful experience going about the house with only candle light. He had many fine candle holders (with large globes which protect them from the wind).

"We came downstairs to a little fire in the sitting room. Had a short talk before dinner and then a deliciously cooked dinner after which we went back to the little sitting room and talked until 11 P.M.

"The radio was off so there was no chance to listen to Byrnes' broadcast. In the course of conversation, McConnell told me many confidential things about his own affairs and the Foundation he had established some time ago to aid charitable work. What he had been doing to assist different organizations. He spoke of my own position and of the problem it represented with advancing years. He wanted me to allow him to give some assistance. I told him that I could not think of anything of the kind as long as I was in office. That he knew of what had been done for me at Laurier House by others. I could manage, I thought, all right. It might be different once I found it necessary to retire. I had no fears for the future as everything had worked out well in the past. Wished him to know how grateful I was for his kind thought. He had spoken to me once before at Kingsmere about allowing him to have some landscape and gardening work done there which I had declined; also at Laurier House before going south by 'plane to Nassau. He urged me not to think of staying on to a point where I would be overtired and exhausted.

"He thought I ought to have, after serving the country through my life, some enjoyment of complete rest and change in the following of one's pursuits. I thanked him for the comfort which his words brought with them and in helping to give a sense of security. Again made it clear to him that I could think of nothing at all while I was in public life."

"McConnell wanted me to know," he added, "that all the profits that had been made from sugar during the war, from beginning to close, had gone into this Foundation, the proceeds of which will be used for charitable purposes. Had not kept for any other purpose a single dollar. When the St. Lawrence Sugar Refinery business was investigated, they would find that nothing had gone to any of the shareholders or to the business. . . .

"Among other things, I told him, and which he said he thought was wholly wrong and unjustified, was that all the entertaining I had done at Laurier House through the years had been from my own pocket – not a dollar from the Government or from the party for any kind of entertainment. This did not, of course, include official entertainment at the Country Club. In the last year or two, I had used hospitality fund to defray expenses of foreign visitors at Laurier House. He agreed that anyone would much prefer dining with the Prime Minister at his residence to going to a club or a hotel or to a banquet however large.

"He spoke of the attention I had paid to acknowledging hospitality and kindness on the part of others. Said that everywhere that was spoken of. He thought, too, that while there were some who were political enemies that I had no personal enemies. That there were few, if any, that he knew of who had any personal feeling.

"He spoke about Meighen being very bitter in heart, particularly since he resigned from the Senate. Ballantyne had tried to get him, McConnell, to support Meighen for the leadership in the Commons but he had refused to lend the *Star* for that purpose.

"He also spoke of Bennett as being at the point of being devoid of any real grace or charm, being very pompous, etc. He spoke about my own courtesy with others as being a tremendous asset. This led him to refer to possible successors. Then he mentioned Pearson's name as the man who he thought possesses more of that kind of innate refinement of nature which in addition to his great knowledge and gifts would make him a real leader of men.

"I found McConnell throughout the conversation exceedingly kind in his references to others and modest about his own benefactions, etc. He certainly is the leading citizen of Montreal and the foremost philanthropist in Canada today."

Next morning (Oct. 19) McConnell "said he wished to speak of something that would necessitate his asking me about how long I thought I might continue in public life and he asked whether it would be over a year. I said I could not say; that I had decided for public reasons to stay on as long as my health would permit and I did not become too tired. I could not say what the strain of another session might mean but felt it was bound to be hard. Nor could I say what my health would be. He then told me that his reason for asking was that he would like me to consider becoming

Chancellor of McGill University. He then outlined the authority and powers which the Chancellor has. Made clear that the duties would be formal and light excepting certain public addresses and referred to it as a crowning position in connection with my public life and work. I recalled to his mind that Beattie and others, himself included, had thought of getting me to accept the position of Principal of McGill. That I had had similar offers from Queen's. In regard to the Chancellorship, I told him I appreciated his thinking of so great an honour. That I was quite sincere in saying that I could not tell how long I would continue as Prime Minister. There were still nearly four years to run if one wanted to take the full time. I did not think an election would come soon as I could see no reason for it nor would any benefit come from a change in government. At any rate, my duty was to stay on as long as I reasonably could."

The visit pleased the Prime Minister very much and led him to reflect in his diary that "the thing now is to become increasingly philosophical and trustful and seek to win back the peace of mind and heart that has been in peril. To drop all thought of giving up public life. Begin anew to make contacts, to endeavour to give more expression in public to my own views and true self. The talk with Mr. McConnell has been helpful toward that end.... What is now needed most is continued concentration."

On November 13 McConnell telephoned to inform Mackenzie King that "at a meeting of the Board of Governors of McGill University it was unanimously agreed I should be asked if I would not accept the position of Chancellor of McGill. He said that every member was favourable; that I might wonder, for example, at one, who was D'Alton Coleman, but said that he had strongly endorsed my appointment. He said that when Morris Wilson was made Chancellor there were two or three against him on the score that he represented St. James Street, Montreal, but that everyone on the Board had voted for me, which he thought was pretty good from the English-speaking element in Montreal. They are pretty generally regarded as the Tory element of the city. I told McConnell I felt deeply honoured. It was something which would have pleased my father immensely, and I would really have been happy to accept did I feel that I could take on additional duties to those which I have in my present position. He mentioned that in England the Chancellors of Oxford and Cambridge were frequently members of the Government. Cited the case of Baldwin when he had been Prime Minister. I told him I did not feel my powers equal to any additional task; also I thought most men made a mistake when they got one position of wanting another and adding to the number. That I felt I must give all the time I had to the office of Prime Minister, if I was to keep on at all. I hoped he would understand. He said he did, but wished very much it had been possible for me. He added that perhaps I would consider it later when I ceased to be in public life. I told him that the future was all too uncertain and not to let any thought of my filling the position interfere with a nomination. It is a very great honour indeed, a very great honour. It is interesting that it should come from McGill University, rather than from my own University of Toronto.... I am very happy to have this expression of regard and, indeed, esteem, on the part of those who govern so great a university as McGill, particularly where most of them are my political opponents."

One of the more minor problems that bothered Mackenzie King in October and November was finding a successor for Albert Matthews who had been Lieutenant-Governor of Ontario since 1937. On October 14 he telephoned Vincent Massey to see "if he would be interested in that particular position."

"Vincent almost at once said he did not think he could consider it. As a matter of fact he and Alice had talked the matter over some little time ago when there was a rumour that the position might become vacant and that they might be asked, and had decided then if the request should come that they would not take on the position. He felt he would be much freer to work independently, if he did not have any official obligations.... It was evident to me that he has something in mind.... No doubt he probably intends to get out a publication recording what he regards as his own contribution to the winning of the war."

R. Y. Eaton was approached next but declined. On November 6 the Prime Minister telephoned General Crerar to test his interest. "I said that in offering the post, I thought the country would feel it was a fitting recognition of his services overseas and that it should fit in with an opportunity for further public service. That with Alexander at Ottawa and himself at Toronto, I thought the country would be safe." As Mackenzie King expected, Crerar also refused to accept the post.

There was one eager candidate, Sigmund Samuel, and the Prime Minister had a talk with him on November 22. Samuel "is eating his heart out in the desire to be made Lieutenant Governor of Ontario," he wrote. "He told me he was prepared to give his house and its contents – house itself worth $250,000 – to the Government as a Chequers – if he was appointed; also would help the party very materially. I told him I was glad he had called for I felt I ought to let him know that, for the present, controversy what it was over Palestine, I could not see any possibility of appointing him Lieutenant Governor. He spoke about the appointment being popular, etc.... The poor man looked as if he had lost ten or fifteen pounds since I saw him last and as though he might not last very long. It was a difficult task to let him know there was no chance of considering him. I said if we appointed him at all, we would appoint him without any consideration of any kind and solely for himself and the place he occupied as a citizen. Hard as it might seem and unjust, I felt that the feeling was too strong to permit me, as head of a political party, to recommend him for the post. He wandered about like one almost dazed after leaving the room and came back again later to make another plea. It was really pathetic. I felt sorry for him. It disclosed what men will give for position."

In the meantime, the Prime Minister had been trying to persuade Ray Lawson to become High Commissioner to Australia but later decided to ask him to become Lieutenant-Governor. They discussed the matter on November 15. Lawson said "he thought he could fill that position as well as it had been by several of those who had held it," and, shortly afterwards, he was appointed.

A more important problem in October was the future direction of federal labour relations policy with the expected lapse of the National Emergency Transitional Powers Act on March 31, 1947, and, with it, the two key war-time orders-in-council, P.C. 1003 and P.C. 4020, which had established new procedures for collective bargaining and union recognition. There were two main issues. First was the problem of defining federal and provincial jurisdiction, in the face of demands from organized labour for a national labour code, and, secondly, what direction a new policy should take.

A meeting of provincial labour ministers had been called for October 15 in Ottawa and, four days earlier, the Cabinet considered the proposals Mitchell intended to place before the conference. Mackenzie King noted that "the Department of Labour was intending to make a new Labour code which would embody the Industrial Investigation Act. This would mean sending the latter more or less into oblivion.

"St. Laurent and Mitchell both said that while the officials would prefer that, they felt the preferable way to deal with the matter in Parliament and otherwise was to restore the Industrial Disputes Investigation Act and add to it amendments in the nature of what would constitute a Labour code. Naturally I felt, being the author of the ... Act, I would prefer the latter. Mentioned special advantage in so doing. Canada setting example to the world in Industrial Investigation and Disputes. The latter was a model of settlement for international disputes and quoted principle of investigation. Was so quoted in Paris and elsewhere as evidence of that as being a model for nations to follow.

"Council seemed of this view which I believe to be the right one. There was much discussion as to how far disclosure should be made at the

Conference of Labour Ministers next week of the federal position. Officials again seemed to favour an appeal from Ontario Regional Boards to a Federal Board. This would mean practically landing all disputes more or less on the Federal Government.

"The Cabinet later felt ... that while disputes came under the Industrial Disputes Investigation Act, they should be dealt with in that way and local disputes should end with regional boards.

"This question was not too simple and Mitchell is always a little vague in the way he speaks...."

In his address at the conference, Mitchell suggested that, to encourage uniformity in both legislation and administration in the labour relations area, the federal government would devise legislation, embodying with some modifications the principles of P.C. 1003, which might be acceptable in whole or in part to the provincial authorities. They would then have to decide to what extent the federal legislation would apply in their own jurisdictions. A national labour relations board would deal with industries under federal jurisdiction and those so designated by the provinces. If a province chose to adopt the federal legislation completely, it would administer the law through its own board for all provincial industries except those specified as being of a national or inter-provincial character. Labour relations problems in these industries would be the responsibility of the national board. In accordance with the Cabinet's decision on October 11, the Minister indicated that, for the present, there would be no system of appeals from provincial bodies to the national board. The provincial ministers accepted in principle and "as far as practicable" the notion of uniform collective bargaining legislation and urged the federal government to prepare a draft bill which could be submitted to the provinces for consideration and advice. A draft bill was circulated in 1947 and, after a great deal of debate and some revision, it was passed in 1948.

Throughout the fall, the question of defence policy appeared regularly on Cabinet agendas. At the meeting on September 26, for example, Mackenzie King "spoke very strongly against permitting the Committee on Defence and the Chief of Staff deciding any matters of importance without the Cabinet being given the fullest opportunity to approve in the first instance.... I complained strongly of attempting any defence in the Arctic without a consideration of the policy of continental defence with the Americans and the British. Abbott claimed that what was being done – experimenting with the tests against cold – was part of routine and was in no way a part of a policy for defence generally. I asked that officials of the Department [of Defence] should survey the whole situation and make a report to us which would enable the cabinet, after discussion of the questions involved, to reach a decision on policy, in conjunction with the British and United States authorities."

At the meeting of Cabinet on October 2, the Prime Minister reported with evident satisfaction, "one good decision reached was to end the association of women with the air force. That body has been pressing for keeping a certain corps to do clerical work and the like. The army and navy have taken a different position. It was clear that all three services would have to act alike. The Cabinet were one with the exception of Gibson, the Minister of Air, in reaching this decision.

"I stressed again in Cabinet the importance of effecting economies in the different services – public expenditures generally."

Connected with this consideration of defence problems was the Prime Minister's trip to New York and Washington in the third week of October. His major reason for going was a desire to spend some time with the Salisburys before they sailed for England but he also attended the opening session of the UN General Assembly and, a few days later, went on to Washington to see President Truman. Canada's delegation to the United Nations was led by St. Laurent and included two other Cabinet members, Paul Martin and Wishart Robertson, John Bracken and M. J. Coldwell. The alternate delegates were Senator J. T. Haig, H. L. Keenleyside, the Canadian Ambassador to Mexico, G. J. McIlraith, the Parliamentary Assistant to the Minister of Reconstruction and Supply, M. W. Mackenzie, the Deputy Minister of Trade and Commerce, and L. D. Wilgress, the Canadian Ambassador to the Soviet Union. Escott Reid of the Department of External Affairs headed a strong team of civil service advisers.

Mackenzie King arrived in New York on October 23 and that afternoon went to Flushing Meadows for the UN session. On the way, his car was "overtaken by a procession of cars from the Waldorf. In one of them, I saw Molotov and his party seated. My car got into the line with the police escort and we arrived at the building before other members of the party. While waiting for them, I met no end of persons whom I had met at San Francisco or Paris or London. Joined our delegation in a large hall. While there, shook hands with many of the delegates including Mrs. Roosevelt.

"Shortly after 4, the President [Truman] arrived along with Mr. Spaak, the President of the Assembly, and Mr. Lie, the Secretary [General]. The Mayor of the community gave a cordial welcome. Mr. Spaak's address was in French; not translated. The President gave, I thought, an excellent address so far as what he said was concerned. Direct, clear and firm statement of America's position.

"Mr. Truman noticed me in the audience before speaking and looked down and smiled. When he had finished his address, I noticed he looked over to Byrnes and smiled cordially at him as much as to say: I made clear our position together against any isolationism. I noticed his remark that he hoped the U.N. would have a permanent home in the United States met with a slight applause. There is increasingly the feeling that a mistake has been made in having this gathering in a great city like New York and having to drive the distances. While listening to the proceedings, I felt a certain solemnity about what was being said and at the same time a great concern that the future of the world should rest so largely in the hands of some of those who are representatives of their countries.

"I returned from the gathering with St. Laurent, Martin and Robertson to the Biltmore. A pleasant talk with them on the way but found the minute we began to discuss some matters of government requiring decision, I felt a sense of returning fatigue and exhaustion. There was no time for any rest before going to the Waldorf Astoria to a reception given by the President and Mrs. Truman.

"On coming into the room, the President saw me and stopped in the procession to shake hands. Later on the platform, we had a word or two about his painting [by Salisbury]. . . . The President asked me if I was coming to see him. He had sent word previously if I would be in Washington, he would like to see me. . . . When he asked when I was coming to see him, I replied that I would be looking forward to that which means that I must go on to Washington before returning to Ottawa. I think perhaps it is good in every way that I should have a talk with the President at this time."

Most of the next two days Mackenzie King spent with the Salisburys but he found time on October 25 to interview Mrs. Gooch, a Scottish cook from Hamilton, who agreed on November 5 to come to Laurier House early in the new year.

On Saturday, October 26, the Prime Minister, accompanied by Mr. and Mrs. St. Laurent and their daughter, drove to the Rockefeller estate at Tarrytown to attend a reception for UN delegates. "It was a beautiful drive, the autumn along the way was quite magnificent. All land on both sides of the road is controlled by the State. We made rapid progress and when I looked at my watch we were near Tarrytown [and] it was exactly ten past two. The approach to Mr. Rockefeller's residence was beautiful. The trees were reflected in the water of a little lake nearby.

"Nelson and his wife were receiving the delegates of the U.N. at what is called the playhouse. I mistook it for the residence that Mr. Rockefeller once occupied himself. He told me subsequently they had taken it down altogether. . . .

"I met a large number of delegates and much enjoyed the talks I had with some of them. Among others either the Counsel for, or the President of Metropolitan Life, who spoke to me about the possibility of the Government acquiring their building if we desired it.

"I said I felt we would be glad to make some arrangement with the Company. They will put up a building of their own in another part of the City. I had a talk of some length with Mr. and Mrs. Watson who were very pleasant and with numerous other delegates. John D. Rockefeller, Jr. had not reached the line when our party came through. Curiously enough we had met the others in line on the way driving out. I subsequently first brought Mr. St. Laurent and Senator Robertson to meet Mr. and Mrs. Rockefeller, and then St. Laurent's wife and Robertson's wife and then later McIlraith, and Wilgress, and still later, Bracken and Coldwell.

"Mr. and Mrs. Rockefeller gave me a very warm welcome. And spoke particularly nicely to all our delegates. Later in the day Mr. Rockefeller told me he did not think much of Bracken's appearance or manner – regarded him as rather a bull-dozer and uncouth. He liked Coldwell's quiet way, – both he and Mrs. Rockefeller liked our delegation very much. They spoke nicely of the ladies as well as the men. Cocktails were served outdoors, which, I am sure, was a trial to John D., Jr. After waiting for some little time for the arrival of all the delegates, there was a procession through part of the grounds to a large building, used as a swimming pool, and on to a tent where luncheon was served for 400 or 500 people at round tables. I was given a seat to the right of John D. III's wife and had the wife of the Philippino delegate, Romulo, to my right, an exceedingly pleasant little lady. I had a very happy talk with her and with Mrs. John D. III – whom I thought particularly charming and sweet. She spoke so nicely of John's life and her own – and their quiet interests.

"It was five o'clock before the luncheon was over. On leaving the building I met Mrs. John D. R. who asked me to drive back with her to the house. The St. Laurents went back in with the car that we came out in. On the way Mrs. R. said to me, she wished I would make John stay and enjoy the party. He had gone home earlier. She said she enjoyed meeting people. We had a nice talk together.

"On reaching the house, we found Mr. Rockefeller taking a rest. She then showed me to my room which was the room Mr. Rockefeller, Sr., had occupied during his life. A fine, large room. Picture of his mother over the mantelpiece. All home pictures on the walls and tables round about. As I looked out of the windows, I was impressed with the great beauty of the scene and landscape gardening about. Glad, however, to get to bed for an hour's rest before dinner. Again the hands of the clock were exactly together in a straight line at 6 as I went for a rest. I dozed off to a partial sleep and had a bath. Was up at 7 at which time Mr. Rockefeller came in to bring me into an adjoining room for a little talk together. It seemed to me he was much more fatigued than when I had seen him last. I could not but feel he was thinking a lot about the afternoon and rather doubtful about some of its features. He is so strong a teetotaler himself that I am sure he was a bit concerned after having cocktails and wines served by Nelson at the luncheon. It would be difficult to see how Nelson could have done otherwise with the people that he was entertaining.

"The gathering was really quite remarkable for it was one at which some 50 nations were represented. It was the Rockefeller family extending hospitality to the representatives of countries from all parts of the world – a fine national gesture – something that could scarcely have been done a half a century ago."

Mackenzie King spent a good part of Sunday morning, while they drove around the estate, persuading Rockefeller to have Salisbury paint his portrait. "Nelson came in just as John and I returned to the house. David and his little son, David, were also present. We had a talk about the United Nations. Nelson feels strongly that the headquarters should be kept at Flushing or somewhere near to New York, but its activities scattered in different countries. He feels that if the United Nations moves from America the people will lose interest in the organization. If kept here they will be kept in the centre of the movement which will help materially. As I came away, Mr. and Mrs. Rockefeller and Nelson and David and David's little boy all stood grouped together at the front of the house, standing there until the car was out of sight. One feels increasingly in all these meetings and partings that one never knows whether one shall see these dear friends again. It seems strange to be talking in terms of forty years and of being now over the age of seventy.

"I could see that as we talked together Mr. Rockefeller found himself unbending more and more. I really think he feels closer to myself than to any other man he knows. In talking together this morning he said how very few men there were on whom you could rely to the very end."

That afternoon the Prime Minister left by train for Washington. During his brief visit he spent a good deal of time looking at houses which might be purchased and used as an Embassy residence and he was vastly relieved when Hume Wrong decided to rent a house for a year. On October 28 he saw Cordell Hull at the Naval Hospital and, after lunch, went to the White House to see President Truman. The "press were waiting and I was shown in the President's executive room. I had with me the photos of the Salisbury portrait. The President immediately unwrapped one and seemed to be quite pleased with it. Left a second one for Ross, his secretary. The President then signed one Salisbury had given to me . . . and placed on it the following inscription: 'To my good friend the Prime Minister of Canada with kindest regards and best wishes, Harry Truman.' Speaking of himself as a friend and saying to me that that was what he meant.

"The President spoke most appreciatively of Salisbury. A fine man. Spoke about his convictions. He suggested we should go out to be photographed. In the grounds there were about twenty photographers. We walked together, talked, shook hands three or four times. The President remarked this was necessary for the public. I said to him I approved strongly all he had said in his speech at New York. Felt he was presenting our point of view as well as that of the United States. That our delegation were all of one view in regard to it. The President emphasized that he meant exactly what he said in every particular. In the course of our conversation we talked of the U.N.O. I said I thought some plan of economy of time and expense ought to be worked out. Also that the people would be astounded at the expenses of these gatherings. I thought arrangements should be made to limit the entertainment. The President said the taxpayers were really paying the entertainment outlays which some other countries were enjoying. I spoke too of the enormous charges of hotels, of the need of some control there through some other way of housing delegations and their members.

"We talked of the Paris Conference. I spoke of Byrnes' stature having become more apparent to the world. The President said yes, he was a very able man. He also said they were quite fond of Bevin. I told him about Molotov's attitude towards myself in Paris. He remarked that he liked Stalin better than Molotov. He said he had had the United States Ambassador in for a talk during the morning. He had told him (the Pres.) that he thought the Russian attitude was due to the problems that Russia herself had within her own country. It would take about five years for them to adjust the differences to which the war had given rise. There was great poverty in Russia. The masses of the people were far from settled. Gave some figure which was astounding of the numbers which are in concentration camps. Said that they were put away – some of them were of the intelligentsia, writers, movie performers and others – so that they could not influence the people. It was almost impossible to get outside ideas into Russia. I told him that Wilgress had given me the same impression about the Five Years Period. He had added that the second Five Years would be used for building up a strong steel industry. The third Five Years might witness Russia more or less defying other parts of the world."

Quite early in their conversation, President Truman "brought up the question of our common interests in Defence. He said he thought it was quite apparent about the U.S. and Canada that each depended in part on the other. There was need for co-ordinating our methods. He said that he had a visit from Field Marshal Montgomery – at first he referred to Alexander – but meant Montgomery of Alamein – and said that he had spoken about the British, themselves and Canada all having their similar standards of weapon. He himself approved of that. I said I also did. It was desirable they should operate together efficiently. The President said that anything in the nature of war between any of us was inconceivable and that war with any one of the three might certainly bring in the others. He then spoke of the United States Chief of Staff feeling that there was need for co-operation in defence and mentioned Goose Bay in particular. He had referred to Iceland and Greenland. He spoke of the U.S. planes having demonstrated that a flight we had in mind would be around the northern regions. He said there was need for meteorological studies so as to direct planes. The purpose would be helping civil aviation quite as much as military.

"When he spoke of Goose Bay I mentioned that one consideration was that it belonged to the Labrador section which belonged to Newfoundland. We would have to work in full harmony with them which meant also working with full knowledge so far as the United Kingdom was concerned. The President said in all of these matters he agreed there should be a most complete understanding and agreement between all three. What he hoped for was agreement on defence matters. I said I hoped for agreement also and believe it should be possible to reach an agreement. We were a small country in population and wealth compared to the United States. They might wish to put in large numbers of men. I understood they were thinking of some 10,000 in Goose Bay. The President said he did not know the numbers or any details, that would have to be worked out with care and with agreement. He believed it could. I said we had to watch particularly the question of our sovereignty. Not that we entertained any fears on that score, but having regard to the years as they went by and to the view the people would take, large numbers of troops from other countries being stationed out of their own country, or would have to be arranged on the basis of agreement to protect national rights.

"Truman spoke about meteorological stations to study the weather. He thought all we might wish to do could be done for several purposes without making any mention of boundaries. I said I thought what had to be most considered was the way in which the public became informed on these matters. The whole publicity should be agreed to in advance, steps to be taken very slowly and surely. Care would have to be taken not to give the

Russians a chance to say we were trying to fight them. The President said there was no aggression in our mind at all. All that we were doing would be to make aggression impossible anywhere.

"I spoke of the enormous expenditures the armed forces had made. I said I thought it would be well in regard to any statement we were making of our conversation to make clear that while we had touched on defence it had been with a view to discussing means of effecting economies and an effective co-operation between the forces. The President said he thought my judgment was right in referring to the matter in this way. I said that one could not take exception in seeking to effect economies in joint defence. The President mentioned that in working out plans he thought further steps should be taken up through Ministers and on a diplomatic level rather than by the services. With this I agreed. In fact a memorandum which I had been given, as well as the one he had been given, had expressed this view in common. It was clear that the purpose of the meeting was to give official sanction in both countries to go ahead and work toward an agreement as a result of which plans for defence would be co-ordinated and developed.

"We talked a little on general subjects. I spoke about the coming elections. He thought there would be difficulty. The party had been long in office. I spoke of how we had lost one or two by-elections. The President stressed particularly the way in which people tried to influence farmers from getting the prices they should. I said I thought the public had liked the way in which he had spoken out about some of the Congressmen being selfish. He said is it not surprising how quickly, after a situation is met, men begin to seek to further their own personal interests. He had said what he believed. That was his method of proceeding. . . .

"I referred to how well he looked. He said he enjoyed politics and felt happy. I confess he does look remarkably well. His whole appearance is that of a business executive who has himself well in hand, completely in training. He has a very disarming smile, very deep dimples in his right cheek when he smiles. Eyes kindly and sympathetic and yet strong. Our conversation ended where it began by further references to joint defence. The President emphasized his friendship for Canada and of it being a particular pleasure to him to talk with me at any time. We must both stay on in our work until the job is finished. He did not indicate just what he had in mind. I assume it was getting back to the normal order of things. Unfortunately I had been late for the appointment, some five or ten minutes. I kept an eye on the clock and when I looked up at one time both hands were together at 3.15. I had been told earlier that the President was keeping plenty of time for the interview and not to hurry. But I felt we would soon be having nearly three-quarters of an hour and as the train left shortly after 4 I had better not stay too long. The President made no move of hastening at the close of the conversation, but re-emphasized the pleasure it had been to him to have had me come and said to do so whenever I was down this way."

Almost immediately after leaving the White House, Mackenzie King left by train for Ottawa.

His attention diverted to other matters, the Prime Minister did not return to the problem of defence policy until Sunday, November 10. He spent the day reading over a number of memoranda and despatches on the subject and felt "a very great and grave concern about the manner in which the services have been pushing their end at the expense of others and the lack of any real supervision over the defence forces and their unification. I feel an even greater concern with the efforts being made to hold the Dominions liable for security of Commonwealth as a whole and to centralize the direction and administration of affairs in London and the manner in which the services are lending themselves consciously and unconsciously to this end. There is I feel a great concern about the tendencies toward conflict in the world itself. On going through the material I could see how carefully planned the whole British programme had been and how deliberately they were seeking to force our hand regardless of any decent feelings or the considerations of which we are bound to take account. I decided, that while it would add to my responsibilities and work, to take the Chairmanship of the Defence Committee, that I would have to assume this task. I regard the defence problem as the major problem of government today. I was pleased to see that at the conference I have not hesitated to register Canada's position very strongly in the most difficult of circumstances."

Still on the scent of centralization the next day, Mackenzie King "was quite incensed when I received a despatch from Attlee, written by the War Office, in a tone which would indicate that Canada had to give an accounting to the United Kingdom as to what she was going to do in the Commonwealth policy – a complete reversal of the order of things which has been the kind of relationship toward different governments in Canada over the last forty years. The worst feature of it all is that after all Canada has done, and before we have been able to begin to meet the obligations arising out of the gifts of money, and the sacrifice of men and materials we have made, that there should come a demand on this country as if it were some Colonial possession of inferior races. I have not been far wrong in sensing the kind of situation which is developing under those at present in control of war policy in London. I can see a battle ahead and I may have to speak

The Shift in External Affairs 365

out pretty plainly. This perhaps will help me to recover some confidence in myself which I have been losing rapidly of late."

On November 12 Mackenzie King dined at Government House and discussed the problem of Anglo-Canadian defence liaison with Alexander. "The conversation," he wrote, "gave me a chance to bring up recent despatches from England, which have caused me a good deal of irritation and feeling. I told His Excellency quite plainly that I thought the Prime Minister's military advisers, whoever they were, were making a mistake. That I had been amazed at what had taken place at the meeting of Prime Ministers, where Ministers had frankly said that they had taken the position that Britain was no longer responsible for her own defence, but that there must be Commonwealth defence, in which each would take a share. No recognition of what had been done or of the success which had attended the flexible method of organization, but an endeavour to get back to centralized control in London. Mentioned the telegram I had received from Attlee speaking of Britain having adopted compulsory training in time of peace and virtually asking us to assume part of the cost of what was involved thereby and in tone taking the position that we were expected to give some accounting to the British Government as to how we proposed to meet our obligations to her. I also spoke about the communications that had appeared to the effect that Britain was sending an officer to the U.S. to work out with the U.S. Government the disposition of some of our own possessions and what was necessary for the defence of Canada, as though we were still a colony, if not a dependency. I let His Excellency know that I deplored this, because of the reaction it was certain to bring, and said quite plainly that if this kind of thing were known publicly it would soon lead to this continent securing its own fortunes independently of Britain altogether and leaving Britain to look after herself. I said I felt entitled to speak in the light of my actions over the years that I have been in office and what I had done to keep Canada united and the Commonwealth united and the relations with the U.K. friendly.

"I found H.E. very responsive. He spoke very nicely of Attlee's government. He said he had thought Attlee had done a darn good job; that he had a difficult position. No doubt these communications were put in his hand and he just sent them on. I said I knew all this and knew how these matters were done. I said that somebody had to be told that that was not the way our defence relations between the different nations were to be carried out. I told him I was simply discussing the matter with him in a very friendly way, not with a view to making representations. He said to me he understood that, but he had his relations with The King and others. Thought he could be helpful in these matters; as G.G. it was part of his duty to help in any way he could. I said I was glad to have him to talk to as I could not talk to some of my colleagues on these matters. It was altogether a most helpful conversation. I found him so fair and reasonable in his attitude. He thought that Monty might be a little over-zealous, and was inclined to stress what Alan Brooke appeared to wish to effect.

"I spoke to him of what the Americans were contemplating at Goose Bay. He told me he did not think that was necessary at all. Indeed, on these things, he has a most sensible and realistic attitude."

The Prime Minister returned home "feeling much refreshed by the evening's conversation and greatly relieved to have someone to talk quite frankly with on the greatest problem which is facing the world today."

The Cabinet and Chiefs of Staff met to discuss the problem the next day, November 13. Mackenzie King "raised many of the questions that are likely to come up in seeking to reach a decision on policy as to what it might be most advisable to do in our relations with Britain and the United States and the forces that we are to maintain in Canada. I was surprised to find that St. Laurent [he had returned to Ottawa for these discussions at the Prime Minister's request], who was very strong this morning in stating that Smuts was all for centralization, and for each of us taking a share in certain proportion of Commonwealth defence, suddenly this afternoon excused the whole British attitude by saying he thought it was just perhaps a method of finding it the most natural way to deal with the problem of Commonwealth defence. I was quite outspoken in saying I felt it was a reversion to the old order of things which sought centralization and control, in London. I read from the record of the Prime Ministers Conference just what Smuts had said at the Conference on that matter, though I know when it comes to something that really matters he joins with the British Government at every turn. I found it pretty difficult to get our Ministers to speak out."

Discussion resumed in Cabinet the next morning with the Chiefs of Staff and other expert advisers again in attendance. "Had the experts of the three Departments give an outline of the strategic concept of the various tasks required of the several forces to meet the situation with which Canada is faced. The presentation of the case took almost two hours and was exceptionally well performed. Major Anderson, head of the Intelligence Branch, directed and interpreted the various phases. Dr. Solandt spoke on the defence research work which is just in its inception. He, too, made a remarkably good presentation.

"I think Members of the Cabinet were profoundly impressed by the exposition as a whole. The information gathered is largely based on American sources. General Foulkes who has discussed the matter with the British authorities stated that their information was virtually identical. The information was of such a strictly confidential character that I do not propose to record any of it.

"We continued our discussions this afternoon from 3.15 until 5.45. The Chiefs of Staff in turn outlined to the Members of the Government as a whole the part which the respective services would be expected to play and were playing at the present time. Dr. Solandt gave another very good description of the defence research side of things.

"I presented to the Cabinet Recommendation 35 of the Joint Defence Board which sets forth the principles in accordance with which representatives of the two countries can be expected to carry on joint planning. Its various clauses were approved by the Cabinet in the presence of the Chiefs of Staff. It was interesting to observe how completely surprised some Members of the Government were at what was disclosed; equally amazing in some particulars how little some of the Members appreciated the military situation today and what it involves in the way of a complete change in the way in which from now on some old-time conceptions will have to be viewed. It is the greatest problem with which the Canadian Government has been faced since the war."

To the Prime Minister, the "world situation is infinitely more dangerous than we have yet believed it to be. It would almost seem that we are headed into an inevitable conflict which will mean either civil war or revolution spreading pretty generally through different countries, or open conflict between East and West with Communism versus Capitalism or Atheism versus Christianity. The war will be in the nature of a religious war as well as a class struggle and may result in a sort of Armageddon. Some changed conditions may intervene to save the situation but there is very much that indicates that in some particulars the movement already is much more rapid than one would have believed had been possible.

"Today's papers announcing the revolt of fifty or more members of Attlee's Government in an amendment to the Speech from the Throne opposing British foreign policy as one inevitably leading to war, and demanding a policy which will favour release of natural resources in all countries of the world, is a symptom of what is going on in Britain itself; a Communistic movement permeating the masses. This, on top of what is taking place in the elections in France and Italy, makes clear how far Communism is sweeping over the face of the Continent of Europe. The appalling truth is the fact that Russia today has enough armed forces to control the whole continent if she should wish to do so."

Mackenzie King was in Cabinet again on November 15 "from 11 until 1, discussing defence matters and again this afternoon from 3 to 5.

"Discussed at length the subject of organization for defence in London the different views and arguments pro and con of centralization versus coordination. Got renewed approval by the Cabinet of the 35th recommendation of the Permanent Joint Board. Agreed British Government should be informed of our intention to accept the recommendation. Took up the statement which President Truman was supposed to have had before him in the course of our interview and which I had since agreed to have used for a basis for discussion. Cabinet put much of today on discussion of its different clauses – a very profitable discussion I thought. I felt much relieved to have Cabinet's view carefully recorded on different paragraphs.

"During the afternoon tried to get some reaction from colleagues in the light of information of the last two days which would be helpful in effecting economies, but none seemed to have very much in the way of definite ideas. They all are inclined to accept in greater or less measure, what is put before them by the officials. I pointed out that while the estimates had been prepared on the basis of the defence forces operating in areas they had been accustomed to operate in, if under the new strategic concept our work was to be related principally to the North – to the Arctic – the percentage increase of costs would not only be 100% but might be several hundred percent. It was necessary therefore to keep down the initial size of the services. I also pointed out that in a few years there would be a depression. I pointed out that what we started with today would be a baseline and that expenditures would increase, not lessen, from year to year. A depression would come a little later on and men would be thrown out of employment. We should so plan now that beginning with smaller numbers we could enlarge the services by transfer of men to these opportunities of public work. I discussed the whole question of organization. Cabinet was agreed it would be desirable to have one Minister in control of the three services.

"After Council Gibson who in Council said he agreed strongly with that point of view, as did Abbott, came to say that if I wanted his resignation as Minister for Air, he of course would be ready to give it. I told him I was not thinking of resignations at all, just of what might be needed when it comes to reorganization of the Cabinet. That I would expect him and Abbott to do what they could meanwhile in the way of getting the joint reports from the services and effecting economies.

"Abbott agreed that we might do away with one of the aircraft carriers which we do not yet own and which the British are loaning to us. Gibson told me of Army arrangements for a fleet air arm and of some fool notion that the army seems to have that it must train its men to fly. The whole business is exceedingly complicated and technical.

"As I said to the Cabinet, we had not, to any extent, discussed the bearing of atomic weapons and bacteriological warfare on the whole business of re-organization of the Defence forces, simply because we were not competent so to do."

During the meeting of the Cabinet, Mackenzie King asked St. Laurent "whether in the light of what he had experienced, he thought the U.N.O. had brought us nearer to war or had helped to keep us further removed from war. He said it was not a light question but one requiring careful consideration. He replied speaking of how greatly some such organization was needed, also pointing out that Britain and the United States, as great powers, were as selfish in some ways as Russia but he did not wholly answer the question. I gave it as my opinion that they had really served to further Russia's purpose, etc., whatever it may be. That I thought Russia had first of all secured the veto which meant that nothing could be decided either at the peace conferences or at U.N. conferences which would not be in her interests. In the second place, she was now operating wholly behind an iron curtain and the rest of the world knew nothing whatever of what she was doing. How far she had progressed in developing her military and other strength. On the other hand, she was using the Paris Conferences and the U.N. Assembly as a springboard from which to develop propaganda to serve her ends. [Russia] was not only discovering but exposing to the world the weaknesses and contentions and conflicts between the big and small powers, and of all [other] powers with herself and her satellites. She was using this means to create dissension to enable her to develop her own imperialistic aims and giving her time for this – for sowing seeds of Communism through the different democracies and also the process of objecting to everything was causing her own people to believe the rest of the world was against Russia. I think there is infinite proof of this. I am really coming to the belief that a third world war is in the making although it may take a decade to bring it on. I spoke about Russia being our nearest neighbour on the North as the U.S. was on the South. Pointed out that it was the self-denying ordinance [the Rush-Bagot Treaty] on the Great Lakes which had prevented competitive arming between the two countries [the United States and Canada] and kept the peace. If we could do something similar with Russia we might be saved endless expense and possibly war in the end. One had to admit that we could not trust her even if she said 'yes,' that she was in agreement. It is an appalling situation. Had the Americans and ourselves not been virtually the same people the Rush-Bagot agreement might never have been made. Differences of race, religion, etc., will operate against any corresponding escape from competitive arming in the North. Once it begins it will not end until there has actually been war. The fight right along between the centralization and the decentralization forces in defence has taken place. I think I was able to make out my whole case with reference to the communiqué to the public at the end of the meeting of the Prime Ministers in London. I must now come out and make out a brief which will serve me when Parliament meets and the question of defence becomes a subject of discussion."

"We had better be careful about constructing bases [in the Arctic]," Mackenzie King wrote on November 22. As "the Governor General says [they] may become bases from which the enemy himself may operate, but would not operate were they not there. It is a difficult problem." With a procedure for examining the problem of defence co-operation agreed upon, the whole issue apparently went back to the Permanent Joint Board on Defence and it was not until February 1947 that the Prime Minister felt able to make public the general guidelines for future defence co-operation between Canada and the United States.

CHAPTER ELEVEN

Dominion-Provincial Battles and Cabinet Shuffles

IN ADDITION to his preoccupation with personal matters and the defence problem in the fall of 1946, Mackenzie King had to face a reorganization of the Cabinet, a task which inevitably took a lot of time and energy. The major problem was J. L. Ilsley. The heavy responsibilities which the Minister of Finance had borne during the war and the immediate postwar period had obviously taken their toll and it had become increasingly clear that he would have to be shifted to a less demanding portfolio or leave the Cabinet altogether.

During a conversation with Ilsley on October 7, the Prime Minister "asked him about himself. Had he found now that he had had a holiday that he was more inclined to remain in the Government. He said to me in a sort of laughing way and then frowning that he was glad I had asked him this question. He had not liked to bring up the subject himself. He thought he would just go ahead and do the best he could, say nothing more about it. However, he had found that he again was suffering from obsessions – the latest was over a matter connected with an egg contract which Gardiner had entered into without his knowledge and which might even lead to an increase of a point in the cost of living index. He said he would wake in the morning, could not free himself of the thought of this thing. His wife told him that no matter what happened, he would have to get out of the Government. This could not go on, living with him suffering as he was in this way.

"He then said to me he did not like to embarrass his colleagues by leaving the Government. . . . I said to him his health was the first consideration. He knew that I did not like to lose a colleague, least of all himself, but that I would not be fair to him if I did not meet his wishes in a matter of the kind. I asked him about his constituency. He said there was a young fellow in the riding he was sure could carry it quite easily.

"I spoke about possible successor [in the Cabinet from Nova Scotia].

He thought Winters [M.P. for Queens-Lunenburg] was the most promising [from] N.S. Macdonald [one of the two M.P.s from Halifax] not so good – in part because of his voice, though seeming ineffective while being a very able lawyer. He did not think that Isnor [the other member for Halifax] would expect a post of the kind. He had not the education. I told him we would leave matters over until the by-election was over. In the meantime, I would have a word with St. Laurent and perhaps the three of us would have a talk when he got back. He said he would like that very much. St. Laurent had mentioned to me earlier he thought Ilsley was anything but well. He had not gotten over his troubles."

At the Cabinet meeting on October 11, "the possibility of having Ilsley made Minister of Justice and Abbott taking his place" was discussed briefly. By October 17, Mackenzie King was even more concerned about the strength of his present Cabinet. "I can see wherein I am being left almost entirely to myself. St. Laurent and Martin will be in New York at the Conference of the U.N.O. Possibly till on in December. Howe is away for some days and will be away for some time. Mackenzie is just back and going to the West in another few weeks. Gardiner has been away much of the time. Is not too helpful when here. Mitchell is leaving on a cruise to the West Indies. Says he needs the rest, this recommended also by his doctors. When I asked him who might be acting as Minister of Labour, he suggested Howe. I said I thought it would be much better to appoint someone else. Abbott is going West and will be absent for several weeks. Ilsley is tired out; does not move in some things and is very difficult in others. . . . How the cabinet is to be strengthened, I don't know, especially in the Defence Departments. . . .

"With St. Laurent away, I shall find myself without anyone with whom to counsel. . . . As I thought over the whole situation, I felt my strength go with the thought of another heavy load and strain."

Later that day, the Prime Minister talked about the party leadership with Grant Dexter of the *Winnipeg Free Press*. "I was amazed to have him tell me that Gardiner had had a set-to with him on the score that the Free Press was trying to prevent him becoming leader of the Liberal party and threatening to make it difficult for anyone that sought to stand in his way. It is amazing to me that any man should be working toward securing the position of leadership for himself. I doubt if Gardiner would ever get the support of the party. Dexter seemed to think that Stuart Garson might come to Ottawa but would want to get the portfolio of Finance. He would be a real strength to the Government. He thought that in this I [was] probably right that if Pearson could be brought into public life, he would make the best of any successor to myself. This, however, is something which only the future can settle and in the circumstances and the times which would make anything of the kind possible. Dexter thought the mistake I had made in public life was saying that I intended to retire. He thinks I should go around and visit different parts of Canada."

As it became clearer that Abbott would be needed in Finance, Mackenzie King was faced with the problem of finding a successor in Defence. He never seriously considered the Air Minister, Colin Gibson, and still intended to move him to another portfolio and consolidate Defence under one minister, as he had hoped to do when Abbott became Minister of National Defence in 1945. When Mitchell left Ottawa for a rest on October 31, the Prime Minister told him that he would have to make some shifts in the Cabinet and "might even think of him for Minister of Defence, and Martin for Labour." Evidently, this was just a passing thought. By November 6 he was "thinking of possibly putting Claxton into defence and to pull the three departments together into one with a single Chief of Staff and three deputies. I do not see any way more effective to bring about consolidation. Claxton has shown that he can stay away for weeks, thereby not being overconcerned with Health and Welfare. They are very extravagant in that Department. He has the organizing ability required for Defence. If given that post, will at least be kept at home and out of the international arena for a time at least. I think he has quite lost his head in the extravagant manner in which he has travelled about, indifferent to the pressure under which all here have been working. I thought he was a man of sounder judgment.

"My own feeling is that he has probably defeated his own chances for the leadership of his party by creating a certain envy on the part of his colleagues in the Government and in the House. The kind of man needed is a man like St. Laurent who will make their immediate job a first concern."

These comments on Claxton seem to have been prompted by recollections of the Paris Conference. On October 16 Mackenzie King had "noticed in the despatches ... that Claxton has given two dinners to which heads of the different delegations have been invited. That is right enough I assume but some day there will be a real outcry in Parliament about these expenditures." The Prime Minister had also listened, with no great pleasure, to a radio broadcast by the Minister on October 3 summing up the results of the conference. "He has got a way of keeping himself before the public and at the same time giving an interesting account of foreign affairs. As I listened to him what struck me was how easy it is to make an address out of the commonplace." On October 22 he came close to blaming the by-election defeats in Toronto-Parkdale and Portage la Prairie on

Claxton. "It makes me sad to see the Liberal party begin to disintegrate," he wrote, "and that for no reason other than the apathy of the men who comprise the present Ministry and its following in the House. The man who is making the greatest mistake is Claxton who, had he stayed at home, or hurried home and taken in hand the whole work of organization as I suggested to him, many months ago, today would have won the approbation of the party in a way which would have made his chances good for selection as a leader later on. Neither Abbott nor Martin have shown inclination or ability in the direction of federal organization. This, too, will prejudice their chances of recognition."

Whatever his private thoughts on the organizational skills of his younger colleagues, Mackenzie King realized that he needed them and on November 12 he discussed with Abbott "the possibility of taking over Finance; also the necessity of having one Minister over the Department of Defence – one head of permanent services. He was very strongly for that. I asked who he thought could handle Defence if he left it. He suggested either Claxton or Bridges. Did not think that Bridges would be too good; Gibson not firm enough; thought Claxton would do the job well. I spoke of Claxton being very extravagant with public money. He said he certainly was, but doubted if he would be in that Department. I stressed on Abbott the seriousness of the problems that lie ahead."

One of the problems which had bothered the Minister of Finance since the end of the war was the gradual dismantling of the complex system of commodity and price controls. It was in this area that Ilsley most frequently came into conflict with the views of his colleagues, particularly the irrepressible Minister of Agriculture. However, one significant set of problems was removed on October 9 with the decision to abolish wage control in November. Mackenzie King was in Cabinet "from 2.45 to 7 P.M. which was much too long. We spent some time over the question of abolishing wage control. It was agreed, with Macnamara and Donald Gordon both present, that the Government would not continue wage control beyond the present year. Gordon thought from the way it was being administered there was less chance of the price ceiling being affected than if it were abolished altogether. He said he had quite changed his views as asserted some days ago – that the price ceiling could only be maintained if the wage ceiling was maintained.

"We also took up the question of meat rationing. A beef contract has been announced by Gardiner. Statement intended to be issued when meat contract was publicized was held back with the understanding that if any question were raised it would be put out as agreed upon between Finance and Agriculture and what was most important of all is that the Government decided to remove wholly meat rationing, at the latest, early in the new year. Donald Gordon doubts if we can expect to hold the price ceiling far into next year and by that time matters will have been fairly well steadied down in the States and begun to adjust themselves here. These were knotty problems on which to get decisions."

The problem which gave Ilsley most trouble and caused frequent disagreement between him and the Prime Minister was the negotiation of tax rental agreements with the provinces. Prince Edward Island had created no difficulty and was disposed of with a flat sum of $2,100,000. Good progress was made during the fall in discussions with Saskatchewan, Manitoba and New Brunswick. The negotiations with Alberta and British Columbia were somewhat more difficult and little, if any, progress was made with Nova Scotia, Ontario and Quebec. Though his distaste for the subject knew few bounds, Mackenzie King had been drawn into the negotiations shortly after his return to Ottawa in September. On September 27 he "worked through the forenoon on revision of letter to Premier Drew closing off Dominion-Provincial Conference for the present. This letter will create a lot of Tory yelping in the press."

Drew, of course, responded with another letter repeating his demand that the conference be reconvened. In his reply, which the Deputy Minister of Finance approved on October 10, the Prime Minister "intimated that until financial relations with the provinces are satisfactorily settled, the Government does not feel anything will be gained by resuming the Conference unless the provinces of Ontario and Quebec in their reaction to the proposed budget make it clear that they are prepared for modifications of their positions which would make it probable that a Conference would succeed.

"During the afternoon, Douglas of Saskatchewan and Mr. Fines, the Treasurer, came in to speak of a settlement, first, of outstanding Treasury Bills and secondly, of amounts due on natural resources – to be made subject to two separate enquiries, the latter by a Commission. I advised strongly that both matters had better be taken up together and a settlement reached at once and a tax agreement effected. With the authority of Ilsley in Council yesterday, I made it clear that their chances of getting the best possible settlement would be effected in this way. I agreed that they could send the two gentlemen they have had recently investigating the natural resources matter, to Ottawa, to discuss with the Finance Department the questions. Spoke to Clark of this. He approved and I undertook to write them to that effect.

"While talking, Douglas said he saw that there was nothing to be gained by another Conference until Drew and Duplessis took a different attitude and financial arrangements were satisfactorily concluded. He asked if once this was done in a general way, the Federal Government would call the Provinces together to discuss social, health and investment questions. I said that had been made quite clear."

On October 18 Mackenzie King spent the morning working on a reply to still another letter "received yesterday from Drew. I had read yesterday to Council and received general approval of a draft made by P. but made many important revisions by myself this morning and later further revisions in company with Pickersgill. One or two slight additional changes by Clark who otherwise had approved the letter which I think is a good one – it is concise and clear."

The morning of October 22 "was taken up seeking to prepare replies to Drew and Angus Macdonald regarding resumption of the Dominion-Provincial Conference. That whole business is a tangled skein which I am thoroughly tired of dealing with. Both Drew and Duplessis have made it a game of the most demagogic type of politics. On the other hand, our Finance Department has been far too rigid in matters of negotiation. I feel, too, that far too much has been left to Skelton to advise upon and he has not a large enough vision or experience to cope with the situation properly. Indeed, there is far too much Bank of Canada influence on the Finance Department and the Finance Department on Government policies. Could I see any possibility of having matters settled without a wrangle and making the last state worse than the first, I would, despite the wishes of the Finance Department, bring the provinces together anew. One needs a clear mind and good judgment to prolong a controversy of the kind. I have, at the moment, neither the heart nor the head for anything of the kind. I felt the hopelessness of the situation in trying to discuss it with what Members of the Cabinet were present at this afternoon's meeting. Finally, I sent off a mere line to Drew, to end the discussion with him, and a somewhat longer letter to Macdonald, which he will not welcome and which will not help matters. He is quite as antagonistic as Drew and Duplessis and more dangerous perhaps because of being more subtle and less in the open. The mistake at the start was ever allowing an issue to arise on centralization versus decentralization. I pointed this out very strongly at the beginning of the whole business." The two letters were approved at the meeting of the Cabinet that day.

Later in the day, the Prime Minister had a talk with Stuart Garson, the Premier of Manitoba, "who says he is getting on well with the agreement he is making with Ilsley. They are satisfied with the attitude the Federal Government is taking with Drew and Duplessis. Thinks we have been entirely in the right and believes once they are forced to levy income taxes

Provinces and Cabinet 377

by their own Government, they will soon come around to making agreements which will permit of some general agreement being entered into. I spoke to him about coming into the Federal Parliament. He thought he should get the tax agreement business out of the way first; also should not be in a hurry in breaking up his coalition. When he said there might be some difficulty in getting a seat, I told him I was sure Glen's seat would be made available at any time. I said I thought his own chances in the party for a leading position later on would be greatly advanced were he here from an early day. I did not feel as a result of our talk together that it was at all probable that he could think of coming in before a year or more and might not even then."

The Cabinet resumed discussion of federal-provincial financial problems on October 29 after the Prime Minister had returned from New York and Washington. "Ilsley seems in a very excited nervous condition. Spoke about the agony and pain of negotiating agreement and said Clark was also nervous. I can see it is Ilsley's condition which would make others highly overstrained. There will have to be a change there but everything is difficult with so many colleagues away."

On November 6, with Gardiner absent, the Cabinet "discussed at some length further terms that Ilsley was considering for Saskatchewan. He has got a settlement which includes the cleaning up of the natural resources matter on basis of award of the majority. I had said in Cabinet I felt sure this could be negotiated in the agreement and that Saskatchewan would wish it. Gardiner had thought the contrary and indeed favoured keeping the issue opened. To make perfectly sure of Cabinet accepting Ilsley's proposal, I asked if there were any opposed and then stated we were unanimous. Ilsley rightly felt were he to try to go further, the matter would have to be referred to Cabinet anew in Saskatchewan but it might open up other questions and lead to a debate that we had been unduly crowding the Government, that he could get a definite and final setlement now on the terms he proposed. In order that Gardiner might not have a grievance, I stated I thought we should keep Fines, of Saskatchewan, here until we had a chance to 'phone Gardiner about the matter itself which I said I would do myself and which relieved Ilsley immensely."

The next day (November 7) Mackenzie King telephoned Gardiner and explained the situation to him. "Later gave the word to Ilsley. I really think that by taking the matter in hand myself in this way, I have succeeded in getting a settlement. Gardiner, I feel certain, will not try to oppose further and will agree. The minute I suggested his return to the Cabinet, he told me that his son Wilfrid was going to leave the farm for law and he had a problem to deal with there. I think he felt he had better go on to

Regina and see Patterson [the provincial Liberal leader]. Would explain matters to him. Would then 'phone Ilsley in a manner which would enable the question to be settled tonight."

During this period, the Prime Minister became concerned about a by-election in Richelieu-Verchères to fill the vacancy caused by Cardin's death. He took charge of arrangements himself. On October 30 he had a long talk with Edouard Simard, a prominent Quebec Liberal, who pointed out that Cardin had carried the constituency in every election since 1911. "That he had not carried it by a lot of speakers [appearing] in the riding. Was usually away. It had been carried by a system of complete organization of the constituency under an organizer named Lachapelle. He strongly advised letting Lachapelle handle the campaign and deciding upon the candidate. He said there was no doubt Cardin's partner would be the one who would be selected. He was a little young but was the best man he thought in the constituency. He mentioned that he himself had been thought of but he recognized that the other man would likely be preferable and he told me that the day of the funeral, Bertrand and some of the Ministers had begun speaking to Lachapelle about the coming elections. Lachapelle said he hoped they would wait until the funeral was over before discussing the matter. Since then, Lachapelle had lost his wife and Bertrand had gone to the funeral. He [Simard] strongly advised against having Bertrand try to take the situation in hand. Other colleagues have done the same.

"While Simard was in the room, I rang up Lachapelle and expressed sympathy to him in the two bereavements. Asked if I might speak about bringing on the by-election on the 23rd of December instead of waiting until the new year. He asked me to leave the matter over; he would discuss it with some of the men there and would let me know later.

"Before 3, he told me it was all right to have an election at that time. He said that he would himself come and see me later on. When he spoke about keeping others away, I said I would keep matters in my own hand. This was all said in the presence of Simard. The latter told me he was relieved to hear me say I would keep matters in my own hand. He said if we would leave the organization to Lachapelle, we don't need to even worry about expenses. He would see that that side was looked after but he did not want others coming in and dealing with that aspect of the situation. . . .

"Simard said he hoped I would stay on in public life. Said that Quebec was more behind me than anyone. Believed the country was, too. Asked me who I thought would be the best one in Quebec as successor were I to drop out. I said St. Laurent. He said St. Laurent was a wonderful man.

There was no better man. When I indicated St. Laurent would not likely continue, he mentioned, as I thought he would, Howe as a possibility. There has always been a close friendship there. I did not say a word one way or another but thought he was the last man who could hold the party together for any length of time."

Mackenzie King telephoned Lachapelle on November 4 and "Spoke about desire of Quebec Ministers to give all help possible but of their wish to be governed by his wishes as largely as possible. They were anxious nothing should be left undone to secure the election.

"Also asked Lachapelle if he was coming to see me this week. He replied he would rather wait until next week as he was busy with his organization. I mentioned that Ministers wanted to plan for the speakers, etc. He said he had arranged for the meeting next week to get a candidate into the field. He could give me the name at once.

"He then mentioned COURNOYER who was Mr. Cardin's partner and his close friend. I told him we were all pleased at the choice and could all be behind him.

"He did not wish anyone to come into the riding at present but agreed that I might have Quebec Ministers present when he comes up to see me next week. He said he felt confident about the results and said not to have any concern."

The following day Simard telephoned "to report on how matters were going in the by-election. He thought everything was well under way. All the committees had been appointed. Arrangements had been made for radio broadcasting. . . .

"I mentioned that Lachapelle was coming up to see me next week. Simard said that he probably would come with him when the whole situation could be explained. I said the Quebec Ministers were anxious that nothing should be left undone and were relying upon me letting them know the wishes of the organization. I asked first if any of them would be wanted for the nomination [on December 10]. Simard said: no. I said they would like to know what would be expected of them in the way of literature, speaking, etc. He said that could all be arranged after the nomination. There would be plenty of time for that.

"He asked if St. Laurent would be away. I said I thought I could get him at any moment. He said there was no need at present but some little differences might arise over some people who still held to the frame of mind that Cardin had, as a consequence of the way he had been treated. That young Cournoyer would come out as a 100% Mackenzie King Liberal. They were anxious to get as many votes as they possibly could and were working earnestly toward that end.

"I said I would try to get the Quebec Ministers together when he and Lachapelle came up. He again expressed his view that everything was well in hand."

A week later, on November 13, the Prime Minister saw Simard and Lachapelle at his office. He "had all of the Quebec Ministers, including St. Laurent, present. I thanked Lachapelle and Simard for their active and well-planned efforts. They assured us that the election would be won. Later, when I was alone with the two of them – other colleagues had left, they pleaded with me very earnestly to continue in the leadership of the party. They said that my name stood higher than that of anyone in the Province of Quebec. It was the real asset that they had. If I dropped out, and Howe and St. Laurent dropped out, it would be like a barrel with the staves separating. They said that the statement I made a day or two ago of being prepared to reconsider staying on had been like putting a ring around the staves so as to hold the barrel together. Simard is full of similes of the kind. I really was deeply touched by the way they spoke and I might say that almost for the first time I began to feel how hard it will ultimately be to get out of harness if the party insists on my staying. I am adamant however in not ever consenting to run another general election. Time can take care of all that will come up between now and then."

Partly because he was a good deal more confident about the prospects for a victory in Richelieu-Verchères, Mackenzie King was shocked to learn that another by-election would be necessary with the death of W. C. Macdonald, one of the Halifax members, on November 19. Macdonald's death not only opened another seat but also complicated the Prime Minister's problem with Ilsley. He brought up the question of a by-election in Cabinet that day, pointing out that there was "no one in any office here who we could ask to go and get particulars re organization. Ilsley said he would 'phone to the organizer in Halifax. He thinks the organization there is in very good shape. I did not wait for Ilsley to send a message but got in touch with him myself, and also with Wishart Robertson in New York. I mentioned to them as I had to Council that I thought we must have the by-election come on before Parliament reassembles. I had 'phoned Castonguay who had given me January 20th as the earliest possible date; that is over two months hence. They all seemed to be hesitant. Council agreed it would be best to have the election over by that time. There were excuses about Christmas vacation, etc. I am sure the quicker the better. The main thing now is the choice of the candidate. He will have to be an Irish Catholic which does not make the choice any easier, as there is apt to be a feud between some of the brethren. Should we lose Halifax I am afraid the party's position would be extremely difficult. If we win, we will have at least two Members to bring into the House, if we win Richelieu-Verchères, as I feel sure we will. Everything is in readiness for that campaign."

The Prime Minister's humour was not improved by a talk he had later that day with J. R. Kirk, the Liberal M.P. for Antigonish-Guysborough. Kirk, who had been seriously injured in an accident some weeks before, asked for an appointment to the Senate. "I felt very sorry for him, but also felt really it was almost ludicrous that he should make this request. I asked him why? He said he might die at any minute and would not be much use in the Commons. But what he had really worked himself into saying was, that as we had lost a couple of by-elections, it would be well to bring one on where we could be sure to win it. If I could appoint him to the Senate he felt we would be sure to carry his seat. He made up his mind to this yesterday. . . . I told him it would hardly be a sound reason to appoint anyone to the Senate; that he was not well enough to be in the Commons. I said it would make it very difficult to refuse openings for others, including members of the Ministry who were anxious to leave the Commons. It seemed to me that the world must be going crazy."

Ilsley had decided to attend the Macdonald funeral in Halifax and use the occasion for a talk with Angus Macdonald who was still taking a belligerent attitude to the federal government's tax rental proposals. After the Cabinet meeting on November 20, he asked to see the Prime Minister. "We remained in the Chamber," Mackenzie King reported. "He said he was wondering whether he should not get out at once; that his seat was perfectly safe, and if we had the two by-elections in Nova Scotia, assuming we lost one, we could be sure of carrying one. I told him in this connection of what Kirk had proposed yesterday. I told Ilsley I thought his name would be needed in the campaign; that he would have to help there. If he got out before the by-election was over, that would cost us heavily in the province. On the other hand, if we carried the by-election, it would be easier to take the step soon. I had spoken to St. Laurent about his going to Justice. St. Laurent quite agreed. Ilsley said to me: I must get out of the Finance Department; I cannot stand the pressure there any longer. He then mentioned one thing after the other, including pressure re exemption of women's income from their husbands' salary, etc. He said it had just got beyond him. He had got now where he was getting cross, talking too loud, and the rest of it, and just could not stand it. I told him I wondered how he stood it as long as he did. I had already spoken to Abbott about taking on Finance and would try to get these adjustments made fairly soon – perhaps before Christmas. He then said that during the session he might get out. This is the farthest point to which he has gone. He asked if the Chief Justiceship of Nova Scotia could be kept open. I told him I saw no reason why it should not. He really has had a very difficult time."

They talked again on November 26 after Ilsley returned to Ottawa. "He thinks Connolly, one of the Ministers in the [provincial] Government, is undoubtedly the best man [for the nomination in Halifax], but he is getting $10,000 and would only get $6,000 at Ottawa. Ilsley hinted at the possibility of having him made a parliamentary secretary. I would not consider this. It would be unfair to men who are already in the House. He said Isnor had volunteered the suggestion of Winters being made a parliamentary secretary. Isnor would like a senatorship later on. Ilsley also told me of his talks with Angus Macdonald. Said they had a pretty hot discussion in Nova Scotia, but he believes that, with some adjustments which he is considering, re gas, that he may be able to work out an agreement with Macdonald. If this had been done while the Conference was on, as I had urged, he would have had agreements with all the provinces. Clark has been the stumbling block and is only just now coming around. Ilsley said he is most anxious to get into the Department of Justice as soon as possible. Felt he could not stand Finance any longer.

"After Council I had a talk with Wishart Robertson, which was along the lines of my talk with Ilsley. I was delighted to hear him say he would go and stay on the job in Nova Scotia until the election was over. Give up N. Y. if need be. He felt they had a good organization.

"Still later, I had a talk with Isnor who had been helpful at the interview between Macdonald and Ilsley. He said that both of them were pretty tense in their conversation together. I advised Ilsley to have Macdonald come at once. Lose no time in trying to settle with him. I am not at all sure that we are going to be able to work matters out on lines suggested, and I am not at all certain that we shall win the seat. However, I told Council that the election must not be later than the last week of January, come what may.

"We cannot wait for questions, debates, etc., in the House, which are likely to further embarrass the situation."

On November 30 both Ilsley and Robertson came to Laurier House for a further talk about the political situation in Nova Scotia, both the by-election problem and prospects for a tax rental agreement. "Ilsley seemed very happy when he came in," the Prime Minister wrote. "When we got on to his talk with Macdonald, he told me it had been very difficult but he was hopeful there would be a successful outcome. He said he had undertaken to meet his wishes on the gasoline tax. Kept going back and forth as to whether this had been best or not. Clark had now come to the opinion he thought it was all right. I could not help saying that if Clark could have made this concession at the right time, with one or two minor things, we would have had the whole business settled months ago. Ilsley rather amazed me. He had agreed with Macdonald to have an annual conference of provinces and Dominion held at a specified date each year. He is the one who has been stronger against conferences than anyone. That caused me to see at once that his judgment was not to be relied on. I said I did not think we could agree to this and gave him the reasons pointing out what had already been said in letters sent to others.

"It is clear Macdonald is simply playing the game for Drew, etc. He said Macdonald had brought a letter with him enumerating various points he was demanding. Was taking it back with the concession indicated. Would probably write raising the points again but they could be answered by him.

"Before we had gone very far, I saw pretty clearly that neither Ilsley nor Wishart Robertson thought we should be issuing the writ for the by-election on Tuesday. They suggested a postponement of a week. In a moment, I saw that Macdonald was probably trying to hold Ilsley up, knowing he was anxious to get matters settled before the by-election. His own difficulty will arise when he has to prepare his budget. I therefore said immediately I thought it would be better to leave the date of the by-election open altogether until we get an agreement. I am sorry for this because delay will certainly mean a more difficult situation later on. There is no chance of having Connolly as I believed there would not be, and Ilsley himself admitted we might lose the by-election though Robertson still hopes that we can carry it. I, myself, am very doubtful. I was sorry to see Ilsley take a second round of Scotch in the course of the conversation. He had said something about having taken a lot of beer at lunch and he was not conscious he had had a mouthful of it. Quite clearly, his nerves have got wholly the better of him.

"I felt that we must complete the change of Ministers next week at the latest. It was 11 when I got to bed. Robertson and Ilsley both spoke of how [Angus] Macdonald would go up to see Alec Johnston [a former M.P. for Nova Scotia and a retired Deputy Minister] who is, of course, a thoroughly bad influence. They both agree that Johnston, Lambert [Senator Norman Lambert], Grattan O'Leary [publisher of the *Ottawa Journal*] and Macdonald all work together. Macdonald's trouble is his disappointment at not having – as he expected he would – succeeded me in the leadership of the party. This little group have always worked together to that end. They say that Macdonald now does not make any mention of myself but turns his feelings against Ilsley and others, trying to find some excuse for what he knows to have been his own mistakes. He has been a great disappointment and may even wreck the Liberal party in his own province as well as help to work injury federally in much the same way that Mitchell Hepburn did in Ontario."

Claxton telephoned the Prime Minister on December 2 with an alarming description of Ilsley's condition. "Mrs. Ilsley had been 'phoning him. Claxton felt Ilsley would have a complete breakdown if he did not get out at once. Mrs. Ilsley said that he is at his worst from 2 until 6 in the morning; does not sleep and is quite beside himself. It is perfectly clear that these agreements with the provinces have brought this to pass, both as affects Ilsley and as affects Clark. I am beginning to think it may be advisable for me, with a new Minister of Finance, to have a Conference, and see if I can clear the whole thing up. If I can get some guarantee in advance from Drew as to how far he would be prepared to go, I may take that course. It is Clark who does not want a conference at any cost and Ilsley is backing Clark, though agreeing with Angus Macdonald to an annual conference, he changed the whole position. It is very serious and indeed well nigh tragic situation, with St. Laurent and others in New York and some away, etc. I shall have to work it out some way this week."

Later that day Mackenzie King had a long talk with John Hart, the Premier of British Columbia, who was in Ottawa for discussions with the Department of Finance. "I could see when we met that Hart was a little put out that he had not seen me sooner.... He began by saying that finality would have to be reached at once with regard to B.C. agreement with Federal Government. Otherwise he would have to go back. Later he told me in confidence that the Premiers of the Provinces that had not received an agreement were going to line up, draw up what they thought would be reasonable terms, would then come in a body, present them to me, demanding that we should have a conference. He told me that Angus Macdonald had been talking to him. Had told him of the demands that he, Angus, was putting forward and had made it plain that Drew, Angus and Manning, all had been working together on the plan to force the situation. That he, Hart, would have to join in with other protesting provinces if what Ilsley had put forward in the budget was the last word. He did not want to do this but had no alternative. He said he would not talk with Ilsley, that he was a sick man, and did not exercise any authority of his own, but was guided solely by Clark, who was an autocrat, telling Ilsley what to do and what not to do. Hart said that he knew, had small concessions regarding the gasoline tax been made, while we were all in conference, the whole question would have been settled at that time. It was the arbitrary stand of the Finance Department which exasperated all the other Premiers. He said he did not come down here to be greeted pleasantly by Ministers and then turned over to Deputies, with all of which I have the utmost sympathy. I did all I could to placate Hart. Told him I would do all I could. Arranged to have Abbott come over in the morning, when we would talk together. He repeated he would talk to me and would be glad to have Abbott present as well; would not go near the Finance Department."

The following morning, December 3, Mackenzie King spent at his office "from 11 to 12.30 . . . with John Hart and Abbott, and from 12.30 until after one with Abbott alone. Hart went over the ground which he thought would make a fair basis of an agreement with B.C. It related to allowing payments on the basis of growth of population, development of resources, etc., in a way that would meet B.C.'s favourable economic position but would not change what was necessary with the other provinces. He told Abbott a good deal of what he had said to me about the other provinces lining up against us, and left in a very good mood. Abbott, himself, sees something of the possible development along the lines Hart had suggested. It was agreed that they would work out the details between Abbott and Hart. When alone I spoke very frankly to Abbott about mistakes I thought there had been in the way our whole side of the case had been handled from the start – mistakes causing the provinces to feel they were losing autonomy and not giving them a little more of what they felt was a return; not being more careful [in] giving back exactly what was taken away, rather than some centralizing alternative. I told him, Abbott, I hoped to make him Minister of Finance within a few days. He himself felt that Ilsley should conclude, if possible, the agreement with Macdonald first. I told him even if it was unpleasant, I would be prepared to call another conference, if we knew definitely in advance what would make the basis of a settlement, without having more squabbling in public. It would have to be on a sound basis. I told him I thought if the trouble with the provinces was allowed to continue it would be a running sore and might ultimately lead to the defeat of the Government. I thought the public were getting sick of these controversies and the sooner they could be gotten out of the way the better."

At the Cabinet meeting that afternoon, "Ilsley spoke of the talk he had had with Macdonald, and something also he had promised that he doubted if he should have, which we all agreed he should not have. He had made the condition he would have to get the consent of his colleagues. He was very worried as to whether he should 'phone at once and to say he had gone too far in that. His whole attitude was that of a man who had come to the end of his tether. I felt extremely sorry for him. I tried to have him say nothing more of what he had discussed and said that everything would be all right. Some question came up on the agenda which had to do with the financing of the National Railways. He turned and asked me if I could leave that until Abbott became Minister. The truth is he is not in shape to battle anything further. I just hope things have not already gone too far. He seemed in poorer shape today than any day I have seen him yet. This telephoning back and forth to Halifax is all nonsense. Conditions Macdonald is trying to exact are perfectly monstrous. They have nothing to do with exact terms and are all an effort to control the Federal Government, wishing no conference and the like with all provinces combined. It was a real tragedy, but is a lesson in the folly of men persisting in doing things that are not sound or politically wise; letting officials run control of their judgment."

The Prime Minister was happy to hear on December 4 that Abbott thought he had been "making real headway with John Hart in working out an agreement with B.C., along the lines we talked over together yesterday. I hope and pray he succeeds in this. If he does it will knock one prop out from under a bit of intrigue which Angus Macdonald, Drew and Manning of Alberta have been busy concocting.

"Poor Ilsley rang me up early in the afternoon to say he had not succeeded in making an agreement with Macdonald. He said that the latter had 'phoned him to say his Cabinet would not accept the terms; also saying he was writing him (Ilsley). Ilsley begged of him to make his letter as moderate as he could, to put it in the form of saying he hoped that consideration would be given, etc., so as not to close the door too tight. Ilsley's voice was almost like that of a woman weeping. I felt deeply sorry for him. Told him he had handled everything all right and not to worry. Things would work out well. I also let him know of the intrigue that I knew of in the whole business which I think rested his mind a little.

"Currie of Nova Scotia [L. D. Currie, Minister of Mines and Minister of Labour in the Macdonald government] had 'phoned earlier in the day to let me be informed that the Cabinet in Nova Scotia were not at all united on the Macdonald stand. That, as a matter of fact, Macdonald and only one or two of his Ministers were holding out against accepting the terms Ilsley offered. The others were strongly for accepting, also were demanding that there should be a caucus of the party which certainly would accept the terms if they were put to them. They felt that Macdonald was holding back something from them and concluded it was some understanding and arrangement he had with Drew of Toronto that he was holding to. This is absolutely correct. Macdonald is in his way just as bad as Hepburn was and may succeed in doing for Nova Scotia Liberalism what Hepburn did for Liberalism in Ontario. Pretty effectively destroy it for a season and with it much of the power of Liberalism in the Dominion as well.

"I shall see to it, however, that he makes no headway with the Dominion through any intrigue with the Tory party in Ontario or the Social Credit party in Alberta. These two parties are lining up together. As Ilsley said, it is tragic indeed that Macdonald should be the one Liberal to help to oppose the Liberal Government here, a Government of which he was a Member, from reaching a settlement of a nationwide problem of first concern. It is all on a par with the way in which Macdonald behaved when in league with Ralston and others to upset the administration in 1944. While I am prepared to consider the calling of another conference, what I now know of what has been going on underground makes me feel that I shall cease to consider that possibility. Take the decision in Parliament, that as a Government, we are answerable to the representatives of the several provinces in the House of Commons. We are not answerable to provincial governments for our policies and the course we may pursue. To adopt any other course is to destroy the independence of the Federal Government and place us at the mercy of the provincial governments. I still feel very strongly at the Finance Department for not yielding in the matter of a few taxes when I fought so strenuously to have them do so at a time when, without any substantial loss of revenue, we would have got this whole business properly settled."

On December 6 Mackenzie King learned from Abbott that "Clark of Finance had come to the conclusion the formula Hart had worked out himself was sound and just – would mean an increase of one or two millions for B.C. over what was originally proposed, but can be justified on revenues, etc. – being raised at the time wartime agreements were made. Just before Abbott came in, I received a letter from Angus Macdonald, along lines anticipated, which I think it will be possible to answer in a way that will enable him to make an agreement, and not unduly embarrass our Government. I am, however, far from believing that we are yet within sight of a final agreement with either B.C. or N.S.

"I sent word today to St. Laurent to be here Monday if possible as Ilsley is deeply concerned over the whole matter, and the possible effect the proposed agreements may have on Quebec. I shall try and settle the portfolio business on Tuesday or Wednesday of next week.

"Hart came in . . . and he and Abbott talked for a little over an hour during most of which time the lights were out, and it had continued to grow increasingly dark. Hart did most of the talking, reviewing his case and telling us something of the telephone calls he was getting from Angus Macdonald, from Manning of Alberta, and Drew of Toronto. What Angus told him of what he hoped to get; of Canada withdrawing from the gas field at present at all events, etc. It was left that he and Abbott would try and reduce in writing the statement that he should make and that I should make if necessary, when he, Hart, leaves for B.C. on Tuesday or Wednesday next."

The Prime Minister talked to St. Laurent on December 9 and discovered that he "had come from New York on Saturday, worked Saturday night with Abbott and Ilsley, and practically all day Saturday and Sunday on the negotiations with Hart of B.C. and what was to have been sent to Macdonald of N.S. in answer to his communication. He went over the ground with me. I agreed to the principles of the communications which were to be sent to both. It was a delight to see how clear his mind was." However, before further progress was made on these problems, the Cabinet changes had been made and Ilsley had gone to the more congenial and calm Justice portfolio.

During these weeks of frantic activity, Mackenzie King had also been busy with a number of other matters. On November 29 he went to Quebec City to speak at a testimonial dinner for St. Laurent. Put into the proper mood by an enthusiastic reception at the railway station, he drove to the Chateau Frontenac and "got to work immediately on the French speech, making several alterations, having learned of the different order of the speeches. I kept practising the pronunciation with E. H. [Handy]. Worked back and forth on this for some time. At 5.30 I went to bed for an hour's rest. After dressing, went over the French again but did not trouble further with the English. Decided on certain pages I would cut out, realizing the time it would take with the French and with the applause to cover.

"Mr. St. Laurent and Senator Dessureault came to the suite at 10 to 8. I met 100 or more members of the party in the lounge and shook hands with all before we went into the large ballroom where every bit of accommodation had been taken. The head table ran the full length of the room, sideways. There was an orchestra on the platform and the ladies gallery was filled with ladies opposite.

"Fafard presided. Godbout, St. Laurent and I were the only speakers. Fafard made a splendid introduction, over-elaborate in what he said in reference to myself. I was given a great ovation on rising. When I began to speak in French the ovation was renewed. It was renewed again after concluding the French and after my speech in English it was quite overpowering. There was singing as well. The applause and the singing took a considerable amount of time. The French seemed to go remarkably well, with only one or two little slips. It certainly was well received. Took nearly six minutes. The entire time was nearly 50 minutes, of which I think 10 at least were applause and singing. I felt the English speech was registering well and the effect pretty direct in places. References to Mr. St. Laurent were magnificently received.

"Godbout made a marvellous speech, without a note. His delivery was extraordinarily good. I felt, however, for the occasion he spoke much too long and also I thought unwisely spent too much time on provincial politics. He should have confined what he had to say on that occasion pretty much to St. Laurent himself. He must have spoken over half an hour. The result was Mr. St. Laurent did not get on until almost 11 P.M. when we went off the air except locally. It was almost midnight when we concluded. He was considerably handicapped on all sides. First the hour being so late, then the radio being off and though I am not sure of this I think the loudspeakers were also off. The air was pretty well charged with smoke and St. Laurent was pretty tired and this affected his throat. However, he delivered what he had to say very effectively and with deep feeling. It certainly was a magnificent demonstration and one merited beyond words. It was quite a task getting away from the dinner, with people who wished to shake hands. I could see Madame St. Laurent was greatly pleased with the evening, also the daughters and the boys. A fine family.

"I must say I enjoyed every moment of the evening, a fine tone about the whole affair, on a high level. I was greatly pleased so many of the Ministers were present and that the welcome from all sides was what it was. He came with me to the train and left about 12.30 A.M."

Back in Ottawa the next afternoon, Mackenzie King telephoned St. Laurent. "He sounded quite pleased about the night; kept saying he thought it would have the effect of letting all present see that we were most sincere in our actions in the war period but that there were more things to be considered than perhaps some of them knew about and that they would really feel that the Liberal Party was THE PARTY for Canadian unity. That, as such, he thought the evening would have a helpful effect.

"I said to him what I had remarked to P. and H. last night thinking of what I had said in the evening and what had been said of the confidence people [had] in me that, looking in a broad way on Dominion and Commonwealth relations, it was I believed true that Quebec had saved the Dominion through what it had contributed, as I had brought out last night, to national unity and that Canada had saved the Empire through what we had done, through developing responsible government and complete and national autonomy. St. Laurent in some way was the stone which the builders rejected in so-called organization and power, etc., and had become the chief stone of the corner, just as Quebec had been rejected by the rest of the Dominion and as the Liberal party of Canada had when rejected by the Imperialists, etc."

The dinner for Mr. St. Laurent was not the only honour received by a member of the Government late in 1946. The Cabinet had decided on September 26 "not to attempt any Honours List for the New Year, apart from possible recommendations of a few names overlooked in the list of July." Two names in this category, the Prime Minister decided, were Mackenzie and Gardiner. On Sunday, December 1, he sent a cable to Norman Robertson, who was seeing Attlee the next morning, asking him to suggest their appointment as United Kingdom Privy Councillors. Gardiner "and Mackenzie are the only two who have been at my side since 1935. In addition to Ilsley and Howe who have P.C.'s, all have rendered real service during the war. Mackenzie too has been acting Leader in the House and is the oldest Member of the Government. I made it clear, if it was embarrassing, not to ask for Gardiner at present. My impression is that Attlee will agree to both. If so I will certainly have done my duty by these two colleagues, despite very much which I have to overlook and am only too happy to overlook. There was a time when Gardiner was ready to go over with Power and a few others – Hepburn and others – in considering the latter for leadership. Was not just as loyal as he should be. Mackenzie has been loyal throughout, but through his weakness has at times been very difficult to control. However I can overlook that. The fact that I was very glad was clear from the fact that I slept from 3.30 till 6 very soundly."

Mackenzie King had an extraordinarily busy day on December 9. At 11.00 A.M. he attended the funeral of his old colleague, Charles Stewart, who had been President of the International Joint Commission. After returning from the cemetery, he voted in the municipal elections and then went to St. Laurent's office for an hour's conversation about the tax rental negotiations with British Columbia. After lunch he attended Malcolm MacDonald's wedding at Christ Church Cathedral and the reception at Government House, where he found time to secure the Governor-General's approval for the Cabinet changes to be made the next day, "Ilsley as Minister of Justice and Abbott as Minister of Finance. I spoke of Claxton as Minister of Defence – combining the three services in one. The Governor was very strong in his view that to combine the services was the right thing to do. He also agreed that Gibson did not seem to be the person who would be strong enough for that work. I did not make any particular comment on Claxton. I spoke about Ray Lawson as Lieutenant-Governor of Ontario, mentioning the efforts I had made to secure first Massey, then Eaton and then Harry Crerar. The Governor said, certainly, the Prime Minister has his problems."

At 5.30 P.M. he returned to Laurier House to prepare for a speech at a Rideau Club dinner that evening where he was to unveil a portrait of Sir John A. Macdonald. "At the Club I felt a very companionable atmosphere – something I think I felt for the first time in that Club. I used to be so sensitive to its Tory complexion. However, it was a great pleasure to meet so many men that I have not seen for years. All seemed most appreciative of the dinner party which filled the large dining room. I sat to the right of Kenneth Greene, who presided, and had Duncan Campbell Scott to his left. I had Fosberry to my right, with Harold Daly immediately beyond. The dinner was a very good one. Kenneth Greene made a first-rate introductory speech in which he recalled the letter I had written in 1918 suggesting an arts committee to arrange for the hanging of pictures in the Club. It was a much better letter than I could write today. Harold Daly spoke, I thought, exceedingly well, telling the history of the painting as Greene had done with relation to the background of the founding of the Club and its members. When it came to my turn to speak, while I had been feeling very tired and was feeling a bit fearful as to getting on, I found to my delight that my mind was quite clear and functioning well. I spoke, I think, for about half an hour. In that time I did not hesitate for a word nor did I look at a note. The latter part of the speech was wholly improvised, taken mainly from the remarks of the President and Daly. I could see that those present were intensely interested and at the conclusion I got one of the finest receptions I have ever had after speaking. There were, of course, about the occasion some features of exceptional interest. One which I mentioned as a subject for conclusion but which I did not care to reflect upon was the fact that at the dinner I was the oldest member of the Club present, not oldest in the matter of years but in the matter of membership – having entered in 1900. There are only some six or eight memberships which go back prior to 1900. I had never expected the day would come when I would hold that position at the Rideau Club. Even more extraordinary was that I should have been the one at the Rideau Club to unveil Sir John's portrait, and more extraordinary still was that I should have been the one who had succeeded Sir John and Sir Wilfrid in the leadership of a political party. I had been in office longer than either Sir Wilfrid or Sir John. My referring to the way in which I got into the Club caused immense amusement and offered a fine opening for what followed. I closed with a reference to the rapidity with which time was passing and of the matter of all doing our utmost in all that we could in the interests of our country in the time left.

"After dinner I received no end of congratulations and when I was leaving the Club, going downstairs with the President, the members gathered at the top of the stairs and gave me a round of applause. It was really a most heart-warming evening and I enjoyed it more than any event in which I have participated in years."

Before going into the Cabinet meeting on December 10, the Prime Minister had "a talk with Graham Towers who has been offered the head position in the International Bank. This time he is wavering in his decision. He is, I think, tempted by the magnitude of the offer and the fact that the man who was secured in the first instance has not thus far made a success of the undertaking. I told him I thought he should consider very carefully where his happiness would lie through the years. He would find living in the States, not being his own master, very different from the position he occupied here and the support of the Department of Finance of Canada. Also that he might well consider whether anyone could make a success of the bank and what a failure to this end might mean. I pointed out how wise Pearson was to stay in Ottawa instead of becoming Secretary-General of the U.N.O. I pointed out there were different standards in the business of politics in the U.S. from those of Canada. He might find a ruthless attitude there which might be anything but satisfactory. I told him that, of course, the Government would not think of putting any obstacle in his way if he felt the call of duty was such as to cause him to accept. The offer was going to be made to Gordon, if Towers would not accept, but he doubted if Gordon would. I shall not be surprised if Towers accepts though I think he will make a grave mistake if he does. In some ways, he has the finest position of any man in Canada." In the event, Towers decided to remain as Governor of the Bank of Canada.

In Cabinet, Mackenzie King announced the new Cabinet posts for Ilsley and Abbott and "spoke of Ilsley's services over the years and how much they were appreciated. Expressed the hope that the duties would be less exacting than Finance.

"Ilsley then began to speak of his own condition; feeling he had not measured up. St. Laurent came along splendidly with a reassuring word and all went off I thought very well. It was five years to the day that St. Laurent had entered the Government." These two changes in the Cabinet were announced to the press later that day.

The Prime Minister discussed a series of diplomatic appointments with St. Laurent on December 12 and "went over . . . what I had in mind of further changes in the Ministry, to be effected by tomorrow night. We both agreed that Claxton would be best for Defence, though we knew he would prefer to stay where he is. However, that appointment would give him a wider experience in government in every way. It seemed obvious that Paul Martin was the person to succeed Claxton in Health and Welfare, he having been immediately interested in social problems and being also a member of the social and economic council of the U.N.O.

"Spoke also of Ian Mackenzie for Secretary of State making Gibson Minister of Veterans' Affairs. I assumed that Mackenzie would welcome this. It would lighten his burden and knowing what will probably be coming to him from Britain, nothing would be better. In that event, I had decided to make Mackenzie Secretary of State and Gibson, Veterans Affairs, he being a veteran, having had a good experience in the Defence Department. I did not think him strong enough for that strong Department but the best available. McCann would, of course, have been the right person either for that Department or Health and Welfare being an exceptionally good administrator but he has not had any service overseas – indeed has had no association whatever with the Defence forces and the Defence services would resent that appointment. Besides he is at the moment doing excellent work in the Revenue Department which needs reform.

"I had sent for Claxton to come to see me before luncheon. Had he not been absent because of his father's death, I would have had him appointed at once when Abbott was appointed. It was my first conversation with him since his father's death. I expressed my sympathy anew and we talked of what his father's life had meant to him. He said the happiest day his father had had was the day we all lunched together at Laurier House.

"When we had opened this conversation, I asked Claxton if he had seen the heading in the Citizen last night. It was to the effect he was likely to be Minister of Defence. He said: yes; what a shameful statement, or words to that effect. I replied that I did not know who had read my mind on the matter. I rather thought that while I had had a conversation with only one or two colleagues, it had been from one of those sources that the matter had leaked out. I did not mention any names but I feel pretty sure that Abbott has found it difficult to resist letting the press know who his successor was likely to be though, in this, I may be quite wrong. Once it was known that Claxton would go to Defence, the other two appointments would be logically deduced. I then said to Claxton that I had come to the conclusion that he was the one I would like to have take over the Department of Defence. I did not see any situation at the moment quite as important and critical as that which pertained to the three services.

"First of all, looking at the question as it related itself immediately to the public service of Canada, these Departments had been running too much on their own. The Ministers who had had control during the war had extravagant notions. Things had gone very far in the way of expenditures. They had left before the elections and the Ministers that have since taken hold, had done so without any feeling that the arrangements would be final. I forgot to speak about McNaughton who really checked up things a bit but referred particularly to Abbott and Gibson but their finding that there were so many watertight compartments, each demanding full equipment and the like that I thought on all things they had in common, great saving should be effected. Also they should be made to reach joint agreements; that could never be done under different Ministers. Each would feel it necessary to defend his own particular Department. I have in mind what had been found necessary in England now with one Minister at the head; also of what Truman said to me about his feeling it best to have one Minister; and also Lord Alexander, that he was sure that that was desirable. I said that I thought the services were continuing to go too far. The army was planning for an overseas army. The navy had no need at all at the present time for aircraft carriers. I had always opposed this from the start as unnecessary. We should have a purely coast defence. I said more important than all this was the shaping of policy in the light of discussions which have taken place in New York at the U.N.O. on disarmament, etc. Relations with Russia. Nothing be done here to give excuse for competitive armament. With Britain, the greatest care should be taken over the question of bases and the like. That we should not go throwing money into the water in the North; breaking holes in the ice in the North, in the light of the atomic age, etc. All of this was a very large problem. A real world problem. I felt it would give him a knowledge and experience that would be more valuable than could be gained anywhere else. I then said to Claxton: You are interested in Health and Welfare, in social questions. You know as well as I do if we are to have money for these purposes, we cannot go on spending what we are on the army, navy and air force. Either one or the other will have to be cut down. I think your task should be to see that the utmost economy consistent with security should be effected in the Defence Department and I look to you for that. I mentioned specifically that St. Laurent was feeling that aircraft carriers should go at once. What nonsense it was to see pictures of waste of money and our men travelling in cities like Mexico, etc. It all irritated the public after the war."

At one stage in the conversation, Claxton expressed a preference to stay where he was. "I said I knew that that was so but I thought he was the one person for this larger task. I reminded him he had said to me in Paris, when he was thinking of possibly having External Affairs though I had never mentioned this specifically, that his own Department of Health and Welfare was well organized. Could get on all right. To remember he had said that. I said to him of course I could make no commitments about the future but I might tell him that St. Laurent was staying only for another session. I might have to make some appointment there later on. Whether it would be Martin or someone else, I could not say and would not say now but in any case such knowledge as he had gained in Defence would be helpful in External Affairs and a knowledge of External Affairs would be pretty helpful in Defence. Really this post offered a chance second to none for a man to make himself indispensable in the Government and give him the largest outlook.

"He expressed his appreciation of the confidence I was showing and said he would do the best he could. I told him that we would probably make the change tomorrow. Claxton spoke about intending to return early to Montreal tomorrow but would wait over till 6. (It amazes me how little some times men see the smaller and more immediate thing which blinds their vision as to the significance of the larger. That is true with most men through life.)"

After lunch, Mackenzie King telephoned Ian Mackenzie in Vancouver. "When I got to Mackenzie, I said to him that, as he knew, I was reconstructing the Government; in so doing, I was thinking of appointing him Secretary of State to relieve him of the heavy burdens of the War Veterans Department and asked if he would let me have his resignation of the War Veterans so as to enable me to make the necessary adjustment. . . .

"To my surprise, Mackenzie's first reaction was he regarded this as a demotion and that I had better count him out altogether. Reminded him that he himself had asked that he might be given the Secretary of State and relieved of the other portfolio on account of his health. His reply was his health was now so much better. He said that he knew the war veterans wanted him in that position. He had brought the Department up to the place it was at, etc. I expressed surprise that he should feel as he did and said I did not wish to discuss the matter further over the 'phone. He asked me to hold matters over until before Christmas when he would be back. I said I could not do that. I had to make changes at once. He then said: Of course, you are the Prime Minister. Added I should do whatever I thought best but he would ask that I count him out altogether. I said to him I had no thought of doing that. He would know with what conversations we had had before wherein I felt I was really doing him a kindness in proposing the change.

"I said nothing about his being made an Imperial P.C. as I had not up to that time had any final word from Attlee nor did I wish to make the one thing in any way conditional upon the other. I knew he would be certain to be appointed Imperial P.C. but I was anxious to see just what his attitude would be without any assurance on this point. I was quite disappointed that he took the line he did but it only confirmed my view that he is anything but himself. He sounded as though he was very much excited. In fact he had quickly been thrown into a rage. Probably only the complex re-asserting itself so I did not try to go any further, simply said I had nothing further to say at this time. I did not ask him to send any word one way or the other. I confess I felt a little incensed myself having been more than patient with Mackenzie over the last year or two. If I had any resentment in my nature I would immediately have cabled Robertson to tell Attlee that I did not wish to urge Mackenzie's appointment, but would ask that the matter be given no further consideration and done the same with Gardiner who I know, at times, has not been too loyal. Is unnecessarily rude and aggressive in his attitude in Council which is pretty testing to all his colleagues and myself. However my spirit is not of that kind. I have never allowed personal feelings to influence what I thought should be done on public grounds; also I am not unappreciative of the services Mackenzie and Gardiner have rendered in the past, nor am I forgetful that when there were difficult places in the government, while others were ready to throw the Government over on account of the issue, they both stood firmly and helped save the administration."

After talking with Mackenzie, the Prime Minister telephoned Paul Martin in New York and told him that he would probably be shifted to Health and Welfare. "He replied at once: Mr. King anything that you wish will be all right as far as I am concerned. I will appreciate whatever you do. Will send you word by telegram at once to give you a free hand in reorganization. He could not have been readier or pleasanter. Of course it really is a much better post for Paul Martin than Secretary of State though in the moment's conversation there was not even time for him to consider that aspect. I then went to the East Block. When I arrived there [Gordon] Robertson handed me a communication. I said to myself I am sure this is from Attlee to say he is agreeable to giving Mackenzie and Gardiner P.C.s. Sure enough that is what it was when I opened it."

Mackenzie King then sent for St. Laurent and told him about his conversation with Mackenzie. "Then showed him Attlee's message. I told him I was quite certain if I told Mackenzie of the message he would at once say he would be glad to take the Secretary of State. I said, however, I would not do that. I thought I ought to hold to my idea of having Gibson take Secretary of State. St. Laurent thought Gibson might not like it and that he would have no feeling if sent to Veterans Affairs. I said my idea was that when Mackenzie went out of Veterans Affairs I should appoint Tucker

[M.P. for Rosthern] to that position. He was best qualified. St. Laurent said he thought Tucker's preference was for the leadership in the Province. I said I doubted that; I thought he had accepted it wholly as a duty, had done good service; anyone could be found to take the leadership in the Province. His work would be all to the good and as a Federal Minister he could continue on helping both the provincial and federal there.

"St. Laurent subsequently said it might be better not to fill Veterans Affairs until Tucker came down. That was my own view and I felt it would be better to leave the matter that way. I have a feeling that Mackenzie is so completely breaking up that it will become apparent he can no longer carry on in any portfolio, certainly not in Veterans Affairs, and that once he was made Imperial P.C. it may be possible for him to step down, without injuring too greatly any of his Highland pride. It is a pity he has not been feeling equally strongly of Highland honour in his own individual life. I pointed out how different Martin's attitude had been."

After his talk with St. Laurent and the decision to keep Mackenzie in Veterans Affairs, Mackenzie King summoned Gibson, outlined the proposed changes in the ministry, and told him that he would become Secretary of State. "I saw at once an expression of intense relief come over Gibson's face. Obviously he had been worrying about where he might have to go; perhaps he had in mind possibility of returning to Revenue but the Secretary of State would make an appeal to him as an easy position and one having a certain social dignity about it which he could enjoy. However, he was very pleasant about it."

With these chores out of the way, the Prime Minister decided that the three additional changes would be announced later that day rather than on December 13 as he had originally intended. "It would be better. Would prevent further speculation in the press and would free one's mind at once.

"I then sent for Heeney and asked him to 'phone the Governor General's Secretary and say I would like to have the two Ministers sworn in this afternoon and that a third would be sworn in when he got back from New York. I told Heeney then to get the Orders ready."

Before going into the Cabinet meeting that afternoon, Mackenzie King had a talk with Gardiner, reviewed the controversy earlier in the year about the appointment of Ilsley and St. Laurent, and told him that Attlee had agreed to recommend his and Mackenzie's appointment to the United Kingdom Privy Council. "Gardiner said he wished it could have been given to him before having fed the British people. I replied that if that were stated, some of the people of Canada might think now he had gone perhaps a little far, making special contracts in Britain, with the difficult situations to be faced here. However I did not think there would be anything specified. It was simply for the services and it gave me much pleasure to know that this honour was coming to him. He expressed his thanks in not any too appreciative a way. He has got into a sort of surly and dogged mood; has little of graciousness in any of his acts. I told him to say nothing of the matter to anyone. I then told him what I was proposing in regard to transfers in the Government. He said he thought what I was suggesting was right.

"Howe, by the way, has not been in the Cabinet the last couple of days so I can easily let him know why it has not been possible to consult him in any way at this time. I did not think it necessary to consult with Ilsley."

In Cabinet, the Prime Minister informed his colleagues of the changes. "There was no discussion; indeed there was no opportunity or inclination for it. All was accepted in the friendliest way. I had sent a little note to Claxton who got the first word at the table that he would be sworn in tonight.

"I then mentioned that I had called in the press and would be glad to have the two Ministers who had taken new portfolios present.

"At 5, I sent word to the press. They were present at 6. I had Claxton and Gibson on either side. I then told the press of the changes and of Ministers being sworn in later. Did not let conversation run on too long and, as I saw there was time to get down to Government House before having Duncan Ross to dinner, I arranged to drive them and have Claxton accompany me. Gibson went down I think in his own car or with Heeney.

"The swearing in ceremony did not take long at Government House."

On December 13 Mackenzie King "was interested in seeing what messages might come from Martin and Mackenzie. From Martin, came an exceedingly well-worded telegram giving me a complete free hand in the reorganization of the Government. H. brought in a message that had been 'phoned to him by Senior [Mackenzie's assistant]. . . . I did not think that Mackenzie would go far in his message to me, knowing that if he did I might very soon see that he received no Privy Councillorship. I was therefore not surprised, though very pleasantly relieved, at the message which came and which stated that he had felt at first my message to him might be considered by the veterans as not being fair to them and what he had done for them, but stating that on consideration he regarded the Secretary of State post as a senior position. I had mentioned to him it had so been viewed by different administrations. He mentioned, of course, that he had asked to be relieved of the Veterans Affairs. He added 'The office of Secretary of State suggested by you today is a senior position in the Cabinet and with your recommendation to the Crown, I would be prepared to accept. Kindest regards.'

"This 'with your recommendation to the Crown,' I could see had reference to the P.C. though so worded as not to make it all too evident. Of course it was what I myself had in mind. I took care not to 'phone Mackenzie till he could see the announcement in the paper of the Secretary of State's position being filled by Gibson. I 'phoned him around 11. Said that he would see by the papers that following our conversation of yesterday, I had not done anything further with respect to his position but had appointed Gibson as Secretary of State. Then mentioned that had been done after our talk in the afternoon. That I had not received his message until this morning. I understood it came in about 11 last night. I said to him, however, that was not my purpose in ringing up at the moment. I wanted to tell him that, after our conversation, I had received a cable from Attlee asking if I would ascertain if he would be prepared to have him, Attlee, recommend him to the King for a P.C. in the New Year. That while I assumed he would accept, I wished to get a definite word from himself. His voice changed in his tone instantly and he said he was most grateful to me. That I had always been so considerate of him. He wanted to thank me very much. Of course he would be only too ready to do whatever I wanted in the matter of government position, etc. Wanted me to feel free to do whatever I liked. I said that all I wished to ascertain at the moment was his acceptance of the P.C. so that I could send word of this at once. I said nothing to him of Gardiner. Could see how immensely relieved he was though I could tell by his voice that he is not in any shape at all. Whether he has been drinking again or not, I cannot say. I personally shall not be surprised if he would break up completely at almost any time. At any rate, all has worked out for the very best.

"What happens now is that I have time to think over what may be best to do as regards a successor to him in Veterans Affairs. If Tucker is agreeable to accepting that position, I would probably find it possible to put him into it, Mackenzie finding it impossible to carry on as a Minister. It will be his own fault that he has not been made Secretary of State and there will be no other portfolio to give him. His action of yesterday may result in his ceasing to be a Minister of the Crown altogether and this because of circumstances for which he himself is wholly responsible. The Secretary of State's position accepted now would have relieved him of much responsibility and as it is, he has determined it with what consequences later on, as the result of his own action will be seen ere long. All of this is an interesting study of men and their behaviour, As Ramsay MacDonald said: 'We have all to make our own roads, and not only our roads, but the homes which we inhabit at the end of our roads.'

"I 'phoned Martin.... I congratulated him and said I thought he would find the new position very much to his liking; thanked him also for his message. He said he hoped the message was what I wanted. He was very pleased. Had read of his appointment in the New York Times of this morning. Was grateful for what I had said. Was most appreciative."

After becoming Minister of Finance on December 10, Abbott had continued the negotiations he had already started on a tax rental agreement with British Columbia. During the afternoon of December 11 Mackenzie King went to his office to meet Premier Hart and Abbott. "Hart looked the picture of happiness itself. An agreement has been reached between the Finance Department and himself on the lines which we discussed earlier and which the Finance Department believe wholly just and equitable. Hart agrees with me that, had the concessions now being made been made when the Conference was first held, the whole business would have gone off amicably. Indeed matters could have been settled at a distinctly less cost to the Dominion. I felt and said at the time that later on the Department would pay for its rigidity. It has pretty nearly cost Ilsley and Clark their lives. Certainly in large part their health. Clark told me that both Drew and Macdonald had been 'phoning him. He had told Drew virtually all about the settlement [with British Columbia] that he had secured. He said Drew seemed to be terribly taken aback and disappointed. He had talked as though Clark had gone back on him. As Hart said, he had never been a party to the scheme that was being planned by Drew and Macdonald to have all the Premiers come and set their own terms and demand another conference. Hart emphasized that Drew was bitterly annoyed as well as disappointed and quite disgruntled. He said that Angus was a changed man. Seemed to be quite different and was now ready to accept what was going to be proposed to him. Hart then said there was no doubt at all that Drew would come in later on. He would probably have his House meet, kick up some sort of a fuss there, but would settle rather than have the job of having double taxation. Hart had told both and had put an arrow into Drew's breast particularly by telling him that he, Hart, had had to think of what double taxation would have meant to his people in B.C.; that he might have pressed for more but felt that the agreement was better than anything which would mean he would have to tax his people on income and corporations in addition to those [taxes] levied by the Dominion."

Somewhat optimistically, the Prime Minister concluded that it "now looks as though by the time our Parliament opens, all provinces will have reached an agreement except Ontario and Quebec. That will put us in a very strong position. However, there is always the possibility of making a slip between the cup and the lip. Getting matters into Abbott's hands is the surest guarantee that a settlement will be reached. Ilsley had got to where members of other governments would not have anything to do with either Clark or himself."

The proposed agreement with British Columbia and the text of another letter to the Premier of Nova Scotia were discussed in Cabinet on December 13. "Ilsley is already greatly improved in health since he went to the Department of Justice," Mackenzie King wrote. "He says he sleeps for the first time all night and for the first time in a long while is not sick from his stomach. I noticed, however, when we began discussing terms and members of Council pointed out certain difficulties he got quite excited and two or three times used the expression: Good God. I said to him on one occasion, which caused people as well as himself to laugh, to remember that he was now Minister of Justice and not of Finance, and later told him that if he kept repeating the expression quoted, we would have to take him from Justice and put him in the ministry. He really has undergone torture in the whole business. I have a feeling that we have now reached the point where both Hart and Macdonald will soon come to terms. The trouble now is with McNair of N.B. who feels the others are getting in some way a better deal than he had. What a mistake a few little changes were not conceded last summer!"

When the terms of the agreement with British Columbia became public, McNair was not the only premier who was upset. Stuart Garson immediately came to Ottawa to protest that the B.C. terms were more favourable than those already accepted by Manitoba. On December 16 Mackenzie King discussed the problem with Abbott. "He told me that Garson had been much upset by the agreement with Hart as likely to cause Manitobans to feel that British Columbia was getting something more than Manitoba. As Abbott points out, the rates of taxes and social services were higher in B.C. than they were in Manitoba at the time the war came on. What we are doing is maintaining the relative level. It was never our intention to try to bring all to a similar level.

"I understand that McNair is quite upset also at the B.C. agreement. The letter to Angus Macdonald had to be re-written. . . . This I got off at noon. The letter was sent by 'plane to be substituted for one in the hands of an officer of the Finance Department today.

"Later I talked with Garson at some length about his coming into the Government. I could see clearly from the way he spoke that he is not at all sure about the wisdom of transferring. He said he had talked to only one person who was the one who might succeed him if he left. He was told that if he left the whole Government would go to pieces; that might perhaps react against us federally later on. He spoke in a nice confidential way about himself not having too much courage or self-confidence. I told him that was natural humility which was all to the good; much better than over-assertion. People liked it better. What was wanted was to establish confidence in character. I told him I could quite understand his feeling about reaching no decision immediately. In any event it would be best to have the whole Dominion-Provincial agreement settled, both in his legislature and in our Parliament, before thinking of any exchange; to keep my suggestion at the back of his mind. He said he was not too sure that he had the qualifications for a leader; that the position of Minister at Ottawa, as against Premier in the Province, would hardly make it advisable for him to come here. I told him that the province was a small affair, but what Canada needed was the best men she could get from all parts. Not to lose sight of the federal arena but to take his time in giving the matter further consideration."

At the Cabinet meeting on December 18, a telegram from McNair was discussed, "in which he now backs out from the agreement he made because B.C. got something better. Colleagues felt the only thing to do was to let matters ride. If provinces begin to back out we shall have to get ahead on the basis of our legislation without agreement. How convincingly this proves the unwisdom of the rigidity of the Finance Department at the time of the conference last year! If the different provinces insist on what they call equality we will never get agreement. There is nothing equal about the provinces themselves in wealth or sources of wealth or opportunity. As I pointed out, B.C. is not only historically but by nature in a better position than all the others."

The Cabinet returned to the subject on December 19. By this time, Macdonald had replied to the Prime Minister's letter, firmly rejecting the latest offer and calling for another full-scale conference, and released his reply to the press. "It is clear that Drew, having spoken in the last couple of nights, and Duplessis having also given interviews within the past day – all re-echoing a demand for another conference – shows they have all been working in concert together.

"I had quite a talk with Abbott, who got off a letter today to Manitoba, Saskatchewan, and N.B., making clear that if they objected to the B.C. agreement we would not go on with it, but would sign with them. It will be known, however, that their objection is responsible for not getting agreement with B.C. . . .

"I told Abbott I thought he ought to have something prepared along the line Macdonald has suggested, setting out exactly what the new offer is and how it stands in relation to all the provinces. I said I thought we should go further and consider, if we could not work out some proposal which, were it to be made public by the Government at the beginning of the new year, would be accepted by all the provinces. I said I was prepared to sink any feelings of personal feeling or other pride, overlook all that Drew and others had said, if I felt that by a step of the kind we would get this bewildering problem out of the realm of contention. He is going to look into that aspect of it. I doubt if Ilsley and St. Laurent would agree to another conference. I myself am quite prepared for it, but I would want to be sure in advance that we are going to succeed. I think I might be able to get that through Macdonald working with Drew, but I am not too sure. Drew's insolence in the last day or two has made thought of any further conference with him almost out of the question. Bracken, too, has been joining in so as to be able to fight on the matter in the House of Commons." Further consideration of the tax rental agreements was postponed to the new year when negotiations resumed on the basis of a modified federal formula.

Mackenzie King greatly enjoyed the messages and tributes he received on his 72nd birthday on December 17. The highlight of the day was "a package that came in from Winston Churchill. It contained one of the souvenir medallions which he had had struck off for his colleagues in the Coalition Government. It was accompanied by a letter mentioning those to whom he was presenting a medallion and making me one of the inner circle that had helped to preserve the world's freedom. He significantly adds to his message: 'For a time.' It was a joy to receive that medallion today. I got off wires to him; also to Attlee and Lord Addison, each of whom sent kindest greetings, and a cable to Frank and Maude Salisbury of thanks for the exceptionally beautiful message received from them today, 'Our affectionate thoughts surround you on this joyous day; may you be greatly blessed in your important work and be spared for many years to the friends who love you – signed Frank and Maude'. As I dictate, my table is covered with telegrams and letters. There has not been time to add a word to the acknowledgments attached to many. I shall have to leave that until morning."

A combination birthday and Christmas gift was an overwhelming Liberal victory in the Richelieu-Verchères by-election. The first word the Prime Minister received on the evening of December 23 was that the Liberals "in some 30 polls . . . had had a majority of over two thousand. During the evening this ran up to over five thousand. Before the results were announced finally it was clear that both the Union des Electeurs (Social Credit people) and the Conservative candidate had lost their deposits.

"I then got into touch with Lachapelle, the organizer. Mr. Edouard Simard who was in Notre Dame Hospital, Montreal, having caught a cold and threatened with pneumonia, and also with Cournoyer, the candidate. I extended congratulations to them all. I was quite delighted with the sound of the voice of the newly elected Member. St. Laurent tells me he was much impressed by him. He really gives promise of being a valuable addition to the House. The results have made me feel very happy and relieved but more annoyed than ever that we should have lost Pontiac and Portage la Prairie. Had we won these and Toronto as well, the Liberal party might have looked forward to completing five years of the present Parliament if they so desired and winning over to its side many of the opposition. Third parties in the House would be certain to disappear if we began getting victories. This happened after the last war and happened time and time again. I would have to make a strong appeal to our party to begin with its work of organization in earnest."

Two issues emerged immediately after Christmas. One was the future of Newfoundland, a subject Mackenzie King had discussed with British officials several times since the end of the war. In December 1945 Attlee had announced that a National Convention would be elected in Newfoundland to make recommendations on alternative forms of government for the colony which would be submitted to the people in a referendum. Debates within the Convention, which was elected in June 1946, were heated and acrimonious, illustrating a deep split between those who favoured a return to responsible government and those who urged that Commission government be continued. Occasional proposals for union with either the United States or Canada made proceedings even more lively. At the Cabinet meeting on December 27, there was "a long discussion on Newfoundland being brought into Confederation. Council generally felt Canada for the present, or even more for the future, would expect us to have Newfoundland made part of the Dominion. Also that the immediate problem was the danger, if we did not keep the way open and encourage the coming in of Newfoundland, that the United States might make an effort to have that Colony join them or perhaps some large American syndicate might get control of the little island, or that the Newfoundland people themselves might seek annexation with the States.

"St. Laurent was quite strong for bringing the island in, believing that if we secure Labrador as part of the Dominion territory in connection with the terms, Canada might come into possession of valuable mineral deposits. These include uranium as well as iron ore. Also timber, etc. He admitted the country would be a liability for some years to come. Its cost way beyond what any revenues would bring.

"Gardiner was strongly for the proposal. Ilsley was perhaps strongest against it as any immediate proposal. The real need for action is that the British Government wish to know what we are likely to do as they propose, if we are ready to take Newfoundland in, to stop assisting the island any further and leave them to themselves. I pointed out that while, in the long run, the objective should be the inclusion of Newfoundland, we had a domestic problem to settle with our own provinces before we began to add another province to the Dominion. I said I thought we should let the British know that, until we were able to settle terms with all our provinces and thereby have some basis on which we could negotiate with respect to bringing in a new province, we could not do other than indicate that we would welcome at the right time the addition of Newfoundland. I pointed out that all the reports we had had from our representatives there had indicated that if we showed an anxiety to bring Newfoundland in, the people there would pull away. I thought we would be better off later on if we waited until they began to feel the need of Confederation to save themselves. I am sure that until we get the Dominion-Provincial matter settled, we would only be adding to our present grief to give to the provinces any cause to complain that they were not getting as good terms as a new province that we were bringing in. I expressed the view that what really should be done was the consolidation of the three maritime provinces into one and to have Newfoundland made a part of that larger whole. Also pointed out that the problem of annexation would not end there. The British Government would wish us later to take in the West Indies and others as a sun-room for the Dominion in the South. I felt that we would have to be pretty cautious about further outlays and expressed the view that I thought we had gone further today in the way of commitments than we would be able to meet. Certainly until we settle the health and welfare matters, we should not go further in anything involving large expenditures by the Federal Government. This seemed to be the general view of Council and External Affairs was told directly to advise accordingly."

A second problem concerned Canada's position in discussions on disarmament and the peaceful uses of atomic energy which, somewhat surprisingly, had come to dominate the proceedings of the UN General Assembly in New York. On December 28 Mackenzie King and St. Laurent met to discuss the role Canada would play in discussion of American attempts to ensure that the "great power" veto would not apply to sanctions imposed by the Security Council for violation of the terms of the Atomic Energy Commission agreement. Canada, which had strongly supported the creation of the AEC, was represented on the Commission by General McNaughton. "Both St. Laurent and I," the Prime Minister reported, "were wholly at one in feeling that Canada should support the American position and that it would be well for Pearson to go to New York to be with McNaughton and others on Monday. He was to let them know that both St. Laurent and myself wished to have the American position supported. As I said to St. Laurent, Canada of all countries concerned had the strongest reason for not allowing information concerning the bomb to be disclosed to Russia, unless she would agree not to apply the veto in the case of herself or some friend of Russia's being responsible for starting a conflict against other countries which might lead to a world war. I pointed out to St. Laurent that I thought there should be no misunderstanding as to what Russia's position should be. Much better to have no agreement at all than one which would admit of subterfuges and interpretations that would fail to effect the real purpose of preserving peace. It would be like building a structural piece on quicksand. What was needed was the solid rock of complete truth and understanding." In a talk with Pearson on January 1, Mackenzie King was "amazed and delighted" to hear that "progress had been made" in the Commission; it left "a different feeling in one's mind and heart" about the United Nations.

The characteristic summing up of the year's activities is missing from the diary for 1946. It had been an extraordinarily busy year but even larger issues, political and personal, loomed ahead for Mackenzie King.

Appendix

CHANGES, MACKENZIE KING MINISTRY
SEPTEMBER 1, 1945 – DECEMBER 12, 1946

December 31, 1945	C. D. Howe ceased to be Minister of *Munitions and Supply* and *Reconstruction* (abolition of the Departments was authorized by law on December 18, 1945)
January 1, 1946	C. D. Howe appointed Minister of *Reconstruction and Supply* (creation of the Department authorized by law on December 18, 1945)
September 3, 1946	Mackenzie King resigned from *External Affairs*
September 4, 1946	Louis S. St. Laurent appointed Secretary of State for *External Affairs*
December 9, 1946	Louis S. St. Laurent resigned as Minister of *Justice and Attorney General*
	J. L. Ilsley resigned as Minister of *Finance and Receiver General*
December 10, 1946	J. L. Ilsley appointed Minister of *Justice and Attorney General*
	Douglas C. Abbott appointed Minister of *Finance and Receiver General*
December 11, 1946	Douglas C. Abbott resigned from *National Defence* and *National Defence for Naval Services*
	Colin Gibson resigned from *National Defence for Air*
	Brooke Claxton resigned from *National Health and Welfare*
	Paul Martin resigned as *Secretary of State of Canada*
December 12, 1946	Colin Gibson appointed *Secretary of State of Canada*
	Brooke Claxton appointed Minister of *National Defence*
	Paul Martin appointed Minister of *National Health and Welfare*

THE MINISTRY, DECEMBER 31, 1946

Prime Minister and President of the Privy Council	W. L. Mackenzie King
Minister of Veterans Affairs	Ian A. Mackenzie
Minister of Justice and Attorney General	J. L. Ilsley
Minister of Reconstruction and Supply	C. D. Howe
Minister of Agriculture	James G. Gardiner
Minister of Trade and Commerce	James A. MacKinnon
Secretary of State of Canada	Colin W. G. Gibson
Secretary of State for External Affairs	Louis S. St. Laurent
Minister of Labour	Humphrey Mitchell
Minister of Public Works	Alphonse Fournier
Postmaster General	Ernest Bertrand
Minister of National Defence	Brooke Claxton
Minister of Mines and Resources	James A. Glen
Solicitor General	Joseph Jean
Minister of Transport	Lionel Chevrier
Minister of National Health and Welfare	Paul Martin
Minister of Finance and Receiver General	Douglas C. Abbott
Minister of National Revenue and Minister of National War Services	J. J. McCann
Minister of Fisheries	H. F. G. Bridges
Minister without Portfolio and Leader of the Government in the Senate	Wishart McL. Robertson

Index

Abbott, Douglas C.: Minister of National Defence, 4–5, 342; Gouzenko affair, 14, 34; relations with WLMK, 103, 202; and Ilsley, 112, 204; on repatriation of Canadian troops, 123, 176; as Acting Minister of Finance, 277, 385–8; and possible Cabinet changes, 372–4, 381; on defence, 368; becomes Minister of Finance, 385–8; Dominion-provincial negotiations, 400–2

Acheson, Dean, Assistant Secretary of State, USA, 37; USA policy on A-bomb and spy inquiry, 39–43, 45, 47, 97; visits Ottawa, 343

Addison, Lord, Secretary of State for Dominion Affairs, 25, 31, 53–4, 271, 403; on Russia, 49–52; meets WLMK, 49–52, 67–8, 82, 92–3, 224–5, 241–3, 245, 250, 287; and Newfoundland, 67, 242; discusses defence, 83, 247–9, 265; honours to Canadians, 105, 118; London Conference (1946), 229; visits Ottawa, 328, 342–3

Africa, and UN, 319

Alaska, 60, 199, 265; highway, 125, 219, 248, 265

Alberta, 55; and federal-provincial negotiations, 375

Alexander, Lady Margaret, 94–5

Alexander, Sir Harold (Viscount Alexander of Tunis), Governor-General, 81–2, 186, 245, 254–5, 362; meets WLMK, 94–5; in Ottawa, 198–9, 354; on USA-UK-Canada federation, 219; opinions on, 240, 243, 251; and Cabinet changes, 336, 390–1, 394; and defence, 365–6, 370

Alexandra Bridge, 190

Algoma Steel Corporation, strike at, 284

Alice, Princess, Countess of Athlone, 68, 94–5; departure ceremonies, 179–80, 187–8; WLMK on, 240

Allied Control Council, 281

American Famine Emergency Committee, 268

Anderson, Major W. A. B., 366

Anderson, Sir John, 58, 82, 97–8

Anglo-Egyptian Treaty (1936), 220

Antigonish-Guysborough (federal riding), 381

Aquitania, 73, 225

Arctic, defence of, 265–6, 356, 368, 370

Argentine, 44, 51

Arlington National Cemetery, 97

Armistice Day (1945), 97

Arsenault, Bona, 21, 275

Atherton, Ray, ambassador of USA to Canada, 19, 36, 38, 42, 268, 335

Athlone, Earl of, 68, 75, 94–5; departure ceremonies, 179–80, 187; returns to England, 240, 245, 255

atomic bomb: object of espionage, 8, 11, 14, 41, 51, 144–5, 147, 282; and the USSR, 17, 19–20, 40, 44, 49, 95, 266, 406; WLMK on, 19–20, 26, 29–30, 47, 55, 58, 91; and Churchill, 19, 59, 236–8; effect on international affairs 26, 57, 96, 219; and Attlee, 43, 57–8, 65–6, 89; use of, 76, 133; discussed at Washington Conference (1945), 80, 83, 98; and Truman, 88; and Eisenhower, 122

atomic energy, 57, 69, 218; and USSR, 46, 52; for war, 70; discussed at Washington Conference (1945), 96–8; and Canada, 405–6

Atomic Energy Commission (USA), 98, 405–6

Attlee, Rt. Hon. Clement, 6, 25, 52, 83, 102, 185, 197, 252–3, 271, 403; espionage and A-bomb policy, 39–43,

50, 55, 58-60, 65-7, 70-1, 75, 80, 89-90; relations with Ernest Bevin, 54, 76; with WLMK, 57-60, 68-74, 82, 89-90, 92-3, 240, 250, 287, 328; and Washington Conference (1945), 68, 88-90, 96-8; and George VI, 77-8; honouring Canadians, 93, 105, 118, 232-3, 235, 245, 255, 390, 395-7, 399; addresses Canadian Parliament, 99; repatriation of Canadian troops, 123, 176; loan negotiations, 160, 172, 175; and India, 188; and London Conference (1946), 202, 217-19, 221, 223-26, 228, 230-1; and Churchill, 234, 241; discusses defence, 247-9, 265, 290-1, 293; Paris Conference, 290-1, 293; Labour party revolt, 367; and Newfoundland, 404
Attlee, Mrs. Clement, 59, 69, 93, 241, 250
Attlee, Felicity, 69
Attlee, Martin, 47-8, 69, 73-4
Australia, 6, 223, 242, 287

Baldwin, Stanley, 69, 73, 267, 353
Balkans, 121-2
Ballantyne, Senator C. C., 21, 352
Banff (Alta.), 120
Bank of Canada, 130, 165, 392; WLMK on, 215, 217; federal-provincial fiscal matters, 376
Bank of England, 241
Barrie (Ont.), 102
Baxter, Beverley, 79
Bayeux, 303-4
Beasley, Rt. Hon. J. A., 249, 252
Beaverbrook, Lord, 64, 251
Belokhvostikov (Russian chargé d'affaires at Ottawa), 139-41, 281
Belokhvostikov, Olga, 13, 141, 180
Bennett, R. B., 253, 287-8, 352
Benning, J. S., arrested as spy, 137
Beny-sur-Mer, 303
Berlin, 25, 81, 296, 306, 316-18; WLMK visits, 313-16
Bernhard of the Netherlands, Prince, 252
Bernières, 302
Bertrand, Ernest, Postmaster General, 5, 27; honours and awards, 112; visit of Léon Blum, 197; Richelieu-Verchères by-election, 378
Bevan, Aneuran, 68
Bevin, Ernest, Foreign Secretary, UK, 31, 80, 82, 246; Canadian spy inquiry, 28, 33, 55, 59, 136, 138, 172; and USSR, 49, 51-2, 54, 57, 87, 297; relations with Churchill, 53, 87; on lend-lease, 56; George VI on, 76, 240; at London Conference (1946), 225-7, 291; and Paris Conference, 287, 306-7, 319-21; Truman on, 361
Bidault, Georges, President of France, 289, 299, 325
Biddle, Mr. Justice (at Nuremberg), 316-17
Blackwell, Leslie E., attorney-general of Ontario, 341
Blair House, 96, 298
Blanchette, J. A., 20
Bland, Charles H., 344
Bloc Populaire, 175, 348
Blum, Léon, former premier of France: visits Ottawa, 196-8; in Paris with WLMK, 295-6
Bonaparte, Napoleon, 326
Borden, Sir Robert, 345
Boyer, Dr. Raymond, arrested as spy, 137
Bracken, John, Conservative party leader, 5, 14, 25, 36, 93, 220, 257, 270, 278, 403; on improvement to national capital, 15; and the spy inquiry, 138-9, 153-4; meets Léon Blum, 197; on price controls, 201; at opening of UN General Assembly, 357-9
Bracken House, 349
Brand (British loan negotiator), 166, 170
Braun, Eva, 313-14
Bretteville-sur-Laize, 300
Briand, Aristide, 289
Briand-Kellogg Pact, 289
Bridges, H. F. G., Minister of Fisheries, 5, 112; and possible Cabinet changes, 374
Brighton, 54, 55
British Columbia, 55; and Alaska, 125; and federal-provincial negotiations, 375, 384-8, 390, 401
British Commonwealth Air Training Plan, Britain's indebtedness for, 167, 171-2, 174
British loan negotiations: Cabinet discusses, 160, 163-9, 172-4; British proposals, 161-2, 164-5; WLMK on, 162, 164-7, 171-2, 175; agreement, 174, 189
British Museum, 17
Brockington, L. W., 120, 334

Index 411

Bronson, Fred, 334
Brooke, Sir Alan, 94, 366
Brown, D. C., 249
Bruce, Stanley M., 252
Buckingham Palace, 75, 84, 239, 322
Bush, Dr. Vannevar, 98
Butter, R. A., 54
Byng, Lord, 94–5, 274
Byrnes, James, Secretary of State, USA, 96, 234, 351; intermediary for Truman on spy inquiry, 13, 15, 19, 28, 33, 59, 60, 80, 97, 136, 146, 150; peace negotiations, 44, 52, 54, 245; Paris Conference, 293, 296–8; USA-UK defence agreements, 320–1; Wallace crisis, 343–4; UN General Assembly, 358; Truman on, 361

Cabinet (federal), 4, 34, 36, 159, 219, 280, 322, 328, 347; composition, 5, 350; on rationing, 20; wheat, 22, 262–4; and indemnity for M.P.s, 34, 37; Attlee meets, 99; jealousies within, 105–9, 111–15, 118, 238–9, 246; discusses honours and awards, 112–13, 116, 119, 231–3, 238–9, 254, 390, 397; and repatriation of Canadian troops, 123, 176; Dominion-Provincial negotiations, 127–31, 203–4, 206, 208, 215–16, 276–7, 376–8, 385–6; learns of Gouzenko affair, 135–7, 149, 151; discusses British loan application, 160, 163–9, 172–4; changes in, 177–8, 371–4, 383, 390, 392–6, 398; national capital improvements, 189; labour relations, 195–6, 356; steel strike, 284–6, 340–1; Liberal caucus, 200; price controls, 200–3, 273–4; 1946 budget, 260; national defence, 264–5, 356–7, 366–9; flag debate, 274–6; on Paris Conference, 284–6, 340–1; changes in External Affairs, 334; and by-elections, 348–9, 380–2; WLMK's relations with, 324, 330; proposals on Newfoundland, 404–5
Cadogan, Sir Alexander, 15, 33, 38–9, 80
Caen, 299, 301–2, 305
Calcutta, riots in, 315
Calgary (Alta.), 134
Canada at Britain's Side, 182
Canada House (London), 274–6
Canada Medal, 116, 119

Canadian Broadcasting Corporation, 28, 34
Canadian Club (Ottawa): Eisenhower at, 120
Canadian Congress of Labour: brief to Cabinet (April 5, 1946), 195–6; and steel strikes, 284, 338–9, 342; and Communists, 340
Canadian National Railways, 386
Canadian Pacific Railway, 118; British securities in, 160
Canadian Press, 73, 329
Canterbury, Eng., 243
Cardin, P. J. A., 350, 378
Carnegie, R. K., 329
Carnegie Corporation, 192
Carr, Sam: spy suspect, 80, 152, 157; arrested, 284
Castonguay, N. J. V., 380
Central Mortgage and Housing Corporation, 192
Chamberlain, Neville, 315
Chamberlain, Mrs. Neville, 65, 88–9, 250
Château Frontenac, 388
Chaudière, Regiment de la, 302
Chequers, 48, 59, 73
Chevrier, Lionel, Minister of Transport, 4, 5, 107, 285; and steel strike, 340; by-elections, 348
Chiefs of Staff (British), 92, 223
Chifley, J. B., Prime Minister of Australia, 223
China, 23; WLMK on, 29, 163, 307; Canadian loans to, 160
Chicago, University of, WLMK at, 345
Chisholm, Sir J. A., 110
Churchill, Clementine (Mrs. Winston), 84, 183, 186
Churchill, Mary, 74, 84
Churchill, Randolph, 84, 183
Churchill, Rt. Hon. Winston, 73, 78, 171, 197, 240, 246, 249, 253–4; on Russia and A-bomb, 19, 59, 85–7, 307; election defeat, 48, 53–4, 76; and Bevin, 56; relations with WLMK, 79, 83–8, 185–6, 234–8, 250, 403; and the Commonwealth, 92, 234, 241; and Eisenhower, 121–2; his "Iron Curtain" speech at Fulton, Missouri, 87, 150, 180–6, 234, 268; WLMK on, 218, 252; and post-war world, 234–8; and George VI, 255; and Eden, 267–8; at Quebec, 274
Citizen (Ottawa), 393

Clarendon, Earl of, 250
Clark, W. C., Deputy Minister of Finance, 111; federal adviser at Dominion-Provincial Conference, 124–5, 128–9, 131–2; and subsequent negotiations, 203–4, 207, 209–10, 212, 216–17, 276–7, 375–7, 382–4, 387, 400–1; British loan negotiations, 160, 162, 165, 168, 170, 172–4; relations with Ilsley, 191–2, 260–1; on prices, 272, 274
Claxton, Brooke, Minister of National Health and Welfare, 4, 5, 16, 27, 349; relations with WLMK, 103, 202; and Ilsley, 109, 112, 384; considered in Cabinet changes, 178, 335, 373–4; Dominion-Provincial negotiations, 206, 210–11, 215–16, 260; accompanies WLMK to Europe, 279–81, 296, 301, 308, 312, 323–4; at Paris Conference, 287, 289, 291, 326, 328; becomes Minister of Defence, 390–1, 393–5, 398
Clay, General Lucius, 315
Clay, Mrs., 315
Cobbold, C. F., 162, 166, 168–70
Coldwell, M. J., CCF leader, 15, 53, 93, 138, 197; WLMK on, 19; in Parliament, 34–6, 99, 257; Eisenhower on, 122; learns of Gouzenko affair, 145–6; arrest of Fred Rose, 153–4; at opening of UN General Assembly, 357–9
Coleman, D'Alton, 353
Commonwealth, 31, 92–3, 126; WLMK on, 163–4, 170, 242, 254; defence of, 181, 249, 256, 364–6; Churchill on, 234
Commonwealth Prime Ministers, Conference of, 202, 223–9, 291; WLMK invited to, 202, 217–19; WLMK on, 217–18, 220–1; Germany-Russia discussed at, 225–6, 228–9; WLMK speaks at, 226–8
Confederation: and Newfoundland, 35, 67
Congo, 54
Connolly, Harold, 382–3
Conroy, Pat, 195–6, 338–42
Conservative party, 5, 22; opposition in Parliament, 15, 20, 328; by-elections, 349, 403; in Ontario, 387
Cooper, Duff, 320
Co-operative Commonwealth Federation (CCF) party, 5, 53, 88, 93, 328; by-elections, 349
Corby (*alias*). *See* Gouzenko
Côté, Philias, 194–5
Council of Foreign Ministers, 6, 25; effect of spy inquiry on, 9, 11, 14, 19; Russians and, 31, 33, 45, 48, 51, 225, 287; deadlocked, 89, 217; convenes Paris Conference (July 1946), 269, 290, 296; New York meeting (Nov. 4, 1946), 327
Council of Nations, 31
Country Club (Ottawa), 352
Cournoyer, G., 379, 403
Courseulles, 302
Craigavon, Lord, 249
Cranborne, Lord, 82, 249
Crankshaw, Sir Eric, 249
Crerar, General H. D. G., Commander, Canadian Army, 13, 81, 180, 302; honours for war service, 116, 230, 235, 244, 254–6; as possible Lieutenant-Governor, 354, 391
Cripps, Sir Stafford, 63, 82, 85
Currie, L. D., 386
Curzon, Lord, 161
Czechoslovakia, 292, 320–1, 326

D-Day, 311
Daily Mail, 249
Dalton, Hugh, 53, 62, 76, 79, 87, 328
Daly, Harold, 391
Davies, J. E. (American ambassador to Russia), 145
Davies, Clement, 79
Davis, Thomas, 269
Defence, Department of, 343; studies Arctic, 356; portfolio offered to Claxton, 393–4
defence, of Canada, 264–7, 356, 362–3
Defence Committee, 356, 364
Defence of Canada Regulations, 14
Democratic party (USA), 343
Dessureault, Senator, J.-M., 338, 388
Désy, Jean, 269
Dexter, Grant, 372–3
Diefenbaker, John, 156
Dieppe: WLMK's speech at, 304, 307–8, 316; visits, 310–13; Canadian memorial at, 312
Dill, Sir John, 97
Dixon, Sir P., 54, 57
Doenitz, Admiral K., 318

Dominion Day: bill to change name, 194–5
Dominion-Provincial Conference, 67, 99–101; Co-ordinating Committee meets Jan. 28–Feb. 1, 1946, 124–33; and April 25–26, 202–8; plenary session April 29–May 3, 208–15; Cabinet review of, 216–17; WLMK on, 260–1; post-mortems, 277, 375–6, 382, 400; demand for recall of, 402
Dominion Steel and Coal Corporation: strike at, 284
Douglas, Sir Sholto, 314–15
Douglas, T. C., Premier of Saskatchewan: Dominion-Provincial Conference, 130, 205, 210–11, 215; and subsequent negotiations, 277, 375–6
Drew, George, Premier of Ontario: Dominion-Provincial Conference, 124–32, 205–16, 261, 375–6, and subsequent negotiations, 383–4, 386, 388; reaction to B.C.'s settlement, 400; demands new conference, 402–3
Dublin, 269, 271
Dunkirk, 251
Dunton, A. D., 28; head of CBC, 34, 37
Duplessis, Maurice, Premier of Quebec: Dominion-Provincial Conference, 124–5, 127, 129, 131, 204–6, 209, 211, 213–16, 375–6; Quebec popularity of, 276; compared to Molotov, 297; demands new federal-provincial conference, 402

Eady, Sir Wilfred, 160–2, 164–71
Earnscliffe, 11, 13, 28, 30, 35, 99, 150, 196, 343, 346
Eaton, R. Y., 354
Eddy paper mill: WLMK tries to remove, 101; fire threatens, 190
Eden, Sir Anthony, 54, 57, 79, 186; Bevin on, 56; George VI on, 77; visits Ottawa, 267
Edmonton, 265, 298
Egypt, 241; British troops and, 220; Churchill on, 235, 251
Eisenhower, Dwight D., 243; visits Ottawa, 119–23
Eisenhower, Mount, 120
Elizabeth, Princess, 75–7, 234, 240, 253
Elizabeth, Queen, of England, 75–7, 234, 239–40, 252, 253
embassies, Canadian, 321–5, 360
Empire Parliamentary Association, 267

Endless Adventure, The, 247
espionage, in Canada, 30; *see also* Gouzenko
Ethiopia, 292
Europe; conditions in, after war, 24–5
Evatt, Herbert V., Australian Minister of Foreign Affairs, 6, 50, 60, 62–3, 67; London conference, 202, 223–6, 228; Paris conference, 290–2
Evening Standard, 88
Exercise Muskox, 265
External Affairs, Department of: spies in, 30; WLMK as minister of, 178, 271; Pearson for, 272; WLMK on, 295; WLMK considers changes in, 330–1; offered to St. Laurent, 333–7; papers to, 344; Claxton and, 394–5; and Newfoundland, 405

Fafard, Senator J. F., 388
Falaise, 301, 305–6
Fauteux, Gerald, 135, 141, 148, 197
Federal Bureau of Investigation, 11–13, 15, 134
Federal District Commission, 189
Federal Labour Board, 356
Feiling, Keith, 88–9
Fielding, W. S., 193
Finance, Department of, 381, 392; and Dominion-Provincial negotiations, 375–6, 384–5; Abbott becomes Minister of, 400–2
Financial Post, 265
Fines, C. M., 375, 377
flag, Canadian: WLMK on, 7, 15, 27; maple leaf for, 104, 274–6; at Beny-sur-Mer, 303
Flushing Meadows, 357, 360
Foch, Marshal, WLMK's speech on, 119
Ford Motor Company, 21, 339
foreign exchange, 273–4
Fort William, 259
Forum Club (Montreal), 156
Fosberry, Ernest G., 391
Foulkes, General C., 176, 342, 366
Fournier, Alphonse, Minister of Public Works, 5; Pontiac by-election, 274, 348
Fournier, Mme, 179
France: Duke of Windsor in, 77–8; conditions in, 197; embassy in Ottawa, 197; and coal, 315, 320; elections in, 367
Frankham, Roger, 345

Fulton (Mo.), 268; Churchill's speech at, 87, 181, 183, 234, 268

Gardiner, Edwin, 37
Gardiner, J. G., Minister of Agriculture, 37, 156, 222, 265, 278, 349; on food situation in Europe, 159; British loan, 163–4, 174; WLMK on, 193; price controls, 200–1; relations with Ian Mackenzie, 238–9, 245, 399; wheat agreement with UK, 263–4; Dominion-Provincial negotiations, 260, 377; in Europe, 308, 328; possible Cabinet changes, 371, 372; rationing, 374–5; appointed Imperial Privy Councillor, 390, 396–7, 389; on Newfoundland, 404
Gardiner, Wilfrid, 377
Garson, Stuart S., Premier of Manitoba: at Dominion-Provincial Conference, 125, 130, 209, 215; as possible federal minister, 221, 372, 377, 401–2; federal-provincial negotiations, 376, 401
Gaulle, General Charles de, 196–7, 302–3
Geneva, 61, 271–2, 289, 292, 313
George VI, King of England, 179, 188, 198, 245, 247, 252–3, 271; WLMK at Buckingham Palace, 75–8, 239–41, 253–5; honours Massey, 230–4; Victory Day celebrations, 252–3
Geographic Board, 120
Georgic, 287
Germany, 142; in World War II, 19, 121, 269, 310, 321; WLMK plans to visit, 25; Russian occupation of, 49, 315; and League of Nations, 57; conditions in, 81, 225, 228–9, 315, 320; Leahy on, 133; WLMK on, 135; Canadian troops in, 176; Churchill on, 183, 241; East Germany, 225, 228; settlement with, 226, 228–9; Russians in, 316
Gibson, Colin W. G., Minister of National Defence for Air, 5, 119, 184, 187, 247; repatriation of Canadian troops, 176; in England with WLMK, 287; by-elections, 348; and RCAF, 357; and defence, 368; possible Cabinet changes, 373–4, 393–4; and combined services, 390; becomes Secretary of State, 178, 396–9
Gibson, F. W., 344–5
Gibson, James, 3, 247, 272

Glen, James A., Minister of Mines and Resources, 5, 112, 120
Glengarry (constituency), 32
Godbout, Adelard, Quebec Liberal leader, 27; Pontiac by-election defeat, 348; speaks on St. Laurent, 388–9
Goebbels, Paul Josef, 313
Goering, Hermann, 313–14; at Nuremberg, 317–19
Golding, W. H., 20, 259
Gooch, Mrs. (cook, Laurier House), 358
Goose Bay (Nfld.), 362, 366
Gordon, Donald, 204, 392; and prices, 200, 272–4, 374–5
Gort, Viscount, 251
Gousev, Fedor T., Russian Ambassador in London, 70, 90–1, 141
Gouzenko, Igor: Russian embassy seeks, 13; reveals espionage network, 14, 16–17, 38, 41, 140, 154, 239, 242; RCMP conceal, 18; Truman learns of, 40; arrests demanded because of, 42, 65, 74–5; WLMK on the defection of, 34, 143–6; public learns of, 133–6, 147–8; commission hears evidence of, 135–8; WLMK meets, 282–3
Government House, 11, 94, 179, 204, 243, 390, 398
Grand Central Station, 35
Gray's Inn, 288, 330
Graydon, Gordon, Conservative House Leader, 178, 189, 220
Greber, Jacques, 45, 189
Greece, 236
"Green Book" Proposals, 124
Greene, Kenneth, 334, 391
Greenland, 266, 362
Greenwood, Viscount, 59, 244, 249, 288
Grey, Edward, 41
Grey, the Earl, 187
Gusev. *See* Gousev

Haig, J. T., 21; at opening of UN General Assembly, 357
Halifax, 225, 257, 332, 386; by-election, 380–2
Halifax, Lord, British Ambassador in Washington, 78; and Gouzenko affair, 39, 47; atomic bomb, 70, 80; and WLMK, 96, 244; and Churchill, 186
Halton, Matthew, 300
Hamilton, 338
Handy, J. E.: and WLMK, 3, 151, 184,

Index

247, 345, 338–9; in Paris with WLMK, 287, 289, 325–6; and Heeney, 331
Harriman, Averill, Ambassador of USA in London, 244–5; appointed Secretary of Commerce, 344
Harris, Walter, 274–5
Hart, John, Premier of British Columbia: at Dominion-Provincial Conference, 130, 205, 210, 213; federal-provincial negotiations, 384–8; agreement, 400–1
Harvard Club, 45
Harvard University, 344–5
Health and Welfare, Dept. of, 393–6
Heeney, Arnold, Clerk of the Privy Council, 4, 187, 239, 336, 397–8; flag debate, 7; and Gouzenko affair, 14; and Ian Mackenzie, 113; relations with WLMK, 142, 329–32, 334; Paris Conference, 270–2, 281, 287, 289, 323
Hepburn, Mitchell F., Ontario Liberal leader, 384, 386, 390; WLMK on, 22
Hess, Rudolf, 317–18
Hindenburg Palace, 314
Hirohito, Emperor of Japan, 44
Hitler, Adolf: and World War II, 34, 49, 52, 184; George VI on, 77; Drew Pearson on, 144; Duplessis compares govt. with, 209; Bevin on, 225; Churchill on, 236–7; WLMK on, 297, 311, 317; and Berlin, 313–14, 319
Hofmeyr, Jan H., 63, 113; appointed Imperial Privy Councillor, 93
Hollywood, 77
Holmes, S. L., 217
Hoover, Herbert, 268
Howe, C. D., Minister of Munitions and of Reconstruction, 4, 5, 103, 189, 398; and Gouzenko affair, 14, 34, 136; meets trade union delegates, 16; on wheat, 23; on tax deductions, 27; WLMK on, 32, 328–9; and atomic bomb, 91; relations with WLMK, 105–9, 111, 113–19; housing, 110, 192; Dominion-Provincial negotiations, 127, 132, 207, 209–10, 214; loan to Britain, 160; appointed Imperial Privy Councillor, 230, 232, 238–9, 245–6, 260; Dominion-Provincial conference, 260; on prices, 273; and St. Laurent, 280; and steel strikes, 284–5, 340–1; by-elections, 349; and possible Cabinet changes, 372; as successor to WLMK, 379–80

Hudd, F., acting Canadian High Commissioner in London, 231; and WLMK in London, 82–3, 249–50; and recognition for Massey, 230–1; proposed as Deputy High Commissioner, 334
Hull, 101, 189–90
Hull, Cordell, 44–5, 360
Hungary, 326
Huron-Perth (constituency), 259

I Chose Freedom, 282, 307
Iceland, 362
Ile de France, 225
Ilsley, J. L., Minister of Finance, 4, 5, 7, 218, 231, 280, 398; Gouzenko affair, 14, 149; on wheat, 21, 23, 263; indemnity for MPs, 25, 31, 34, 37; as acting Prime Minister, 26–7, 99, 221–2, 239, 260, 278; relations with WLMK, 31–2, 109–12, 116–17; becomes Imperial Privy Councillor, 93, 104–8, 113, 118, 189, 230, 397; British loan negotiations, 25, 160, 163–5, 167–8, 170–5; Dominion-Provincial negotiations, 125–9, 131–2, 203–12, 214–17, 260, 276–7, 375–7, 400, 403; and World Bank offer, 190–4; on US domination, 191–4; price controls, 200–1, 272–4, 374; budget, 260–2, 277; strikes, 284, 329; his health, 277–9, 371, 401; tours Europe, 294, 313, 323, 328; wishes to resign portfolio, 371–2, 380–2, 384; on political situation in Nova Scotia, 380–3, 385; becomes Minister of Justice, 388, 390, 392; on Newfoundland, 404
Imperial Conference (1923), 161
Imperial Council of Defence, 92
Income Tax Act: amendments to, 111
indemnities for MPs, 25, 31, 37, 102
India, independence for, 188, 217; Churchill on, 235, 241, 251; at Paris conference, 290; Calcutta riots, 315
India, 188, 217, 241; independence for, 235; Churchill on, 251; at Paris conference, 290; Calcutta riots, 315
Industrial Disputes Investigation Act, 355–6
Industrial Relations Committee, 339; strike inquiry, 285
Industry and Humanity, 7, 46, 69, 185, 195, 285, 294
Inns of Court, 288
Intelligence service: British, 10, 14, 80; Canadian, 366

International Bank for Reconstruction and Development, 190-1, 193-4, 392
International Joint Commission, 185, 390
International Labour Conference, 51
Iran, 150, 217
Iraq, King of, 252
Ireland, 94, 217; Northern Ireland, 249
Ismay, Major-General Sir Hastings, 248, 251; discusses defence with WLMK, 247, 265
Isnor, Gordon B., 372, 382
Italy, 19, 25, 57, 244, 293, 306, 311; elections in, 367

Jackson, C. S. (trade union official), 16
Jamaica, 176-7
Japan, 3, 19, 34, 41, 44, 57, 133, 142, 251
Jean, Joseph, Solicitor General, 5, 112, 348
Johnston, Alec, 383
Joint Chiefs of Staff, 87
Joint Defence Board, 181-2, 219, 248, 370; on Arctic defence, 265-6; on UK-Canada defence planning, 367-8
Jones, Walter, Premier of PEI; Dominion-Provincial Conference, 210, 213
Journal (Ottawa), 99, 383
Jowitt, Sir William, 249-50
Juliana, Princess, 252
Justice, Dept. of, 333, 381

Kaltenbrunner, General, 317
Keenleyside, Hugh, Canadian Ambassador to Mexico, 133; at opening of UN General Assembly, 357
Keitel, General Wilhelm, 318
Kellock, R. L., Commissioner to look into Gouzenko affair, 135, 141, 151
Kenora–Rainy River (constituency): by-election in, 274
Keynes, J. M., 194, 203
Kilbourn, F. B., 284
King, Max, 294
King, Rt. Hon. William Lyon Mackenzie: end of the war, 3-5; and the new Parliament, 6-7; Igor Gouzenko defects, 8-14, 16-19, 28-31, 33-4, 38-41, 47-9, 58, 65, 69-70, 74-5, 79-80, 83, 86, 90; discussions with labour representatives, 15-16, 21, 29, 195-6, 201, 284-6, 338-42, 355-6; on wheat, 21-3, 262-4; plans trip to UK, 24, 34; and indemnity for MPs, 27, 31, 35-7; and Newfoundland, 35, 67, 362, 404-5; visits Washington, 37-45; talks with Truman, 37, 39-42, 358, 360-4; and Lord Halifax, 43-4; in England, 47-95, 223-56, 287-8, 328-9; with Attlee, 48, 57-60, 65, 68-73, 83, 89-93, 247-50, 287; and Lord Addison, 49-52, 67-8, 92-3, 224-5, 241-3, 245, 247-50, 287; and Bevin, 54-7, 225-7; repatriation of Canadian troops, 72-3, 81, 123, 126, 176-7; and George VI, 75-8, 239-40, 253-5; plans spy arrests, 74-5; relations with Montgomery, 80-2, 198, 254, 342-3; and Churchill, 83-8, 180-3, 185-6, 234-8, 250-2, 254; and Viscount Alexander, 94-5, 198-9; attends Washington conference, 96-8; Dominion-provincial negotiations, 99-100, 124-33, 202-17, 260-1, 375-6; rationing, 100-1, 374-5; tariffs, 101-2; Canadian flag, 104, 274-6, 337; Cabinet problems, 105-11, 113-18, 245-6; reconstruction, 106; Gouzenko affair, action in, 133-41, 145-58, 181, 199, 237, 239; Parliament and spy inquiry, 153-7; British loan negotiations, 159-75; Churchill's "Iron Curtain" speech, 180-86; improvements to national capital, 189-90; advice to Ilsley, 190-4; housing crisis, 193; and price policy, 21-3, 200-2, 272-4, 374-5; London Conference, 202, 217-21, 223-56; discusses UK–Canada exchange of military information, 247-9; Victory Day celebrations, 250, 252-3; decides not to run for re-election, 258-9, 337, 380; 1946 budget, 260-2; and national defence, 264-7, 320, 356-7, 362-70, 394; Gouzenko affair, conclusion of, 281-4, 307; appointed Bencher of Gray's Inn, 288, 330; Paris Conference, 289-94, 296-7, 319-20, 323-4, 326; and Bevin, 306-7, 319-21; visits Dieppe, 308-13; Berlin, 306, 313-16; Nuremberg, 306, 316-19; Cabinet changes, 330-1, 333-7, 387-8, 390, 392-400; by-elections, 348-51, 363, 373-4, 378-83, 403-4; federal-provincial fiscal problems, 375-8, 381-4; at opening of UN General Assembly, 357-8; meets John D. Rockefeller, 358-60; returns to Ottawa, 364

Index

—OPINIONS ON:
Communists in Canada, 16, 19, 29, 340; atomic bomb, 19–20, 29–30, 47, 58, 91, 96, 98; Conservative party, 22, 25, 88, 112, 349; Liberal party, 27, 157, 199, 374, 390; C.C.F., 88; health and welfare, 132; communism, 30, 132, 164, 172, 227, 367; the UN, 31, 46, 61–2, 163, 319, 358; Japan, 44; socialism, 112, 122; Russia, 46, 49–53, 55, 57, 133, 143–4, 146, 148, 163, 184, 224, 227, 298; USA, 56, 142–3; defence, 92, 248–9, 256, 266; Germany, 228, 313–19; France, 288, 299–306, 309–13
—Canada and Russia, 60, 71–2, 133, 136, 143, 155, 163, 256; Canada and USA, 60, 72, 133, 143, 155, 163, 219, 242, 248–9; Commonwealth Air Training Plan, 171; Canada and Britain, 171–2, 202, 220–1
—Abbott, 112, 202, 374; Attlee, 77, 95, 253; Léon Blum, 197–8, 296; Bracken, 25; Claxton, 112, 202, 373–4; Duplessis, 211, 214, 297; Eisenhower, 120–23; Gardiner, 193, 372, 396, 398; Garson, 402; George VI, 78–9; Gouzenko, 146, 283; Howe, 32, 108–9, 116, 328, 379; Ilsley, 31–2, 93, 109, 116, 129, 192–3, 207, 277; Angus Macdonald, 383–4; Ian Mackenzie, 104–5, 109, 111, 114–17, 246, 390, 396–7; McNaughton, 394; Paul Martin, 374, 397; Vincent Massey, 233–4, 354; Molotov, 50, 298; Pearson, 332, 372; Pickersgill, 333; Norman Robertson, 270–1; St. Laurent, 32, 93, 109, 112, 167, 193, 328, 332, 351, 373, 390; Towers, 165; Truman, 363; Vanier, 325
—PUBLIC SPEECHES:
Liberal caucus (Sept. 12, 1945), 20; Quebec Liberals (Sept. 19, 1945), 26; members of British Cabinet (Oct. 24, 1945), 82–3; in praise of Eisenhower (Jan. 10, 1946), 120; public statement on Gouzenko affair (Feb. 15, 1946), 141–2; in House of Commons on spy inquiry (March 18, 1946), 154–5, 157; on departure of Lord Athlone (March 18, 1946), 179–80; Liberal caucus (March 20, 1946), 188–9; at 10 Downing Street (June 7, 1946), 249–50, 254; to House of Commons (June 17, 1946), 257–8; to Liberal caucus on his retirement (June 21, 1946), 259; at Paris Conference (Aug. 2, 1946), 293–4; in Normandy (Aug. 10–11, 1946), 301–2, 303–4; at Dieppe (Aug. 19, 1946), 308, 311–12; press conference (Sept. 4, 1946), 337; at dinner for St. Laurent (Nov. 29, 1946), 388–90; at Rideau Club (Dec. 9, 1946), 391–2
—PERSONAL:
intuition, 8; piety, 88, 163, 236, 250, 258, 318, 348; loneliness, 63; portrait, 64–5, 82, 288, 346–7, 358, 360; retirement, 15, 21, 258–9, 352; health, 23–4, 60, 76, 109, 297, 337, 352; memoirs and private effects, 133, 257, 344–7; career, 184–5, 258; family life, 184, 342; and Louis Pasteur, 325–6

Kingsmere, 12–13, 26, 99, 199, 269, 296, 333, 342, 351; disposition of, 344, 346–7
Kirk, J. R., 381
Komura, J., Count, 41
Krotov, Ivan I., 90
Kuriles Islands, 29, 60, 307

Labelle (constituency), 259
labour, relations with, 21, 29, 195–6, 284–6, 338–42, 355–6
Labour, Dept. of, 16, 345, 355; meets steel unions, 338
Labour Ministers, conference of, 356
Labour party (UK), 69
Labour-Progressive party, 152
Labrador, 248, 362, 404
Lachapelle, M. (Liberal organizer), 378–80, 403
LaCroix, W., 275
La Guardia, Fiorello, 272, 280
Lalonde, M., 259
Lambert, N. P., 264, 383
Lanctot, Gustav; and WLMK's papers, 344–6
Lapointe, Hugues, 259
Lapointe, Ernest, 351
Larkin, P., 343
Lascelles, Sir Alan, 198, 249; and Massey, 230–1; and Gouzenko affair, 242; and WLMK, 250; on honouring McNaughton, 253–5
Laurier House, 11, 13, 26, 34, 36, 99, 104, 109, 114, 123, 133, 177, 196, 199, 200, 252, 343, 345, 351–2, 382,

391, 393; WLMK and provincial premiers at, 126; as gift to nation, 298, 344, 346–7
Laurier, Sir Wilfrid: WLMK on, 26, 167, 170, 186, 189, 191, 257, 336, 346, 350, 391
Lawson, Ray, Lt.-Governor of Ontario, 355, 391
Lay, H. M., 102
Leader, Harry, 349; death of, 221
League of Nations, 57, 183, 319; WLMK on, 31
Leahy, Admiral, 96–7, 234; visits Ottawa, 133
Legal and Drafting Commission (Paris Conference), 326
Lend Lease, 159
Liberal party, 53, 156–7; by-elections, 348–9, 403; in Nova Scotia, 387; in Ontario, 387; St. Laurent on, 389; WLMK on, 390
Lie, Trygve, UN Secretary-General, 357
Life of Christ, 243
Life of Pasteur, 294
Light, Heat and Power Company (Quebec), 204
Lincoln, Abraham, 211
Lives of a Thousand Irishmen, 342
loans, by Canada; *see* British loan negotiations
London, 17–18, 57, 271–2, 275–6, 330, 334–5
London Conference; *see* Commonwealth Prime Ministers, Conference of
Lotbinière (constituency), 259
Low, Solon, 34–5, 99
Ludwig, Emil, 315, 344; biographer of WLMK, 44
Lunan, Captain Gordon, arrested as spy, 137
Luxembourg Palace, 292
Lybia, 324
Lyttelton, Oliver, 79

McArthur, General Douglas, 251
McCann, J. J., Minister of National Revenue, 5, 348; possible Cabinet changes, 107, 393; on honours and awards, 112; federal-provincial negotiations, 129, price controls, 274; steel strike, 340
McConnell, J. W., 177; WLMK visits, 351–4
Macdonald, Angus L., Premier of Nova Scotia: Dominion-Provincial Conference, 129–30, 206, 208–9, 211, 215, 376; and subsequent negotiations, 276, 381–6, 388, 402–3; reaction to B.C. settlements, 400–1
Macdonald, Gordon, Governor of Newfoundland, 242
Macdonald, Sir John A., 247, 249, 257, 344, 346, 350, 391
MacDonald, Malcolm, British High Commissioner in Ottawa, 224; spy inquiry, 13–14, 29, 31, 43, 137; Newfoundland, 35; honours to Canadians, 93, 114, 118, repatriation of Canadian troops, 123; British loan negotiations, 161, 166, 168–9, 171–2; departure, 196; marries, 390
MacDonald, Ramsay, 73, 196, 314; quoted, 399
Macdonald, Ross, 36
Macdonald, W. C., 372, 380–1
Macdonnell, J. M., 22
Machtig, Sir Eric, 249
McGill University: spies and A-bomb research at, 17, 91; Montgomery receives honorary degree, 81, 243; WLMK offered chancellorship, 353–4
McIlraith, George, 107; at opening of UN General Assembly, 357, 359
McInnis, Angus, 35
McIvor, Dan, 259, 263
Mackenzie, Dr. C. J., 13
Mackenzie, Ian, 4, 5, 26, 37, 257, 285, 328; tenders resignation, 104–5, 108–9, 245–6; relations with WLMK, 110–11, 113–16, 119, 230, 238–9, 260, 278–80, 329; St. Laurent's opinion of, 333; to be made Imperial Privy Councillor, 390, 395–6, 398; considered in Cabinet shuffle, 372, 393, 395–9
Mackenzie, M. W., at opening of UN General Assembly, 357
Mackenzie, William Lyon, 143, 179–80, 184, 258, 296, 303, 342
MacKinnon, J. A., Minister of Trade and Commerce, 4, 5; British loan negotiations, 160; budget, 204; wheat policy, 262
Mackintosh, W. A., 124–5, 131, 162
McLarty, Norman, death of, 23
McNair, J. B., Premier of New Brunswick: Dominion-Provincial Conference, 130, 209, 215; reaction to B.C. settlement with federal government, 401–2
Macnamara, Arthur, 340–1, 374

Index

McNaughton, General A. G. L., 76, 105, 116, 394; WLMK on recognition of, 231, 235, 243-4, 253-6; on Atomic Energy Commission, 405
Malaya, 196, 307
Manchuria, 150
Manitoba, 101, 124, 401-2; and federal-provincial negotiations, 375
Manning, Ernest, Premier of Alberta: at Dominion-Provincial Conference, 130, 210-1, 213, 215, 261; and subsequent negotiations, 276, 384, 386, 388
Marlborough House, 68
Marshall, General G. C., 251
Martin, Paul, Secretary of State, 4, 5, 16, 180, 253, 344; and possible Cabinet changes, 178, 373-4; at opening of UN General Assembly, 357-8, 372; becomes Minister of Health and Welfare, 393, 395-6, 399-400; compared to Ian Mackenzie, 397-8
Martin, Mrs. Paul, 180
Martin, Ross, 4, 348
Mary, Queen, of England, 68, 240, 252-3
Massey, Alice, 223, 229, 233-4
Massey, Vincent, Canadian High Commissioner in London, 94; resignation, 177-8; departure from England, 223, 229; awarded CH, 230-4; retirement, 269; as possible lieutenant-governor, 354, 391
Matapedia-Matane (constituency), 194
Matte, Gideon, 4
Matthews, Albert, 354
Mauretania, 328
May, Professor A. N. (*alias* Primrose): spies for Russia, 14, 17-18; 33, 38, 41, 47, 58, 65, 69, 91, 144; plans to arrest, 71, 74; detained, 138-9, 145, 149-50; confesses, 147; arrested, 151; sentenced, 284
Mazaryk, Jan, President of Czechoslovakia: at Paris Conference, 292-3
Mazerall, S. W., arrested as spy, 137
Mediterranean Sea, 319
Meighen, Arthur, 253, 352
Mexico, 283, 394
Miami, 180, 182
MI5. *See* Intelligence service (British)
Millard, Charles, 338-41
Missouri, University of, 87
Mitchell, Humphrey, Minister of Labour, 4, 5, 16, 112, 118; steel strike, 285; WLMK on, 328; and mediation, 338-41; on labour code, 355-6; and possible Cabinet changes, 372-3
Molotov, V. M., 84; behaviour at Council of Foreign Ministers criticized, 33, 48-9, 77; and at San Francisco, 51; WLMK on, 50, 320; and Bevin, 54, 226; and Harriman, 244; and Truman, 361; at Paris Conference, 292, 296-8; opening of UN General Assembly, 337
Montgomery, Field Marshal Sir Bernard, 49, 254, 362, 366; chats with WLMK, 80-2, 243; visit to Canada, 198, 243, 342-3
Montreal, 14, 27, 308
Montreal Gazette, 142, 153
Montreal Research Laboratories, 138
Montreal Star, 177, 351-2
Moran, Lord, 68
Morrison, Herbert, 82, 249-50
Mosher, A. R., President of CLC, 195, 338-9
Mountbatten, Lord, 73
Mulock, Sir William, 64, 177, 336
Mulock, W. P., 180
Mundell, D. M., 135, 141
Munich, 259, 320
Munitions and Supply, Dept. of, 116-18
Munro, Ross, 300, 314
Murphy, E. P., 45, 190
Mussolini, Benito, 145
Mutual Aid Programme, 159, 174

NKVD, 139
Nash, Walter: London Conference, 202, 223, 227, 229; at dinner in WLMK's honour, 245, 249, 252
National Defence, Dept. of, "Exercise Muskox," 265
National Emergency Transitional Powers Act, 355
National Gallery, 346
National Housing Act, 192
National Research Council, 13; arrest of spies in, 137
Navy Island (1838), 303
Neal, W. M., president of the CPR, 118
Nelson, H.M.S., 302
Neurath, Konstantin von, 318
New Brunswick, 402; and federal-provincial negotiations, 375
New York, 35, 45, 134-5, 163, 182, 186, 192, 238, 289, 321, 327, 360, 380, 384, 394, 396-7
New York Times, 400

Newfoundland, 35, 67, 242; US bases for, 362; debates future, 404–5
Nippon Supply Company, 74
Normandy, 315; WLMK visits, 299–306
North Africa, 311
Nova Scotia, 387–8; and federal-provincial negotiations, 375; by-elections in, 382
Nuremberg trials, 316–19, 324, 326

Official Secrets Act, 284
Ogdensburg Agreement, 182, 184
O'Leary, Grattan, 383
Ontario, 400; and federal-provincial negotiations, 375
Ontario Hydro, 204
Ontario Regional Labour Board, 356
Order in Council: invoked to detain spy, 14; and steel strike, 341; labour relations, 355–6
Ottawa, 15–16, 19; WLMK and improvements to, 189–90
Ouimet, Marcel, 300

Pacific Council, 50
Palestine, 56, 89, 217, 354; American attitude to, 287; UK policy toward, 306–7, 321
Paris, 272, 279, 286, 288, 297, 306, 325, 330, 355, 394
Paris Conference (1946): planned, 224–5, 227, 269; preparations for, 270, 272, 279; WLMK on, 280, 308, 337, 361; preliminary discussions, 289–91; opening sessions, 293, 296–7, 301, 306, 311; procedural difficulties, 313, 319–20, 323–4; conclusion, 326–7; Russian manipulation of, 369; Claxton's assessment of, 373
Parker, W. J., 264
Parkman, Sir Francis, 94
Parliament, 3, 6, 24, 34, 325, 330, 400; first meets (Sept. 6, 1945), 7; on wheat, 22; St. Laurent on, 25; debate on Address (Sept. 27), 36; passes UN charter, 68; WLMK on rationing, 101; wartime emergency powers, 101; prorogued, 102, 324, 332; debates spy inquiry, 153–7; vote on British loan agreement, 175; External Affairs Act, 178; Dominion Day bill, 194–5; and price controls, 200–1; 1946 budget debate, 261–2, 285; awaits WLMK's return from Europe, 328; by-election,

348–50; on labour code, 355; and Liberal by-elections, 382; WLMK on, 387; and federal-provincial relations, 403
Parliamentary Association (UK), 53
Pasadena, 61
Pasteur, Louis, 69, 294; WLMK at tomb of, 325–6
Patterson, N. M., 264
Patterson, W. J., 378
Patteson, Mrs. J., 64, 119
Pavlov, Vitali G., 139–41
Peacock, Sir Edward, 241
Pearson, Drew, 134–6, 142, 144
Pearson, Lester B., Canadian ambassador to the USA, 28, 182, 352; WLMK in Washington, 37, 39, 42, 75; and UN, 60, 405–6; suggested as UN Secretary-General, 62, 123–4, 392; at Washington Conference, 96–8; and American reaction to Gouzenko case, 150; future political career of, 177–8, 221, 269–72; and wheat negotiations, 263–4; appointed Under-Secretary of State for External Affairs, 4, 294–5; in Germany, 313; relations with WLMK, 329–32; to Ottawa, 334, 336; WLMK's possible successor, 372
Penn Station, 36
Pétain, Marshal Henri Philippe, 197
Petawawa, 91
Pickersgill, J. W., Special Assistant to WLMK, 4, 210; and Canadian flag, 104; and Howe, 117; and Mount Eisenhower, 120; arrest of Rose, 152; in Fulton, 184; and farewell address for Athlone, 187; and Dominion-Provincial conference, 206; relations with WLMK, 247, 333–5, 389; honouring McNaughton, 256; and WLMK's papers, 344; federal-provincial negotiations, 376
Pitt, William, 224
Pittsburgh (Pa.), 219, 238
Poland, 324
Pontiac (constituency); by-election, 274, 348–9, 404
Pope, Major-General Maurice, 248, 281, 306, 313–14, 327
Popov (Russian military attaché), 134, 137, 140
Portage la Prairie, 211; by-election, 348–9, 373, 404
Potsdam Conference, 17, 54, 81, 226, 267

Power, C. G., 156, 180, 390
price control policy, 200–2, 272–4, 374
Prince Edward Island, 260; and federal-provincial negotiations, 375
Public Archives of Canada, 344–5
Public Secrets Act, 151
Puys, 309–10

Quebec, 26, 387, 390, 400; and federal-provincial negotiations, 375; support of WLMK, 378, 380; WLMK on, 389
Queen Elizabeth, 73, 76
Queen Mary, 45, 47, 68, 74, 80, 222, 225, 239, 241, 256, 329, 332

Raeder, General Erich, 318
Ralston, J. L., 105, 387; WLMK on, 22
Rand, Ivan C., 339
Red Army Day, 145
Red Cross (Canadian), 303
Red Ensign, 7, 27, 104, 274–5
Regina, 138, 378
Regional Labour Board, 339
Reid, Escott, 357
Reid, Thomas, 20
Remembrance Day, 274
Renaud, Vallery, 294
repatriation, of Canadian troops, 72–3, 81, 123, 126, 176–7
Republican party, 344
Ribbentrop, Joachim von, 316–18
Richelieu-Verchères (constituency): by-election, 378–81, 403
Rideau Club (Ottawa), 391–2
Ritchie, Charles, 272
Roberts, General, 312
Robertson, Gordon, 4, 231, 247, 272, 396
Robertson, Norman, Under-Secretary of State for External Affairs, 4, 34, 182, 202, 348; and WLMK, 6, 53; advises WLMK on Gouzenko affair, 7–14, 16–19, 33–4, 38–40, 74–5, 79–80, 83, 134, 136–41, 145–50, 152–3, 281–2; on Communists, 19; WLMK proposes European trip, 24–5; Washington trip planned, 28, 35–6; spy arrests, 32–3; in Washington with WLMK, 37–9, 42, 45; on atomic bomb, 46–7, 51; in England with WLMK, 51–2, 54, 59–60, 62–3, 65–6, 74–5, 79–80, 83, 88–92; mentioned for UN Secretary-General, 62; at Washington Conference (1945), 96–7; on British loan, 162; proposed High Commissioner in London, 177, 269, 271–2; on trade with France, 197; London Conference (1946), 222–4, 230–2, 247, 249–50, 264; appointment as High Commissioner in London, 4, 294–5, 328, 334–6; Paris Conference, 281, 296, 320, 323; accompanies WLMK to Europe, 287, 289; in France with WLMK, 322; relations with WLMK, 329–30, 332; Pickersgill on, 344; in London, 390, 396
Robertson, Sir Brian, 315
Robertson, Wishart McL., Senator and Minister without Portfolio, 5; at opening of UN General Assembly, 357–9, 380; political situations in Nova Scotia, 380, 382–3
Rockefeller, David, 360
Rockefeller, David, Jr., 360
Rockefeller, John D., Jr., 359–60
Rockefeller, John D., Sr., 359
Rockefeller, Nelson, 44, 358–60; offer to WLMK, 191
Rodney, H.M.S., 302
Rogers, Norman, 210, 344
Romulo, General Carlos P., 359
Roosevelt, Eleanor, 357
Roosevelt, President, Franklin Delano, 50, 315; and Russia, 19, 59, 146, 268, 307; portrait of, 39–40, 64; WLMK on, 42, 218; death of, 51; at Yalta, 251; at Quebec, 274
Roosevelt, Theodore, 41, 244
Rose, Fred, 139; a spy, 30, 80; arrest for spying, 152–3; attends debate on spy inquiry, 154; detention of, 188; sentenced, 284
Ross, Duncan, 398
Ross, Frank: threatens to resign, 109, 111, 115; WLMK on, 115–18
Rosthern (constituency), 259
Roumania, 236, 324
Rouyn, 348
Rowan, L. (secretary to Attlee), 66, 89, 97, 233
Rowley, Mrs. John, 196
Royal Canadian Air Force, 77, 176, 265, 357
Royal Canadian Mounted Police, 18, 47, 134; holding of Gouzenko, 10–11
Royal Commission on Espionage, 141, 147–8, 183; first report, 149–51; second report, 152–4; third report, 156–8; final report, 281–4, 307, 320
Royal Military College (Kingston), 198

422 *Index*

Royal Regiment of Canada, 309
Ruhr, 81
Russia. *See* USSR

St. Aubin, 302
St. Jean Baptiste Society, 175
St. Laurent, Louis, Secretary of State for External Affairs, 4, 5, 25–6, 270; the Gouzenko affair, 8, 9, 34, 74, 99, 136–7, 147–8, 151–2, 156–7; made Imperial Privy Councillor, 93, 104–5, 107–8, 113, 118, 189, 230, 397; at UN General Assembly, 111, 126, 357–9, 372, 384; WLMK on, 32, 192; and Ilsley, 112, 191; wants to retire, 103, 106, 395; Dominion-Provincial negotiations, 127–8, 204–5, 209–13, 260, 387–8, 390, 403; British Loan negotiations, 160–4, 166–9, 172–3; on honours and awards, 231–3, 238–9, 245–6, 396; prices, 273; flag debate, 276; labour relations, 285, 355; defence, 369; by-elections, 348, 404; and atomic energy, 405–6; as acting prime minister, 278–80, 328–9, 332; Cabinet changes, 350, 381, 392–3; becomes Minister of External Affairs, 177–8, 333–7; testimonial dinner for, 388–90
St. Laurent, Mme, 358, 389
St. Lawrence Sugar Refinery, 352
St. Paul's Cathedral, 301
Salisbury, Frank, 49, 360; paints WLMK's portrait, 63–5, 80, 82; relations with WLMK, 223, 288, 329–30, 358, 403; visits Ottawa, 346–7; Truman's opinion of, 361
Salisbury, Maude, 223, 329–30, 346–7, 358, 403
Samuel, Sigmund, 354–5
San Francisco, 40, 44, 61, 163, 274, 321
San Francisco Conference, 3, 57, 60, 134, 185, 291, 298; Wrong on, 26; Russia at, 31; Molotov at, 50–1
Sandwell, B. K., 138
Saskatchewan, 55, 402; and federal-provincial negotiations, 375, 377
Savannah (Ga.), 190, 193
Saturday Night, 138
Schacht, H., 318
Scott, Duncan Campbell, 391
Seigniory Club, 10
Selassie, Haile, 292
Sequoia, 97
Seyss-Inquart, Dr., 318

Sicily, campaign in, 311
Simard, Edouard, 350; Richelieu-Verchères by-election, 378–80, 403
Simonds, Lt.-General Guy G., 243
Skelton, A.: studies federal-provincial fiscal matters, 124–5, 129, 131–2, 376; consulted, 204, 209; WLMK critical of, 276
Smith, Arthur, 155, 285
Smith, Durnford, arrested as spy, 137
Smuts, General J. C., 180, 186, 244, 246; WLMK compares himself to, 184, 252; at London conference, 202, 223–5, 228–9; Churchill on, 235; dinner in honour of WLMK, 245, 249, 251; George VI on, 255; Paris conference, 319–20; on Commonwealth defence, 366
Social Credit party, 5; by-elections, 348, 403; in Alberta, 387
Solandt, O. M., 366–7
Soong, T. V., Chinese ambassador to Canada, 23, 25
South Africa, 113, 239, 242
South America, 6, 44, 61
South Pacific, 223
Southeast Asia, 223
Spaak, Paul-Henri, 292; as president of UN General Assembly, 357
Spain, 51
Stacey, Charles, 299, 300
Stalin, Josef, 13, 17, 84, 95, 278; British view of, 48, 50, 52, 59, 226, 242, 267, 320; reputed to be ill, 71, 76–7; Churchill on, 85, 236–7; and WLMK, 143, 155, 218; at Yalta with FDR, 244, 251; Gouzenko on, 283; and Truman, 361
Stalingrad, 311
Star (Toronto), 210
Steel Company of Canada, 340; strike at, 284–5; violence at, 338; settlement, 341–2
Steel Workers Organizing Committee, 284, 338
Stephenson, Sir William, 10–12, 28
Stettinius, Edward, 8, 11, 44, 61–2, 134
Stewart, Charles, 390
Strachey, E. J., British Minister of Food, 262–4
Strang, Sir William, 315
Streicher, Julius, 317–18
Stresemann, G., 289
Study in the Principles Underlying Industrial Reconstruction, 294

Index

Suez Canal, 242
Sunday Times, 71
Switzerland, 40, 269, 272, 280

Tarrytown, 358
Taschereau, R., Commissioner to look into Gouzenko affair, 135, 141
tax agreements, 260-2, 276-7, 375-7, 384-8, 400-3
Teheran Conference, 226
Témiscouata, 162, 259
Tennyson, Alfred Lord, 314
Thornton, Sir H. W., 322
Thorson, J. T., 180
Times, The, 57, 316
Toronto, 102, 140, 181, 338, 347, 386
Toronto, University of, 354; Montgomery at, 243
Toronto-Parkdale (constituency); by-election, 348-9, 373, 404
Towers, Graham, Governor of Bank of Canada, 27, 128; British loan negotiations, 160, 162, 165, 168; relations with Ilsley, 131, 192, 216; World Bank offer, 190, 193-4, 392; on prices, 272; and American-Canadian dollar parity, 273-4
Trans-Canada Airlines, 108, 118
Transitional Powers Act, 355
Truman, President Harry S., 52, 235, 394; Russian espionage and A-bomb policy, 18, 28, 35, 39-42, 46, 50, 55, 58-9, 65-7, 71, 88-9, 134, 138, 237; talks with WLMK, 37, 39-42, 46, 358, 360-4; Washington Conference (1945), 88-9, 96-8; Churchill speaks at Fulton, Missouri, 87, 150, 183, 185-6, 234; commercial policy, 101-2; and famine relief, 268; proposes Ilsley and Towers for World Bank, 193-4; Wallace crisis, 344; opening of UN General Assembly, 357-8, 361; on US-Canada defence, 362-3, 368
Tucker, W. A., 259, 396-7
Turgeon, W. F. A., 60, 269
Turnbull, Walter, 4

Union des Electeurs, 403
Union Jack, 274-5
USSR: embassy in Canada, 5, 8-14, 16-17, 137-9, 144-6, 148-9, 151, 281; espionage network, 11, 16-18, 29-30, 38, 40, 44, 59-60, 66-7, 75, 80, 83, 86, 90, 134-5, 137-8, 143-4, 147, 150, 227, 244, 282; and United Nations, 33, 46; and atomic bomb, 34, 58-9, 90, 95, 266, 406; relations with Western powers, 42, 55; foreign policy of, 49, 52, 54, 85-6, 163, 225-7, 282, 363, 369, 394; influence in Europe, 122; Lord Alexander on, 94; confronted with Gouzenko's evidence, 139, 142; embassy in Washington, 145; acknowledges spying, 148; in Iran, 150; in Manchuria, 150; attacks on WLMK, 151; WLMK on, 155; in Germany, 226, 228-9, 315-16; Gouzenko on, 282-3; and Paris Conference, 290-1, 297, 306, 328; in Far East, 307; and satellites, 320-1; conditions in, 361
United Kingdom: and Gouzenko affair, 8, 12, 28, 33, 38; and wheat, 22-3, 262-4; espionage in, 30, 147; and defence, 356, 362, 365-6
United Kingdom Privy Council, 390, 397
United Nations, 33; founding of, 3; WLMK on, 31, 46, 48, 51, 311, 319, 361; Security Council: 41, 138, 217, Hull on, 44, WLMK on, 46, 48, 51, 311, 319, 361, Attlee on, 48, Palestine and, 56; site for, 51; General Assembly, 60-1, 111, 126, 144, 217, 307, 326, 333; Secretary-General, 62, 122-4, 392; Canada approves charter, 68; on atomic energy, 98, 405-6; conference of trade and employment, 102; in New York, 289, 372; opening session, 357-8; Russian manipulation of, 369; social and economic council, 393; on disarmament, 394
UNRRA (United Nations Relief and Rehabilitation Administration), 272, 280, 322
United States, 8, 335; relations with Russia, 12, 227; atomic bomb and, 14; communism in, 16; and wheat, 21-3; Gouzenko affair, 28; Russian espionage in, 30, 33, 38, 40-1, 143-4, 146-7, 150; lend lease, 56; meat rationing, 100-1; loan to Britain, 160, 162, 166, 168-9, 172-3; absorption of Canada by, 219; defence, 265-6, 356, 362-3, 366; possible annexation of Newfoundland, 404

Vancouver, 41, 273
Vanier, Georges, 272, 281; in Paris with WLMK, 288-9, 295; with WLMK in

France, 301, 308, 311–12; relations with WLMK, 321–5
Vanier, Pauline, 288, 324–5
Van Kleffen, of the Netherlands, 62
V-E Day, 274
Veterans Affairs, Dept. of, 393–6, 397, 399
Victoria, Queen, of England, 179
Victory Day (London), 250, 252–3
Vienna, 61
Vinson, F. M., 190–1

Wallace, Henry, 343
Walpole, Sir Robert, 224, 241, 247, 258
War Measures Act, 47, 136–7
War Office (UK), 364
Ward, Barrington, 59
Wartime Information Bureau, 137
Wartime Prices and Trade Board, 20, 200–1, 204, 284, 338
Washington, 186, 197, 321; WLMK to go to, 28, 33, 35–6, 52, 88, 358, 360; WLMK in, 37–8; Attlee visits, 90; Churchill to visit, 181–2, 186; WLMK on, 330; Wrong appointed ambassador to, 334–6
Washington Conference, 93; WLMK at, 96–8; press release of, 98; agreement, 218
Webb, Sidney, 314
Weir, Gibb, chief whip of Liberals, 20
Welland (Ont.), 68
Westminster College (Fulton, Mo.), 183
Weston, Garfield, 101, 190
Wheat Board, 21–2, 263
wheat policy, 22–3, 262–4
White, Harry, 194

White House, 78, 96, 98
Wilgress, L. Dana, Canadian ambassador to Moscow, 269; and Gouzenko affair, 141; Paris Conference, 272, 281; opening of UN General Assembly, 357, 359; on Russia, 361
William the Conqueror, 301, 304, 305
Williams, E. K., 47; and Gouzenko affair, 134–5, 137, 141; WLMK advises on Gouzenko affair, 147–8
Willsher, Kathleen: arrested as spy, 137; spy for Russia, 149–50; sentenced, 284
Wilson, Morris, 353
Winant, J. G., 78
Windsor, Duke of, King George discusses, 77–8
Winnipeg Free Press, 372
Winnipeg Rifles, 305
Winnipeg Wheat Pool, 264
Winters, Robert H., 372, 382
Woikin, Emma, 137, 149, 157
Wolfe, General, 342
World Bank; *see* International Bank
Wrong, H. H., 26; and WLMK, 6, 28, 75, 172, 269; and Gouzenko affair, 7, 8, 34, 40; Washington Conference (1945), 96–7; and Fred Rose, 152; Canadian ambassador in Washington, 272, 294, 334–7, 360

Yalta Conference, 51, 244, 251
Yugoslavia, 292, 320

Zabotin, Colonel Nicolai, 11, 134, 145
Zaroubin, George N., Russian ambassador to Canada, 13, 145, 148
Zaroubin, Mrs., 180. 281

www.ingramcontent.com/pod-product-compliance
Lightning Source LLC
Chambersburg PA
CBHW020238030426
42336CB00010B/524